A BIOGRAPHICAL DICTIONARY OF WOMEN ECONOMISTS

A Biographical Dictionary of Women Economists
is dedicated to the memory of
Michèle Pujol
who, with great scholarship, commitment, and courage,
was an outstanding pioneer of the study of the history of women in
economics.

A Biographical Dictionary of Women Economists

Edited by

Robert W. Dimand

Brock University, St Catharines, Ontario, Canada

Mary Ann Dimand

Salinas, California, USA

and

Evelyn L. Forget

University of Manitoba, Winnipeg, Manitoba, Canada

Edward Elgar

Cheltenham, UK • Northampton, MA, USA

Published by
Edward Elgar Publishing Limited
Glensanda House
Montpellier Parade
Cheltenham
Glos GL50 1UA
UK

Edward Elgar Publishing, Inc.
136 West Street
Suite 202
Northampton
Massachusetts 01060
USA

A catalogue record for this book
is available from the British Library

Library of Congress Cataloguing in Publication Data

A biographical dictionary of women economists / edited by Robert W. Dimand, Mary Ann Dimand, and Evelyn L. Forget.
    Includes bibliographical references.
    1. Women economists—Biography.   I. Dimand, Robert W. (Robert William)
II.Dimand, Mary Ann, 1960–   III. Forget, Evelyn L., 1956–

    HB76 .B535   2000
    330'082'0922—dc21
    [B]   00–028842

ISBN 1 85278 964 6

Typeset by Manton Typesetters, Louth, Lincolnshire, UK.
Printed and bound in Great Britain by MPG Books Ltd, Bodmin, Cornwall.

Contents

Contributors to the volume and their entries

G. Abraham-Frois, MODEM, Paris X-Nanterre, France
Haguette Biaujeaud

Judith A. Alexander, The Ontario Workplace Safety and Insurance Tribunal, Canada
Agatha Louisa Chapman; Irene M. Spry

Robin L. Bartlett, Denison University, Granville, Ohio, USA
Katharine Coman

Giandomenica Becchio, Università degli Studi di' Torino, Italy
Margaret Cole

Alexandra Bernasek, Colorado, State University, USA
Ruth Alice Allen

Michael H. Best, University of Massachusetts, Lowell, USA, and Judge Institute of Management Studies, Cambridge University, UK
Edith Tilton Penrose

Krishna Bharadwaj, formerly Jawaharlal Nehru University, Delhi, India
Krishna Bharadwaj

Gudrun Biffl, Austrian Institute of Economic Research (WIFO), Vienna, Austria
Hilde Behrend

Ronald G. Bodkin, University of Ottawa, Ontario, Canada
Anna Koutsoyiannis

Mauro Boianovsky, University of Brasilia, Brazil
Maria da Conceição Tavares

Michael D. Bordo, Rutgers University, New Jersey
Anna Jacobson Schwartz

Felix Butschek, Austrian Institute of Economic Research (WIFO), Vienna, Austria
Maria Szecsi

Bernard Corry, Queen Mary and Westfield College, University of London, UK
Marian E.A. Bowley

Anne Innis Dagg, University of Waterloo, Ontario, Canada
Mary Quayle Innis

John B. Davis, Marquette University, Milwaukee, Wisconsin, USA
Helen Stuart Campbell

Mary Ann Dimand, Salinas, California, USA
Charlotte Perkins Gilman

Robert W. Dimand, Brock University, St Catharines, Ontario, Canada
Emily Greene Balch; Caroline Wells Healey Dall; Caroline Augusta Foley Rhys Davids; Minnie Throop England; Theresa Schmid McMahon; Michèle A. Pujol; Lise Salvas-Bronsard; Mabel Frances Timlin; Priscilla Wakefield

Zohreh Emami, Alverno College, Milwaukee, Wisconsin, USA
Joan Robinson

Magda Fontana, Università degli Studi di' Torino, Italy
Costanza Costantino

Evelyn L. Forget, University of Manitoba, Winnipeg, Manitoba, Canada
Mary Jean Bowman; Dorothy Stahl Brady; Ann Fetter Friedlaender; Alice Hanson Jones; Harriet Martineau; Mary Meynieu; Margaret Gilpin Reid; Clémence-Auguste Royer; Marguerite Thibert; Phyllis Ann Wallace

Graziella Fornengo, Università degli Studi di'Torino, Italy
Vera Cao Pinna

Aurora Gamez, University of Malaga
Marjorie Grice-Hutchinson

Susan H. Gensemer, Syracuse University, New York, USA
Emilia Jessie Boucherett; Elizabeth Beardsley Butler; Susan Myra Kingsbury; Virginia Penny

Peter Groenewegen, University of Sydney, Australia
Helen Dendy Bosanquet; Clara Elizabeth Collet; Amy Hewes

Deborah Haas-Wilson, Smith College, Northampton, MA, USA
Selma J. Mushkin

Harald Hagemann, University of Hohenheim, Stuttgart, Germany
Fanny Ginor; Cläre Tisch

Claire Holton Hammond, Wake Forest University, Winston-Salem, NC, USA
Edith Abbott; Sophonisba Breckinridge; Katherine Bement Davis; Hannah Robie Sewall

J. Daniel Hammond, Wake Forest University, Winston-Salem, NC, USA
Rose Director Friedman

Indra Hardeen, Brock Centre for Social and Economic Research on Niagara, Ontario, Canada
Eleanor Lansing Dulles; Barbara Wootton

James P. Henderson, Valparaiso University, Indiana, USA
B.L. Hutchins; Beatrice Potter Webb

Ingrid Henriksen, University of Copenhagen, Denmark
Ester Boserup

Rolf Henriksson, Stockholm University, Sweden
Karin Kock

M.C. Howard, University of Waterloo, Ontario, Canada
Raya Dunayevskaya; Natalie Moszkowska

Jane Humphries, All Souls College, Oxford University, UK
Edith Tilton Penrose

Prue Hyman, Victoria University of Wellington, New Zealand
Kate Sheppard

Aiko Ikeo, Kokugakuin University, Shibuya-ku, Tokyo, Japan
Koko (Takako) Sanpei; Setsu Tanino; Kikue Yamakawa

Christine Ivory, University of Manitoba, Winnipeg, Manitoba, Canada
Julie-Victoire Daubié

Joyce P. Jacobsen, Wesleyan University, Connecticut, USA
Margaret Gordon; Ursula Hicks

Niels Kærgård, Royal Danish Agricultural University, Denmark
Ester Boserup; Kirsten Gloerfelt-Tarp; the Philip Family

Morton I. Kamien, Northwestern University, Evanston, Illinois, USA
Nancy L. Schwartz

Vibha Kapuria-Foreman, Colorado College, USA
Selma Evelyn Fine Goldsmith

Sherryl Davis Kasper, Maryville College, Maryville, Tennessee, USA
Eveline Mabel Richardson Burns

J.E. King, La Trobe University, Australia
Raya Dunayevskaya; Natalie Moszkowska

Susan King, The University of Sydney, Australia
Clementina Black

Douglas Kinnear, Colorado State University, USA
Ruth Alice Allen

Richard Kleer, University of Regina, Canada
Lucy Barbara (Bradby) Hammond; Rosa Luxemburg

Claus-Dieter Krohn, University of Hamburg, Germany
Käthe Bauer-Mengelberg; Cora Berliner

Tatiana E. Kulakovskaja, Mathematics, St Petersburg State University, Russia
Olga Nikolajevna Bondareva

Frederic S. Lee, De Montfort University, Leicester, UK and University of Missouri at Kansas City, USA
Caroline Farrar Ware

Margaret Lewis, College of Saint Benedict, St Joseph, Minnesota, USA
Jean Trepp McKelvey

Barbara Libby, Niagara University, New York State, USA
Anna Pritchett Youngman

Richard A. Lobdell, University of Manitoba, Winnipeg, Manitoba, Canada
Hazel Kyrk; Jessica Blanche Peixotto; Elizabeth Boody Schumpeter; Helen Laura Sumner Woodbury

Christopher McDonough-Dumler, US Department of the Treasury, Washington, DC, USA
Shirley Ann Montag Almon

Gary Mongiovi, St John's University, New York, USA
Frieda Wunderlich

Natalia I. Naumova, Mathematics, St Petersburg State University, Russia
Olga Nikolajevna Bondareva

Jürgen Nautz, University of Kassel, Germany and University of Vienna, Austria
Martha Stephanie Browne; Helene Lieser; Gertrud von Lovasy; Ilse Schüller Mintz

Chris Nyland, Monash University, Australia
Elizabeth Faulkner Baker; Mary Abbey Van Kleeck

Spencer J. Pack, Connecticut College, New London, Connecticut, USA
Maxine Bernard Yaple Sweezy Woolston

Henk W. Plasmeijer, University of Groningen, The Netherlands
Elisabeth Caroline van Dorp

Bette Polkinghorn, California State University, Sacramento, USA
Jane Haldimand Marcet

Michalis Psalidopoulos, Panteion University, Greece
Marina Goudi; Maria Negreponti-Delivani; Irini (Rena) Zafiriou

Michèle A. Pujol, formerly University of Victoria, British Columbia, Canada
Millicent Garrett Fawcett; Harriet Hardy Taylor Mill

Shyamala Raman, Saint Joseph College, West Hartford, Connecticut, USA
Dorothy C. Goodwin

Mark Rix, Centre for Social Change, University of Wollongong, Australia
Elizabeth Faulkner Baker; Mary Abby Van Kleeck

Christopher K. Ryan, Iowa City, Iowa, USA
Elizabeth Read Brown; Barbara Ward

Warren J. Samuels, Michigan State University, USA
Caroline Farrar Ware

Philine Scholze, Humboldt-Universität, Berlin, Germany
Charlotte Leubuscher

Janet A. Seiz, Grinnell College, Iowa, USA
Millicent Garrett Fawcett; Eleanor Rathbone

Jean Shackelford, Bucknell University, USA
Mabel Newcomer; Flora Tristan

Karen Shopsowitz, independent film-maker, Ottawa, Ontario, Canada
Irene M. Spry

Kathryn Kish Sklar, History, State University of New York, Binghampton, USA
Florence Kelley

William D. Sockwell, Berry College, Georgia, USA
Barbara Bodichon

Lewis A. Soroka, Brock University, St Catharines, Ontario, Canada
Rosalind (Hyman) Blauer

J.J. Thomas, London School of Economics, UK
Elizabeth Waterman Gilboy

Alison Comish Thorne, formerly Utah State University, USA
Elizabeth Ellis Hoyt

Hans-Michael Trautwein, University of Oldenburg, Germany
Marie Dessauer

Rita McWilliams Tullberg, Stockholm International Peace Research Institute, Sweden
Mary Paley Marshall

Ramakrishna Vaitheswaran, Coe College, Cedar Rapids, Iowa, USA
Barbara Ward

Brenda Spotton Visano, Atkinson College, York University, Toronto, Ontario, Canada
Margaret Good Myers

Theresa Wobbe, Institute für Soziologie, Freie Universität Berlin and Berlin-Brandenburg Academy of Sciences, Berlin, Germany
Käthe Leichter; Charlotte Leubuscher

Introduction

When we began this project, we suspected that there had been more women contributing to the development of our discipline than economists knew about. William Baumol's 'Digression: On Earlier Writings by Women', in an article on the centenary of the American Economic Association, reported that 'before World War I, as today, a (distressingly) few women *were* contributing to the literature' (Baumol, 1985, p. 11), noting that his research assistant had found seven articles (one in two parts) by four women. We knew that they missed at least one. Katharine Coman's article filled the first 19 pages of volume 1, number 1, of the *American Economic Review*. We knew of Barbara Libby's quantitative studies of the participation of women in the American economics profession (Libby, 1984, 1987, 1990). And we had some sympathy for Baumol's research assistant because we knew how easy it is to miss women who use initials rather than first names, especially if you search using the *Index of Economic Journals. Economica*, vol. 1, no. 2 (May 1921), for example, includes not only an article by Mabel C. Buer, but also an article by Miss E.T. Kelly and Miss M.L. Haskins (Kelly and Haskins, 1921, pp. 116–31), while vol. 1, no. 3 has an article by Margaret S. Miller, but also an article by Miss W.A. Mackenzie (Mackenzie, 1921, pp. 211–30). The *Index* omits the honorific 'Miss'.

Since we began the research leading up to this volume, there has been a tremendous amount of new work on the subject. We soon learned that the proportion of women among contributors to the 'Old Palgrave', R.H. Inglis Palgrave's *Dictionary of Political Economy*, was slightly higher than that of *The New Palgrave* (Eatwell et al., 1987), published almost a century later (see Dimand, 1999). Barbara Libby's (1998) analysis continues. Peter Groenewegen and Susan King (1994) published an important working paper that listed 112 women (6.78 per cent of contributors) who published 222 articles (5.3 per cent of the total) in five core British and American economics journals from 1900 to 1939. Robert Dimand extended this search to the 1890s, and found 44 articles by 30 women in the *Quarterly Journal of Economics* (founded 1886), the *Economic Journal* (1891) and the *Journal of Political Economy* (founded 1892). The other two journals used by Groenewegen and King, *Economica* and the *American Economic Review*, did not exist in the 1890s. The only essays co-authored with a man were two that Beatrice and Sidney Webb published (Dimand, 1999). Michèle Pujol (1996) and Kirsten Madden (1998) presented papers on the contributions of women economists to History of Economics Society conferences. The preparatory work for a Routledge anthology of economic writing by women before 1900, undertaken by Pujol before her death, is being completed by Janet Seiz. Groenewegen published the results of a symposium on women economists in Australia held at the University of Sydney in 1997 (1998, cf. Groenewegen, 1994). N.G. Butlin, V.W. Fitzgerald and R.H. Scott (1986) reported on the activity of women in *The Australian Economist* in the 1890s, and Judith Alexander (1995) survey their participation in Canada. We also began to develop a new appreciation for women whose contributions to economics appeared in books rather than in the journal literature, and whose analysis challenged our understanding of how the discipline of economics ought to be conceived. Charlotte Perkins Gilman's institutional analysis published in *The Home: Its Work and Influence* (1903) and *Women and Economics* (1898) is an example of such work (see M.A. Dimand, 1995).

We began to trace these leads, and discovered that looking for women economists is like pulling on a loose thread. Every woman we discovered led us to two or three more whose work they cited, or with whom they co-authored articles or books. They led us to others they mentored, or with whom they studied or worked. Women economists kept appearing in the oddest places. Looking back, it now seems almost inevitable that the project would grow beyond our expectations, as we rather belatedly began to follow the lead of other disciplines and take notice of the women who contributed to our history. Mary Jo Deegan's *Women in Sociology* (1991) and Mary Ellen Waithe, the editor of the four-volume *A History of Women Philosophers*, also began modestly: 'I decided to attempt to restore women's contributions to the history of philosophy, and initially believed that the subject would make an interesting article for, say, the *Journal of the History of Philosophy*' (Waithe, 1987, vol. I, p. x). And so we faced our first decision: how should we decide whom to include? Some of our decisions were necessarily arbitrary. We chose not to include the relatively large generation of women economists currently active in the profession. Most of our subjects are either dead or retired, although some of the more prolific continue to produce articles well into their nineties. We chose to focus on economists who were important, either because they made a substantive contribution to the field or, in a few cases, because they were historically important, such as being the first woman (of whom we were aware) in a particular country to contribute to the discipline. We tried to extend the coverage to non-anglophone traditions, but we were very dependent upon the willingness of collaborators to assist us. We were more successful in some languages, such as Japanese because of Aiko Ikeo's work and German thanks to Harald Hagemann and Claus-Dieter Krohn, than in others. Chinese and Latin American economists are virtually absent from this book. Indeed, we wish we knew more about such women as Mabel

Ping-Hua Lee (born 1897), whose book *Economic History of China* (1921) was her Columbia University Ph.D. dissertation.

We also had to decide how to delimit the discipline of economics. We are editing this volume primarily for the use of economists, hoping that some will be sufficiently intrigued by the stories we have collected to do further work on these women and on their insights. Therefore, we wanted to define the discipline in such a way that present economists would recognize it. But we are mindful of the relatively recent domination of our discipline by pure theory, or what He Qinglian called 'techniques of dragon slaying' in her bestselling and controversial book entitled *China's Pitfall* (1996; see Liu and Link, 1998). We did not want to define economics so narrowly that we eliminated virtually all of the women and most of the men working in the past. The further back we go, the less clearly is economics distinguished from sociology and the related disciplines. So we decided to include individuals who were intentionally working in what would, at the time they wrote, have been considered economics. We included, for example, the consumer economists working in departments of home economics and government departments of agriculture early in this century. But we excluded people who were primarily social activists or journalists who, occasionally, wrote on topics related to economic reform. Many of the women attached to the Saint-Simonian movement in nineteenth-century France, such as Suzanne Voilquin, were excluded, while Julie-Victoire Daubié, the first woman baccalaureate in France (in 1862), was included. Her articles in the *Journal des Économistes* (1862, 1863) and her 1866 book on women and poverty, works which systematically examined economic issues, justified her inclusion.

The most difficult decision we faced, however, was to send the manuscript to the publisher. This project was beginning to take on the air of Scheherazade's *Tales*. Some contributors submitted a piece, and then sent rather desperate messages begging to revise because they found new and really interesting material. Others became so intrigued by their subjects that one- to two-thousand-word articles turned into much longer pieces, only some of which were successfully shortened. Some kept turning up new names and new people who ought to be included. And others ran into difficulty finding material on women who ought to have been included, or were so meticulous that the articles never appeared. We do not present this volume as an exhaustive account of women's contributions to the discipline. We know that there are women who really ought to have been included and yet, for one reason or another, were not. We have also developed enough humility to know that there are many women in the history of our discipline of whom we remain ignorant. This volume is produced with the hope that some readers will be inspired to help us fill the gaps in our institutional memory.

What have we learned?

The nineteenth century
Priscilla Wakefield's criticism of Adam Smith's *Wealth of Nations* is our earliest inclusion (Wakefield [1798], 1817). She faulted Smith for insufficient coverage of the economic activity of women, both in the sphere of household production (which he had excluded from economic analysis on the grounds that it was not governed by considerations of rational self-interest) and in the realm of wage work and market activity. Sophie de Grouchy, the marquise de Condorcet, had translated Smith's *Theory of Moral Sentiments* into French in 1798, and appended eight letters on the subject of sympathy which constitute a significant treatise on moral philosophy. She did discuss economic issues and, for example, was much more critical of inequality of wealth than was Smith, but this was not primarily a work in economics. Wakefield, by contrast, protested against the exclusion of women from Smith's *Wealth of Nations* raising at the time concerns that feminist scholars have more recently emphasized (Pujol, 1992; Rendall, 1987). 'Does it matter to the relevance of his doctrine', Michèle Pujol asked (1992, p. 22), 'that at least half of the human race is not allowed to be freely guided by self-interest?' In his unpublished Glasgow lectures, Smith had followed Montesquieu in discussing the social status of women in different historical stages of economic development (Chris Nyland, 1993), but they disappear from the *Wealth of Nations*.

The classical neglect of women's economic contributions continued. Neither David Ricardo's *Principles of Political Economy and Taxation*, nor T.R. Malthus's *Principles of Political Economy* mention women. Jean-Baptiste Say, by contrast, developed a patriarchal analysis of women's social roles alongside his market analysis (Forget, 1997). Robert Owen and John Bray, British Utopian socialists, presented an analysis 'infused with paternal imagery' (Nancy Folbre, 1993, p. 97), a criticism that could be levelled with equal justice against Barthelémy-Prosper Enfantin, the Saint-Simonian theorist who argued that women were inherently different from men and ought to retire from active participation in economic activity until the new world to be created by Saint-Simonian activities comes about.

But there were women economists writing during the classical period. Frances (Fanny) Wright, one of the women mentioned in Dorfman's monumental *The Economic Mind in American Civilization* was a popular lecturer and leading figure in Utopian communities at Nashoba, Tennessee (where she helped to resettle slaves whose freedom she had purchased) and, with Robert Owen, at New Harmony, Indiana. She was a social reformer with outspoken views on religion, marriage and education rather than an economist systematically contributing to economic analysis. The same can be said of Anna Wheeler, sometime collaborator with the British Utopian socialist William

Thompson (Folbre, 1993, p. 98), and of Saint-Simonians such as Suzanne Voilquin (Moses, 1984).

More familiar to most economists are the popularizers, Jane Marcet and Harriet Martineau. Since Marcet (1816) and Martineau (1832–34) sold better than the monthly instalments of Dickens's novels, it is perhaps not necessary to mention that they also outsold classical theorists such as Ricardo (Polkinghorn, 1993, 1995). Marcet is often written of as making Ricardo accessible, a considerable feat since her book appeared the year before his (Dimand, 1995, pp. 12–13). While she knew Ricardo, who recommended her book to his daughter, her value theory was actually closer to Say's utility theory than to Ricardo's, and she was less concerned than Ricardo or Malthus about population growth and natural resource scarcity (Polkinghorn, 1993, pp. 52–5). Martineau's *Illustrations of Political Economy* (1832–34) also helped to popularize political economy, but she distanced herself from this early dogmatism in her autobiography (1877, vol. I, pp. 194–5). Martineau questioned those aspects of factory legislation that limited women's opportunities for employment (1855). Her *Society in America* ([1837], 1962) included a chapter on the status of women in America, contrasting their low wages and restricted property rights with the American ideology of equality (Frawley, 1992).

Barbara Leigh Smith Bodichon drafted the petition to Parliament that led to the Married Women's Property Act (1857) and the petition for women's suffrage that John Stuart Mill presented to Parliament in 1866 (Robson and Robson, 1994, pp. xxvi–xxviii). She also founded the Society for Promoting the Employment of Women and the *English Woman's Journal*, and wrote on *Women and Work* (1857) and on laws affecting women. In the 1860s, Bodichon and her Langham Place associates were introduced to John Stuart Mill by his stepdaughter, Helen Taylor. Mill's views on the social and economic roles of women were influenced by his wife, Harriet Taylor. Pujol (1992, 1995), however, argues that Taylor's views were more radical than those of Mill. Millicent Garrett Fawcett (1892, 1918) was also a visitor to Langham Place and, by the time of her *Economic Journal* articles, widow of Henry Fawcett (who had been MP for Brighton and Professor of Political Economy at Cambridge).

Women were active in the National Association for the Promotion of Social Science, from its founding meeting in 1857 until its dissolution in 1886 (Cobbe, 1861; Rogers, 1952; Martel, 1986). Indeed, women were seen as changing the very nature of economic discourse. In 1876, Sir Francis Galton attempted to have Economics removed from Section F of the British Association for the Advancement of Science, and the following year the Adam Smith Centennial Dinner of the Political Economy Club broke into an acrimonious discussion of the nature of economics. Following the dinner, the *Pall Mall Gazette* reported that:

the natural philosophers have been frightened out of their wits by the ladies who flock to the Section of 'Economic Science and Statistics' and who insist on reading papers and starting discussions which are not only not scientific but which savour of the singular antipathy to science for its own sake common to all the feminine movements of the day. (*Pall Mall Gazette*, 22 August 1878, p. 1, quoted in Jevons *Papers & Correspondence*, iv, pp. 272–3n5)[1]

In France and America, women were also making their presence known.

Mary Meynieu wrote a popularizing *Eléments d'économie politique* (Elements of Political Economy) (1839) and *Paupérisme anglais* (English Pauperism) (1841). She published in the *Journal des économistes* in 1859 and, the following year, produced a pamphlet on women's work. Clémence-Auguste Royer published a two-volume *Théorie de l'impôt, ou la dîme sociale* (Theory of Taxation) (1862). She was primarily an anthropologist and writer on scientific issues such as Darwin's *Origin of Species*, which she translated in 1862, but published on broad sociological topics in the *Journal des économistes* in the 1870s. Julie-Victoire Daubié won a prize from the Academy of Lyons in 1859 with an essay on 'La femme pauvre au XIXe siècle' (The impoverished woman of the nineteenth century), which she published as a series of articles in the *Journal des économistes* in 1862 and 1863, and then as a book in 1866. Her work was accepted as part of the conversation of political economy, while Flora Tristan's criticisms of classical economics in her *London Journal* (1840) were treated as the work of an outsider. Ekelund and Hébert (1999, p. 427) note a letter from Walras to Mlle Guillaumin, 'who took over her father's publishing business on his death [in 1864] and acted as *de facto* editor of the *Journal des économistes*'. Palgrave's *Dictionary*, in an article on Urbain Gilbert Guillaumin, noted that 'Guillaumin's two daughters, of whom the eldest, Félicité died in 1885 at the age of fifty-six, inherited both his administrative ability and his devotion to economic science'.

Caroline Healey Dall considered the economic role of women in a series of public lectures in Boston, published as 'Women's Right to Labor' (1860). She served on the executive committee of the American Social Science Association from its foundation in 1865 until 1905, initially as a director and then, from 1880, as vice-president. Virginia Penny published *The Employments of Women: A Cyclopaedia of Woman's Work* (1863). The second printing was entitled *Five Hundred Occupations Adapted to Women; with the Average Rate of Pay in Each* and the third, *How Women Can Make Money, Married or Single*. The book reported on wages, gender pay differentials (both as stated by employers and as understood by the author), necessary skills and education, time needed to learn the job, seasonality, paid or unpaid apprenticeship, and openness to women. *Think and Act: A Series of Articles Pertaining to Men and Women, Work and Wages* (Penny, 1869) considered married women's property rights, domestic labour, market work, human capital, poverty rates of women relative to men and economic consequences, especially for women, of the Civil War.

Consumer economics and the household

From the time of Adam Smith, the household was customarily seen as outside the sphere of rational calculation and self-interest. A line of research initiated at Iowa State College and the University of Chicago by Elizabeth Ellis Hoyt (1928, 1938), Hazel Kyrk (1923, 1933) and Margaret Gilpin Reid (1934), however, attempts to bring concepts of economic efficiency to considerations of the allocation of time and other resources within the household. The 'new home economics' of Nobel Laureate Gary Becker builds on this tradition.

Women were also intensely involved in the empirical studies upon which postwar theories of consumption were based. Dorothy Stahl Brady and Rose Director Friedman (1946) anticipated the relative income hypothesis, for which the later publications of James Duesenberry are usually cited (Dimand, 1995, pp. 13–14). The permanent-income hypothesis of Milton Friedman (1957) and the life-cycle theory of Franco Modigliani were explicitly based upon empirical studies conducted by Dorothy Brady, Rose Friedman and Margaret Reid, a debt that both Friedman and Modigliani acknowledge. For these contributions, Reid was the first woman named Distinguished Fellow by the American Economic Association.

Twentieth-century continental economics

Rosa Luxemburg's 1897 University of Zürich doctoral dissertation in political science was published in 1898 as *The Industrial Development of Poland*, a year before V.I. Lenin's *Development of Capitalism in Russia* (1899). *The Accumulation of Capital* ([1913], 1951) was her major work, and a significant contribution to growth theory and Marxian macroeconomics. Natalie Moszkowska won her doctorate at the University of Zürich in 1917, with a dissertation on workers' savings banks in the Polish coal and steel industries. She worked as a tutor and wrote for the trade union and socialist press. Moszkowska criticized Marx's theory, of the tendency of the profit rate to fall in *Das Marxsche System* (1929) and *Zur Dynamik des Statkapitalismus* (1943). She offered an underconsumptionist theory of crises in *Zur Kritik Moderner Krisentheorien* (1935), and published three articles in a mainstream economics journal, *Schmoller's Jahrbuch* (1959, 1963, 1965). In the first, she compared Marx to Keynes, unfavourably, on crisis theory.

The study of peasant economies was a feature of Russian economics from the early 1890s. Two women economists contributed significantly to this area of study. F.A. Scherbina was the most prominent writer in the field, and S. Platova was one of the authors of *Methods of Quantitative Calculation of the Effectiveness of Land*, a 1925 study edited by A.V. Chayanov (Jasny, 1972).

Chayanov's Institute for Peasant Studies was destroyed, along with N.D. Kondratieff's Business Cycle Institute, after the arrest and disappearance of Chayanov and Kondratieff. Associated with Kondratieff's Business Cycle Institute was another woman, O.E. Pryakhina, who was credited by Nikolai Kondratieff for the careful and critical statistical work upon which his *The Long Wave Cycle* was based (Kondratieff, 1984, pp. 34–5). When serious scholarly activity resumed in the Soviet Union after Stalinism, Olga Bondareva became a game theorist of international stature, the author of 70 papers and a book, and a member of the editorial board of *Games and Economic Behavior*.

Frieda Wunderlich earned her doctorate at the University of Freiburg in 1919 and became a professor at the University of Berlin before emigrating to be a professor of economics at the New School for Social Research in New York from 1933 to 1954. She published an article in the *Quarterly Journal of Economics* in 1928 on German unemployment insurance, and another in 1938 on 'Germany's defense economy and the decay of capitalism', 14 articles between 1934 and 1953 in the New School's journal *Social Research* on women's work in Germany, unemployment insurance, health insurance and the Beveridge plan, as well as books on *German Labor Courts* (1946) and *Farm Labor in Germany, 1810–1945* (1961). Marie Dessauer earned a doctorate at the University of Frankfurt in 1933, with a doctorate on major English deposit banks. She emigrated to study at LSE (1934–36) and became a research assistant to T.E. Gregory and Friedrich Hayek (1937–41). She contributed articles on banking and unemployment to the *Review of Economic Studies*, *Economic History Review* and *Economica*.

Ilse Schueller Mintz, who earned a doctorate at the University of Vienna in 1927 under Ludwig von Mises' supervision, earned a second doctorate at Columbia in 1951. She taught at Columbia from 1948 to 1969, and from 1951 to 1973 was Senior Research Associate at the National Bureau of Economic Research, which published four books she authored.

Huguette Biaujeaud received a doctorate from the University of Paris in 1933 with a thesis on Ricardian value theory. She did not pursue her academic work further. This may well have been due to limited opportunities for academic employment in France: the only woman to hold a professorship in any discipline in interwar France was Marie Curie (appointed after her first Nobel prize). The *Revue d'économie politique* reveals only two articles by women between 1921 and 1934, one of which was written by the Swedish economist Karin Kock. French women economists such as Marguerite Thibert were, however, involved in international economic agencies such as the International Labour Office.

Karin Kock's Stockholm dissertation was published in English as *A Study of Interest Rates* (1929). She published primarily in Swedish, but did publish internationally on monetary economics and trade policy. She collaborated on the construction of retrospective national income accounts for Sweden. Kock became Sweden's first female cabinet minister, was head of the Central Bureau of Statistics from 1950 to 1958 and of the Swedish delegation to the UN Economic Commission for Europe from 1947 to 1960.

Aiko Ikeo's work on Japanese political economy brings to us the insights of such economists as Sumiko Takahara, who criticized the assumption of methodological individualism while arguing for the inclusion of women's household labour in economic analysis in a 1979 book entitled *Challenging Male Economics* (Ikeo, 1999, p. 590).

Surveying women economists
This introduction has not come close to mentioning all of the people and all of the stories contained in this volume, let alone all women contributors to our discipline. One of the things of which we have become aware is the incredible diversity in the writing of women economists. They did pay far more attention, proportionately, than did men to 'women's issues'. From Priscilla Wakefield [1798] and Julie-Victoire Daubié (1862, 1863) to Michèle Pujol (1992) to Heidl Hartmann (1981), critics have argued that economic theories, whether neoclassical, classical or Marxist, exclude the important work of household production and reproductive work from their analysis. Women labour historians, such as Edith Abbott, Alice Clark, Elizabeth Dexter, Bessie Leigh Hutchins, Annie Meyer, Ivy Pinchbeck, Helen Sumner and Caroline Ware, offer analyses of the past work experience of half the population, both in the household and in the marketplace.

Women devoted more interest than did men to social policy and gender pay differentials (Helen Campbell), but they also wrote on topics as diverse as Marxian macroeconomics (Rosa Luxemburg, Natalie Moszkowska), income distribution (Mary Jean Bowman, Selma Goldsmith), the economics of education (Mary Jean Bowman. Sophie Willock Bryant), the economics of racial and gender discrimination (Phyllis Wallace), exchange rates (Elisabeth Caroline Van Dorp, Joan Robinson), international trade theory (Marion Crawford Samuelson), monetary economics (Anna Schwartz, Helen Makower, Eleanor Lansing Dulles, Sara McLean Hardy, Margaret G. Myers), the theory of the firm (Joan Robinson, Edith Penrose), capital theory (Joan Robinson, Krishna Bharadwaj, Ruth Cohen (of the Ruth Cohen curiosum)), public finance (Ursula Hicks. Mabel Newcomer, Selma Mushkin), development (Elizabeth Boody Schumpeter, Irma Adelman. Ester Boserup, Polly Hill, Cynthia Taft Morris, Barbara Ward, Vera Smith Lutz), institutional economics (Charlotte Perkins Gilman) and the history of economic thought (Marian Bowley, Marjorie Grice-Hutchinson and Jacqueline Hecht).

Consumer economics, both in the form of the 'new home economics' and in empirical work behind innovations in the theory of the consumption function, owe much to Margaret Reid, Dorothy Brady. Rose Friedman, Elizabeth Hoyt, Hazel Kyrk and Ruby Turner Morris.

Economic history has always attracted the attention of women: Mabel Ping-Hua Lee's *Economic History of China* (1921), Margaret Stephenson Miller's *Economic Development of Russia* (1925), Vera Anstey's *Economic Development of India* (1929) are worthy of note. Mabel Buer, Ivy Pinchbeck and Elizabeth Gilboy wrote on topics related to the Industrial Revolution. Miriam Beard's *History of Business* (1938), Alice Hanson Jones's magisterial study of wealth distribution in colonial America, Anne Bezanson's work in price history, and, especially, Elizabeth Boody Schumpeter's work on commercial statistics, are significant pieces of work.

The political range of women economists was equally vast, ranging from the revolutionary Marxism of Rosa Luxemburg and Raya Dunayevskaya to Vera Smith Lutz's case for the free banking alternative to a central bank in a doctoral dissertation supervised by Hayek (Smith, 1936), and the anti-statist views of Suzanne LaFollette (1926). He Qinglian's dismissal of Chinese academic economics as either 'toady writing' (the construction of economic justifications for political decisions) or 'techniques of dragon slaying' (pure economic theory with no political or social referents), in a scathing criticism of recent Chinese economic history, reminds us of the territory we have not covered in this volume. Her *China's Pitfall* was published to critical acclaim in Hong Kong (1996) and was eventually published (under the less provocative title *A Pitfall of Modernization* (1998)) in China (see Liu and Link, 1998).

An invitation
The stories we have collected are fascinating. Enjoy. And keep looking …

Note
1. We would like to thank Sandra Peart for drawing this article to our attention.

References
Alexander, Judith A. (1995), 'Our ancestors in their successive generations', *Canadian Journal of Economics*, **28**(1): 205–24.
Anstey, Vera (1929), *The Economic Development of India*, London: Longmans, Green.
Baumol, William J. (1985), 'On method in U.S. economics a century earlier', *American Economic Review*, **75**(6): 1–12.
Beard, Miriam (1938), *A History of Business*, 2 vols. Reprinted Ann Arbor: University of Michigan Press, 1962.
Butlin, N.G., V.W. Fitzgerald and R.H. Scott (eds) (1986), *The Australian Economist 1888–1898*, 2 vols. Sydney: Australian National University Press.
Cobbe, Frances Power (1861), 'Social science congresses and women's part in them', *Macmillan's Magazine*.
Daubié, Julie-Victoire (1862), 'Quels moyens de subsistence out les femmes', *Journal des économistes*, 2nd series (34).
Daubié, Julie-Victoire (1863), 'Travail manuel des femmes', *Journal des économistes*, 2nd series (38 and 39).

Deegan, Mary Jo (ed.) (1991), *Women in Sociology: A Bio-Bibliographical Sourcebook*, New York: Greenwood Press.

Dimand, Mary Ann (1995), 'The Economics of Charlotte Perkins Gilman', in Dimand, Dimand and Forget (1995): 124–49.

Dimand, M.A., R.W. Dimand and E.L. Forget (eds) (1995), *Women of Value: Feminist Essays on the History of Women in Economics*, Aldershot, UK, and Brookfield, VT: Edward Elgar.

Dimand, Robert W. (1995), 'The neglect of women's contributions to economics', in Dimand, Dimand and Forget (1995): 1–24.

Dimand, Robert W. (1999), 'Women Economists in the 1890s: journals, books and the Old Palgrave', *Journal of the History of Economic Thought*, **21**(3).

Dorfman, Joseph (1946–59), *The Economic Mind in American Civilization*, 5 volumes, New York: Viking.

Eatwell, J., M. Milgate and Peter Newman (eds) (1987), *The New Palgrave: A Dictionary of Economics*, 4 vols. London: Stockton Press.

Ekelund, Robert B. Jr and Robert F. Hébert (1999), *The Secret Origins of Modern Microeconomics: Dupuit and the Engineers*, Chicago: University of Chicago Press.

Fawcett, Millicent Garrett (1892), 'Mr. Sidney Webb's article on wages for women', *Economic Journal*, **2**(1): 173–6.

Fawcett, Millicent Garrett (1918), 'Equal pay for equal work', *Economic Journal*, **28**(1): 1–6.

Folbre, Nancy (1991), 'The unproductive housewife: her evolution in nineteenth-century economic thought', *Signs: Journal of Women in Culture and Society*, **16**(3): 463–84.

Folbre, Nancy (1993), 'Socialism, feminist and scientific', in Marianne Ferber and Julie Nelson (eds), *Beyond Economic Man*, Chicago: University of Chicago Press.

Forget, Evelyn L. (1997), 'The market for virtue: Jean-Baptiste Say on women in the economy and society', *Feminist Economics*, **3**(1): 95–111.

Frawley, Maria H. (1992), 'Harriet Martineau in America: gender and the discourse of sociology', *Victorian Newsletter*, **81**: 13–20.

Gilman, Charlotte Perkins (1898), *Women and Economics: The Economic Factor Between Men and Women as a Factor in Social Evolution,* Boston: Small, Maynard. Reprinted (with an introduction by Carl Degler) New York: Harper Torchbooks, 1996. Reprinted Amherst, NY: Prometheus Books, 1994.

Gilman, Charlotte Perkins ([1903] 1970), *The Home: Its Work and Influence*, New York: New York Source Book Press.

Groenewegen, Peter D. (ed.) (1994), *Feminism and Political Economy in Victorian England*, Aldershot, UK, and Brookfield, VT: Edward Elgar.

Groenewegen, Peter D. (1998), 'Women economists in Australia', *Economic Papers*, **17**(1).

Groenewegen, Peter D. and Susan King (1994), 'Women as producers of economic articles: a statistical assessment of the nature and extent of female participation in five British and North American journals 1900–1939', University of Sydney Working Papers in Economics no. 201.

Hartmann, Heidi (1981), 'The unhappy marriage of Marxism and feminism: towards a more progressive union', in Lydia Sargent (ed.), *Women and Revolution*, Boston: South End Press: 1–41.

Hoyt, Elizabeth Ellis (1928), *Consumption of Wealth*, New York: Macmillan.

Hoyt, Elizabeth Ellis (1938), *Consumption in Our Society*, New York: McGraw-Hill.

Ikeo, Aiko (1999), 'Japanese political economy', in Phillip A. O'Hara (ed.), *Encyclopedia of Political Economy*, London and New York: Routledge.

Jasny, Naum (1972), *Soviet Economists of the Twenties: Names to be Remembered*, Cambridge: Cambridge University Press.

Kelly, E.T. and M.L. Haskins (1921), 'Foundations of industrial welfare', *Economica*, **1**(2): 116–31.

Kondratieff, Nikolai (1984), *The Long Wave Cycle*, translated by Guy Daniels with an introduction by Julian M. Snyder, St Moritz, Switzerland: International Moneyline.

Kyrk, Hazel (1923), *A Theory of Consumption*, Cambridge, MA: Houghton Mifflin, The Riverside Press.

Kyrk, Hazel (1933), *Economic Problems of the Family*, New York: Harper and Brothers.

LaFollette, Suzanne (1926), *Concerning Women*, New York: Albert and Charles Boni.

Lee, Mabel Ping-Hua (1921), *The Economic History of China, with Special Reference to Agriculture*, New York: Columbia University Press.

Libby, Barbara (1984), 'Women in economics before 1940', *Essays in Economic and Business History*, vol. 3: 273–90.

Libby, Barbara (1987), 'Statistical analysis of women in the economics profession', *Essays in Economic and Business History*, vol. 5: 179–89.

Libby, Barbara (1990), 'Women in the economics profession 1900–1940: factors in declining visibility', *Essays in Economic and Business History*, vol. 8: 121–30.

Libby, Barbara (1998), 'As time goes by: a chronological study of women in the economics profession', *Essays in Economic and Business History*, vol. 16: 261–76.

Liu Binyan and Perry Link (1998), 'A great leap backward?' (review of He Qinglian's *China's Pitfall*), *New York Review of Books*, **45**(15): 19–23.

Mackenzie, W.A. (1921), 'Changes in the standard of living in the United Kingdom, 1860–1914', *Economica*, **1**(3): 211–30.

Madden, Janice F. (1972), 'The development of economic thought on the "women problem"', *Review of Radical Political Economics*, **4**(3): 21–39.

Madden, Kirsten (1998), 'Female economists in the history of economic thought: methodological issues and a case study in consumption theory', Millersville University, presented to History of Economics Society.

Marcet, Jane Haldimand (1816), *Conversations on Political Economy*, London: Longman.

Martel, Carol F. (1986), 'British women in the National Association for the Promotion of Social Science, 1857–1886', unpublished Ph.D. dissertation, Arizona State University.

Martineau, Harriet (1832–34), *Illustrations of Political Economy*, 9 volumes, London: Charles Fox.

Martineau, Harriet ([1837] 1962), *Society in America*, abridged and edited by Seymour Martin Lipset, Garden City, NY: Doubleday Anchor. Reprinted New Brunswick, NJ: Transaction Books, 1981.

Martineau, Harriet (1855), *The Factory Controversy: A Warning Against 'Meddling Legislation'*, Manchester: Ireland and Company and the National Association of Factory Operators.

Martineau, Harriet (1877), *Autobiography*, 2 volumes, M.W. Chapman (ed.), London: Smith, Elder.

Miller, Margaret S. (1925), *Economic Development of Russia*, London: P.S. King & Son.

Moses, Claire G. (1984), *French Feminism in the 19th Century*, Albany: State University of New York Press.

Nyland, Chris (1993), 'Adam Smith, stage theory, and the status of women', *History of Political Economy*, **25**(4): 617–40.

Palgrave, R.H. Inglis (ed.) (1894–99), *Dictionary of Political Economy*, 3 vols. London: Macmillan.

Polkinghorn, Bette (1993), *Jane Marcet: An Uncommon Woman*, Aldermaston, Berkshire: Forestwood Publications.

Polkinghorn, Bette (1995), 'Jane Marcet and Harriet Martineau: motive, market experience and reception of their works popularizing classical political economy', in Dimand, Dimand and Forget (1995): 71–82.

Pujol, Michèle (1992), *Feminism and Anti-Feminism in Early Economic Thought*, Aldershot, UK, and Brookfield, VT: Edward Elgar (paperback edn, with preface by Janet A. Seiz, Cheltenham, UK, and Northampton, MA: Edward Elgar, 1998).

Pujol, Michèle (1995), 'The feminist economic thought of Harriet Taylor (1807–58)', in Dimand, Dimand and Forget (1995): 82–102.

Pujol, Michèle (1996), 'Nineteenth century economic writing by women', paper presented to History of Economics Society, Vancouver.

Qinglian, He (1996), *Zhongguo de xianjing* (*China's Pitfall*), Hong Kong: Mingjing chubanshe.

Reid, Margaret Gilpin (1934), *Economics of Household Production*, New York: John Wiley.

Rendall, Jane (1987), 'Virtue and commerce: women in the making of Adam Smith's political economy', in Ellen Kennedy and Susan Mendus (eds), *Women in Western Political Philosophy: Kant to Nietzche*, Brighton: Wheatsheaf Books.

Robson, Ann P. and John M. Robson (eds) (1994), *Sexual Equality: Writings by John Stuart Mill, Harriet Taylor Mill and Helen Taylor*, Toronto: University of Toronto Press.

Rogers, Brian (1952), 'The Social Science Association, 1857–1886', *The Manchester School*, **20**(3).

Smith, Vera (1936), *The Rationale of Central Banking: And the Free Banking Alternative*, London: P.S. King & Son. Reprinted with an introduction by Leland Yeager, Indianapolis: Liberty Fund, 1990. (Later Vera Smith Lutz.)

Wakefield, Priscilla ([1798] 1817), *Reflections on the Present Condition of the Female Sex, with Suggestions for its Improvement*, 2nd edn, London: Darton, Harvey, and Darton.

Waithe, Mary Ellen (ed.) (1987), *A History of Women Philosophers*, 4 vols. Dordrecht: Martinus Nijhoff.

Acknowledgements

The editors are grateful for permission to reprint:

Krishna Bharadwaj's autobiography, reprinted from Philip Arestis and Malcolm Sawyer (eds), *A Biographical Dictionary of Dissenting Economists*, Aldershot, UK, and Brookfield, VT: Edward Elgar Publishing Ltd, 1992. Reprinted by permission of the publisher.

'Olga Nikolajevna Bondareva' by Tatiana E. Kulakovskaja and Natalja I. Naumova with the assistance of Joseph V. Romaovsky, *International Journal of Game Theory*, 1992, pp. 309–12. Reprinted by permission of the *International Journal of Game Theory*.

'Anna Jacobson Schwartz' by Michael D. Bordo, from David Glasner (ed.), *Business Cycles and Depressions: An Encyclopedia*, New York and London: Garland Publishing, Inc. Reprinted by permission of the author.

'Nancy L. Schwartz' and 'Publications of Nancy L. Schwartz' by Morton I. Kamien, from Donald P. Jacobs, Ehud Kalai and Morton I. Kamien (eds), *Frontiers of Research in Economic Theory: The Nancy L. Schwartz Memorial Lectures, 1983–1997*, Cambridge, UK, and New York: Cambridge University Press, 1998, pp. xvii–xxv. Reprinted by permission of the author.

Robert W. Dimand thanks Brock University's President's Fund for the Advancement of Scholarship for course relief for work on this project.

Edith Abbott (1876–1957)

After earning her Ph.D. in economics from the University of Chicago in 1905 (the second woman to do so), Edith Abbott built a successful academic career for herself, first, as a labour economist and economic historian and, later, as Professor and Dean of the University of Chicago Graduate School of Social Service Administration and as long-time editor of the *Social Service Review*.

Abbott was born in Nebraska in 1876 to the small-town prairie lawyer, Othman Abbott, and his wife, Elizabeth Griffin. Both believed in equal rights for women and in education for their daughters, Grace and Edith. (Grace grew up to become a nationally recognized social reformer and Chief of the US Children's Bureau.) Edith was a natural scholar and did well in her studies, although her undergraduate college years were punctuated with family financial difficulties stemming from the long Nebraska drought and depression of the 1890s. For seven years Abbott worked to combine high-school teaching with summer and correspondence courses, and eventually full-time studies, to earn her undergraduate degree at the University of Nebraska in 1901.

In 1903, Abbott won a fellowship to study political economy at the newly established University of Chicago, which she had seen under construction during a visit to the World's Columbia Exposition in 1893 and which she knew had admitted women from its inception. There she came under the influence of Professors J. Laurence Laughlin and Thorstein Veblen and the work of erstwhile Veblen student, Wesley Clair Mitchell. In addition, she took courses with Professor Sophonisba Breckinridge (*q.v.*), with whom she established a close, life-long professional association.

Abbott showed an early aptitude and interest in labour statistics and employment trends, topics that would dominate her writings until the 1920s. In 1904 she published her first article, 'Wage statistics in the twelfth census', in the *Journal of Political Economy* (*JPE*), a critique of the imprecise statistical methods used in a report by Davis Dewey on the wage and employment trends of the 1900 census. An important article based on her dissertation, 'Wages of unskilled labor in the United States, 1850–1900', was published in the *JPE* the following year. This was the first statistical study of the wages of unskilled labour in the USA and documents a 50 per cent increase in the wages of such workers over the last half of the nineteenth century. According to Abbott, such a study was a 'first step toward a complete history of wages' (p. 325).

Eventually Abbott would write a large portion of the history of US wages and employment, centring particularly on women. Breckinridge's course on the legal and economic position of women had prompted Abbott to wonder about the history of women in the labour force. Her research into this

1

question resulted in many articles and her seminal book, *Women in Industry* (1910).

Her first effort in this direction was a joint paper with Breckinridge, 'Employment of women in industries – twelfth census statistics', which appeared in the *JPE* in 1906. In quick succession she published 'History of the industrial employment of women in the United States: an introductory study' (JPE, 1906), 'Harriet Martineau and the employment of women in 1836' (*JPE*, 1906), 'Employment of women in industries: cigar-making – its history and present tendencies' (*JPE*, 1907), 'Employment of women in cotton mills, parts I, II, and III' (*JPE*, 1908 and 1909), 'Study of the early history of child labor in America' (*American Journal of Sociology*, 1908) and 'Women and industry: the manufacture of boots and shoes' (*American Journal of Sociology*, 1909). Several of these articles formed the basis of chapters in *Women in Industry*. In 1911, she co-authored, with Breckinridge, 'Women in industry: the Chicago stockyards' (*JPE*, 1911) and two years later she published 'Women's wages in Chicago: some notes on available data' (*JPE*, 1913).

There are many and enduring contributions from this body of work. Abbott documented the work lives of seventeenth- and eighteenth-century American women, showing that the field of employment for women was broader than had generally been supposed, so much broader that she concluded that the rate of labour market participation of working-class women had remained substantially unchanged over the last century. Women had always dominated certain trades, such as spinning and weaving, and a significant result of the Industrial Revolution was not the advent of women's employment, but the movement of women's work out of the home into the factories. She traced this transformation for women from home manufacture to factory work and attributed it to the development of specialized machines and to the economies of scale and division of labour that followed mechanization. She discovered that, contrary to contemporary popular opinion, women were not displacing men in factories. She showed that women formed a smaller proportion of the total number of persons employed in manufacturing in 1900 then they had 50 years earlier. She attributed ongoing labour shifts and adjustments, not to a sort of Gresham's law in which cheap women's labour drove out men's, but instead to a complex mixture of supply and demand forces that varied from industry to industry. These included immigration, workplace monopolization by men's unions, and technological innovations that sometimes enabled women to do physical work previously too hard for them (for example, in boot- and shoe-making) or made jobs they had held too physically taxing for women (for example, in cotton mills). She compared women's wages to men's over time and found them very much lower but attributed this to the fact that women did more unskilled work then men, partly because of ability (not enough strength or endurance), partly because of restrictions (women had limited access to trade apprenticeships), and partly because of societal mores (some work was considered unsuitable for women, for example butchering).

After she graduated from the University of Chicago in 1905, Abbott moved to Boston to work for the Women's Trade Union League and as research assistant to labour economist Carroll Wright. Soon she earned full-time support from the Carnegie Institution for her work on women's industrial history. In 1906, the Carnegie Institution along with the Association of Collegiate Alumnae financed a year's study at the London School of Economics and Political Science. There she studied under Beatrice (*q.v.*) and Sidney Webb and developed an interest in British employment statistics and experiments with British poor relief. This new interest resulted in another research programme and a string of publications.

In 1907, Abbott published 'Municipal employment of unemployed women in London' (*JPE*), which discussed the effect on British women of artificial government work provided by the Unemployed Workman Act of 1905. In her 1913 *American Economic Review* article, 'Public pensions to widows with children', she applied the findings of the Royal Commission on the Poor Laws in England to a series of bills under consideration in the USA. She touted the potential benefits from a British minimum wage law in two 1915 articles, 'A forgotten minimum wage bill' (*Life and Labour*) and 'Progress of the minimum wage in England' (*JPE*). She investigated the effects of World War I on British employment, wages and poverty in a series of articles published in the *JPE* from 1917 to 1925 ('The war and women's work in England' (1917), 'The English Census of 1921' (1922), 'English statistics of pauperism during the war' (1925)). Her statistical documentation of the exodus from the workhouse and the disappearance of the pauper that occurred during the war was particularly noteworthy.

After her year studying in London, Abbott took a job teaching at Wellesley College. This was a plum academic job for a woman Ph.D. but did not satisfy Abbott, who longed to return to Chicago. She got her chance in 1908 when Sophinisba Breckinridge, then Director of Social Research at the independent Chicago School of Civics and Philanthropy, offered her a job teaching statistics in the Department of Social Investigation. (She also taught part-time at the University of Chicago beginning in 1913.)

When Abbott returned to Chicago, she moved into Hull House, where she lived until 1920. She had lived in settlements before, at Denison House in Boston and St Hilda's Settlement in London. Jane Addam's Hull House, with its thriving reform-minded resident community, was a mecca for educated women in the early twentieth century and had the added attraction for Abbott that her sister already lived there. Over the years, Grace and Edith Abbott would become well-known residents of Hull House: Grace for her social reform advocacy; Edith for her scholarship and strong commitment to statistical research.

Abbott's professional partnership with Breckinridge came to fruition during their years together at the School of Civics and Philanthropy. Both were keenly interested in careful statistical investigations of contemporary social problems as a precursor to reform advocacy. During the first 12 years of their collaboration at the Department of Social Investigation they jointly produced 'The housing problem in Chicago', ten articles in the *American Journal of Sociology* (1910–15) reporting the results of their major survey of tenement conditions in Chicago (a follow-up study, *The Tenements of Chicago, 1908–1935*, was published in 1936); *The Delinquent Child and the Home* (1912), a study of Chicago's juvenile court; and *Truancy and Non-Attendance in the Chicago Schools* (1917), an investigation which led them to support compulsory school attendance and child labour legislation.

Abbott was a prolific researcher and over the years published several books and scores of articles in both scholarly and popular journals on her ongoing research into a variety of social problems and her opinions on social welfare laws. Notable titles include *The Real Jail Problem* (1915); 'Crime and the war' and 'Recent statistics relating to crime in Chicago' (*Journal of the American Institute of Criminal Law and Criminology*, 1915 and 1922); 'Are women a force for good government?' (*National Municipal Review*, 1915); 'Statistics in Chicago suffrage' (*New Republic*, 1915), *The Administration of the Aid-to-Mothers Law in Illinois* (1921); Poor people in Chicago' (*New Republic*, 1932); and *Public Assistance* (1941).

Abbott also developed a national reputation as an educator after she and Breckinridge persuaded the University of Chicago to bring the underfunded Chicago School of Civics and Philanthropy under its auspices. In 1920, the University of Chicago's Board of Trustees voted to rename the School the University of Chicago Graduate School of Social Service Administration. It was the first graduate school of social work in the country affiliated with a major research university.

Abbott was hired as an Associate Professor of Social Economy, and as one of the driving forces behind the Graduate School she rose quickly in rank and was named Dean in 1924. Because of Abbott's and Breckinridge's training in economics and political science, they shared a vision of social work education that was unique at the time. Over the years, they fashioned a rigorous curriculum that played down the treatment and clinical side of social work. For them social work should rightly be considered a new field in the social sciences. Consequently, their curriculum placed a heavy emphasis on social statistics and on the historical, legal, economic and political underpinnings of social problems and public welfare efforts. In addition, they fought for the professional status of social work. In 1931, Abbott collected many of her papers, addresses and speeches on social service education into a single volume entitled *Social Welfare and Professional Education* (1931, revised and enlarged in 1942).

Abbott believed strongly that graduate students should have access to primary sources in their research and studies. Noting a particular difficulty in obtaining original documents on immigration issues, she set out to become an expert on contemporary and historical immigration documents and edited two important collections, *Immigration: Select Documents and Case Records* (1924) and *Historical Aspects of the Immigration Problem: Select Documents* (1926).

In 1927, Abbott and Breckinridge jointly established the distinguished academic journal, *Social Service Review*, published by the University of Chicago Press. The Review was dedicated 'to the scientific and professional interests of social work'. Abbott and Breckinridge were co-editors of the *Review* from 1927 to 1934, when Grace Abbott was named editor upon her resignation as Chief of the Children's Bureau. Edith Abbott resumed as editor after her sister's death in 1939. She retained the position until 1952.

Throughout the 25 years Edith Abbott was associated with the *Review* it provided a scholarly outlet not only for the research of the School's graduate students, but also for articles that were often multidisciplinary, historical or international in scope. The articles often took an activist position and the *Review* became known for its support of public welfare legislation and its bias against articles on psychiatric casework. Abbott wrote many articles for the *Review* that are representative of the *Review*'s content under her editorship. These include 'The Civil War and the crime wave of 1865–70' (1927), 'The Webbs and English poor law' (1929), 'Abolish the pauper laws' (1934), 'Evictions during the Chicago rent moratorium established by the relief agencies, 1931–35' (1935), 'Unemployment relief a federal responsibility' (1940), and 'Juvenile delinquency during the First World War: notes on the British experience, 1914–18' (1943). In addition, Abbott wrote a series of articles for the *Review* on her memories of Hull House, Jane Addams, her sister Grace, and Sophinisba Breckinridge (1939, 1948, 1950 and 1952).

Over her 40 years at the University of Chicago, Abbott became a university institution. Her retirement in 1953 marked the end of an era at its Graduate School of Social Service Administration. Her death in 1957 marked the passing of a certain type of professional woman economist who had flourished in the first part of the twentieth century. Abbott was typical of a small group of extremely talented American women who pursued their education in the first years after the opening of US colleges and universities to women. Abbott, like most of the early women who earned Ph.Ds in economics, was deeply interested in problems of social welfare. To her, poverty was 'the most intriguing and tormenting problem of political economy' ('The promise and practice of social legislation', p. 1) and its victims cried out for a cure. In this she was not unlike many male economists of the time. However, as economics developed into a professional discipline, social reform advocacy by economists lost its legitimacy within the profession. Abbott, and many other women economists, did not comply with the profession's growing trend away from reform activity. For them, social science and social reform advocacy could mix in a productive and professional way. Abbott's efforts at the School of Social Service Administration were an attempt to show that it could be done. In this she succeeded brilliantly. But she did not influence the economics profession in this direction. Abbott is remembered today as a labour economist and economic historian who turned away from economics to pursue an academic career in social work.

CLAIRE HOLTON HAMMOND

Bibliography

Selected writings by Edith Abbott

(1904), 'Wage statistics in the twelfth census', *Journal of Political Economy*, **12**, June, 339–61.

(1905), 'Wages of unskilled labor in the United States, 1850–1900', *Journal of Political Economy*, **13**, June, 321–67. (Ph.D. dissertation.)

(1906), 'Employment of women in industry: twelfth census statistics', *Journal of Political Economy*, **14**, January, 14–40.

(1906), 'The history of industrial employment of women in the United States: an introductory study', *Journal of Political Economy*, **14**, October, 461–501.

(1906), 'Harriet Martineau and the employment of women in 1836', *Journal of Political Economy*, **14**, December, 614–26.

(1907), 'Employment of women in industries: cigar-making – its history and present tendencies', *Journal of Political Economy*, **15**, January, 1–25.

(1907), 'Municipal employment of unemployed women in London', *Journal of Political Economy*, **15**, November, 513–30.

(1907), 'Women in manufactures: a supplementary note', *Journal of Political Economy*, **15**, December, 619–24.

(1908), 'Study of the early history of child labor in America', *American Journal of Sociology*, **14**, July, 15–37.

(1908), 'Employment of women in cotton mills', *Journal of Political Economy*, **16**, November, 602–21.

(1908), 'History of the employment of women in the American cotton mills, Part II: Early mill operatives, conditions of life and work', *Journal of Political Economy*, **16**, December, 680–92.

(1909), 'History of the employment of women in the American cotton mills, Part III: Early mill operatives, the period of transition', *Journal of Political Economy*, **17**, January, 15–37.

(1909), 'Women in industry: the manufacture of boots and shoes', *American Journal of Sociology*, **15**, November, 335–60.

(1910, rev. 1919), *Women in Industry: A Study in American Economic History*, New York: D. Appleton Co. 1919.

(1910–1915), 'The housing problem in Chicago', Ten articles in *American Journal of Sociology*, **16–21**.

(1911), 'English poor-law reform', *Journal of Political Economy*, **19**, January, 47–59.

(1911), 'Women in industry: the Chicago stockyards', *Journal of Political Economy*, **19**, October, 632–54.

(1913), 'Women's wages in Chicago: some notes on available data', *Journal of Political Economy*, **21**, February, 143–58.

(1913), 'Public pensions to widows and children', *American Economic Review*, **3**, June, 473–8.

(1915), 'A forgotten minimum wage bill', *Life and Labor*, **5**, January, 13–16.

(1915), 'Progress of the minimum wage in England', *Journal of Political Economy*, **23**, March, 268–77.

(1915), *The Real Jail Problem*, Chicago: Juvenile Protective Association.

(1915), 'Are women a force for good government?', *National Municipal Review*, **4**, 437–47.

(1915), 'Statistics in Chicago suffrage', *New Republic*, **3**, 12 June, 151.

(1917), 'Charles Booth, 1840–1916', *Journal of Political Economy*, **25**, February, 195–200.

(1917), *Truancy and Non-Attendance in the Chicago Schools: A Study of the Social Aspects of the Compulsory Education and Child Labor Legislation of Illinois*, Chicago: University of Chicago Press.

(1917), 'The war and women's work in England', *Journal of Political Economy*, **25**, July, 641–78.

(1918), 'Crime and the war', *Journal of the American Institute of Criminal Law and Criminology*, **9**, May, 32–45.

(1921), *The Administration of the Aid-to-Mothers Law in Illinois* (Children's Bureau Publication no. 82), Washington, DC: Government Printing Office.

(1922), 'Recent statistics relating to crime in Chicago', *Journal of the American Institute of Criminal Law and Criminology*, **13**, November, 329–58.

(1922), 'The English Census of 1921', *Journal of Political Economy*, **30**, December, 827–40.

(1924), *Immigration: Select Documents and Case Records* (Social Service Series), Chicago: University of Chicago Press.

(1925), 'English statistics of pauperism during the War', *Journal of Political Economy*, **33**, February, 1–32.

(1926), *Historical Aspects of the Immigration Problem: Select Documents* (Social Service Series), Chicago: University of Chicago Press.

(1927), 'The Civil War and the crime wave of 1865–70', *Social Service Review*, **I**, June, 212–34.

(1929), 'The Webbs on the English poor law', *Social Service Review*, **3**, June, 252–69.

(1931, rev. and enl., 1942), *Social Welfare and Professional Education*, Chicago: University of Chicago Press.

(1932), 'Poor people in Chicago', *New Republic*, **72**, 5 October, 209.

(1932), 'Fallacy of local relief', *New Republic*, **72**, 9 November, 348–50.

(1934), 'Abolish the pauper laws', *Social Service Review*, **8**, March, 1–16.

(1935), 'Evictions during the Chicago rent moratorium established by the relief agencies, 1931–33', *Social Service Review*, **9**, March, 34–57.

(1936), *The Tenements of Chicago 1908–1935* (University of Chicago Social Service Monographs), Chicago: University of Chicago Press.

(1939), 'Grace Abbott: a sister's memories', *Social Service Review*, **13**, September, 351–408.

(1940), 'Unemployment relief a federal responsibility', *Social Service Review*, **14**, September, 438–52.

(1941), *Public Assistance*, Chicago: University of Chicago Press.

(1943), 'Juvenile delinquency during the First World War: notes on the British experience, 1914–18', *Social Service Review*, **27**, June, 192–212.

(1948), 'Sophonisba P. Breckinridge: over the years', *Social Service Review*, **23**, December, 417–23.

(1950), 'Grace Abbott and Hull House, 1908–21', *Social Service Review*, **24**, September and December, 374–94 and 493–518.

(1952), 'The Hull House of Jane Addams', *Social Service Review*, **26**, September, 334–8.

(n.d.), 'The promise and practice of social legislation', speech to the University of Chicago Alumni Association, box 5, folder 2, The Papers of Edith and Grace Abbott.

Other sources and references
The Papers of Edith and Grace Abbott, The University of Chicago Archives.

Costin, Lela B. (1971), 'Abbott, Edith', in Edward T. James (ed.), *Notable American Women 1607–1950: A Biographical Dictionary*, Cambridge: Harvard University Press, pp. 1–3.
Costin, Lela B. (1983), *Two Sisters for Social Justice: A Biography of Grace and Edith Abbott*, Urbana: University of Illinois Press.
Diner, Steven J. (1977), 'Scholarship in the quest for social welfare: a fifty-year history of the *Social Service Review*', *Social Service Review*, March, 1–66.
Fitzpatrick, Ellen (1990), *Endless Crusade: Women Social Scientists and Progressive Reform*, New York: Oxford University Press.
Kerr, P. (1987), 'Abbott, Edith', in John Eatwell, Murray Milgate and Peter Newman (eds), *The New Palgrave: A Dictionary of Economics*, Vol. 1, London: Macmillan, p. 1.
Marks, Rachel (1958), 'The published writings of Edith Abbott: A bibliography', *Social Service Review*, March, 51–6.
Muncy, Robyn (1990), 'Gender and professionalization in the origins of the U.S. welfare state: the careers of Sophonisba Breckinridge and Edith Abbott, 1890–1935', *Journal of Policy History*, 2(3), 290–315.

Ruth Alice Allen (1889–1979)

Born in Cameron, Texas in 1889, Ruth Alice Allen was a life-long Texan. She received her BA in 1921 and her MA in 1923, both from the University of Texas at Austin, before going to the University of Chicago for her Ph.D. degree. At the University of Chicago her adviser was H.A. Millis, and her committee included Frank Knight, the distinguished labour economist (and later US Senator) Paul Douglas, and Lloyd Mints. After receiving her Ph.D. Allen returned to the University of Texas, where she taught until her retirement in 1959.

During her tenure at Texas, Allen served for a short stint as department chair (1942–43) and a longer term, encompassing most of the 1940s and 1950s, as the department's graduate adviser. Her devotion to education and her concern for racial equality is evidenced by the fact that she spent six years of her retirement at Huston-Tillotson College, a predominantly black school in Texas, in order to preserve its accreditation. In 1968, at the age of 79, Allen began her final retirement; in 1979 she died at the age of 90. Upon her death, the University of Texas faculty passed a memorial resolution noting that Allen 'made her way to the professorship in times when this was close to impossible for a woman'.[1] In the process, Ruth Allen undoubtedly helped break down some of the barriers to women who followed her into the profession.

In addition to her contribution as a role model for women economists, Allen offered what was probably one of the first courses in the country that examined the economic position of women, entitled 'The Economic Status of Women'. Her interest in this topic went back even further, at least to her dissertation, *The Labor of Women in the Production of Cotton* (1933). This work, later published as a monograph, utilizes a socioeconomic approach that methodologically fits in with the institutionalist tradition of labour studies as pioneered by John R. Commons. In this work, Allen investigated the role of farm women's labour in the production of cotton and its implications for the price of cotton and the living standards of cotton-farming families. Allen's method of inquiry was a survey of women in farm households in Texas. She designed the questionnaire herself and conducted the majority of the interviews personally; this allowed Allen to compile not just impersonal data, but also her own observations and reactions to the women she met and to the conditions of their lives and work.

Allen's research work led her to the conclusion that the type of work done by farm women (for example, field work in cotton production versus non-field work in the home) was influenced more by tradition and custom than by economic costs and benefits. Allen found that tradition led women to provide unpaid field labour in cotton production, and that this process depressed the wages of paid farm workers and led to overproduction of cotton, which kept the price of cotton artificially low and perpetuated depressed farm incomes. Allen's recommended solution was the expansion of the wage system to include farm women's labour; this would create value for their work as well as make the price of cotton a more accurate reflection of the true costs of production, which would enhance farm incomes.

The Labor of Women in the Production of Cotton, like Allen's subsequent works, is characterized by a wealth of extremely detailed information peppered with her insights, which were often more sociological than strictly economic. One of the themes of the work is the effect of economic change on the lives of the women in the study; for example, Allen predicts that the growth of the urban population will draw girls and women into the city to work in factories, and she points out that knowledge of their backgrounds would provide some understanding of 'the place women will fill as workers and as bargainers in the new system' (Allen, 1933, p. 14).

Ruth Allen was at the University of Texas Department of Economics at a time when it was one of the USA's leading centres of institutionalism. With her empirical, fact-based methodology Ruth Allen presumably fitted in quite well. Additionally, Allen shared the institutionalists' view of work as a normal human drive, in Allen's words a 'personal assertion' (Allen, 1933, p. 94), that is clearly at odds with the mainstream view of work as an inherently distasteful activity. In this, as in Allen's later studies, the neoclassical theory of wage determination is nowhere to be found. By looking at the social relations of production she goes beyond the neoclassical to explain the allocation of women's labour to field work.

Apart from *The Labor of Women in the Production of Cotton*, *East Texas Lumber Workers* (1961) is Allen's most original and important work. The book's subtitle, 'An Economic and Social Picture, 1870–1950', aptly describes this work. Again Allen displayed her talent for amassing copious quantities of information, this time in the process of thoroughly illuminating the economic conditions of the Texan lumber country. Again her approach was eclectic and fundamentally institutionalist in that she viewed the people's physical, social and economic environment as the most important influence on their behaviour.

Ruth Allen's other works have been less influential. *Chapters in the History of Organized Labor in Texas*, a University of Texas monograph published in 1941, is merely a collection of archival information amassed from court records, newspaper articles, library archives and so on, pertaining to the labour history of Texas. Allen apparently intended this as a record to be used for other research projects. Similarly, her 1942 monograph *The Great Southwest Strike* is a historical account of a famous rail strike that rocked the region in 1886. Allen again displayed her ability to present large amounts of information coherently and, in this case, to organize it into a surprisingly compelling story. This work also demonstrates Allen's support for organized labour and her general advocacy for labour, which again places her in accord with the traditional institutionalist affinity for productive effort.

Allen's ten entries in the *Handbook of Texas*, published in 1952, reflect her interest in labour issues in Texas specifically and the southwest generally, and again seem intended to provide archival information for later scholars.

Allen's achievements as a woman in academia – long service as a professor and graduate adviser at a major economics programme – were remarkable for her time. Her teaching of a course on the role of women in the economy similarly placed her ahead of her time. Her research continues to resonate with modern scholars. As feminist scholarship has expanded in recent years it is not surprising that Allen's pioneering work on women should be rediscovered. *The Labor of Women in the Production of Cotton* has been referenced in several recent works on home production.[2] Looking to the broader influences of Ruth Allen's work, we can discern two distinct themes: her analysis of family and gender relations *vis-à-vis* labour markets, and her efforts to leave a historical record of issues pertaining to the southwest's labour history. In the first case, Allen's work qualifies her as one of the first, along with women like Margaret Reid (*q.v.*) and Charlotte Gilman Perkins (*q.v.*), to place women's production at the centre of economic analysis. In the second case, Allen's rather unglamorous and painstaking compilation of historical information, while not containing much analytical insight, has preserved an important record of the southwest's labour history from which researchers can continue to draw today.

ALEXANDRA BERNASEK
DOUGLAS KINNEAR

Notes

1. Gordon, Wendell, Forest Hill and C. Patton Blair, 'In Memorium: Ruth Alice Allen', *Documents and Minutes of the General Faculty*, University of Texas at Austin, 1980.
2. See for example Joan M. Jensen, 'Cloth, Butter, and Boarders: Women's Household Production for the Market', *Review of Radical Political Economics*, vol. 12, no. 2 (1980); Susan A. Mann, 'Slavery, Sharecropping, and Sexual Inequality', *Signs*, vol. 14, no. 4 (1989); and Carolyn E. Sachs, *The Invisible Farmers: Women in Agricultural Production* (1983). Additionally, Allen has also been referenced recently for her historical/archival work particularly *East Texas Lumber Workers* and *The Great Southwest Strike*.

Selected writings by Ruth Alice Allen

(1933; repr. 1975), *The Labor of Women in the Production of Cotton*, New York: Arno Press (reprint of Allen's 1933 doctoral dissertation).
(1941), *Chapters in the History of Organized Labor in Texas*, Austin: The University of Texas Publication, 15 November.
(1942), The Great Southwest Strike, Austin: The University of Texas Publication, 8 April.
(1961), *East Texas Lumber Workers: An Economic and Social Picture, 1870–1950*, Austin: University of Texas Press.

Shirley Ann Montag Almon (1935–75)[1]

The pioneer of the applied econometric technique known as the 'Almon distributed lag' was born on 6 February 1935 and died on 27 September 1975. Born in Saxonburg, Pennsylvania, to Harold and Dorothea Pflueger Montag, Shirley Almon graduated from Goucher College, Baltimore in 1956 and from Harvard University in 1964 with a Ph.D. in economics. Her first appointment was teaching at both Harvard and Wellesley College as an instructor from 1964 to 1966. She subsequently moved to the Council of Economic Advisors when her husband, Clopper Almon, Jr received an appointment at the University of Maryland–College Park. She died in 1975 from a brain tumour that was discovered in 1967 and that left her paralysed before her death.

Her Ph.D. thesis (1964) provides the basis for her two sole published works: 'The distributed lag between capital appropriations and expenditures' (1965) and 'Lags between investment decisions and their causes' (1968). The first article introduces the Almon distributed lag and applies it to predicting future capital investments by firms, while the second investigates the determinants of investment decisions. The economics literature largely passed over these empirical investigations of the determinants of investment. However, the econometrics in both articles helped to stimulate a reinvestigation of lag operators in econometrics. And her work provided an early example of data-determined estimation techniques which are now becoming more popular.

Almon (1965) and (1968) applied the econometric technique developed in Almon (1964). Neither of the applications to investment is embedded in a formal economic model, but instead uses either an atheoretical description of the data (1965) or a simple accelerator model of investment decisions (1968). In modelling the timing of investment decisions by firms, Almon (1965) decomposes the effect of expenditures on future appropriations and finds that the effect is strongest several quarters in the past. In Almon (1968), cash flow was the only variate which affected decisions over several quarters, indicating that retained earnings were the most important sources of investment, and not the capital markets. Even though the within-sample fits of the model were very good, Almon (1968) did not contain comparisons between the proposed model and other competing explanations for investment, and no out-of-sample forecasting was done. In Jorgenson (1971) such comparisons indicate that the Almon distributed lag models did not compete well against other neoclassical explanations such as the Modigliani–Miller theory of investment.

In contrast, the econometric technique in her dissertation received immediate acceptance by the econometric community, so much so that by 1973 two econometricians had to note with caution that the 'technique has caught on amongst empirical investigators to such an extent that it appears on the verge of being used with the same unquestioning reverence as the five percent significance level, or the assumption of normality' (Schmidt and Waud, 1973: 11). Ten years after this, *Econometrica* researchers had cited the 1965 article over 180 times. By 1991, more than 370 citations appeared in the economics, sociology, and political science literature – as well as in the sciences. Numerous authors described the estimation of the lag structure and refined the estimation technique so that researchers could correctly specify and easily estimate the model.[2]

The Almon distributed lag starts with the assumption that many commonly observed economic variables can be represented with a distributed lag; that is, it is possible to think of an economic time series as a function not only of current variables, but past ones as well. An autoregression is an example of a series which is a function of lagged values of itself. More complex models represented series such as investment through four to eight quarters' lagged variates of debt, retained earnings, interest rates or other variables.

While the distributed lag representation had theoretical support, data limitations prevented effective practical implementation of many lag models. The distributed lag representation was popular in the 1950s and 1960s as several prominent economists advocated such models (Eisner, 1960; Koyck, 1954; Solow, 1960) as natural representations of such adjustment models as the accelerator theory of investment. All these models shared the assumption of relatively long distributed lags, resulting in low degrees of freedom because of limited data. Further, the distributed lag parameters were non-linear functions of the data, so computing power often limited estimation as well. As many macroeconomic variables are highly correlated with their past observations, collinearity often plagued the macroeconomic implementation of distributed lag models. These caveats left researchers unable to estimate models efficiently with theoretical support because of econometric or computational limitations.

Almon (1965) proposes a method which assumes that the weights of the distributed lag function lie on a Lagrangian interpolation polynomial. That is, the weights of a distributed lag are some function of the coefficients on a low-degree-approximating polynomial. This assumption allows estimation of a model with eight or nine lags using a two- or three-degree polynomial. With one third or one half the number of parameters, a researcher could focus attention on a more richly specified economic model. The technique was a success with the applied econometric community for its ease of estimation and parsimonious representation of the data. It was possible to estimate the parameters in the distributed lag through ordinary least squares, and then through a simple analytical transformation. A commonly cited reference in Kmenta (1971; 492–3) provides a clear exposition of how to estimate the parameters in her distributed lag model.

In the original work, Almon (1965) assumes that it would be possible for the polynomial approximation to be approximate. However, later researchers demonstrate that this is not correct. A desirable feature of the Almon distributed lag estimator is that it always has lower variance than the least squares estimator. However, if the weights of the distributed lag do not lie on the polynomial, then the estimators are biased and inconsistent. Teräsvirta (1976) and Schmidt and Sickles (1975) derive this bias.

While it is true that the bias is not severe when the distributed lag weights are approximately on a polynomial, researchers need to specify the length of the distributed lag and the polynomial degree in an Almon lag model. By requiring both specifications there are now three avenues open for misspecification: the length of the distributed lag, the degree of the interpolation polynomial, and whether there is a distributed lag.

Godfrey and Poskitt (1970) and Teräsvirta (1976) provide statistical tests to determine both the lag length and polynomial degree. In most distributed lag models it is possible to nest this test in a null hypothesis of no distributed lag versus an alternative of a distributed lag. Such a nesting is impossible with the Almon lag as, if one wants to estimate a one-degree or higher polynomial, one needs the lag length to be at least one.

Proper specification is important, as Schmidt and Waud (1973) demonstrate in investigating two attempts at answering the debate about the efficacy of monetary versus fiscal policy. Andersen and Jordan (1968) use the Almon lag to claim that fiscal policy is nearly ineffectual, and monetary policy provides the only lasting impact on the economy. In a rejoinder Corrigan (1970) uses an alternative specification to the Almon lag on different data to arrive at the opposite conclusion. Schmidt and Waud resolve this debate and demonstrate that both papers are sensitive to the assumptions about the lag length and polynomial degree. Simple changes to either the degree of the polynomial or lag length can lead to a reversal of the conclusions in either paper.

However, since there are statistical tests to test for the appropriate lag length and polynomial degree, one could still use the Almon distributed lag with an appropriate search algorithm if it were not for the undesirable statistical properties of coefficients estimated using a search routine. Frost (1975) investigates their properties and finds that they have a non-normal distribution and serious biases. Hence the conventional test statistics do not have the standard distributions, and hypothesis tests based on these test statistics will not be valid.

Because of these problems with the Almon lag procedure, applied econometricians relied on the technique with less frequency so that, by the 1980s, few researchers were using the Almon distributed lag in empirical macroeconomics. The data limitations which motivate Almon (1965) no longer apply as often. However, the technique's ease of estimation still draws people to its use, and several articles every year appear using it or citing it as the basis for future work. Further, the Almon distributed lag estimator receives theoretical support for its use, as Shiller (1971) demonstrates that this estimator is a special case of a Bayesian distributed lag estimator which attempts to incorporate a researcher's prior beliefs about the degree of smoothness in the distributed lag. If the variance of the prior distribution approaches zero, the Bayesian estimator becomes the Almon distributed lag estimator. So the estimator is a limiting case where the researcher believes in the absolute smoothness of the distributed lag.

As not all distributed lag estimators are a special case of this Bayesian estimator, the Almon lag estimator deserves special attention. More importantly, the estimation routine in Shiller (1971) contains a suggestion for using the data to determine the degree of smoothing – removing the arbitrariness of previous applications of the Almon distributed lag estimator. And in a survey article Sims (1974) recommends a modification of the Shiller approach to provide a Bayesian analysis of multicollinearity.

While no longer commonly used, the Almon distributed lag estimator helped to simulate a full analysis of distributed lag models in later work. As distributed lag models are a generalization of autoregressions, these models were the early attempts by investigators to summarize the data efficiently, much as vector autoregressions are a natural implement in the toolkit of applied macroeconomists. And as witnessed by its immediate acceptance, this estimation routine demonstrates how applied researchers appreciate simple estimation techniques of complex models.

CHRISTOPHER MCDONOUGH-DUMLER

Notes

1. Many thanks to Peter C.B. Phillips for his suggestions and comments on the historical link between the smoothness priors and the Almon distributed lag.
2. The total numbers of citations come from the *Social Science Citation Index*, various years.

Bibliography

Selected writings by Shirley Almon

(1964), 'The distributed lag between capital appropriations and expenditures', Ph.D. dissertation, Cambridge: Harvard University.
(1965), 'The distributed lag between capital appropriations and expenditures', *Econometrica*, **33**(1), January, 178–96.
(1968), 'Lags between investment decisions and their causes', *The Review of Economics and Statistics*, **50**, May, 193–206.

Other sources and references

Andersen, L.C. and J.L. Jordan (1968), 'Monetary and fiscal actions: a test of their relative importance in economic stabilization', *Review of the Federal Reserve Bank of St. Louis*, November, 11–24.
Corrigan, E.G. (1970), 'The measurement and importance of fiscal policy changes', *Monthly Review, Federal Reserve Bank of New York*, June, 133–45.
Eisner, Robert (1960), 'A distributed lag investment function', *Econometrica*, **28**, 1–29.
Frost, Peter A. (1975), 'Some properties of the Almon lag technique when one searches for degree of polynomial and lag', *Journal of the American Statistical Association*, **70**(351): 606–12.
Godfrey, L.G. and D.S. Poskitt (1970), 'Testing the restrictions of the Almon lag technique', *Journal of the American Statistical Association*, **70**, March, 105–8.
Jorgenson, Dale W. (1971), 'Econometric studies of investment behavior: A survey', *Econometrica*, **9**(4), December, 1111–47.
Kmenta, Jan (1971), *Elements of Econometrics*, New York: Macmillan.
Koyck, L.M. (1954), *Distributed Lags and Investment Analysis*, Amsterdam: North-Holland Publishing Company.
Schmidt, Peter and Robin Sickles (1975), 'On the efficiency of the Almon lag technique', *International Economic Review*, **16**(3), October, 792–5.
Schmidt, Peter and Roger N. Waud (1973), 'The Almon lag technique and the monetary versus fiscal policy debate', *Journal of the American Statistical Association*, **68** (341), March, 11–19.
Shiller, Robert J. (1971), 'A distributed lag estimator derived from smoothness priors', *Econometrica*, **41**(4), July, 775–88.
Sims, Christopher A. (1974), 'Distributed lags', in Michael D. Intriligator and David A. Kendrick (eds), *Frontiers of Modern Quantitative Economics, Vol. 2*, Amsterdam: North- Holland Publishing Company.
Solow, Robert M. (1960), 'On a family of lag distributions', *Econometrica*, **28**, 393–406.
Teräsvirta, Timo (1976), 'A note on the bias in the Almon distributed lag estimator', *Econometrica*, **44**(6), November, 1317–21.

Elizabeth Faulkner Baker (1885–1973)

Brief overview of Baker's life

Elizabeth Faulkner Baker was born in Abilene, Kansas on 10 December 1885 and died in Seattle, Washington, on 30 January 1973. Baker received a bachelor of laws degree (major in English) from the University of California in 1917. She went on to receive a master's degree in economics from Columbia University in 1919 and a doctorate in economics from the same university in 1925. In addition to her four main publications, which are briefly considered below, Baker had numerous articles and book reviews published in academic and professional journals, including the *American Economic Review, Industrial and Labor Relations Review* and *Annals of the American Academy*.

Before undertaking graduate studies, Baker was Dean of Women and Instructor in Economics at Lewiston State Normal School in Idaho (1915–17) and subsequently Dean of Women at Ellensberg State Normal School in Washington State (1917–18). From Ellensberg she went on to Barnard College where she took up the position of Instructor in Economics, where she served from 1919 to 1926. She was promoted to Assistant Professor of Economics at Barnard College in 1926 and stayed in that position until 1939 when she was made Associate Professor of Economics. In 1948 Baker was appointed Professor of Economics at Barnard where she remained until her retirement in 1952, serving as Chair of the Department of Economics from 1940 through 1952.

Elizabeth Baker also led an active life outside the walls of the academy. During World War II she was Hearing Officer and Panel Chairman representing the public, National War Labor Board, Region II (New York). In the late 1920s she joined the Taylor Society, an international body for the promotion of the science and art of administration and management that was deeply committed to the diffusion and development of the management principles pioneered by Frederick Winslow Taylor. In 1935 the Society was renamed the Society for the Advancement of Management, and Baker served as Director of its New York section (the country's largest) from 1944 to 1946. That she became Director of the New York section suggests that her involvement in the Taylor Society was not only of long standing but also active and enthusiastic. She was attracted by the conviction, central to the Taylorists' programme and activities, that friendly cooperation between workers and managers was possible and desirable and that organized labour could play a positive role in the management of industrial and commercial enterprises – a sentiment that found eloquent expression in several of her major publications (Nyland, 1996, 1998).

Besides her active involvement in the scientific management movement, Baker was a member of the American Economic Association, the Industrial

16

Relations Research Association, the National Planning Association and a participating member of the Labor Discussion Group, a body composed of teachers of industrial relations who worked in and around New York. According to the 1950–51 edition of *Who's Who in America*, Elizabeth Baker was a Democrat.

Major works

Baker's doctoral thesis was on protective labour legislation with special reference to the experience of women in the state of New York. It was published by Columbia University Press in 1925 as part of its 'Studies in History, Economics and Public Law' series (and republished by AMS Press in 1969). Titled *Protective Labor Legislation, with Special Reference to Women in the State of New York*, the book was published at a time when the women's movement was deeply divided over this issue. Baker began with an examination of the scope of protective labour legislation as applied to both men and women in the USA. As part of this examination, the constitutionality of specific legislation as tested by the US Courts was considered. The book then proceeded to examine the growth of protective legislation for men and women in New York as a prelude to an analysis of special legislation for women in that state. Particular attention was paid to the influences that prompted the enactment of special legislation, the history of enforcement and the effects of such legislation on the women the sale of whose labour it was designed to regulate. The book ended with a review of the arguments both of those who supported labour laws that limited what employers could demand of their women employees and those who opposed special legislation on the grounds that it was prejudicial to women's interests and who insisted they should have no more assistance from the state than that available to men.

From this review Baker concluded that working women were advantaged by the existing sex-specific laws even if such laws meant that a small minority of women suffered disadvantage. She believed that both men and women should be free to work in any occupation they chose, but that a raft of progressive legislation was needed to protect the most helpless and vulnerable workers, with these laws applying to both sexes wherever possible. At the same time her commitment to the methodology advocated by the scientific management movement, which emphasized detailed and case-specific analysis rather than a wide-sweeping universalism and/or singular emphasis on deduction, led her to concede that in some instances a case existed for sex-specific labour laws. Thus she observed that while generally there was no reason to distinguish between men and women workers when formulating labour law, where scientific analysis could prove that one particular sex was especially disadvantaged and could be assisted by laws peculiar to that sex, then such laws should be enacted. As regretful as was the fact that some women might be disadvantaged by such laws, failure to do otherwise would be at the expense of the overwhelming majority of working women and hence of social as well as economic progress.

Baker also urged the need to strengthen the bargaining power of men and women workers and encouraged women to organize more vigorously and extensively than they had done in the past. She called for the advancement of intelligent women into skilled trades, and for a comprehensive system of health insurance. To take any other action than the whole range of measures that she advocated, Baker urged, would be 'fraught with the danger of restriction instead of protection'.

Published in 1933, that is in the depth of the Depression, Baker's second book also dealt with a highly controversial topic, that of technological unemployment. *Displacement of Men by Machines: Effects of Technological Change in Commercial Printing* reported the findings of a study conducted into commercial printing in New York and Chicago over a five-year period ending in winter 1929. It was republished by Arno Press in 1977 as part of its 'Work: Its Rewards and Discontents' series.

The study had begun with the aim of tracing the economic and social fate of manual press-feeders who had been displaced by mechanical feeders. In the process of technical change in the pressroom, manual feeding of the presses was transformed into a relatively low-skilled occupation. Perhaps the most important finding of the study was that, far from displacing skill, improved pressroom techniques in fact stimulated an increase in demand for skilled labour and the displacement of unskilled and semi-skilled workers. This left unanswered the question of what had become of the displaced manual feeders. In seeking answers to this question, Baker concluded that the unemployment which plagued the industry was not simply the inevitable result of technological change. She dispensed with the notion of 'technological unemployment' and coined the phrase 'technocultural unemployment' in recognition of the fact that the displacement of workers was as much a cultural, sociological and economic phenomenon as an effect of technical advance. In particular, she pointed to problems of management and union leadership, especially lack of sufficient foresight on the part of both, to help explain the difficulties experienced by industry and personnel in adjusting to the introduction of new machines and techniques.

In summing up the findings of the study of technological change in the commercial printing industry, she astutely observed:

> If this investigation of a specific branch of industry teaches any lesson it is this: Until we devise a method of absorbing displaced workers in self-respecting occupations without serious or protracted periods of unemployment, we cannot speak of social progress and the substitution of men by machines in the same breath. As productivity increases it is becoming more glaringly evident that cultural services

are as badly needed as material goods, and that judgment and foresight, informed by the mistakes and omissions of the past, are imperatively required in solving the problems presented by each new technical advance.

Baker's interest in the labour market consequences of technological change was carried over into her next major work, *Printers and Technology: A History of the International Printing Pressmen and Assistants' Union*, published by Columbia University Press in 1957. In the Foreword, Baker noted that the book was a documentary account of the emergence and development of the Pressmen's Union which traced the Union's adaptations to new machines and changing techniques. The account paid close attention to the Union's evolving relations with employers and other unions and to the attempts by unions outside the commercial printing industry to poach its members. Of most interest were the changing demands of the Union's membership, which was composed of a greater diversity of crafts than any other printing union. This diversity demanded great adaptability and flexibility from the Union in responding to the introduction of new technology. On this score, Baker concluded that the history of the International Printing Pressmen and Assistants' Union had shown it to be an 'alert and socially minded organization' which had been disciplined by rapidly changing economic and technical circumstances to assume responsibility not only to its membership but also to the printing employer for their continued welfare and prosperity. Adaptability to the introduction of new machines and techniques came with rewards *and* penalties, but the Union had demonstrated that it was capable of taking the good with the bad, thus exhibiting 'how usefully American trade unionism can work'.

Baker's final major work brought together her long-established interest in the place of women in industry and concern with the effects of technological change. Titled *Technology and Women's Work*, and published by Columbia University Press in 1964, the book presented a comprehensive account of how technological advances, ranging from the steam engine to automation and computers, had altered the working and domestic lives of American women. In presenting this account, Baker considered the transition from home to workplace and paid work which many women had experienced over the previous 160 years.

Standardization, mechanization and the development of scientific management practices had opened many occupations to women and girls. In a great many cases their opportunities were confined to the performance of repetitive tasks which required little training, but these influences also generated a wide range of new occupations which required relatively high levels of education, training and skill. A junior high-school education was the generally accepted standard of attainment for filers, multigraph operators, and bill stock, payroll and mail clerks. Senior high-school education was the norm for stenographers, dictating-machine operators, bookkeepers and bookkeeping-machine operators. The secretarial stenographer usually had a college diploma. On the other hand, while the introduction of bookkeeping and billing machines had led to the displacement of men by women, managerial and administrative positions were still usually reserved for men.

In *Technology and Women's Work*, Baker never lost sight of the fact that for many women the transition from home to work was only partial in the sense that they were generally unable to divest themselves entirely of domestic and family responsibilities. Indeed, the constraints imposed by domestic responsibilities forced many women to accept part-time or casual employment. For many others who made the transition, the 'traditional' women's professions of schoolteaching, nursing, office work and sales assistant were all that were on offer or could realistically be aspired to. Often, women's secondary and post-school education prepared them for this limited range of occupations. Moreover, in the expectation that in a relatively short time after taking up a job they would leave work to have a family, many young women who did secure full-time employment failed to be appointed to the higher positions or receive the more advanced training available to their male colleagues of a similar standing.

While the book focused on the consequences of technological and scientific development, it also looked at the far-reaching impact of the 'driving forces' of war and improved educational opportunities on women's work-force participation. In the two world wars, women proved that they were often as capable as men of doing 'men's jobs' in the office and factory. This was particularly true of those jobs that required high levels of dexterity, skill and education, but entrenched attitudes and prejudices quickly rose to the surface again during peacetime, pushing women back into their traditional occupations. Nevertheless, World War II, in particular, had brought about 'great technological changes' which called for 'more brain power, more scientific training, more engineers'. Traditional myths about women and their capabilities largely evaporated in the face of the demands and pressures occasioned by these changes. The war, in short, had acted as a catalyst accelerating the positive effect that technological development was having on the nature of women's work. Thus while many obstacles and prejudices remained to be overcome,

> [a] multitude of women have nevertheless made their mark in the professions and arts – as teachers, nurses, social workers, entertainers. Without sacrificing femininity they were everywhere in the office, at the switchboard, behind the counter, some in highly responsible and well-paid positions. More women are entering the field of science, and now we have witnessed a Russian woman astronaut orbiting the globe 42 times. Coeducation in America has gained almost complete public acceptance; and in many directions the sex line is blurred.

Baker's studies of protective labour legislation, the challenge to organized labour presented to technological change in the workplace, and women in industry demonstrated a strong conviction that economics must be relevant and useful in the analysis of social, political and industrial problems. However, they also reveal that she was convinced that to be relevant and useful, economics needed to develop methods and practices which were holistic and that brought together analysis of factor markets, culture studies, management and industrial relations. An approach to social research and analysis which combined insights and perspectives drawn from these fields would preserve the requisite checks and balances between theory and *praxis* and ensure that economic analysis kept its feet on the ground.

CHRIS NYLAND
MARK RIX

Bibliography

Selected writings by Elizabeth Faulkner Baker

(1925), *Protective Labor Legislation with Special Reference to Women in the State of New York*, New York: Columbia University Press (AMS Press, 1969).

(1933), *Displacement of Men by Machines*, New York: Columbia University Press (Arno Press, 1977).

(1957), *Printers and Technology: A History of the International Printing Pressmen and Assistants' Union*, New York: Columbia University Press.

(1964), *Technology and Women's Work*, New York: Columbia University Press.

Other sources and references

Nyland, Chris (1996), 'Taylorism, John R. Commons, and the Hoxie Report', *Journal of Economic Issues*, **30**(4) December, 985–1016.

Nyland, Chris (1998), 'Taylorism and mutual gains', *Industrial Relations*, **37**(4): 519–42.

Who's Who in America: A Biographical Dictionary of Notable Living Men and Women 1950–1951, Chicago: The A.N. Marquis Company.

Emily Greene Balch (1867–1961)

Emily Greene Balch, co-winner of the 1946 Nobel Peace Prize, was born in Jamaica Plain, Massachusetts, on 8 January 1867, the second of six surviving children of Francis Vergnies Balch, a lawyer who had been secretary to the abolitionist Senator Charles Sumner, and of Ellen Maria Noyes Balch, a former schoolteacher. Emily entered Bryn Mawr College in 1886, earning her AB in 1889 with Bryn Mawr's first graduating class. As the first winner of the Bryn Mawr Fellowship for European Study, she spent 1890–91 at the Sorbonne, researching her monograph on *Public Assistance of the Poor in France*, which was published by the American Economic Association in 1893. In the summer of 1892, she met Jane Addams of Hull House and the economic historian Katharine Coman (*q.v.*) of Wellesley College while attending the Summer School of Applied Ethics at Plymouth, Massachusetts, convened by Felix Adler, founder of the Ethical Culture Society. Regretting that in France she had studied the poor without meeting them, Emily became active in social work. In December 1892, she joined in founding Denison House, a Boston settlement house patterned on Chicago's Hull House, and served as Headworker for a year until her Bryn Mawr classmate Helena Dudley was available for the post. In 1894, she attended the national convention of the American Federation of Labor as a delegate of Boston's Central Labor Union. Emily Balch studied economics for a semester at the Harvard Annex (later Radcliffe) in 1893, under the influence of the historical economist William Ashley, and spent a quarter taking courses in economic theory and sociology at the University of Chicago in 1895. Together with another of Ashley's graduate students, Mary Kingsbury (later Simkhovitch), Balch spent 1895–96 at the University of Berlin, attending the seminars of Adolf Wagner and Gustav Schmoller: 'As [the University] was not regularly open to women students I got permission from the Reich Cultus Minister, the Rector of the University, and separately from each professor with whom I was to study. My friend, Mary Kingsbury and I were curiosities', although they found other women among the graduate students in economics, notably Fräulein von Dyhrenfurth, who had just published on 'Working Women in England' in *Schmoller's Jahrbuch*, and Frau Daszynska, later a labour leader in Poland. Balch and Kingsbury attended the International Socialist Workers and Trade Union Congress in London in July 1896 (Balch, 1972, pp. 40–47).

Balch hoped to complete a Ph.D. at the Massachusetts Institute of Technology, but at that time MIT's degree requirements included chemistry, which she had not studied. However, she returned home from Germany on the same ship as Katharine Coman, then teaching economics single-handedly at Wellesley (and later the author of the lead article in the first issue of the *American Economic Review*). Coman invited Balch to join Wellesley, initially grading student papers, but teaching courses from the second semester. Balch taught economics and, from 1900, sociology at Wellesley during her time there from 1896 to 1918. Balch taught pioneering courses on the history of socialism, labour problems, social pathology, immigration, consumption and the economic role of women (see Balch, 1910b, 1914) as well as introductory economics (taking a marginalist approach based on the writings of Böhm-Bawerk), sociology, statistics and economic history. She chose to live solely on her earnings, giving away her unearned income from her father's estate. In 1899 Balch lent $200 to a striking shoe-makers' union in Marlboro, Massachusetts, and was later 'told by President Caroline Hazard of Wellesley that this loan was the reason that she had been kept on as a mere assistant without normal promotion' (Randall, 1964, p. 109). Balch helped found the Women's Trade Union League in 1903, and later served as president of its Boston branch. Like Coman, she was active in the Consumers' League. Balch was promoted to Associate Professor in 1903, and in 1913 received a five-year contract as Full Professor and Head of the Department of Economics and Sociology, succeeding the ailing Coman. She declared herself a socialist in 1906 (and accepted reappointment at Wellesley only on condition of the president knowing this), and, together with her Wellesley colleague Vida Scudder, organized a three-day conference on 'Socialism as a World Movement' in Boston in 1909. Balch served on the Massachusetts Factory Inspection Commission and chaired the Massachusetts Minimum Wage Commission (established 1913).

Emily Balch spent 1904–5 on sabbatical in Austria–Hungary, visiting the sources of Slavic immigration to the USA (becoming a close friend of Thomas and Charlotte Garrigue Masaryk) and 1905–6 on unpaid leave, visiting centres of Slavic immigration in the USA. Her *magnum opus* of 536 pages, *Our Slavic Citizens* (1910a), was a scholarly but passionate defence of the social, cultural and economic benefits of free immigration, a cause she upheld in many venues, including the *American Journal of Sociology*, the *American Economic Review* (1912) and in a 1939 leaflet on *Refugees as Assets*. Among economists, she was the outstanding opponent of the Immigration Restriction League, in which such economists as John R. Commons and Irving Fisher were prominent.

A pacifist since the Spanish–American War, Balch joined Jane Addams among the American delegates to the International Congress of Women at The Hague in 1915, urging mediation to resolve World War 1. In support of this plan, she visited Scandinavia and Russia, and lobbied President Woodrow Wilson, who had been one of her teachers at Bryn Mawr. She spent several months with the International Committee on Mediation in Stockholm in 1916. Balch wrote for *The Nation* in New York City during a sabbatical (1916–17) and unpaid leave (1917–18), opposing conscription and defending civil liberties, including those of conscientious objectors and the foreign-born. Her Wellesley contract expired in 1918, and the next year the board of trustees narrowly refused to reappoint her, despite protests by the college president, alumnae trustees, and Balch's department. At the age of 52, Balch lost her academic position for the same antiwar activism for which she was to share the Nobel Peace Prize in 1946.

Raised a Unitarian, Balch joined the Society of Friends in 1921. At about the same time, Balch rejected socialism, as having become too closely identified with Marxism. She was active in the International Congress of Women in Zürich in May 1919 and was the founding international secretary–treasurer (until 1922) of the Women's International League for Peace and Freedom (WILPF), the Geneva-based permanent organization established by the Congress. She succeeded Jane Addams as president of the American section in 1931 and as honorary international president in 1937. With five other Americans (including two African-American women and the economist Paul Douglas), Balch investigated conditions in Haiti in 1926, and urged the removal of the Marines who had occupied Haiti since 1915 (Balch, 1927; cf. Balch, 1926). Appalled by Nazi Germany's threat to dominate Europe and persecution of the Jews, Balch supported the US war effort in World War II as the lesser evil, but remained in the WILPF and urged its members to aid the interned Japanese-Americans. In 1946, she shared the Nobel Peace Prize with John R. Mott of the Student Christian Movement. The only previous American woman to win the prize had been Balch's friend, Jane Addams. After World War II, Balch's writings emphasized internationalization of waterways, air routes, polar regions, and strategic bases, and an international reconstruction corps (Balch, 1972, Part V; Pois, 1995). She died in Cambridge, Massachusetts, on 9 January 1961, after four years in a nursing home.

ROBERT W. DIMAND

Bibliography

Selected writings by Emily Balch

Papers, Swarthmore College Peace Collection.
(1893), 'Public assistance of the poor in France', *Publications of the American Economic Association*, first series, **8**(4–5), 1–180.
(1910a), *Our Slavic Fellow Citizens*, New York: N.Y. Charities Publication Committee; excerpts from ch. XVIII, pp. 396–425 are in Balch (1972), pp. 52–9.
(1910b), 'The education and efficiency of women', *Annals of the Academy of Political Science*, **1**, 61–71.
(1912) (et al.), 'Restriction of immigration: discussion', *American Economic Review* Supplement, **2**, March, 63–78.
(1913), 'What the poor need is income', *Survey* (American Association for Labor Legislation), **30**, September, 755–6.
(1914), 'The economic role of the housewife', *Home Progress*, **4**, September, 620–24.
(1915), 'The effects of war and militarism on the status of women', *Publications of the American Sociological Society*, pp. 39–55.
(1924), 'Economic aspects of a new international order', *Report of the Fourth Congress of the Women's International League for Peace and Freedom*, Washington, DC, pp. 72–7, reprinted in Balch (1972), pp. 110–15.
(1926), 'Economic imperialism with special reference to the U.S.', *Pax International*, **2**(1) (November), and in *Report of the Fifth Congress of the Women's International League for Peace and Freedom*, Dublin, pp. 92–7, reprinted in Balch (1972), pp. 140–44.
(1927) (ed.), *Occupied Haiti*, New York: The Writers Publishing Company.
(1939), *Refugees as Assets*, Women's International League for Peace and Freedom, revised 1940, leaflet reprinted in Balch (1972), pp. 60–62.
(1972), *Beyond Nationalism: The Social Thought of Emily Greene Balch*, ed. Mercedes M. Randall, New York: Twayne Publishers.

Other sources and references

Pois, Anne Marie (1995), 'Foreshadowings: ecofeminist/pacifist feminism of the 1980s', *Peace and Change*, **20**(4), 439–65.

Randall, Mercedes M. (1964), *Improper Bostonian: Emily Greene Balch, Nobel Peace Laureate, 1946*, New York: Twayne Publishers.
New York Times (1961), Obituary of Emily Greene Balch, 11 January.

Käthe Bauer-Mengelberg (1894–1968)

Born 23 May 1894 at Krefeld, died 22 April 1968 at New York, Käthe Bauer-Mengelberg was one of the representatives of the Heidelberg School. After starting her studies at Munich in 1914, as a student of Lujo Brentano, she switched to the University of Heidelberg, where she graduated in political economy and sociology in 1918, with a dissertation on the *Financial Policy of the Social Democratic Party* supervised by Salomon P. Altmann. Subsequently she worked, first, as assistant and later, after her habilitation in 1923 with a study *On the Theory of Job Evaluation*, as private lecturer at the Department of Economics at the Commercial College at Mannheim. In 1930, she was offered a Chair at the State Institute of Vocational Education at Frankfurt am Main, at which teachers for vocational schools were trained. In accordance with Paragraph 6 of the so-called National Socialist Law on the Restoration of the Civil Service, enacted in April 1933, she was dismissed on 1 March 1934, for reasons of 'administrative rationalization'; however, this also mirrors the National Socialist aim of restricting women's work. At the same time, she lost her *venia legendi* due to the break-up of the Commercial College at Mannheim. Because she had been a civil servant only for a short period of time, she was entitled to draw a pension for a transitional period of merely two years.

Bauer-Mengelberg's decision to leave Germany – a decision taken in 1934 – and her actual emigration as late as January 1939 point to the precarious situation of this woman scientist. While in Germany, she tried in vain to get an academic position in a foreign country. The international relief committees, however, could only act on behalf of scientists who had already fled their home country. As a single parent with two school-age children – her marriage with a Jewish lawyer, who was by then living in Paris as a destitute emigrant, had ended in 1930 – she did not want to leave Germany for an uncertain future. Thanks to recommendations by prominent advocates already living in emigration, such as Emil Lederer and Karl Mannheim, different colleges in both Great Britain and Australia had shown an interest; however, they had made no offers because they assumed that Bauer-Mengelberg would hardly be mobile because of her parental responsibilities. From 1936 to 1938, she earned her living as an assistant at the Chamber of Commerce at Wuppertal, before being offered a temporary position at Iowa State College of Agriculture and Mechanic Arts, financed by funds from the Emergency Committee in Aid of Displaced German Scholars and from the Oberländer Trust. This job was followed by further short-term contracts – in the summer of 1943 at New York University, from the autumn of 1943 until 1946 at the New Jersey College for Women at Rutgers University – before she was finally offered a permanent post as Professor of Sociology at Upsala College at East Orange, New Jersey, where she worked until her retirement in 1964.

Bauer-Mengelberg's academic work in the German period illustrates the interdisciplinary scientific approach of the Heidelberg School which, following the end of World War II, aimed at educating future democratic élites for the new Weimar Republic. Bauer-Mengelberg's work focused not so much on original economic analysis, but rather – determined by her experiences while training practitioners at the School of Commerce and at the Institute of Vocational Education – on the clarification of basic socioeconomic relations. In accordance with her political convictions, she started out, in her dissertation and her habilitation thesis, with analyses of the Social Democratic economic and social theories; these were followed by different essays on the sociology of class analysis ('Soziologie und Sozialpolitik', *Soziale Praxis*, 1925; 'Stand und Klasse, Der Bürger', *Kölner Vierteljahreshefte für Soziologie,* 1924 and 1929), before she turned towards agrarian policy, because of her teaching commitments at Mannheim. On this subject she wrote a textbook in 1931, followed by essays on suburban housing development, the German market for fats, and the world market for wheat, which were published between 1932 and 1934 in the *Wirtschaftskurve*, edited by the *Frankfurter Zeitung*, and which discussed the chances of the National Socialist autarky policy.

These publishing activities were disrupted by her dismissal and she was not able to pick them up again after emigration. With a short work on the agrarian cultivation of the USA during World War II ('Economic Analysis of the Food Stamp Plan', *Journal of Farm Economics*, 1941), she tried to revive these earlier agrarian–political studies; however, these were but isolated attempts. In contrast to her colleagues and companions in misfortune in Iowa, Gerhard Tintner and Adolf Kozlik, she suffered badly from her uprooting. In her insecure position, she imputed to every American that he or she assumed every emigrant to be a 'fifth columnist'. Such an attitude was by no means beneficial to her academic productivity. In addition, there were the immense teaching commitments at American colleges, which made personal research more difficult. As a writer, she distinguished herself only once more when, years later, she translated Lorenz von Stein's *History of the Social Movement in France*, for which she also wrote an introductory commentary.

CLAUS-DIETER KROHN

Bibliography

Selected writings by Käthe Bauer-Mengelberg
(1919), *Die Finanzpolitik der sozialdemokratischen Partei in ihren Zusammenhängen mit dem sozialistischen Staatsgedanken*, Mannheim–Berlin–Leipzig (diss.).
(1926), 'Zur Theorie der Arbeitsbewertung', *Archiv für Sozialwissenschaft und Sozialpolitik*, vol. 55: 680–719; vol. 56: 129–59.
(1926), 'Die liberalen Tendenzen in der ökonomischen Theorie des Sozialismus', *Archiv für die Geschichte des Sozialismus und der Arbeiterbewegung*, **12**, 199–212.
(1931), *Agrarpolitik in Theorie, Geschichte und aktueller Problematik*, Leipzig–Berlin.
(1964) (translation, introduction, and editing of) Lorenz von Stein, *The History of the Social Movement in France, 1789–1850*, Totowa, NJ.

Other sources and references
Society for the Protection of Science and Learning, Oxford; Emergency Committee in Aid of German/Foreign Scholars, New York.

Hilde Behrend (1917–2000)

Hilde Behrend was born on 13 August 1917 in Berlin. At the age of 19 she emigrated to Great Britain. She first earned her living as a secretary but decided in 1941 to enter the London School of Economics to study economics. After finishing her studies she took up a job as grammar school teacher of German and French. The deep understanding of the working life of teachers, which she acquired at that time, resurfaces in her later scientific research when she stresses the motivational differences of workers in various labour markets. In 1949 Behrend abandoned her job in the secondary education system for a position as Assistant Lecturer and Research Fellow at the University of Birmingham. She continued her studies and acquired a Ph.D. from the University in 1951. Three years later she accepted a job as Lecturer at the University of Edinburgh, where she remained for the rest of her academic life. In 1973, at the age of 56, she became Professor of Industrial Relations there, and in 1982, Professor Emeritus. Hilde Behrend died on 11 January 2000, at the age of 82.

Behrend's scientific work centres on the analysis of human behaviour patterns and decision processes. In 'Normative factors in the supply of labour' (1955) she points out that there are systematic differences in job fluctuation between workers in manufacturing industries and secondary education due to differing behavioural patterns. She demonstrated empirically that social norms (codes of professional conduct) represent a powerful independent, constraining, regulating, determining force which limits people's response to market forces and thus the effectiveness of the price mechanism.

Another research topic which Behrend started to focus on in 1959, and which she kept returning to throughout her academic life, is voluntary absence from work. She identified personal characteristics as well as work conditions to account for high absence rates. Her conclusion from extensive empirical work is that jobs rather than people are associated with high turn-over or absenteeism. Apart from the results of her empirical studies, which are interesting *per se*, Behrend shows the way for further research. The tremendous non-random variation in individual absence behaviour affords a differentiation of analysis, for example going beyond the calculation of age-standardized percentage distributions of absence rates in occupations and industrial sectors and analysing the dispersion of absences over the working week and year (one-day absences versus sickness), the correlation with the wage rate, status, duration of employment, working hours, overtime and so on.

Behrend endeavoured to identify, define and analyse the complexity of the problems of industrial relations, that is, the relationship between interest groups and the state. Industrial relations are multidimensional in that they have to focus on attitudinal, economic and institutional interactions and processes. Behrend concentrated on the analysis of the behaviour of consumers, their perception of prices and price developments, the adaptation of price images in the course of inflation – a topic scarcely touched upon before. Furthermore she illuminated the perception of the layman as well as managers and trade union members in pay negotiations of the wage–price adjustment mechanisms. She demonstrated by empirical research that the limited knowledge that exists on economic interrelationships has severe implications for the acceptance rate of a national incomes policy. If one wants incomes policy to work one must provide a realistic picture of prices (provision of information by an independent institution and a relevant reference system for price developments, that is income and income developments. Behrend pointed out that price-critical purchasing by consumers is a prerequisite for success in making consumers play their part in the fight against inflation. She pointed out that in the case of Great Britain prices are judged in terms of past prices and learned expenditure patterns are not a question of income but of social group identity.

GUDRUN BIFFL

Bibliography

Selected writings by Hilde Behrend
(1955), 'Normative factors in the supply of labour', *The Manchester School of Economic and Social Studies*, **23**(1), 62–76.
(1959), 'Voluntary absence from work', *International Labour Review*, **79**(2), 109–40.
(1961), 'A fair day's work', *Scottish Journal of Political Economy*, **8**(2), 102–18.
(1966), 'Price images, inflation and national incomes policy', *Scottish Journal of Political Economy*, **13**(3), 273–96.
(1969), 'Have you heard the phrase "productivity agreements"?' (with A. Knowles and J. Davies), *Scottish Journal of Political Economy*, **16**(3), 256–70.

(1971), 'Public acceptability and a workable incomes policy', in *An Incomes Policy for Britain*, London: National Institute of Economic and Social Research and Social Science Research Council.

(1974), 'The Impact of Inflation on Pay Increase Expectations and Ideas of Fair Pay', *Industrial Relations Journal*, **5**(1), 5–10.

(1974/75), 'A new approach to the analysis of absences from work', *Industrial Relations Journal*, **5**(4), 4–21.

(1975), 'Pay negotiations and incomes policy. A comparison of views of managers and trade union lay negotiators' (with A.I. Glendon and D.P. Tweedie), *Industrial Relations Journal*, **6**(3), 4–19.

(1976), 'Absence and the individual: a six-year study in one organisation' (with S. Pocock), *International Labour Review*, **114**(3), 311–27.

Other sources and references
'Obituary: Hilde Behrend', *Royal Economic Society Newsletter*, 109(April 2000), p. 14.

Cora Berliner (1890–?1942)

Cora Berliner was born on 23 January 1890 at Hanover, was deported to Theresienstadt on 19 June 1942, and died in the Holocaust. After graduation from the Leibniz-Gymnasium at Hanover in 1909. Cora Berliner initially studied mathematics for two semesters at Freiburg and at the Technical University of Hanover. Subsequently she switched to political economy at Berlin. Having stayed for six semesters in the German capital, she moved to Heidelberg, where she finished her studies in 1916 as a student of Emil Lederer with a dissertation on the organization of Jewish youth in Germany: *Die Organisation der jüdischen Jugend in Deutschland. Ein Beitrag zur Systematik der Jugendpflege und Jugendbewegung.* This topic clearly had its roots in her social and sociopolitical commitments. Even as a high-school student, Berliner had already worked in the Jewish Travellers' Aid Society, which supported, above all, Jewish refugees from Russia following the pogroms at the beginning of the century – subsequent to the lost war against Japan and to the revolution against tsarism of 1904–5 – on their way to the USA and to Palestine (in the 2nd Alija, the second wave of Jewish immigration to Palestine). During her student days, she participated in the girls' work of the non-Zionist Jewish youth movement. At that time, she wrote numerous articles, mostly based on lectures, on the Jewish self-image in the hectic internal debate challenged by the Zionist movement.

Berliner continued to work in Jewish social security in an honorary capacity when, having finished her studies, she entered the municipal administration of Berlin-Schöneberg where she dealt with questions of food supply during the final phase of World War I. At the end of 1919, she was appointed to the young Weimar Republic's new Ministry of Economics as a temporary worker, where she was responsible for consumer protection and for the cooperative system. One year after her appointment as Senior Executive Officer in 1923, President Ernst Wagemann called her to the Statistical Office of the Reich, where she stayed in the department of commercial statistics until 1933.

In those years, Berliner published her few works in economics. After the disastrous hyperinflation of 1923, during which money had completely failed as a standard of value, her works focused, for example, on the rebuilding of ordered foreign trade statistics under stable monetary conditions. Her writings reflect the problems Berliner had to deal with in her practical work. In 1927, she spent a few months at the German embassy in London, in connection with her research on German–British trade relations, before being offered a part-time professorship in economics at the State Institute of Vocational Education in Berlin. Details concerning her work there – the training of vocational teachers – are not known, because she produced no publications on this topic.

Following the seizure of power by the National Socialists and her dismissal from the civil service in accordance with the so-called Law for the Restoration of the Civil Service of April 1933, Berliner took over the administration of the economic and sociopolitical department of the Reich Representative of German Jews (Reichsvertretung der deutschen Juden), established in September 1933. And as deputy chairwoman of the Jewish Women's League she also organized the emigration of Jewish women and children. Furthermore, she launched into numerous other activities within the framework of the ever more tightly drawn limits set by the National Socialists for Jewish organizations. Among other things, she continued her training of social workers under the roof of the central Jewish welfare institution; furthermore, she contributed to the publication of the *Philo-Lexikon*, of which a new edition appeared in 1935.

After the pogrom night of 1938, her emigrant siblings, two sisters and two brothers, as well as several friends urged her to leave Germany. However, Cora Berliner refrained from taking this step as long as those she looked after still needed her help, although she would have had the chance to do so on her exploratory journeys relating to Jewish emigration to Palestine, in 1936, and to Sweden, in 1939. In 1942, Cora Berliner was deported to Theresienstadt together with other representatives of the Jewish Agency; the circumstances of her death in the National Socialist genocide are not known.

CLAUS-DIETER KROHN

Bibliography

Selected writings by Cora Berliner
(1916), *Die Organisation der jüdischen Jugend in Deutschland. Ein Beitrag zur Systematik der Jugendpflege und Jugendbewegung*, Berlin (diss.): Verlag d. verbandes d. jüd. Jugendvereine Deutschland.

(1925), 'Probleme der Handelsstatistik', *Magazin der Wirtschaft*, **1**, 1158–67.
(1929), 'Die Reform der deutschen Außenhandelsstatistik', *Weltwirtschaftliches Archiv*, **29**, 320–333.
(1930), 'Die Handelsbilanz im Rahmen der Zahlungsbilanz', *Die Bank*, **23**, 1161–4.
(1932), 'Englands Abkehr vom Goldstandard', in *Deutschland-Jahrbuch für das deutsche Volk*, Leipzig, pp. 30–37.

Other sources and references
Hildesheimer, E. (1984), 'Cora Berliner, Ihr Leben und Wirken', *Leo Baeck Institute Bulletin*, **67**, 41–70.
Kaplan, M.A. (1981), *Die Jüdische Frauenbewegung in Deutschland*, Hamburg, pp. 150–51.
Lowenthal, E.G. (ed.) (1966), *Bewährung im Untergang. Ein Gedenkbuch*, Stuttgart, pp. 23–7.

Krishna Bharadwaj (1935–1992)

I was born, the youngest of six children, on 21 August 1935 at Karwar, a small coastal town resting in the foothills of Sahyadri on the western coast of India. My father, Maruti Chandawarkar, was a highly motivated educationalist who actively supported the education of the deprived, particularly women and child-widows. When I was two, my family moved to Belgaum, a multilingual town, a place of confluence of north and south Indian cultural traditions known particularly for its music, dramatic arts and folk culture. It was also a politically alive place, a frontier town on the borders of the Portuguese colony of Goa. As part of the nationalist freedom movement, the young socialists were active in the town. One of the important achievements of Gandhi's strategy of nationalist struggle was the space it created for the active involvement in the liberation movement of women and children, of all ages and ranks. The movement had a profound impact during my youth in instilling an urge for social and economic action towards independent self-reliant development.

In 1951, I moved to Bombay for college education. Although fascinated by mathematics and sciences, it was mainly the mundane consideration of combining employment with study that prompted me towards the 'Arts'. After the death of my father in 1952, I began the study of economics specifically for the potentialities it held for employment. Once I took up the subject at the University of Bombay, however, I found it fascinating partly because of the lively social context it acquired just when independent India was launching upon the path of planned development.

In my graduate years, while the theory of value remained essentially a theory of competitive equilibrium with smatterings of monopolistic competition, what held our interest was macroeconomic theory, predominantly Keynesian (a little less of Kaleckian), together with the inter-industry studies which followed Leontief's pioneering work. Strategies of development and analytical techniques of planning dominated the professional debates. A general consensus among social scientists seemed to be that in order to accelerate the pace of development, transcending the protracted colonial interregnum, planned interventions of the state were imperative. This was the generally accepted view even among the big industrialists. Strong debates arose, however, on the diagnosis of backwardness and on the strategies of investment, particularly with the Second Five-Year Plan commencing in 1956, the planning policy having been launched in 1951.

My critical orientation towards economic theory began with my involvement in development theory as a doctoral student at the University of Bombay. Early attempts at theorizing on problems of development emerged mainly as an adaptation of the competitive equilibrium framework of resource allocation. This maintained that efficient resource utilization would occur in a competitive market economy composed of individual agents maximizing their return, given their endowment of primary resources, the technological possibilities of transformation and the set of preferences. The nature, source and hence the diagnosis of underdevelopment was thus attributed to limited availability of primary resources, adverse proportions of factor supplies or their limited substitutability, biased preferences and imperfections or non-formation of markets which explained 'market failures' of various kinds. The state of underdevelopment was viewed as a departure from the competitive resource utilization model. A remedial policy widely discussed was the use of 'shadow' or implicit prices derived from the setting up of optimal programmes. A critique of this position was presented in my early paper 'The Logic of Implicit Prices' (1965).

The other strand in my early doctoral work emanated from the interdependent production models inspired by Leontief, on the basis of which consistency plan models were being constructed in India. My doctoral dissertation, submitted to the University of Bombay in 1960, was on 'Techniques of Transportation Planning, with Special Reference to Railways'; in it I discussed the special problems of investment decisions relating to such a critical social-oriented sector in the context of the ongoing debates on plan strategies. I also used the first inter-industry transactions table constructed by the Indian Statistical Institute in Calcutta for projecting the rail-transport requirements of the plan.

The critique of neoclassical theory, particularly of distribution, was sharpened during my visit to Cambridge, Massachusetts. Accompanying my husband, Ranganath Bharadwaj, who was on a postdoctoral fellowship at Harvard, I joined the Center for International Studies at MIT. Then under the directorship of Professor Rosenstein Rodan, the Center was engaged in organizing research on developing countries, including India. I continued to consider problems of planning and development, but with greater critical perceptions. Apart from working on issues emerging from my doctoral dissertation, I examined the arguments emanating from Hirschman's strategy of development which stressed structural factors of 'backward' and 'forward' linkages to identify 'key' sectors. I was critical of the excessive emphasis placed on material linkages, with the relative neglect of the problem of effective demand. In 'Structural Linkages in the Indian Economy' (1962), I discussed Hirschman's notion of key sectors in planned development, pointing out the analytical weaknesses of the statistical measure of linkages. I also argued that the strategy based on structural interdependence was more workable with reference to choice between alternative programmes than for priority ranking of individual sectors.

During my stay at Cambridge, Professor Joan Robinson (*q.v.*) arrived on her famous trip to launch her attack on the aggregate production function and the neoclassical theory of distribution, and to debate with Professors Samuelson, Solow and other neoclassical theorists. At that time my approach to neoclassical theory was primarily formed in the context of the theory of development – siding against its static resource-allocative, individual-centred analysis. My interest in the distribution theory was rekindled by this controversy between the two Cambridges. As a critic of the marginal productivity theory of distribution, I became more pointedly aware of the capital-theoretic debate. I did not then know of the more fundamental critique of economic theory heralded by Piero Sraffa's work.

While finding that the input–output techniques gave an insight into the intersectoral material connections as transactions, I had two reservations about the predominantly production-based analysis as used in planning strategies. First, in plan models there was an excessive reliance on technologically induced quantity relations. At the same time, the technological relations were presumed to operate under constant returns to scale so that the dynamic scale economies and 'externalities' that characterized the key sectors in history were left out of account. Secondly, the excessive – sometimes exclusive – emphasis on technological interdependence tended to ignore forces operating on income and demand formation. The use of inter-industry analysis needed to be supplemented by a theory of growth of output, consumption and investment, and also by appropriate characterization of exchange systems. The supreme importance given to technological linkages tended to neglect aspects of the formation of demand and the play of market forces. With entry into planning, the problem of development in India was perceived not merely as one of efficient allocation of given resources, but also as one of resource creation and market formation.

The Second Five-Year Plan adopted the Mahalanobis strategy of accelerating investment in heavy industry to lead eventually to a higher rate of income growth. Important debates on strategy ensued between the proponents of industrialization and those of 'agriculture first'. The Bombay School, where I was then a research student, supported the latter, advocating priority to agriculture (wage goods) in the interest of promoting capital formation through the use of surplus labour. The arguments drawn from the Lewis model of promoting industrialization in a dual economy on the basis of transferring surplus labour from agriculture to industry at a constant subsistence wage also appeared in the forefront of debates. A critique of these models was developed by me in 'Notes on Political Economy of Development: The Indian Case' (1972). By constructing a countercase I argued that even when the capitalist sector is supplied with labour at a constant subsistence wage, there could still be internal limitations on the growth of the capitalist industrial sector, due to the peculiar forces of differentiation (in production, exchange and distribution) that prevail in this non-competitive sector. This argument, appearing in 1965 and emphasizing the internal contradictions emerging from the industrial sector even when all constraints emanating from agriculture were held in abeyance, appeared counter-intuitive at that time. For the failure of agriculture to grow had created pressures on the government to review its earlier strategy of promoting investment in heavy industry and instead to sponsor the green revolution. When later in the 1970s the agriculture sector in the aggregate had shown remarkable buoyancy, industry experienced a deceleration and a different set of contradictions appeared to have emerged. I was to return to this theme again to deal explicitly with the question of differentiation in agriculture and industry within a political-economy framework (see below).

During the interval there was a sea-change in my approach to the critique of economic theory. Although I had always opposed neoclassical theory, in this earlier phase my criticism was much more directed against its static, resource-allocational efficiency bias; against its symmetrical explanation of wages, profits, rent and interest as 'factor prices' on the same principle as commodity prices; against the individual-centric perception of choice, and against the fallacy of composition involved in treating social welfare as a simple aggregation of individual welfares. It was not until I discovered through the Sraffian critique the structural contrasts between the two alternative theories – classical and demand-and-supply equilibrium (less appropriately termed neoclassical) – that my approach changed. Although I had been introduced to the capital theory debate through the Robinsonian onslaught, neither the full critical implications of the debate nor the reconstructive aspects of the controversy were clear to me until, on my return to Bombay from MIT, I came upon Piero Sraffa's *Production of Commodities*.

On my return to India in 1962, I joined the Department of Economics, Bombay University, as a lecturer. The turn in my research interests was quite drastic. Sachin Chowdhury, the editor of *The Economic Weekly* who was a close friend of the Cambridge scholars Joan Robinson and Maurice Dobb and an admirer of Piero Sraffa, invited me to his office to extract – as was his style – a contribution to his *Weekly*. Knowing my interest in theory, he drew out of his drawer this slim volume: Sraffa's *Production of Commodities* and offered the book for review, suggesting it would be a feast for thought. Leafing through this, I agreed to review it in a month or so! Mr Chowdhury suggested – enigmatically, I thought then – that I could take my own time since the author had been writing it over decades and had published it even then only as a prelude to something more substantial. Thus I set upon reading the little book. My acquaintance with Marx was mainly from a cursory reading of *Capital* and with Smith and Ricardo mainly secondhand through history of thought compendiums. My interest in radical thought had been mainly nurtured on reading the left-Keynesians, Kalecki and the political arguments for state interventionist planning. Sraffa's book fascinated me and inspired me to read the originals in depth.

The review did not appear for two years (1964). It was a novice's effort to state in simple terms what appeared to me to be astonishingly and challenging original. I was most taken by surprise when I received complimentary letters from Joan Robinson, Maurice Dobb, Ronald Meek and many other Indian and European scholars and from Piero Sraffa himself. It was through the efforts of Joan Robinson that Clare Hall generously offered me a fellowship to work at Cambridge in 1967. This gave me the unique opportunity to communicate with Piero Sraffa and with other scholars including Joan Robinson, Maurice Dobb, Richard Kahn, Nicholas Kaldor, Luigi Pasinetti, Pierangelo Garegnani and with a group of young economists from England and Europe interested in the revival of classical and Marxian theory. My association with Piero Sraffa until his death in 1983 radically altered my theoretical perspective in economics.

When I arrived in Cambridge, a major controversy had erupted over the neoclassical theory of profit. This followed Sraffa's demonstration of the possibility of reswitching of techniques and, more generally, the challenge to the existence of a normal demand function for capital (implying a monotonic inverse relation between capital intensity and the rate of profit). A major attack on the neoclassical theory of distribution appeared in the series of articles in the symposium on 'Paradoxes in Capital Theory' (*Quarterly Journal of Economics*, November 1966, pp. 503–83). I did not take part directly in the debate although I shared exciting discussions with its main participants and with the Sraffian scholars in Cambridge. I also wrote a paper (1970) to bring out the analytical significance of Sraffa's basic–non-basic commodity distinction which (having been identified with the more familiar matrix classification of decomposability and indecomposability) had led to misinterpretations of the Sraffian arguments.

The main task I undertook was to elaborate the Sraffian critique of economic theory which, as I understood it, brought out the distinctive differences in the theoretical approaches and the methodological frameworks of the two streams of economic theory. These were the classical or surplus-based theories (represented by Smith, Ricardo and Marx) and the currently dominating demand-and-supply equilibrium (DSE) theories spearheaded in the writings of Jevons, Menger and Walras. I saw Sraffa's work as achieving a two-fold task: reconstructing the long-submerged approach of the classical writers in economic theory and developing a critique of marginalist theory which had acquired dominance since the 1870s. Inspired by Sraffa's framework. I proceeded to take up certain debates in the history of political economy arising out of the works of Smith, Ricardo and Marx, and particularly concerning the questions of value and distribution. These revealed the particular framework that underlay the manner in which such problems were formulated, analysed and debated.

Some of the essays written over several years appear in *Themes in Value and Distribution: Classical Theory Reappraised* (1989) and share a certain thrust of analysis. The general critique of theory is advanced through three themes. One is the attempt to determine the basic common elements in the analytical approach of classical theory and to trace their development through the critical debates which resulted from the writings of Smith, Ricardo and Marx. Following Sraffa's unravelling of the classical approach in his masterly edition of Ricardo's works, I attempted to analyse the critical controversies in classical theory, to investigate the formation and evolution of the basic theoretical framework they shared and the specific concepts and categories they evolved. The attempt was to discover the explicit or implicit theoretical setting in which they analysed questions of value and distribution as basic to their theory of accumulation. Even when such explicit statements on the structure of theory are not available, if is possible, as Sraffa's analysis of Ricardo indicates, to discover the rational foundations of their propositions, for instance, by recognizing the peculiar framing of their theoretical questions, the specific forms in which logical difficulties are perceived and encountered, and their resolution attempted. Sraffa's reconstruction of Ricardo's system illustrates the method of inquiry. In parallel, I have also attempted to draw out the basic structure shared in neoclassical theory.

The second strand in my research is the unravelling of the differences in theoretical structure between classical and DSE theories in their explanation of prices, quantities and distribution. A general position of the methodological contrast between the two alternative schemes of theorizing was presented from a Sraffian perspective in my Dutt Memorial Lectures delivered in 1976 and published in 1978. In these, I laid out the structure of classical theory shared by Smith, Ricardo and Marx and compared it with the demand-and-supply-based equilibrium theory. My central argument was that DSE theories resort to a method which is restrictive in its ability to incorporate the variety of conditions under which changes in output, methods of production, consumption and distribution take place, and that these limitations arise from the assumptions that are imposed for validating the theory. Secondly, the basis on which the well-behaved demand-and-supply functions are constructed throw up a number of logical difficulties such as the one raised in the capital-theory debate.

The classical theory, on the other hand, allows openness for diverse factors to influence the determination of quantities (production, distribution and consumption). Moreover, prices are treated as compatible with the required circular reproduction of the system consistent with the rules regarding the generation, appropriation and distribution of surplus. The two theories thus differ in their structures in explaining prices and quantities. It is the elaboration of this difference that explains, first, the relative openness of the classical theory to deal with historical change and, second, the restricted conception of change and choice presumed in the DSE theory (in order that it remain internally consistent with the theory of market equilibrium). By emphasizing the limitations of the DSE theory flowing from its logical structure and methodological approach, I have tried to lend accuracy and sharpness to earlier critiques directed against the utilitarian and subjective basis of DSE, the lack of realism of its assumptions and so on. With the structural critique inspired by Sraffa, there is now an opportunity to give these criticisms a sounder logical basis.

The third strand in my studies is to focus on the different analytical structures of the two theories and to investigate attempts to assimilate and synthesize classical into DSE theory. I examine certain commonly adopted concepts like demand, supply and competition to show how concepts and notions placed in different theoretical frameworks acquire different connotations and roles. I use this argument to counter the 'continuity thesis' of unidirectional improvement of ideas that some DSE theorists hold in order to argue that the classical framework is at best only a partial scheme or a subsystem of the more general DSE theory. I have argued that original concepts like demand and supply, transplanted into a different theory, change not only their connotations but also their content. The danger is all the greater when abstract theoretical concepts like supply, demand and market are used unwarily in common parlance. A clear understanding of how the structures of various theories differ becomes essential for a careful interpretation of commonly used concepts and the theoretical propositions derived from them.

The viewpoint emerging in my work, greatly influenced by Sraffa, is the critique of theories on the basis of their structures, their logical coherence and their ability to give consistent answers to questions of social change.

While these investigations mainly address questions of value and distribution, they can be extended to the theory of accumulation and change. While attempting to extend the Sraffian interpretation of the classical approach to the problem of effective demand, I have also tried to develop the surplus approach to problems of accumulation in developing countries like India. Thus my effort has been to provide a link between the resurgence of classical theory and the exploration of problems of development.

My first work to extend classical political economy into development theory attempted to analyse production conditions in Indian agriculture as reflected in the newly published farm management studies. This was undertaken at the Department of Applied Economics, Cambridge, when I was a Senior Research Officer during 1968–69. The farm management surveys primarily recorded information about production and business conditions according to different centres, farm sizes and crops. Most economists used these data to discuss conventional equilibrium-theoretic questions. I set out to explain the observed differences in production performance, input-utilization patterns and the differing terms of transactions on the basis of the differential involvement in markets of a differentiated peasantry. I proposed a classification of peasantry according to access to land, as well as to the nature of exchange involvement in the agrarian situation where competitive capitalist markets had not yet fully emerged. I attempted to stratify the peasants according to their status in production and their corresponding involvement in exchange under conditions of uneven commercialization. The output markets were more commercialized whereas those in labour, credit and land were not fully formed. In the paper I tried to relate the production status of the households to their involvement in different discriminatory exchange systems. In this work (completed in 1968 but published in 1974) the idea of interlinked markets and their consequences for the exploitative processes was offered for the first time.

It was after my return to Delhi to join the Jawaharlal Nehru University in 1971, however, that my endeavours to combine my work in the reconstruction of classical political economy with the problems of development took concrete shape. With the help of some other economists, the university offered me an opportunity to launch a programme in postgraduate studies for the newly constituted Centre for Economic Studies and Planning. Over these last years [written in 1991] we have attempted to build postgraduate and research degree programmes that promoted critical thinking in economic theory, in development theory and policy. It is in my endeavours to combine theory and historical experience that I have found teaching and interactions with colleagues the most rewarding.

In the initial period I continued to work on the problems of agriculture. My idea of interlinked markets was taken over by game theorists who set up a variety of models of contractual markets. However, my main interest was in the differential dynamics that arise due to the coexistence of different exchange systems corresponding to a differentiated peasantry. In 'A View of Commercialization in Indian Agriculture' (1985), I extended these ideas on interlinked markets, emphasizing the varied dynamics generated by the different patterns of differentiation and the corresponding patterns of exchange involvements. A major difference in my analysis from the game-theoretic approach dominating formal analysis was that the latter continued to ask the standard neoclassical static efficiency questions and to explain the coexistence of different exchange systems rather than their transitions or their effects on the aggregate patterns of growth. My focus was on the macrodynamics that the processes of differentiation generated within the coexisting but interacting exchange systems. The differential patterns of accumulation generated in regions with different structures of production and exchange were discussed in the 1985 paper. I also reformulated my earlier essay on the political economy of development by proposing a differentiated production and exchange system in agriculture, adopting a wider differentiation of commodity sectors and introducing a wider categorization of income classes (1979).

What emerged out of my several studies on the production and exchange processes at work in the Indian economy was neither the simple scenario of dualism (reflected in an agriculture–industry dichotomy) nor the dynamic advance of capitalist accumulation drawn in the image of Britain as the home of capitalism. In my 1988 Daniel Thorner lecture, I discussed the genesis and consequences of the peculiar patterns of development experienced in India wherein, despite substantial changes in national product and its composition since the launching of planned development, no significant shift has occurred in the proportion of population depending on agriculture for bare survival or even in the numbers subsisting below the 'poverty line'.

In considering the dynamics of developments in India, with its colonial past and within changing international conjunctures, I have found classical and Marxian theory much more open and flexible than neoclassical theory in dealing analytically with the processes of differentiation in production, distribution and exchange. I have thus attempted to combine my critique of economic theory and the reconstruction of the classical (including Marxian) approach with the analysis of historical change in the course of development. In a plenary address delivered at the Indian Economic Association's conference, I argued the methodological *superiority* of the classical approach over the neoclassical to deal with the problems of accumulation and change (1990). In other related publications (1988b, 1988c), I have tried to draw upon the classical theory to derive conceptual frameworks for the handling of development problems, particularly in relating exchange conditions to production relations.

It is thus that my work in analysing the history of theory and reconstructing classical and Marxian theory (inspired by the Sraffian perspective) has converged with my parallel interest in the problems of accumulation in developing countries.

KRISHNA BHARADWAJ

Editors' note: Krishna Bharadwaj died 7 March 1992.

Bibliography

Selected writings by Krishna Bharadwaj

(1962), 'Structural linkages in the Indian economy', *The Economic Week*, August. Reprinted as 'A note on structural interdependence', *Kyklos*, **25**, 1972.
(1964), 'Value through exogeneous distribution', *Economic Weekly*, August. Reprinted in G.C. Harcourt and N.F. Laing (eds), *Capital and Growth*, Penguin, 1977.
(1965), 'The logic of implicit prices', *Indian Economic Journal*, **12**.
(1970), 'On the maximum number of switches between two production systems', *Schweizerische Zeitschrift für Volkwirtschaft und Statistik*, no 4.
(1974), *Production Conditions in Indian Agriculture as Reflected in the Farm Management Studies*, Cambridge: Cambridge University Press.
(1978), *Classical Political Economy and the Rise to Dominance of Supply and Demand Theories*, Orient Longmans; second revised edition, Calcutta: University Press India Ltd, 1986.
(1979), 'Towards a macroeconomic framework for a developing economy: the Indian case', *Manchester School Journal*, **47**.
(1985), 'A view of commercialization in Indian agriculture', *Journal of Peasant Studies*, **13**.
(1988a), 'Dynamics of development and the formation of labour markets', Daniel Thorner Lecture submitted at Dhaka, December.
(1988b), 'Production and exchange in price formation economic transition', in M. Baranzini and R. Scazzieri (eds), *Foundations of Economics*, Oxford: Basil Blackwell.
(1988c), 'The analysis of agriculture-industry relation', in K.J. Arrow (ed.), *The Balance between Industry and Agriculture in Economic Development*, London: Macmillan.
(1989), *Themes in Value and Distribution: Classical Theory Reappraised*, London: Unwin Hyman.
(1990), 'Paradigms in development theory: plea for a labour-ist approach', *Economic and Political Weekly*, 27 June.
(1994), *Accumulation, Exchange, and Development: Essays on the Indian Economy*, New Delhi: Sage.

Other sources and references

Harcourt, Geoffrey C. (1993), 'Krishna Bharadwaj, 21 August 1935–7 March 1992: a memoir', *Journal of Post Keynesian Economics*, **16**(2).
Robinson, J., *Collected Economic Papers*, Oxford: Basil Blackwell, vol. IV, 1973; vol. V, 1979.
Roncaglia, Alessandro (1993), 'Krishna Bharadwaj, 1935–1992: in memoriam', *Metroeconomica*, **44**(3), 187–94.
Sraffa, P. (ed.) with M. Dobb (1951), *The Works and Correspondence of David Ricardo Vol I*, Cambridge: Cambridge University Press.
Schefold, Bertram (1998), 'The creation of economic theories and the history of economic thought. Reflections on the work of Krishna Bharadwaj', *History of Economic Ideas*, **6**(1), 7–25.
Sraffa, P. (1960), *Production of Commodities by Means of Commodities*, Cambridge: Cambridge University Press.

Huguette Biaujeaud (*c.* 1910–90)

Biaujeaud's *Essai sur la Théorie Ricardienne de la Valeur* (1934), which offers an interpretation of Ricardo similar in many respects to the later work of Sraffa, is the single publication of an author who chose not to follow a career as an economist. This work was originally presented as a doctoral thesis to the Faculty of Law at the University of Paris on 2 December 1933 under the supervision of Gaëton Pirou, one of the leading historians of economic thought of the day. It was subsequently published by Sirey in 1934 with a preface by Pirou, and reissued by Economica in 1988 with a preface by G. Abraham-Frois. This was very much an independent investigation; Biaujeaud's contacts with Piero Sraffa, whom she met once, and Jacob Hollander took place, according to Biaujeaud, 'when my work was already very advanced ... I had submitted to them my ideas and essential conclusions. It seems to me, and I am almost certain, that they accepted them without great controversy.'[1] These contacts permitted the author to correct a few errors in Ricardo's correspondence.

Biaujeaud's work passed almost unnoticed in France, despite the preface by Pirou, who also emphasized the significance of the work in his *Introduction à l'Étude de l'Économie Politique* (1939, p. 241) and in *La valeur et les prix* (1948, p. 21). There were virtually no significant references to this work in France until very much later (Vidonne, 1982, 1986; Béraud, 1986).

Nevertheless, the importance of Biaujeaud's contribution seems incontrovertible. Although only 200 copies of the original work were printed, well-known specialists cited it. Sraffa, editor of the monumental edition of the *Works and Correspondence of David Ricardo*, cited Biaujeaud in his 1951 preface. Stigler took note of her work in his 'Ricardo and the 93 per cent labor theory of value' (1958). Mark Blaug included her as the only French author among the 12 references he cited in his article on Ricardo for the *International Encyclopedia of the Social Sciences*. Contemporary specialists such as Alessandro Roncaglia cited her work in a 1985 conference presentation. But for French specialists, this work had taken on the character of a myth, particularly since it was virtually inaccessible until its reissue.[2]

Biaujeaud's book contained a comparative analysis of the three editions of Ricardo's *Principles*, and especially the variations in the important first chapter dedicated to value. She developed an original and interesting position on a 'duality' between value determined as a cost of production and value as determined by labour in Ricardo's theory, a point to which I shall return. But her analysis of the influence of the agricultural sector must also be noted.

Sraffa introduces the 'corn model' in his 1951 preface to the first volume of Ricardo's *Works*. He argues that in Ricardo's 1815 'Essay on profits' and in his correspondence of 1814 and 1815, the general rate of profit is determined by the rate of profit in agriculture. In the 1951 preface, Sraffa recognized that in Ricardo's subsequent work the determining role of agricultural profit is weakened and that there is no longer any trace of it in the *Principles* (Sraffa, 1951, p. xxxi).

Similarly, Biaujeaud claims that Ricardo 'bases his system on a theory of profits elaborated long before the *Principles* ... [It emerges] in his 1813 correspondence ... and blossoms in the *Essay*' (Biaujeaud, 1988, p. 64). Moreover, Biaujeaud also notes that 'the general rate of profit is determined by the profit of the farmer ... The rate of profit depends on the difficulty of growing wheat, which regulates the rate of wages' (p. 66).

Both Sraffa and Biaujeaud note in parallel fashion the limitations of Ricardo's analysis: Sraffa claims that Ricardo never specified the 'rational foundation' by means of which agricultural profits played a determining role (Sraffa, 1951, p. xxxi). Biaujeaud claims that 'Ricardo, in his first letters, never explains the connection' between agricultural profits and wages (Biaujeaud, 1988, p. 66). Moreover, Biaujeaud and Sraffa both cite the same letter to Malthus (2 June 1814) as the source of their assertions (Sraffa, 1951, p. xxxii; Biaujeaud, 1988, p. 65).

According to both authors, there was a 'moment' (a few months, perhaps) when Ricardo seemed to believe that the general rate of profit was determined independently of the value of commodities, by the ratio between the physical quantity of corn produced by the farmer and that necessary for the support of farm labour. A letter to James Mill (30 December 1815), in which Ricardo recognized that he must deal with the problem of value before he could continue, signalled the end of this phase. And here again, both Sraffa and Biaujeaud recognize the progressive movement of Ricardo away from a determining role for corn on the rate of profit, towards a theory based in value (Sraffa, 1951, p. xxxii; Biaujeaud, 1988, pp. 68, 70, 73).

It seems clear that there is a striking similarity between the interpretations of Huguette Biaujeaud and Piero Sraffa. The latter, however, went much further in Appendix D of *Production of Commodities by Means of Commodities* (1960) in which he argued, in contradiction with his analysis of 1951, that Ricardo afforded a determining role to the profit of the farmer in the *Principles*.[3]

The analyses of Biaujeaud and Sraffa are, however, not identical; the latter is much more systematic. Nevertheless, it would be hard to dispute a certain anticipation in Biaujeaud's work. Perhaps we ought to recall, in this context, George Stigler's analysis of the nature and role of originality in scientific progress, in which he notes the extreme difficulty of identifying the first formulation of a hypothesis or concept. It seems the corn model is another illustration of his point.

But Biaujeaud's work attracted Sraffa's attention for another reason (Sraffa, 1951, p. xxxviii). She examined the changes introduced into the chapter on value in the second and third editions of the *Principles* and, like Sraffa, argued that the theory of value expounded in the third edition did not represent a retreat from a labour theory of value (Biaujeaud, 1988, pp. 39, 154). This view opposed the then widely accepted claims of Jacob Hollander and Edwin Cannan that, in successive editions of the *Principles*, Ricardo had weakened his original argument that embodied labour is the foundation of value. But unlike Sraffa, who held that, in the *Principles*, value is essentially determined by embodied labour, Biaujeaud argued that, from the first edition, value is regulated by cost of production (Biaujeaud, 1988, pp. 36–9). Indeed, she claims, there is less an evolution in Ricardo's theory than a continuous strengthening, in which the idea of cost of production becomes more and more precise and the related notion of a measure of value is clarified (ibid., pp. 154f.).

Biaujeaud's overturning of received opinion becomes even more complete when she argues that, if anything, it is in 'the third edition ... where Ricardo demonstrates for the first time that value depends on labor' (Biaujeaud, 1988, p. 168). If there is any evolution at all, she argues, it is not away from a labour theory of value, but towards one (ibid., p. 103).

Biaujeaud notes that Ricardo determined value by cost of production as early as the first edition of the *Principles*. For example, he argued that a general reduction in wages would cause an increase in the prices of those commodities produced with the assistance of fixed capital (Biaujeaud, 1988, p. 70; Sraffa, 1951, pp. xxiii–xxiv). A few pages earlier, Biaujeaud noted that 'to establish these results, which Ricardo recognized were not in accord with received doctrine, he had imagined the extreme case of commodities produced solely by fixed capital and others produced solely by circulating capital, by a machine working without human assistance, or by human work exclusively' (Biaujeaud, 1988, p. 58).

According to Biaujeaud, this recognition of the difficulty caused by differing capital–labour ratios in the first edition is sufficient to reject the thesis that Ricardo had increasing doubts about the labour theory of value as time passed. In fact, by the second edition, this example was considerably modified, and by the third edition it disappeared entirely, to be replaced by the passage that gave birth to George Stigler's notorious 'Ricardo and the 93 per cent labor theory of value' (1958) (cf. Biaujeaud, 1988, p. 125). Stigler distinguished between an analytical labour theory of value, which he claimed not to find in Ricardo, and an empirical labour theory of value, for which he cites textual evidence. But in fact, the 93 per cent labour theory of value exists only because of modifications that appeared in the third edition, as Wilson and Pate have recognized (1968) and as Biaujeaud had much earlier noticed.

Biaujeaud's book is therefore important because it demonstrates that the problem of differing capital–labour ratios was present from the first edition of the *Principles*; Ricardo had, from the beginning, a theory of value founded on cost of production. Labour was, by contrast, a 'measure', or means of estimating, value, and this role was essential to the author of the *Principles*.

Biaujeaud's position is quite original. On the one hand, she disputes Sraffa's claim by recognizing that the modifications introduced into the third edition of the *Principles* are important (Sraffa, 1951, pp. xxxix–xv). But on the other, she claims that it is not, therefore, necessary to conclude, as did Cannan and Jacob Hollander, that Ricardo weakened his position on the labour theory of value. In fact, she sees in them the point of departure for a deepening of Ricardo's thought (Biaujeaud, 1988, pp. 120–21), but claims that the innovations introduced into the third edition are much less important than the introduction of fixed capital in the first edition. Far from a weakening of Ricardo's recognition of the role of labour, the third edition represents reinforcement or, at least, greater precision.

Many authors have claimed that Ricardo had a theory of value founded on cost of production: Alfred Marshall in Appendix I of the *Principles*, George Stigler (1958) and Samuel Hollander (1979) argue as much. Biaujeaud's originality is to argue that 'the labor theory of value and the cost of production theory of value coexisted parallel to one another in Ricardo's thought' (Biaujeaud, 1988, pp. 69f.). In fact, she argues that 'the true interest of the Ricardian system lies in the duality of these two theories' (ibid., p. 185).

G. Abraham-Frois

Notes

1. Mme Biaujeaud made this claim in personal correspondence with the author (cf. Abraham-Frois, 1997, p. 2).
2. Biaujeaud's lack of impact in French is probably related to the more general problem of the non-diffusion of Ricardian thought in France (cf. Abraham-Frois, 1997, p. 3).
3. Controversy in the secondary literature related to the corn model is extensive. See Samuel Hollander (1979), Gilbert Faccarello (1982) and Paul Vidonne (1986).

Bibliography

Abraham-Frois, Gilbert (1997), 'Huguette Biaujeaud, Piero Sraffa et David Ricardo', Colloque: 'La tradition économique française 1848–1939', Lyon.

Béraud, Alain (1986), 'Note sur certaines interprétations récentes de la pensée ricardienne', Contribution à la table-ronde: 'Production de marchandises par des marchandises ...', Nice: Latapses.

Biaujeaud, Huguette (1988), *Essai sur la Théorie de la Valeur*, Paris: Economica.

Blaug, Mark (1968), 'Ricardo, David', in *International Encyclopedia of the Social Sciences*, New York: Macmillan.

Cannan, Edwin ([1929]1964), *A Review of Economic Theory*, with an introduction by B.A. Corry, New York: A.M. Kelley.

Faccarello, Gilbert (1982), 'Sraffa versus Ricardo: the historical irrelevance of the "Corn-profit" model', *Economy and Society*, **11**(2). Reprinted in Ben Fine (ed.), (1986) *The Value Dimension*, London and New York: Routledge and Kegan Paul, pp. 188–203.

Gide, Charles and Charles Rist (1909), *Histoire des doctrines économiques*, Paris: Sirey.

Hollander, Jacob H. (1904), 'The development of Ricardo's theory of value', *Quarterly Journal of Economics*, **18**: 455–91.
Hollander, Samuel (1979), *The Economics of David Ricardo*, Toronto: University of Toronto Press.
James, Émile (1955), *Histoire sommaire de la pensée économique*, Paris: Montchrestien.
Pirou, Gaëton (1939), *Introduction à l'étude de l'Economie Politique*, Paris: Sirey.
Pirou, Gaëton (1948), *La valeur et les prix*, Paris: Sirey.
Pribram, Karl (1986), *Les fondements de la pensée économique*, Paris: Economica.
Ricardo, David (1951), *Works and Correspondence of David Ricardo*, ed. P. Sraffa, Cambridge: Cambridge University Press.
Sraffa, Piero (1951), 'Preface', in Ricardo (1951).
Sraffa, Piero (1960), *Production of Commodities by Means of Commodities*, Cambridge: Cambridge University Press.
Stigler, George J. (1955), 'The nature and role of originality in scientific progress', *Economica*, new series, **22**: 293–302.
Stigler, George J. (1958), 'Ricardo and the 93 per cent labor theory of value', *American Economic Review*, **48**: 357–67.
Vidonne, Paul (1982), 'Essai sur la formation de la pensée économique, Nature, rente, travail', thesis, Université de Paris X-Nanterre.
Vidonne, Paul (1986), *La formation de la pensée économique*, Paris: Economica.
Wilson, George W. and James L. Pate (1968), 'Ricardo's 93 per cent labor theory of value: a final comment', *Journal of Political Economy*, **76**.

Clementina Black (1853–1922)

Social investigator, staunch women's rights activist, art lover and critic, romantic novelist and economist, Clementina Black was born in Brighton, the eldest child of eight to David Black, the town coroner, and Clara Patten. Her paternal grandfather, Peter Black, was naval architect to Tsar Nicholas I. Her maternal grandfather was George Patten, ARA, portrait painter to the Prince Consort. Little is known of the early education of the Black family, but several of the children displayed remarkable talent. Clementina was a proficient linguist (in particular French and German) and her books reveal a comprehensive knowledge of art, literature, politics and economics. She wrote her first novel (*A Sussex Idyll*) at the age of 24. This was followed by *Orlando* (1880), a three-volume epic, *An Agitator* (1894), *The Princess Desiree* (1896), *Pursuit of Camilla* (1899), and *Caroline* (1908), presumably a useful source of income over these 20 years. Her writing career, which began in earnest after she moved to London in 1882, also produced biographical works (*Frederic Walker*, 1902; *The Linleys of Bath*, 1911), an edition of *The Cumberland Letters* (1912) and translations of biographical studies on Rembrandt, Rodin and Millet. Her younger sister received a first at Cambridge in the Classical Tripos and later became well known as Constance Garnett for her translations from Russian of over 70 novels. Carolyn Heilbron (1961, p. 169) claimed that Constance was tutored by her brothers, one of whom became a brilliant mathematician and another a doctor.

In 1875 Clementina's father was struck down with locomotor ataxia (leaving him paralysed until his death 20 years later). Her mother died in the same year, giving Clementina the responsibility of the Black household. In 1882 she felt free to move to London with her sisters and this undoubtedly became the most formative period of her life. She and Constance entered fully into the intellectual life of the day. Significant for her later interests, Clementina first met Charles Booth when Constance was hired as a tutor of Greek and Latin to the Booth children. Both girls were active in Fabian circles and Constance was a member of the executive committee. Heilbron (1961, p. 71) reports that both Constance and Clementina 'detested the Potter sisters and throughout their lives distrusted the sort of state socialism which owed so much to the Webbs'. Clementina also established some social contact with the family of Karl Marx. Kapp (1977, p. 226) reports that Clementina spent time reading to the ill Jenny Marx and assisted Eleanor Marx when she was on the verge of a nervous breakdown. A Keynes connection is also possible since Constance was a close friend of Florence Keynes (Maynard Keynes's mother) when they studied together at Newnham.

The last two decades of the nineteenth century were a time of social and political upheaval. These were the years of the new unionism, Charles Booth's investigation of London life, labour and poverty including the sweated female labour of its East End. This turned Black into a labour reform activist. In 1886 she became Secretary of the Women's Protective and Provident League (later to be called the Women's Trade Union League). Founded by Emma Ann Patterson, it aimed to protect women via the lobbying of political parties for the passage of protective legislation. For the next three years Black's work involved much travelling to assist in establishing women's trade unions. Her visit to Scotland in 1887 led to the formation of a Women's Trade Council under the leadership of Margaret Irwin (Lewenhak, 1977, p. 122). Her concerns now centred on women working at home, in sweated workshops or in domestic service. Her leadership of the League between 1886 and 1888 led to the formation of a Consumers' League. Success was minimal and confined to a few provincial cities. The concept of a 'fair' wage, however, crystallized through this work and became her basic economic argument for social reform. She delivered a strongly critical speech on the treatment of match-girls to the Fabian Society in June 1888. Annie Besant, who was present, described it as a 'capital lecture on female labour' (Kapp, 1977, II, p. 268). The subsequent successful 'match-girl' strike for better wages and working conditions, including the abolition of fines and deductions, provided her with a significant opportunity to demonstrate her organizing talent.

At this point Clementina Black may have experienced qualms about the direction being taken by the leadership of the League. She resigned her position as Secretary in 1889 and joined the newly formed Women's Trade Union Association (WTUA – later the Women's Industrial Council) which enjoyed considerable support from male trade unionists including Tom Mann, Ben Tillett and John Burns for its objective of organizing women in the East End of London. Black (1889), just before her resignation from the League, outlined the pitiful working conditions in the East End and likened them to slavery, unimaginable to the 'average well-to-do'. While summarizing the case of a woman with starving children, she asked: 'Is there any one of us to whom it does not give a thrill of horror to think that such a woman working steadily with useful work ... should not be able to keep her children in food?' Society's responsibility was to alleviate these conditions as soon as possible and her economic solution was formalized: 'Low pay appears to me to be at the root of most wrongs and sufferings of women in this country' (Black, 1889, pp. 698–9). As the driving force and President of the WTUA, Black's main objective was to found unions for women workers. The Association's funds would not be used for strike purposes – a dictum which Mappen (1985, p. 16) maintains indicated the middle-class bias of Black, since the strike 'was viewed as a radical and working class weapon and not as a tool for an organisation led by primarily middle class women'.

Within a year the WTUA was heavily embroiled in the ten-day chocolate-makers' strike and concluded only after considerable and lengthy negotiations between Black, John Burns and the company. By 1894 she had moved the WTUA's activities towards providing a systematic and thorough investigation of working conditions of women. This may have reflected lack of success in organizing female unions which Strachey (1928, p. 238) claims was due to women's 'obedient apathy', or it may have been a realization on the part of Black that publication of appalling working conditions to middle-class Victorian consciousness was likely to have more effect than unionization. Mappen (1985, p. 17) maintains that Black was more comfortable with this form of activity than 'standing in front of a sweated workshop distributing handbills to working class women and girls'. It is difficult to ascertain how fair this assessment is, but Black was indeed successful in the role of social investigator, as the following 15 years indicate. By 1915 the Council under Black's guidance had investigated more than one hundred trades centred on home work and the work of married women; it had published numerous pamphlets, held conferences on female labour and provided witnesses for parliamentary inquiries and commissions. It also provided a rich source of female sanitary and factory inspectors, medical officers and school board members such that members of the executive came to be regarded as public experts on female labour.

An exhibition in 1904 of sweated labour in Berlin caught the imagination of leading Fabians in Britain, leading to a similar exhibition in London.

Black was a chief contributor and speaker, together with Mary Macarthur, Margaret Irwin and G.B. Shaw. The experience influenced Black profoundly. She became an executive member of the Anti-Sweating League (and later its Vice-President). It led to her first real economic work *Sweated Industry and the Minimum Wage* (1907), followed two years later by the *Makers of Our Clothes: A Case For Trades Boards*. As a result of the agitation of the League, the Trades Boards Act was passed in 1909 (extended and amended in 1916). Black's services to women were recognized by the grant of a Civil List pension in 1913 – a very rare occurrence at the time, for a woman. The intense activity of these middle years is contrasted to the quieter life she led in the last dozen years of her life. She still published: *Married Women's Work* (1915) and in 1918 her last book *A New Way of Housekeeping*.

Black's economic works are an attempt at dispassionate social investigation of working and living conditions of women in late Victorian and Edwardian England. Underneath her social philosophy lies an economic framework based on the assumptions of the inequity of competition in the labour market which needed to be removed by a minimum wage and trade unionism. She viewed wages as the result of the interaction of the supply and demand for labour but argued that the return to labour should be sufficient to live comfortably with some added return for expenditure of the life force involved in such labour. 'The cost then of labour as a commodity is the cost of the worker's existence, a cost paid by the worker not in money, but in exhaustion, in hunger, in actual flesh and blood' (Black, 1907, p. 165). Unencumbered free competition leads to the cheapest selling price for all commodities but when this includes labour it causes 'the impoverishment of the seller, deterioration of the product and increase of human misery' (ibid., p. 166). This was not to say that manufacturers benefited from the exploitation of labour. Black maintained that given unfettered competition and lack of combination among sellers, the consumer was the one who ultimately gained in the form of lower prices. This 'profit' was eroded in the long run by the need of a benevolent society to support those who were indigent as a result of low wages. The benevolent, in turn, by providing charitable relief, enabled employers to pay below subsistence wages: 'charitable donations can only be, in effect, a rate in aid of wages and therefore in the end a force towards the reduction of wages' (ibid., p. 703). She neither subscribed to Helen Bosanquet's (*q.v.*) view that wages were a payment determined by the quality of work nor that the best method to erase poverty was to make the poor more efficient. Poverty was caused by an excess of labour in the market, not inefficiency, and 'ill nourished, ill clothed and ill taught (labour) cannot be made efficient'. Further, 'it is difficult to believe that the poor are the architects of their own poverty and they must themselves be its physician' (ibid., pp. 158–9). The first solution was interference in the market mechanism for labour by the establishment of a minimum wage, which would be administered by various trades boards. Higher wages would not necessarily lead to higher prices since manufacturers would respond by improving technology and management techniques. Improved efficiency would undoubtedly raise productivity. She cited the cotton industry where increased wages had, via the inducement to implement new technology, increased output and productivity. Higher wages and therefore income would increase the level of consumption, which would in turn stimulate the economy and growth. The second solution to poor working conditions was unionization. Low wages reflected a large pool of unorganized surplus labour. Black argued in *Sweated Industry* that labour was unlike any other commodity and therefore unionism was justified even if this opposed prevailing laws of political economy. Intervention in the process of competition was socially and economically beneficial. *Laissez-faire* economics was in any case unrealistic since a number of sectors in the economy experienced situations from a 'modified feudalism to an almost undiluted socialism' (Black, 1907, p. 193). At the end of her career Black focused on the economic role of women as distinct from the economic consequences of women working. Black (1918) explores the theme that women's right to work should be enhanced by improved methods of child care, provision of crèches at work and more efficient housekeeping methods. She also provides a sustained argument for the release of women from domestic chores to higher endeavours via the provision of constructive domestic science. She viewed housework as a form of 'penal servitude' and makes a distinction between 'vital labour – the labour that does and makes and deadening labour – that labour that merely repeats without producing anything' (Black, 1918, p. 38).

Absence of biographical information means that Black's personality and character can only be gauged by her work. Social consciousness and compassion are evident in the haunting and graphic descriptions given of the poverty encountered in her investigations. As a highly intelligent, educated and articulate woman with varied interests, she became an acknowledged expert in the field of female labour who seemed equally adept at door-knocking in the working-class domain and in discussions with ministers and politicians. Her economic contribution consists of detailed investigations of female sweated labour. While she worked with the need for a minimum wage and could justify this theoretically, she did not provide an original theoretical framework for her labour economics. Her empirical revelations were of sufficient impact to provide the impetus for legislative change. Black can therefore be ranked as one of the most proficient and significant investigators of women's labour of her era.

SUSAN KING

Bibliography

Selected writings by Clementina Black
(1880), *Orlando*, 3 vols, London: Smith Elder and Co.
(1883), 'Harriet Martineau (1802–1876)', *Encyclopaedia Britannica*, Edinburgh: ninth edition,
   XV, pp. 583–4.
(1889), 'Organisation of Working Women', *Fortnightly Review*, **46**, 695–70.
(1890), 'On Marriage', *Fortnightly Review*, **47**, 586–94.
(1890), 'Chocolate Makers Strike', *Fortnightly Review*, **48**, 305–14.
(1902), *Frederic Walker*, London: Duckworth and Co.
(1907), *Sweated Industry and the Minimum Wage*, London: Duckworth and Co.
(1909), *Makers of Our Clothes: A Case For Trade Boards* (with Mrs Carl Meyer), London:
   Duckworth and Co.
(1911), *The Linleys of Bath*, London: Martin Secker.
(1915), *Married Women's Work*, London: Bell and Sons.
(1918), *A New Way of Housekeeping*, London: W. Collins and Son.

Other sources and references
Collette, Christine (1989), *For Labour and For Women*, Manchester: Manchester University
   Press.
Garnett, David (1954), *The Golden Echo*, London: Chatto and Windus.
Heilbron, Carolyn G. (1961), *The Garnett Family*, London: Allen and Unwin.
Kapp, Yvonne (1977), *Eleanor Marx: Vols 1–3*, London: Lawrence and Wishart.
Lewenhak, Sheila (1977), *Women and Trade Unions*, London: Ernst Benn.
Mappen, Ellen (1985), *Helping Women at Work – The Women's Industrial Council: 1889–1914*,
   London: Hutchison.
Soldon, Norbert (1978), *Women and British Trade Unions: 1874–1976*, Dublin: Gill and
   Macmillan.
Strachey, Ray (1928), *The Cause*, London: G. Bell and Sons.

Rosalind (Hyman) Blauer (1943–73)

Rosalind Blauer's career was brief, cut short by her tragic death at the age of 30. She none the less made significant contributions to both social policy and our understanding of inflation and income distributions.

Rosalind Hyman was born in Montreal on 24 January 1943. She was an outstanding student in high school, and considered entering the accounting programme at McGill University. Her father, an experienced chartered accountant, discouraged her. It was no job for a woman, he explained; no matter how good she was, she would spend her life out of sight in a back room. So in 1959 she entered McGill's economics programme, which provided an outlet for both her intellect and her growing social awareness. She graduated in 1963 with first-class grades, and moved to the University of Rochester for her MA, which she completed in 1965. Her husband, Marvin Blauer, accompanied her to Rochester to enter the graduate programme in political science. The Blauers then returned to McGill to enter Ph.D. programmes in economics and political science. In the autumn of 1966 they both moved to St

Catharines, Ontario, to take up faculty positions at the newly established Brock University. Rosalind Blauer was the founding faculty member in the Department of Economics.

Rosalind Blauer completed her Ph.D. thesis in 1971 under the supervision of Jack Weldon, an economist noted for both his powerful analytic abilities and his brilliance as a teacher. Her topic was 'Inflation and the redistribution of income and net worth of Canadian households, 1950–1967'. Most inflation studies up to that point estimated changes in functional income shares or dealt with inflation's effects on those with institutionally fixed incomes. Analyses of changes in wealth usually distinguished between net creditors and net debtors, but little else. Blauer extended these analyses to consider the effects of inflation on individual households, which may have individuals with various sources of income, who work in different industrial sectors and hold different types and amounts of wealth. In the final stages of the analysis, she considered the effects of inflation on the overall distribution of household income.

Her analysis required detailed income information for the years 1945–67, much of which was not easily available. Monthly and quarterly data such as industrial wage rates and the many different interest rates were available from the Dominion Bureau of Statistics (now Statistics Canada) and from firms in the financial sector. Other earnings, ranging from professional fees to teachers' salaries to entertainers' fees, were more problematic. Blauer collected these data through painstaking correspondence with many different industry associations, trade unions, government departments and individual companies. With these data she was able to create time series for different forms of income, assets and liabilities.

She then turned to customized data tapes from the 1961 Census and to balance sheets from the 1964 Dominion Bureau of Statistics survey of consumer finances. Using these household data she was able to calculate changes in income and net worth for individual households, based on the assumption that the household's factor supplies and asset holdings remained constant over time.

The period from 1945 to 1967 was divided into periods of 'mild inflation', 'strong inflation' and periods of constant prices. (It is interesting to note that, from the perspective of the late 1960s, an annual increase in the Consumer Price Index of 2.5 per cent per annum was considered 'strong inflation'!) Changes in income distributions were then compared for periods of similar and periods of dissimilar inflation rates.

Her results were, at the time, rather startling. She summarized them in an invited paper, 'Fixed Income and Asset Groups in Canada', which she presented at a special conference at Queen's University in June 1970. The paper was later published in the conference volume, *Inflation and the Canadian*

Experience (1971). Her first of many conclusions was that 'inflation was not accompanied by any major changes in income distribution over broad socio-economic categories that did not also occur during periods of price stability' (Blauer, 1971b, p. 146). Further, 'Inflation was accompanied by increasing equity in the distribution of wealth, whereas price stability was accompanied by increasing inequality' (ibid.). In addition, she found that the costs of anti-inflation policies, through their effects on labour markets, weighed more heavily on lower-income households.

Blauer's results were of great interest because they called into question the benefits of the anti-inflationary policies which many considered to be important. She, on the other hand, suggested that 'the cost to society of curbing inflation might well be higher than the cost of the inflation itself' (Blauer, 1971b, p. 148).

Blauer's concern with income distributions and social welfare extended beyond her scholarship. She and her husband were active in provincial and federal politics, supporting candidates for Canada's social democratic party, the New Democratic Party (NDP). They were active in other local community organizations, and they adopted a son, Daniel. In 1972 they both took leave of absence from Brock University to join Jack Weldon in Winnipeg as policy analysts for the province of Manitoba's new NDP government. Rosalind Blauer served as the Director of Economic Analysis in the Cabinet Policy Secretariat. She represented Manitoba in discussions on revisions to the Canada Pension Plan and was especially concerned with the treatment of women by the Plan.

Rosalind Blauer gave birth to Andrew in 1973. Shortly after his birth she underwent what was to be minor surgery, lapsed into a coma and passed away a month later. Her death was a personal tragedy; it was also a tragedy for the wider community, which lost one of its most promising young scholars and social activists.

While at Brock, Rosalind Blauer was instrumental in founding a day care centre, primarily to assist women with children who wanted the opportunity to attend university. The thriving Rosalind Blauer Centre for Child Care is a lasting memorial to her many contributions.

LEWIS A. SOROKA

Selected writings by Rosalind Blauer

(1971a), 'Inflation and the redistribution of income and net worth of Canadian households, 1950–1967', PhD thesis, McGill University, Montreal.

(1971b), 'Fixed income and asset groups in Canada', in N. Swan and D. Wilton (eds), *Inflation and the Canadian Experience*, Kingston, Ontario: Industrial Relations Centre, Queen's University, pp. 127–48.

(1972), 'Inflation in Canada', in John Chant, Keith Acheson, Parzival Copes and Gilles Paquet (eds), *Canadian Perspectives in Economics*, Don Mills, Ontario: Collier-Macmillan.

Barbara Bodichon (1827–91)

Barbara Bodichon is most noted for her role during the 1850s and 1860s in initiating in Britain a movement to gain economic and political independence for women. She was the inspirational, if not always actual, leader of a group of women who were among the earliest to agitate for women's property, marriage and voting rights, as well as better-quality education for women and their improved access to the workplace. Her major written contributions to economics generally supported the ideas of the classical economists, but emphasized women's rights.

Bodichon's early unconventional life, in which her father treated her equally with his sons, provided her with a good education and endowed her with enough income for financial independence (see Herstein, 1985; Burton, 1949). She used her financial resources to attend Bedford College, one of the few colleges then open to women. When she was 22 her education led her to read with great interest John Stuart Mill's *Principles of Political Economy*. Although she absorbed most of the ideas of the classical economists, she was critical of Mill for neglecting the plight of women and the laws concerning them.

Convinced of the importance of educating women, in 1854 she opened her own coeducational school for children. In 1860 she presented a paper on the deficiencies of education for middle-class women and girls to the National Association for the Promotion of Social Sciences, which was printed in the *English Woman's Journal* later in the year (Herstein, 1985, p. 63). Her school and later activities laid the groundwork for the more inclusive public system that was created in 1870.

In 1854 Bodichon authored a pamphlet, *A Brief Summary, in Plain Language, of the Most Important Laws Concerning Women*, that created quite a sensation. This pamphlet was a short and direct explanation of the legal status of women in England, primarily with respect to the lack of property rights for married women. Bodichon urged a repeal of the laws that were restraining women and she asked that the same laws regarding property rights be applied to both men and women. *Brief Summary* 'clearly reflected a strong belief in an individualistic, noninterventionist mode of government' (Herstein, 1985, p. 73).

Although others had recognized the legal problems of married women, no organized movement for change existed until Bodichon organized the Married Women's Property Committee in December 1855. The committee collected over 24 000 signatures to a petition asking for property rights for married women; Bodichon herself collected 3000. With the help of the Law Amendment Society, a bill was presented in Parliament in 1857 that eventually led to the passage of the Marriage and Divorce Bills of 1857 and 1858, which made divorce more accessible and gave women the right to separate with their children and the right to keep any future earnings or inheritance (Strachey, 1928, pp. 73–6; Burton, 1949, pp. 66–71; Herstein, 1985, pp. 78–93).

Bodichon also addressed women's problems in the workplace, writing her most important pamphlet concerning economics, *Women and Work* (1857). Despite being poorly arranged, the essay raised important points and presented one of the earliest accounts of the overcrowding theory of women's pay.

Bodichon suggested that 'Women want work both for the health of their minds and bodies. They want it … *for all the reasons that men want work*' (1857, in Lacey, 1987, p. 63). Yet she noted that many positions were closed to women because they were poorly trained and unskilled. Bodichon blamed parents for not recognizing that their daughters needed to be educated, pointing out that for 'women at the age of twenty and upwards, forty-three out of the hundred in England and Wales are unmarried' (ibid., p. 40). She also argued that it was wrong to think of women as less feminine if they worked, and wrong to be prejudiced against women who worked for money. Bodichon warned against the belief that only women of the lower classes worked for money and that all others should work for free, primarily for charities.

Another fallacy she noted was the common belief 'that ladies should not take the bread out of the mouths of the poor working-man or woman by selling in their market'. She refutes this fallacy in the best tradition of Say's Law: supply creates its own demand:

> The riches and material well-being of the country consist in the quantity of stuff in the country to eat and wear, houses to live in, books to read, … etc. Anyone who puts more of any of these things into the country, adds to its riches and happiness. … This is why we bless steam-engines; this is why we would bless women. Steam engines did at first take the bread out of a few mouths, but how many thousands have they fed for one they have starved! (Ibid., pp. 62–3)

Because women were poorly trained and because of societal prejudice, few jobs were open to women and competition for these jobs was intense, causing wages in those occupations to be abysmally low. If only the impediments preventing women from working and attaining education could be removed, Bodichon argued, women and society would be enhanced as productivity and output increased. Throughout *Women and Work* she noted numerous occupations women could profitably and easily pursue with the proper training. Aiding women in this task turned out to be a major task of Bodichon and her cohorts in the years ahead.

Bodichon's Married Women's Property Committee was a catalyst that spawned a women's movement encompassing a large network of women who were involved in numerous activities. Strachey (1928, p. 94) suggests that they 'dealt with everything which could be connected with the Women's Movement with a moderation, a seriousness, and tact which deserved the utmost praise'. The activities of the Committee and other interested women gradually 'coalesced around the office of the [*English Woman's*] Journal', which was started in 1858 by Bodichon and her friend Bessie Rayner Parkes (1829–1925), and was located at Langham Place (Herstein, 1985, p. 134). The women who worked at Langham Place should be recognized as the first group in England actively to promote women's issues. The major outlet for their written views was the *English Woman's Journal*, but their major legacy was the agencies they created to seek change.

The women at Langham Place focused their efforts on activities that would enhance the independence of women, including securing educational opportunities and improving job opportunities. Soon after the *Journal* was launched women began to come into its offices to inquire about jobs at the *Journal* or leads for jobs elsewhere. To meet the demands for jobs, the women at Langham Place founded the first employment bureau and later formed the Society for the Promotion of the Employment of Women in 1859. One of its early successes was in training women in the printing profession. Among the activities started by the Society were a law engrossing office, a telegraph school, and a business school for young women to help them attain the training necessary for many business-related jobs that had been closed to them. The Employment Society and its related affiliates were successful at finding many other jobs for women and eventually opened branch offices across England. By the 1860s the women of Langham Place were also pressing for more and better higher education for women. While progress was slow, their activities set in motion the process of gaining equal access for women to higher education.

Barbara Bodichon and her cohorts based their economic arguments and justified their activities principally on the simple principles of *laissez-faire*, Say's Law, and the equitable concept that females should be able to own and dispose of property to the same extent as males. In this they were very comfortable with the ideas of the classical economists, such as John Stuart Mill, in whose parliamentary election they campaigned vigorously. Bodichon best exemplified this view in *Women and Work*. Along with Mill, she developed the notion of overcrowding of women, arguing that the surplus of women workers drove down their wages, but only because of the laws, rules and customs that restricted women's entry into the workforce. Consistent with these views, she and her colleagues concentrated on ensuring that women were able to own property and had access to better education and thus more jobs. Although their later activities were increasingly centred around obtaining the vote for women, they continued to write about and participate in activities designed to promote economic independence for women and, in doing so, created a lasting legacy.

WILLIAM D. SOCKWELL

Bibliography
Bodichon, Barbara Leigh Smith (1854), *A Brief Summary, in Plain Language, of the Most Important Laws Concerning Women: Together with a Few Observations Thereon*. Reprinted in Lacey (1987), pp. 23–35.
Bodichon, Barbara Leigh Smith (1857), *Women and Work*. Reprinted in Lacey (1987), pp. 36–73.
Burton, Hester (1949), Barbara Bodichon, London: John Murray.
Herstein, Sheila R. (1985), *A Mid-Victorian Feminist, Barbara Leigh Smith Bodichon*, New Haven, CT: Yale University Press.
Lacey, Candida Ann (ed.) (1987), *Barbara Leigh Smith Bodichon and the Langham Place Group*, New York and London: Routledge and Kegan Paul.
Strachey, Ray (1928), *The Cause: A Short History of the Women's Movement in Great Britain*, London: G. Bell and Sons; reprinted London: Virago, 1978.

Olga Nikolajevna Bondareva (1937–91)

Olga Nikolajevna Bondareva was born in Leningrad (now again called St Petersburg) on 27 April 1937. She spent her childhood in the Ukraine. In 1944 her family returned to Leningrad and the remaining part of her life was passed in this city.

Beginning in 1950, she joined a mathematical 'kruzhok' (circle) led by Georgij Vladimirovich Epifanov. (This circle was organized on an experimental basis: the members spent extended periods of time together focusing not only on mathematics but also on cultural self-education, sports activities, camping excursions, and so on.)

In 1954 Olga finished her university education and joined the mathematical faculty of the Leningrad State University. She became a member of the chair of probability which was headed by Yu. V. Linnik. Simultaneously she became interested in the theory of games (thanks to the lectures of Nicolaj N. Vorobiev who for a long time acted as her scientific adviser).

In 1963 she received her Ph.D. degree in mathematics at Leningrad University. The title of her thesis was 'Theory of the Core in an n-Person Game'. The main results of this work are nowadays included in various textbooks on game theory and its applications in mathematical economics.

In 1984 she received a Dr. Sci. degree in mathematics at the University of Moscow. The title of her thesis was 'Methods of solving cooperative games and their applications'.

Olga Bondareva held the following positions, all at Leningrad State University:

October 1959 to April 1972: Junior Research Fellow, then Associate Professor in Operations Research, then Senior Research Fellow of the Mathematical Faculty.
June 1972 to July 1984: Senior Research Fellow of the Economics Faculty.
July 1984 to March 1989: Senior Research Fellow at the Institute of Physics.
In October 1989 she returned to the Mathematical Faculty as a leading research fellow and remained in this position until her death.

(The changes in the place of employment within the University of Leningrad were related to an incident in 1972 which was very typical for that time. One of Olga's students decided to emigrate to Israel, and the student organization 'Komsomol' was ordered to expel him. This was a natural procedure but in addition was considered to give reason to organize a political 'hate lesson' for his class mates. Olga, as their tutor, appeared on this show and stated that 'we should feel sorry rather than hate a person who leaves his native country'. Thereafter the students' decision was not unanimous, and Olga, as the alleged source of this trouble, was expelled from the mathematical faculty. Her return to this faculty was a result of 'perestroika'.)

Following the example of Epifanov, Bondareva arranged a mathematical 'kruzhok' herself in 1959, and three girls from this group later on became her long-time colleagues (Tatiana Kulakovskaja, Natalia Naumova and Natalia Sokolina – the first two continue to work in the mathematical faculty).

Olga Bondareva was an adviser to seven Ph.D. students. She was a member of the American Mathematical Society and the Leningrad Mathematical Society as well as a member of the editorial board of *Games and Economic Behavior*. Beginning in 1968, she was invited to almost all international conferences on game theory but only in 1988 did she obtain permission to participate, after which whe went to conferences in Columbus, Brussels, Oberwolfach, Ulm, Bielefeld, New Delhi and Stony Brook.

She wrote 70 papers, a chapter in an edited collection (reference no. 6 below) and a popular book on the theory of games (reference no. 3 below).

She named the following papers as her main publications:

1. 'Some applications of linear programming to the theory of cooperative games', *Problemy kibernetiki*, **10**, 1963 (in Russian, see English translation in *Selected Russian Papers in Game Theory 1959–1965*, Princeton University Press, 1968).

   The paper provides a necessary and sufficient condition for the core of a cooperative game with side payments to be non-empty. This condition is formulated in terms of balanced sets (a notion that was introduced independently later on by L.S. Shapley). The paper also contains conditions for the core to be a solution in the sense of von Neumann–Morgenstern.

2. 'Solution for a class of games with empty core', *Soviet Doklady*, **185** (2), 1969.

A sufficient condition that some solutions of a game may be presented as Cartesian products of solutions of games with smaller sets of players, constructed from the given game.

3. *On game-theoretic models of economy*, Leningrad University, 1974.
    The main topics of the theory of cooperative games are presented in a popular form.

4. 'Acyclic games', Vestnik (Review) of Leningrad University, no. 7, 1975.
    Acyclic games are cooperative games endowed with an acyclic dominance relation. The following results are proved in this paper: if a game is acyclic then the set of all imputations can be divided into a system of 'pyramidal' components with an acyclic dominance relation. Moreover, if the dominance relation allows for a solution on each compact pyramidal subset of the set of imputations, then the acyclic game has a solution.

5. 'Convergence of space with a relation and game-theoretical consequences', *Zhurnal Vych. Math. i Math. Phys.*, **18**(1), 1978.
    Here Bondareva considers a topological space endowed with a binary relation. Various definitions of continuity of such relations are discussed and the resulting continuity properties of cores and solutions of games with respect to the initially introduced topology are treated. These results are then applied to obtain sufficient conditions for the existence of Nash equilibrium points and non-strict Pareto optimal points in problems of vector optimization.

6. 'Development of game theoretical methods of optimization in cooperative games and their applications to multi criterial problems', in N. Moiseev (ed.), *Sovremennoe sostojanie teorii issledovanija operatskij* (State of the art in the theory of operations research), Moscow: Nauka, 1979.
    The problem of finding a core in a cooperative game, Nash-equilibrium point in games in normal form, and existence of Pareto-optimal points in the problem of vector optimization are considered from the point of view of finding the set of maximal elements of binary relation.

7. 'Extensive coverings and some necessary conditions of existence of solutions in cooperative games', Vestnik of Leningrad University, no. 19, 1983.
    Extensive coverings constitute a generalization of balancedness. Using this definition the paper presents necessary conditions for a cooperative game to have a core solution and a solution with discrimination.

8. 'Finite approximations of choice on infinite sets', Izvestija AN SSSR, *Tekhnicheskaja kibernetika*, no. 1, 1987.
    Axioms of revealed preferences are considered: heritage condition, Condorcet condition, independence of irrelevant alternatives. If the choice function satisfies these axioms on finite subsets of the set of alternatives, then the axioms are not necessary satisfied on infinite sets. The

conditions of such expansion are given in terms of continuity of the choice function and revealed preferences.

9. 'Game theoretical analysis of one product market with similar utilities', *Kibernetika*, no. 5, 1990.

   The paper deals with a market with n participants and one undivisible commodity. Every participant can be both a seller and a buyer. This market is modelled as an n-person cooperative game. For this game the Shapley value and the nucleolus are constructed.

10. 'Revealed fuzzy preferences', in *Multiperson Decision Making Models Using Fuzzy Sets and Possibility Theory*, Kluwer Academic Publishers, 1990.

    In this paper it is proved that there exists a one-to-one mapping between the class of all anti-reflexive binary non-fuzzy relations and a class of choice functions with certain properties. For example, the maximal elements of a binary relation, or the set of those elements which are internally and externally stable, constitute a choice function corresponding to a certain binary relation. The paper then continues to provide a 'fuzzy extension' of these notions and to show analogous results with respect to a 'fuzzy' social choice theory.

The list so far was provided by Olga herself. We would like to extend it by several titles as follows:

11. 'Solution of an arbitrary four-person game', Vestnik (Review) of Leningrad University, no. 7, 1979 (joint work with T.E. Kulakovskaja and N.I. Naumova).

    It is stated that each cooperative four-person game has a von Neumann–Morgenstern solution.

12. 'On solution of classical cooperative four-person games with non-empty cores (general case)', Vestnik of Leningrad University, no. 19, 1979.

    A von Neumann–Morgenstern solution is constructed for an arbitrary four-person game with a non-empty core and for one class of games with an empty core as well.

13. 'Extensive coverings and exact core bounds', University of Twente, Department of Applied Mathematics, Memo no. 915, December 1990 (joint work with T.S.H. Driessen).

    The topic of this paper is the determination of exact bounds for non-empty cores of cooperative games. The exact lower and upper bounds are determined in terms of extremal excesses with respect to reduced upper and lower coverings.

14. 'Domination, core and solution (brief survey of Russian results)', Discussion paper no. 185, IMW, University of Bielefeld, 1989.

This is a survey written with the intention of making some literature accessible only in Russian available to English-speaking readers.

TATIANA E. KULAKOVSKAJA
NATALIA I. NAUMOVA

Editors' note: The assistance of Joseph V. Romanovsky in the preparation of this contribution is acknowledged.

Helen Dendy Bosanquet (1860–1925)

Helen Dendy Bosanquet was the fifth of nine children of John Dendy (1824–94) and Sarah Beard (1831–1922). She grew up in the confines of one of those nonconformist clergyman's families which created 'an aristocracy of talent' in Victorian England. Four of the children fit this description. Older brother John was a successful lawyer and amateur writer of travel books and lay sermons, oldest sister Mary became a teacher and social worker, while Arthur, the second youngest son, became a noted botanist. As prominent social worker, Royal Commissioner and fairly prolific author, Helen Dendy became the most famous in this talented family. When her youngest brother graduated in 1885, Helen Dendy, who until then had been involved in house-keeping for her large family, decided to acquire some higher education for herself to supplement the limited education she had received from her mother and a German governess. In 1886, she entered Newnham College, Cambridge, taking the Moral Sciences Tripos and specializing in political economy studies. Her period as a student therefore coincided with the return of Alfred Marshall to Cambridge, as its new Professor of Political Economy. She attended his classes from 1887 to 1889, including his Advanced Political Economy Class in Michaelmas term 1888 as the only woman in the company of gifted male economics students such as Flux and Chapman. She gained a first in the Tripos examinations and, in later correspondence, Marshall addressed her as a fellow economist, a status which meant that he had to respond to her criticism of part of his *Principles* in her book, *The Strength of the People* (Bosanquet, 1902 [1903], p. 70, correspondence reproduced in its preface; Groenewegen, 1995, pp. 521–3). A career in teaching economics being highly unlikely for a gifted woman, she followed her older sister's example and went to London as a social worker.

There she made contact with the Charity Organization Society (COS), befriending its Secretary Charles Loch and his wife, and in October 1890 gaining the salaried position of COS District Secretary for Shoreditch. She held this position until her marriage in 1895 to Bernard Bosanquet, whom she met at meetings of the London Ethical Society. He encouraged her to become a university extension lecturer, which she did for a short period despite opposition from Foxwell (Burrows, 1978, p. 8). He also gave her advice on suitable teaching techniques, and gained her the assignment of translating Von Sigwart's two-volume work, *Logik*, important for its detailed examination of the induction theories of Bacon, Hume and John Stuart Mill, which she had studied at Cambridge as part of the Moral Sciences Tripos syllabus. It was published in 1895, the same year in which she published seven previously published essays in *Aspects of the Social Problem* (Bosanquet, 1895). Topics included 'Children of Working London', 'The Position of Women in Industry', 'Marriage in East London', 'Old Pensioners', 'The Industrial Residuum', 'The Origins and History of the English Poor Law' and 'The Meaning and Methods of True Charity'. These were themes to which she returned over and over again in her writings.

Marriage did not halt these activities of social work and writing. Her position as social worker became an honorary activity. In 1896 she published *Rich and Poor*; in 1898 *The Standard of Life and Other Studies*, in 1902 *The Strength of the People. A Study in Social Economics*, in 1906 *The Family* and in 1914 a history of the COS entitled *Social Work in London 1869–1912*. In 1909 she became editor of *Charity Organisation Review*, after serving with great distinction on the Royal Commission on the Poor Laws (1905–9), discussed at length in McBriar (1987) and of which she produced a summary (Bosanquet, 1909). After World War I, when both her own health and that of her husband started to decline, she continued publication at a reduced rate. A slim volume of verses and German translations called *Zoar* (1919), a brief biographical memoir of her husband following his death (Bosanquet, 1924a) and an essay, *Free Trade and Peace in the Nineteenth Century* (Bosanquet, 1924b) which defended the liberal economic policies she had espoused for nearly the whole of her working life, were her final publications.

Bosanquet's work as an economist concentrated on what she later described as social economics, 'an applied science ... directly useful to those engaged in public administration' (Bosanquet, 1902 [1903], p. xiv). Nearly all her published work, including her ten articles for the *Economic Journal*, can be described in this way and was in itself informed by her long, active association with the COS. That association, which lasted until its demise, is another strong manifestation of her staunch liberal values of individualism and limited government intervention. These principles defined her economic perspectives from her first economic publications onwards. They also made her an obvious candidate for the role of early historian of the COS. Bosanquet (1914) has become a classic on its origins and evolution, a status recognized by the fact that it was reprinted in full in 1973 in the Harvester Press series on society and the Victorians. It chronicles the losing battle fought by the defenders of self-help and controlled charity (as an avenue towards enabling the privileged classes to carry out their social obligations) against the 'class warriors' of socialism who sought, in the end victoriously, to place that obligation in the hands of the state. With private charity regaining prominence at the end of the twentieth century as part of a sustained attack on the welfare state, the rules of the COS and their practice have a contemporary as well as historical interest.

The Strength of the People, perhaps Bosanquet's major work, is a clear enunciation of the COS philosophy of self-help and independence by which the poor and underprivileged can lift themselves to a higher standard of life through education, example and a minimum of government regulation. Increased wealth and income for the poor are not necessarily blessings unless it is clearly demonstrated to them how best to use their new resources – otherwise the new wealth may lead to degradation through strong drink and other unwise use of leisure (Bosanquet, 1902 [1903], p. 82). Freedom, self-help and education are therefore the keys to the elimination of poverty, which release the innate strength of the population (ibid., pp. 95, 340). The old Poor Law with its unsystematic charity is decried; the new Poor Law of 1834 is extensively praised. Redistributional policies inspired by Bentham's utilitarianism principles are criticized as potentially wasteful, unless the people are taught how to consume with greater effect. A balance has to be created between government regulation and assistance for special cases, and the policy of inculcating principles of self-help which strengthen character and independence, a lesson illustrated by discussion of the appropriate treatment of children and the aged (ibid., chs 7, 8). In the context of work and wages, raised income from greater efficiency is praised and contrasted with wage rises gained through strikes, an almost invariably wasteful activity. Unions are beneficial for their friendly-society activities and similar responsibilities. Minimum wage laws are decried as a waste of time if set low enough that all can find work to earn them; or as unfair when they are set too high to create an underclass of unemployed who will never find work at such a wage (ibid., pp. 292–3). Bosanquet's social economics is a science of human nature and its reactions to certain factors; it is a science of exerting influence over society as a whole, in which political economy can assist because it involves the study of causes and consequences of wealth. Unemployment captures this dual dimension. 'The fact that a man is out of work may be explained mainly by his own character, or mainly by the conditions of trade; but in the majority of cases both causes will be involved' (ibid., pp. 319–20).

Bosanquet's (1909) summary of the Poor Law Commission Report reiterates these views on unemployment. Unemployment is ascribed to manifold causes of which two stand out: lack of demand for a particular labour service and defects in personal character (Bosanquet, 1909, pp. 90–91). Remedies are emigration and encouragement of interregional labour mobility (ibid., pp. 140–41), while public works were not sympathetically entertained by the majority of the Commission. Helen Bosanquet also wrote a substantial part of the Majority Report, probably with some assistance from her husband. One of her fellow commissioners described her 'as having the best-balanced mind of the whole lot of us' while its chairman saw her as his 'right hand' in executing the difficult task (McBriar, 1987, pp. 282–5).

A good indication of Helen Bosanquet's traditional liberal free-trade principles is given in her last contribution for the *Economic Journal* (Bosanquet, 1920). Taking for her title a remark from a speech by Cobden about the impact on demand for British cotton if every Chinaman annually bought a cotton nightcap, she portrayed post-World War I commercial rivalry as 'the race for the Chinaman's nightcap'. This race, she argued, should be conducted on free-trade rather than protectionist lines, as is easily shown from the lessons of nineteenth-century protectionist literature. Irrespective of the potential for financing necessary social expenditure from the boost to tariff revenue due to increased protection, which the leading European protectionist statesmen dangle in front of their electorates, free trade should be universally embraced. Its promises of gains from specialization and economy of production are not the major reason for this, in Bosanquet's opinion. 'It is the imperative need for a real international harmony which forms the strongest argument for complete freedom of trade' (ibid., p. 320). She returned to this classical Manchester School theme in her final economic monograph for the Norwegian Nobel Institute (Bosanquet, 1924b), which paraded the lessons of history from the nineteenth century in this respect. She remained an old-fashioned, nineteenth-century economic liberal to the last.

Bosanquet's published work also included discussions of women's education, women's work and women's wages. Her stress on the value of women's education is captured in the following. Although education greatly raised the 'commercial value' of women in the labour market, as demonstrated by the many women earning an independent living from 'thorough and honest work', thereby indicating the good investment it was, the more important benefit of this development for Helen Bosanquet was social. This arose from the widening of the female mind to broad issues of life and thought which good education entailed, together with the expansion of the power of concentration generated, and would ultimately open up the ability for women to do original work in defiance of contemporary male opinion on this subject (Bosanquet, 1898, p. 148). Equally, she valued the consequences of women's industrial training as a way to raise women's effective remuneration and job opportunities (ibid., pp. 157–73) and condemned the unfair competition from well-meaning charities which lowered women's rates of remuneration, as was also the result of the supplementation of women's incomes by their families and of poor relief (Bosanquet, 1902, pp. 42–9). Her support of the family and its values never detracted from her understanding of the fact that many women needed to be able to support themselves, and sometimes their children, from paid work as independent persons or households.

Although not strictly an economic text, her book on *The Family* (Bosanquet, 1906) needs to be briefly mentioned here. It depicted the family as a crucial institution 'in human society', all too frequently ignored by statesmen and economists, yet deeply significant for social and political movements. It contains two parts, one analysing the history of the family, the other examining the modern family in respect of its economic functions and evaluating its psychology and constituents. Although the historical part draws heavily on what is now seen as unsatisfactory anthropology, the book as a whole is still of considerable interest. It stresses marriage as real partnership (ibid., pp. 274, 280) and emphasizes that proper education for women makes the marriage arrangement even 'higher and more beautiful' and that 'the noblest harmonies of life arise when two disciplined and independent wills combine ... ' (ibid., p. 282). Given contemporary evidence on the subject, the book is naïve on the incidence of domestic violence – 'except among the roughest and most uncivilised classes, public opinion and the law are too strongly against the man who cannot maintain his authority without recourse to violence ... ' (ibid., p. 261). Her argument that the weakening of family life is caused by 'excessive reliance' on external, that is, government sources of maintenance (p. 339), is a typical expression of her COS philosophy.

Helen Bosanquet cannot be described as an analytical economist, involved in the advancement of theory. She was, however, an interesting and well-informed writer on social economics, contributing to the academic journal literature (especially the then new *Economic Journal*) and publishing collections of articles on this topic. Her work drew on the economics and other moral sciences she had learned at Cambridge and was frequently applied to the amelioration of the poor so dear to the heart of her economics mentor, Alfred Marshall. For her, as for him, 'the standard of life [formed] the basis of economic progress' (Bosanquet, 1898, p. v). This entailed an optimistic belief in the sense that it favoured good wages, because 'in the long run, it is the Standard of Life aimed at by any class which determines what the wages in that individual class will be' (ibid., p. 53). This is social economics pure and simple; it supplements a simplified labour market analysis based on the laws of supply and demand. Her social economics was combined with the defence of nineteenth-century liberal values: free trade, anti-socialism and, in the sphere of social work, the remedies of self-help and private, regulated charity to aid the deserving poor. These positions were elegantly, persistently and very firmly put in the many writings she produced over nearly three decades as a social economist of note and in her position as a Royal Commissioner on the Poor Law and dedicated official of the COS.

PETER GROENEWEGEN

Bibliography

Selected writings by Helen Dendy Bosanquet
(1895), *Aspects of the Social Question*, London: Macmillan.
(1896), *Rich and Poor*, London: Macmillan.
(1898), *The Standard of Life and Other Studies*, London: Macmillan.
(1902), 'A Study in Women's Wages', *Economic Journal*, **12**(49), March, 42–9.
(1902 [1903]), *The Strength of the People: A Study in Women's Wages*, London: Macmillan, second edition.
(1906), *The Family*, London: Macmillan.
(1909), *The Poor Law Report of 1909. A Summary*, London: Macmillan.
(1914), *Social Work in London 1869–1912*. Reissued Brighton: Harvester Press, 1973.
(1920), 'The Race for the Chinaman's Nightcap', *Economic Journal*, **30**(123), September, 308–20.
(1924a), *Bernard Bosanquet: A Short Account of his Life*, London: Macmillan.
(1924b), *Free Trade and Peace in the Nineteenth Century*, Kristiania: H. Ashehoug & Co., Publications de l'Institut Nobel Norvégien, vol. 6.

Other sources and references
Burrows, John (1978), 'The Teaching of Economics in the Early Days of the Extension Movement in London 1876–1902', *History of Economic Thought Newsletter*, no. 20, pp. 8–14.
Groenewegen, Peter (1995), *A Soaring Eagle: Alfred Marshall (1842–1924)*, Aldershot, UK and Brookfield, US: Edward Elgar.
McBriar, A.M. (1987), *An Edwardian Mixed Double. The Bosanquets versus the Webbs*, Oxford: Clarendon Press.

Ester Boserup (1910–99)

The Danish economist Ester Boserup (née Børgesen) participated for more than 50 years in the Danish and international debate on economics and other social topics. She was an economist with forceful points of view, and since the 1930s her observations have been regarded as important contributions to the economic debate. From early on, she was a noted academic Marxist participant in the Danish debate; later she became internationally known in the field of development theory, women's issues and agricultural economics. An important characteristic of Ester Boserup is her independence – she was for many years a freelance researcher, and it is impossible to classify her as a member of any of the orthodox economic or political schools.

She was born in 1910 into an upper-class family in Copenhagen, but even before she entered university she had become a member of the Danish Marxist high-school movement. It was in this movement that she met Mogens Boserup. Both began their economic studies at the University of Copenhagen in 1929; they were married in 1931, and worked closely together until Mogens's death in 1978.

Both Ester and Mogens Boserup were prominent members of the intellectual Marxist circles in Denmark in the 1930s. Ester Boserup was from 1931 editor of the Marxist journal *Monde* (which changed its name to *Plan* in 1932). Later in the 1930s they were closely involved with the Marxist student movement's journal *Clarte*. The Boserup group were Marxist and communist, but independent of the Danish Communist Party. Areas of conflict existed in these circles in regard to the relationship to the Communist Party and, with respect to the journals, the balance to be maintained between cultural and social subjects. A number of the intellectuals in these circles were mainly interested in literary and artistic questions. The Boserup group represented a social and political interest, and were completely independent of the Communist Party (see Larsen, 1986; Bredsdorff, 1982).

The internationally known Danish communist author Hans Scherfig, in his novel about the 1930s, *Idealister* (published in Sweden in 1944 and after the war a bestseller in many countries), wrote about a student and his sister who published a journal called *Academic Intelligence Pages*. The couple (clearly a caricature of the Boserups) were too intellectual to be important for the class struggle. Scherfig's attitude was probably common in the Communist Party. But the Boserups were not pure theorists; they did much practical work for German refugees in Denmark during the 1930s (Larsen, 1986).

Ester Boserup obtained her degree in economics in 1935. From 1936 to 1947 she worked in the Danish Central Bank in the exchange control department; from 1938 she was head of section. But she was still very active in publishing her work in the Marxist journals.

She was one of the first to notice the importance of J.M. Keynes's *General Theory*. At a Nordic meeting for younger economic researchers in 1936 she presented a paper about Keynes and Marx (the paper was published in the Danish economic journal *Nationaløkonomisk Tidsskrift* in 1936; see Boserup, 1936; Topp, 1986; Larsen, 1986). Ester Boserup's main point was the similarity between Keynes and Marx: she saw Keynes's *General Theory* and Marx's ideas as parallel criticisms of the view that the market economy is a self-regulating mechanism which automatically creates a harmonious equilibrium. Furthermore, she saw the book and its stress on the aggregated demand as expressing an argument that was relevant in the then current political debate on the level of the wages. Many considered wage cuts to be a necessary policy to combat the Depression; Ester Boserup saw Keynes's book as providing support for the Marxist arguments against such wage reductions.

The article also gave a clear indication of what sort of Marxist economics she liked. 'The Marxist system is most often seen as a theological system whose followers did not really do economic research, but carried out dogmatic exegeses and examinations of the master's revelation' (translated from Danish). For Ester Boserup, however, the Marxist system was a framework for debate and research.[1]

In 1947 Ester and Mogens Boserup left Denmark in order to work for the United Nations, from 1947 to 1957 for the Research Division of the Secretariat of the Economic Commission of Europe in Geneva (Nicholas Kaldor was director of this institution at the time), and from 1957 to 1960 in India. ECE work was not published in the names of the authors but was produced as team work; consequently, there are very few publications by the Boserups in their own name during this period. The largest-scale research project to which they contributed was Gunnar Myrdal's *Asian Drama – An Inquiry into the Poverty of Nations*, in three volumes and with a total of 2284 pages; its publication was one of the main reasons for giving Myrdal the Nobel prize in 1974. Myrdal himself wrote about the Boserups in the preface to the book:

> When in the autumn of 1957 I took up my work in New Delhi, I was accompanied by two senior colleagues from the Research Division of the secretariat of the E.C.E., Mogens and Ester Boserup. The study had been planned to take two and a half years, and the Boserups left me, as we had agreed, in the spring of 1960. Because my own views about the kind of book I wanted to write were at that time gradually changing, the text in its final version contains comparatively little of what Mr. and Mrs. Boserup produced during their term of duty. Nevertheless, the further work on what are now Chapters 22 and 26 on labour utilization in agriculture and agricultural policy could build on early drafts for several sections by Ester Boserup, and a large part of Chapter 10 on population and development of agricultural resources is in the main founded on a manuscript by Mogens Boserup; he also wrote the very first sketch of Chapter 27 on population prospects. In some other chapters of the book there are passages that go back to the early association of the Boserups with the study. (Myrdal, 1968, p. xiv)

The time in Geneva brought the Boserups into contact with many leading European economists, such as Gunnar Myrdal, Nicholas Kaldor and Jan Tinbergen, and when Mogens Boserup was appointed to a post at the University of Copenhagen in 1966, these people visited Copenhagen and contributed to the research milieu there with inspiring lectures for the students (as a Ph.D. student in the early 1970s, I personally remember a tea-party with Ester and Mogens Boserup, Jan Tinbergen and a few others at the Boserup's home – NK).

In 1960 the Boserups came back to Denmark, and from then on Ester Boserup worked as freelance researcher on different projects and jobs. She published a number works that became internationally known. The first and perhaps most important of these was the book entitled *The Conditions of Agricultural Growth – the Economics of Agrarian Change under Population Pressure* (1965). The book is an analysis of the development process in primitive agriculture past and present. It explains how agricultural intensity changes with different systems of land use:

(1) *Forest-fallow cultivation.* Under this system of land use, plots of land are cleared in the forests each year and sown or planted for a year or two, after which the land is left fallow for a number of years sufficient for the forest to regain the land.

(2) *Bush-fallow cultivation.* Under this system the fallow is much shorter, usually somewhere between six and ten years. No true forest can grow up in so short a period, but the land left fallow is gradually covered with bush and sometimes also with small trees.

(3) *Short-fallow cultivation.* The fallow lasts one year or a couple of years only. In such a short fallow period, nothing but wild grasses can invade the fallow, before the cultivator returns to the same plot or field.

(4) *Annual cropping.* This is usually not considered a fallow system, but may be classified as such, because the land is left uncultivated, usually for several months, between the harvest of one crop and the planting of the next.

(5) *Multi-cropping.* This is the most intensive system of land use, since the same plot bears two or more successive crops every year. (Boserup, 1965, pp. 15–16)

The main idea propounded in the book is that the shift from less intensive forms of farming to more intensive production is driven by the pressure of increasing population. According to Ester Boserup, the growth in population is thus the main reason for economic developments in agriculture. Malthus and the Neo-Malthusians argue that the exogenous capacity of food production is the main restriction on population growth. As Thomas Malthus wrote in the well-known extract from his *Essay on Population*,[2]

I say, that the power of population is infinitely greater than the power in the earth to produce subsistence for man.

Population, when unchecked, increases in a geometrical ratio. Subsistence increases only in an arithmetical ratio. A slight acquaintance with numbers will shew the immensity of the first power in comparison of the second.

By that law of our nature which makes food necessary to the life of man, the effects of these two unequal powers must be kept equal ...

The race of plants, and the race of animals shrink under this great restrictive law. And the race of man cannot, by any efforts of reason, escape from it. (Boserup, 1976, p. 88)

But Ester Boserup's point of view is just the opposite:

Therefore, it seems implausible to explain upwards changes in rates of population growth as a result of this type of agrarian change. It is more sensible to regard the process of agricultural change in primitive communities as an adaptation to gradually increasing population densities, brought about by changes in the rates of natural population growth or by immigration.

According to the explanation offered here, population increase leads to the adoption of more intensive systems of agriculture in primitive communities and an increase of total agricultural output. This process, however, can hardly be described as economic growth in the generally accepted sense of this term, since the proximate effect upon output per man-hour is to lower it. But sustained growth of total population and of total output in a given territory has secondary effects which – at least in some cases – can set off a genuine process of economic growth, with rising output per man-hour, first in non-agricultural activities and later in agriculture ...

The important corollary of this is that primitive communities with sustained population growth have a better chance to get into a process of genuine economic development than primitive communities with stagnant or declining population, provided of course, that the necessary agricultural investments are undertaken. (Boserup, 1965, pp. 117–18)

Ester Boserup's theory is based on careful studies, in particular of the labour cost per produced unit. If exogenous technical progress causes the changes, the changes should be followed by falling labour costs. If Ester Boserup's theory of population pressure provides the reason for changes, however, labour costs should increase, and this is indeed what she found.

Ester Boserup's book has been extensively discussed among development economists and economic historians. Some argue for the theory; others are sceptical. Ester Boserup seems sure, however, that she is right. On the occasion of her 85th birthday, the Danish newspaper *Politiken* carried out a major interview with her. To the journalist's great surprise, she expressed no fear about overpopulation: 'I am considerably more afraid of being too few,' she said. The importance of the book can be judged by the fact that it has been translated into Spanish in 1967, into French in 1970, into Swedish in 1973, and into Japanese in 1975.

Ester Boserup continued her work by analysing the role of women in the development process. The book *Women's Role in Economic Development* was published in 1970 (Swedish translation 1971, Danish 1972, Italian 1982, German and French 1983, Indonesian 1984 and Spanish 1993). In this book, she describes how the farming system changes during the development process from a female farming system (where women support themselves and their families, and tend to be independent), first to a male farming system, and later to a mixed system, where women are subordinate non-waged labourers in their husbands' fields under the supervision of men.

Ester Boserup is of the opinion that the Europeans played an important role in this process in the developing countries. The European has in mind the idea of an active male farmer working on his own land:

European settlers, colonial administrators and technical advisers are largely re-sponsible for the deterioration in the status of women in the agricultural sectors of developing countries. It was they who neglected the female agricultural labour force when they helped to introduce modern commercial agriculture to the over-seas world and promoted the productivity of male labour ... Their European acceptance that cultivation is naturally a job for men persuaded them to believe that men could become far better farmers than women, if only they would aban-don their customary 'laziness' ... and it then seemed to follow that for the development of agriculture male farming ought to be promoted to replace female farming. Many Europeans did all they could to achieve this. (Boserup, 1970, pp. 53–4)

In 1981 Boserup published the book *Population and Technological Changes*. The book was a continuation of the 1965 book. The author explained the relation between the two books:

> In both books, I focus on those types of technology which are related to population changes, while I ignore or only occasionally mention types which seem to me to have little, if any relationship to demographic changes. But while in my earlier book the focus was on agricultural technology, here I also include other population-linked technologies. I use a broad definition of technology, including, for instance, agricultural methods, sanitary methods, administrative techniques, and literacy. (Boserup, 1981, p. ix)

The conclusion is, however, unchanged:

> It should be said that this book is not a revision of the theory I put forward in *The Conditions of Agricultural Growth*, but only an attempt to broaden and deepen it. My earlier book provoked much comment from scholars belonging to many disciplines. A number of them have attempted to test the theory, either by reinvestigation of already existing information, or by gathering new data. A sufficient number of these studies have come out in support of my theory to make me confident that I was on the right track and have nothing to regret, so far as the theory is concerned. (Ibid., p. x)

This book was also translated – into Spanish in 1984 and into Japanese in 1991.

These three books are, as the number of translations indicates, already modern classics, and it is they that establish Ester Boserup's reputation; but she has a number of other publications to her name, for example *Economic and Demographic Relationships in Development* (1990), and a number of articles and chapters in different journals and books.

Her contributions have been widely recognized and appreciated. She was made an honorary doctor of the Dutch Agricultural University in Wageningen (1978), of the University of Copenhagen (1979) and of Brown University, Rhode Island (1985). She also received a number of awards (among them an award from the Danish broadcasting service for popular lectures).

Modern economics publications are written for specialists, appear in specialized journals, and are typically formulated in a combination of mathematical expressions and English – which is the language of international economic researchers, but is incomprehensible to non-specialists. Ester Boserup is one of the few whose contributions are of interest both to economics specialists and to a wider audience, including people who do not speak English (as can be seen from the number of translations made of her books).

It is possible to identify a theme running throughout the whole body of Ester Boserup's works, from her Marxist writings as a young student to her international publications as an established authority. Sophisticated elaboration of the detail of various theories, which is so common in modern mainstream economics, has never formed her topic. It is difficult to place her in any theoretical school, but she was always a classical economist (like Karl Marx, for example) in the sense that she worked on the main lines of the development process and on the distribution of income and power. Her interest was the distribution of wealth and poverty among people, genders and societies. But in contrast to other 'classical' economists, aggregated demand played a major role in her thinking. This can be seen in her very early acceptance of Keynes in 1936 and in her own theory of development, where population growth and food demand are the crucial factors for agricultural growth. Ester Boserup died in late 1999.

NIELS KÆRGÅRD
INGRID HENRIKSEN

Notes

1. This remained the view of Ester and Mogens Boserup in the period after 1968, and Mogens Boserup in particular was seen by many 1970s-style Marxists as being an old conservative professor representing the establishment.
2. The quotation is taken from Mogens Boserup's *Deres egne ord* (*Their Own Words*), a 327-page collection of extracts from the main arguments of famous economists from Plato to Keynes. The reading of original texts formed a major part of Mogens Boserup's teaching in the history of economic ideas.

Bibliography

Selected writings by Ester Boserup

(1936), 'Nogle centrale økonomiske Spørgsmaal i Lys af den marxistiske Teori' (Some central economic problems in the light of the Marxian theory), *Nationaløkonomisk Tidsskrift*, **74**, 421–35.
(1965), *The Conditions of Agricultural Growth – The Economics of Agrarian Change Under Population Pressure*, London: George Allen & Unwin (second edition London: Earthscan, 1993).
(1970), *Woman's Role in Economic Development*, London: Allen & Unwin.
(1981), *Population and Technological Change*, Oxford: Basil Blackwell.

Other sources and references

Boserup, Mogens (1976), *Deres egne ord* (*Their Own Words*), Copenhagen: Akademisk Forlag.
Bredsdorff, Elias (1982), *Revolutionær humanisme – En introduktion til 1930ernes venstreorienterede kulturtidsskrifter* (*Revolutionary humanism – An Introduction to the Leftwing Intellectual Journal of the 1930s*), Copenhagen: Gyldendal.
Larsen, Steen Bille (1986), *Mod strømmen: Den kommunistiske 'højre' -og 'venstre'-opposition*

i 30ernes Danmark (*Against the tide: The Communist 'Right'- and 'Left'-Wing Opposition in 1930s' Denmark*), Copenhagen: Selskabet til Forskning i Arbejderbevægelsens historie.

Myrdal, Gunnar (1968), *Asian Drama – An Inquiry into the Poverty of Nations*, Harmondsworth, UK: Penguin Books.

Topp, Niels Henrik (1986), *Udviklingen i de Finanspolitiske ideer i Danmark 1930–1945* (*The Development of Ideas about Fiscal Policy in Denmark 1930–1945*), Copenhagen: DJØF Press.

Emilia Jessie Boucherett (1825–1905)

Emilia Jessie Boucherett, known by her middle name, was born in 1825 in Willingham, Lincolnshire, England, to a landed family. She was educated at Stratford-upon-Avon. During a period in which she was, in her words, 'consuming her soul in solitary desire to help women to better economic conditions' (Holcombe, 1983, pp. 122–3), Boucherett happened to see an issue of the *English Woman's Journal*, the first English journal to focus on women's issues. Intrigued by this issue on widening employment opportunities for women, she met the journal's founders, Barbara Leigh Smith Bodichon (*q.v.*) and Bessie Rayner Parkes (Belloc) in London, and received advice concerning her plan to found an organization to help women obtain employment; according to Boucherett, Harriet Martineau's (*q.v.*) 1859 article 'Female Industry' in the *Edinburgh Review* was the inspiration for this idea. Boucherett became part of what has been called the Langham Place Group and was instrumental in founding the Society for the Promotion of Employment for Women. She wrote articles for the *English Woman's Journal*; then, in 1866, she essentially resurrected it after its 1864 demise by establishing, funding and editing the *Englishwoman's Review of Social and Industrial Questions: A Journal of Woman's Work*. Her writings on women in the labour market appeared there and elsewhere. Finally, Boucherett was active in the movement to expand the property rights of wives.[1]

Almost from its inception, the Society for the Promotion of Employment for Women was housed at Langham Place with the *English Woman's Journal*, and was affiliated with the National Association for the Promotion of Social Science, which was described in the *English Woman's Journal* as offering the only forum 'open to women for public discussion' (National Association for the Promotion of Social Science, 1862, p. 60). The Society's purpose was 'to introduce women into new employments' (Boucherett, 1884, p. 97). Accordingly, it became involved in many activities. It operated a school for practical education and training (for example, in arithmetic, bookkeeping, and glass engraving), financed by Boucherett. It worked to improve labour market information directly related to women by housing material about employment opportunities and positions sought by women workers. It sometimes created employment opportunities; for example, the Victoria Press, operated by Emily Faithfull, was created due to the Society's goal of illustrating women's possibilities as printers. In addition, it encouraged women's emigration to countries with attractive labour opportunities. Finally, the Society actively encouraged women's employment by others and promoted the formation of local employment societies.[2]

Boucherett's first writings appear in the *English Woman's Journal*.[3] Most of her writing there focuses on practical training for women with an eye towards enlarging their employment opportunities. She argued that women should obtain such training and schools should exist to provide it for them; women would then be prepared to enter the labour markets not traditionally female, thereby easing crowding in women's markets. She suggested some non-traditional occupations for women. She made the point that, even 'setting aside all considerations of justice and humanity, ... exclusion of women from obtaining a good education is disadvantageous to the community at large' (1862b, p. 27). She protested the idea that women's entrance into labour markets would necessarily 'throw men out of work' (1860, p. 372), but, none the less, she insisted that 'men ought not to shrink from taking their share of the misery' (ibid., p. 374). She disputed the idea that the difficulty for self-dependent, single women in making a living was a 'fact of modern origin' (1864, p. 269) in England. She proposed remedies for the situation, including more male emigration, and made a plea to 'lay the burden of poverty as equally as possible' (ibid., p. 275) on both men and women.

In the first issue of the *Englishwoman's Review*, Boucherett clearly presented her purpose in reviving the defunct *English Woman's Journal* when she stated 'that even the first principles of that branch of political economy which relates to women ... are not laid down, or ... not generally admitted ... [T]herefore, ... a periodical is imperatively required ... in which the subject shall be less superficially treated than usual' (1866, p. 4). Her writings there show her concern with the generation and evolution of labour markets for women.[4] She regularly provided opinions about fields of employment hitherto unexplored by women and monitored women's progress on the labour front; some of her articles contain her speculations about new and potentially remunerative areas of employment for women (for example, agricultural tenancy) or her analysis of government employment statistics. She registered opinions on government policies toward women's labour markets; in particular, she was an outspoken opponent of legislative restrictions (for example, limiting number of hours worked or eliminating night work) in such markets. In 1899 she founded and essentially funded the Freedom of Labour Defence Association, an anti-protectionist organization. She edited the journal until 1871.

Boucherett registered her concerns about women's progress in labour markets in outlets other than the two journals. She wrote a number of other articles and two books, one of which was co-authored by Helen Blackburn, who edited the *Englishwoman's Review* for some time.

Boucherett was an advocate for changes in the law relating to the property of married women; she has been credited as one of the three most important women whose efforts led to a formal request to the National Association for the Promotion of Social Science for support in favour of changes in the law. The agitation which followed, the second of the nineteenth century, led to alterations in the law in 1870, which were not altogether successful from women's point of view (Holcombe, 1983, pp. 122–5, 178–83).

Boucherett's advocacy for a woman's right to earn an independent living was manifested in writings over the course of about forty years, until the turn of the century. She retained proprietorship over the *Englishwoman's Review* until her death in 1905; its demise followed in 1910.

SUSAN H. GENSEMER

Notes

1. The sources for the biographical information on Boucherett are: Boucherett (1884); *Englishwoman's Review* (1979), Introduction by Murray and Stark; Holcombe (1983), pp. 122–5; Stanton (1884), pp. 90–91.
2. The material regarding the Society for the Promotion of Employment for Women was taken from the following sources: Association for Promoting Employment of Women (1860); Boucherett (1861, 1862a, 1884); *Englishwoman's Review* (1979), Introduction by Murray and Stark; Holcombe (1983), pp. 122–5; Lacey (1987), pp. 11–12; Society for Promoting Employment of Women (1863); Stanton (1884), pp. 90–91. Further activities of the Society are recorded in both the *English Woman's Journal* and the *Englishwoman's Review*.
3. The writings summarized here are Boucherett (1860, 1861, 1862b, 1863, 1864).
4. The articles summarized here are Boucherett (1873, 1874, 1879, 1894a, 1894b, 1894c, 1895a, 1895b, 1898).

Bibliography

Selected writings by Emilia Jessie Boucherett

Note: The *English Woman's Journal* is abbreviated *EWJ*; the *Englishwoman's Review of Social and Industrial Questions* is abbreviated *EWR*.

(1860), 'On the obstacles to the employment of women', *EWJ*, **IV**, 361–75.

(1861), 'On the education of girls, with reference to their future position', *EWJ*, **VI**, 217–24.

(1862a), 'Local Societies', *EWJ*, **VIII**, 217–23.

(1862b), 'Endowed schools, their uses and their shortcomings', *EWJ*, **IX**, 20–28.

(1863), *Hints on Self-help: A Book for Young Women*, London: S.W. Partridge.

(1863), 'On the choice of business', *EWJ*, **X**, 145–53; also appears as a chapter in Boucherett, *Hints On Self-Help: A Book for Young Women*, London: S.W. Partridge, 1863.

(1864 [1987]), 'On the cause of distress prevalent among single women', *EWJ*, **XII**. Reprinted in Candida Ann Lacey (ed.), *Barbara Leigh Smith Bodichon and the Langham Place Group*, New York: Routledge & Kegan Paul, 1987, pp. 268–77.

(1866), 'The work we have to do', *EWR*, no. I, 1–5.

(1867), 'The condition of women in France', *Contemporary Review*, **5**, 98–113.

(1869), 'How to provide for superfluous women', in Josephine E. Butler (ed.), *Woman's Work and Woman's Culture*, London: Macmillan and Co.

(1873), 'Legislative restrictions on woman's labour', *EWR*, no. XVI, 249–58.

(1874), 'Occupations of women', *EWR*, no. XVIII, 85–90.

(1879), 'Agriculture as an employment for women', *EWR*, no. LXXIX, 481–4.

(1884), 'The industrial movement' in Theodore Stanton (ed.), *The Woman Question in Europe*, New York: G.P. Putnam's Sons, pp. 91–107.

(1894a), (1894b), (1894c), (1895a), (1895b), 'The report on the employment of women by the Assistant Lady Commissioners', *EWR*, nos CCXX, 1–9; CCXI, 73–9; CCXXII, 149–56; CCXXIV, 10–17; CCXV, 77–90; respectively.

(1896), *The Condition of Working Women and the Factory Acts* (with Helen Blackburn), London: Elliot Stock.

(1898), 'The fall in women's wages', *EWR*, no. CCXXXVII, 73–81.

Other sources and references

Association for Promoting Employment of Women (1860), *EWJ*, **IV**, 54–60.

Englishwoman's Review of Social and Industrial Questions (1979); reprinted by Garland Publishing with an introduction by Janet Horowitz Murray and Myra Stark.

Holcombe, Lee (1983), *Wives and Property: Reform of the Married Women's Property Law in Nineteenth Century England*, Toronto: University of Toronto Press.

Lacey, Candida Ann (ed.) (1987), *Barbara Leigh Smith Bodichon and the Langham Place Group*, New York: Routledge & Kegan Paul.

National Association for the Promotion of Social Science (1862), *EWJ*, **VIII**, 52–61.

Society for Promoting Employment of Women (1863), *EWJ*, **XI**, 419–25.

Stanton, Theodore (ed.) (1884), *The Woman Question in Europe*, New York: G.P. Putnam's Sons.

Marian E.A. Bowley (b. 1911)

Marian Bowley was born in April 1911, one of three daughters of Sir Arthur Bowley, the distinguished economist and statistician. Marian was educated at Berkhamsted school, at the London School of Economics (1928–31) and at the University of Frankfurt (1931), as the holder of an Anglo-German Academic Board Scholarship. She then held a succession of temporary academic posts – at the University of South Wales (Aberystwyth), at Birmingham and at Oxford. Then came two years as a lecturer at the University of Dundee (1938–40). During World War II she held a number of civil service posts in the Ministry of Works and the Ministry of Supply. She joined University College London in 1946 and remained there for the rest of her academic career. Starting as a lecturer she became successively reader (1950) and professor (1965); she retired in 1974. She was also a founding member of the board of editors of the *Review of Economic Studies* (1932).

Marian Bowley is perhaps best known for her work in the history of economic thought and especially for her classic study of Nassau Senior. She did, however, do important work in applied economics, as we shall see below. *Nassau Senior and Classical Economics* (1937) was a published version of her Ph.D. thesis which she studied for at the London School of Economics under the supervision of Lionel Robbins. This was the first major study of Senior who, until then, had been regarded as rather a secondary figure and somewhat neglected in studies of the classical economists. As she put the matter, 'If in the field of pure theory Senior has either been ignored or put a little on one side with a note of interrogation, in the sphere of the application of economic analysis he has received unenviable and quite unjustified recognition as the crude exponent of extreme *laissez-faire*' (Bowley, 1937a, p. 238). She was also able in this study to make use of the then recently published Senior manuscripts discovered by Leon Levy. A major theme of the first part of the book ('Economic Theory') was to argue that there had been an overconnection of classical economic theory and policy with Ricardo and the Ricardians. Rather, she argued, we should think of two parallel streams of thought in classical economics and Senior was a major player in the other – non-Ricardian – stream. Briefly, she suggested, although she later modified this view, that this alternative 'classical' stream had a strong utility base to its theory of value, was against cost of production theories, and was anti-Malthusian. In part 2 ('Problems of Social Policy') she argued forcibly that Senior did not adhere to crude *laissez-faire* policy proposals. Whilst some of his policy stance, for example his opposition to any legislation to limit working hours, could be construed as crude dogma, she points out that when we look at his attitude towards poverty, trade unions and to the role of government in general in economic and social life his approach is more one of welfarism than *laissez-faire*.

In her other major contribution to the history of economic thought, *Studies in the History of Economic Theory before 1870* (1973), she modified some of the views stated in *Nassau Senior* and explains these changes as a by-product of her approach to the study of the history of economic ideas. She here adopts 'an approach which I think is not used as often as it profitably could be. This involves trying to discover some of the actual questions that some of the economists of the pre-classical and classical periods were asking, why they formulated them in the way they did and how this influenced their answers and, also, what assumptions they made implicitly as well as explicitly' (Bowley, 1973, p. viii).

As an example she points out that a misinterpretation – including that by herself – of Smith's dictum that things that have 'no value in use' may have value in exchange led to a completely wrong assessment of Smith's theory of value and of his influence on future developments in value theory. Another good example of Marian Bowley's later approach to the writing of histories of economic thought is to be found in her essay on 'English Theories of Interest in the Seventeenth Century', also in *Studies*. Here she demonstrates that the emphasis on the growing importance of (low) interest rates as opposed to the money supply was 'due to the peculiar institutional and analytical background' and the fact that 'investment was singled out for … the first time in the English literature, as the mainspring of activity and growth' (Bowley, 1973, p. 60).

Her work in applied economics mainly revolved around the economics of the building industry and she was regarded as one of the British experts in what was, at the time that she was actively researching it, a somewhat neglected area. Her numerous contributions include several studies of the relationship between fluctuations in building construction and the trade cycle. These appeared in the *Review of Economic Studies* (1937–40). In 1945 she produced *Housing and the State* (1945) and then, after she had returned to academia from wartime economic policy involvement in the civil service, she produced two volumes, *Innovations in Building Materials – an Economic Study* (1960) and *The British Building Industry – Four Studies of Response and Resistance to Change* (1966). In both of these studies she was highly critical of the UK building industry, finding faults in all aspects of the industry including problems connected with 'innovations, rationality of design, organization of expert knowledge, stimuli to efficiency, the sizes of building projects, contractional relationships, and opportunities for informed choice by building owners' (Bowley, 1966, p. 440). Some might well argue that the faults she itemized are still prevalent in the industry.

Marian Bowley was also a much respected and highly admired teacher. She played an important part in the life of University College London and in her retirement she is still remembered with great affection by her ex-colleagues in the department of economics.

BERNARD CORRY

Selected writings by Marian Bowley

(1937a), *Nassau Senior and the Classical Economists*, London: Allen and Unwin.
(1937b), 'Fluctuations in housebuilding and the trade cycle', *Review* of *Economic Studies*, **4**: 167–81.
(1945, 1947), *Housing and the State*, London: Allen and Unwin.
(1960), *Innovations in Building Materials – An Economic Study* (Industrial Innovations Series), London: Duckworth.
(1966), *The British Building Industry – Four Studies* of *Response and Resistance to Change*, Cambridge: Cambridge University Press.
(1973), *Studies in the History of Economic Theory before 1870*, London: Macmillan.

Mary Jean Bowman (b. 1908)

Mary Jean Bowman was born in New York City in 1908. She graduated Phi Beta Kappa from Vassar in 1930, earned an MA from Radcliffe in 1932 and a Ph.D. from Harvard in 1938. Her career combines academic appointments at a number of universities with appointments at government statistical agencies. In 1932 she was City Supervisor of the US Bureau of Labor Statistics in New York. In 1935, she joined Iowa State University's Economics Department as an instructor and stayed as an assistant professor until 1943, spending the academic year 1935–36 as Director of the Northwest Central Region

Consumer Purchases Survey conducted by the US Department of Agriculture and 1941 as a visiting professor at the University of Minnesota. In 1944, she joined the US Bureau of Labor Statistics as Senior Economist, a post she held until 1946. She spent 1956–57 as a Fulbright Research Fellow in Sweden, and then returned to the USA where she was a contract researcher for the Resources for the Future Program until 1959. In 1958, she joined the University of Chicago as Professor of Economics and Education. She has held visiting appointments in Yugoslavia, Brazil, the London School of Economics, Sweden and the World Bank, editorial appointments with the *Journal of Political Economy* (1959–60), the *International Journal of Social Economics*, and *The Economics of Education Review*. In 1982, she received the Distinguished Service Medal from Columbia University Teacher's College (Blaug, 1986, pp. 111–13).

Bowman's work includes ten books and well over one hundred articles, most of which deal with the economics of education. Her earliest work is largely expository and descriptive, culminating in the production of a textbook (1943), co-authored with G.L. Bach and aimed at teachers of introductory economics and at students of intermediate theory, of which the focus was income distribution and resource allocation. From this developed her interest in measures of income inequality and their implications (1945).

Much of her later work deals with expectations and decision-making under uncertainty. *Expectations, Uncertainty and Business Behavior* (1958) was an attempt to bring some order to the field of business decision-making, particularly as it applies to investment decisions. She adapted concepts drawn from the writing of G.L.S. Shackle to a treatment of educational decisions in 'Expectations, uncertainty and investments in human beings' (1972). This last piece, and others in which she applied concepts from research in business behaviour to investment in human capital, were collected in a book entitled *Educational Choice and Labor Markets in Japan* (1981).

Many of her contributions deal with the effects of education on economic development and income distribution using US, Japanese, Malaysian and Mexican data. She has also emphasized the relationship between fertility and technological change, arguing that high rates of human capital formation and high rates of population growth are incompatible, unless supported by technological change and high rates of out-of-school learning (Ghez, 1987, p. 271).

A hallmark of Bowman's work is its multidisciplinary nature. Her work on the spread of schooling in developing countries, for example, combines elements of the 'new home economics' that specify the options faced by individuals and families, with the idea of 'information fields' drawn from the education and sociology literature, a concept that specifies the data available to decision-makers.

EVELYN L. FORGET

Bibliography

Selected writings by Mary Jean Bowman

(1943), *Economic Analysis and Public Policy* (with G.L. Bach), New York: Prentice-Hall.
(1945), 'A graphical analysis of personal income distribution in the United States', *American Economic Review*, **35**(3), 607–28.
(1958) (ed.), *Expectations, Uncertainty and Business Behavior*, New York: Social Science Research Council.
(1963), *Resources and People in East Kentucky: Problems and Prospects of a Lagging Economy* (with W.W. Haynes), Baltimore: Johns Hopkins University Press.
(1964), 'Schultz, Denison, and the contribution of "Eds" to national income growth', *Journal of Political Economy*, **72**(5), 450–64.
(1965) (eds), *Education and Economic Development* (with C.A. Anderson), Chicago: Aldine.
(1966), 'The costing of human resource development', in E.A.G. Robinson and J. Vaizey (eds), *The Economics of Education*, London: Macmillan.
(1967), 'Schooling, experience, and gains and losses in human capital through migration' (with R.G. Myers), *Journal of the American Statistical Association*, **62**(3), 875–98.
(1968) (ed.), *Readings in the Economics of Education*, Paris: UNESCO.
(1972) (ed.), *Where Colleges Are and Who Attends* (with C.A. Anderson and V. Tinto), New York: McGraw-Hill.
(1972a), 'Expectations, uncertainty and investments in human beings', in C.F. Carter and J.L. Ford, *Uncertainty and Expectations in Economics*, London: Basil Blackwell.
(1972b), 'Time-series changes in personal income inequality in the United States from 1939, with projections to 1985: comment', *Journal of Political Economy*, **80**(3), Part II, S67–S71.
(1973), *Elites and Change in the Kentucky Mountains* (with D. Plunkett), Lexington: University of Kentucky Press.
(1974), 'Postschool learning and human resource accounting', *Review of Income and Wealth*, **20**(4), 483–99.
(1978), *Learning and Earning* (with A. Sohlman and B.-G. Ysander), Stockholm: National Board of Universities and Colleges.
(1981), *Educational Choice and Labor Markets in Japan* (with the collaboration of H. Ikeda and Y. Tomoda), Chicago: University of Chicago Press.
(1982), 'Choice in the spending of time', in W.H. Kruskal, *The Social Sciences, their Nature and Uses*, Chicago: University of Chicago Press.
(1984), 'An integrated framework for analysis of the spread of schooling in less developed countries', *Comparative Education Review*, **28**(4), 563–83.
(1985), 'Education, population trends and technological change', *Economics of Education Review*, **4**(1), 29–44.
(1986) 'An adult life cycle perspective on public subsidies to higher education in three countries' (with B. Millot and E. Schiefelbein), *Economics of Education Review*, **5**(2), 135–45.
(1990), 'Views from the past and the future: an overview essay', *Economics of Education Review*, **9**(4), 283–307.
(1993), 'The economics of education in a world of change', in E.P. Hoffman (ed.), *Essays on the Economics of Education*. Kalamazoo, MI: Upjohn Institute for Employment Research: pp. 163–74.

Other sources and references

Blaug, M. (ed.) (1986), *Who's Who in Economics, a Biographical Dictionary of Major Economists 1700–1986*, Cambridge, MA: The MIT Press, pp. 111–13.
Ghez, G. (1987), 'Bowman, Mary Jean', in J. Eatwell, M. Milgate and P. Newman (eds), *The New Palgrave: A Dictionary of Economics*, London: Macmillan, p. 271.

Dorothy Stahl Brady (1903–77)

Dorothy S. Brady was a statistician who devoted most of her research efforts to the design and interpretation of survey data on household income and expenditures. Her career combined academic appointments with appointments in US federal agencies. She spent two extended periods at the Bureau of Labor Statistics, from 1943 until 1948 and then from 1951 to 1956 (Reid, 1987, p. 272).

The large 1935–36 surveys of income and expenditures in rural and in urban households had provided data to test Commerce Department estimates of the distribution of national income, consumption and savings. Brady examined price and consumption data in the context of efforts to control inflation, and designed the statistical method to price urban household budgets to assess geographic differences in the cost of living.

She participated in the Conference on Income and Wealth of the National Bureau of Economic Research, and was instrumental in making participants aware of data limitations. Using statistical techniques to randomize the effects of omitted variables, she demonstrated that the percentage of income saved by households increases along with relative position in an income distribution. She also found that the inequality of measured income distribution tends to increase as the income of a population increases secularly because the age at which children leave home, often with financial assistance from parents, tends to decrease as incomes rise.

EVELYN L. FORGET

Bibliography

Selected writings by Dorothy Stahl Brady

(1940) (et al.), *Family Income and Expenditures. 5 Regions, Part 2*, Department of Agriculture: Miscellaneous Publication no. 396.

(1945), 'Family spending and saving in wartime', *US Bureau of Labor Statistics Bulletin*, No. 872, Appraisal of survey data: 45.

(1948), 'The city worker's family budget' (with L.S. Kellog), *Monthly Labor Review*, **66**(25), 133–70.

(1948), 'Family budgets, a historical survey', *Monthly Labor Review*, **66**(23), 171–5.

(1949), 'The use of statistical procedures in the derivation of family budgets', *Social Service Review*, **23**(2), 141–57.

(1952), 'Family savings in relation to changes in the level and distribution of income', *Studies in Income and Wealth*, vol. 15, New York: National Bureau of Economic Research, pp. 103–28.

(1956), 'Family savings, 1880–1950', part II in R.W. Goldsmith, D.S. Brady and H. Mendershausen (eds), *A Study of Savings in the United States, vol. III: Special Studies*, Princeton: Princeton University Press, pp. 188–213.

(1957), 'Measurement and interpretation of the income distribution in the United States', in *Income and Wealth*, series VI, London: International Association for Research in Income and Wealth.

(1958), 'Individual incomes and the structure of consumer units', *American Economic Review (Papers and Proceedings)*, **48**(2), 269–78.

(1965), 'Age and the income distribution', *Research Report no. 8*, US Social Security Administration.

(1966), 'Price deflators for final product estimates', *Studies in Income and Wealth, vol. 30: Output, Employment, and Productivity in the United States After 1800*. Conference on Research in Income and Wealth, New York: National Bureau of Economic Research.

(1971), 'The statistical approach: the input–output system', in G.R. Taylor and L.F. Ellsworth (eds), *Approaches to American Economic History*, Charlottesville: University Press of Virginia.

Reference
Reid, M. (1987), 'Brady, Dorothy Stahl', in J. Eatwell, M. Milgate and P. Newman (eds), *The New Palgrave: A Dictionary of Economics*, London: Macmillan.

Sophonisba Breckinridge (1866–1948)

Sophonisba Breckinridge, scion of two distinguished Kentucky families and the first woman to pass the Kentucky bar, was also the first woman to earn a Ph.D. in political science and economics at the University of Chicago (in 1901), and the first woman to earn a Doctor of Jurisprudence degree (in 1904) from the University of Chicago School of Law. Armed with these degrees she went on to forge a remarkable career for herself at the University of Chicago, beginning in 1902 teaching one economics course in the Department of Political Economy and retiring in 1942 as Professor of Social Economy and the Samuel Deutsch Professor of Public Welfare Administration. Along the way she was instrumental in transforming and integrating the independent Chicago School of Civics and Philanthropy into the University of Chicago Graduate School of Social Service Administration. She co-founded the distinguished journal *Social Service Review*, which she edited from 1927 until 1934. She became well known in local and national reform movements. In 1933 President Roosevelt appointed her as a delegate to the Pan America Conference, the first woman to represent the US government at an international conference (see her obituary, *Chicago Daily Tribune*, 31 July 1948). In 1934 she was elected President of the American Association of Schools of Social Work. Her teachings and writings were influential in promoting a role for the federal government in social welfare programmes and in achieving professional status for the field of social work. At the time of her death in 1948 Breckinridge was a venerable and venerated University of Chicago institution. Her career is notable because of what she accomplished, but also because it illustrates how the powerful forces which severely limited academic opportunities for women economists in the first several decades of the twentieth century were counteracted by certain brilliant and tenacious women.

Breckinridge was born in Kentucky in 1866 to Issa Desha and Col. William Campbell Preston Breckinridge, a lawyer and US Congressman. Breckinridge graduated from Wellesley College in 1888 and taught high school in Washington, DC before returning to Kentucky to help with family duties and to read law in her father's law offices. She passed the Kentucky bar in 1895, a feat that earned national attention. When her law practice did not prosper she visited a Wellesley classmate at the University of Chicago who introduced her to Dean of Women Marion Talbot. Talbot offered Breckinridge a job as her assistant and found her a fellowship to enrol at the University to study political science and economics. Breckinridge earned her Ph.M. degree in political science in 1897 and her Ph.D. in political science and economics in 1901.

During the early years of her graduate work, Breckinridge concentrated her studies on political science, working closely with Ernst Freund, Professor of Jurisprudence and Public Law. Later, in her economics studies, she was guided largely by J. Laurence Laughlin, the primary professor for her dissertation, *Legal Tender: A Study in English and American Monetary History*. This was published as one of the 'Decennial Publications' of the University in 1903. Money is legal tender when it may be used in payment of a debt, and the laws governing legal tender are a portion of the law of contracts. In *Legal Tender* Breckinridge examined the historical record to trace what organs of the state in the USA and England have had the power to bestow upon money the status of legal tender and how, when, and why that power has been exercised.

After completing her Ph.D. in 1901, Breckinridge sought academic employment. She wanted to teach but at that time academic positions for women economists were exceedingly scarce (although Laughlin asked her to teach one course, 'The State in Relation to Labor'). Economics (and other social sciences) departments were hesitant to hire women, in part because of the 'separate spheres' gender ideology of the time. The feminine was seen as soft, passive and domestic and therefore inappropriate for the academic setting in which economists were trying to gain a reputation for being rational, hard and scientific. Moreover, fear of effeminization of the whole university further weakened support for hiring women in the traditional departments. (See Hammond, 1993.) As Breckinridge writes in her unfinished autobiography,

> Although I was given the degree Ph.D. magna cum laude no position in political science or in Economics was offered me. The men in the two departments, Boyd and Willis and Ferty and Wesley Mitchell and S.J. Mitchell and others went off to positions in College and University faculty … I earned my room and board at Green Hall [a women's residence hall] as Assistant Head and in 1904, having been given some credit for the Political Science Work, I was granted the degree of J.D. by the Law School in its first graduating class. (*Autobiography*, box 1, folder 8)

By 1904 Marion Talbot had been successful in getting approval for a Department of Household Administration at the University of Chicago. Such interdisciplinary, 'feminine' departments were cropping up at universities as a vehicle for women academics to bypass the gender discrimination rampant in science and social science departments. Breckinridge was offered an instructorship in the new department to teach courses dealing with the legal and economic aspects of family life. She became an assistant professor in the department in 1909 and in 1912 co-authored a book on household administration with Marion Talbot (*The Modern Household*).

Breckinridge always considered Talbot's offer her 'great chance'. She organized courses on 'Consumption', the 'Retail Market', 'Public Aspects of the Household', the 'State and the Child', and the 'Legal and Economic Position of Women', the last a course that also offered economics credit. Breckinridge revelled in the fact that these courses 'gave an opportunity to use every kind of material of which I could make use. The legal, the economic, the historical and the social implications were all appropriately considered' (*Autobiography*, box 1, folder 10). Teaching these courses also introduced Breckinridge to important women intellectuals. Foremost among them was an economics Ph.D. student who was to become Breckinridge's colleague and collaborator for over forty years. Edith Abbott (*q.v.*) took Breckinridge's course on the 'Legal and Economic Position of Women' in 1904. This course piqued Abbott's interest in the historical role of women in the workforce, a topic she began to research under the tutelage of Professor Breckinridge. This was the beginning of their long and productive professional partnership.

At the beginning of her teaching career Breckinridge's research interests centred on labour law and employment of women. Between 1905 and 1915 she published six articles in the *Journal of Political Economy* (1905, 1906a, 1906b, 1910, 1911, 1915) and one article in the *Annals of the American Academy of Political and Social Science* (1914b) on these topics. Two of the articles ('Employment of women in industry: twelfth census statistics' and 'Women in industry: the Chicago Stockyards') were co-authored with Edith Abbott, with the former article serving as the basis for the first chapter in Abbott's book *Women in Industry* (1910), for which Breckinridge wrote the introduction.

During these same years Breckinridge became associated with Chicago's burgeoning reform community. She joined the Chicago Women's Trade Union League and began to live part of each year at Jane Addams's Hull House, a practice she continued into the 1920s. In 1907, in addition to her position at the University of Chicago, she began teaching in the Department of Social Investigation of the Chicago School of Civics and Philanthropy. (The School had been established in 1903 with a loose association with the University of

Chicago's extension division but became independent in 1906.) In 1908 Breckinridge became Director of the Department and hired Edith Abbott away from Wellesley College to teach statistics. In 1909, Breckinridge became Dean of the School (Fitzpatrick, 1990, p. 196). In the ensuing years, Breckinridge, in partnership with Abbott, transformed the school according to her and Abbott's shared vision of professional education for social workers. In 1920 Breckinridge was instrumental in bringing the school back under the auspices of the University of Chicago as the Graduate School of Social Administration, the first such school associated with a major university. In 1925, Breckinridge was promoted to Professor of Social Economy at the University, and in 1929 she was named the Samuel Deutsch Professor of Public Welfare Administration.

Breckinridge and Abbott envisioned social work as a profession like law or medicine, requiring a professional education and an advanced degree. After the merger of the School of Civics and Philanthropy with the University of Chicago, Breckinridge and Abbott wrote, 'We have believed that we should give a broad professional education and, as the Law School, for example, educates lawyers instead of "training" men for criminal law or patent law we have tried to give a similarly broad preparation for professional work in the social administration field' (1924b, p. 4). From the beginning of their association with the School of Civics and Philanthropy, Breckinridge and Abbott de-emphasized the casework and vocational training approach to social work education then in vogue. They restructured the curriculum of the school, emphasizing statistics, empirical research and the scientific method, and making it increasingly like the graduate training in economics, political science and law that they themselves had received. 'Emphasis is laid upon the close relationship between the work of the School and the graduate work of the social science departments ... Sound social policies can be developed only on the basis of a sound knowledge of fundamental principles' (1924b, p. 4).

Yet the school was distinct in its emphasis on social reform. According to a description of the school written in 1924,

> In the departments of Arts, Literature and Science, the chief emphasis is placed on knowing – upon understanding the causes of Poverty and other social ills, just as the physiologist and pathologist study the body and its disease. But to help the poor, or to prevent crime, as to cure the sick, or administer justice, is an active art; it is a doing as well as a knowing. A professional school [of social work] makes this 'doing' aspect prominent. (Tufts, 1924, p. 4)

After they took over leadership of the School of Civics and Philanthropy and its Department of Social Investigation, Breckinridge and Abbott embarked on several exhaustive research programmes that earned them national recognition. Their first major study involved a door-to-door survey of

Chicago's tenement housing. Their findings were summarized in ten articles published in the *American Journal of Sociology* between 1910 and 1915. Breckinridge was responsible for the inclusion of black neighbourhoods in the housing study, and made her case for doing so in an article ('The color line in the housing problem') published in *The Survey* in 1913.

Their next major study was an investigation of Chicago's juvenile court. They collected socioeconomic data from the records of the thousands of cases that had come before the court between 1899, when it was established, and 1909, and from interviews with most of the children brought to court during the year 1903–4. Their book *The Delinquent Child and the Home* was published in 1912. Their third major empirical study of urban school attendance also resulted in a book, *Truancy and Non-Attendance in the Chicago Schools*, published in 1917.

Each of these research efforts led Breckinridge and Abbott to conclude that poverty and 'civic neglect' were the underlying causes of many urban problems. Their work downplayed the role of the individual and the family as sources of social pathology, shifting the blame to the urban environment. To solve the problems of poverty, they supported legislative and other government intervention in the form of housing codes, sanitary and health standards, child labour laws, compulsory school attendance laws and public education. Their research provided some of the earliest justifications for the social welfare reform initiatives of the Progressive era (Fitzpatrick, 1990, pp. 183–8).

In 1927 Breckinridge and Abbott founded the scholarly journal, *Social Service Review*, published by the University of Chicago Press. Breckinridge served as co-editor of the journal with Abbott until 1934. Their purposes in founding the journal were threefold. They hoped to strengthen the professional reputation of social work by having an academic journal from a prestigious press associated with the field; they wanted to give their students a publishing outlet for the empirical research that they emphasized; and they wanted a forum for their views promoting a role for the federal government in social welfare reform. They were enormously successful in all these dimensions. A history of their contributions to the *Review* is detailed in Diner (1977).

Over the years, Breckinridge's reputation as a scholar, educator and social reformer grew. She was a key participant in the Consumers' League, the Immigrants' Protective League, the NAACP, the Progressive Party, the American Association of University Women, the Woman's Peace Party, and the National American Woman's Suffrage Association (Lasch, 1971, pp. 234–5). By the 1920s she was recognized as an expert on women's and children's labour law, property rights of women, women's employment issues, immigration law, delinquent children and public welfare. Her important writings on these subjects include articles in the *Journal of Political Economy* (1923b), the *Annals of the American Academy of Political and Social Science* (1923a), the *Proceedings of the National Conference of Social Work* (formerly *Charities and Corrections*) (1914a, 1925, 1932), and the *Social Service Review* (1927a, 1927b, 1930a, 1930b, 1936, 1943a, 1943b).

Breckinridge also wrote many books. *New Home for Old* (1921) is a study of the living conditions and economic problems of immigrant women. *Marriage and the Civic Rights of Women* (1931) details the relationship between marital status, citizenship and property rights. *Women in the Twentieth Century: A Study of Their Political, Social, and Economic Activities* (1933) was one of a series published under the auspices of President Hoover's Research Committee on Social Trends, chaired by her old classmate Wesley C. Mitchell. In it she documented the developments in the first three decades of the twentieth century with respect to women's employment, voting habits and volunteer activities in clubs and organizations. Her books *Family Welfare Work in a Metropolitan Community* (1924a), *Public Welfare Administration* (1927, revised in 1938), *The Family and the State* (1934a), and *Social Work and the Courts* (1934b) are innovative compilations of documents and case records that are considered to be landmark volumes in social work education (Deegan, 1991).

Breckinridge is remembered today, not as an economist, but as one of the pioneers of academic social work. In collaboration with Abbott, she sought to transform social work from a vocation with modest training standards to a profession requiring an advanced degree, a broad education in research methods and the social sciences, and with a role to play in researching and advocating social welfare policy. Her efforts to professionalize social work are a unique part of the professionalization movement that swept economics and the social sciences in the early part of the twentieth century (see Muncy, 1990).

The process of professionalization of the social sciences involved limiting access to the newly forming professions to those deemed experts and specialists. An expert came to be defined, by the turn of the century, as someone with a Ph.D. who held an academic position in one of the mainstream social science departments and who published in scholarly, specialized journals. In economics, the title professional economist also meant that one subscribed to the scientific method and rejected social reform advocacy, which was seen to lack objectivity. (See Ross, 1991, for a history of the professionalization of economics and the social sciences.)

By earning her Ph.D. Breckinridge met the first criterion for professional status as an economist. When a position in economics did not materialize, her moves, first to the Department of Household Administration and then to the School of Civics and Philanthropy, allowed her to use her economics training

and to perform all the duties of her male colleagues in economics departments, but they also ensured that she would not be considered a professional
economist. Professional economists taught in economics departments, not in
social work or interdisciplinary, 'feminine' departments.

Marginalized from economics by the professional standards of that community, Breckinridge sought to impose many of the same kinds of professional
standards on the field of social work. She transformed the School of Civics
and Philanthropy into a degree-granting institution with the Ph.D. as its
highest degree. She stressed the scientific method in its curriculum. She
emphasized research and founded the scholarly journal, *Social Service
Review*. However, unlike her colleagues in economics departments, she never
believed that a professional social scientist should not directly advocate
social reform. Instead, she sought to develop and promote solutions to social
problems, as well as to determine their causes. Because she was a trained
economist and scholar, as well as a dedicated reformer, this gave economics a
role in the progressive-era social welfare movement that it would not otherwise have had (Muncy, 1990; Fitzpatrick, 1990).

CLAIRE HOLTON HAMMOND

Bibliography

Selected writings by Sophonisba Breckinridge
(1903), *Legal Tender: A Study in English and American Monetary History*, Chicago: The
  University of Chicago Press.
(1905), 'Two decisions relating to organized Labor', *Journal of Political Economy*, **13**, 593–7.
(1906a), 'Employment of women in industry: twelfth census statistics' (with Edith Abbott),
  Journal of Political Economy, **14**, January, 14–40.
(1906b), 'Legislative control of women's work', *Journal of Political Economy*, **14**, February,
  107–9.
(1910), 'The Illinois Ten-Hour Law', *Journal of Political Economy*, **18**, June, 465–70.
(1910–15), 'The housing problem in Chicago' (with Edith Abbott). Ten articles in *American
  Journal of Sociology*, **16–21**.
(1911), 'Women in industry: the Chicago stockyards' (with Edith Abbott), *Journal of Political
  Economy*, **19**, October, 632–54.
(1912), *The Modern Household* (with Marion Talbot), Boston: Whitcomb and Barrows.
(1912, reprinted 1970), *The Delinquent Child and the Home* (with Edith Abbott), New York:
  Charities Publication Committee. Reprinted in the Rise of Urban America Series, New York:
  Arno Press.
(1913), 'The color line in the housing problem', *The Survey*, **29**, February, 575–6.
(1914a), 'The family in the community, but not yet of the community', *Proceedings of the
  National Conference of Charities and Corrections*, **41**, May, 69–75.
(1914b), 'Political equality for women and women's wages', *Annals of the American Academy
  of Political and Social Science*, **56**, November, 122–33.
(1915), 'A recent English case on women and the legal profession', *Journal of Political Economy*,
  23, January, 64–70.
(1917), *Truancy and Non-Attendance in the Chicago Schools: A Study of the Social Aspects of
  the Compulsory Education and Child Labor Legislation of Illinois* (with Edith Abbott),
  Chicago: University of Chicago Press.

(1921), *New Homes for Old*, New York: Harper and Brothers.

(1923a), 'Summary of the present state systems for the organization and administration of public welfare', *Annals of the American Academy of Political and Social Science*, **105**, January, 93–103.

(1923b), 'The home responsibilities of women workers and the "equal wage"', *Journal of Political Economy*, **31**, August, 521–43.

(1924a), *Family Welfare Work in the Metropolitan Community*, Chicago: University of Chicago Press.

(1924b), 'The Graduate School of Social Service Administration: material submitted to Dean Tufts' (with Edith Abbott), The University Presidents' Papers 1889–1925, The University of Chicago Archives, Box 61, Folder 13.

(1925), 'The family and the law', *Proceedings of the National Conference of Social Work*, **52**, June, 290–97.

(1927, revised 1938), *Public Welfare Administration of the U.S.*, Chicago: University of Chicago Press.

(1927a), 'Frontiers of social control in public welfare administration', *Social Service Review*, **1**, March, 84–99.

(1927b), 'Widows' and orphans' pensions in Great Britain', *Social Service Review*, **1**, June, 249–57.

(1930a), 'Separate domicil for married women', *Social Service Review*, **4**, March, 37–52.

(1930b), 'Public welfare organization with reference to child welfare activities', *Social Service Review*, **4**, September, 376–422.

(1931), *Marriage and the Civic Rights of Women*, Chicago: University of Chicago Press.

(1932), 'Children and the Depression', *Proceedings of the National Conference of Social Work*, **59**, May, 126–35.

(1933), *Women in the Twentieth Century: A Study of Their Political, Social, and Economic Activities*, New York: McGraw-Hill Book Co. Reprinted in the American Women: Image and Realities Series, New York: Arno Press, 1972.

(1934a), *The Family and the State*, Chicago: University of Chicago Press.

(1934b), *Social Work and the Courts*, Chicago: University of Chicago Press.

(1936), 'New chapters in the history of the courts and social legislation' (with Grace Abbott), *Social Service Review*, **10**, December, 483–99.

(1939), *The Illinois Poor Law and Its Administration*, Chicago: University of Chicago Press.

(1943a), 'Legal problems of the juvenile court', *Social Service Review*, **17**, March, 12–14.

(1943b), 'The law of guardian and ward with special reference to the children of veterans' (with Mary Stanton), *Social Service Review*, **17**, June, 265–302.

(n.d.), *Autobiography* (unpublished, holographic, unnumbered), The Papers of Sophonisba P. Breckinridge, University of Chicago Archives.

Other sources and references

Breckinridge Family Papers, Library of Congress.

The Papers of Sophonisba P. Breckinridge, The University of Chicago Archives.

University Presidents' Papers, 1889–1925, The University of Chicago Archives.

Abbott, Edith (1948), 'Sophonisba Preston Breckinridge: Over the years', *The Social Service Review*, **22**, December, 417–23.

Deegan, Mary Jo (1991), 'Sophonisba Breckinridge', in Mary Jo Deegan (ed.), *Women in Sociology: A Bio-Bibliographic Sourcebook*, New York: Greenwood Press, pp. 80–89.

Diner, Steven J. (1977), 'Scholarship in the quest for social welfare: a fifty-year history of the *Social Service Review*', *Social Service Review*, **51**, March, 1–66.

Fitzpatrick, Ellen (1990), *Endless Crusade: Women Social Scientists and Progressive Reform*, New York: Oxford University Press.

Hammond, Claire (1993), 'American women and the professionalization of economics', *Review of Social Economy*, **51**, Fall, 347–70.

Lasch, Christopher (1971), 'Sophonisba Breckinridge', in Edward T. James (ed.), *Notable*

American Women 1607–1950: A Biographical Dictionary, Cambridge: Harvard University Press, pp. 233–6.

Lenroot, Katharine (1949), 'Sophonisba Breckinridge, social pioneer', *Social Service Review*, **23**, March, 88–92.

Muncy, Robyn (1990), 'Gender and professionalization in the origins of the U.S. welfare state: the careers of Sophonisba Breckinridge and Edith Abbott, 1890–1935', *Journal of Policy History*, **2**(3), 290–315.

Ross, Dorothy (1991), *The Origins of American Social Science*, Cambridge: Cambridge University Press.

Tufts, James L. (1924), 'The relationship of the professional Schools of Commerce and Administration and Social Service Administration to the social science Departments of Arts, Literature and Science', The University Presidents' Papers 1889–1925, The University of Chicago Archives, Box 61, Folder 13.

Wright, Helen R. (1954), 'Three against time: Edith and Grace Abbott and Sophonisba P. Breckinridge', *Social Service Review*, **28**, June, 41–53.

Elizabeth Read Brown (1902–87)

Elizabeth Read Brown was born on 8 April 1902 in Michigan. Her parents were J. Herbert and Eva Lumley Read. She received bachelor's degrees from what are now Eastern Michigan and Case Western Reserve Universities. Her master's degree in library science was from the University of Michigan. As a librarian she held positions at the following libraries: Royal Oak, Michigan (1928–37), Michigan State University (1937–46), Albion College (1946–51), University of Michigan (1952) and the University of Mississippi (1952–53).

At this last posting she met and married the economist, Harry Gunnison Brown (1880–1975). He was Professor Emeritus of the University of Missouri (1916–51). In his profession Brown was well known for his views on railroad regulation, tax incidence, free trade and land value taxation, among others. She shared his Georgist views on land value taxation, as she would demonstrate in her writing in the ensuing years. While her husband completed his teaching career at Franklin and Marshall College and for five further years, they were active in the promotion of local tax reform throughout the state of Pennsylvania until they returned to his home in Columbia, Missouri in 1965. There, they continued their writing collaboration until his death in 1975. Elizabeth joined the editorial board of the *American Journal of Economics and Sociology* in 1977. She felt that her husband's contributions to economics were not fully appreciated. Due in part to her inquiries, the University of Chicago Press reprinted in 1979 *The Economics of Taxation* (1924). In Missouri she campaigned for more equitable taxation and was active locally in public safety concerns about children. The 83rd General Assembly of the Missouri State Legislature adopted a resolution recognizing her work for a better society. She died on 10 February 1987. After her death, C. Ryan acknowledged her assistance in the preparation of a biographical study of her husband (1987). Will Lissner, founder and long-time editor of the *American Journal of Economics and Sociology*, contributed a warm 'In Memoriam' (1987), concluding: 'Beth, like Harry, made her life an important contributor to the well-being of her fellow citizens and to American culture. We shall miss her sorely.'

Elizabeth Read Brown wrote 19 articles and edited one for the *American Journal of Economics and Sociology*. Six were co-authored with her husband; five were their last submissions to the journal, indicating his deteriorating health. All but four of the articles or reviews deal in one manner or another with land value taxation. The four exceptions advocate free trade against contemporary calls for more protection. She wrote other articles concerning history and library science.

A central theme of her writing on economic matters was the relevance of land value taxation to contemporary problems, along with attention to the existing evidence of its successful application. Alternative tax policy, in particular the effects of introducing variants of land value taxation (lowering of rates on buildings while raising the rates on the value of land, both used and idle), was explored in many of her articles. Could localities adopting such measures attract more industry, achieve their zoning objectives and attain more efficient commercial development? Elizabeth Read Brown argued that offering differential tax rates could provide a profit incentive for firms to settle in the locality. Further, the objective of maintaining or improving the quality of residential or commercial property would be facilitated were capital improvements not taxed. Writing in the late 1950s and 1960, she saw urban obsolescence and decay as in part a result of a general property tax. Finally, she pointed out that a heavier taxation of land values would pressure the use of land sites and reduce speculative holdings. Vacant or underused lots in cities would be fewer, and the inefficient chequerboard land use patterns would not have occurred to the extent that has been observed. She frequently cited in her articles the experience of Australia, New Zealand and the State of Pennsylvania in land value taxation.

In her most detailed article (1961) Elizabeth Read Brown surveyed contemporary economic textbooks for the attention given to land value taxation, and what views of it were presented. When the subject was not mentioned in a text, she further examined it for consideration of Henry George, the single tax, *Progress and Poverty*, and so on. She initially noted that only 41 of the 76 general or introductory texts she consulted made mention of George, his proposal or his famous book. Of those in which mention was more than incidental, she found, with few exceptions, presentation of the single tax idea to be so biased that no appreciable number of students could come to see what she believed to be the relevance of land value taxation to present-day problems.

As the author of this note and many others can attest, Elizabeth Read Brown was in no way discouraged by this state of affairs. She should be, like her husband, remembered as an enthusiastic, persevering advocate of tax reform.

CHRISTOPHER K. RYAN

Bibliography

Selected writings by Elizabeth Read Brown
(1954), 'Plant Location and Community Tax Policy' (with Harry Gunnison Brown), *American Journal of Economics and Sociology*, **14**(1), October, 55–7.
(1957), 'Tax Policy: Its Effects on Housing and Slums', *American Journal of Economics and Sociology*, **16**(3), April, 327–8.
(1958), *The Effective Answer to Communism* (with Harry Gunnison Brown), New York: Robert Schalkenbach Foundation.
(1958), 'Zoning Objectives and Tax Policy', *American Journal of Economics and Sociology*, **18**(1), October, 55–6.
(1959), 'Growing Urban Obsolescence and Tax Policy', *American Journal of Economics and Sociology*, **19**(1), October, 96–8.
(1961), 'How College Textbooks Treat Land Value Taxation', *American Journal of Economics and Sociology*, **20**(2), January, 147–67.

Other sources and references
Lissner, Will (1987), 'In Memoriam: Elizabeth Read Brown', *American Journal of Economics and Sociology*, **46**(3), 383–4.
Ryan, Christopher K. (1987), *Harry Gunnison Brown: Economist*, Boulder and London: Westview Press.

Martha Stephanie Browne (1898–1990)

Martha Stephanie Braun (née Hermann) was born in Vienna 12 December 1898, and died in New York on 2 March 1990. She changed her name to Browne when in the USA. She studied national economy, first in Freiburg, Breisgau (Germany), and then in Vienna, where she obtained her doctorate in 1921 (Dr rer. pol.). After her studies she worked as a freelance journalist. In 1938 or 1939 she emigrated to Great Britain and, in the same year, travelled to the USA. She spent the years 1941 and 1942 at Columbia University, deepening her knowledge of statistical methods. Between 1942 and 1944 she was Assistant Professor of Economics and Geography at the University of Cincinnati, and then worked as an analyst for the State Department until 1947, when she became Assistant Professor of Economics at Brooklyn College. She was an associate professor there between 1954 and 1962, and Professor from 1963 to 1971. She was also a lecturer at Hunter College (1948–49). After World War II she became an honorary member of the Nationalökonomische Gesellschaft der Universität Wien (National Economic Society of Vienna University).

Browne was part of the Mises circle that included the economists Ilse Schüller-Mintz, Gertrud Lovasy, Helene Lieser, Marianne von Herzfeld and Elly Spiro. Her name became known through her publications that appeared during the interwar period. Among other works, she contributed regularly to political currency questions in the *Mitteilungen des Verbandes österreichischer Banken und Bankiers* (*Communications of the Association of Austrian Banks and Bankers*), published in Vienna.

Her main work, *Theorie der staatlichen Wirtschaftspolitik* (*Theory of State Economic Policy*), published in Vienna in 1929, received international attention. Gerhard Winterberger describes her as the 'first important national economist' (1984, p. 398). Hers was the first general theory of economic policy to have originated in Austria. The theoretical basis of this study constitutes the value and price theory of the Viennese School. Browne argues that the entities 'public associations' and 'state institutions' should be included in economic analysis only in so far as they influence pricing institutions. For Browne it is the main task of a science of economic policy that goes beyond historical and legal description to show the consequences of the disturbances of the market equilibrium by state intervention.

In 1930 Browne, together with other women, published the anthology *Frauenbewegung, Frauenbildung und Frauenarbeit in Österreich* (*The Women's Movement, Women's Education and Women's Work in Austria*), under the auspices of the Bund österreichische Frauenvereine (League of Austrian Women's Organizations). Her contribution to this collection is an essay on the causes and consequences of job discrimination against women. We have no way of knowing from this, however, whether Browne was engaged in the feminist movement at this point.

In the USA the main emphases of her research lay in the following areas: theory of economic planning, forecasting developments in energy requirements, regional development, transport and location questions, prerequisites of continuous growth of industrialized regions, as well as economic/geographical problems. In addition, Browne did research for the State Department, including an essay on the role of foreign trade in Japan.

JÜRGEN NAUTZ

Bibliography

Selected writings by Martha Stephanie Browne
(1923–34), contributions to *Mitteilungen des Verbandes österreichischer Banken und Bankiers*, Vienna.
(1929), *Theorie der staatlichen Wirtschaftspolitik* (Wiener Staats- und Rechtswissenschaftliche Studien Neue Folge der Wiener Staatswissenschaftlichen Studien). (Edited with Hans Mayer and Othmar Spann von Hans Kelsen. Vol. XV), Leipzig and Vienna.
(1930), *Frauenbewegung, Frauenbildung und Frauenarbeit in Österreich* (edited with Ernestine

Fürth, Dr Marianne Hönig, Prof. Dr Grete Laube, Dr Bertha List-Ganser, Dr Carla Zaglits), Vienna.
(1930), 'Volkshochschulen', in Browne et al. (1930), pp. 203–6.
(1946), *The Place of Foreign Trade in the Japanese Economy* (co-author), Office of Research & Intelligence, US Department of State, HF 3826.
(1962), 'The Future of US energy supply', *Österreichische Zeitschrift für Nationalökonomie.*
(1981), 'Erinnerungen an das Mises-Privatseminar', *Wirtschaftspolitische Blätter*, **28**, part 4, 110–20.

Other sources and references
Ariadne.
IWK Dokumentations- und Forschungsstelle österreichische Wissenschaftsemigration.
American Men and Women of Science, A biographical directory founded in 1906.
Social and Behavioral Science, vol. 1, New York and London, 1973, p. 288.
Craver, Earlene (1986), 'The emigration of Austrian economists', *History of Political Economy*, **18**(1), 1–32.
Mises, L. von (1978), *Erinnerungen von Ludwig v. Mises mit einem Vorwort von Margit v. Mises und einer Einleitung von Friedrich August von Hayek*, Stuttgart and New York: Fischer.
Mises, L. von (1978), *Notes and Recollections*. Foreword by Margit von Mises. Translation and Postscript by Hans F. Sennholz, South Holland, IL: Libertarian Press.
Mises, M. von (1981), *Ludwig Mises. Der Mensch und sein Werk*, Munich and Vienna. German translation of *My Years with Ludwig von Mises*, New Rochelle, NY: Arlington House.
Nautz, J. (1997), 'Zwischen Emanzipation und Integration. Die Frauen der Wiener Schule für Nationalökonomie', in L. Fischer and E. Brix (eds), *Die Frauen der Wiener Jahrhundertwende*, Vienna, Cologne and Weimar: Boehlau Verlag.
Die Presse, Vienna, 17–18, March 1990.
Winterberger, G. (1984), 'Generationen der österreichischen Schule der Nationalökonomie', *Schweizer Monatshefte für Politik, Wirtschaft und Kultur*, **64**, p. 391–403.
Wirtschaftliche Nachrichten, **15**(34), 21 October 1932.

Eveline Mabel Richardson Burns (1900–1985)

Eveline Mabel Burns played a significant role in establishing the social security system in the USA. She helped to design legislation that provided economic security for various groups in society. She explained the fine points of that legislation to a variety of audiences from academic economists to politicians to professional social workers to the public. She developed a method of public policy analysis that she applied to study the evolution of social security legislation in numerous countries. Finally, she worked to broaden the curriculum in schools of social work to equip students with the tools necessary to accomplish public policy analysis.

During the 1920s, Eveline Burns worked to find her place as an economist. She studied the discipline from several perspectives, including labour economics, economic theory and methodology, and in different roles, including graduate student, bureaucrat, teacher and editor. Like many young women, she was struggling to find the direction to take in her personal and professional life. The issues she pondered were recorded in an extensive correspondence with Oskar Morgenstern, begun when both travelled across the USA as Laura Spelman Rockefeller Fellows during the late 1920s. First, she and her husband, economist Arthur R. Burns, faced the challenge of finding two professional appointments. While a graduate student at the London School of Economics (LSE), she served as a lecturer in economic theory. But the faculty would not agree to hire both her and Arthur at the end of their fellowships. At one point, Morgenstern, somewhat tongue in cheek, advised her to give Arthur her job and remain at home as a housewife and researcher. Burns retorted:

> Of course I dont [*sic*] agree with you about giving up my work ... I'm sorry that you havent [*sic*] understood more about my attitude to work which is really a very important part of my make up. I have no doubt that I should make a very efficient housewife and probably a successful hostess but I have no ambition in that direction and there are plenty of other women who can do that and ther [*sic*] are not so many who can think. Writing is all very well but you know that I must have some stimulus to write, and the necessity of giving lectures provides that. Still more important is the meeting of my contemporaries, a thing which is almost impossible when one is not 'of' the academic world, especially if one is a woman. No Sir: your proposal is not for me. When I find that I cant [*sic*] com[p]ete with men in the academic world I will go home and have babies and become domestic and charming and be a 'wife' and perhaps write from time to time. All the while I can hold my own I'm going to show these disgusting anti-feminists that there are some women who are keen on their career, who can permanently be interested in those branches of hitherto regarded as men's, and that the old view of a woman giving up her job becaus [*sic*] she is married isnt [*sic*] necessarily the true one. (Oskar Morgenstern Papers, 11 November 1927)

After several years of searching, she and her husband were able to obtain appointments at Columbia University, but with feelings of bitterness at their treatment by former colleagues at LSE and frustration with their hiring at lower ranks than Burns believed they deserved.

Eveline Burns also pondered the future direction of her research. During the 1920s, the bulk of her published writings focused on issues related to economic security, including the French minimum wage (1923), publicly and privately funded allowances for children (1925), and a comparative study of the extent and institutional context of wage regulation in Europe, Australia, New Zealand, Canada and the USA (1926). During her travels in the USA, she also explored the methodology of economics with practitioners of mathematical economics, including Henry Shultz and Jacob Viner, statistical economics, including Wesley C. Mitchell and Mordecai Ezekial, and institutional economics, including Walton Wade Hamilton and John Commons. For a time, at the prompting of Morgenstern, Shultz and Viner, Burns also read extensively in the area of economic theory with the intention of applying Shultz's work on the supply and demand curves to study the elasticity of the supply of capital. Ultimately she did not complete this project. The Morgenstern correspondence reveals two possible reasons for her abandonment of this line of research. In part, she repeatedly questioned her ability to complete research in the area of mathematical economics. But her abandonment also reflected her frustration with the wastefulness of mathematical economists using their talents to build abstract models unrelated to real-world problems and, more importantly, to reiterate the shortcomings of each others methods of analysis. In a paper presented at the 1930 annual meeting of the American Economic Association, she outlined what she characterized as a pragmatic method which studied 'the interaction between social institutions on the one hand and economic relationships and the economic aspects of behavior on the other' (Burns, 1931, p. 82). This paper predicted the approach that she would apply to the analysis of issues related to social security for the next five decades. She used marginal analysis to think about the problem of allocating society's scarce resources and an institutional approach to take into account the effect of social institutions on the various public policies she developed and championed. Her 1933 article 'The Economics of Unemployment Relief' provides an early example of this methodological approach.

Eveline Burns committed herself in earnest to her life's work on social security in 1934 when President Franklin Roosevelt appointed her as a consultant to the Committee on Economic Security. As a member of this committee she helped to design the Social Security Act of 1935. In *Toward Social Security* (1936), she made explicit the values that guided this and subsequent work. First, she believed it the responsibility of government to provide for the economic security of all citizens. Second, she believed that members of a democratic society could choose more intelligently 'when they are fully informed as to the implications of the various alternatives' (Burns, 1936, p. vi). Third, ever the pragmatist, she supported the passage of even incomplete legislation if it helped to move the public in the direction of more radical changes in the future.

Eveline Burns proceeded to study social security in a variety of contexts over the next two decades. In the late 1930s she travelled to Europe to complete a comparative study of social security in other institutional contexts. Her book *British Unemployment Programs, 1920–1938* (1941) highlighted the difficulties of combining insurance, transitional payments and public assistance to take care of the unemployed, the important role of the institutional context in determining the success or failure of unemployment programmes, and the universal focus on maintenance of the unemployed rather than the social inadequacy of existing wage systems in Europe, Australia and the USA. From 1939 to 1943, she served as the chief of the Economic Security and Health section of the National Resources Planning

Board. Under her direction, the Board issued a controversial report entitled *Security, Work and Relief* (1943), which outlined the problems and prospects for the postwar economy. The report received much attention from the public and the press, but members of Congress did not view it favourably because it recommended extending the New-Deal philosophy of active government involvement in the economy after the war. From 1943 to 1945 Eveline Burns served as a consultant on social security to the National Planning Association. While there she prepared *Discussion* and *Outline on Social Security* (1944). Her book *The American Social Security System* (1949) provided a detailed outline of the social security system as it had evolved during the postwar years. In 1954 she served as one of a group of consultants to the Secretary of Health, Education and Welfare, whose recommendations led the way to the extension of coverage of Old Age Survivor's Insurance. In 1956, she published *Social Security and Public Policy* in which she outlined the methodological approach she recommended for public policy analysis and applied it to provide yet another analysis of the social security system.

Burns also worked diligently to explain social security to a variety of audiences. She wrote *Toward Social Security* in 1936 to provide a detailed explanation of the provisions of the Social Security Act to the public. She gave testimony about social security to numerous Congressional committees. And she taught generations of students about social security from both an economic and a public policy perspective. She wrote both *The American Social Security System* (1949) and *Social Security and Public Policy* (1956) in part to serve as texts in the field.

Beginning in 1945, Burns also became interested in social work education. She was concerned that schools of social work focused solely on the preparation of students to serve as caseworkers for individual clients. As the role of government in the life of the community increased, she recommended that schools of social work also teach students the methodological approach to policy analysis she used, so that they could gain a system-wide view of the impacts of public policy. She chose schools of social work as the best place for this type of education, because she did not think members of the economics profession with their increasing use of mathematical techniques would be receptive to this approach to policy analysis.

Burns was born on 16 March 1900 in London, the daughter of Frederick Haig and Eveline Maud Falkner Richardson. She attended Streatham Secondary School. She studied at the London School of Economics (LSE), receiving a BS degree in economics with first-class honours in 1920 and a Ph.D. in 1926. From 1917 to 1921 she began her long career of service to the government and social welfare agencies as an administrative assistant in the British Ministry of Labour. From 1921 to 1926 she began her distinguished teaching career as a lecturer in economic theory at the LSE. She also served as assistant editor of *Economica* from 1923 to 1926. From 1926 to 1928, she and her husband, economist Arthur R. Burns, received Laura Spelman Rockefeller Fellowships to meet with and lecture to economists across the USA, including the prominent faculty at Harvard University, the University of Chicago, Stanford University and Columbia University. In 1928, she was appointed as the first female member of the graduate school faculty at Columbia University, where she remained until 1942. In 1942 she left Columbia University to work full-time at the National Resources Planning Board. In 1946 she returned to Columbia as a professor in the School of Social Work, remaining in this post until 1967. After her retirement she continued to advise the government and social welfare agencies about issues related to social security. She served on the executive committee of the American Economic Association from 1945 to 1948; she was elected vice-president of the organization in 1953 and 1954. She was elected President of the National Conference on Social Welfare for the 1957–58 term. In addition to the Laura Spelman Rockefeller Fellowship, she was awarded the Adam Smith medal for outstanding economic research in 1926, and a Guggenheim Fellowship for travel in Europe in 1954–55. In 1960 she received the Florina Lasher Social Work Award.

SHERRYL DAVIS KASPER

Bibliography

Selected writings by Eveline Mabel Burns
(1923), 'The French Minimum Wage Act of 1915', *Economica*, **3**, 236–44.
(1925), 'The Economics of Family Endowment', *Economica*, **5**, June, 155–64.
(1926), *Wages and the State: A Comparative Study of the Problems of State Wage Regulation*, London: P.S. King and Son.
(1931), 'Does Institutional Economics Complement or Compete with Orthodox Economics?', *American Economic Review*, **21**, March, 80–87.
(1933), 'The Economics of Unemployment Relief', *American Economic Review*, **23**, March, 31–43.
(1936), *Toward Social Security: An Explanation of the Social Security Act and a Survey of Larger Issues*, London: Whittlesey House and New York: McGraw-Hill.
(1941), *British Unemployment Programs, 1920–38*, Report prepared for Committee on Social Security. Washington, DC: Social Science Research Council.
(1943), *Security, Work, and Relief Programs*, Report of the Committee on Long-Range Work and Relief Policies to the National Resources Planning Board. (Eveline M. Burns, Director of Research) Washington, DC: US Government Printing Office.
(1944), *Discussion and Study Outline on Social Security*, Washington, DC: The Planning Association.
(1949), *The American Social Security System*, Boston: Houghton Mifflin.
(1956), *Social Security and Public Policy*, New York: McGraw-Hill.

Other sources and references
Correspondence by and to Eve M. Burns (1926–1939), Oskar Morgenstern Papers, Perkins Library, Duke University.

The Oral History Research Office, Butler Library, Columbia University, holds three transcripts of interviews with Burns. A 1965 interview with Peter A. Corning forms part of the social 'security project. A 1979 interview with Patrick D. Reagan contains reminiscences about her professional life. A 1981 interview by Evangeline C. Cooper forms part of the unemployment insurance project.

'Eveline M. Burns' (1960), in Charles Moritz (ed.), *Current Biography*, New York: The H.W. Wilson Co., pp. 64–6.

'Eveline M. Burns' (1986), in Hal May (ed.), *Contemporary Authors*, Detroit, Michigan: Gale Research Co., p. 71.

Shlakman, Vera (1969), 'Eveline M. Burns: Social Worker', in Shirley Jenkins (ed.), *Social Security in International Perspective*, New York and London: Columbia University Press, pp. 3–25. (Contains a complete list of the writings of Eveline M. Burns from 1923 through 1968.)

Elizabeth Beardsley Butler (1885–1911)

Born in 1885, Elizabeth Beardsley Butler was educated at the Packer Collegiate Institute and Adelphi College and in 1905 graduated from Barnard College in New York, USA. She was Executive Secretary of the Consumers' League of New Jersey; she also held positions with the New Jersey Child Labor Committee, the Bureau of Social Research of the New York School of Philanthropy, and the Rand School of Social Science.[1]

Butler was responsible for the first of six volumes of the Pittsburgh Survey, which was designed as 'a careful and fairly comprehensive study of the conditions under which working people live and labor in a great industrial city', according to John Glenn, General Director of the Russell Sage Foundation, which financed the study (Butler, 1984, Introductory to original (1909) printing by Glenn, p. 1). She was recommended for the job by Florence Kelley (*q.v.*), member of the survey's advisory committee and executive secretary of the National Consumers' League. Butler's volume, entitled *Women and the Trades: Pittsburgh, 1907–1908*, was 'the first general survey of women employing trades of an American city' in the words of Paul Kellogg, the director of the survey (Kellogg, 1911, p. 744). The ten-month-long study encompassed 22 185 Pittsburgh wage-earning women, who were distributed across 449 factories, shops and stores, which were all visited. Butler attempted to provide a general characterization of the workers, at least according to categories defined by the industry and specific job. Throughout, the results were described in an interesting way; a reviewer for the *Economic Journal* said that '[t]he descriptions ... are graphic and convincing' (Reinherz, 1910, p. 80).

The book begins with a brief discussion of the relationship between the job distribution of women across ethnic groups and the groups' immigration histories. Then much of the book provides a disaggregated look at the women workers. Specifically, it surveys different jobs within a number of industries (for example, canning, cracker, and cleaning industries) and presents the following job statistics: number of workers, wage range, number of hours worked, seasonality of work and overtime hours. It also gives some information on male workers and makes interesting comparisons of distributions across jobs by sex of the workers. It describes the social life of women inside and outside the place of employment.

Butler summarized the findings and provided a number of conclusions. For example, she used the data to test economists' hypotheses explaining female–male wage differentials (for example, lack of women's unionization, relative lack of productivity, women's transience in the labour market); she concluded that while some of the hypotheses may have been partially true, they did not entirely account for the observed differentials, and then she suggested other explanations for the differential (for example, the traditional view that women were viewed as others' financial dependants). Butler investigated the extent to which women could make a living wage; on the basis of the data and cost-of-living figures she derived, she concluded that 60 per cent of the women did not earn a subsistence wage and noted this as a possible reason for them to enter prostitution. Finally, based on her analysis, she suggested some changes in public policy (for example, shorten the workday, improve the environment of the workplace) and changes in the women themselves (for example, invest more in their own human capital), which would improve their condition.

Following her Pittsburgh investigation, Butler produced the study *Saleswomen in Mercantile Stores: Baltimore, 1909* (Butler, 1912) commissioned by the Maryland Consumers' League. She again formed a disaggregated set of data, this time dealing with female workers at a group of mercantile establishments in Baltimore. She provided information on the organization structure, including chains of command; furthermore, she determined the distribution of females and males within the hierarchy and made some comparisons and contrasts. She compared the extent to which men's and women's jobs were seasonal; she viewed the degree of women's job seasonality over men's to be 'striking' (p. 84). She recorded wages, including bonuses, fines and overtime wages. She then estimated cost-of-living and concluded that 81 per cent of the women did not earn a subsistence wage. She listed some reasons for the low wage; furthermore, she viewed these wage-lowering conditions to be 'operative in Baltimore ... to an unusual degree' (p. 120).

Butler succumbed to tuberculosis on 2 August 1911, at Saranac Lake, New York. Some insight into her impact on those around her was given by John Glenn, who said that '[s]he was thoughtful and thorough ... and ... made friends in all ranks ... [Her death] has taken from ... [her co-workers] a valued friend and from society a valuable worker' (Butler, 1912, Preface by Glenn, p. vi).

In her short life of 26 years, Butler showed an impressive professional publication rate: two books and numerous articles. Through her work, Butler showed herself to have been a vigorous, persistent and precise researcher; after her death, Paul Kellogg described her as an individual who 'mapped out her field with rare deftness and held to her working scheme with a marvelous fund of buoyant energy' (Kellogg, 1911, p. 743).

An enormous amount of work was involved in the collection of the statistics and in the summary of qualitative results; her results are well argued and sometimes provocative. Her work conveys a sense of the possibilities of an individual who is inspired to expose and clarify the truth, at least as far as he/she understands it. In fact, Kellogg said that 'in her splendid courage we catch a glimpse of the power which the woman who works is to be in the day that lies ahead' (Kellogg, 1911, p. 744).

Susan H. Gensemer

Note

1. Biographical material for Butler is taken from Butler (1984), Introduction by Greenwald; Chambers (1976), pp. 34–5; Kellogg (1911).

Bibliography

Selected writings by Elizabeth Beardsley Butler

(1907), 'New Jersey Children in the Trades', *Charities and the Commons*, **17**, 16 March, 1062–4.

(1907), 'Sweated Trades in Hudson County', *Charities and the Commons*, **19**, 21 December, 1257–64.

(1909 [1984]), *Women and the Trades, 1907–1908*, vol. 1 of the Pittsburgh Labor Series, Paul U. Kellogg (ed.), New York: Charities Publication Committee; reprinted by University of Pittsburgh Press, 1984, edited and with an introduction by Maurine Weiner Greenwald.

(1912), *Saleswomen in Mercantile Stores: Baltimore, 1909*, New York: Charities Publication Committee, Russell Sage Foundation.

Other sources and references

Chambers, Clarke A. (1976), *Paul U. Kellogg and the Survey: Voices for Social Welfare and Social Justice*, Minneapolis: University of Minnesota Press.

Kellogg, Paul U. (1911), 'Elizabeth Beardsley Butler', *Survey*, **26**, 743–4.

Reinherz, H. (1910), 'Review of *Women and the Trades*, vol. 1 of Pittsburgh Labor Series', *Economic Journal*, **20**, 77–80.

Helen Stuart Campbell (1839–1918)

Born Helen Campbell Stuart on 4 July 1839 in Lockport, New York, died on 22 July 1918 in Dedham, Massachusetts, Helen Stuart Campbell was a social reformer and first-generation muckraker, active in the settlement movement, an influential feminist, active popular lecturer, an early home economist and home economics professor, theorist on the nature of women's work in the market and the home, and an author of popular fiction on the struggles of women and of children's stories at the turn of the century. She was married in 1861 to a surgeon in the Grand Army of the Republic, Grenville Mellen Weeks, divorced in 1871, and henceforth assumed her mother's maiden name.

In the late 1870s Helen Campbell became involved in the early home economics movement after having taken lessons from Juliet Corson of the New York Cooking School, and began teaching in 1878 in the Raleigh (North Carolina) Cooking School. Campbell wrote a home economics textbook, *The Easiest Way in House-Keeping and Cooking* (1881), and associated with Anna Lowell Woodbury in founding a mission school and diet kitchen in Washington, DC. Later she helped to organize the short-lived National Household Economics Association in 1893.

Concern with the diet of the poor led her to write her first major muckraking work, *The Problem of the Poor. A Record of Quiet Work in Unquiet Places* (1882), which described the work of a city mission on the New York waterfront with which she was associated (run by Jerry McAuley), and which dealt with poverty in New York, especially in connection with the unfortunate effects of low wages on women. As many of her works, the book first appeared serially in popular magazines. At this time she also wrote a number of financially successful novels, including *Mrs. Herndon's Income* and *Miss Melinda's Opportunity*, which emphasized women's struggles with the low (and often falling) wages.

As a result of the reputation she acquired as a social critic and reformer, Campbell was commissioned by Horace Greeley's *New York Tribune* to write weekly articles beginning on 24 October 1886 on the conditions among women in the needle trades and department stores of New York. She documented how even well-intentioned employers were driven by competition to drive down wages and raise piece rates, and how difficult it was for women and their children to survive on women's wages as low as three dollars per week. The *Tribune* articles were later collected as *Prisoners of Poverty: Women Wage-Workers, Their Trades and Their Lives*. This work was immediately followed by *Prisoners of Poverty Abroad*, a sequel written after travel to Europe and a visit arranged by Florence Kelley (*q.v.*) to Friedrich Engels in England.

Campbell's best-known achievement was that she helped attract the attention of middle-class audiences to the plight of poor women wage-earners at the outset of the period of early Progressive era social reform. But she also pioneered as an early social economist in applying new methods of social science, such as the use of official reports and government documents and the analysis of earnings and family budgets to explain the living and working conditions of women. Her methodology of writing was to examine closely individual cases that were representative of the circumstances of many women, and then generalize about larger issues affecting working women.

In 1891 her monograph, *Women Wage-Earners*, a survey of conditions of working women in America and Europe, received an award from the American Economic Association. Subsequently published in an expanded version as *Women Wage-Earners: Their Past, Their Present, and Their Future* (1893; reprinted 1972) with an introduction by Richard T. Ely, it argued for workers' associations and consumers' unions as means of seeking better wages and improvements in working conditions, and vividly described factory work as preparation 'for the hospital, the workhouse, and the prison', given that workers were regularly 'inoculated with trade diseases, mutilated by trade appliances, and corrupted by trade associates' (p. 213).

Ely had founded the American Economic Association in 1885 to oppose Social Darwinism and *laissez-faire* individualism, and had become a popular figure at the University of Wisconsin in Madison. Campbell studied with Ely in 1893 at Wisconsin, and the following year Ely persuaded the regents of the University to invite Campbell to deliver two courses of lectures for the spring of 1895, 'Household Science' and 'Social Science', arranging for their remuneration himself. The lectures, however, did not lead to a permanent position for Campbell at Wisconsin as was hoped, but did result in another textbook, *Household Economics* (1897), which concerned 'the connecting link between the physical economics of the individual and the social economics of the state'. The election of a populist governor led to Campbell's appointment as a professor of home economics at Kansas State Agricultural College in 1897, but she resigned the following March on account of ill health and charges of conflict with subordinates. She then returned to freelance writing and lecturing for the rest of her life.

Campbell was a member of the First Nationalist Club of Boston, a group following Edward Bellamy's 1888 *Looking Backward* ideas, and also wrote for the Bellamyite publication, *Nationalist*, as well as for the *American Fabian* and Benjamin O. Flower's social reform periodical *Arena*, including for the latter such pieces as 'Certain Convictions as to Poverty' (1889–90), 'White Child Slavery' (1889–90), and 'The Working-Women of To-day' (1891). She was also an influential close friend and 'mother figure', according to Charlotte Perkins Gilman, whose *Women and Economics: A Study of the*

Economic Relation Between Men and Women as a Factor in Social Evolution (1898) has been called 'the most important work of feminist theory in the emerging Progressive Era' (Sklar, p. 305).

JOHN B. DAVIS

Bibliography

Selected writings by Helen Campbell
(1881), *The Easiest Way in House-Keeping and Cooking*, New York: Fords, Howard and Hulbert.
(1882), *The Problem of the Poor. A Record of Quiet Work in Unquiet Places*, New York: Fords, Howard and Hulbert.
(1886), *Mrs. Herdon's Income*, Boston: Roberts Bros.
(1886), M*iss Melinda's Opportunity*, Boston: Roberts Bros.
(1887), *Prisoners of Poverty: Women Wage-Workers, Their Trades and Their Lives*, Boston: Roberts Bros. reprinted Westport, CT: Greenwood Press, 1970.
(1889), *Prisoners of Poverty Abroad*, Boston: Roberts Brothers.
(1889–90), 'Certain Convictions as to Poverty', *Arena*.
(1889–90), 'White Child Slavery', *Arena*.
(1891), 'The Working-Women of To-day', *Arena*.
(1893), *Women Wage-Earners: Their Past, Their Present, and Their Future*, Boston: Roberts Bros. reprinted New York: Arno, 1972.
(1897), *Household Economics*, New York: G.P. Putnam's Sons.

Other sources and references
Bremner, Robert H. (1972), *From the Depths: The Discovery of Poverty in the United States*, New York: New York University Press.
Gilman, Charlotte Perkins (1898), *Women and Economics: A Study of the Relation Between Men and Women as a Factor in Social Evolution*, Boston: Small, Maynard.
James, Edward T., Janet Wilson James and Paul S. Boyer (1971), *Notable American Women, 1607–1950. A Biographical Dictionary*, Cambridge, MA: Belknap.
Shapiro, Laura (1986), *Perfection Salad: Women and Cooking at the Turn of the Century*, New York: Henry Holt and Co.
Sklar, Kathryn Kish (1995), *Florence Kelley and the Nation's Work: The Rise of Women's Political Culture, 1830–1900*, New Haven and London: Yale.

Agatha Louisa Chapman (1907–63)

Agatha Chapman was one of a number of Canadian women economists active during the 1930s and 1940s.[1] They include Irene M. Spry (*q.v.*), Beryl Plumptre, Alison Kemp-Mitchell, Phyllis Turner-Ross, Sylvia Ostry, Mary Quayle Innis (*q.v.*) and Lucy Morgan (see Alexander, 1995). Some were Canadian-born, others, although born outside the country, adopted Canada through marriage or through living there. For many who worked in the government or the private sector, their work was, and is still, unattributed. In Agatha Chapman's case, this phenomenon, combined with her short working life, resulted in only one book to her credit. Nevertheless, the account of her life raises interesting questions for women economists.

Agatha Chapman was born in 1907 in England to a Canadian mother and a father who spent many years as a judge of the High Court of India. Her great-grandfather was Sir Charles Tupper and one of her great-uncles a lieutenant governor of Manitoba. Her family moved to Vernon, British Columbia in 1918. She attended Cheltenham Ladies' College and the University of Toronto, where she received a master's degree in economics in 1931. After spending several years with Sun Life Assurance in Montreal, she joined the federal government in 1940, first at the Bank of Canada and then at Dominion Bureau of Statistics. A newspaper photograph from that time shows an elegant, spectacled woman in her thirties.

In the early 1940s Canada was overhauling its national income accounts, following reforms made in Great Britain under Meade and Stone. Chapman worked on these under the supervision of Claude Isbister. She travelled with Isbister to the meeting of the League of Nations Subcommittee on National Income Statistics held at Princeton in 1945. There she met Richard Stone who, amongst his other duties, was recruiting for the newly established Department of Applied Economics at Cambridge. She receives an acknowledgement in the publication that came out of that conference.

In 1947, on the strength of that encounter with Professor Stone, she moved to Cambridge, England, where she remained until 1949. During her tenure at the Department of Applied Economics, she produced a study on national income in Great Britain, *Wages and Salaries in the United Kingdom, 1920–1938*. This was described in the *American Economic Review* as 'a work of admirable and indefatigable scholarship' (Lebergott, 1953). The study, part of a series from the National Institute for Economic and Social Research, estimated wages, salaries and average annual earnings for all classes of employees in Britain. The study forms a pair with that by Stone (1954) on expenditure, and they were reviewed in tandem by R.G.D. Allen (1954). Allen notes that Stone emphasizes the teamwork required for this type of enterprise. Thus we should treat Chapman's work as one piece in a very technical puzzle. Much of this early work has been superseded by changing computational techniques, and indeed some of Chapman's work was dated, even as it appeared, by changes in employment classifications.

Chapman returned to Montreal in the early 1950s, married a refugee from the McCarthy investigations in the USA, Richard Edsall, and, with him and Kayyam Paltiel, set up a consulting firm specializing in labour economics. She died in the 1960s in a fall from her apartment window, an apparent suicide. She was buried in the cemetery of Mount Royal in Montreal.

This brief synopsis omits what was probably the defining event of Chapman's life. The beginning of the cold war can be traced to the defection of Igor Gouzenko in Ottawa in 1945. His defection, and the resulting report of the Kellock–Taschereau Commission, released in Ottawa in 1946, had repercussions in Great Britain, the USA and indeed most of the western world. It figured in the trials of Alan Nunn May, Klaus Fuchs and the Rosenbergs, and influenced indirectly the events of the McCarthy era in the USA. Only recently has the international regime introduced by the cold war loosened its grip, yet many of us have forgotten, or never knew, the events that precipitated it.

The Kellock–Taschereau Royal Commission investigated Gouzenko's allegations of widespread spy rings in Canada. Chapman was implicated, although she consistently denied any involvement. This investigation and her public trial changed her life and arguably contributed to her early death. She certainly lost her civil service position on account of this case. Many of those implicated by the Commission suffered untimely deaths, not necessarily suicides, but from other causes such as alcoholism and illness.

Chapman had, for many years, belonged to left-wing organizations, in particular the League for Social Reconstruction, and hosted study groups at her home. This group began amongst left-wing League intellectuals in Toronto and Montreal in 1931 or 1932, led by Frank Underhill and the lawyer and poet, F.R. Scott. The League was critical of monopoly capital and demanded change through parliamentary means. Disillusion with socialism led to its 'quiet demise' in the early 1940s. Professor Rosenbluth wrote that Chapman was 'probably a communist sympathizer ... a not unreasonable position for a progressive person' at that time. Many of those involved in the affair had, at one time or another, been to her home at 282 Somerset Street, in Ottawa (the house still stands and is now the Embassy of Madagascar). Agatha Chapman was not named in Gouzenko's documents. The immediate link was made by another woman, ultimately convicted of espionage, who belonged to the study group and who claimed that she received information about her contacts directly from Agatha Chapman.

The Commission first interviewed Chapman, and then she was tried in court and acquitted of 'giving information to a foreign power during time of war'. She had been suspended from her job at the Dominion Bureau of Statistics as soon as the affair became public and after the acquittal she announced in a press release that she did not feel comfortable going back to work. She may well have been pressured to resign. Several months later, in April 1947, she left for England and the appointment at Cambridge.

Chapman's life and career raise several questions. There are two compelling reasons for her obscurity. The first is the general lack of information about government employees of that era, much of whose work was not attributed. The second was the disinclination of people to talk about the Gouzenko affair, and also the secrecy surrounding the case. Many of the documents in the case, and the transcript of the Commission's hearings itself, were not made public until the 1980s. This point was made by John Sawatsky, who tried to interview those interviewed by the Commission 30 years after the event and found that most were not willing to speak and that those who did were still visibly upset by their memories.

Chapman was not, at any time, accused of spying. The Commission found her association with others who were accused, and in some cases convicted, of offences against the state incriminating. One wonders how her career in the civil service might have developed if she had not been connected to the Gouzenko case. Without commenting on her possible involvement, we now know that individuals involved in various front organizations, leftist and peace movements ran the gamut from the completely unwitting and innocent to the most knowing. If her study groups provided a place where people could meet, then she may have been an unwitting dupe, although that theory is inconsistent with her apparent character and intelligence. It is also possible that her study groups were exactly what she thought they were – meetings of friends to discuss contemporary social issues. Her career seemed to hold so much promise, one cannot escape the feeling that her life was blighted.

Agatha Chapman is still remembered among older economists, but neither the Bank of Canada nor Statistics Canada retains a corporate memory of her. Very soon, all who knew her will have died and her story will be lost.

JUDITH A. ALEXANDER

Note
1. Two economists, Anthony Scott and Gideon Rosenbluth, gave me invaluable help with background information for this article. Scott (1993) mentions Agatha Chapman in his paper; Alexander (1995) contains a review of Canadian women economists.

Bibliography
Alexander Judith A. (1995), 'Our ancestors in their successive generations', *Canadian Journal of Economics*, **XXVIII** (1), February, 205–24.
Allen, R.G.D. (1954), 'Studies in national income and expenditure', *Economic Journal*, **LXIV** (1), March, 124–9.
Bothwell, Robert and J.L. Granatstein (1982), *The Gouzenko Transcripts*, Webcom Ltd, Canada.
Chapman, Agatha, assisted by Rose Knight (1952), *Wages and Salaries in the United Kingdom 1920–1938*, Studies in National Income and Expenditure of the United Kingdom, no. 5, Cambridge: Cambridge University Press.
Lebergott, Stanley (1953), 'Review of *Wages and Salaries in the United Kingdom 1920–1938* by Agatha Chapman', *American Economic Review*, **43** (1), March, 192–5.
Royal Commission on Spy Activities in Canada (1946), The Honourable Mr. Justice Robert Taschereau and the Honourable Mr. Justice R.L. Kellock, Ottawa: Edmond Cloutier.
Sawatsky, John (1984), *Gouzenko: The Untold Story*, Toronto: Macmillan.
Scott, Anthony (1993), 'Does living in Canada make one a Canadian economist?', *Canadian Journal of Economics*, **XXVI** (1), February, 26–38.
Stone, Richard (1954), *The Measurement of Consumers' Behaviour and Expenditure in the United Kingdom, 1920–1938*. Studies in National Income and Expenditure of the United Kingdom, no. 7, Cambridge: Cambridge University Press.
Stone, Richard (1947), *The Measurement of National Income and the Construction of National Accounts*, Geneva: The United Nations.

Margaret Cole (1893–1980)

Margaret Isabel Postgate Cole was one of the most important personages of the English cultural milieu during the first half of the twentieth century. She played a leading role in the history of English socialism, especially in relation to the Labour Party and Guild Socialism, of which she was a tireless organizer rather than a theorist *tout court*. Raised in Cambridge, she belonged to a family in which every member was as interested in international political events as in national ones. During her childhood and youth she learnt to appreciate and love poetry and literature and wrote verses and short stories, that were later published. She became a teacher in London, at Saint Paul's Girls' School, until the outbreak of World War II. In 1917 she became a member of the Fabian Research Department (FRD), where she met G.D.H. Cole. They married the following year – 'a promising union of two devoted fellow workers', said Beatrice Webb (*q.v.*). After her marriage, she moved to Oxford, where she began working as a tutor at the Workers' Educational Association and at Morley College, and wrote many pamphlets for the Labour Research Department (LRD) in *The Nation* and in *Labour Monthly*. During the 1920s she analysed the rise and the fall of Guild Socialism, a new English syndicalism whose founder was her husband, and followed the development of the Labour Party up to its first electoral victory.

In the 1930s, after her return to London, Margaret Cole was very involved in politics: the most ambitious project for which she worked, together with Beatrice Webb, was the renovation and the reorganization of the Fabian Society (for which she became Honorary Secretary). Her aim was to turn the Fabian Society into an organization to promote the success of the Labour Party. In that period Cole studied Soviet and fascist political economy. Another great interest of hers was the reform of the English educational system: she always blamed the presence of expensive public schools alongside state schools, because such a double system maintained social class differences.

In 1946, Margaret Cole wrote *The Rate for the Job*, a pamphlet in which she argued for the necessity of reaching real equality between men and women, not only in political fields, but also in the working environment. In her opinion, universal suffrage wasn't enough to build a just society that would guarantee the same opportunities for everybody, without sexual discrimination. Unequal wages between men and women and the barriers to women seeking to pursue a career were the most urgent economic and social problems in that period. Cole underlined that the difficulties for women in reaching a high working level were exacerbated by the fact that women often chose a lower working level in order to spend more time in housekeeping. This mental attitude, historically imposed on them, was undoubtedly strengthened in England by Victorianism, of which Margaret Cole always was an implacable enemy.

After World War II, Cole became an active journalist; she wrote her most important books, *The Story of Fabian Socialism* (1961) and *The Life of G.D.H. Cole* (1971). Her books give an account of the history of English Socialism: in the former she dealt with the Fabian Society (since its foundation in 1883); in the latter she described – through her husband's life – the evolution and the fall of Guild Socialism. Cole's aim was to show the unity of Fabianism and Guild Socialism – two socialist movements that moulded the Labour Party.

Cole was the biographer of labourism: in *Makers of the Labour Movement* (1948) she wrote the biographies of 15 'pioneers of labourism' – from Tom Paine and Robert Owen to Sidney Webb and H.G. Wells – and she edited Beatrice Webb's writings. During the last period of her life she assisted in compiling the *Dictionary of Labour Biography* (the second volume contains her long contribution on Sidney and Beatrice Webb, with an excellent bibliography of their works). She was also active in founding the Labour History Museum and the Society for the Study of Labour History.

Margaret Cole wasn't an economist in the classical sense. She was on one hand a passionate chronicler of labourism and on the other a socialist. Though she lacked G.D.H. Cole's theoretical originality and Beatrice Webb's intellectual charm, she stood out because of her organizing capacities: a tireless worker with a practical mind (typically English), neither theorist nor political philosopher, she was a clever observer of the national and international political scene, which she analysed from the socialist perspective. Her contribution to the introduction of women's rights in English society shouldn't be forgotten.

GIANDOMENICA BECCHIO

Bibliography

Selected writings by Margaret Cole
(1933), *Twelve Studies on Soviet Russia*, London: Gollancz.
(1936), *Roads to Success*, London: Methuen.
(1937), *The New Economic Revolution*, London: Gollancz.
(1938), *Women of Today*, London: Nelson.
(1938), *Marriage*, London: Dent.
(1939), *Democratic Sweden* (with Charles Smith), New York: The Greystone Press.
(1945), *Beatrice Webb: a Memoir*, London: Longmans Green.
(1946), *The Rate for the Job, a pamphlet prepared for the Fabian Women's Group and based on the Evidence of the Group before the Royal Commission on Equal Pay*, London: Gollancz.
(1948), *Makers of the Labour Movement*, London: Longmans Green.
(1953), *Robert Owen of New Lanark*, New York: Kelley.
(1956), *Servant of the County*, London: Dobson.
(1961), *The Story of Fabian Socialism*, London: Heinemann Educational Books Ltd.
(1966), *What I Believe*, London: Allen and Unwin.
(1971), *The Life of G.D.H. Cole*, London: Macmillan.
(1971), *Essays in Labour History 1886–1923* (edited by Asa Briggs and John Saville), London: Macmillan.

(1977), *Essays in Labour History, 1918–1939*, (edited by Asa Briggs and John Saville), London: Croom Helm.

Other sources and references
Betty Vernon (1986), *Margaret Cole, 1893–1980*, Croom Helm, London.

Clara Elizabeth Collet (1860–1948)

Clara Elizabeth Collet, British feminist, social economist and statistician, was born on 10 September 1860, the second daughter of Collet Dobson Collet and Jane Collet, née Sloan. Her father was a radical reformer, rationalist and student of the law, editor of *The Diplomatic Review*, and author of several books. One of his friends, the socialist reformer and labour historian Jacob Holyoake, wrote in the introduction to Collet's *History of Taxes on Knowledge* that its author was an 'unusual man ... incessant in promoting public causes ... with absolute disinterestedness'. Collet was also an acquaintance and occasional correspondent with Marx and Engels during the 1870s. Clara Collet's diary mentions visits with her father to the Marxes for Shakespeare readings and in June 1878 she recorded that 'the Marxes and the Oswalds are the only people I care for now' (Collet, 1876–1914, pp. 12, 13, 15). Clara Collet was educated at North London Collegiate School, later did her BA at University College London (1880), and took her MA in 1885. She became University College's first woman Fellow in 1896. Collet (1945) recorded that her introduction to political economy was due to the fact that it was a compulsory subject for the London MA. Her economics essays were corrected by William Ashley and J.E. Symes, while Jevons examined her on philosophy in 1880. Her lectures on economics were given by Foxwell, who became a life-long friend (Collet, 1936). During her political-economy studies, she read Adam Smith, John Stuart Mill (whom she thought 'dull') and Ruskin's *Unto this Last*, which, she thought, grossly misinterpreted Smith and Mill. Both Mill and Ruskin introduced her to social questions; ministers of religion, including Philip Wicksteed, a family friend, reinforced this interest, as did attendance at a lecture by Arnold Toynbee in March 1882 on 'Are Radicals Socialists?', a lecture which she recorded as much less impressive on further reflection than when she first heard it. She also frequented meetings of the suffragettes. During this formative period, she earned her living as Assistant Mistress at Wyggeston's Girls' School, Leicester (1878–85), which entitled her to join the Association of Assistant Mistresses in Public Secondary Schools. She became its president in 1891 and was made an honorary member from 1894. Some of her later essays reflect this experience.

Her calling to social inquiry began in earnest when Charles Booth invited her to join his team of social investigators for the Greater London Survey he was conducting. She worked for him from 1888 to 1892, contributing a number of chapters to his reports (Collet, 1889, 1891a), which rank among her first publications. She also published in the *Quarterly Journal of Economics* (Collett, 1891c). Her presence in London for the work enabled her to pursue other activities, such as the formation of the London Junior Economic Club in 1890 which brought her the friendship of Henry Higgs (Collet, 1940), and foundation membership of the British Economic Association (later the Royal Economic Society). In the context of the last, as Arthur Bowley (1950) mentioned, she was the only person who contributed to both the first volume of the *Economic Journal* and its 50th Jubilee volume in 1940 while her name, appropriately enough, is also recorded in the centenary volume of journal and society (Hey and Winch, 1990). She was elected member of the Royal Economic Society Council in 1918, retiring from this position in 1941, aged 81; in 1894 she had been elected as Fellow of the Royal Statistical Society and served on its council from 1919 to 1935 (Thorburn, 1948). Her work in the last anticipated her remarkable economic and statistical career in public service from the early 1900s onwards. During 1892 she served with distinction as one of four assistant commissioners for the Labour Commission (Bulley, 1894, pp. 43–5; Collette, 1989, pp. 12–13), which led to her appointment as Labour Correspondent for the Board of Trade (1893–1903), Senior Investigator, Board of Trade (1903–17), and Ministry of Labour (1917–20), her last official full-time public service position. She continued her official duties as a member of trade boards (1921–32) on a part-time basis. During these years of semi-retirement she wrote the chapter on domestic service for a *New Survey of London Life and Labour* (Collet, 1931), a final contribution to another long-standing interest in labour economics.

Her effective retirement from 1933 was not inactive, and in part was devoted to research on family history. The Collet name is an old one, which came to England not long after the Norman Conquest from Rouen traders' stock. In 1933, this research produced an edition of *The Private Letter Books of Joseph Collet*, a great-great-great-uncle, who had been an official of the East India Company and a governor of Madras in 1717. Merchants were therefore conspicuous in her family, which also produced the occasional colonial governor, such as her elder brother Sir Wilfred Collet, who was Governor of British Guiana and British Honduras. The British Library Catalogue reports a typewritten four-volume work written together with Henry Haines Collett, *Collett. Memorials relating to various branches of the family, with pedigrees and accompanying biographical notes, together with miscellaneous data*, dated 1935, another product of her interest in family history. The Modern Records Centre (Warwick University Library) records other subsequent unpublished work among her papers, including a statistical survey of pre-Victorian novels, a proposal for an edition of the Higgs–Foxwell correspondence, mainly on currency questions, and a pamphlet (rejected by Allen and Unwin) on the extension of church establishment.

No wonder she was described as being of a 'lively disposition' (Thorburn, 1948) and a fine raconteur, capable of producing 'many amusing, and sometimes surprising anecdotes, racily told' about her friendship with interesting individuals (such as one of Marx's daughters, Eleanor Marx-Aveling and the Gissings), her participation in Edgeworth's 'tramping parties' and her encounters with Philip Wicksteed, Marshall and other distinguished speakers at the Junior Economics Club. The flavour of these is at least partly preserved in her obituary of Higgs (1940) with its extracts from her diaries; a number of footnotes in Keynes's (1972, pp. 137 n.4, 138 n.1) essay on Jevons in *Essays on Biography* and her own obituary by the Indian statistician, P.C. Mahalanobis (1948), who was also one of her many Indian friends.

Clara Collet's economic work falls largely into the category of labour economics with special emphasis on the analysis of working women. Her only book (Collet, 1902a) on the subject addressed problems for a special segment of the women's labour market, namely educated working women, which capitalized on her former work as teacher and office-bearer in a teachers' association. More generally, she studied problems of working women as a whole, including their wages, working conditions, composition of the workforce within a particular occupational group (Collet, 1931) or in a specific location (Collet, 1891a and b, 1898a and in her earlier work for Booth – Collet, 1889, 1891a). Both her official appointments and her great skills in handling statistical evidence made her an authority in her field and a person, throughout her active working life in public service, to whom 'one naturally turned for help, if one was concerned with any problem of women's work and wages' (Bowley, 1950). Such public recognition of her expertise did not only come after her death. By the mid-1890s her authority was sufficiently apparent for her to be asked to contribute the articles on female labour and female earnings in the original *Palgrave Dictionary* (Collet, 1896a and b).

Collet (1902) reprints a number of papers largely published during the 1890s. The first offered a comparative view of the economic situation of working women at the start of the 1890s relative to that prevailing at the mid-point of the nineteenth century. This indicated some improvement, especially from the growth in absolute numbers of female university graduates. However, relative to numbers of women teachers employed (the main employment opportunity for women graduates) and women within the educational age cohort of 5–20 years, women graduates were but a drop in the bucket. This contradicted widespread belief about an excess supply of women graduates which justified the payment to them of lower salaries. Collet's data induced two conclusions. First, women graduates should not work for salaries below an agreed minimum; second, standards in women's education should be raised by increasing the demand by business for women graduates. The latter measure would give women workers greater choices in seeking employment and raise the standards of life, and eventually the salaries, of female secondary schoolteachers. More adequate payment would also enable unmarried educated women to live independently without relying on family support. Other essays in the volume addressed the issue of marriage prospects for middle-class women, the influence on wages of the standard of living for single, working women, the effective age span of a woman's working life, reviewed a book on women and economics, and evaluated the degree of economic progress women had achieved during the second half of the nineteenth century on the basis of literary evidence from novels. These essays tend to illustrate Collet's clever use of statistics to make her points, and her generally cautious tone in assessing problems and progress in women's work. A review of the book by Mary Paley Marshall (*q.v.*) (1902) links many of its findings with her husband's economic principles: the capacity for economic independence is an essential part of individual self-respect and hence of character; and rising standards of life contribute effectively to women's efficiency as workers. During World War II, Collet (1915) analysed the opportunities for professional women, including married professional women, for gaining employment in the changed labour market conditions the war had generated. The opportunities for, and the plight of, the educated woman worker was a topic of continuing concern for Clara Collet, whose own career personified the possibilities in this rather small but crucial segment of the labour market for women.

In her statistical and economic work on the female labour market, Collet used census returns, reports from government factory inspectors, surveys of women employees and her own fieldwork. Skilfully combined, these sources provided deeper insights into the prevailing atmosphere in the female workplace together with data on sources of labour supply, general hiring practices in the relevant industries, as well as wage data. She had undoubtedly absorbed this wide form of social and economic investigation during the experience gained while working with Charles Booth on the London Life and Work project (Collet, 1889, 1891a) and consolidated it during her work as lady assistant commissioner for the Labour Commission. Collet (1891b) illustrates this method and the broad conclusions it could produce. The Leeds textile industry had initially opened up opportunities for women's work through the introduction of the power loom, which enabled the substitution of women for men as part of the deskilling process when handwork was replaced by machines. In the ready-made clothing industry, on the other hand, skilled work proliferated, with women's skills benefiting in particular from the external economies of the local presence of a skilled male labour force which enabled them to gain higher wages, often on equal terms with men. This situation could not endure. Men would eventually be substituted for women, because past experience with sexual substitution in the clothing industry suggested that 'women were employed because wages were low, and not *vice versa*' (Collet, 1891b, p. 462). As in her work for the Labour Commission (cf. Collette, 1989, pp. 14–15), none of this work on women workers attempted to prove social dangers in particular female occupations or sought to jeopardize the independent status of women wage-earners. Much of her official work as a public servant employed in the Labour Department of the Board of Trade and subsequently in the Department of Labour falls into this category.

More forcefully, Collet (1898b) combated views on the alleged detrimental consequences of married women's work in terms of infant mortality. Her data provided no real evidence of any significant statistical association between the employment of married women and infant mortality, though the available data themselves were not really adequate for the task. Improvements in data collection, such as requiring information on mother's occupation before and after marriage on the death certificates of infants, would be one way to remedy this unsatisfactory situation. This part of Collet's work provided implicit criticism of economists such as Jevons (see White, 1994, esp. pp. 64–5), who had tried to associate infant mortality with married women's factory work on the basis of demographic data. Hence Collet defended not only the right to work of middle-class professional women like herself but also that of those women whose employment options were confined to factory work.

Her published contributions to labour economics all fell within the research programme on women's labour issues which she had set out in her *Palgrave* contribution on the subject (Collet, 1896a, p. 49). This included investigating female competition for employment with men, the effects of such competition on male wages and on family income, and the consequences of married women's employment in factories for the welfare of their families. Where possible these issues were investigated on a statistical basis in an attempt to ascertain the facts before positing a conclusion. Her factual analysis was invariably conducted in a critical way; she never drew conclusions which the data did not warrant and she never refrained from drawing conclusions from the evidence even if they were incompatible with her beliefs. For this reason, she found it very difficult to generalize about wage growth for women, particularly relative to male wages, and on the effects of women's wages on family income, both highly controversial issues in labour economics (Collet, 1898a, 1919).

Although for much of the twentieth century a 'neglected daughter of Adam Smith' (see Groenewegen, 1994), in the period of her life as an active economist she was not ignored, nor was she forgotten at her death by the learned societies to which she belonged and contributed for a long part of her busy life. Her work deserves clearer recognition as a fine example of careful, applied research in an important area of economics. Without personally contributing to theory, the premises in her research were always grounded in economic theory, the contemporary findings of which she ruthlessly applied to the specific problems she was analysing. For example, Marshall's notion of an efficiency wage was used to good effect in making the case for a more adequate salary scale for women schoolteachers, as Marshall's wife recognized in her review of Collet's essays. Statistical analysis was her main tool of research, used both in the construction of hypotheses and in their testing. Here she was a loyal daughter of Adam Smith, worthy of emulation, because she was sceptical and critical of the sometimes fantastical claims made in support of inferences drawn from inconclusive data. Her cautious, common-sense thinking and wider social perspectives when putting forward positions on issues such as marriage, equality of the sexes and women's education, also bear imitation. A plea (Collet, 1903) that knowledge and tolerance are essential parts of the armament of the social investigator doubling as advocate for particular remedies reveals the attitudes of this authoritative labour economist at their best

PETER GROENEWEGEN

Bibliography

Selected writings by Clara Collet

(1876), Diary 1876–1914, unpublished, Clara Collet Papers, Modern Records Centre, University of Warwick Library.

(1889), 'Women's work', in Charles Booth (ed.), *Labour and Life of the People in East London*, London: Williams and Norgate, Part II, ch. VIII, pp. 406–77.

(1891a), 'West End tailoring – women's work', in Charles Booth (ed.), *Labour and Life of the People of London* (continued), London: Williams and Norgate, Part II, ch. II (3), pp. 310–21.

(1891b), 'Women's work in Leeds', *Economic Journal*, **1**(3), September, 460–73.

(1891c), 'Wages and the standard of living', *Quarterly Journal of Economics*, **5**(2), April, 365–8.

(1896a), 'Female labour', *Palgrave Dictionary of Political Economy*, London: Macmillan, vol. 2.

(1896b), 'Females and children, earnings of', *Palgrave Dictionary of Political Economy*, London: Macmillan, vol. 2.

(1898a), *Changes in the Employment of Women and Girls in Industrial Centres*, London: HMSO, Cmnd 8794.

(1898b), 'The collection and utilisation of official statistics bearing on the extent and effects of the industrial employment of women', *Journal of the Royal Statistical Society*, **62**(2), June, 229–60.

(1902), *Educated Working Women*, London: P.S. King and Sons.

(1903), 'Review of *The Strength of the People*', *Economic Journal*, **13**(43), March, 81–4.

(1915), The professional employment of women', *Economic Journal*, **25**(100), December, 627–30.

(1919), 'Comment on Dorothea Barton', *Journal of the Royal Statistical Society*, **82**(4), July, 547–9.

(1931), 'Domestic service', in *The New Survey of London Life and Labour*, under the direction of Sir Hubert Llewellyn Smith, London: P.S. King & Son, vol. 2, ch. VIII, 427–69.

(1936), 'Professor Foxwell and University College', *Economic Journal*, **46**(184), December, 614–19.

(1940), 'Obituary of Henry Higgs', *Economic Journal*, **50**(200), December, 546–61.

(1945), 'Charles Booth, The Denison Club and H. Llewellyn Smith', *Journal of the Royal Statistical Society*, **108**, Pts I–II, 482–5.

Other sources and references

Bowley, Arthur L. (1950), 'Obituary of Clara E. Collet', *Economic Journal*, **60**(238), June, 408–10.

Bulley, A. Amy (1894), 'The employment of women: The Lady Assistant Commissioner's Report', *Fortnightly Review*, n.s. **55**, January–June, 39–48.

Collette, Christine (1989), *For Labour and for Women. The Women's Labour League 1906–18*, Manchester: Manchester University Press.

Groenewegen, Peter (1994), 'A neglected daughter of Adam Smith: Clara Elizabeth Collet (1860–1948)', in Peter Groenewegen (ed.), *Feminism and Political Economy in Victorian England*, Aldershot, UK and Brookfield, US: Edward Elgar, pp. 147–73.

Hey, John D. and D. Winch (eds) (1990), *A Century of Economics. 100 Years of the Royal Economic Society and the Economic Journal*, Oxford: Blackwell.

Keynes, J.M. (1972), *Essays in Biography*, in *Collected Writings of John Maynard Keynes*, London: Macmillan for the Royal Economic Society, vol. X.

Mahalanobis, P.C. (1948), 'Clara E. Collet', *Journal of the Royal Statistical Society*, Series A, **111**(3), 254.

Marshall, Mary Paley (1902), 'Review of "Educated working women", by Clara E. Collet', *Economic Journal*, **12**(46), June, 252–7.

Thorburn, Catherine (1948), 'Clara Elizabeth Collet', *Journal of the Royal Statistical Society*, Series A, **111**(3), 252–3.

White, Michael. (1994), 'Following strange gods: women in Jevons's political economy', in Peter Groenewegen (ed.), *Feminism and Political Economy in Victorian England*, Aldershot: Edward Elgar, pp. 46–78.

Katharine Coman (1857–1915)[1]

Katharine Coman was born in 1857 in Newark, Ohio, at the corner of Sixth and Locust Streets, to Martha Seymour Coman and Levi Parsons Coman. Levi Coman was a graduate of Hamilton College and was a teacher, storekeeper and lawyer. He was an abolitionist and led his own company during the Civil War. After the war he moved his family ten miles north to Hanover, Ohio, where he established a church and its schools. Martha Coman graduated from an Ohio seminary founded by an alumnae of Mount Holyoke.

Katharine's parents believed that their daughters should be as educated as their sons. When the principal of the Steubenville Female Seminary would not give Katharine advanced work, her parents sent her to a high school at the University of Michigan. After high school, she entered the University of Michigan and received a B.Ph. in 1880. At the time women could only major in health-related or teaching fields.

After graduating from the University of Michigan, she acquired a position as an instructor of rhetoric at the newly founded Wellesley College. Because of her interest in economics, she became a professor of political economy in 1883. At the turn of the century, she organized the Department of Economics and Sociology, which she chaired until her retirement in 1915.

In 1911 Katharine Coman wrote the first article in the first issue of the *American Economic Review*. 'Some Unsettled Problems of Irrigation' is a fascinating history of the development of the western third of the USA. Coman examines the physical, legal and financial problems of developing the desert regions. Her economic history of the region begins with Brigham Young and his 140 'devoted saints' who began to plough the earth within two hours of their arrival at the Great Basin area. The earth was so dry and hard that their ploughs broke. The settlers carried water from the Great Salt Lake to soften the land. As Coman points out, the Mormons and later settlers of the West learned that water was more important than capital or labour.

Coman traces two legal battles relevant to development. First, she examines the battle over ownership and control of water rights. She traces this battle from California's Riparian Rights (a first come, first serve rule) to Colorado's Doctrine Appropriation (a claim that every stream and natural waterway belongs to the people and is for all to use) to Wyoming's 1890 water law (a law that made water rights and land ownership one and the same). Second, she examines the battle over land ownership. Coman discusses the various attempts by the government to develop huge tracts of land for the common farmer. For example, the Carey Act, passed in 1894, and the Reclamation Act of 1902 gave homesteaders rights to land once they met capital and residence requirements. Generally, wealthy farmers benefited from this legislation. While the land was cheap, the capital needed to acquire expensive irrigation equipment or build irrigation ditches was considerable.

The residence requirement also hurt the common farmer. The law required homesteaders to live on the land with their families for five years before they became eligible for the title. Coman acquired primary data from a federal employee that showed that only 43 per cent of the homesteaders were successful. Of the 57 per cent who failed, 71 per cent did so because of the long residence requirements. Few financiers would lend money to homesteaders without titles to their lands. Coman saw this impediment to development as contrary to the government's intention. She recommended that land improvements be the measure of commitment to the homestead and not the length of stay:

> In this way, the man with small capital but possessing those more valuable qualities of brains, pluck, and endurance, would be enabled to earn a farm by the labor of his hands, as truly as did his forbears in the humid states east of the Missouri River. (Coman 1911, p. 19)

Her main concern was for the development process and factors that impeded it. Katharine Coman went directly into the field to gather data. She spent four years travelling through the west, traversing the routes of the fur traders and railroaders. She interviewed anyone who knew anything about either topic. Those she wrote about were central to the economic issues of the time: capital accumulation, growth and the determination of income and its distribution. Her work was published in some of the most prestigious journals: *American Statistical Association, New Series, Bulletin of the American Economic Association* and *The Journal of Political Economy.*

Despite Coman's extensive studies of the developing west, her work was largely ignored by contemporaries. For example, in a study commissioned for the 100th anniversary of the American Economic Association, William Baumol (1985) commented on works of several prominent economists at the turn of the century. The works of such luminaries as J.B. Clark, Irving Fisher and Thorstein Veblen were included. Katharine Coman's work was noticeably missing from the list.

At the conclusion of Baumol's study, he thanks his female graduate assistant for pointing out that no women were reviewed in his essay. He justifies this omission by suggesting that the early women economists tended to concentrate on 'women's issues'. Although Baumol's critique might be accurate for some early female economists, the following list of Coman's publications does not substantiate his claim:

- *The Industrial History of the United States*
- *Economic Beginnings of the Far West*, vols 1 and 2
- 'The Railroads as an Advanced Agent of Prosperity'
- 'Government Factories: An Attempt to Control Competition in the Fur Trade'
- 'Unemployment Insurance: A Summary of European Systems'
- 'The Negro as a Peasant Farmer'
- 'Wages and Prices in England'

Contrary to Baumol's claim, Coman mentions women only tangentially in these works.

Coman was self-taught in economics and did not have a Ph.D. Her work would meet the same criticism that Baumol levelled at the early male economists. Her work was definitely 'opinionated, tainted with preconceptions of virtue, and devoid of algebraic symbols'. However, it was filled with history, data and economic models. She was as scholarly and scientific as her contemporaries.

ROBIN L. BARTLETT

Note

1. The author would like to thank Carolyn Shaw Bell, the Katharine Coman Professor of Economics, Wellesley College, for providing much of the archival material used in this article. Katharine Coman is of particular interest to me because she was born in Newark, Ohio, just eight miles east of Denison University.

Bibliography

Selected writings by Katharine Coman
(1893/94), 'Wages and prices in England, 1261–1701', *Journal of Political Economy*, **2**, December/September, 92–4.
(1904), 'The negro as a peasant farmer', *American Statistical Association*, new series, **66**, June, 39–54.
(1905), *Industrial History of the United States*, New York: Macmillan.
(1908), 'The railroads as an advanced agent of prosperity', *Review of Reviews*, **38**, November, 591–2.
(1911), 'Some unsettled problems of irrigation', *American Economic Review*, **1**(1), March, 1–19.
(1911), 'Government factories: an attempt to control competition in the fur trade', *Bulletin of the American Economic Association*, fourth series, **1**(2), April, 368–88.
(1912), *Economic Beginnings of the Far West*, vols 1 and 2, New York: Macmillan and August M. Kelley, 1969.

Other sources and references
Baumol, William J. (1985), 'On Method in US. Economics a century earlier', *American Economic Review*, **75**(6), December, 1–2.
Halsey, Olga S. (1915), 'Katharine Coman 1857–1915', *The Survey*, 23 January, 450–51.

Costanza Costantino (1913–92)

The contribution of Costanza Costantino is most significant within the debate on the business cycle and on the national revenue in relation to the fluctuations of the economic trend which took place in Italy between the two world wars. However, the direction of her research is quite varied and complex, as can be seen from an analysis of her publications and academic career.

Costanza Costantino was born in Turin, Italy, in 1913. In the same city, she earned her doctor's degree in economic and commercial sciences with a thesis on long-term economic fluctuations. This work contains the theory of the business cycle which lies at the basis of her future work and which reveals her methodological approach: in it she argues for the necessity of a dynamic approach to economic analysis, which should make use of such instruments as the study of historical facts and comparison.

The same elements can be found in one of her main works on the business cycle (*Sulle fluttuazioni economiche di lunga durata* [On long-term economic fluctuations], 1939) published after a thorough study of the history of economics during the years 1935 and 1936. This research concerns the trend of the European and US economies from 1790 to 1892. In it, Costantino first examines the phenomenon of the long waves and then attempts a critical explanation of the phenomenon itself. She draws attention to some of the most significant theoretical contributions, which find the causes of the fluctuations in the dynamics of the capitalist system (Kondratieff, Van Gelderen); in the variations of the quantity of precious metals (Cassel, Simiand); in the interaction between demand and supply (Lescure, Saint Germès); and, finally, she expounds her theory of the economic cycle. It is a realistic theory with some elements taken from the monetary hypothesis. In other words, if the first cause of the long waves must be looked for in the interaction between demand and supply, the variations in the production of gold give one of the indispensable elements: the metal basis.

The originality of Costantino's approach lies in the role played by technological change and the entrepreneur in determining the events in an economic system. Periods of growth are induced by the introduction of radical innovations, while periods of decline are times of intensive development brought about by the entrepreneur. The first type of period leaves to the entrepreneur a widened field of activity, new enterprises, wider industrial exploitation, and extended commercial relationships. During periods of decline, however, the entrepreneur tries to maintain the previous situation in far less favourable conditions by improvement of the firm's organization, of techniques, and through investments in research.

In spite of her exclusion from the University of Turin in 1938, due to anti-Semitic laws, she continued her studies autonomously, focusing her interest on the problems of the freedom to work, particularly with reference to women (*Di alcuni aspetti del problema del lavoro femminile nel quadro della ricostruzione europea*, 1941).

After the war, Costanza Costantino gained the cooperation of the University of Torino where, in the Department of Jurisprudence, she taught finance and financial law for many years. In these years, her collaboration with Attilio Garino Canina (whose biographer she later became), director of the Finance Institute of the Department of Economics and Commerce, revealed itself as being particularly fruitful: she started a series of both theoretical and empirical comparative research into the sensitivity of taxation to the phases of the business cycle (*Imposte e Congiuntura*, 1951; *Finanze Pubbliche in Danimarca*, 1956). In these works, Costantino suggests a policy that controls the business cycle, based upon the natural sensitivity of taxation. While the work that contains the first formulation of her opinions regarding finance in its different phases of the business cycle was in publication, Parliament enacted Law no. 25 of 1951 on the equal distribution of national revenue and on taxation in which her recommendations were largely applied. In the same period, she worked, still within the framework of her studies in finance, with

Professor Scotto of the Department of Economics and Commerce of the University of Genoa.

In 1956, Costanza Costantino was granted a scholarship from the Ministry of Foreign Affairs that allowed her to complete her studies in Denmark on active and passive sensitivity of taxation. At the same time, she was able to complete laborious research on the relevance of taxes, begun towards the end of 1955, in which she set out a thorough critical examination of the literature on the subject up to the theory of Jenkins on the flow of money.

In February 1960, with unanimous consent, she qualified for university teaching in finance and financial law.

In 1961, the Honourable Member of Parliament Tremelloni, president of Parliament's committee of inquiry on the limits to competition in the economic field, asked her to report to the committee on the sugar beet industry. The resulting study proved very laborious and complex, involving problems of economic, financial and tax policy, and, in conclusion, it denounced the inadequacy of the state's economic policy. According to Costantino, years of protectionism and of controlled prices had prevented not only the formation of a competitive market, but also, and above all, the attainment of efficiency in this industry.

In December 1967, she was awarded the professorship of finance and financial law at the Department of Economics and Commerce of the University of Turin. She kept this chair until the academic year 1969–70, when it was offered to Professor Reviglio.

Meanwhile, work to reform the revenue system (1971) was in full operation. Costantino followed it closely and published, as early as 1972, a short critical description of the new system, with successive yearly editions that kept track of the numerous amendments enacted through Acts of Parliament. These critical studies were organized into a collection, published in 1981 with the title *Il Sistema Tributario Italiano. Esposizione Critica* [The Italian taxation system: a critical exposition].

In 1970, Costantino was assigned the professorship of economics of transportation, which she kept without interruption until 1990. She died in August 1992

MAGDA FONTANA

Selected writings by Costanza Costantino

(1939), 'Sulle fluttuazioni economiche di lunga durata' ('On long-term economic fluctuation'), *Rivista Internazionale di Scienze Sociali*, 794–809.

(1941), 'Di alcuni aspetti del problema del lavoro femminile nel quadro della ricostruzione Europea' ('On certain aspects of women's labour in the course of European reconstruction'), *Rivista di Politica Economica*, pp. 677–84.

(1951a), *Imposte e Congiuntura* (*Taxation and the Business Cycle*), Turin: Giappichelli.

(1951b), 'Finanze Pubbliche e congiuntura in Italia' ('Public finance and the business cycle in Italy'), *Rivista Italiana di Scienze Commerciali*, pp. 3–18.

(1952), 'Piani di Sviluppo e Finanze Pubbliche' ('Development planning and public finance'), *Rivista Internazionale di Scienze Sociali*, 156–70.

(1952b), 'L'impôt italienne sur le revenu global et sa sensibilité conjoncuturelle' ('The Italian tax on aggregate income and its cyclical sensitivity'), *Public Finance*, no. 3, 259–78.

(1955), 'Ancora sulla Divergenza di Opinioni intorno alla Traslazione dell'Imposta Generale sul reddito', *Giornale degli Economisti*, 253–79.

(1956), 'Finanze Pubbliche in Danimarca' ('Public finance in Denmark'), *Rivista di Politica Economica*, 1123–40.

(1958a), 'Sulle moderne dottrine relative all'incidenza dell'imposta sulle vendite' ('On the modern doctrine concerning the incidence of a sales tax'), *Giornale degli Economisti*, nos 5–6, 265–92.

(1958b), 'Ancora sulle moderne dottrine relative all'incidenza dell'imposta sulle vendite' ('More on the modern doctrine concerning the incidence of a sales tax'), *Giornale degli Economisti*, nos 7–8, 406–39.

(1965), 'Il Settore dello Zucchero', – Camera dei Deputati, Doc. XVII, no. 1 – *Atti della Commissione Parlamentare di Inchiesta sui Limiti Posti alla Concorrenza nel Campo Economico, Studi e Monografie*, vol. VII, Rome: Servizio Studi Legislazione e Inchieste Parlamentari.

(1976), *Elementi di Scienza delle Finanze* (with M. Fanno), 38th edition, Turin: Lattes.

(1981), *Il sistema tributario italiano. Esposizione critica* (*The Italian tax system*), Turin: Lattes.

(1990), *Lezioni moderne di finanza pubblica* (*Modern lessons on public finance*), Turin: Società Editrice Internazionale.

Caroline Wells Healey Dall (1822–1912)

Caroline Dall was born in Boston on 22 June 1822, the daughter of Caroline Foster Healey and of Mark Healey, an India merchant. She was educated at home by tutors and attended a nearby school for girls. Margaret McFadden's article 'Boston Teenagers Debate the Woman Question, 1837–1838' (1990) gives a fascinating account of the origins of Dall's feminism in a correspondence between Caroline, aged 15, and her friend Ednah Dow Littledale (later Cheney), in which Caroline Healey was then an opponent of women's rights. The correspondence was influenced by Harriet Martineau's (*q.v.*) chapter on 'The Political Non-Existence of Women' and by what Littledale termed 'a brave address on Women's Rights at the Lyceum' by Amasa Walker, an 'underground railway' activist and soon to be professor of political economy at Oberlin. From the age of 13, Caroline published essays on moral and religious topics, which were collected in her first book, *Essays and Sketches* (1849). Ironically, that book, including essays expressing disinterest in women's rights, was not published until 1849, the year that she first wrote in favour of women's rights in the abolitionist journal *The Liberator*. In the 1840s she was attracted to the transcendentalist ideas emerging within Unitarianism, and in 1841 she attended a weekly series of conversations led by the feminist author Margaret Fuller. For at least 60 years from around 1840, she conducted Unitarian Sunday school classes.

When her father suffered financial reverses, Caroline Healey worked as vice-principal of Miss English's School for Young Ladies in Georgetown, DC, from 1842 to 1844, when she married Charles Appleton Dall, a Unitarian minister and Harvard classmate of Thoreau. They lived in Baltimore and Toronto, where he was a minister. She undertook the first census of free blacks in the District of Columbia, in order to organize schools for them, and was the Toronto agent for a society aiding fugitive slaves. In 1854, while still in Toronto, she became a contributing editor for *Una*, Paulina Wright Davis's women's paper based in Providence, Rhode Island. Following his breakdown in Toronto in 1854, Rev. Dall returned to Boston with his family. He sailed for India as a Unitarian minister-at-large in 1855, remaining there until his death in 1886, but Caroline Dall remained in Boston with their children (born in 1845 and 1849).

Caroline Healey Dall reported to a women's rights convention in Boston in 1855 on the legal status of women, following with a series of annual reports on that status. She organized the New England Women's Rights Convention in Boston in 1859. A precursor of Charlotte Perkins Gilman (*q.v.*) among American feminists, Dall went beyond the suffrage question and unequal laws on property rights to a critique of the economic role of women in a series of three public lectures in Boston in November 1859, published as

'Women's Right to Labor': or Low Wages and Hard Work (1860). Together with two series of lectures on women's rights to education and on *Women's Rights under the Law* (1861), this series was incorporated in Dall's *The College, the Market, and the Courts; or Women's Relation to Education, Labor, and the Law* in 1867. As Stephen Nissenbaum (1971) notes, Dall ([1867] 1972, p. 179) went beyond calling for educational and legal equality, attributing women's discontent to restricted opportunities for paid employment, for it was no longer the case that 'every woman found, in spinning, weaving, and sewing, in the active life of a ... household, full employment for time and thought'. Dall also published *Historical Pictures Retouched* (1859), vindicating notable women such as Aspasia, Sappho and Mary Wollstonecraft, and a *Life of Marie E. Zakrzewska, M. D.* (1860).

Dall served on the executive committee of the American Social Science Association from its foundation in 1865 until 1905 (seven years before her death at the age of 90, and four years before the dissolution of the ASSA), initially as a director and from 1880 as a vice-president. The entry on Dall in *Moulton's Women of the Century*, reprinted in Dall (1914, p. xv), stated that 'She was the original mover for the Social Science Association with Governor Emery Washburn and Dr. Samuel Eliot as helpers, and has read many papers before that body.' James Redpath's 'Caroline Healey Dall', first published about 1866, according to the reprint in Dall (1914, p. xii), also reported that 'She was the first to move the formation of the Social Science Association.' This claim goes beyond the statement by Rose (1999) that Dall was a founding member of the ASSA (cf. Dall, 1914, p. xvii, for an 1875 biographical sketch mentioning 'her agency in the formation of the Social Science Association'). Dall had been in contact with the secretary and assistant secretary of Britain's National Association for the Promotion of Social Science, founded in 1857 (cf. ibid., pp. 336–7, on 'the noble usefulness for women' of that 'out-of-door Parliament'). Dall (ibid., p. 379) noted that the ASSA was organized with two women on its board of directors, and that the Boston Association for the Promotion of Social Science was subsequently established with seven departments and seven women on its board of directors, one assigned to each department. At the founding meeting of the ASSA, Dall and Amasa Walker worked together to oppose creating a separate department to study crime prevention and reformation of criminals. The American Economic Association was founded (with six women among the first 185 members) at the 1885 ASSA annual meeting with the support of the secretaries of the ASSA's Finance and Social Economy sections (and with Amasa Walker's son, Francis Amasa Walker, as the AEA's first president). The sociologists established their own professional association in 1905, and the political scientists in 1909.

After 1879, Dall lived in Washington, DC, with her son, the Arctic explorer William Healey Dall, who worked at the Smithsonian Institution. She taught adult classes in philology, biblical criticism, Shakespeare and Herodotus before moving to Washington, where she continued to offer private adult classes on literature and morals, with 40 students by 1898. Anne Rose (1999, pp. 26–7) notes that

> most of her later work was ephemeral in nature, such as a series of children's books entitled *Patty Gray's Journey to the Cotton Islands* (1869–1870), a travel account of *My First Holiday; or Letters Home from Colorado, Utah, and California* (1881), and *What We Really Know about Shakespeare* (1886). It is possible that as intellectual life became professionalized and as male-dominated universities increasingly monopolized serious thought, an informally educated and aging woman such as Caroline Dall was subtly pushed toward popular subjects.

One would, however, wish to know more about the many papers she read to the American Social Science Association. Her 'holiday' in the western states was a lecture tour. In her seventies, Dall turned to her past, publishing *Margaret and her Friends* (1895), her notes taken in her teens at ten weekly 'Conversations' led by Margaret Fuller in 1841, a reminiscence of *Transcendentalism in New England* (1897), a memoir of her childhood entitled *Alongside* (1900), and a *Memorial to Charles Appleton Dall* (1902).

President A.A. Allen of Alfred University, Alfred, NY, writing on the occasion of the University's award of an LL.D. to Dall in 1877, declared that

> Her work on Women's Rights has been so exhaustive in logic and facts that it has been a golden fountain from which most of the later writers and lecturers have drawn, often without so much as 'By your leave, Madam.' Her labor has been very influential in opening the doors of colleges to woman; but still she says, 'It is true that the mere means of education is open to some extent to woman, but education *itself* is not won for her till it brings her precisely the same blessings that it bears to the feet of man; till it gives her honor, respect, and bread; till position becomes the rightful inheritance of capacity, and social influence follows a knowledge of mathematics and languages'. (Reprinted in Dall, 1914, p. xxiv)

ROBERT W. DIMAND

Bibliography

Selected writings by Caroline H. Dall

Papers, Massachusetts Historical Society, Boston, and Schlesinger Library, Radcliffe College, Cambridge, MA.

(1860), *'Women's Right to Labor'; or Low Wages and Hard Work: In Three Lectures Delivered in Boston, November, 1859*, Boston: Walker, Wise and Company.

(1867), *The College, the Market, and the Court, or Women's Relation to Education, Labor, and Law*, Boston: Lee and Shepard. Reprinted New York: Arno Press, 1972.

(1914), *The College, the Market, and the Court, or Women's Relation to Education, Labor, and the Law*, Boston Memorial Edition, Concord, NH: The Rumford Press.

Other sources and references

Furner, Mary O. (1975), *Advocacy and Objectivity: A Crisis in the Professionalization of American Social Science, 1865–1905*, Lexington, KY: University of Kentucky Press.

Haskell, Thomas L. (1977), *The Emergence of Professional Social Science: The American Social Science Association and the Nineteenth Century Crisis of Authority*, Urbana, IL: University of Illinois Press.

McFadden, Margaret (1990), 'Boston teenagers debate the Woman Question, 1837–1838', *Signs: Journal of Women in Culture and Society*, **15**(4), 832–47.

Nissenbaum, Stephen (1971), 'Dall, Caroline Wells Healey (June 22, 1822–Dec. 17, 1912', in Edward T. James, with Janet Wilson James, assisted by Paul S. Boyer, *Notable American Women*, vol. 1, Cambridge, MA: Belknap Press of Harvard University Press, pp. 428–9.

Rose, Anne C. (1999), 'Dall, Caroline Wells Healey (22 June 1822–17 Dec. 1912)', in John A. Garraty (ed.), *American National Biography*, vol. 6, New York: Oxford University Press, pp. 26–7.

Welter, Barbara (1969), 'The merchant's daughter: a tale from life', *New England Quarterly*, **42** (March), 3–22.

Julie-Victoire Daubié (1824–74)

Julie-Victoire Daubié was born into a working-class family, the daughter of a bookkeeper for an ironwork factory in the Vosges. Daubié received minimal formal schooling, attending a primary school for girls until she earned her *brevet élémentaire*. She first worked as governess for a family of manufacturers. Continuing her studies on her own, she eventually became a teacher.

In 1861, Daubié applied for authorization to take the baccalaureat examination (the entrance exam for all post-secondary education in France), an exam that was, at the time, the exclusive right of male students. A diligent woman, she had asked her brother, a priest, to teach her Latin and Greek, which were requirements for the baccalaureat, and omitted from the women's curriculum. The application was received by Roulard, the Minister of Public Instruction, who disregarded her letter on the basis of the applicant's gender. The following year, when the Minister received yet another application from Daubié, he was strongly urged by the Empress Eugénie, a strong advocate of higher education for women, to look into the matter.

The Minister was surprised by the small investigation he made on the applicant. Daubié was a teacher well into her thirties, the author of a prize-winning essay on the social and economic situation of French women. *La femme pauvre au XIXe siècle* (*Poor Women in the Nineteenth Century*) was awarded a prize by the Academy of Lyons in 1859, and published in 1866.

After considerable public demonstration in support of Daubié's application, and with the strong recommendation of the Empress Eugénie and the influential support of the well-known Saint-Simonian François Barthélemy Arlès-Dufour, who had been one of the adjudicators who awarded her prize in Lyons, Minister Roulard granted Julie-Victoire Daubié authorization to take the baccalaureat examination. She became the first woman in France to pass the examination and was granted her baccalaureat from the University of Lyons in 1862. Arlès-Dufour escorted her to Paris to enable her to gain physical possession of her degree from the hands of the bitter and recalcitrant minister, and urged her to continue her education (Bidelman, 1982, p. 39). In 1871, just three years before her death, she became the first *bachelière* to receive a degree from the Sorbonne, which awarded her a *license ès lettres*. Daubié's achievement encouraged hundreds of young women to apply to universities and to hold public demonstrations in support of equal opportunity in education.

In 1871, Daubié founded L'Association pour l'émancipation de la femme (The Association for Women's Emancipation). Her friend and mentor, the elderly Arlès-Dufour, was named President of the Association. Unfortunately for both Arlès-Dufour and Daubié, their Association was abandoned with Daubié's death in 1874. Although short-lived, the Association was known as a haven for young socialist women such as the well-known radical Hubertine Auclert.

Daubié was dedicated to the social and economic welfare of women. The purpose of *La femme pauvre au XIXe siècle*, her most significant and influential work, was to examine the desperate situation of women in nineteenth-century France and to reveal the economic and social problems which impoverished them. Daubié tied social ills to the economic situation. She saw 'a connection between the economic order and the moral and civil code', and argued that 'true notions of a social economy are lost in states where the conditions of women and children are left to the discretion of man's passions' (Daubié, 1866, p. 286).

Daubié examined the legal, social and economic situation of women by travelling throughout the country in search of empirical evidence to help support the reforms she advocated. The scenes she witnessed all over France confirmed her belief that the position of women had deteriorated since the Revolution and the Second Empire. In feudal times, she noted, women could inherit and manage property and were often chosen by the king to become ambassadors. During the eighteenth century, educated women could practise medicine and study in the academies. Furthermore, civil service jobs were also typically offered to the widows of military men. Ironically, with the Declaration of the Rights of Man of 1789, the jobs available for women began to disappear. The nineteenth century closed the newly restored academies to women, even excluding midwives from medical schools. Daubié traced the narrowing of public jobs for women from the First to the Second Empire. In 1810, women still held positions in the post office, governmental offices and clerkships; by the time Daubié was writing her book women no longer had the opportunity to work in any administrative position. Little by little, women were even excluded from the health sector and education. Male workers were favoured in hospitals even though their lack of experience was, according to Daubié, detrimental to patients (Robertson, 1982, p. 327).

Daubié strongly urged the state to restore rights that women had begun to lose during the First Empire and during the Restoration, including the rights to the same education, training and admission process as men for all adminis-trative positions. She dedicated an entire chapter to a detailed examination of restrictions tying women to lower-paying jobs, studying industries on a case-by-case basis, and produced data on apprenticeship programmes show-ing this discrimination against women.

Daubié came to the conclusion that women could not support themselves economically because of discrimination in the workplace, low wages and sexual exploitation. Poverty would continue to plague women until society allowed them to be self-sufficient and independent. Daubié advocated three required economic and social reforms: to raise women's wages to those of men when the work or services were identical; to open new careers to women, especially outside the manufacturing and textile industries; and to examine and eliminate the economic, social and judicial consequences of the unequal public and private rights of men and women (Daubié, 1866, p. vi). She believed the greatest improvements for women would be access to new careers, apprenticeships and professional training. The economic reforms Julie Daubié suggested were centred on the reopening of positions for women in all sectors of work. She strongly urged that women be allowed back into the administrative positions they held before the Revolution of 1848.

Daubié opposed the virtual monopoly that the Church held on all jobs in the sector of social assistance, including health care, education and pastoral work, which she considered uniquely suited to the maternal nature of women. Secular organizations could not compete with religious orders as long as the latter subsidized the salaries of their members and continued to have an influx of new members. Providers of cheap women's labour, convents domi-nated employment in areas such as hospitals, prisons, orphanages, retirement homes, welfare agencies and charity organizations. Furthermore, if positions were available to the laity, the state typically sent firefighters or policemen to work in hospitals and nurseries.

The exclusion of secular women from these salaried positions, Daubié suggested, left two types of employment to absorb women's labour – domes-tic service and prostitution. The latter was often a last recourse for women denied more honourable means of sustenance:

> The inadequate pay of the urban working woman sometimes drives her, even during a period of industrial prosperity, into meeting her budget by selling her

body ... this is called the fifth quarter of the day [and] during periods of unemployment, this kind of right to work fills the entire day. (Daubié, 1866, p. 271)

Daubié proposed to reform the law in ways that would end women's sexual vulnerability. This required not only that the issue of prostitution be addressed, but that paternity suits be permitted, legal equality for illegitimate children ensured, and freedom to marry for all of legal age (including those in the military who were currently prevented from marrying) be granted.

During the 1860s, Julie Daubié campaigned strongly to put an end to state-regulated prostitution; she wanted to see the purchasers of sexual services charged for the same crimes as the prostitutes and public officials held accountable for allowing offences against public morality. She also advocated changes to the civil and penal code to protect domestic workers from economic and sexual exploitation at the hands of unscrupulous employers.

In addition to changes in legal institutions, Daubié saw education as vital to the economic security of individual women. She blamed the religious orders for their poor education. Daubié believed that the convent exploited the poor student, because without a significant dowry a child had no alternative but to undertake menial work in order to buy her way into redemption. A poor student had no choice but to accept employment offered by the convent if she was to have any access to education. Daubié was a strong supporter of mixed education. She boasted of the success of American mixed primary schools and noted that all Catholic schooling in parishes, as opposed to convents, was open to boys and girls. She stated that 'boys would acquire subtlety with their manners and learn to express their emotions, while girls would gain judgment, energy and will' (Daubié, 1866, p. 191). Although she emphasized the need for mixed education, Daubié realistically recognized that this attempt to revolutionize primary education would be futile until society could respect the human dignity of women.

Daubié advocated equal opportunity in both vocational training and university education. The absence of women from universities was not her only concern. Daubié saw weaknesses in the level of freedom accorded to professors. She came to the conclusion that university professors were restricted in their methods as compared to industrial workers because their liberties were not respected in the same way. The reforms Daubié suggested were meant to help the case of universities until a time when it would be safe to practise 'free' education. She wanted to extend the freedom granted entrepreneurs to the academies, ensuring freedom from government repression and control.

Daubié was a strong and active advocate of universal suffrage. In 1871, the same year she organized L'Association pour l'émancipation de la femme, she also published several pamphlets on the question. Shortly before her death, Daubié wrote to the mayor of her *arrondissement* in Paris in order to inform him that she intended to enrol in the electoral registers of the district. In *La femme pauvre au XIXe siècle*, Daubié devoted an entire chapter to political rights. Her definition of universal suffrage meant equal representation by gender and social class.

Julie-Victoire Daubié is remembered today for her exceptional research on the economic situation of women during the nineteenth century. More than a century after her death, Daubié's work continues to be one of the most reliable sources for studying the conditions of women in the 1800s.

CHRISTINE IVORY

Bibliography

Selected writings by Julie-Victoire Daubié
(1862), *Du progrès dans l'instruction primaire: justice et liberté*, Paris: impr. de Mme Claye.
(1862), 'Quels moyens de subsistance ont les femmes?', *Journal des économistes*, 2nd series, **34**.
(1863), 'Travail manuel des femmes', *Journal des économistes*, 2nd series, **38** and **39**.
(1865), 'De l'enseignement secondaire pour les femmes', *Journal des économistes*, June.
(1866), *La femme pauvre au XIXe siècle*, Paris: Guillaumin.
(1871), *L'émancipation de la femme en dix livraisons*, Paris: E. Thorin.
(1872) (ed.), *Manuel du jeune homme*, by Silvio Pellico. Paris: E. Thorin.
(1872), 'French Morality under the Regulation System', in Josephine Butler (ed.), *The New Era: A Collection of Twenty-five Pamphlets Relating to the Contagious Diseases Act of 1864, 1866 and 1869*, London.

Other sources and references
Bidelman, Patrick Kay (1982), *Pariahs Stand Up! The Founding of the Liberal Feminist Movement in France, 1858–1889*, Westport, CT: Greenwood Press.
Moses, Claire Goldberg (1984), *French Feminism in the 19th Century*, Albany: State University of New York Press.
Robertson, Priscilla (1982), *An Experience of Women, Pattern and Change in Nineteenth-Century Europe*, Philadelphia, PA: Temple University Press.
Scott, Joan (1987), '"L'ouvrière! Mot impie, sordide …": women workers in the discourse of French political economy, 1840–1860', in Patrick Joyce (ed.), *The Historical Meanings of Work*, Cambridge: Cambridge University Press, pp. 119–42.

Caroline Augusta Foley Rhys Davids (1857–1942)

Caroline A. Foley, MA, was the daughter of Caroline Windham Foley and Rev. John Foley, vicar of Wadhurst, Sussex. She studied at home before going to University College London, from which she graduated in philosophy. She was one of the founding staff members of the *Economic Journal* from 1891 to 1895, and several *Economic Journal* articles from 1892 to 1900 were translated by her from French, Italian and German, including Carl Menger's well-known article 'On the Origin of Money'. She also published a volume of

Kant in translation. Foley contributed 17 articles to Palgrave's *Dictionary of Political Economy*. Twelve of these were biographical, but her contributions also included 'Famine', 'Rent of ability', 'Science, Economic, as distinguished from art', 'Statics, Social, and social dynamics', and 'Fashion, Economic influence of'. This last article was based on her remarkable 1893 *Economic Journal* article, 'Fashion', which called for 'a study of the consumer as such', argued for the existence of 'a taste for change', and stressed the inter-subjective and non-additive nature of individual demands (see Fullbrook, 1998). She attributed the neglect of fashion by male economists to their identification of changes in fashion with women and irrationality. Alfred Marshall cited her article in later editions of his *Principles of Economics*, but did not pursue her positing fashion as an instance where one agent's preferences depend on the tastes of other agents.

In 1894, Foley married Thomas William Rhys Davids, the Pali scholar who wrote the Palgrave article on 'Caste', and was one of the original Fellows of the British Academy. They had a son, who was killed in action in World War I, and two daughters. Sharing her husband's interests, she became 'The most eminent of women Orientalists' (Jayawardena, 1995, p. 159). Her publications fill seven columns in the *National Union Catalog of pre-1956 Imprints*. Kumari Jayawardena (1995, pp. 159–61) reports that

> She took on work in the Pali Text Society in 1900, becoming its Secretary in 1907 … She taught Indian philosophy at the University of Manchester from 1910 to 1913, and from 1918 to 1931 was lecturer in the History of Buddhism at the School of Oriental Studies in London. After her husband's death in 1922 she succeeded him as president of the Pali Text Society. Caroline Rhys Davids was also a committed feminist. From 1890 to 1894 she worked in societies concerned with the welfare of working women and children, and from 1896 to 1914 was active in the women's suffrage movement. The Buddhist Society, under her influence, spoke out for women's rights … She was a typical 'new woman' of the period, moving in feminist circles, involving herself in women's struggles, doing academic work, raising three children, and writing about Buddhism up to her death in 1942 … the feminist analysis that Rhys Davids brought to her Pali scholarship gave fresh meanings to the old texts and made known the 'new women' of the past to audiences in the East and West.

In 1901, she published in the *Economic Journal* on 'Economic Conditions in Ancient India', closely related to her later chapter on 'Economic Conditions according to Early Buddhist Literature' in the *Cambridge History of India* (1922). With these exceptions, her distinguished academic career was entirely outside economics after 1900.

ROBERT W. DIMAND

Bibliography

Selected writings by Caroline A.F. Rhys Davids
(1893) 'Fashion', *Economic Journal*, **3** (September), 458–74.
(1901), 'Economic conditions in ancient India', *Economic Journal*, **11** (September), 305–20.
(1922), 'Economic conditions according to early Buddhist literature', *Cambridge History of India*, vol. 1, pp. 198–219.

Other sources and references
Fullbrook, Edward (1998), 'Caroline Foley and the theory of intersubjective demand', *Journal of Economic Issues*, **32**(3), 709–31.
Jayawardena, Kumari (1995), *The White Woman's Other Burden: Western Women and South Asia During British Colonial Rule*, London and New York: Routledge.
Palgrave, R.H. Inglis (ed.) (1894–99), *Dictionary of Political Economy*, London: Macmillan.

Katherine Bement Davis (1860–1935)

In 1900 Katherine Bement Davis became the first woman to earn her Ph.D. in economics at the University of Chicago. By 1922 she was acclaimed by the National League of Women Voters as one of the 12 greatest living American women. Her journey from Chicago to national prominence is one of commitment to science and to the idea that the best way to approach society's problems is via social and economic research into their underlying causes.

Davis was born in 1860 in Buffalo, New York, the daughter of Oscar and Francis Bement Davis. She graduated from Rochester Free Academy in 1879 and taught at Dunkirk High School to pay her way through Vassar where she studied science and mathematics. She graduated with honours in 1892.

After graduation Davis spent a year studying food chemistry at Barnard and Columbia Colleges. In 1893 she was named director of the 'New York State Working Man's Model Home' at the World's Columbian Exposition in Chicago. The purpose of the model was to demonstrate that two adults and three children could be adequately housed, clothed and fed on an annual income of $500 (a typical working man's income). Davis's exhibit with its experimental house and furnishings, exacting nutritional standards and on-display family was the most ambitious domestic exhibit at the fair. Davis systematically measured and recorded every aspect of the experiment and concluded that if one were very frugal, an acceptable standard of living was just possible.

The Model Home experiment sensitized Davis to the hardships of the poor and she decided to enter settlement work. She served as Headworker of the Philadelphia College Settlement from 1893 to 1897. While there she further explored housing reforms by converting four tenements into model homes.

In 1897, at the age of 37, Davis won a fellowship in economics to the University of Chicago. She explained in a 1896 letter to chairman J. Lawrence Laughlin,

> I feel more and more as time goes on the need of further study in Economics and Sociology. Here [at the Settlement] our practical efforts crowd any very system-atic study to the wall ... I'd like to study for the Ph.D. doing my major work in Economics and my minor in Sociology for the reason that I am more deficient in the former.

This move to further her education was in line with her goal to use science to improve the lot of the working class, but it signified a shift in interest from household and nutritional management to wage and price determination.

Davis enjoyed a successful career at Chicago as a student of Thorstein Veblen. She published four articles in the *Journal of Political Economy* (*JPE*) during her tenure there. Each article displays her strengthening belief that painstaking data collection was a requisite to understanding economic conditions.

In the December 1892 *JPE* Veblen had published a study of the price of wheat from 1867 through 1891. In the 1898 volume, Davis continued this study in her article 'Tables Relating to the Price of Wheat and Other Farm Products since 1890'. She compiled data on output and prices of the world and US wheat crops, and argued on the basis of her data that the US market was a price-taker in the world market.

Davis took advantage of recent relaxations of the ban on women students at European universities and, in accordance with the practice common for male graduate students at the time, spent 1898–99 studying political economy at the Universities of Berlin and Vienna as a European Fellow of the New England Women's Educational Association. In Europe she began her disser-tation work on the economic conditions of Bohemians. She spent 1899–1900 back at Chicago finishing her dissertation, *Causes Affecting the Standard of Living and Wages*, and in 1900 she became the first woman to earn her Ph.D. in economics from the University of Chicago (and only the fourth woman to earn a Ph.D. in economics from a US institution).

Her dissertation led to two articles in the *JPE*. In the first, 'An error in Austrian wages statistics' (1899) she reported that the unexplained but widely accepted notion that there had been a large drop in wages in Austria between 1859 and 1860 followed by a correspondingly large rise in wages in 1865–66 was based on a simple mistake of misplaced columns. She concluded, 'this illustrates the dangerous character of statistics as a basis of economic deduc-tion, unless one takes some pains to see that the facts fit the figures' (p. 105).

In 'The modern condition of agricultural labor in Bohemia', Davis reviewed the conditions of feudalism and the restrictions on peasant proprietorship that led, in part, to the Austrian Revolution of 1848 and the reform of 1869 which made peasant properties divisible for the first time. Objections to the change had been based on the ideas that divisibility would lead to excessive absorption of land into the large (and still indivisible) estates and the splitting up of land into parcels too small to support a family, thereby giving rise to an increase in wage-seeking farm labourers.

Davis gathered evidence to test these hypotheses. With data on landholding from 1861 to 1890 she found that the indivisible portion of property had not increased significantly. She reported a decrease in the number of agricultural labourers despite population growth over the period. She theorized that the primary cause was the rapid opening of the region to other markets which provided non-farm opportunities for workers.

The article included a study of the age and sex distribution of Bohemian farm labour, their in-cash and in-kind wages, terms of contracts and hours of work. Measuring real wages as the number of days required to earn a hectolitre composed of equal parts of three foodstuffs, she found an increase in real wages since the Revolution.

Her next *JPE* publication, 'The condition of the Negro in Philadelphia' (1900), was an article-length review of the study conducted by W.E.B. DuBois for her former employer, the Philadelphia College Settlement, in conjunction with the University of Pennsylvania. Davis reported DuBois's findings on jobs, unemployment, education and training, union participation, income and earnings and property ownership for the blacks of the seventh ward in Philadelphia, an area which Davis knew intimately from her settlement days. Davis praised DuBois's work, as an example of the sort of data-gathering she believed was important to understanding and ultimately solving economic problems.

After graduation Davis took the competitive New York civil service examination and won appointment as superintendent of the newly opened Reformatory for Women at Bedford Hills, New York. Her move into prison work was unusual for a newly minted Ph.D. economist. However, Davis had a long history of interest in scientific investigation coupled with reform, and women's prisons offered her a concrete way to put some of her ideas into practice. Her appointment was noted by the emerging economics profession. In the December 1900 issue of the *JPE* editor Laughlin reported Davis's new job and commented that 'the passing of educated and highly trained economic students into this field is a sign of the times worth recording' (p. 121) .

During her 13 years at the Reformatory, Davis was responsible for two major innovations that brought her, through her numerous writings and speeches, widespread attention both at home and abroad. The first was her educational initiatives for inmates and the second her establishment of a research laboratory at Bedford Hills.

Since the Civil War prison reformers had been successfully lobbying for separate prisons for women where prisoners could be rehabilitated in a home-like atmosphere, learning womanly domestic chores. At the new Reformatory at Bedford Hills, Davis expanded on these ideas. She implemented an educational programme that went beyond training in domestic jobs to prepare inmates for varied employment after release. Her programmes, which attracted considerable journalistic comment, included cooking, sewing and cleaning, but also hatmaking, machine knitting, stenography, chair caning, cobbling, bookbinding, painting, carpentry, masonry, road building, ice harvesting, and vegetable, poultry, beef and hog farming.

Her second major initiative, the establishment of the Laboratory for Social Hygiene at Bedford, grew out of Davis's penchant for systematic study. Mental testing of criminals was the latest variation in the eugenics movement and the idea that mental deficiency, or feeblemindedness, caused crime was currently in vogue. Davis hired two psychologists to investigate this theory using the women inmates at Bedford Hills. Given her economics training, however, the unicausal determinism linking mental condition and crime was not compelling to Davis. She believed that

> The woman offender is divided into two general classes. The first class includes those who are delinquent on account of ... various degrees of feeblemindedness ... The second class includes those for whom environment is largely responsible ... For this class society is directly responsible. Crowded and unsanitary conditions in our cities, the lack of enforcement of city ordinances, the failure to enforce compulsory education laws, inefficient methods in our public school system, unjust economic conditions and the low moral standard among men which prevails in our cities, all of these are the things which are directly controlled by society and which are largely responsible for the making of the delinquent women who fall into this class. (Davis, 1910, p. 37–8)

In 1910, after a decade at Bedford, Davis wrote a pamphlet for the Charity Organization Society entitled *A Plan for the Rational Treatment of Women Convicted in the Courts of New York City* (1917) in which she argued that since women prisoners were not homogeneous, a system of classification was important to determine each prisoner's proper place of commitment. Her pamphlet persuaded John D. Rockefeller to fund the Laboratory for Social Hygiene at Bedford Hills as an activity of his Bureau of Social Hygiene which he was organizing to study prostitution. The Laboratory gave Davis her opportunity to develop a classification methodology and also to collect the socioeconomic data which she thought would be as important as psychological data to help in understanding causes of female delinquency.

The Laboratory was a unique institution both for its location at a reformatory with inmates as its experimental (and involuntary) subjects and for the breadth of its investigations. Studies conducted by the Laboratory under Davis's direction were among the earliest to test the explanatory power of mental condition. Under Davis's influence the Laboratory also maintained a department of sociology to complement its department of psychology. In Davis's 1913 'Study of prostitutes committed from New York City to the State Reformatory for Women at Bedford Hills', she applied the methodology she had used in her economics work on New York prostitutes. She collected data on their birthplace, age, parents occupation, family size, education, previous occupation, earnings, marital status, number of children, religion, and the reasons they gave for entering prostitution. With these data, Davis tested several popular notions. For example, one idea was that native-born Americans, having enjoyed the advantages of their country, would contribute proportionately less to the population of prostitutes than the foreign-born. Davis's data indicated the opposite. Birth data countered the accepted belief that prostitutes were largely recruited from naïve country-girls. Data on family size were used to test whether prostitutes were apt to be members of large families driven to prostitution because of economic pressures.

By 1913, Davis's name was well known across the country for her work at the Reformatory. Her public recognition had been widened by the publicity she received for her 1909 earthquake relief work in Italy, where she was on vacation. She was honoured by the Red Cross, the king of Italy and the Pope for the clothing and shoe factories she organized to employ the survivors.

In December 1913 she was selected to be Commissioner of Corrections by the Mayor-elect of New York City, John Purroy Mitchel. She was the first woman to hold a commissionership in that city and the only woman Commissioner of Corrections in the country. Her two-year tenure was often controversial. In the beginning, newspaper commentary centred on her ability to handle a 'man's job'. Then, in July 1914, she won acclaim for her unprecedented handling of the Blackwell Island riot when her personal visit calmed the 700 rioting men. In other noteworthy actions she abolished striped clothing for prisoners, instituted a model young men's reformatory farm in rural New York State, and improved conditions at the women's prison, including securing the first woman superintendent and a woman resident physician. She was instrumental in writing and securing the passage of the Parole Commission Act of New York City which enabled prisoners, for the first time, to earn parole before the expiration of their sentences. In 1916 she resigned as Commissioner to become the first chairman of the Parole Commission. Her role ended in 1917 when Mayor Mitchel was not reelected.

From 1918 until her retirement in 1928 Davis was the General Secretary of Rockefeller's Bureau of Social Hygiene. (She served as Chairman of the Women's Section of the Social Hygiene Division of the Commission on

Training Camp Activities during World War I.) In her years at the Bureau she was directly responsible for two major studies. The first was a study of the relationship between rents, housing and wages of employed women of Manhattan (*Housing Conditions*, 1922). The second, a study of the sexual practices of normal women, consumed the rest of her career and resulted in numerous scholarly publications and a book, *Factors in the Sex Life of Twenty-Two Hundred Women*, published in 1929 and reprinted in 1972.

For many years Davis had been interested in women and crime, and, at the time, much female crime was directly or indirectly associated with prostitution. Davis had come to believe that education rather than enforcement of laws was the way to reduce vice. Yet, she wrote, 'In no part of the field of education is there greater difference of opinion than in that which deals with sex. This is largely because ... sex is scientifically an unexplored country' (Davis, 1929, p. ix). In typical Davis fashion, she set out to begin systematic exploration. 'Her studies reported age, education, health, age at marriage, occupation before and after marriage, length of time employed, number of pregnancies and childbirth, use of contraceptives, frequency of intercourse, sterility rates, number of abortions, auto-erotic and homosexual practices, and periodicity of sex desires for 1000 married women and 1200 unmarried women with college degrees. Hers was the first statistical study of auto-eroticism and the extent of homosexuality in normal, adult women in the USA.

Davis died on 11 December 1935. She is characterized today as a prototypical feminist and prison reformer of the Progressive era. But this characterization is incomplete for it neglects her large body of scholarly work that, from her study of prostitution in 1913 to her studies of sex practices in the 1920s, marks the beginnings of what has become the field of economics and crime. Unlike her contemporaries, who approached criminal behaviour as deterministic, Davis was an inductivist who argued that criminal behaviour could be the result of a wide variety of socioeconomic factors that needed measuring. As she remarked at the time of her retirement, 'I have a statistical mind that always has to count noses before I draw a conclusion' (Coster, 1928).

CLAIRE HOLTON HAMMOND

Bibliography

Selected writings by Katherine Bement Davis
(1895), *Report on the Exhibit of the Workingman's Model Home as Exhibited by the State of New York at the World's Columbian Exposition*, Albany: J.B. Lyon.
(1898), 'Tables relating to the price of wheat and other farm products since 1890', *Journal of Political Economy*, **6**, June, 403–10.

(1899), 'An error in Austrian wages statistics', *Journal of Political Economy*, **8**, December, 102–6.

(1900), 'The condition of the Negro in Philadelphia', *Journal of Political Economy*, **8**, March, 248–60.

(1900), 'The modern condition of agricultural labor in Bohemia', *Journal of Political Economy*, **8**, September, 491–523.

(1905), 'The fresh air treatment for moral disease', *Proceedings of the Annual Congress of the National Prison Association of the U.S.*, 205–11.

(1909), 'Outdoor work for women prisoners', *Proceedings of the National Conference of Charities and Corrections*, 289–94.

(1910), 'Reformation of women – modern methods of dealing with offenders', *Annals of the American Academy of Political and Social Science*, **36**, July, 37–42.

(1911), 'The New York State Reformatory for Women', *Survey*, **25**, 851–4.

(1913), 'A study of prostitutes committed from New York City to the State Reformatory for Women at Bedford Hills', in George Kneeland (ed.), *Commercialized Prostitution in New York City*, New York: The Century Co., pp. 163–251.

(1915), 'The Department of Corrections', *Proceedings of the Academy of Political Science*, **5**, April, 564–80.

(1916), 'Introduction', in Jean Weidensall (ed.), *The Mentality of the Criminal Woman*, Baltimore: Warwick and York, pp. ix–xiv.

(1917), 'Plan for the rational treatment of women convicted in the courts of the County of New York (or City)', in Burdette G. Lewis (ed.), *The Offender and His Relation to Law and Society*, New York: Harper and Brothers, pp. 358–71.

(1920), 'Introduction', in Mabel Ruth Fernald et al. (eds), *A Study of Women Delinquents in New York State*. Reprinted Montclair, NJ: Patterson Smith, 1968.

(1922), *Housing Conditions of Employed Women in the Borough of Manhattan*, New York: The Bureau of Social Hygiene.

(1928), 'Why they failed to marry', *Harper's Monthly Magazine*, **156**, March, 460–69.

(1929), *Factors in the Sex Life of Twenty-Two Hundred Women*, New York: Harper and Brothers. Reprinted New York: Arno Press and The New York Times, 1972. See also *Journal of Social Hygiene*, 1922, 1923 and 1925; *Journal of Mental Hygiene*, 1924 and 1925; and *American Journal of Obstetrics and Gynecology*, 1926 and 1927.

(1933) , 'Three score years and ten', *University of Chicago Magazine*, **26**, December, 58–61.

Other sources and references

Bureau of Social Hygiene, Rockefeller Family Archives.

University President's Papers 1889–1925, University of Chicago Archives.

Vassar College Library Alumnae Archives.

Barnes, Joseph W. (1981), 'How to raise a family on $500 a year', *American Heritage*, **33**, December, 91–5.

Coster, Esther (1928), 'Katherine B. Davis to devote time to book on "Sex Life of Normal Woman" on retirement', *Brooklyn (N.Y.) Eagle*, 1 January.

Edwards, Davis (1912), 'To make punishment fit the criminal, not the crime (an interview with Katherine Bement Davis)', *Vassar Alumnae Monthly*, October, 123–8.

Fitzpatrick, Ellen (1990), *Endless Crusade: Women Social Scientists and Progressive Reform*, New York: Oxford University Press.

Freedman, Estelle B. (1981), *Their Sisters' Keepers: Women's Prison Reform in America, 1830–1930*, Ann Arbor: University of Michigan Press.

Gordon, Lynn (1986), 'Davis, Katherine Bement', in William Trattner (ed.), *Biographical Dictionary of Social Welfare in America*, New York: Greenwood Press, pp. 207–10.

Herald Tribune (1935), 'Obituary', 11 December.

Large, Jean (1934), 'A man's job', *University of Chicago Magazine*, **27**, January, 105–8.

Lekkerkerker, Eugenia C. (1931), *Reformatories for Women in the U.S.*, Netherlands: J.B. Wolters.

Lewis, W. David (1971), 'Davis, Katherine Bement', in Edward T. James (ed.), *Notable American Women 1607–1950: Biographical Dictionary*, Cambridge: Harvard University Press, pp. 439–41.
New York Times (1922), 'Twelve greatest women', 25 June.
New York Times (1935), 'Obituary', 11 December.
Rafter, Nicole Hahn (1990), *Partial Justice: Women, Prisons, and Social Control*, second edition, New Brunswick, NJ: Transaction Publishers.
Reed, Amy (1936), 'Katharine Bement Davis', *Vassar Alumnae Magazine*, February.
Tarbell, Ida M. (1912), 'Good will to woman', *The American Magazine*, **75**, December, 45–53.

Marie Dessauer (b. 1901)

Little is known about the life of Marie Dessauer, apart from the following facts. She was born on 28 April 1901 in Bamberg, Germany. In the 1920s and early 1930s she worked for the Chamber of Commerce in Frankfurt am Main. In 1929 she spent a few months at the London School of Economics. Four years later she received her doctoral degree from the University of Frankfurt, where Eugen Altschul was her Ph.D. supervisor. The title of her thesis was *The Big Five. On the Characteristics of English Deposit Banks* (1933).

In 1934 Dessauer emigrated to the United Kingdom; her surname suggests Jewish ancestry, so the Nazis may have made life difficult for her in Germany. During her first years in emigration she visited the seminars of Friedrich August Hayek and Lionel Robbins at the London School of Economics. From July 1937 onwards Dessauer worked as a research assistant for Hayek and Theodore Gregory, who held the chair of Banking and Currency. In the 1920s Gregory had been the driving force in acquainting LSE economists with the richness of the 'Continental literature' of the interwar years, thereby helping to overcome the 'splendid isolation' of English economics (see Shehadi, 1991). He and Hayek had been opinion-leaders at the LSE at different times, but when Dessauer worked for them, both had largely lost their influence at the School.

During her years at the LSE Dessauer published a few short articles on the German Bank Act of 1934 (1935) and on English unemployment records of the nineteenth century (1940a and 1940b). In August 1940 she married and took the name Meinhardt. Her activity at the LSE ended when the School was exiled to Cambridge in 1941, due to German bomb raids on London. In the 1960s Marie Meinhardt, now living in Bournemouth, published a long and a short article for a German readership in which she described the legal status and accounting practices of British joint-stock companies (1965 and 1967).

Marie Dessauer's expert knowledge of limited companies in the UK can be traced back to her major work, the dissertation of 1933. In *The Big Five*, she described in great detail (and in German) the development and activities of the five English joint-stock banks that had formed in a huge merger wave in

1918. Comprising Barclays Bank, Lloyds Bank, the Midland Bank, the National Provincial Bank of England, and Westminster Bank, those Big Five dominated the deposit transfer and short-term lending business in the United Kingdom for a long time. Their 'trade names' still exist, even though the merger of National Provincial and Westminster, forming NatWest, has reduced the club to the Big Four that nowadays share the domain of retail banking with a former savings bank, the Trustee Savings Bank (TSB), and a former building society (Abbey National). Considering this continuity, Dessauer's thesis may attract readers as an early chronicle of the current Big Four.

The most interesting aspect of her study is, however, that it is a snapshot of the English system of special banking in the Great Depression, at a time when Britain had just left the gold standard. *The Big Five* stands in remarkable contrast to comparative studies of banking systems in the 1980s. Dessauer described the English system of special banking as a result of an evolutionary market process in which joint-stock banks competed successfully with private banks on the one hand and the privileged Bank of England on the other. The joint-stock banks established control of short-term lending and deposit transfers in a three-tier system that was characterized both by regional segmentation between City banks and country banks, and by sectoral segmentation between deposit banking and investment banking. Due to its 'firewalls', this system proved to be much more resistant to contagious insolvencies and bank runs in the 1920s and 1930s than the German system of universal banking or the US system of mixed banking. With reference to the comparative robustness of the English system, the Glass–Steagall Act of 1933 introduced a similar system of special banking in the USA.

In the 1970s and 1980s the market segmentations of special banking were largely eroded by waves of financial innovation and deregulation, both in the USA and in the UK. With hindsight, many economists have criticized the regulatory separation of deposit banking, short-term lending and the payment system from other branches of financial intermediation as legal restrictions that are inefficient, 'purely political' and incompatible with market forces. The bursting of credit bubbles in the early 1990s exposed much of that hindsight as shortsightedness. Even though nobody seriously pleads for a return of the Big Four to the earlier restrictions of deposit banking, it remains feasible to analyse the specific institutional framework of banking systems in which the systemic risk of a severe shortage of liquidity is kept comparatively small. Dessauer's history of English deposit banking provides rich material for such analysis.

However, Dessauer did not claim to have produced a comprehensive study of banking systems, from which banking theories or policy proposals could be distilled. *The Big Five* is an accurate description of the history and practice of English banking, no more and no less. The robustness of that system notwithstanding, Dessauer doubted whether it could be transferred to other economies, as it was the outcome of very specific historical developments. She emphasized the differences between the institutional links that exist, for example, between the financial and industrial sectors in Germany and in the UK, and she concluded that the English banking system could not be imported to Germany without disrupting long-term credit relations between banks and industrial firms.

In her review of the German Banking Act of 1934 (1935) Dessauer pointed out that the German system of universal banking, on the other hand, was susceptible to 'the authoritarian influence of the government', even though the Act gave the impression to many observers that it could not but help to re-establish the principles of sound banking. More than six decades have passed since Dessauer's prediction, but new information about the dark sides of the long-term credit relations between German banks, industrial firms and Hitler's government still keeps coming to light.

HANS-MICHAEL TRAUTWEIN

Bibliography

Selected works by Marie Dessauer
(1933), *Die Big Five. Zur Charakteristik der englischen Depositenbanken*, Stuttgart: C.E. Poeschel.
(1935), 'The German Banking Act of 1934', *Review of Economic Studies*, **2**, 214–24.
(1940a), 'Unemployment Records, 1848–59', *Economic History Review*, **10**, 38–43.
(1940b), 'Monthly Unemployment Records, 1854–1892', *Economica*, **7**, 322–6.
(1965), 'Der Jahresabschluß von Aktiengesellschaften in Großbritannien', in *Der Jahresabschluß von Aktiengesellschaften in Europa und USA, I. Teil*, edited by Ausschuß für wirtschaftliche Verwaltung (AWV), Berlin, pp. 59–105.
(1967), 'Das neue Aktienrecht in Großbritannien', *Außenwirtschaftsdienst des Betriebsberaters*, **13**, 433–5.

Other sources and references
Alsthin, J.M. (1992), (London School of Economics), Letter of 18 February.
Shehadi, Nadim (1991), 'The London School of Economics and the Stockholm School in the 1930s', in Lars Jonung (ed.), *The Stockholm School of Economics Revisited*, Cambridge: Cambridge University Press, pp. 377–89.

Elisabeth Caroline van Dorp (1872–1945)

Elisabeth van Dorp was the first female economist in the Netherlands. Her contributions to economic theory up to 1931, in particular in the fields of monetary and international trade theory, were highly regarded by the Dutch profession. In 1931 she alienated the mainstream because of her criticism of the Austrian theory of capital and income distribution.

Van Dorp was born in Arnhem on 5 September 1872, and grew up in a well-to-do family. She started her studies at Leiden University in literature, but took a degree in law studies. From 1903 to 1915 she practised as a lawyer in The Hague. When in her twenties she became involved in the Women's Suffrage Association. In 1903 her thesis brought her into conflict with one of its leading members, Aletta Jacobs (1854–1929), who had pleaded for economic self-reliance for married women. According to Van Dorp this demand was too radical. The goal of the suffragette movement ought to be making women conscious of their female identity and letting them develop this identity in freedom. In 1906 she dissociated herself from the 'ultra-feminism' of the Association and organized the 'moderate' feminists in a newly founded League for Female Suffrage. In 1910 she presented at the annual meeting of what is now called the Royal Netherlands Economic Association her views on the wage labour of married women and on whether government should interfere in this. (For the Dutch debate on protective legislation, see Jansz, 1995.) She told her audience that the undesirable consequences for family life are to be found in the working class, in which the mother's wage labour is an economic necessity.

Between 1922 and 1925, shortly after women had been enfranchised, she was a Member of Parliament as a one-woman faction for a liberal party. In Parliament she voted with the two other liberal parties and the socialists against the government's proposal to expand the Dutch fleet and to raise armament expenditure enormously.

From 1910 onwards Van Dorp concentrated on economics. In 1918 she was accepted as a *privaatdocent* (lecturer without salary) in economics at the law faculty of the University of Utrecht. In her inaugural lecture Van Dorp pleaded for an analytical approach to economics. She held this position until 1929, but stopped lecturing in 1922. Her courses did not appeal to the law students. In 1922 she applied for a full professorship at the agricultural polytechnic in Wageningen, but was passed over by the minister. However, Dutch economists, most of who belonged to the old Austrian School, had accepted her for her work on monetary theory and foreign trade.

When in 1916 Van Dorp published her first articles on monetary theory, Dutch monetary thought was taking a new direction. (For a comprehensive treatment see Fase, 1992.) The metallist view, which regards the link between (paper) money and precious metals as essential, was rapidly losing ground among Dutch economists. The prevailing view became the nominalist one, which stresses the legal foundation of money. Van Dorp argued that the gold standard is a poor institution to establish confidence in the value of money. The reason she gave is that the function of money is as a generally accepted means of exchange, for this clearly shows that the essence of money is the claim on the goods and services offered in the market. An effective and trustworthy control of the quantity of money can do the job. Van Dorp's work in this field was highly regarded. In 1929 she was asked by the Royal Netherlands Economic Association to present her views on price stability at the annual meeting.

In the field of foreign trade theory she was the main defender of the purchasing power parity (PPP) theory of exchange rates in the Netherlands. She opposed the balance of payments theory 'with arguments which still seem modern today' (Fase, 1992, p. 161). She must have been unpleasantly surprised when in 1918 G. Cassel, who was at the time the leading advocate of the PPP theory, argued that the Swedish crown was above parity in London because of British impediments to Sweden's imports, which gave rise to huge export surpluses. He considered this an exception to the PPP theory. Van Dorp, however, sensed a relapse into the balance of payments theory. She argued in the *Economic Journal* that neutrality during World War I had added to the relative strengths of the Swedish and Dutch economies and that the foreign exchange rates of the crown and the Dutch guilder reflected postwar PPP. The German mark had fallen against the guilder because of an inflationary monetary policy in Germany and because of a drop in German production to about 60 per cent of the prewar level. The Dutch export surpluses were the result of a huge German demand for loans.

Until 1931 Van Dorp had shown no particular interest in the theory of value, capital and income distribution. She accepted the prevailing views in the Netherlands. At the time these were the views of the old Austrian School, which stressed subjectivism in value theory and which relied on Wieser's imputation procedure for determining the value of capital and on Böhm-Bawerk's time premium theory for determining the rate of interest. In 1928, however, Van Dorp was asked by the editors of the Dutch professional journal *De Economist* to review two books by Willem Lodewijk Valk which dealt with the so-called Cassel–Walras system. In these books Valk argued that, now Cassel's simplifications had made Walras's system accessible to non-mathematical economists, Walrasian general equilibrium analysis should supersede Austrian subjectivistic reductionism. It took Van Dorp five years to review Valk's books, but in 1931 it had already become clear that she had left the Austrian ranks. In one publication after another she criticized the Austrian theory of capital and presented her own alternative, which was a remarkable literary version of a Walrasian temporary equilibrium approach.

Van Dorp left the Dutch Austrian School rather tumultuously. In 1931 her first critical article was published in the *Festschrift* for the dean of the Dutch Austrians, C.A. Verrijn Stuart (1865–1948). The same year she published a modified German translation of this article. In 1933 she continued her criticism with a pamphlet and the long-overdue review of Valk's books. She came into conflict with R. van Genechten (1895–1945), a co-editor of *De Econo-*

mist who had disqualified her alternative theory as a 'theory of exploitation'. Van Genechten's own interpretation of the Austrian theory of capital was criticized by Van Dorp, first in an article in German (Van Dorp, 1933) and next in an article in Dutch which was refused by *De Economist* and subsequently published as a pamphlet. Van Dorp cancelled further cooperation with this journal, which at the time implied that she stopped all further communication with the leading members of the Dutch Austrian School. In 1937 Van Dorp published a monograph in English, in which she could not refrain from remarking that in the Netherlands Böhm-Bawerk's time premium theory had the quality of a gospel. The same year K.E. Boulding published a rather reticent but amiable book review in *The Economic Journal*, in which he assessed her criticism of Böhm-Bawerk as 'excellent' and as going 'a long way towards clearing up the muddle which has enlivened the pages of our journals for so many decades'.

Van Dorp developed her criticism on Austrian subjectivism systematically from a Walrasian 'market-clearing' point of view. She used a down-to-earth style, which for a theorist may not be wholly satisfactory, but which clearly elucidates why for the little Walrasian girl in the crowd the Austrian emperor has no clothes. Entrepreneurs, for example, do not impute values to capital goods on the basis of the natural values of final commodities, as Wieser would have it. In 'reality' they go to the market, perceive prices of capital goods and try to maximize profits. Her list of criticisms is quite extensive (see Plasmeijer, 1998) and in many instances a modern reader will regret that she did not push further, for example when she mentions some problems for Böhm-Bawerk's average period of production arising out of the heterogeneity of capital. But she did push further when developing her own ideas.

Van Dorp came to fascinating results, although her work in the 1930s clearly shows that she worked as an isolated scientist. She presented a literal Walrasian temporary equilibrium model, at the time called a 'this week, next week approach'. She believed that Böhm-Bawerk was right when specifying production technology as roundabout processes, but maintained that entrepreneurs cannot vary the length of the production period. She introduced the notion of the choice of techniques. The implication of such a Walrasian model with strict roundabout processes is that, as in Adam Smith, consumption is not inversely related to investment. Van Dorp pointed out that this bears a striking resemblance to the old *wages fund* doctrine, which can also be found in Böhm-Bawerk's work. She stressed the time structure of the model and came up with two notable non-neoclassical propositions:

1. Since labourers spend what they get and entrepreneurs get what they spend, profit is a residual income.
2. The relationship between capital intensity and factor rewards is not unique.

These propositions foreshadow in many ways the capital controversies in the 1960s, for it can be shown that they carry over to a Sraffa–Leontief model (see Plasmeijer, 1998).

Van Dorp's work on capital theory and income distribution left hardly any trace in the Netherlands. After World War II the Austrian School was dead and buried and for the new generation Van Dorp's stinging criticism of that school was no longer relevant. And Elisabeth Caroline van Dorp was no longer among them to defend her Walrasian views. In 1939 the threat of war with Germany induced her to move to Indonesia, which at the time was still a Dutch colony. During the Japanese occupation she was interned. She died on 6 September 1945, shortly after the Japanese capitulation, in the women's concentration camp at Ambarawa near Banjoe Biroe on Java.

HENK W. PLASMEIJER

Bibliography

Selected writings by Elisabeth Caroline van Dorp
(1919), 'The deviation of exchanges', *The Economic Journal*, **29**, 497–503.
(1919–20), 'Die Bestimmungsgründe der intervalutarische Kurse', *Weltwirtschaftliches Archiv*, **15**, 29–39.
(1920), 'Abnormal deviations in international exchanges', *The Economic Journal*, **30**, 411–14.
(1931), 'Agio oder Lohnfonds?', *Archiv für Sozialwissenschaft und Sozialpolitik*, **66**, 284–319.
(1933), 'Löhne und Kapitalzins', *Zeitschrift für Nationalökonomie*, **4**, 254–66.
(1937), *A Simple Theory of Capital, Wages, Profit and Loss, a New and Social Approach to the Problem of Economic Distribution*, London: P.S. King & Son.

Other sources and references
Author unknown (1938), 'Elisabeth Caroline van Dorp', in *Persoonlijkheden in het Koninkrijk der Nederlanden in Woord en Beeld*, with an introduction by Prof. Dr H. Brugmans, Amsterdam: Holkema en Warendorf N.V., pp. 380–81.
Fase, M.M.G. (1992), 'A century of monetary thought in the Netherlands', in J. van Daal and A. Heertje (eds), *Economic Thought in the Netherlands: 1650–1950*, Aldershot: Ashgate, pp. 145–81.
Fase, M.M.G. (1994), 'Elisabeth Caroline van Dorp (1872–1945)', in J. Charité and A.J.C.M. Gabriels (eds), *Biografisch Woordenboek van Nederland, Volume 4*, Amsterdam, 114–16.
Jansz, U. (1995), 'Women or workers? The 1889 Labor Laws and the debate on protective legislation in the Netherlands', in U. Wikander, A. Kessler-Harris and J. Lewis (eds), *Protecting Women, Labor Legislation in Europe, the United States and Australia, 1880–1920*, Urbana and Chicago: University of Illinois Press, pp. 188–209.
Laar, H.J.M. van de (1992), 'Elisabeth Caroline van Dorp, een strijdlustige juffrouw', in J.F.E. Bläsing and H.H. Vleesenbeek (eds), *Van Amsterdam naar Tilburg en toch weer terug*, Leiden, pp. 123–37.
Plasmeijer, H.W. and M. Haan (1992), 'Via Von Böhm-Bawerk terug naar de klassieken; over de campagne van Mevr. E.C. van Dorp in de jaren dertig', *Tijdschrift voor Politieke Ekonomie*, **14**(4), 22–46.
Plasmeijer, H.W. (1998), 'Elisabeth Caroline van Dorp, between Austrian and Walrasian thought', in W. Samuels (eds), *European Economists of the Early 20th Century, Vol. 1: Studies of Neglected Thinkers of Belgium, France, The Netherlands and Scandinavia*, Cheltenham, UK and Northampton, US: Edward Elgar.

Eleanor Lansing Dulles (1895–1996)

Eleanor Lansing Dulles, the 'Mother of Berlin' was famous for her work as a diplomat and instrumental in the rebuilding of Europe after World War II, but she also had a distinguished career as an economist. She published several books, did scholarly work on the theory of money, was a prominent member of the American delegation at the Bretton Woods International Monetary Conference and advocated economic policy as a means to assist the refugees of both world wars.

Dulles was born on 1 June 1895 in Watertown, New York, the fourth of five children born to Allen Macy Dulles and Edith Foster. Allen was a Presbyterian minister and Edith was the daughter of a civil war general who also served as Secretary of State. She was born into a hard-working, high-achieving family: the children were expected to be successful while making a contribution to society. Dulles was not especially close to her brother Foster (a future Secretary of State), but did maintain a fluctuating relationship with her brother Allen (a future director of the Central Intelligence Agency). One of the most important things she received from her family was a love of travel. Her maternal grandfather had been chief diplomatic representative in Mexico, Russia and Spain, and he had also been to India, China and Japan. She spent hours at a time reading travel books and listening to travel stories. This provided her with a window to the world that ignited her desire to travel, which she did extensively.

In 1913, at the age of 18, she started attending Bryn Mawr College. Dulles dreamed of being a writer, but these hopes were dashed when her writing was severely criticized by her professors. Also, her marks were mediocre; this was a bitter disappointment for someone who had such high expectations of herself. Since her academic writing failed to impress, she joined the school newspaper, where she had more success. Writing, however, was still secondary to her main ambition of being a missionary to China; the best route to this goal was to become a doctor. This was also dealt a severe blow in her second university year when she failed her chemistry exam, and as a result, switched her major to psychology and graduated in 1917.

In April 1917, the USA declared war on Germany, while her uncle, Robert Lansing, was Secretary of State. She saw this as an opportunity, and in June of that year, went to France to work with the refugees of Europe. By 1918, after the war had ended, she was helping with the rebuilding effort, by running a store where supplies were sold for a nominal amount. This was to be the forerunner of a plan she would propose 25 years later for the United Nations Relief and Rehabilitation Administration, and would be used after 1948 in the Marshall Plan.

She returned to the USA in 1919 and was offered a fellowship at Bryn Mawr in the Social Economy Department. By now she was looking forward to a career in industrial management, as the idea of heavy industry appealed to her. She took field trips to Philadelphia factories, and did work terms in various industrial settings, even working as a payroll clerk in a hairnet factory. These experiences only served to dissuade her from a career in industry, as they did not allow for much creativity, and she wanted to exert more influence than a career in industry could provide. In 1921, she went to the London School of Economics to study for a Ph.D. in economics.

By that time, the LSE had begun teaching a combination of classical and theoretical economics, but by 1923 she decided she wanted a Radcliffe–Harvard degree and took five courses at Harvard. She passed her oral exams, and felt for the first time she had proved herself as an economist. Her thesis topic was the study of the decline of the French franc and her first Ph.D. grant was given on the understanding that her thesis would be published as a book. In 1925, she returned to Paris to resume her research.

At the time, the theory of monetary value was based on the quantity of money, especially notes in circulation, with little attention on the velocity of money and psychological factors. Dulles's research showed that notes in circulation increased after the value declined and that the psychological effects of political uncertainty determined the rate of inflation. She concluded that the increase of money in circulation resulted from an increase in the rate of spending and that velocity of circulation depended on expectations of inflation. Dulles (1980, pp. 101–2) recounts that Professors Robert Murray Haig and James Harvey Rogers of Columbia University visited her in France to suggest that she hand over her thesis and notes to be used in a book by Rogers, but she persevered in writing her own book, published in 1929 as *The French Franc, 1914–1928*. Keynes even commented favourably on the book in a letter to Dulles, saying it was an outstanding contribution to monetary theory.

Although Dulles enjoyed her work in economics, and her book was well received, she felt that contemporary economics was becoming too dependent on mathematics, to the exclusion of psychological factors. In 1928 she was granted a new fellowship from Radcliffe and Harvard's research bureau which resulted in the book *The Bank for International Settlements at Work*. She went to work in Bonn where she consulted with Professor Joseph Schumpeter and then to Basel, Switzerland, to work for the newly established Bank for International Settlements (BIS).

In 1932, she returned to the USA and married David Blondheim (he committed suicide while Dulles was pregnant with their first child in 1934). In 1933, she published another book, *Depression and Reconstruction*. She was on the faculty at Bryn Mawr from 1928 to 1930 and from 1932 to 1936.

In 1936 she started working at the newly established Social Security Board, where she stayed for seven years. The Social Security Act became law in 1935 and there were three main branches to the system. Old age insurance was administered federally and financed from payroll taxes, unemployment insurance was administered by the states, and public assistance was financed in part by Washington and the states. She campaigned to simplify the system, while vigorously defending it, but she met resistance from other board members. A subtle campaign was initiated against Dulles, and believing she had completed all her useful work at the Board, she resigned.

In 1942, she accepted a job with the Board of Economic Warfare, but by September of that same year she transferred to the State Department in the Special Division, which consisted of economists and political scientists. They were responsible for preparing papers on political structure, education, finance, transport, industry, power, refugees, labour and other major aspects of postwar life in Europe and Asia. Some members proposed creating the United Nations Relief and Rehabilitation Administration (UNRRA) to prevent starvation and provide for refugees. Dulles acted as secretary for the interdepartmental committee on plans for the refugees, where she recommended the development of counterpart currencies. This was based on the system used after World War I, in which goods were sold for nominal amounts in local currencies, and the funds used to buy more goods for sale.

Dulles also worked on the problem of international banking and exchange control in terms of Bretton Woods. She called for an inclusive international bank to stabilize exchange rates and smooth the flow of funds between money markets, but her ideas were eclipsed by the Bretton Woods Conference in 1944, when the International Monetary Fund and the International Bank for Reconstruction and Development were created and a system of fixed exchange rates between currencies established. She did participate in Bretton Woods as a member of the conference's international secretariat, but it was to be the only international conference the State Department would ask her to attend.

In 1943, Dulles became a member of the German committee in the State Department. She believed in a strong Germany, ruled by moderates and free of extreme ideas, whereas others on the committee wanted a weak Germany in the belief that a weak country was not a dangerous country; she believed her work on the German committee was the most important of her life. Dulles also helped in the reconstruction of Austria while living in Vienna, and was instrumental in getting the Austrian economy back on its feet. In 1952, after a brief stint in the Department of Commerce, she organized the 'Berlin desk', where she was responsible for the planning and administering of the many programmes assisting the reconstruction of Berlin. In 1953 she went to work on reducing unemployment, which she believed could be done by rehabilitating basic production industries such as iron and steel. She secured one billion dollars in aid for Berlin. At the end of 1959 she was given the personal diplomatic rank of minister.

Dulles was forced to leave the State Department in 1962 due to the antagonism between the Dulles family and President Kennedy (particularly with Allen Dulles over the Bay of Pigs fiasco). She regretted that she was not on the 'Berlin desk' when the Berlin Wall went up, as she felt she would have been of great use during that time of crisis. She taught at Duke University for a brief time and then spent seven years at Georgetown University. Dulles was a consultant to the State Department's Bureau of European Affairs from 1971 to 1977.

Because of her spectacular career as a diplomat, Dulles's contributions to economics are sometimes overlooked. Her book *The French Franc* was part of a new way of thinking and was even admired by Keynes; she attended Bretton Woods where her ideas were adopted if not recognized as being hers; and she helped rebuild the postwar European economy.

Eleanor Lansing Dulles died on 30 October 1996, at the age of 101.

INDRA HARDEEN

Bibliography

Selected writings by Eleanor Lansing Dulles
(1929), *The French Franc, 1914–1928*, with an introduction by Allyn Young, New York: Macmillan.
(1932), *The Bank for International Settlements at Work*. New York: Macmillan.
(1933), *The Dollar, the Franc and Inflation*, New York: Macmillan.
(1936a), *Depression and Reconstruction*, Philadelphia: University of Pennsylvania Press.
(1936b), 'The French Franc in 1935', *Harvard Business Review*, **14**(2), 146–60.
(1936c [1937]), *Financing the Social Security Act*, Washington, DC: Bureau of Research and Statistics, Social Security Board, Bureau Memoranda nos 4, 10.
(1938a), 'Social Security Program: discussion', *American Economic Review Supplement*, **28**, March, 136–40.
(1938b), 'The Bank for International Settlements in recent years', *American Economic Review*, **28**, June, 290–304.
(1940), 'War and investment opportunities: an historical analysis', *American Economic Review Supplement*, **32**, March, 112–28.
(1980), *Eleanor Lansing Dulles, Chances of a Lifetime: A Memoir*, Englewood Cliffs, NJ: Prentice-Hall.

Other sources and references
'Eleanor L. Dulles of State Dept. Dies at 101', *New York Times*, 4 November 1996, p. B10.
Mosley, Leonard (1978), *Dulles: A Biography of Eleanor, Allen and John Foster, and Their Family Network*, New York: Dial Press.

Raya Dunayevskaya (1910–87)[1]

More philosopher and political theorist than economist, Raya Dunayevskaya is best known for her humanist interpretation of Marxism and her characterization of Soviet society as a form of 'state capitalism'. Born in a small Ukrainian village near the Romanian border on 1 May 1910, she emigrated to the USA with her family in 1922 and soon became active in the revolutionary movement in Chicago. Dunayevskaya was expelled from the youth section of the US Communist Party in 1928, and joined the Trotskyists. In 1937–39 she served as Trotsky's Russian-language secretary in his exile in Mexico, breaking with him in 1939 on the question of the class nature of the Soviet Union. Under the pseudonym of Freddie Forest she was associated with C.L.R. James (J.R. Johnson) in the Johnson–Forest Tendency, which constituted the state capitalist opposition fraction in American Trotskyism during the 1940s. Dunayevskaya later established her own political organization, propagating the ideas of Marxism–Humanism in a series of books and pamphlets and in the monthly paper *News and Letters*. She died in Chicago on 9 June 1987. Fourteen volumes of her personal papers were issued on microfilm in 1988–89 as *The Raya Dunayevskaya Collection* by Wayne State University Archives of Labor and Urban Affairs.

Based on her early reading and translation of Marx's 1844 *Economic and Philosophical Manuscripts*, which were not widely available in the west until the 1960s, Dunayevskaya argued that there was a profound continuity in Marx's thought, from his initial, openly Hegelian phase through to the mature political economy of *Capital* and *Theories of Surplus Value*. This placed her at the opposite end of the spectrum from the Althusserians, who claimed to have discerned a sharp epistemological break in the mid-1840s, when Marx is supposed to have abandoned humanist philosophy in favour of structuralist materialism. In this Dunayevskaya was certainly right, though whether continuity extends to the 'late' Marx of the Zasulich letter and the 1870s ethnographical notebook is more doubtful. She was also right to emphasize the central role, throughout Marx's writings, of the related concepts of alienation and fetishism, and to view his work in its entirety as an elaboration of the dialectics of human liberation. Significantly, the preface to her first major book, *Marxism and Freedom* (1958), was by Herbert Marcuse. Dunayevskaya also maintained, controversially, that Lenin's philosophical notebooks reveal the Bolshevik leader to have taken a similar position. She was never able, however, to reconcile Lenin's supposed humanism with his Jacobinism on organizational matters or the extreme brutality of his years at the head of the Soviet state.

More fundamental to an appraisal of Dunayevskaya's economics is her assessment of Marx's *Capital*. Here she took an uncompromisingly essentialist position, very similar to that originating with the independent Polish Marxist Henryk Grossmann and subsequently taken up by other mavericks such as Roman Rosdolsky (with whom Dunayevskaya was associated for a time) and the Council Communist Paul Mattick. This led to her aggressively uncritical support for the falling rate of profit theory set out by Marx in volume III, which she regarded as an inexorable law of capitalist development. Thus she became a severe critic of those strands of Marxism which located the sources of economic crises directly in deficiencies of aggregate demand. Dunayevskaya insisted that underconsumption was a consequence rather than a cause of crises, which originated in production and not in exchange, and attacked even those Marxists to whom she was otherwise sympathetic (such as Rosa Luxemburg *q.v.*) for their revisionist errors. This doctrinaire approach to Marxian political economy was initially characteristic of anti-Stalinist streams of thought, but in the 1970s it became the hallmark of Communist orthodoxy; it is very largely discredited today.

If Dunayevskaya had very little to contribute as a theorist of the western economies, her writings on the Soviet Union carry much more weight. She was one of the first Marxian theorists to explain the degeneration of the Russian Revolution as one aspect of a new phase of world capitalism, in which private ownership and control of the means of production was increasingly irrelevant and the state had taken over more and more of the functions of the traditional capitalist. The notion that Nazi Germany, New Deal America and Stalin's Russia were tending to converge was common to a wide range of heretical thinkers, from Friedrich Pollock of the Frankfurt School, through theorists of 'bureaucratic collectivism' such as Bruno Rizzi and Max Shachtman, to the ex-Trotskyist James Burnham and his concept of a 'managerial revolution'. Dunayevskaya was one of the few to employ the term 'state capitalist' not merely as a slogan but also as a theoretical tool with which to analyse the Stalinist mode of production.

Identifying socialism with state property, she argued, was to confuse legal form and social substance. As she wrote in 1941, in her first statement of the state capitalist position:

> The determining factor in analysing the class nature of a society is not whether the means of production are the *private* property of the capitalist class or are state-owned, but whether the means of production are *capital*, that is, whether they are monopolized and alienated from the direct producers. The Soviet Government occupies in relation to the whole economic system the position which a capitalist occupies in relation to a single enterprise. Shachtman's designation of the class nature of the Soviet union as 'bureaucratic state socialism' is an irrational expression behind which there exists the real economic relation of state-capitalist-exploiter to the propertyless exploited.[2]

After the disintegration of the Soviet system it is much harder to view the bureaucracy as a 'collective capitalist', as Dunayevskaya asserted: no genuine ruling class abandons power so easily. And she was forced into some quite untenable positions in defence of the state capitalist thesis, including the claims that the Marxian law of value applied in the USSR no less than in the west, and that the Soviet economy was equally dominated by the tendency for the rate of profit to fall. Joan Robinson's (*q.v.*) reaction to this latter proposition is contained in her handwritten comments on an early outline of *Marxism and Freedom* submitted to Oxford University Press in 1947: 'This all seems to me to be very great nonsense, if you excuse me saying so' (*Rada Dunayevskaya Collection*, vol. I, p. 492).

It was in this context, however, that Dunayevskaya made her first and only appearance in a mainstream economic journal. In September 1944 she published a translation of 'Teaching Economics in the Soviet Union', an official article from the Soviet theoretical journal *Under the Banner of Marxism*, together with her critique. According to the Soviet authors, the Marxian law of value applied in a socialist economy, not just under capitalism. For Dunayevskaya, who identified the theory of value with the theory of surplus value, this 'startling reversal' of Soviet political economy (1944, p. 534) was no accident. The Soviet article had exposed the ideas and the methodology of the new exploiting class, with its hunger for surplus value. Her own brief paper, written by an unknown political activist with no academic credentials and no university affiliation, brought a sharp and immediate reaction from two of the most influential Marxian economists of the twentieth century, Paul Baran and Oscar Lange (there was also an uninteresting apology for Stalin from Leo Rogin). Their responses are extremely revealing. Baran (1944) expressed doubts that 'commodities' were produced in Soviet Russia, denied that anything resembling the law of value could conceivably apply in an economy where exchange ratios were set by the state, and dismissed Dunayevskaya's class analysis of the USSR as 'entirely gratuitous'. Lange (1945), however, argued that Marx himself had – rightly – considered the law of value to be the guiding principle of a socialist economy. Thus the Soviet authors were simply restating classical Marxian doctrine; their error lay in their failure to recognize the inadequacy of labour values for planning purposes, and the need to introduce marginalist methods into Soviet economics.

In her rejoinder Dunayevskaya (1945) restated her original position. The theory of Marxist–Humanism, though, was her real reply to her academic critics.

M.C. HOWARD
J.E. KING

Notes

1. The authors are grateful to Leslie S. Hough of the Walter P. Reuther Library, Wayne State University, for biographical information on Dunayevskaya.
2. This comes from an unpaginated supplement, contained in a pocket at the end of Dunayevskaya (1992), 'The Union of Soviet Socialist Republics is a Capitalist Society', published on 20 February 1941 under the pseudonym Freddie James.

Bibliography

Selected writings by *Raya Dunayevskaya*

(1944), 'A new revision of Marxian economics', *American Economic Review*, **34**(3), September, 531–7.

(1945), 'Revision or reaffirmation of Marxism? A rejoinder', *American Economic Review*, **35**(3), September, 660–64.

(1958), *Marxism and Freedom ... from 1776 to Today*, New York: Twayne Publishers; second edn 1964; third edn, New York: Pluto Press, 1971.

(1973), *Philosophy and Revolution: from Hegel to Sartre, and from Marx to Mao*, New York: Delacorte Press.

(1982), *Rosa Luxemburg, Women's Liberation and Marx's Philosophy of Revolution*, New Jersey: Humanities Press.

(1992), *The Marxist–Humanist Theory of State-Capitalism*, Chicago: *News and Letters*, 1992.

Other sources and references

Anderson, K. (1988), 'Raya Dunayevskaya, 1910 to 1987, Marxist economist and philosopher', *Review of Radical Political Economics*, **20**(1), Spring, 62–74.

Baran, P.A. (1944), 'New trends in Russian economic thinking?', *American Economic Review*, **34**(4), December, 862–71.

Howard, M.C. and J.E. King (1992), *A History of Marxian Economics, Volume II, 1929–1990*, Princeton: Princeton University Press and London: Macmillan, ch. 3.

Lange, O. (1945), 'Marxian economics in the Soviet Union', *American Economic Review*, **35**(1), March, 126–33.

Rich, A. (1986), 'Living the Revolution', *Women's Review of Books*, **3**(12), September, 1–4.

Minnie Throop England (1875–1941)[1]

Minnie Throop England presented her analysis of entrepreneurial promotion of new enterprises as the cause of crises and the business cycle in four major articles in the *Quarterly Journal of Economics* and the *Journal of Political Economy* from 1912 to 1915, and in earlier monographs in the University of Nebraska *University Studies*. Unusually for a woman economist of her time, she taught at a state university and worked on monetary and business cycle theory rather than on stereotypical 'women's issues'. Her work attracted favourable notice from Irving Fisher, Wesley Mitchell and Joseph Schumpeter, but her promising career was cut short following political upheavals at the University of Nebraska during World War I.

Minnie Throop England, a native of Lincoln, Nebraska, graduated from Nebraska Wesleyan University, Lincoln, and married a classmate, who became a farmer. She received a Ph.D. from the University of Nebraska at Lincoln and taught economics there as an assistant professor from 1906 until 1921. Her dissertation, 'Church Government and Church Control', was never published, and was unrelated to her later scholarship. At the University of Nebraska, she studied with the economist W.G. Langworthy Taylor, whose opinion of her work was presumably responsible for her hiring, for her publication in *University Studies* while she was still a student, and for a term she spent studying at the University of Chicago, with whose economics faculty Taylor had connections. Her 1907 *University Studies* essay on the influence of credit on the price level was reviewed the following year in the *Yale Review* by Irving Fisher, who hailed it as an 'able little monograph', and in 1909 Joseph Schumpeter reviewed England (1906).

England (1912) criticized the monetary theory of economic fluctuations presented in Fisher's *Purchasing Power of Money*, arguing that there was no more empirical evidence for lagged adjustment of the nominal interest rate than for lagged adjustment of any other price. Fisher acknowledged but evaded this critique. In the preface to the 1913 second edition, Fisher ([1911] 1913, p. xiii) stated that, were it not for the cost of altering the printing plates, 'I should have liked to modify somewhat the statement of the theory of crises ... to make use of the helpful criticism of Miss Minnie Throop England of the University of Nebraska ... also to meet a criticism of Mr. Keynes'.'

England (1913a, 1913b, 1915) went on to expound her own theory of business cycles driven by promotion of new enterprises, drawing on her 1906 monograph. Wesley Mitchell ([1913] 1960, p. 165) reported that 'While the proofs of this chapter were in my hands, Mrs. Minnie Throop England's preliminary sketch of her projected theory of crises appeared [England, 1913a]. Mrs. England seems to have formulated the problem in much the same way that I have done, to have employed like methods, and to have reached broadly similar conclusions.' Mitchell (1927, p. 22) recognized, however, that her approach was closer to that of Schumpeter ([1913] 1934), noting that 'the "promotion theory" of business cycles, developed by Professor Minnie T. England of the University of Nebraska, rests upon the same foundations as Schumpeter's theory of innovations. While less complete in its formal logic, Mrs. England's exposition runs in more realistic terms and cites more evidence. It should be studied by those who feel that Schumpeter's sketch lacks substance.' Discussing theories of the business cycle as an investment cycle in his *History of Economic Analysis*, Schumpeter (1954, p. 1128) wrote that 'Mrs. England, with a keener sense of the necessity for a more convincing cause, pointed to the activity of promoters or, more generally, to the intrusion into the horizon of entrepreneurs of new technological or commercial possibilities.' Despite these acknowledgements in well-known books by leading business cycle theorists, England's contributions were forgotten by the profession.

In 1917, England and her senior economics colleagues, W.G. Langworthy Taylor and J.E. LeRossignol, were swept up in the patriotic fervour surrounding US entry into World War I, and questioned the loyalty of several of their colleagues. Eleven faculty members were investigated, and three lost their jobs, two for involving the university in public criticism and one for halting loyalty. However, the Board of Regents also provisionally demanded the resignations of England and a history professor for spreading suspicion about their colleagues (but took no action against either of the full professors of economics). Although the demand was withdrawn on 1 August 1918, England's career faded: she never published again, and in 1921 she left the university. Other business cycle theorists lost track of her: Wesley Mitchell (1927) wrote of her as still teaching at the University of Nebraska, which she had left six years before. In November 1941, the *Nebraska Alumnus* reported, under notes on the class of 1906, that 'Minnie T. England, 66, former instructor in the University, died Sept. 13 at Norfolk, Nebr. She taught for 15 years, until 1921, in the business administration department. Surviving are an adopted son, a sister, and two brothers' (Tomiska, 1941).

ROBERT W. DIMAND

Note

1. The author is grateful to David Laidler for biographical information on M.T. England.

Bibliography

Selected writings by Minnie Throop England

(1906) 'On speculation in relation to the world's prosperity', University of Nebraska *University Studies*, **6**(1), January, 21–107.

(1907), 'Statistical inquiry into the influence of credit on the level of prices', University of Nebraska *University Studies*, **7**(1), January, 41–123.

(1910), 'Trade and the flag', University of Nebraska *University Studies*, **10**(3), November, 177–234.

(1912), 'Fisher's theory of crises: a criticism', *Quarterly Journal of Economics*, **27** (November), 95–106.

(1913a), 'Economic crises', *Journal of Political Economy*, **21** (April), 345–54.

(1913b), 'An analysis of the crisis cycle', *Journal of Political Economy*, **21** (October), 712–34.

(1915), 'Promotion as the cause of crises', *Quarterly Journal of Economics*, **29** (August), 748–67.

(1916), 'The Chinese colonies', *The Mid-West Quarterly*, **4**(1), October, 42–62.

(1918), 'Race contact and mixture in colonies', *The Mid-West Quarterly*, **5**(3), April, 163–81.

Other sources and references

Dimand, Robert W. (1999) 'Minnie Throop England on crises and cycles: a neglected early macroeconomist', *Feminist Economics*, **5**(3).

Fisher, Irving with Harry G. Brown ([1911] 1913), *The Purchasing Power of Money*, second edn, New York: Macmillan.

Manley, R.N. (1969), *Centennial History of the University of Nebraska, I. Frontier University (1869–1919)*, Lincoln, NE: University of Nebraska Press.

Mitchell, Wesley C. ([1913] 1960), *Business Cycles and Their Causes*, Berkeley and Los Angeles: University of California Press.

Mitchell, Wesley C. (1927), *Business Cycles*, New York: National Bureau of Economic Research.

Schumpeter, Joseph A. ([1911] 1934), *The Theory of Economic Development*, trans. Redvers Opie, Cambridge, MA: Harvard University Press.

Schumpeter, Joseph A. (1954), *History of Economic Analysis*, ed. Elizabeth Boody Schumpeter, New York: Oxford University Press.

Tomiska, V. (1941), 'Alumni paragraphs', *The Nebraska Alumnus* (November).

Millicent Garrett Fawcett (1847–1929)[1]

Millicent Garrett Fawcett is best known as the foremost leader of the women's suffrage movement in Britain. She was active in the movement almost from its inception, making her first suffrage speech in 1868. By the 1880s her speeches and writings had made her the movement's intellectual leader, and from 1907 to 1919, she was President of the National Union of Women's Suffrage Societies (NUWSS, which represented the movement's 'moderate' wing, as distinguished from the 'radical' wing led by the Pankhursts). Although suffrage was Fawcett's primary focus, she also campaigned to increase women's access to education, employment and the professions, and to make laws on property, marriage and divorce fairer to women.

Millicent Garrett received little formal education but came from a family of strong-minded individuals active in the liberal circles of the time. Her father was a wealthy grain and coal merchant in Suffolk, and her mother raised ten children while also helping with family business affairs. Millicent's older sister, Elizabeth Garrett (Anderson), was the first British woman to pursue a career as a physician. Millicent was initially educated at home, reading voraciously and taking part in the household's energetic discussions of politics and world affairs. She attended a girls' boarding school from the ages of 12 to 15.

At 19, Millicent married Henry Fawcett (1833–84), the blind professor of political economy at Cambridge University, who was a Member of Parliament, a disciple and friend of John Stuart Mill, and a feminist. Becoming Henry Fawcett's 'eyes and hands', she developed an interest in economics which soon led her to writing in the field. Although she lacked formal credentials (as did many writers on economics at this early stage of the field's professionalization), she achieved some recognition as an economist: she lectured on political economy at Queen's College, London in 1879 and 1889, for instance, and was listed in 1891 as a member of the British Economic Association (founded in 1890).

In addition to her economic works discussed below, Fawcett wrote hundreds of articles on varied topics, and nine books, including biographies, memoirs, a history of the suffrage struggle and an unsuccessful novel. Her writing and activism were guided by a complex set of values, including strong patriotism (she led in persuading the NUWSS to suspend the suffrage campaign during World War I); a leaning toward *laissez-faire* government and individual self-help (she opposed free public education, believing it would weaken parental responsibility); support for trade union organization, alongside vehement opposition to unions' efforts to bar women from industry; and an unwavering commitment to feminism.

Fawcett's principal economic writings fall into two groups: books and essays on political economy in the 1870s, and feminist economic articles written after 1890. Her 1870 *Political Economy for Beginners*, an introductory text designed for use in boys' and girls' schools, was conceived while she was helping her husband prepare a third edition of his *Manual of Political Economy*. The text went through ten editions and was still in demand in the 1920s. It covered the standard topics, for example land, labour and capital in production, exchange, values and prices, money and credit, income distribution, foreign trade and taxation, in a highly accessible way. Like Henry Fawcett's *Manual*, it was strongly influenced by Mill, although it departed from Mill in significant respects. Millicent Fawcett supported the wage-fund doctrine, emphasized the defects of socialism, and invited students in an end-of-chapter question to 'Prove from the propositions enunciated in this chapter that the capitalist is the real benefactor of the wages-receiving classes, and not the spendthrift or the alms-giver' (third edition, 1874, p. 37). Her 1874 *Tales in Political Economy*, also intended for young readers, used entertaining stories (for example 'The Shipwrecked Sailor') to illustrate central principles of political economy such as the benefits of free trade and the advantages of money and credit. It was not as successful as the earlier text.

Fawcett's early writings were not solely aimed at 'popularizing' political economy, however, and some of her early essays were strongly feminist. An 1872 collection, *Essays and Lectures on Social and Political Subjects*, included eight pieces by Millicent and six by her husband, mostly previously published. Her essays discussed free public education (she opposed it), the national debt (she feared that the state withdrew too much capital from industry), proportional representation schemes for government, girls' and women's education, and the case for women's suffrage. The two essays on female education decried the tendency of parents and educators to provide education to females that was deficient in both quantity and quality. She noted that parents' motivation in educating sons better than daughters was in large part economic, since only the education of sons would 'pay'. And she decried the ideology of domesticity that confined most women to the home: '[A]s long as women are considered useful members of society in proportion to the number of their children, so long will their intellectual and moral faculties be neglected' (p. 201). Her two essays on women's suffrage provided eloquent arguments for giving women equal political voice.

Beginning in the 1890s, Fawcett wrote several significant articles (1892, 1916, 1918a, 1918b) on women's employment and wages, two of which appeared in the *Economic Journal*. In doing so, she engaged in debate with two prominent social reform leaders: Sidney Webb, the Fabian Society founder devoted to building the labour movement, and Eleanor Rathbone (*q.v.*), an important feminist activist who led the campaign for family allowances (see Pujol, 1992 for more detail on these debates).

In an 1891 article in the *Economic Journal*, Sidney Webb examined data collected by the Fabian Society on women's and men's occupations and wages. The data showed that women and men rarely performed the same jobs in the same workplaces, and that in virtually all occupations, women earned substantially less than men. Webb speculated that while wage inequality had many causes, 'Where the inferiority of [women's] earnings exists, it is almost always coexistent with an inferiority of work. And the general inferiority of women's work seems to influence their wages in industries in which no such inferiority exists' (Webb, 1891, p. 657). The alleged 'inferiority' of women's work referred both to lower physical productivity and to cases in which women and men did equally difficult work but the market placed lower value on women's products. And women's wages, Webb suggested, were often 'set less by their efficiency ... than by comparison with what women earn elsewhere' (p. 658). While he concluded that the most important negative influences on women's wages were 'custom and public opinion', he also observed that women workers demanded less because most received partial support from husbands or other male relatives, and that women were much less likely than men to belong to trade unions.

In Fawcett's response (1892), she accepts Webb's assertion that women's productivity (in value terms) is generally lower than men's. But she argues that this should be seen as a result of labour market structure rather than of distinct characteristics of women workers, and she offers an early theory of 'segregated' or 'dual' labour markets.[2] In her account, the key fact is the presence of 'non-competing groups' in the labour market, 'limited both industrially and geographically', with 'the equalizing effect of competition in wages only operat[ing] within each of these groups' (ibid., p. 173). Wage gaps persist because workers are unable to shift from low-wage to high-wage areas of employment. Thus women's lower wages are explained by their lack of direct competition with men, in a situation in which 'the most wealth-producing of men's industries, such as engineering, mining, banking ... are more wealth-producing than the most wealth-producing of women's industries, such as cotton spinning and weaving, schoolkeeping, etc.' (pp. 174–5).

Because occupational segregation is so widespread, when women and men do meet and perform similar work, their pay remains unequal. While many feminists were calling for 'equal pay for equal work' to remedy this situation, Fawcett here opposes the demand (her position would later be reversed):

> I have always regarded it as an error, both in principle and in tactics, to advise women under all circumstances to demand the same wages for the same work as men ... The cry 'the same wages for the same work' is very plausible, but it is proved impossible of achievement when the economic conditions of the two sexes are so widely different. (p. 176)

It is crowding that makes it difficult to apply the equal pay principle. Fawcett cites the experience of the London School Board: female teachers flock towards job opportunities, and are paid less than the rare males who apply for the posts. 'Under these circumstances,' she says, 'no one can accuse the Board of injustice to their women teachers.' When one school did decide to pay women and men teachers equally, it was able to hire 'exceptionally well qualified' female teachers and 'mere average' male ones, so the 'equality therefore was only nominal; the same money bought a better article in the female labour market than it did in the male labour market' (p. 176).

While Fawcett agrees with Webb that the unionization of women is impor- tant, she places more emphasis on the need to alleviate crowding by allowing women into a wider range of jobs. 'What women most want', she insists, 'is more training, to enable them to pursue more skilled handicrafts and a large number of professional occupations' (ibid.).

Fawcett changed her stance and became a forceful advocate of 'equal pay' during World War I. In an essay on 'The Position of Women in Economic Life' (1917), she draws on wartime experience to argue for the removal of barriers to women's employment and for equal pay. Due to women's substan- tial contribution to the war effort, she notes, their productive power has at last been 'discovered' – although, she adds, 'the great mass of our countrywomen always have worked for their living; whether as wage-earners or as home- keepers, and sometimes as both' (p. 191).[3] Yet women receive for their market work 'less than half of what men are paid, women's wages being often set 'below subsistence level' (p. 193). Quoting a recent Fabian Women's Group study showing that a large proportion of wage-earning women had dependants and/or were wholly supporting themselves,[4] she denounces the common rationale offered for women's low pay: 'The extraordinarily low level of women's wages before the war cannot therefore be explained either on the "pocket money" theory or by the fiction that they have no one dependent upon them' (p. 196).

Fawcett attributes women's low pay to trade union and professional asso- ciation practices that exclude women from most of the skilled trades and professions. By denying women access to training and credentials, these organizations contribute to the crowding of women into a small group of unskilled occupations. Fawcett denounces this as 'a hideous tyranny, which has kept huge masses of industrial women in a sort of serfage' (p. 199).

The war, she argues, 'has destroyed the fiction that women were incapable of skilled work' (p. 198). Abundant evidence demonstrates that women are highly productive in their new jobs, sometimes more productive than men had been (since unionized men often intentionally restricted output). Fawcett calls upon trade unions to accept that women in industry 'have come to stay' (p. 199). The unions can best protect their interests, she urges, not by trying to push women out, but rather by helping to organize the women and supporting the feminist demand for equal pay. Only a rise in women's wages will remove 'the temptation to employers to cease to employ men and take women in their place' (p. 197). Analogous arguments apply to the professions, which she says have been even more exclusionary than the unions.

Employment barriers lead to underuse of women's capacities as industrial workers and professionals, a 'gross waste of national resources' that must cease. Women's underpayment and overwork in the crowded industries, often so severe as to endanger their health, are likewise inefficient as well as unfair. Thus Fawcett's case for equal opportunity and equal pay is based on the evidence of women's equal – or higher – productivity, when allowed to receive training to perform 'men's work', and the improvement in women's health and welfare that would derive from wages providing more than bare subsistence.

The strongest voice against 'equal pay' within the women's movement was that of Eleanor Rathbone, who argued in a 1917 *Economic Journal* article that in demanding 'equal pay' feminists were ignoring the many 'disadvantages' of female labour to employers; in practice, 'equal pay' would merely further women's exclusion from skilled jobs. In Rathbone's view, the main cause of the wage gap was the fact that it was men who were seen as responsible for supporting families. Only if workers received 'family allowances' determined by the number of their dependants, removing this rationale for higher pay for men, would it be possible to equitably raise women's wages.[5]

Fawcett responded to Rathbone in the *Economic Journal* in 1918. Her response is short and does not address Rathbone's arguments on family allowances. Instead she focuses entirely on equal pay, reiterating arguments she had made earlier.

Rathbone's article characterized the feminist demand for 'equal pay' as 'vague and ill-defined'. Fawcett contests this, insisting that the demand has never meant that women should be paid the same as men when they are less efficient. Rathbone's preferred interpretation of 'equal pay' as 'securing for women a fair field of competition with men, their work being accepted or rejected on its merits, recognising that any permanent disadvantage that adheres to women workers as such should be allowed for by a pro rata reduction in their standard rates' is, Fawcett states, an 'admirably clear' definition that would be widely accepted among feminists (1918a, pp. 3–4).

Fawcett criticizes Rathbone for 'assum[ing] too much that women are always industrially less advantageous to their employers than men and that their lower wages to a large extent merely reflect this lower value' (ibid., pp. 2–3). Rathbone has not taken sufficient account, she says, of women's wartime experience, which 'has stiffened the conviction of many feminists that a large proportion of supposed feminine disadvantages exist more in imagination than in reality' (ibid., p. 4). If allowed training, women could acquire the skills that would make them as efficient as male workers. No one knows what women ... can do until they have had an opportunity of learning how and trying' (ibid., p. 5).

For Fawcett, the causes of women's inferior pay are clear: women's exclusion from most trades and the sweated conditions women face in the trades into which they are crowded. What women need in order to achieve equal pay, therefore, is 'a free entry into skilled industries and the opportunities of training, the organization of women either in men's trade unions or in trade unions of their own and political power to support their industrial claims' (p. 4).

'Equal pay' for women was not (to put it mildly) achieved in Fawcett's lifetime: the depression of the 1920s in fact led to a worsening of women workers' economic situation. Still, she could find solace in the triumph of the suffrage struggle which had occupied most of her life: the extension of voting rights to all adult women occurred in 1928, just a year before Fawcett's death.

MICHÈLE A. PUJOL
JANET A. SEIZ

Notes

1. At the time of Michèle Pujol's tragic death in 1997, she had begun to draft this entry but it was very incomplete. Janet A. Seiz is grateful to Bob Dimand for the invitation to complete the piece.
2. The economics profession has wrongly attributed to Edgeworth the development of the 'crowding' theory of women's pay, ignoring earlier formulations by Fawcett and others. See Pujol (1992).
3. Fawcett notes here that to describe homemakers caring for children as 'unoccupied' is 'one of the little jokes of the Census Department' (p. 192).
4. For more detail on the Fabian Women's Group study of *Wage-earning Women and Their Dependents* (published in 1915), see Pujol (1992).
5. For more on this, see the Rathbone entry in this volume and Pujol (1992). Fawcett strongly opposed family allowances, believing that they would encourage high fertility and weaken parents' sense of responsibility and incentive to work. She believed it would be far better to give women a legal right to a portion of their husbands' incomes.

Bibliography

Selected writings by Millicent Garrett Fawcett

(1870), *Political Economy for Beginners*, London: Macmillan & Co. Reprinted in *Works of Henry and Millicent Fawcett*, London: Routledge/Thoemmes, 1995.

(1874), *Tales in Political Economy*, London: Macmillan. Reprinted in *Works of Henry and Millicent Fawcett*, London: Routledge/Thoemmes, 1995.

(1872), *Essays and Lectures on Social and Political Subjects* (with Henry Fawcett), London: Macmillan. Reprinted in *Works of Henry and Millicent Fawcett*, London: Routledge/Thoemmes, 1995.

(1892), 'Mr Sidney Webb's article on women's wages', *Economic Journal*, **2**(5), March, 173–6.
(1917), 'The position of women in economic life', in William Harbutt Dawson (ed.), *After-War Problems*, London: Allen & Unwin.
(1918a), 'Equal pay for equal work', *Economic Journal*, **28**(109), March, 1–6.
(1918b), 'Equal pay for equal value', *Contemporary Review*, **114**, 18 October, 387–90.
(1924), *What I Remember*, London: T. Fisher Unwin.

Other sources and references
Oakley, Ann (1983), 'Millicent Garrett Fawcett: duty and determination', in Dale Spender (ed.), *Feminist Theorists*, London: Routledge.
Pujol, Michèle A. (1992), *Feminism and Anti-Feminism in Early Economic Thought*, Aldershot, UK and Brookfield, VT: Edward Elgar.
Rathbone, Eleanor (1917), 'The remuneration of women's services,' *Economic Journal*, **27**(105), March, 55–68.
Rubinstein, David (1991), *A Different World for Women: The Life of Millicent Garrett Fawcett*, Columbus, OH: Ohio University Press.
Strachey, Ray (1931), *Millicent Garrett Fawcett*, London: John Murray.
Thomson, Dorothy Lampen (1973), *Adam Smith's Daughters*, Jericho, NY: Exposition Press.
Webb, Sidney (1891), 'Alleged differences in wages paid to women and men for similar work', *Economic Journal*, **1**(4), December, 639–58.

Ann Fetter Friedlaender (1938–92)

Ann Fetter was born in Philadelphia on 24 September 1938 to Ferdinand Fetter and Elizabeth Head. She married Stephen Friedlaender on 28 December 1960, the same year she graduated from Radcliffe College with a BA, and subsequently became the mother of two sons, Lucas Ferdinand and Nathaniel Marc.

After earning her BA from Radcliffe College, Friedlaender was a Woodrow Wilson fellow from 1960 until 1962 and earned a Ph.D. from MIT in 1964. Friedlaender was a Fulbright lecturer in Finland in 1964, and accepted a position as assistant professor at Boston College in 1965. She had been promoted to full professor by the time she left to join MIT permanently as a professor of economics and civil engineering in 1974. She had been a visiting professor in 1972 and 1973. Friedlaender became the first woman chair of an academic department at MIT, when she accepted the responsibility of chairing the Economics Department in the academic year 1983–84. In 1984, she became dean of the School of Humanities and Social Sciences, the first woman to become an academic dean at MIT, a post she held until 1990. Among other directorships, she was a member of the board of trustees of Rand Corporation and a member of the board of directors of Consolidated Rail Corporation.

Friedlaender was the chair of the American Economic Association's Committee on the Status of Women in the Economics Profession from 1978 until 1980, on the executive committee of the American Economic Association from 1982 until 1984 and vice-president of that organization in 1987. She died of cancer on 19 October 1992, at the age of 54, in Cambridge, Massachusetts.

Friedlaender's academic interests were largely in the area of transport economics. The author and co-author of many papers, her most important work included *The Dilemma of Freight Transportation* (1969), *Freight Transport Regulation* (1981) with R.H. Spady, and *Government Finance* (1981) with John F. Due. Evidence of her continuing influence on the field is provided by the many citations and reprints of her empirical studies of transport regulation.

EVELYN L.FORGET

Bibliography

Selected writings by Ann Fetter Friedlaender
(1965), *The Interstate Highway, System: a Study in Public Investment*, Amsterdam: North-Holland.
(1969), *The Dilemma of Freight Transport Regulation*, Washington: Brookings Institution.
(1971), 'The Social Costs of Regulating the Railroads', *American Economic Review*, **61**(2), 226–34.
(1973), 'Macro policy goals in the postwar period: a study in revealed preference', *Quarterly Journal of Economics*, **87**(1), 25–43.
(1976), *Econometric Estimation of Cost Functions in the Transportation Industries* (with R.H. Spady), Cambridge, MA: Center for Transportation Studies.
(1981), 'Price distortions and second best investment rules in the transportation industries', *American Economic Review*, **71**(2), 389–93.
(1981), *Freight Transport Regulation: Equity, Efficiency and Competition in the Rail and Trucking Industries* (with R.H. Spady), Cambridge, MA: MIT Press.
(1981), *Government Finance: Economics of the Public Sector* (with J.F. Due), Homewood, IL: Irwin.
(1986), 'Macroeconomics and microeconomics of innovation: the role of the technological environment', in Ralph Landau and Nathan Rosenberg (eds), *The Positive Sum Strategy: Harnessing Technology for Economic Growth*, Washington, DC: National Academy Press, pp. 327–32.
(1991), 'Fair rates and rates of return in a deregulated rail industry', MIT Working Paper 576.
(1992), 'Coal rates and revenue adequacy in a quasi-regulated rail industry', *Rand Journal of Economics*, **23**(3), 376–94.

Other sources and references
Who Was Who In America?, vol. XI (1993–96).

Rose Director Friedman (b. 1911)

Rose Director Friedman's most important legacy to economics is her collaborative effort with her husband Milton Friedman on political economy topics in *Capitalism and Freedom* (1962), *Free to Choose* (1980) and *Tyranny of the Status Quo* (1984). In these three books and the television series that preceded *Free to Choose* the Friedmans made a compelling case for competitive capitalism. Theirs was an argument cutting very much against the *status quo* in western intellectual circles that favoured large and active government. With clear and powerful prose and relatively simple economic theory, the Friedmans laid a key part of the intellectual foundation for a turn away from the statist presumptions that had guided public policy since the 1930s.

Capitalism and Freedom is based on a series of lectures that Milton Friedman gave at a Volker Foundation conference held at Wabash College in 1956. Rose Friedman was in fact co-author of the book, though she is listed as assisting Milton Friedman. She transformed his notes for the lectures into the book manuscript. The first two chapters make an argument for limited government and identify principles for determining where the limits should be. The rest of the chapters apply the principles to public policy areas such as monetary and fiscal problems, education, poverty and discrimination. Rose Friedman was co-author in name as well as fact for their sequel, *Free to Choose*, in which the Friedmans supplemented the evaluation of public policies and added a new element that was only in the shadows in the earlier book – public choice analysis. In *Tyranny of the Status Quo*, for which she was again co-author, the Friedmans developed a public choice explanation of why reform in the direction of greater reliance on private initiative and markets is so difficult to achieve, and recommended constitutional changes to break the 'iron triangle' of groups receiving state subsidies, politicians who confer the subsidies, and government professionals who administer the programmes.

A second important contribution is Rose Friedman's work in the 1940s on the economics of saving and consumption. She and Dorothy S. Brady (*q.v.*), developed the relative income hypothesis in their 1947 paper, 'Saving and the Income Distribution'. Using family budget data from the Consumer Purchases Study of the National Resources Committee and the Study of Spending and Saving in Wartime of the Bureau of Labor Statistics, they showed that much of the theretofore unexplained differences in savings rates for families with similar incomes in different cities and regions could be explained by controlling for the families' position in the income distribution. For example, families with a given absolute income in regions with high average income tended to have lower savings rates than families in regions with lower average income. Brady and Friedman found that this could be accounted for by the fact that in the high average income region the same absolute income was further down in the income distribution. Families with similar relative incomes within their region tended to save similar proportions of their income. Their finding implied that a general increase in income would reduce the marginal effect of income on saving (increase for consumption) below that which was postulated in the absence of the relative income effect. They also found that farm families saved a larger proportion of their income than non-farm families, both in absolute and relative income terms. This they attributed to farm families being more entrepreneurial and therefore having experienced wider fluctuations in income.

In addition to the direct contribution of the paper by Brady and Friedman to knowledge of household spending and saving behaviour, Rose Friedman's work on the topic also played a key role in preparing the way for Milton Friedman's much-acclaimed study, *A Theory of the Consumption Function*. Her work and ongoing interest in the subject were instrumental in drawing Milton Friedman back in 1951 to a field that he had done no work in since the mid-1930s. Both she and he did their first work on consumption economics at the National Resources Committee, where they worked on the Consumer Purchases Study. Rose Friedman was on the staff there for three months, and then moved to the Bureau of Home Economics of the US Department of Agriculture to continue work on the Consumer Purchases Study. Later, in 1941, she was again on the staff of the Bureau of Home Economics, where much of the work on consumption budget studies was being done. Rose Friedman's only publication in the field was the 1947 paper with Brady. But through her friendship with Brady and with Margaret G. Reid (*q.v.*), who was appointed Head of the Family Economics Division of the Bureau of Human Nutrition and Home Economics of the Department of Agriculture in 1944, Rose Friedman kept in touch with research in consumption economics. Milton Friedman joined in their conversations, which by the late 1940s often took place at the Friedmans' summer home in New England. From the discussions there emerged the permanent income hypothesis. Margaret Reid first put the hypothesis to an empirical test, and Milton Friedman became directly involved in the work in 1951 when he wrote an explication of the underlying theory. So Rose Friedman's research in consumption economics with Dorothy Brady and her friendship with Brady and Margaret Reid were Milton Friedman's *entrée* to what may be his most important theoretical achievement, *A Theory of the Consumption Function*.

Rose Director was born in Russia in December 1911, two years before her family emigrated to the USA. She grew up in Portland, Oregon and attended Reed College in Portland. After her second year at Reed she transferred to the University of Chicago, where her brother Aaron Director was on the faculty. Though she arrived at Chicago just after Robert Maynard Hutchins's curriculum reform, Director elected to major in economics under the old curriculum. She took her Bachelor of Philosophy degree in 1932 and remained at the University of Chicago to enrol in the economics Ph.D. programme. It was as first-year graduate students at the University of Chicago that Rose Director and Milton Friedman met. A year later George J. Stigler and W. Allen Wallis arrived. They became life-long friends of the Friedmans as well as intellectual soul-mates, and later as members of the faculty helped give postwar

Chicago economics the distinctive cast most commonly identified with Milton Friedman.

After taking off part of the 1933–34 academic year, Rose Director returned to her studies in the autumn quarter of 1934. Frank H. Knight arranged for her to receive an assistantship from the Social Science Research Committee. She worked as Knight's research assistant for a project on the history of capital theory. She also began her Ph.D. dissertation on the same subject under Knight's tutelage. She produced two papers, 'Fixed Capital in the Ricardian System' and 'Senior's Theory of Capital and Interest', though she never finished the dissertation.

In the autumn of 1936 Rose Director left Chicago for Washington to work for the National Resources Committee on the nationwide Study of Consumer Purchases. After a short stint working on this study, Director left for the Federal Deposit Insurance Corporation, where she worked in the Research Division until she and Friedman were married in June 1938. She then moved to New York, where Friedman was on the staff at the National Bureau of Economic Research. She joined the National Bureau, participating in a study of bond markets, until they departed New York for Wisconsin.

The Friedmans moved in 1940 to Madison, Wisconsin, where he joined the faculty of the University of Wisconsin on a visiting basis, and she took time off to start a family. Over the course of the year Milton Friedman's reappointment to a permanent position became an issue in an internecine struggle in the Wisconsin Economics Department. This prompted the Friedmans to leave Madison at the end of the academic year. They spent the summer of 1941 in Vermont and then moved to Washington, DC. There Rose Friedman returned to work at the Bureau of Home Economics with Dorothy Brady. Her employment at the Bureau of Home Economics turned out to be short-lived, as the Friedmans moved again in 1943 to New York, but it later bore important fruit in the Brady and Friedman paper on the relative-income hypothesis.

Along with the political economy books on which they collaborated, Rose and Milton Friedman have written their memoirs. *Two Lucky People* (1998) tells the story of their shared lives in a unique format. Each of them wrote separate accounts of their experiences, and these accounts are woven together through the book's chapters. Along with her co-authored work with Milton Friedman and with Dorothy Brady, Rose Friedman published *Poverty: Definition and Perspective* (1965), and 'Milton Friedman: husband and colleague' (serialized, May 1976–August 1977). She also edited the 'Bibliography of articles on price theory' in the American Economic Association's *Readings on Price Theory* (1952).

J. Daniel Hammond

Bibliography

Selected writings by Rose Director Friedman

(undated), 'Senior's theory of capital and interest', mimeo, Box 48, Folder 19, Frank H. Knight Papers, Joseph Regenstein Library, University of Chicago.

(1936), 'Fixed capital in the Ricardian system', mimeo, Box 48, Folder 18, Frank H. Knight Papers, Joseph Regenstein Library, University of Chicago.

(1947), 'Savings and the income distribution' (with Dorothy S. Brady), *Studies in Income and Wealth*, **10**, New York: National Bureau of Economics Research, 247–65.

(1952), Bibliography of articles on price theory', in K.E. Boulding and G.J. Stigler (eds), *Readings in Price Theory*, Chicago: Richard D. Irwin, pp. 527–53.

(1965), *Poverty: Definition and Perspective*, Washington, DC: American Enterprise Institute.

(1976–77), 'Milton Friedman: husband and colleague', *The Oriental Economist* (serialized May 1976 to August 1977).

(1980), *Free to Choose: A Personal Statement* (with Milton Friedman), New York and London: Harcourt Brace Jovanovich.

(1984), *Tyranny of the Status Quo* (with Milton Friedman), New York and London: Harcourt Brace Jovanovich.

(1998), *Two Lucky People: Memoirs* (with Milton Friedman), Chicago: University of Chicago Press.

Other sources and references

Friedman, Milton (1956), *A Theory of the Consumption Function*, Princeton: Princeton University Press for the National Bureau of Economic Research.

Friedman, Milton (1962), *Capitalism and Freedom*, Chicago: University of Chicago Press.

Elizabeth Waterman Gilboy (1903–73)

Biography

Elizabeth Lane Waterman was born in Boston on 24 September 1903, the daughter of Arthur John and Amy (Lane) Waterman. After attending Boston Girls' Latin School, where she took courses in English, Greek, Latin, mathematics and physics, she studied for her first degree at Barnard College (Columbia University) . She took her AB in 1924 with honours in economics and sociology and was elected to Phi Beta Kappa. After obtaining an AM from Radcliffe College in 1925, she began work on her Ph.D. thesis at Radcliffe College, researching wages in eighteenth-century England under the supervision of Edwin F. Gay. She was awarded a Whitney Travelling Fellowship in 1926–28 to visit England and collect data and during this period she was registered as a graduate student at the London School of Economics and Political Science. She obtained her Ph.D. in 1929, having been an instructor in economics at Wellesley College during 1928–29.

She married Glennon Gilboy on 19 April 1930 and they divorced in November 1953. Glennon Gilboy, who was a professor of engineering at MIT from 1925 to 1937 before going into private practice, died on 18 August 1958. There were no children.

Elizabeth Waterman Gilboy was Secretary of the Committee on Research in the Social Sciences at Harvard University during 1929–30 and Executive Secretary from 1930 to 1941. She was also Graduate Adviser at Radcliffe College from 1930 to 1941.

She saw service in Washington during World War II, when she was a member of the Economic Division, Office of Strategic Services, 1942–43 and she was a consultant to the US Bureau of Labor Statistics from 1960 to 1964.

She held the post of Associate Director of the Harvard Economic Research Project from 1950 until she became Acting Director in 1964–65. This project, which was known informally as the 'Leontief Project', was largely devoted to the development of input–output analysis.

Both before and after her retirement, she lived in the house of Elizabeth Boody Schumpeter, a friend from her graduate school days at Radcliffe. Towards the end, her health deteriorated and she died in Waltham, Massachusetts on 9 October 1973.

Academic Contributions

Gilboy's published work falls into five areas.

Wages in eighteenth-century England

At the time that Gilboy began her research into this topic, there was considerable disagreement over what had happened to the standard of living of workers during the Industrial Revolution in the United Kingdom. At one extreme it was argued by some writers, such as the Webbs (Webb and Webb, 1927), that the eighteenth century was a 'golden age' for the labourer. At the other extreme, writers such as the Hammonds (1918, 1919, 1920) painted a much more pessimistic picture of a progressive degradation of labouring-class standards, especially after 1760.

In the course of her researches, Gilboy drew on a number of sources of data on wages, ranging from the records of the statutory fixing of wages by justices of the peace in Gloucestershire, Kent and Middlesex (Gilboy, 1928) to the account book of Thornborough estate in Yorkshire (Gilboy, 1932b). This geographical spread enabled her to build up a statistical picture of what had happened to wages during the eighteenth century. Beveridge's data on wheat prices enabled her to construct estimates of real wages, and a comparison for different areas of England showed a more varied pattern than either of the extreme positions suggested, with low, relatively unchanging wages in Gloucestershire and high, *increasing wages* in Yorkshire. Later work (Gilboy, 1936) with improved price indices did suggest falling real wages in London, but confirmed high and rising real wages in the north of England. Her work showed 'how wage differentials between north and south and between town and country provided the stimulus for labour migration into the growing industrial areas of the eighteenth century' (Hartwell, 1971, p. 101).

Gilboy's other contribution to the debate was to examine the extent to which increasing demand (both domestic and international) contributed to the Industrial Revolution. She concluded that '[c]hanging consumption standards, the increase of population and shifting of individuals from class to class, and a rise in real income provided a stimulus to the expansion of industry that must not be underestimated' (Gilboy, 1932d, p. 639). See also Gilboy (1930c and 1934a).

Demand studies
Gilboy's emphasis on the importance of demand in explaining the Industrial Revolution led to a number of studies of demand. The majority were theoretical (Gilboy, 1930a, 1930b, 1931, 1939a) and were concerned – post Working (1927) – with the problem of reconciling empirical data that changed over time to the concept of the Marshallian static demand curve. Her articles concentrated on the interpretation of the elasticity of demand in a dynamic context and argued for a movement away from the idea of the static demand curve towards the estimation of expenditure–income functions (Gilboy, 1939a).

In addition to her theoretical contributions, Gilboy also carried out empirical demand studies. The first (Gilboy, 1932a) is an exercise in estimating expenditure–income and expenditure–price functions based on a sample of 50 Harvard economists and may have been stimulated by the work of Jessica B. Peixotto (*q.v.*) whose studies (Peixotto, 1927 and 1929) are referenced in Gilboy's article. The other empirical studies are of the demand for milk and butter in Boston, using monthly data from 1899 to 1926 (Gilboy, 1932c) and the demand for coffee and tea in the USA using annual data from 1850 to 1930 (Gilboy, 1934b) . These two studies combine economic theory with an economic historian's concern with understanding the data and explaining them in more than a purely statistical or mathematical sense: 'There should be no attempt to force empirical results into a neat theoretical structure, no matter how beautifully it may lend itself to mathematical development' (Gilboy, 1939a, p. 73).

Consumer behaviour and the consumption function
While she was familiar with statistical techniques, such as ordinary least squares, Gilboy tended to analyse data on expenditure and income by plotting the data on double logarithmic paper and fitting simple functions by eye. She found that in general straight-line (constant-elasticity) functions did not fit well for higher-income families or individuals and that curves that allowed for changing expenditure with rising income gave a better fit. This evidence led her into an early exchange with Keynes over the assumptions about the 'fundamental psychological law' underlying his concept of the marginal propensity to consume (Keynes, 1936, ch. 8), which she criticized on the grounds that he did not take changes in the distribution of income sufficiently into account in his theoretical analysis (Gilboy, 1938a) – see Thomas (1992) for an account of this exchange.

While she backed down and printed a letter from Keynes in her next contribution to this debate (Gilboy, 1939b), she remained unconvinced and returned to the question of the importance of the distribution of income for the propensity to consume in Gilboy (1940b, 1941), where she presented expenditure–income elasticities for the USA in 1935–36 and showed that they varied across the distribution of family and individual income levels.

Her final contribution in this area was her book *A Primer on the Economics of Consumption* (1968) in which, according to Wassily Leontief's preface to the book, she 'interprets the principal elements of theoretical and factual analysis in the field of the economics of consumption and presents them in a form accessible not only to the student of economics but to an interested general public as well' (Gilboy, 1968, p. iii). The book does indeed draw on her skills as an economist and economic historian to blend a non-technical discussion of consumer behaviour with tables of statistical data to illustrate the main trends in US consumer behaviour from the 1930s to the 1960s.

The effects of the recession in Massachusetts
Gilboy was involved in a research exercise begun in 1934 in a collaboration between Harvard University and the Massachusetts Emergency Relief Agency

(ERA) to study the conditions of the unemployed in that state and the effects of the work relief programme set up to help the unemployed. This linked back to her earlier work, since the New England states were still dominated by the Elizabethan concept of poor relief, the system that was in operation during the Industrial Revolution in Britain.

Three articles were based on this study: Gilboy (1937, 1938b) showed that the average expenditure of those on relief programmes exceeded average incomes, with the gap being bridged by liquidating insurance policies, running down savings and increasing debts – particularly to landlords, doctors and grocers, while Sorenson and Gilboy (1937) examined the diets of those on relief programmes and showed evidence of poor diets and malnutrition. They were critical of 'the existence of embarrassing agricultural surplus concurrently with food shortages' (ibid., p. 679).

The research culminated in Gilboy (1940a), a book that provided both a detailed statistical analysis of over 2000 work relief cases and a broad evaluation of the programme. She was sympathetic to the unemployed and defended them from critics who regarded them as 'idle' or 'work-shy', by setting the general recession in the context of declining industries in Massachusetts. Her evaluation of the work relief programme was positive: cyclical and technological unemployment would not be controlled in the short term and work relief seemed to her to be the best way of providing support to the unemployed.

Input–output analysis
Gilboy's long association with Wassily Leontief began during this period and he acknowledged her editorial input into his classic book *The Structure of the American Economy, 1919–1939*, see Leontief (1941, p. viii). Her duties within the Harvard Economic Research Project were partly administrative and she was responsible for managing the budget and looking after visitors to Harvard. However, she also had an academic input into the project, in which she concentrated on the analysis of consumption within input–output models. She wrote on that subject for the project's annual research reports – see Gilboy (1955, 1956b, 1957, 1959), presented a paper at the 1955 American Economic Association Meeting in New York summarizing work on consumption being carried out at Harvard (Gilboy, 1956a) and contributed to a technical paper presented to a conference on consumption and saving at the Wharton School of Finance and Commerce (Danière and Gilboy, 1959).

Having worked closely with Wassily Leontief, Gilboy was appointed Secretary-General to an international conference on input–output techniques, held in Geneva in 1961.

Conclusions

Elizabeth Waterman Gilboy's academic career illustrates the difficulties under which women academics operated in the first half of the twentieth century. Women studied at Barnard College and Radcliffe College in order to obtain access to the all-male professoriate teaching the male-only students at Columbia University and Harvard University respectively. Although her Ph.D. was supervised by a Harvard professor, it was awarded by Radcliffe College. Her long association with Harvard University (where she was known as 'Mrs' Gilboy) involved some teaching, but was mainly administrative, whereas she taught and advised in an academic capacity at Radcliffe College as 'Dr' Gilboy.

Gilboy's publishing career spanned four decades, from her first article published in 1928 while she was still working on her Ph.D., to her *Primer on the Economics of Consumption* in 1968. Between 1928 and 1941, she published two books and 19 articles (one joint), an average of 1.36 articles per year. While this may seem low in the current Stakhanovite era of 'publish or perish', it represented a high rate of publication at a time when quality counted for more than quantity, particularly as her articles were published in top-quality journals.

She made academic contributions to the English Industrial Revolution debate, the development of applied demand analysis and the analysis of consumer behaviour. For a number of years, she made both academic and administrative inputs into the development of input-output analysis at Harvard.

Of her various academic contributions, the most lasting were those she made to the English Industrial Revolution debate. Thus Hartwell (1971) refers to Gilboy (1932d) as 'a stimulating essay' (p. 113) and 'an important and neglected essay, partly, no doubt, because of the rarity of the volume in which it is published' (p. 139) and Gilboy (1934a) is currently listed as recommended reading in economic history at the London School of Economics and Political Science.

J.J. Thomas

Bibliography

Selected writings by Elizabeth Waterman Gilboy

(1928), 'Some new evidence on wage assessments in the Eighteenth Century', *English Historical Review*, **171**, July, 398–408.

(1930a), 'Methods used in price forecasting – discussion', *Journal of Farm Economics*, **12**, January, 133–6.

(1930b), 'Demand curves in theory and in practice' , Quarterly Journal of Economics, **44**, August, 601–20.

(1930c), 'Wages in eighteenth century England', *Journal of Economic and Business History*, **2**, August, 603–29.

(1931), 'The Leontief and Schultz methods of deriving "demand" curves', *Quarterly Journal of Economics*, **45**, February, 218–61.

(1932a), 'Demand curves by personal estimate', *Quarterly Journal of Economics*, **46**, February, 376–84.

(1932b), 'Labour at Thornborough: an eighteenth-century estate', *Economic History Review*, **3**, April, 388–98.

(1932c), 'Studies in demand: milk and butter', *Quarterly Journal of Economics*, **46**, August, 671–97.

(1932d), 'Demand as a factor in the Industrial Revolution', in *Facts and Factors in Economic History: Articles by Former Students of Edwin Francis Gay*, Cambridge, MA: Harvard University Press.

(1934a), *Wages in Eighteenth Century England*, Cambridge, MA: Harvard University Press.

(1934b), 'Time series and the derivation of demand and supply curves: a study of coffee and tea', *Quarterly Journal of Economics*, **48**, August, 667–85.

(1936), 'The cost of living and real wages in eighteenth century England', *Review of Economic Statistics*, **18**, August, 134–43.

(1937), 'The unemployed: their income and expenditure', *American Economic Review*, **27**, June, 309–23.

(1937), 'The economics of low-income diets' (with H.L. Sorenson), *Quarterly Journal of Economics*, **51**, August, 663–80.

(1938a), 'The propensity to consume', *Quarterly Journal of Economics*, **53**, November, 120–40.

(1938b), 'The expenditure of the unemployed', *American Sociological Review*, **3**, December, 801–14.

(1939a), 'Methods of measuring demand or consumption', *Review of Economic Statistics*, **21**, May, 69–74.

(1939b), 'The propensity to consume: reply', *Quarterly Journal of Economics*, **53**, August, 633–8.

(1940a), *Applicants for Work Relief: A Study of Massachusetts Families under the FERA and WPA*, Cambridge, MA: Harvard University Press.

(1940b), 'Income–expenditure relations', *Review of Economic Statistics*, **22**, August, 115–21.

(1941), 'Changes in consumption expenditures and the defense program', *Review of Economic Statistics*, **23**, November, 155–64.

(1955), 'Structural relations between consumer expenditure and income, Part I: status for research', Harvard Economic Research Project, *Report on Research for 1954*, February, pp. 136–45.

(1956a), 'Elasticity, consumption and economic growth', Papers and Proceedings of the 68th Meeting of the American Economic Association, *American Economic Review*, **46**, May, 119–33.

(1956b), 'The structure of consumption, Part I: analytical problems', Harvard Economic Research Project, *Report on Research for 1955*, March, pp. 53–8.

(1957), 'Household consumption, Part I: the status of consumption research', Harvard Economic Development Project, *Report on Research for 1956–57*, December, pp. 129–34.

(1959), 'Household consumption: introduction', Harvard Economic Research Project, *Report on Research for 1958–59*, July, pp. 150–51.

(1959), 'A multivariate analysis of selected items of consumer expenditure' (with A.L. Danière), paper presented at the Conference on Consumption and Saving, Wharton School of Finance and Commerce (mimeo).

(1968), *A Primer on the Economics of Consumption*, New York: Random House.

Other sources and references

Hammond, J.L. and B. Hammond (1918), *The Town Labourer, 1760–1832: The New Civilisation*, London: Longmans Green.

Hammond, J.L. and B. Hammond (1919), *The Village Labourer, 1760–1832: A Study in the Government of England Before the Reform Bill*, London: Longmans Green.

Hammond, J.L. and B. Hammond (1920), *The Skilled Labourer, 1760–1832*, London: Longmans Green.

Hartwell, R.M. (1971), *The Industrial Revolution and Economic Growth*, London: Methuen.

Leontief, W. (1941), *The Structure of the American Economy, 1919–1939: An Empirical Application of Equilibrium Analysis*, New York: Oxford University Press.

Peixotto, J.B. (1927), *Getting and Spending at the Professional Standard of Living: A Study of the Costs of an Academic Life*, New York: Macmillan.

Peixotto, J.B. (1929), 'How workers spend a living wage: a study of eighty-two typographers' families in San Francisco', University of California Publications in Economics no. 5.

Thomas, J.J. (1992), 'Income distribution and the estimation of the consumption function: an historical analysis of the early arguments', *History of Political Economy*, **24**, Spring, 155–81.

Webb, S. and B. Webb (1927), *English Local Government, Volume 7. English Poor Law History, Part I. The Old Poor Law*, London: Longmans Green.

Working, E.J. (1927), 'What do "statistical demand" curves show?', *Quarterly Journal of Economics*, **41**, May, 212–35.

Charlotte Perkins Gilman (1860–1935)

Although Charlotte Perkins Gilman was a notorious public figure in her day and despite a review article in the *Journal of Political Economy* (Hill, 1904), her work was neglected from her death in 1935 until her rediscovery in 1956 by historian Carl Degler, and has only recently become a focus of interest for feminist economists. Margaret O'Donnell (1985, 1994), Ulla Grapard (1996), Dimand (1995) and others have examined her writing, which consists of valuable and original economic analyses of economic institutions constraining women, as well as early contributions to environmental thought and market solutions to monopoly extraction of rent.

Life

Charlotte Perkins (Stetson) Gilman was born a collateral member of the Beecher family through her father, Frederick Perkins, but while this heritage brought her the fruits of her father's learning, she was raised in substantial poverty once her parents had separated. Like many poor women with children, her mother moved relatively frequently, and this as well as lack of funds impeded Charlotte's formal education. She constructed a curriculum (including gymnastic training) for herself with the aid of readings her distinguished father recommended and that of 'The Society for the Encouragement of Studies at Home' (1935–72, pp. 27–30, 36–8). While she attended the Rhode Island School of Design for a few years, she did not take a degree, and this ended her formal schooling.

Gilman married the artist Walter Stetson in 1884, and her attempt to fulfil the conventional roles of wife and mother resulted in a temporary mental deterioration which only increased under the treatment of the fashionable 'nerve doctor' S. Weir Mitchell. Gilman's psychological horror story 'The yellow wall-paper' (1892) notoriously draws on this experience. She separated relatively amicably from Stetson, who later married Gilman's close friend Grace Ellery Channing, with whom he raised Katharine, his daughter by Charlotte.

Living initially in California and supporting both Katharine and her own mother, Gilman ran a boarding house as she began to make a name for herself in suffrage and progressive circles as a writer and speaker. She was to lecture before an enormous variety of audiences in the USA and England: suffrage groups, Iowa farmers (male and female), guests at austere American health spas, and an astonishing variety of church congregations. The periodicals through which she published were equally varied, from the *American Journal of Sociology* to the *Woman's Journal*, official organ of the American Woman Suffrage Association, but also *Mother's Magazine*, *Century Magazine*, *Ainslee's* the *Saturday Evening Post*, and the *Puritan*. Her most famous book, *Women and Economics* (1898/1966) was published as a free-standing work, but most of her other monographs and novels appeared first in the one-woman magazine, *The Forerunner*, which she published without monetary profit for over eight years (1909–17/1970).

The style Gilman developed to communicate with these eclectic groups informed much of her work, especially her shorter essays and stories. She wanted to produce work to interest and persuade them, and found that they responded to wit more than to careful argument. Even her more serious treatises overflow with amusing examples from the animal world to discredit bland assertions about the 'natural role' of human females. She was also expert in selecting extracts from the utterances of venerated men, to dissect, skewer and label their assumptions and contradictions.

Gilman was to write repeatedly about how little and badly she wrote, attributing this to the after-effects of her illness and also to the nature of her education. Her canards about her own work have been casually picked up by later writers, who have not felt it necessary to support this assertion with argument. This carelessness in today's readers is understandable up to a point: the popular nature of Gilman's knowledge of biology, history and anthropology which contrasts with our standards no doubt stems in part from her sources. In fact, her learning in these areas was that of the educated non-specialist of the early twentieth century. Gilman's lack of citation and use of 'factual' material as illustration are also in marked contrast to the rigorous economic argument she produced directly from her thought. It would, however, be easy to exaggerate Gilman's weaknesses relative to the scholarly style of her time, when few writers cited sources or used any careful form for citation. Moreover, the notion that Gilman might have been a sluggish and unproductive writer is a terrifying one, given her output. Gilman was by no means exempt from the pressures on women about which she wrote.

By the time Charlotte Perkins Stetson married her cousin Houghton, she had established herself as a writer and lecturer. She was to continue to support herself and, increasingly, her husband, but declining demand for public speakers in the 1920s, coincident with the rise of radio, cut into her income badly, as Lane (1990, pp. 341–2) notes. (Gilman's stress on work as a source of pleasure and her feminism, which de-emphasized sexual emancipation, may also have contributed to decreased demand for her services.) She committed suicide in 1935 when an inoperable cancer reached an advanced and painful stage at which she could no longer work. (Details of Gilman's life are available in Gilman, 1935, Hill, 1980 and Lane, 1990.)

Though Gilman's notoriety had subsided in her later years, the *New York Times* (1935) thought it worthwhile to focus on an alleged recantation of her life-long opinions. The last chapter of Gilman's autobiography, written shortly before her death, gives no sign of recantation, and I have encountered none save in that obituary.

Economics

Gilman's economics is a little hard for today's readers to classify. This is due in part to substantial changes in classification systems for scholarly politics. Popular but educated understanding of Darwinian evolution moved late nineteenth- and early twentieth-century thinkers in strange ways – in the spirit of the time it was difficult not to envision change in terms of improvement, and thus the evolutionary path as deterministic movement toward The Best. Communism and socialism differentiated into a variety of factions as they gained adherents. The eugenics movement was the purview of liberals, and American Progressives felt themselves to be socialist by virtue of their opposition to monopoly. Gilman was involved with each of these movements to some extent, and her thought also paralleled that of other nascent schools, such as institutional economics.

Gilman felt herself to be profoundly influenced by the sociologist Lester Ward, a Social Darwinist who assigned a central role to the concept of gynaecocentrism. Ward's Social Darwinism might be summarized as the belief that, like other species, humans are subject to evolution, but that, unlike them, humans can consciously influence the direction of evolutionary change by choosing the institutions in which they live. Gynaecocentrism, the concept of women as the 'race type' of the human species, implies that institutions affecting women's development crucially determine the growth of the human race. As a feminist Social Darwinist, Gilman herself analysed the roles of the home and the housebound woman in the evolution of humanity, validating them as economically 'necessary' at past stages of development, yet arguing in favour of market-supplied house-service and the freeing of women from merely familial roles.

Andrew Sinclair (1965, p. 272) has compared Gilman with her contemporary Thorstein Veblen, who is claimed as a progenitor of institutional economics, and with Karl Marx. Perhaps Sinclair meant to convey the centrality of her thought to the women's movement, or to comment on the style of her prose. Gilman's first work was in fact coincident with that of Veblen, and the writers covered some of the same territory. Veblen wrote on the sociology of the leisure class, on education, on the economic and social role of the firm and on the socioeconomic position of women in America for a general, educated constituency. So did Gilman, with different emphasis and very different success. Veblen's work has never slipped entirely out of print and has always been recognized by economists. Almost all of Gilman's output has been more out of print than in print, with the exception of 'The yellow wall-paper'. Gilman was to acknowledge and recommend Veblen's work, while Veblen was content to enjoy Gilman's work when their mutual friend Edward A. Ross introduced him to it.

Comparison of Gilman with Marx is more problematic, although both writers analysed the extraction of surplus value – in Marx's case in a waged and in Gilman's in an unwaged sector of the economy. Politically, Gilman seems to have thought of herself as a socialist. In California she worked with Progressives, who as opponents of monopolies and their power were often considered socialist or communist. Moreover, the *American Fabian* selected her as a contributing editor, though she does not seem to have contributed a great deal. But while Marxists tend to see the development of markets as the rise of opportunities for extraction, Gilman saw their development and extension as a source of betterment for society. Whereas socialists typically see social benefit in public ownership and public enterprise, Gilman stressed the incentives offered by private ownership, and seems to have felt that externality problems, in which A's actions affect B's life without agreement between the parties, are best resolved through elevated social consciousness.

Many of Gilman's conceptual methods are now a part of the mainstream economist's standard toolbox. She preceded the North American economics profession, for example, in developing the idea of an activity's opportunity cost – the value of its next-best substitute. She was early to think of environmental and public health issues as externality-producing areas, though her solutions would not seem very practical to most economists. Gilman really shone, however, in her thought on market and non-market activity, market development and economic growth, careful consideration of contracts, and analysis of the incentives offered not only by particular contracts but by an entire economic system. Her insights in this realm – particularly her applications to women's economics status – still yield substantial revelations to today's economists.

Gilman's tour de force was based on recognizing the home as a centre of production which, like others, could be analysed by economists. Her best-known non-fiction work, *Women and Economics* (1898/1994) argued that women were simultaneously managers and labourers who operate under peculiar contractual conditions which were not well acknowledged. The soundness of her analysis and its applicability today are notable to the point of being shocking.

To Gilman, 'house-service' (including meal provision, house cleaning, clothes cleaning, child care and entertainment) differ from primarily market industries in an evolutionary sense – unlike (for example) architecture and house-construction, they have simply not evolved into market enterprises yet. Once production became commercialized, the desire of producers to achieve the highest possible profits would lead to increased efficiency in (lowered cost of) production. Only people who were relatively better at producing the product would go into the business; they would want to hire others with the same sort of comparative advantage in production. Gilman also saw economies of scale – the ability to produce more of an output like cooking per hour of effort (or unit of resources) spent on producing, as the scale of production increases – as a potential source of efficiency for a new industry. Then the decrease in resources needed to produce in one industry frees them to produce more output in that or another sector. To a current economist, this increased output of the economy as a whole can serve as a source of payment to any parties who would otherwise prefer to block the establishment of the new industry. Gilman did not extend her analysis in quite this way, but she did feel that a typical household would benefit by increased income should women have the same access to labour markets (and to the education useful for many occupations) as men.

For Gilman, a substantial reason for house-service's arrested development was precisely that women, who were sociologically specialized in this set of activities, were typically not paid and typically had little access to paid work. These factors created the crowding of women into unpaid household production, lowered the opportunity cost of house-service, and thus tended to result in overproduction of house-service relative to other things. At whatever production level, Gilman perceived waste which was the flip side of the efficiencies which would result from industrializing this sector.

> The performance of domestic industries involves, first, an enormous waste of labour. The fact that in nine cases out of ten this labour is unpaid does not alter its wastefulness ... We are so accustomed to rate women's labour on a sex-basis, as being her 'duty' and not justly commending any return, that we have quite overlooked this tremendous loss of productive labour. (1903/1970, pp. 117–18)

Moreover, since women as a class were confined to a set of household tasks, she thought it nearly impossible that they were all working at what they were best at. The variety of tasks made this unlikely in itself. Some tasks, such as the education of children and the provision of sanitary, nutritious food, seemed to her clearly to require specialized training few women had, were they to be performed well. In addition, providing separate equipment (physical capital) for cooking and cleaning in each house clearly resulted in excessive cost of production. Gilman performed a convincing thought-experiment showing the reduction in labour required to provide house-service if returns to scale were exploited, beginning by describing costs incurred by two hundred traditional families:

> First, the 'plant' is provided. For our two hundred families there are two hundred stoves, with their utensils. The kitchen, and all that it contains, with dining-rooms, etc., ... should be held firmly in mind as a large item in rent and furnishing. Next, there is the labour. Two hundred women are employed for about six hours a day each, – twelve hundred working hours, – at twenty cents an hour. This means two hundred and forty dollars a day, or sixteen hundred and eighty dollars a week, that the block of families is paying to have its wastefully home-purchased food more wastefully home-cooked. Of course, if these cooks are the housewives, they do not get the money' but the point is, that this much labour is *worth* that amount of money, and that productive energy is being wasted. What ought it to cost? One trained cook can cook for thirty, easily; three, more easily, for a hundred. The thousand people mentioned need, in largest allowance, thirty cooks – and the thirty cooks, organised, would not need six hours a day to do the same work, either. Thirty cooks, even at ten dollars a week, would be but three hundred dollars, and that is some slight saving as against sixteen hundred and eighty! (1903/1970, pp. 132–3)

While I have quoted Gilman (1903/1970) above, for its greater terseness, this area was initially and carefully explored in *Women and Economics* (1898/1994). In this work, she also deconstructed the traditional justifications for women's subordinate role in the household so thoroughly that one marvels that they are still heard. Were females as such adjudged incapable of doing 'work' – that is, work remunerated in the market? As Gilman later wrote, 'We have woven an iridescent web of sentiment about the sordid fact that practically half the citizens were house servants. See it we must, but we cheerfully assumed that it was not only "natural", but also that there was something in the very sex of women which endowed them at birth with magical skill in this kind of work, and an innate desire for it' (Gilman, 1929, p. 125).

That women's gender alone is no sign of endowment with such magical skill is shown by an examination of the animal kingdom. '[I]n other species of animals, male and female alike graze and browse, hunt and kill, climb, swim, dig, run, and fly for their livings'. Yet the motherhood function of female humans, like that of mammals and unlike that of the queen bee, does not incapacitate them for other work. If it did, each woman would be 'modified entirely to maternity, ... unfit for any other exertion and a hopeless dependent'. This is not the case, as we both see and expect to see human mothers working hard for their families and churches. Women are simply not paid for this work, and are 'falsely denied independence on the ground that motherhood prevents [them] from working' (1898/1994, pp. 18–21).

Men and women were not economically independent, and men clearly did not pay women for the house-service they performed. Instead, women received financial resources based on their husbands' economic class:

> the salient fact in this discussion is that, whatever the economic value of the domestic industry of women is, they do not get it. The women who do the most work get the least money, and the women who have the most money do the least work. Their labour is neither given nor taken as a factor in economic exchange. (ibid., pp. 14–15)

In fact, Gilman wrote, human institutions have transformed human females into the property of male humans, and simultaneously made men women's 'food supply' (ibid., p. 22). While it has frequently been lightly said that women are men's partners, this is no more true than in the case of men's horses, which are also of economic importance to them (ibid., pp. 12–13).

In *The Home: Its Work and Influence* (1903/1970), Gilman not only reiterated and strengthened her earlier arguments, but analysed the plant in which house-service was performed. She considered the house as a plant designed for too many kinds of work, particularly combined with consumption activities.

> The eating-room then confronts [the domestic architect] … We do not wish to eat in the kitchen. We do not wish to see, smell, hear, or think of the kitchen while we eat. So the domestic architect is under the necessity of separating as far as possible these discordant purposes, while obliged still to confine them to the same walls and roof.
>
> Then come the bedrooms. We do not wish to sleep in the kitchen – or in the dining-room. Nothing is further from our ideals than to confound the sheets with the tablecloths, the bed with the stove, the dressing-table with the sink. So the domestic architect, whose kitchen-tendency was so rudely checked by the bedroom-tendency, its demand for absolute detachment and remoteness, and the necessity for keeping its structural limits within those same walls and roof.
>
> Then follows the reception-room tendency – we do not wish to receive our guests in the kitchen – or the bedroom – or exclusively in the dining-room. So the parlour-theme is developed as far as may be, connected with the dining-room, and disconnected as far as possible from all the other life-themes going on under that roof.
>
> When we add to these the limits of space, especially in our cities, the limits of money, so almost universal, and the limits of personal taste, we may have clearly before us the reasons why domestic architecture does not thrill the soul with its beauty. (Ibid., pp. 146–7)

Viewed strictly as a workplace, it was inefficient – its structure embedded too many disparate sorts of production. Moreover, the existence of houses constructed for particular gender roles tends to perpetuate those gender roles, by lowering the cost to households of performing house-service on a private basis in each household. Even though it is wasteful for society for meals, washing, child-rearing, and so forth to be performed multiply on such a small scale, a rational household will typically acquire most of these services on a non-market basis. When such tasks are allocated to a (usually) female domestic partner, women's cost of market work is raised, keeping them from labour markets, and thus creating the impression that women simply don't do market work as much as men. Thus more homes are built for the in-house production of these services, and the cycle continues.

Many current readers of Gilman fail to understand the sweeping nature of her critique of institutions. They cite McDonald's and dry-cleaners, and suggest that she advocated the creation of a servant underclass. Gilman criticized the institutions surrounding employment of servants in her time from both economic and sociological points of view. She specifically did *not* advocate extending the use of family servants, and particularly not live-in domestic employees – she felt that this merely extended the inefficiencies and exploitations already present in the organization of household labour. Similarly, the existence of fast-food establishments and dry-cleaners would not satisfy her. We can tell that these are not establishments filling the bulk of food and laundering needs. Very few homes are built without kitchens, and washers and dryers abound, as do vacuum cleaners and other specialized cleaning tools, household by household, spending most of their time in closets. 'Working mother' is a phrase still heard, used to distinguish such women from 'regular' mothers.

Rather, Gilman championed a change in society, whereby the industries of food preparation, the bulk of child care and education, and the provision of hospitality would be delegated to the market. Afterwards, 'Inside the home are love, marriage, birth, and death; outside the house are agriculture, manufacture, trade, commerce, transportation, art, science, and religion' (1903/ 1970, p. 190). The house itself, liberated of kitchen, parlour and laundry, would function as a place for repose and a family life more concentrated on the family, rather than on the care of family bodies. These changes would emancipate women to specialize in the areas of their comparative advantage, *whether in house-service or in other industries*, facilitating greater social welfare.

Even though Gilman tended, in my view, to underestimate the human taste for custom-prepared food, she knew that the sort of institutional change she envisioned would be revolutionary:

> The change of woman's position from that of an unpaid domestic servant to that of a
> paid social one, involves such wide upheaval of social customs, such thwarting of

habits so long indulged that they have become race instincts, such shattering of old ideals, that it is no wonder we are slow to accept it. Nevertheless, into the world's thought is being forced by circumstances a growing doubt if our 'domestic economy' is economical, efficient, or conducive to social progress. (1929, p. 124)

It was probably (at least in part) to prepare American society for such major changes that Gilman wrote several of her novels. The realistic *What Diantha Did* (1909–10) depicted Diantha's construction of a firm successfully grow-ing to provide a considerable variety of house-service to a California community. It not only incorporates explicit economic analysis novel for its period, but seems almost to have been intended as a 'how-to'. *Moving the Mountain* (1913) and the famous *Herland* (1915/1979) portray two different Utopian societies in each of which women are an integral part of the labour force – in *Moving the Mountain* as integral as men. (The parthenogenic society of *Herland* contained no men but the western observers, including the narrator.)

If we are persuaded by Gilman's powerful arguments about the improved efficiency of a society with truly equal rights to market work and with much or most house-service industrialized, we are none the less left with a prob-lem. The two Utopian novels depict societies embodying these principles, but the transitions which led to them are not to be emulated. The revolution in social, market and household structure leading to *Moving the Mountain* was achieved in 20 years through mass conversion to a religion called 'Life'. The transition to *Herland*'s Utopian and uniformly female society came about when a community was isolated from the rest of the world, all males died of a sex-specific disease, and one woman turned out to have parthenogenic abili-ties. While *Diantha* presents the aspiring house-service entrepreneur with something of a development plan, food-delivery services and communities of kitchenless homes attempted in part because of Gilman's polemics failed as soon as food prices rose and the cost of market provision of meals increased somewhat (Hayden, 1979, 1981). Such industries were up against not only the taste for custom-produced food, but the infrastructure built into most homes, and so ably analysed by Gilman. (1903/1970).

Gilman's analysis remains challenging and inspiring. Her dreams remain unfulfilled.

MARY ANN DIMAND

Bibliography

Selected writings by Charlotte Perkins Gilman
(1892), 'The yellow wall-paper', *New England Magazine*, Vol. 5 (January): 647–59. Reprinted in Charlotte Perkins Gilman, *The Yellow Wallpaper and Other Writings*, New York: Bantam Books, 1989.

(1898), *Women and Economics: The Economic Factor Between Men and Women as a Factor in Social Evolution*, Boston: Small, Maynard. Reprinted with introduction by Carl N. Degler, New York: Harper & Row, 1966; Amhert, NY: Prometheus Books, 1994.

(1898), 'Economic basis of the Woman Question', *Woman's Journal*, 1 October. Reprinted in Aileen Kraditor (ed.), *Up from the Pedestal: Selected Writings in the History of American Feminism*, Chicago: Quadrangle Books, 1968.

(1903), *The Home: Its Work and Influence*, New York: McClure, Phillips. Reprinted New York: The New York Source Book Press, 1970.

(1909–17), *The Forerunner*, 7 volumes, New York: Charlton Company. Reprinted New York: The New York Source Book Press, 1970.

(1909–10), *What Diantha Did*, serialized in *The Forerunner*, Vol. 1.

(1910–11), *Our Androcentric Culture*, serialized in *The Forerunner*, Vol. 2. Reprinted New York: The New York Source Book Press, 1970.

(1913), *Moving the Mountain*, serialized in *The Forerunner*, Vol. 4.

(1915), *Herland*, serialized in *The Forerunner*, Vol. 6. Reprinted as *Herland: A Lost Feminist Utopian Novel*, ed. with introduction by Ann J. Lane, New York: Pantheon Books, 1979.

(1929), 'Feminism and social progress', in Baker Brownell (ed.), *Problems of Civilization*, Vol. 7 of *Man and His World*, New York: D. Van Nostrand Company.

(1935), *The Living of Charlotte Perkins Gilman: An Autobiography*. Reprinted New York: Arno Press, 1972; Madison, WI: University of Wisconsin Press, 1991.

Other sources and references

Dimand, Mary Ann (1995), 'The economics of Charlotte Perkins Gilman', in Mary Ann Dimand, Robert W. Dimand and Evelyn L. Forget (eds), *Women of Value: Feminist Essays on the History of Women in Economics*, Aldershot, UK, and Brookfield, VT: Edward Elgar.

Dimand, Robert W. (2000), 'Nineteenth century American feminist economics: from Caroline Dall to Charlotte Perkins Gilman', *American Economic Review (Papers and Proceedings)*, **90**(2).

Grapard, Ulla (1996), 'The trouble with women in economics: a postmodern perspective on Charlotte Perkins Gilman', in S. Cullenberg (ed.), *Postmodernism, Economics and Knowledge*, London and New York: Routledge.

Hayden, Dolores (1979), 'Charlotte Perkins Gilman and the kitchenless house', *Radical History Review*, No. 21 (Fall): 225–47.

Hayden, Dolores (1981), *The Grand Domestic Revolution: A History of Feminist Designs for American Homes, Neighborhoods, and Cities*, Cambridge, MA: MIT Press.

Hill, Caroline (1904), 'The economic value of the home', *Journal of Political Economy*, **12**: 408–19 (review article on Gilman 1903).

Hill, Mary A. (1980), *Charlotte Perkins Gilman: The Making of a Radical Feminist 1860–1896*, Philadelphia: Temple University Press.

Knight, Denise D. (ed.) (1994), *The Diaries of Charlotte Perkins Gilman*, 2 volumes, Charlottesville, VA, and London: University of Virginia Press.

Lane, Ann J. (1990), *To Herland and Beyond: The Life and Work of Charlotte Perkins Gilman*, New York: Pantheon Books.

New York Times (1935), 'Charlotte Perkins Gilman dies to avoid pain', Tuesday 20 August, 44:2.

O'Donnell, Margaret (1985), 'Charlotte Perkins Gilman's economic interpretation of the role of women at the turn of the century', *Social Science Quarterly*, **69**(1): 177–92.

O'Donnell, Margaret (1994), 'Early analysis of the economics of family structure: Charlotte Perkins Gilman's *Women and Economics*', *Review of Social Economy*, **52**(2): 86–95.

Sheth, F.A. and Robert E. Prasch (1996), 'Charlotte Perkins Gilman: reassessing her significance for feminism and social economics', *Review of Social Economy*, **54**(3): 323–35, with reply by Margaret O'Donnell: 337–40.

Sinclair, Andrew (1965), *The Emancipation of the American Woman*, New York: Harper & Row.

Fanny Ginor (b. 1911)

Fanny Dulberg, born in Otynja, Galicia, was two years old when her family removed from the then Danube monarchy to Stuttgart where she received a classical education at a secondary school. From summer 1930 onwards she studied economics and civil law at the Universities of Frankfurt, Heidelberg and Munich where she wanted to gain her Ph.D. with Otto von Zwiedineck-Südenhorst after finishing her diploma exam. When a group of uniformed Nazis under the leadership of Rudolf Hess marched into the great hall during one of Adolf Weber's lectures shortly after Hitler's appointment to Chancellor, Ginor, who meanwhile had become the chairwoman of the Zionist students' club, decided to continue her studies in Switzerland. There she was one of many émigré economists from Nazi Germany who did her Ph.D. with Edgar Salin at the University of Basel. Immediately after finishing her doctorial thesis on *Der Imperialismus im Lichte seiner Theorien* (*Imperialism in the Light of its Theories*) (1936) in summer 1934 Ginor emigrated to Palestine.

At first Ginor, who was deeply rooted in German culture and literature, suffered from the 'Crisis of Transition into another Cultural Civilization' which she later presented impressively (1997). She became acquainted with Hebrew culture and literature only slowly, and earned her living as a farm worker, bank clerk and book-keeper in a small factory between 1934 and 1943. After that she was a close collaborator of David Horowitz and Eliezer Kaplan in the Economics Department of the Jewish Agency where she studied the problems of transition from a war to a peace economy. After the decision of the United Nations in November 1947 to divide Palestine into a Jewish and an Arabic part, Ginor assisted Hoffien, the Director of the Anglo-Palestine Bank, in the preparation of a new currency for the State of Israel which was founded in May 1948. With the formation of the government of Ben Gurion many departments of the Jewish Agency were transformed into offices and ministries. Kaplan became the first Finance Minister of Israel and Horowitz Director-General in this ministry. It was then a natural development that Ginor – after a short period as a counsellor in the new Israeli embassy in Washington – worked as an economist in the Ministry of Finance from March 1949 until the end of 1953. Here she primarily had to deal with the great problems of inflation, shortage of foreign exchange, the rationing of consumption goods and the integration of the numerous immigrants which characterized those years. In particular she became a specialist in the calculation of the Israeli claims for reparation and restitution payments which were paid by Germany after the agreement of Luxembourg from September 1952. The analysis of the impact of these payments on the Israeli economy became one of her central fields of research.

When Horowitz was appointed the first Governor of the Bank of Israel in 1954 Ginor became his economic adviser. She stayed there until 1971, only interrupted by a period as an economic counsellor to the Permanent Mission of Israel to the United Nations in New York from 1962 to 1964. Ginor was repeatedly a member of the Israeli delegation at the meetings of international organizations, such as the United Nations General Assembly, the UNCTAD, UNESCO, the World Bank and the IMF. When Golda Meir was Foreign Minister in 1957, Ginor became Israeli representative in the Second Committee of the United Nations General Assembly in which economic and financial issues were in the foreground, in particular problems of developing countries with which Ginor now dealt intensively. So she prepared the report on *The Economy and Agriculture of Israel* (1959) for the Mediterranean development project of the Food and Agricultural Organization (FAO).

After entering the Bank of Israel Ginor started extensive university teaching and intensified her research work. From 1954–1959 she was a lecturer at the High School for Law and Economics in Tel Aviv. After 1955 she also lectured at the Faculty of Agriculture of the Hebrew University in Rehovot. When in 1959 the Department of Economics of the Hebrew University founded a Tel Aviv branch, Ginor became an associate lecturer until she left for New York in 1962. After her return to Israel she wrote the major study *Reparations and Their Impact on the Israeli Economy* (1965), together with J. Tishler, for the Bank of Israel. In early 1966 she resumed teaching at the University of Tel Aviv where meanwhile a Department of Economics had been established within the Faculty of Social Sciences. Abba Lerner, then Dean of the Faculty, hired Ginor as a senior lecturer and assigned her to the Department of Developing Countries. When Horowitz retired as the Governor at the end of 1971, Ginor, too, left the Bank of Israel and took over a full position at Tel-Aviv University where she was promoted to Associate Professor in 1974 and stayed until her retirement in 1978. Besides her own major research areas, development economics and the problems of the Israeli economy, she now focused her attention on social policy and issues of income distribution. Her studies culminated in the book *Socio-Economic Disparities in Israel* (1979), in which she analysed the socioeconomic differences between and within the Jewish and the Arabic part of the population, the impact of the participation of women on family incomes and the effects of the economic growth process on the development of income distribution since the 1920s.

The main problems of the Israeli economy were always at the centre of Ginor's research. In one of her earlier contributions she analysed comprehensively the economic effects of the import of some of the US agricultural surpluses on the Israeli economy (1963). She came to the conclusion that the main advantages for Israel consisted of the anti-inflationary effect and in particular of the saving of foreign currency reserves which could be used instead for the import of modern machinery for industry and agriculture.

Ginor's analyses of the economic consequences of the German reparations and restitution payments on the Israeli economy are of particular importance. In their main study Ginor and Tishler (1965) showed that these payments, which were made from the end of 1953, had been a substantial aid in a critical phase, an insight which for quite some time was limited to a Hebrew circle of readers (see Ginor, 1990, p. 202). Only after her retirement from the Bank of Israel could Ginor publish an updated English summary (1972–73). She made it clear that between 1953 and 1971 the reparations, which were paid mainly as investment goods transferred in accordance with an agreed schedule based on Israel's needs and Germany's available products, and the personal restitution payments as a source of foreign currency, on average covered 27 per cent of the annual Israeli trade deficit. Ginor calculated that directly and indirectly about 80 per cent of the German payments were used for investment purposes. Thus their contribution to the process of capital formation and economic growth was considerable. Ginor computed 12 per cent of the additional capital and 6 per cent of the additional GNP for the period 1953–66 (see Ginor, 1972–73, p. 40). In particular in the first phase after the mass immigration in the early 1950s, when Israel suffered from a severe lack of capital and foreign currency reserves, the German payments contributed to overcome the balance-of-payments constraint on the growth process of the Israeli economy. On the same issue Chenery and Bruno (1962) calculated that, with the inclusion of the personal restitution payments made in money to victims of the Holocaust which promoted the process of private savings formation, the contribution of the reparation receipts amounted to 36 per cent of the additional GNP in the first three-year period 1954–57.

In two further papers Ginor analysed the impact of capital imports on the process of growth and structural change in developing countries (1969) and the structural dynamics in the Israeli economy (1970). She emphasized that capital imports have two main functions: to speed up investment activity by supplementing internal savings and to enable the import of more investment goods to accelerate the process of economic growth by the financing of trade deficits. Nevertheless, the danger exists that the import surplus economy becomes structurally dependent on capital imports. Ginor's studies elucidate the importance of an enlightened long-run economic policy which promotes domestic savings and structural change to increase the share of tradable goods and services in GNP so that it can overcome this danger via export diversification and import substitution and thus achieve a reduction of trade deficits.

HARALD HAGEMANN

Bibliography

Selected writings by Fanny Ginor

(1936), *Der Imperialismus im Lichte seiner Theorien*, Basel: Philographischer Verlag.

(1959), *The Economy and Agriculture of Israel*, prepared for FAO in participation with the Ministry of Agriculture, Jerusalem.

(1963), *Uses of US Agricultural Surpluses – Their Economic Effect in Israel*, Jerusalem: Bank of Israel.

(1965), *Reparations and Their Impact on the Israeli Economy* (in Hebrew, with J. Tishler), Tel Aviv: Bank of Israel.

(1969), 'The impact of capital imports on the structure of developing countries', *Kyklos*, **22**, 104–23,

(1970), 'Structural changes in a developing economy: the case of Israel', *Weltwirtschaftliches Archiv*, **105**, 188–218.

(1972–73), 'The Impact of German reparations and restitution payments on the Israeli economy', *The Wiener Library Bulletin*, **26**, 38–45.

(1979), *Socio-Economic Disparities in Israel*, Tel Aviv and Rutgers University, NJ: Transaction Books.

(1990), 'Ein Leben im Schatten der Geschehnisse' (A life in the shadow of events), autobiography, unpublished manuscript, Tel Aviv.

(1997), 'Krise des Übergangs in einen anderen Kulturkreis', in H. Hagemann (ed.), *Zur deutschsprachigen wirtschaftswissenschaftlichen Emigration nach 1933*, Marburg: Metropolis, pp. 437–58.

Other sources and references

Chenery, H.B. and M. Bruno, (1962), 'Development alternatives in an open economy: the case of Israel', *Economic Journal*, **72**, 79–103.

Kirsten Gloerfelt-Tarp (1889–1977)

The Danish politician and economist Kirsten Gloerfelt-Tarp was born in 1889. She obtained a master's degree in economics from the University of Copenhagen in 1915. From 1916 to 1958 she worked in the Danish Factories Inspectorate: from 1921 to 1938 as a factory inspector, and from 1938 as head of section. It was typical of her that she genuinely wanted to discover what life was like for female industrial workers, so that even though she came from an upper-class family and had a university education, she took a job herself in a sheet-metal factory for a time.

She participated as an expert in the Danish government delegation to the ILO conferences in Geneva (1927–38) and again after the war. She was opposed to any special protection for female workers (for example a ban on women working night shifts) and in favour of publicly financed, not company-financed, maternity leave. She feared that special protection and rights for female workers would make it impossible for them to get the best jobs.

She was active in the feminist movement, and from 1925 she was a member of the Danish Women's National Council, being its chair from 1931 to

1945. In this role she fought for women's position in the labour market during the mass unemployment of the 1930s, a period when some people wanted to reserve the few jobs available for male workers. The Women's Council and Kirsten Gloerfelt-Tarp were active in humanitarian activities for Spanish children during the Civil War, for Jewish children in Central Europe in 1939, for Finnish children during the Finnish–Russian War and in general social work in Denmark during World War II.

In Denmark, women got the right to vote in local government elections in 1908, and in national parliamentary elections in 1915. For many years the result was a disappointment for women – out of 140–49 Members of Parliament, only 3–4 of those elected were women. But in 1945 this number doubled to 8, and one of the new members was Kirsten Gloerfelt-Tarp. (In 1998, 67 out of 179 members of the Danish parliament were female.) She was elected to the small, but influential, centre Social–Liberal Party 'Det radikale venstre'. She was a Member of Parliament until 1960. In 1945 she was the only woman representing her party in Parliament, and from the start she was active on committees and commissions working on social and women's issues. In 1957–60 she was vice-president of the Social–Liberal Party's group in Parliament. Gloerfelt-Tarp's example inspired a number of women in the intellectual circles in Denmark: Else Zeuthen, 1897–1975 (teacher of English and married to the leading Danish economist of this century, Frederik Zeuthen) and Else Merete Ross, 1903–76 (teacher of German and married to the leading Danish jurist of the century, Alf Ross) were both Members of Parliament for the Social–Liberal Party, as was the economist Grethe Philip.

Kirsten Gloerfelt-Tarp wrote a number of articles in journals and newspapers, and in 1937 she edited and co-authored a book entitled *Kvinden i Samfundet*, published in an English version entitled *Women in the Community* in 1939. In 1943 she was co-author of a book about labour protection, and in 1965 of a book published on the occasion of the 50th anniversary of female enfranchisement.

In 1927 she married her former fellow student of economics, Bror Gloerfelt-Tarp, who died in 1958. She herself died in 1977.

NIELS KÆRGÅRD

Selma Evelyn Fine Goldsmith (1912–62)

Selma Goldsmith was born on 17 January 1912 in New York City, the only child of Abraham Fine and Lena Schwartzman. She graduated from Morris High School in New York City. She earned a BA from Cornell University in 1932 and attended Harvard Graduate School, earning a Ph.D. from Radcliffe in 1937. Her dissertation dealt with business cycles in England in the seventeenth and eighteenth centuries. She spent most of her career in the US federal government, beginning with stints at the Department of Agriculture and the National Resources Planning Board. She then served as chief of the Income Section of the National Income Division of the Department of Commerce and subsequently as chief of the Income and Statistics branch of the Bureau of the Census of the Department of Commerce.

Goldsmith specialized in the analysis of changes in the distribution of income in the USA. Her earliest published work on income distribution is an article with Enid Baird (1939) evaluating the use of income tax data in the National Resources Committee estimate of the size distribution of income. Thereafter she wrote numerous articles on the changing size distribution of income and in 1956 received a Rockefeller public service award to study the methodology used in developing estimates on the size distribution of income in Great Britain and Canada. She was the only woman among the group of 16 recipients. In addition, she was honoured with the Distinguished Service Award by the Department of Commerce in 1955.

According to Joseph Pechman, 'The work on income distribution after World War II was carried forward mainly by Selma Goldsmith and her associates Maurice Leibenberg and Hyman Kaitz in the Department of Commerce' (Pechman, 1990, p. 416). In a series of studies Goldsmith and her associates examined the changing distribution of income in the USA and attempted to understand the nature and causes of these changes. What is characteristic of these studies is Goldsmith's attempt to generate series comparable to those of other investigators, her emphasis on analysing and explaining changes in definition and coverage over time, and the careful explanation of the nature of income distribution changes.

During the late 1930s Goldsmith was on the consumption research staff of the National Resources Committee and thus worked on the NRCs report on *Consumer Incomes in the United States: Their Distribution in 1935–36*. In an article with Enid Baird (1939), she explained the adjustments made to income tax data before they could be used for analysis of income distribution. First, the definition of net income employed in sampling for the study of consumer purchases differed from the concept of net income applicable under the 1934 Revenue Act. The value of owner-occupied housing and the value of home-produced goods were excluded from taxable income, capital gains and losses were treated differently in the two income concepts, and adjustments had to be made to the taxable income for various deductions and tax-exempt earnings. In addition, tax returns had to be reclassified since the income distribution data were restricted to families and single individuals. Finally, the data were adjusted for the 1935–36 fiscal year (instead of the 1935 calendar year) and for non-reporting and understatement of income. These adjustments made possible a clearer understanding of the nature of income distribution in the upper tail, a group under-represented among the sample collected in the Study of Consumer Purchases.

In 'Statistical information on the distribution of income by size in the United States' (1950), Goldsmith discussed the results obtained in various measures of the size distribution of income. She compared the results obtained from surveys for 1935–36, 1941, each of the years 1944–48, and for 1945–48 by various government agencies. Before analysing the changing distribution of income, she reconciled the differences in definition and coverage used by the different surveys. The reduction in income inequality between 1935–36 and 1944 was described using Lorenz curves, quintile distributions, and Pareto coefficients and also examined in terms of its sources. She concluded that the movement towards greater equality occurred due to the rising shares of the lowest 40 per cent and the falling shares of the highest 20 per cent and the greater rate of increase in average income of the bottom quintiles. This trend towards greater equality occurred because of increasing employment and the resulting larger share of total income comprising wages and salaries, and the declining importance of interest and dividends. She argued that the movement towards greater equality would be even stronger when account was taken of the change in family size over this period.

In 'Appraisal of basic data available for constructing income size distributions' (1951), Goldsmith discussed 'the problems encountered in reconciling and integrating the various types of data used in constructing income size distributions' (p. 267). After describing the nature and coverage of sample field surveys, individual income tax returns, reports on workers filed by employers with the Bureau of Old Age Survivors' Insurance, estimates of income by the National Income Division of the Department of Commerce, and the estimates of population prepared by the Bureau of the Census, Goldsmith outlined the adjustments made to derive consistent income distribution data. She derived an estimate of aggregate consumer money income and

> After a series of adjustments made with admirable precision and appalling comprehensiveness, these data are then compared with those derived from the Department of Commerce estimates of personal income. The disparities are substantial, and carry serious implications for the use of size distributions based on unadjusted survey data, as so many in this field are. (Lebergott, 1951, p. 373)

In studies reported in a series of articles, Goldsmith analysed the changes in the US income distribution since the 1930s. In 'Changes in the size distribution of income' (1957), 'Size distribution of personal income' (1958), and, with George Jaszi, Hyman Kaitz and Maurice Leibenberg, 'Size distribution of income since the mid-thirties' (1954), Goldsmith described the nature of changes in income distribution, the causes of these changes, and the extent to which the figures employed and results obtained were influenced by the concepts and definitions employed. Between 1929 and 1955 (Goldsmith, 1957, pp. 504–5) and in the decade 1947–57 (Goldsmith, 1958, p. 11), average family income increased steadily. In addition, there was a marked decline in the proportion of income accruing to the top income group, most of the change occurring by the end of World War II (Goldsmith, 1957, pp. 504–5).

This change in income appears in both the population income distribution series developed by Simon Kuznets and the family income series developed by Goldsmith and her colleagues. The decline in the share of the top 5 per cent of the income distribution was offset by gains in the shares of all the other income groups. This appearance of reduced income inequality after 1929 and especially after 1939 is supported by the dramatic increase in the proportion of personal income consisting of wages, salaries and transfer payments, and the marked reduction in the share of investment income. This was reinforced by decreasing dispersion in wage and salary incomes, a narrowing of income differences between the farm and non-farm population, and a reduction in regional income inequality.

Goldsmith et al. (1954) employed Lorenz curves and concentration ratios to track changes in income distribution between the mid-1930s and 1950, being careful to describe the data difficulties associated with making these comparisons due to changes in enumeration procedures between the pre- and post-war surveys, their coverage and the concepts employed.

Goldsmith did not take findings of changing income distribution at their face value. She expended considerable effort on scrutinizing the data and evaluating the results in light of the limitations of the income statistics. These shortcomings included conceptual problems (income for a single year is not a satisfactory measure of income inequality; when income shares of a given quintile are compared in two periods the group of families being compared has changed) and statistical problems (separate cost-of-living indexes were not available for each income group, data for the number and composition of families at the lower end of the income scale were particularly inadequate). Finally, she discussed the imperfections of the income measures employed in determining relative income shares – the under-recording of deferred income and income in kind, the effect of changes in the tax code on the way income is reported, under-reporting, the exclusion of capital gains, and so on – and estimated the effect of better measurement of these items on the reported decline in income inequality.

'Size distribution of income since the mid-thirties' also examined the effect of the federal income tax on income distribution. The authors concluded that progressivity declined between 1941 and 1950 in the sense that proportionately larger percentage increases in tax rates were experienced by the lower income groups. However, because of the combination of changes in income distribution and in the tax structure, the income tax reduced income inequality somewhat more in 1950 than in 1941.

'The relation of Census income distribution statistics to other income data' (1958) provided comparisons of the results obtained in census income data with those obtained from the income series developed by the Office of Business Economics as well as other sources. It summarized major differences in income coverage between surveys and among major types of income. Most importantly, Goldsmith provided for the first time complete distributions covering the period from 1929 to 1953 on a comparable basis and analysed their results in terms of the short-term and long-term changes in income distribution.

In 'Low-income families and measures of income inequality' (1962), Goldsmith focused on the number, composition and structure of low-income families, and investigated the implications of her findings for common assessments about changes in US income inequality. On the basis of findings on the changing characteristics of low-income families, Goldsmith concluded that the figures may have understated the share of low-income families and recommended, 'In our future work in this field, we should plan to incorporate in our measures of income shares adjustment factors to allow for these and other changes in family composition' (Goldsmith, 1962, p. 19).

In addition to the works described above, Goldsmith and George Jaszi prepared a study of income distribution that was published as a supplement to the *Survey of Current Business*. In addition, she assisted Lawrence H. Seltzer in the preparation of *The Nature and Tax Treatment of Capital Gains and Losses*.

> Mrs. Goldsmith not only assembled, coordinated, and refined the figures on capital gains and losses from *Statistics on Income* but also, with great skill and resourcefulness, filled gaps and revealed many significant relations or their absence. Nearly all the statistical appendix is her work. She contributed also a preliminary draft of a substantial segment of Chapter 5, in which the figures are reviewed, as well as related materials used in several other chapters. (Lawrence Seltzer, 1951, p. vii)

Goldsmith was the co-author of the *Standard Study on Capital Gains and Losses*, published by the NBER in 1951, and was engaged in bringing it up to date at the time of her death. Her career was tragically cut short when she died of cancer in Washington on 15 April 1962. She was 50 years old and was survived by her husband, Raymond W. Goldsmith (died 1988), then Professor of Economics at Yale University, and three children, Jane, Donald and Paul.

VIBHA KAPURIA-FOREMAN

Bibliography

Selected writings by Selma Evelyn Fine Goldsmith

(1939), 'The use of income tax data in the National Resources Committee estimate of the distribution of income by size' (with Enid Baird), *Studies in Income and Wealth*, vol. 3, New York: NBER.

(1950), 'Statistical information on the distribution of income by size', *American Economic Review*, **40** (May), pp. 321–41.

(1951), 'Appraisal of basic data available for constructing income size distributions', *Studies in Income and Wealth*, vol. 13, New York: NBER.

(1953), 'Income distribution in the United States by size, 1944–50' (with George Jaszi), supplement to the *Survey of Current Business*, Washington, DC: US GPO.

(1954), 'Size distribution of income since the mid-thirties' (with George Jaszi, Hyman Kaitz and Maurice Liebenberg), *The Review of Economics and Statistics*, **34** (February), 1–32.

(1954), 'Inequality of income distribution – discussion', *American Economic Review*, **44**, May, 271–3.

(1956), 'Reply to Dr. Clyman', *The Review of Economics and Statistics*, **38** (May), 227.

(1957), 'Changes in the size distribution of income', *American Economic Review*, **47**, May, 504–18.

(1958), 'Size distribution of personal income', *Survey of Current Business*, April, 10–19.

(1958), 'The relation of Census income distribution statistics to other income data', *An Appraisal of the 1950 Census Income Data, Studies in Income and Wealth*, vol. 23, Princeton: Princeton University Press.

(1960), 'Size distribution of income and wealth in the United States' in Helmut Arndt (ed.), *Die Konzentration in der Wirtschaft*.

(1962), 'Low-income families and measures of income inequality', *Review of Social Economy*, **20** (March), pp. 1–19.

Other sources and references

Lebergott, Stanley (1951), 'Comment [on Goldsmith 1951]', *Studies in Income and Wealth*, vol. 13, New York: National Bureau of Economic Research, pp. 373–7.

Pechman, Joseph (1990), 'Comment', in Ernst R. Berndt and Jack E. Triplett (eds), *Fifty Years of Economic Measurement, Studies in Income and Wealth*, vol. 54, Chicago: University of Chicago Press.

Seltzer, Lawrence H. (1951), *The Nature and Tax Treatment of Capital Gains and Losses*, New York: NBER.

Dorothy C. Goodwin (b. 1914)

Dorothy C. Goodwin's multifaceted professional life is composed of three phases: government 'quasi' economist, academic economist and policy economist. While Goodwin attributes the shape of her career to chance, luck, serendipity and timing, she must be credited for her bold embrace of unexpected opportunities. One thread that runs throughout Goodwin's career is a concern with land use and agriculture.

Born into a privileged and well-known Hartford, Connecticut family, Dorothy Goodwin attended Oxford School in Hartford and Milton Academy in Milton, Massachusetts. She graduated *magna cum laude* from Smith

College in 1937 with an undergraduate degree in sociology. While at Smith, she took four courses in economics and became interested in the field.

Goodwin began her career by working for the federal government. During World War II, she was sent to India by the Board of Economic Warfare and its successor agencies. The task of her group was to collect intelligence on vulnerabilities in the Japanese economy and on strategic minerals required for the war effort. After the war, Dorothy Goodwin headed off to Japan as a bureaucrat in General Macarthur's Occupation of Japan staff. There she worked on land-reform issues during the Allied Occupation. She describes the occupation as basically benign, remarking that the intent of the USA was not to have a permanent occupation but rather to work closely with the Japanese to eradicate feudal land-owning practices and to ensure the renewal of Japan. These experiences as a government economist prepared the young Ms Goodwin to reflect on and to address issues with impact beyond a local or narrow sphere.

When her work in Japan had ended, Goodwin returned to Hartford, Connecticut in 1952. Her mother had just died and her father was alone, and her filial piety led her to stay in Connecticut. She took over the management of the household while her father was recovering from a stroke. Never one to waste time, Goodwin enrolled in the doctoral programme in agricultural economics at the University of Connecticut in Storrs, Connecticut. She was the only woman among the first group of three graduate students in the newly instituted Ph.D. programme in agricultural economics. Strongly endowed with academic talent, Dorothy Goodwin received her Ph.D. in 1957.

Dorothy Goodwin's stint as an academic economist began in the autumn of 1957 with her appointment as Assistant Professor in the Department of Economics at the University of Connecticut in Storrs. She notes that this opportunity arose when a professor resigned at the last minute. Goodwin taught the whole gamut of introductory and intermediate courses in microeconomics, macroeconomics, applied price theory, money and banking. She also taught a graduate course in state and local finance. After seven years of teaching she was called into administration by Dr Homer Babbidge, then President of the University of Connecticut, who offered her a position as Director of Institutional Research. Goodwin accepted. She considers herself a teacher of undergraduate economics and enjoyed the contact with students. Yet, on the basis of previous administrative experience she recognized that she would enjoy decision-making with a broader, university-wide scope. Goodwin received tenure – her case backed by her extensive public service.

When asked to comment on the methodology of economics, Goodwin declared, 'It is an elegant fairy tale.' In explanation, she points out that the initiative in economics during her lifetime has been deductive; and, while she likes the elegant logic inherent in the equilibrium models, she argues that they are unrealistic and have very little relevance to the real world. Goodwin believes everyone should have some training in economics, but she would discourage students from going directly into graduate school for economics without having had some real-world experience. Her advice is that one should get the widest variety of experience one can.

After holding a number of unpaid positions in local government in Mansfield, in 1975 Dorothy Goodwin was elected to the first of her five terms as a democratic state representative from Storrs and Mansfield. In her role for at least three terms as House Chair of the Legislature's Joint Education Committee, she made productive use of her academic interests in state and local finance, in order to craft legislation aimed at the equalization of educational opportunity and at tax equity. She took on the issue of local schools being funded by property tax, and led the highly lauded effort on the school equalization formula through the House. A frequent participant in debates in the House, she gave 76 speeches in one three-month period. Goodwin was also noted for her role in the reorganization of public higher education in the state of Connecticut. She has been recognized as a Regent Emeritus of the Board of Trustees of the University of Hartford, and has served on the Board of Trustees, since the 1950s, of the Hartford College for Women. Dorothy Goodwin is the recipient of a steady stream of accolades. Notable among them are the Wilbur Cross Award of the Connecticut Humanities Council for her career teaching, scholarship and service, and her induction into the Connecticut Women's Hall of Fame.

Dorothy Goodwin's contribution as a woman economist is characterized by a subtle resistance to the received career path of an economist. Certainly her teaching, service, and work in public policy have not been driven by narrow cost–benefit analyses. Her decisions and activities reflect a fine attunement to real-world problems and reveal a steady, flexible responsiveness to the needs and opportunities she has encountered within her several communities. Goodwin's career as an economist is that of a humane public scholar and an indefatigable, cooperative activist in the cause of public education. As such it illustrates an unspoken but clearly substantiated commitment to a life's work determined by factors beyond the pleasure–pain calculus.

SHYAMALA RAMAN

Sources

Interview with Dorothy C. Goodwin, 24 June 1999.
http://www.cwhf.org/browse/inductees/goodwin.htm

Margaret Gordon (1910–94)[1]

Margaret Gordon (née Shaughnessy) was born on 4 September 1910 in Wabasha, Minnesota. Her father, a physician, and mother had both been raised in Ashland, Massachusetts, and the family moved back to the Boston area, to Framingham, in 1919. She received her BA (in economics) from Bryn Mawr in 1931, her MA in 1933, and her Ph.D. in 1935, both from Radcliffe College. She married Robert Aaron Gordon, then an instructor at Harvard and a Harvard economics Ph.D., in 1936, and had two sons – Robert, born in 1940, and David, born in 1944, both of whom went on to receive degrees from Harvard and become academic economists. She died on 28 June 1994, at the age of 83.

Gordon's early academic interests lay in the area of international trade. While at Harvard, she was influenced by Joseph Schumpeter and Gottfried Haberler. Her doctoral dissertation, entitled 'A pre-war cycle in British trade, 1885–1896', her first published paper (1940), first major paper (1946), and first book (1941) were all on trade topics.

However, rather than rising through the academic ranks in the field of international trade, Gordon found her career in economics to be hindered by two forces: the general unavailability of academic positions in the 1930s; and her sex. This limitation on her aspirations had not necessarily been apparent during her college and postgraduate years; Bryn Mawr at the time was considered the major college for producing future female doctoral degree holders. And while she received a Radcliffe degree in name, it represented a Harvard education, identical in content to that received by the men. But after finishing her degree, no tenure-track positions were forthcoming. She was an instructor in economics at Wellesley College from 1935 to 1936, and then spent three years as a research fellow of Radcliffe College.

In 1938 her husband Robert was offered a tenure-track position at the University of California at Berkeley. The University did not offer Margaret any employment, and even if an offer had been forthcoming from the Economics Department, the anti-nepotism rule in force at the time would have prevented her from taking the position. Nevertheless, the couple were glad that Robert had received this offer, and they moved to Berkeley and remained there for the rest of their lives, except for a stint in Washington, DC during World War II.

Other than a short affiliation with the Office of Price Administration (1942–43), Margaret did not have a formal position from 1939 until 1950, although she did receive financial assistance for her research in international trade from the Trade Regulation Project at the University of California. She then began a long affiliation with the Institute of Industrial Relations at the University of California at Berkeley. She was an assistant research economist from 1950 to 1954, and then served as Associate Director of the Institute from 1954 to 1969. She was a member of the editorial board (and managing editor for the first two years) of *Industrial Relations*, the Institute's scholarly journal, from its foundation in 1961 through 1982 (and continued through 1987 as an editorial advisory board member). During this time she wrote and edited several books related to projects sponsored by the Institute alone or in conjunction with the Ford Foundation. These include *Employment Expansion and Population Growth: The California Experience: 1900–1950* (1954); *The Economics of Welfare Policies* (1963), which contains some international comparisons, but mainly considers social security and unemployment insurance in the USA; and *Occupational Disability and Public Policy* (1963), which she co-edited as well as contributing two chapters on the foreign experience with industrial injuries insurance, one for the period before and one for the period after World War II.

During the latter part of this affiliation Margaret also served as member of several federal committees: The Department of Labor's Advisory Committee on Unemployment Insurance (1962–64); the Social Security Administration's Advisory Committee on Research Development (1965–68); and the President's Task Force on Older Americans (1967–68). She was also a member of President Johnson's Commission on Income Maintenance Programs (also known as the Heineman Commission) (1968–69), which generated the well-known Heineman Report: *Poverty Amid Plenty: The American Paradox* (1969).

Gordon then became Associate Director of the Carnegie Commission on Higher Education, and then Associate Director of its successor, the Carnegie Council on Policy Studies in Higher Education. During her affiliation with these two organizations from 1969 through 1979, she bore a large portion of the administrative burden, a not inconsiderable one: the two organizations combined sponsored 120 studies and generated 40 reports, of which she drafted over a dozen. The most influential of these reports was *Higher Education and the Nation's Health* (1970), which was converted almost intact into the Health Manpower Act of 1972 (policies for subsidizing medical and dental education). The range of topics covered by these reports is considerable, including policies for community colleges, classification of institutions of higher education, affirmative action in higher education, and general student financial aid issues. Gordon also served as general editor of a series of monographs on youth education and employment in other countries. The series culminated in her book, *Youth Education and Unemployment Problems: An International Perspective* (1979), which sums up the results from the country-specific studies.

While Margaret's husband was supportive of her work, they did not routinely work together; however, there were important exceptions. When Margaret went to Europe to do research for her monograph *Retraining and Labor Market Adjustment in Western Europe* (1965), she travelled around interviewing sources in tandem with Robert, who was studying full employment policies in Western Europe. She also edited two proceedings volumes for conferences in which they both participated, *Poverty in America* (1965) and *Prosperity and Unemployment* (1966); he is co-editor of the second.

Although Margaret's writings are mainstream in tone and content, she was well aware of the economics discipline's slighting of issues concerning women's labour force participation. In her concluding chapter in *Higher Education and the Labor Market* (1974), she writes: 'As the only female contributor, I mildly chastised the authors, when we met for a discussion of our first drafts in the fall of 1971, on their exclusive preoccupation with data relating to men.' Several of her works are concerned with women and the labour market, including the Carnegie Commission report *Opportunities for Women in Higher Education: Their Current Participation, Prospects for the Future and Recommendations for Action* (1973), 'Women and work: priorities for the future' (1979), and (with Clark Kerr) 'University behavior and policies: where are the women and why?' (1978).

Ironically, given that her initial interest in labour economics came about because of the availability of a job in this area, Gordon's academic reputation rests on her contributions to labour economics and public finance issues rather than on her work in international trade. However, all Gordon's works display great attention to detail and an interest in international comparisons of such details. Her final book, *Social Security Policies in Industrial Countries: A Comparative Analysis* (1988), is a particularly masterful compilation of information about social security programmes, which she defines broadly to include pension, health benefit, unemployment, manpower, child allowance, family policy, and public assistance programmes. It includes details for 28 countries, discussing the programmes' major features, including scope and adequacy of benefits and structure of financing provisions.

While Gordon did not achieve the conventional measure of academic success of a tenured professorship, she none the less had a scholarly career that included a substantial share of public notice and influence. But Gordon's life is also illuminating because of the panoply of other outlets she found for her substantial intellectual energies. Clark Kerr, her colleague of many years at the Institute and the Carnegie Council, paraphrased the *Iliad* to describe her in his remarks at the 1987 Benjamin Ide Wheeler Award Luncheon in her honour: 'she has been one of those rare people "to be both a speaker of words and a doer of deeds"'.

The Gordons were active campaigners for racial justice and Margaret was one of the organizers (in 1953) of Berkeley's chapter of the National Association for the Advancement of Colored People (NAACP). She was also very active in the League of Women Voters and in Democratic Party activities, including serving as co-chair from 1948 to 1950 of the Alameda County Democratic Central Committee.

Margaret was also a force in Berkeley city politics, serving as an appointed member of the city's personnel board from 1961 to 1965, and as an elected member of the city council from 1965 to 1969. She wrote a detailed essay on her experiences in Berkeley city politics during the tumultuous 1960s: 'From Liberal Control to Radical Challenge' (1978). The Gordons were early members of the Berkeley Coop, a pathbreaking consumer purchasing cooperative, and Margaret served as its president from 1982 to 1985 (as had her husband three decades earlier). She also served on the board of Stiles Hall, the University's community service centre for placing student volunteers in local service positions, for three years during the 1980s. The cap to her civic career was receiving the 1987 Benjamin Ide Wheeler Service Medal, awarded biannually to 'Berkeley's most useful citizen'. Award recipients had to have distinguished themselves either in the City of Berkeley or on the Berkeley Campus; very few distinguished themselves in both arenas, but Margaret Gordon was counted among those few.

While one might wonder if Gordon's energies would have been diverted into so many directions away from purely academic pursuits had she received more formal encouragement in her early career, it is clear that she none the less carried out a well-lived life, notable for its balance as well as for its depth.

JOYCE P. JACOBSEN

Note

1. The author gratefully acknowledges the assistance provided by Robert and David Gordon.

Bibliography

Selected writings by Margaret Gordon

(1940), 'Japan's balance of international payments, 1903–31', in Elizabeth B. Schumpeter (ed.), *The Industrialization of Japan and Manchukuo*, New York: Macmillan, pp. 865–925.

(1941), *Barriers to World Trade: A Study of Recent Commercial Policy*, New York: Macmillan.

(1946), 'International aspects of American agricultural policy', *American Economic Review*, **36**(4), part 1, September, 596–612.

(1954), *Employment Expansion and Population Growth: The California Experience: 1900–1950*, Berkeley: University of California Press.

(1963), *The Economics of Welfare Policies*, New York: Columbia University Press.

(1963), *Occupational Disability and Public Policy* (edited with Earl F. Cheit), New York: John Wiley & Sons.

(1965), *Retraining and Labor Market Adjustment in Western Europe*, Washington, DC: U.S. Government Printing Office.

(1965) (ed.), *Poverty in America*, San Francisco: Chandler Publishing.

(1966), *Prosperity and Unemployment* (edited with R.A. Gordon), New York: John Wiley & Sons.

(1974) (ed.), *Higher Education and the Labor Market*, New York: McGraw-Hill.

(1978), 'From liberal control to radical challenge', in Harriet Nathan and Stanley Scott (eds), *Experiment and Change in Berkeley: Essays on City Politics 1950–1975*, Institute of Governmental Studies, University of California, Berkeley, pp. 269–316.

(1978), 'University behavior and policies: where are the women and why?' (with Clark Kerr), in Helen S. Astin and Werner Z. Hirsch (eds), *The Higher Education of Women: Essays in Honor of Rosemary Park*, New York: Holt, Rinehart & Winston, pp. 113–32.

(1979), 'Women and work: priorities for the future', in Clark Kerr and Jerome M. Rosow, (eds), *Work in America: The Decade Ahead*, New York: Van Nostrand Reinhold, pp.111–37.

(1979), *Youth Education and Unemployment Problems: An International Perspective* (with Martin Trow), Berkeley: Carnegie Council on Policy Studies in Higher Education.

(1988), *Social Security Policies in Industrial Countries: A Comparative Analysis*, Cambridge: Cambridge University Press.

Other sources and references

Berkeley Historical Society (1984), transcription of interview of Margaret Gordon by Therese Pipe, for the Consumers' Cooperative of Berkeley Oral History Collection, Berkeley Oral History Project.

Marina Goudi (1914–86)

Marina Goudi was born in Athens in 1914. After completing her primary education she entered the Law School of the University of Athens and took her first degree in politics and economics in 1939. She then proceeded to take the degree in law in 1940.

Her graduation coincided with the outbreak of World War II and the occupation of Greece by the Axis powers. After the liberation of Greece, Goudi entered the central bank of the country, the Bank of Greece, at first as an employee paid on an hourly basis. She quickly proceeded to occupy positions of responsibility. She was in charge of the bureau of the Deputy Prime Minister and Governor of the Bank of Greece, K. Varvaressos, in 1945. In 1955 she was promoted to the position of consultant to the new Governor of the Bank, Professor X. Zolotas, a position that she kept until her retirement.

Her duties at the Bank of Greece didn't prevent her from pursuing her academic endeavours. From 1946 until 1967 she was editor of the journal *Epitheoressis Politikon ke Economikon Epistimon (Review of Political and Economic Sciences)*. In 1947 she gained her Ph.D. from the University of Athens. From early 1948 to mid-1949 Goudi went on a leave of absence to the USA. She took a master's degree at Harvard under the supervision of A. Hansen. She also visited the University of Chicago.

In 1954 she submitted a research monograph (*ifigessia*) at the University of Athens, the first woman to do so in Greece. From the academic year 1959–60 onwards she started teaching at the Department of Economics of the University of Athens on a permanent basis. In December 1970 she was elected full

Professor for Political Economy and she continued to be an inspiring teacher to new generations of students until her retirement in 1981. She passed away in 1986. She didn't marry and didn't have any children.

Goudi was not a prolific writer; her publications nevertheless were of high quality. She worked on monetary theory and policy and on questions of macroeconomic management. As an economist close to Professor Zolotas she must be credited with sound advice that kept the inflation rate as low as 2 per cent per year between 1955 and 1970, when the rate of growth of GNP was 6.2 per cent per year for the same period. She was not, however, a monetarist and allowed psychological and behavioural explanations into her analysis of inflation.

It must be stressed that for long periods of time, especially between the years 1966 and 1980, Goudi taught a wide range of courses in most subfields of economics at the University of Athens, a fact that partly explains her low publication record.

MICHALIS PSALIDOPOULOS

Bibliography

Selected writings by Marina Goudi
(1946), 'Keynes' General Theory as an explanation of the economic cycle', *Epitheorissis Politikon ke Oikonomikon Epistimon (Review of Political and Economic Sciences)*, Vol. 1: 205–23 (in Greek).
(1947), 'Indifference curve analysis according to J.R. Hicks', *Epitheorissis Politikon ke Oikonomikon Epistimon*, vol. 2: 297–333 (in Greek).
(1950), *Observations on the Problem of Exports after the Readjustment [of the Exchange Rate]*, Athens (in Greek).
(1953), *The Readjustment of the Currency*, Athens (in Greek).
(1967), *On Money*, Athens: Sakkoulas (in Greek).

Marjorie Grice-Hutchinson (b. 1909)

Marjorie Grice-Hutchinson was born at Eastbourne, England on 26 May, 1909, the daughter of a London solicitor, George William Grice-Hutchinson and his wife, Edith Louise. Her parents enjoyed travelling, and by the time she was 16 Marjorie had visited France, Switzerland, Italy, the Scandinavian countries and the USA, sometimes spending long periods in each. She was educated by a series of governesses who were chosen for their knowledge of languages and their interest in music, art and history. She thus had an incomplete education which paid little attention to science, but even as a child she was an avid reader in English, French and Spanish, to which she later added German and Latin.

In 1924 Mr Grice-Hutchinson's legal work took him to Madrid, and a few years later he bought the small country estate of San Julian, near Málaga, where he continued to reside after his retirement. Thereafter Marjorie's life was divided between San Julian, London and (since she had become a good cross-country skier) Switzerland. She formed a wish to improve her somewhat unorthodox education, and eventually studied for an honours degree in Spanish at London University.

From July 1936 to March 1939 the peaceful life of San Julian was disrupted by the Spanish Civil War, in which George William Grice-Hutchinson played a distinguished part by rescuing some sixty Spanish people who were in danger and taking them to Gibraltar in his small yacht, the *Honey-bee*. He also took an active interest in charitable work among the poor, especially those of his own village of Churriana (Málaga). For all these activities he was awarded several Spanish decorations.

Scarcely had the Civil War ended than World War II broke out in the rest of Europe. Marjorie's name had been included in the British Government's 'Central Register' of people whose qualifications would fit them for specialized work in the war effort. In February 1941 she was drafted into a department of the Foreign Office that dealt with economic intelligence, and she spent the next four years working as a linguist in Bletchley and later in London. Soon after her release she was offered a teaching post in the Department of Spanish at King's College, London. During her years in the Foreign Office she had become interested in economics and had studied the subject. She now spent part of her day at the London School of Economics, teaching the translation of economic material from and into Spanish. She also acted as examiner in Spanish for the London Chamber of Commerce. In 1948 she was appointed as Full Lecturer and Head of the new Department of Spanish that was in course of foundation at Birkbeck College, another of the colleges of London University.

At the London School of Economics Marjorie came across a collection of works by some of the Spanish economists of the eighteenth and early nineteenth centuries. She decided to write an article or perhaps a thesis based on this hitherto unstudied material and approached Professor Friedrich von Hayek, a future Nobel scholar, for his advice. He agreed to direct her investigation, and she took up the study of economic thought in Spain that was to make her name and occupy her for some years with the scholastic authors of the sixteenth and seventeenth centuries. After the departure of Hayek for Chicago in 1950 her work was directed by Professor R.S. Sayers. The results were embodied in a short book, *The School of Salamanca. Readings in Spanish Monetary Theory, 1544–1605*, which was published in 1952 by the Clarendon Press.

In 1951 Marjorie married Baron Ulrich von Schlippenbach, a farmer and the owner of the estate of Santa Isabel, near Málaga. For the next 30 years she and her husband lived at Santa Isabel, where they incidentally founded a school for some 120 poor children of the neighbourhood. At the same time Marjorie helped her father with his philanthropic activities until his death in 1959. She did not, however, give up her work as a Hispanist. Her second book, *Málaga Farm*, published in 1956, was a portrayal of the Andalusian countryside and its people, and her third, *Children of the Vega* (1962), written at the request of the Ministry of Education in New Zealand for use in its schools, described the life of children in a Mediterranean community. She also published a brief history of the English Cemetery in Málaga (1962).

In later years Marjorie returned to the subject of the history of economic thought in Spain, basing her investigations on material not used for the *School of Salamanca* and on new material gathered in the British Library and in those of Madrid and Salamanca. *Early Economic Thought in Spain* (1978) is probably her best-known contribution to the subject. Inspired by the work of Americo Castro, it takes the student back to the Middle Ages, traces the part played in business life and thought by the Christian, Islamic and Jewish communities who lived side by side in the Peninsula, and shows how the economics of Plato and Aristotle was transmitted by way of Spain to the Latin West. The second half of the book deals with 'Salamancan' ideas and with the views of the mercantilist writers who preceded the Enlightenment. The book was translated into Spanish in 1982 and published by the prestigious firm of Barcelona, Crítica.

In 1979 Marjorie was invited to become an honorary member of the Department of Economic History and Theory in the recently founded University of Malaga. This appointment encouraged her to continue her researches and to write a short book in Spanish on the development of economic thought in Andalucía, *Aproximación al pensamiento económico en Andalucía: de Séneca a finales del siglo XVIII* (1990). She also presented a number of papers at congresses held in Spain and elsewhere. These were translated into English and edited by the American economists, Professors Laurence S. Moss and Christopher Ryan, and published in book form in 1993. A Spanish edition appeared in 1995.

In 1984 Marjorie donated her old property of San Julian to the University of Málaga for use as a centre of scientific research and a botanical garden.

In 1959 Marjorie was awarded the 'Cinta de Dama' in the Spanish Order of Civil Merit, and in 1975 she was appointed member of the Order of the British Empire. She was awarded honorary doctorates in economics by the University of Málaga and by the Complutensian University of Madrid in 1992 and 1993 respectively. In 1994 the History of Economic Society awarded her a Distinguished Fellowship in recognition of her efforts to promote knowledge of the development of economic thought in southern Europe and more especially in Spain.

Marjorie's work may be said to have played an important part in evoking the present interest in the history of European thought outside the already intensively studied English tradition, and in bringing the ideas of the Spanish economists to the attention of the international community of scholars.

AURORA GAMEZ

Selected writings by Marjorie Grice-Hutchinson

(1952), *The School of Salamanca: Readings in Spanish Monetary Theory, 1544–1605*, Oxford: Clarendon Press.

(1978), *Early Economic Thought in Spain 1177–1740*. London: George Allen & Unwin. Spanish translation, Barcelona: Editorial Crítica, 1982.

(1990), *Approximación al pensamiento económico en Andalucía: de Séneca a finales del signo XVII*, Málaga: Editorial Librería Agora.

(1993), *Economic Thought in Spain: Selected Essays of Marjorie Grice-Hutchinson*, edited with introduction by Laurence S. Moss and Christopher K. Ryan, translated by Christopher K. Ryan and Marjorie Grice-Hutchinson. Aldershot, UK, and Brookfield, US: Edward Elgar.

Lucy Barbara (Bradby) Hammond (1873–1961)

Little is known of the life of Barbara Hammond. Though her correspondence is preserved at the Bodleian Library, only a few details have found their way into the published record (see Tawney, 1960 and especially Clarke, 1968). The daughter of a headmaster, she took a First in Greats at Oxford. She was for a while a Fellow of Lady Margaret Hall, where she distinguished herself as an early feminist. She abandoned the post to become active in social work at London. In 1901, she married Lawrence Hammond, then a rising liberal journalist. It was a very close relationship without any children. On the advice of her doctors after she was diagnosed with tuberculosis in 1905, the pair moved to the rural setting of Hampstead Heath. In 1912 they acquired a more comfortable dwelling ('Oatfield') in a similar environment near Hemel Hempstead. In both places they lived a spartan existence with a fanatic devotion to fresh air (sleeping out of doors and keeping windows open year round). Forced by poor health to retire from journalism in 1907 (he was to return to the field again after 1919), Lawrence accepted a bureaucratic appointment that left him ample time to pursue an interest in history – a life-long project in which Barbara became a full and willing participant. The result was six large jointly authored books, appearing between 1911 and 1930, on the social history of nineteenth-century England. She was responsible for most of the research (until 1913, when ill health forced her to stop, she spent long hours in the archives of the Public Record Office in London) and organizing the large amounts of information into some sensible order. He did the actual writing; his fine journalistic talents account for the books' vivid and often moving style. Throughout these years they kept close contact with a small circle of radical intellectuals such as Hobhouse, Hobson, Tawney, Wallas and key staff members of the two main papers for which Lawrence wrote, the *Nation* and the *Manchester Guardian*. It was to this group and liberals in general that the Hammonds' books spoke and were addressed. Lawrence's health seriously deteriorated during the 1930s. After his death in 1949, Barbara remained alone at Oatfield until the onset of senility in 1957.

Their first book, *The Village Labourer, 1760–1832* (1911), has four main themes. First, because the associated legislative process was thoroughly dominated by the landed interest, the enclosures proved disastrous for smaller landholders, cottagers, squatters and labourers. Second, the aristocracy rejected in turn all sensible expedients for excessively low real wages in agriculture in 1795 (a minimum wage, Poor Law reform, allotments) and adopted instead the disastrous Speenhamland system, which only impoverished workers still further by lowering their market wage. Third, landlords and clergy regularly evaded their social obligations; for instance, they devoted enormous resources to upholding the game laws at a time when many were close to starvation. Finally, judicial proceedings for the 1830 Swing riots were a mockery of justice; because the ministry had decided to come down hard, those accused had little or no chance of a fair trial or sentence. Not a work of detached historical curiosity, the *Village Labourer* spoke to the current debate on land reform. To liberals it suggested an impoverished agricultural population was by no means an unavoidable necessity but could be traced to the self-serving mindset of the aristocracy. This implied that real improvements were possible but for the government's conservative outlook. Perhaps this is why the book proved immensely popular. It sold over a thousand copies in the first six months and went through four editions in the Hammonds' lifetime. As late as the 1970s, one scholar thought it might still be 'the most widely read work of English agrarian history' (Mingay, 1978, p. viii). On the specific subject of enclosures it drew numerous criticisms from economic historians of their own (Clapham) and later generations (Chambers and Mingay), which is perhaps a measure more of its success than of its failings.

In *The Town Labourer* (1917) and *The Skilled Labourer* (1919), the Hammonds gave their assessment of the Industrial Revolution. Built largely around Barbara's mining of the Home Office papers, they focused on the attitudes of rulers toward their subjects. Originally conceived as a single work, the material had to be split up when the initial manuscript grew too long. Into the first book went the broader themes on which Lawrence tended to concentrate: the political and legal devices with which the aristocracy tried to maintain order, the philosophies by which English rulers justified their power to themselves, and the reactions of the poor in the form of trade unions and Methodism. The second book was more Barbara's field: detailed studies of the mining, cotton, wool and silk industries and the Luddite uprisings. The industrial histories emphasized that in each case government authorities made a deliberate choice to support machine-based production, after which the former handicraft workers descended into poverty and misery. There are three main themes in the chapters on Luddism: (i) in most cases Luddites were objecting not to new machinery but to the use of existing machines in a way that harmed their livelihood; (ii) there was very little violence or revolutionary intent – workers were mostly interested in protecting their incomes; and (iii) where violence or revolutionary activity did erupt, it was almost always due to the government's own *agents provocateurs*. The two books were not intended as a scholarly escape into history. They fitted right into Lawrence's work in the Ministry of Post-war Reconstruction by helping combat the common prejudice that mechanized industry was an inevitable feature of modern economic living. The Industrial Revolution had occurred only because the ruling classes of the time made deliberate choices to facilitate it. True, nineteenth-century economic doctrines strongly suggested that there had been no real choice in the matter. But fatalism was merely a religion of convenience; it helped soothe aristocratic consciences troubled by the decision to support a new institutional arrangement which had clearly added to their own power and wealth at the expense of the working classes. These books too proved very popular; many readers were particularly moved by the account of the Swing riots – an English tragedy then little known. The Hammonds pressed Longmans to price the *Town Labourer* so that it would be accessible to the typical client of the Workers' Educational Association; they also urged a publication date calculated to maximize its influence with the public (June 1917). Wallas wrote to them that it would 'have a real and important effect on the temper of the governing classes after the War. When the average Oxford don thinks of scores of W.E.A. classes reading your book he won't find it possible to be perfectly complacent' (cited in Clarke, 1968, p. 188). Ramsay (1929) initiated a particularly ugly exchange of views on its historical accuracy. The *Skilled Labourer* was the first of the Hammonds' books to be afforded coverage in the *English Historical Review*. In attacking its thesis that English workers suffered a fall in their standard of living during the Industrial Revolution, Clapham's *Economic History of Modern Britain* (1926) started a debate that was to remain on the agenda of economic historians for decades.

Lord Shaftesbury and *The Rise of Modern Industry* lacked the stature and popularity of the labourer trilogy. Perhaps this is because they were written largely to fulfil commitments to friends and distracted the Hammonds from their first love during the 1920s, the impending study of Chartism. The first book was a biography of Ashley, a key advocate of the 1848 Ten Hours' Act that put new limits on child labour in English mines and factories. It seemed to stress the power of exceptional individuals to liberate themselves from the preconceptions of their age. And in the details of its account of the Ten Hours' Act (divided opinions among the aristocracy, strong support from some leading manufacturers) it implicitly rejected class-based analyses of capitalism. 'There were distracting forces in English social life, of which Karl Marx's simplifying philosophy failed to take full account' (Hammond and Hammond, 1936, p. 88). The second book, their most formal and academic (it had good success as a university textbook), offered a more comprehensive history of the Industrial Revolution. It set the long-term historical context for industrialization, surveyed the new inventions and techniques and, drawing upon their earlier works, summarized the social consequences. Its central conclusion: industrialization conformed to a historical pattern that also held when Rome fell to the Caesars and South America was colonized by Spain – an initial catastrophe that men of good hearts and minds overcame and turned to the benefit of humanity. From the chaos of the Industrial Revolution emerged Factory Law, the civil service and the trade unions. And between the lines the book made a case for liberal reform over socialist revolution, for spiritual freedom over material determinism. For instance, English towns were allowed to become ugly and impoverished only because 'men still saw with the eyes of their grandfathers'; 'a race that was free and vigorous in its mind could have put an end to it' (Hammond and Hammond, 1926, p. 228).

In *The Age of the Chartists, 1832–1854* (1930) the Hammonds reverted to form: extensive, careful historical research presented in a vivid and engaging style. In its abridged form, *The Bleak Age* (1934, Pelican edn 1947), it became after the trilogy their best-known work. Its professed aim was to disclose the grievances lying beneath the Chartist movement. Conceding a point to critics of their Industrial Revolution studies, they were willing to rule out poverty; the statisticians, they admitted, had clearly shown wealth was rising. The real motive force of Chartism was a deep sense of exclusion and injustice – the net result of oligarchic town governments, the new Poor Law of 1834, crowded and filthy living conditions, the absence of public parks and walks, insufficient controls on the supply of liquor, woefully inadequate provision for public education, and churches that made workers feel lowly and out of place. The movement faded away after 1848 in part because of an emerging counter-movement to the intense individualism of the Industrial Revolution. The new trend was evident in the creation of legal powers relating to urban health and sanitation, the emergence of many new Friendly Societies offering a carefully crafted social life dedicated to equality, a *rapprochement* between workers and the churches, the growth of public libraries and museums, and growing support for public parks and leisure time for workers. The moral of the story: any society based solely on the love of money will give rise to discontent; as the Romans knew, governments must be prepared to spend liberally on public facilities – 'common enjoyments to create and foster the kind of communication between man and man which makes a stable State' (Hammond and Hammond, 1930, p. 361). Clearly, the book was an advertisement of sorts for the political programme of Lloyd George and the Liberals, which called for large-scale expenditures on public works to relieve the country's most pressing problems of unemployment, poverty and worker unrest. There is no published record of its contemporary reception; the book later drew criticism from Marxist social historians like E.P. Thompson.

RICHARD KLEER

Bibliography

Selected writings by Lucy Barbara Hammond

(1911), *The Village Labourer, 1760–1832: A Study in the Government of England Before the Reform Bill* (with John Lawrence le Breton Hammond), London: Longmans, Green.

(1917), *The Town Labourer, 1760–1832: The New Civilisation*, London: Longmans, Green.
(1919), *The Skilled Labourer, 1760–1832*, London: Longmans, Green.
(1923), *Lord Shaftesbury*, London: Constable.
(1926), *The Rise of Modern Industry*, New York: Harcourt, Brace.
(1928), 'Urban Death-Rates in the Early 19th Century', *Economic Journal, Economic History Series No. 3*, 1, January, 419–29.
(1930), *The Age of the Chartists, 1832–1854: A Study of Discontent*, London: Longmans, Green.
(1934), *The Bleak Age* (with J.L. Hammond), London and New York: Penguin Books, 1947.
(1936), *Lord Shaftesbury*, 4th edn, London: Longmans, Green.

Other sources and references
Clarke, Peter (1968), *Liberals and Social Democrats*, Cambridge: Cambridge University Press.
Mingay, G.E. (1978), 'General Introduction' to Barbara and Lawrence Hammond, *The Village Labourer*, reprint of 1911 edn, London: Longman.
Ramsay, Anna A.W. (1929), 'A Socialist Fantasy', *Quarterly Review*, **252**(449), 32–65.
Tawney, Richard (1960), 'J.L. Hammond, 1782–1949', *Proceedings of the British Academy*, **46**, 267–94.

Amy Hewes (1877–1970)

Amy Hewes was born at Baltimore, Maryland, the daughter of Ewin and Martha Gardner Gover-Hewes on 8 September 1877. Nothing is known of her early life until she began her university education. She gained a BA from Groucher College in 1897, then studied at the University of Berlin for a year before entering the University of Chicago's Sociology Department as a Fellow, the only woman to have that distinction between 1892 and 1920. In 1903 she gained her Ph.D. for a dissertation on *The Part of Invention in the Social Process*. In 1905, after two years of unemployment, she was appointed Instructor of Economics and Politics at Mount Holyoake College for Women, becoming Professor in 1907, a post she held until 1943. Over these years, she served on many other public bodies. These included the first Massachusetts Minimum Wage Commission (1913–15), the Committee of Women in Industry, Council of National Defence (1917–19), supervisor of research for the Women's Education and Industrial Union in Boston, the Advisory Council of State Employment Offices, the Advisory Board of the Massachusetts Consumer League, the Advisory Council of the Massachusetts Unemployment Compensation Commission and the Bryn Mawr summer schools for workers. In 1962, her contributions through the Department of Labor in fostering, promoting and developing the welfare of US wage-earners was officially recognized in a citation by the then Secretary of Labor (Deegan, 1991).

Nearly all of Amy Hewes's published writings dealt with labour economics, often and more specifically with the organization of labour in the form of trade unions (Hewes, 1920, 1922a, 1922b, 1924 and 1932). This material was frequently combined with the study of socialism in some of its interwar forms: that is, socialism as it was being constructed in the Soviet Union under Lenin and Stalin, as well as the Guild Socialism which for a brief period captured the imagination of sections of the British working class involved in the cooperative movement (Hewes, 1922b). Her strong interest in labour practices and organization in the Soviet Union explains her visits to that country in 1927 and 1931, the first as part of a sabbatical spent partly in Western Europe. Some of her work combined an interest in labour economics with industry studies. Her research direction of a study on Massachusetts industrial home work (Hewes, 1913) is an early example, as is her first, and only, book on the topic (Hewes, 1917) presenting a study of women munition workers during World War I. An article on the English Coal Commission (Hewes, 1926a) provides some details on the English coal industry and the world competitive pressures it was likely to face. Her edited volumes on Bryn Mawr summer schools for working women dealt respectively with women workers and family support, changing job opportunities, and women workers in the Depression (Hewes, 1925, 1926b, 1933). Her lectures on the contributions of economics to social work (Hewes, 1930), a pamphlet on *Labor's Aims in War and Peace* (Hewes, 1944) and a contribution to an American Economic Association round-table discussion on teaching economics (Hewes, 1940) constitute her final economic work.

Much of this work was also descriptive and institutional, and its occasional foundation in survey work as well as the range of that inquiry to include workplace, home and social amenities (especially Hewes, 1917) is probably why her work has been claimed by sociologists (Deegan, 1991). However, at the time, some of her work at least was considered worthy of being published in major journals, likewise reflecting the broad tolerance to institutional and semi-sociological inquiry by their editorial boards. This applies particularly to the *Journal of Political Economy* and *American Economic Review* of the 1920s and early 1930s. Her one contribution to the *Quarterly Journal of Economics* (Hewes, 1924), an international comparison of union amalgamation is, however, one of the relatively few contributions by women to appear in that journal (see Groenewegen and King, 1994, pp. 4–10). Its summation of the evidence on union and amalgamation in countries as diverse as England, Belgium, Germany, Australia, Russia, France and the USA, together with its explanations of the various trends, reveals the solid analytical mind of the author, a characteristic equally visible in her other longer journal articles. In addition, she was a committed author, dedicated to the causes of working women and men, but never biased as a result of this when making inferences from the data. Her work stands as a set of interesting factual contributions on labour organization and labour conditions, often with an internationally comparative slant, always clearly and economically written and often based on original research. The papers in this genre also reveal a strong analytical bent and an awareness of economic theory which never is allowed to dominate the discourse. That, and their interdisciplinary nature, make them a typical example of the work on this topic done by Chicago graduates of her vintage.

PETER GROENEWEGEN

Bibliography

Selected writings by Amy Hewes
(1915) (ed.), *Industrial Homework in Massachusetts*, Boston: Women's Educational and Industrial Union.
(1917), *Women as Munition Makers*, New York: The Russell Sage Foundation.
(1920), 'Labor conditions in Soviet Russia', *Journal of Political Economy*, **28**, 774–81.
(1922a), 'Russian wage systems under Communism', *Journal of Political Economy*, **30**, 274–8.
(1922b), 'Guild Socialism: a two years' test, *American Economic Review*, **12**, 209–37.
(1924), 'The changing structure of the bargaining unit of labour', *Quarterly Journal of·Economics*, **39**, 612–34.
(1925) (ed.), *Women Workers and Family Support: A Study made by Students in the Economics Courses at Bryn Mawr Summer School*, Washington: Government Printing Office.
(1926a), 'The task of the English Coal Commission', *Journal of Political Economy*, **34**, 1–12.
(1926b) (ed.), *Changing Jobs: A Study made by the Students in the Economics Courses at the Bryn Bawr Summer School*, Washington: Government Printing Office.
(1930), *The Contribution of Economics to Social Work*, New York: Columbia University Press for the New York School of Social Work.
(1932), 'The transformation of Soviet trade unions', *American Economic Review*, **22**, 605–19.
(1933) (ed.), *Women Workers in the Third Year of the Depression: A Study made by Students in the Economics Courses at the Bryn Mawr Summer School*, Washington: Government Printing Office.
(1940), 'Round table on problems in the teaching of economics', *American Economic Review*, **30**, 107–9.
(1944), *Labor's Aims in War and Peace*, New York: Commission to Study the Organization of Peace.

Other sources and references

Deegan, Mary Jo (1991), 'Amy Hewes (1877–1970)', in Mary Jo Deegan (ed.), *Women in Sociology: a Bio-Bibliographical Source Book*, New York: Greenwood Press, pp. 164–71.
Groenewegen, Peter and Susan King (1994), 'Women as producers of economic articles: a statistical assessment of the nature and the extent of female participation in five British and North American journals 1900–1939', Sydney: University of Sydney, Department of Economics, Working Paper No. 201.

Ursula Hicks (1896–1985)[1]

Ursula Kathleen Hicks (née Webb) was born in 1896 in Dublin, Ireland, the only child of Quaker parents from Ulster. It appeared at the outset as if her adult life was to be a quiet one spent in the service of others. After receiving a BA in modern history at Somerville College, Oxford, she spent a short stint working for the British Ministry of Agriculture, followed by years of taking care of her parents. During this time, she did volunteer work for the Workers' Educational Association in Kent and Sussex (where the family had moved), which kindled her interest in economics. After her father's death, she went to the London School of Economics to study economics.

This move, undertaken in Ursula's early thirties, turned out to be the pivotal point in her life. Ursula stayed at LSE for seven years, during which time she received a B.Sc. in economics, wrote her MA thesis under the guidance of Lionel Robbins, and fell in with the lively young group of economists that had coalesced at the LSE, including Abba Lerner, Paul Sweezy, Nicholas Kaldor – and John Hicks, whom she married in 1935. During this period she founded, along with Lerner and Sweezy, the *Review of Economic Studies*, for which she served as managing editor for 28 years, from its first issue in October 1933, through October 1961.

In 1935 John Hicks was appointed to a Fellowship at Caius College, Cambridge, and the couple moved to Cambridge in early 1936. They stayed there until 1938, when Ursula was asked to head the Economics Department at the University of Liverpool and John was appointed to the Jevons Chair of Political Economy in Manchester. They remained in these positions during the war years. After a year of visiting professorships in 1946 at Chicago and Harvard, the couple moved to Oxford. John took a Fellowship in 1947 at newly founded Nuffield College, the first of the mixed graduate colleges at Oxford, while Ursula was appointed by the University to the newly created post of University Lecturer in Public Finance. She was associated with Nuffield College until becoming a senior member of Linacre House, an international graduate centre, upon its founding in 1962. Linacre then became a College and Ursula one of its Fellows in 1964, and she stayed in this post until taking Fellow Emeritus status in 1966. The Hickses retired to their country home, Porch House, in Blockley, Gloucestershire. Ursula continued to be active in economics and in Oxford life until her death in 1985, predeceasing her husband by four years.

All of Ursula Hicks's writings are in the area of public finance. However, within this area, her work encompasses a wide range of topics. While some of her work is retrospective in nature, in others she concerns herself with current public policy matters. Her published work may be divided roughly into two phases – domestic, developed country issues before 1955 and international, developing country issues subsequently. However, her work is unified by the concern that traditional ways of conducting public finance were inadequate to an age in which governmental organizations were greatly increasing in size and complexity. Therefore financial accounting rules needed to be clarified and standardized and principles of economics understood by the public administrators who were in charge of devising new tax systems.

Her first book, *The Finance of British Government, 1920–36* (1938), is based upon her thesis. In the introduction to this volume, she sets the style for all of her future work by writing that she 'endeavours to refrain from the use of economic jargon' (p. vi) as much as possible, a trait which makes her findings readily accessible to the generally educated reader. That book was followed by one co-written with her husband and another author, *The Taxation of War Wealth* (1941). This book resulted from a 1940 grant by the National Institute of Economic and Social Research, and is a comparative study of excess profits taxes and capital levies in the UK and abroad. These books were followed by a set of three papers, co-written with her husband (one with a third co-author), that dealt with the nitty-gritty of local public finance in the UK. These papers, written between 1943 and 1945 for the London-based National Institute of Economic and Social Research, consider tax and spending incidence variations in Great Britain and offer recommendations for rationalizing the system.

Ursula continued her interest in improving the domestic system of tax collection in an influential paper, 'The Terminology of Tax Analysis' (1946). She discusses the various uses of the terms 'direct', 'indirect', 'incidence', and 'burden', finding their usage vague and suggesting the use of 'effective incidence' in place of the latter two terms. Her work on domestic public finance was capped by two additional books: the authoritative textbook *Public Finance* (1947), which was published as one of the influential series of Cambridge Economic Handbooks and went into three editions with multiple reprints; and *British Public Finances: Their Structure and Development 1880–1952* (1954).

The beginning of Ursula's formal interest in the public finance of underdeveloped countries dates from 1950, when she had three major assignments abroad: a visiting professorship at the Delhi School of Economics; a consultancy assignment to the United Nations in India; and, during the summer, a consultancy to the Revenue Allocation Commission in Nigeria. These were followed by a number of additional governmental assignments and consultancy missions for the World Bank. She served, along with her husband, on a two-person commission in Jamaica for two months in 1954, examining the revenue system of the island and making recommendations for its improvement in their *Report on Finance and Taxation in Jamaica* (1955). In 1957 she worked with the Central Bank in Ceylon. In 1962 she served as Fiscal Commissioner in Uganda, and also as Fiscal Commissioner in the Caribbean, investigating on behalf of the Colonial Office the prospects of federation among the smaller islands. In 1964 she was an adviser to the Government of Eastern Nigeria. These interests were reflected in her scholarly work as well in particular in two books published in 1961: *Federalism and Economic Growth in Underdeveloped Countries: A Symposium*, which is the report from a 1959 Working Party conference, for which Hicks wrote the introduction and epilogue; and *Development from Below: Local Government and*

Finance in Developing Countries of the Commonwealth. Her broader interest in the workability of federalism is addressed in her final book, *Federalism: Failure and Success, A Comparative Study* (1978).

The Hickses also travelled extensively on the scholarly circuit. Ursula held visiting professorships at several points during the 1960s, at Delhi, Osaka, Buenos Aires, Northwestern, Purdue, and Australian National Universities. In 1969 the Hickses made a lecture tour of centres of advanced economic study in India, and in 1970–71 they toured various Italian universities. Ursula was clearly well travelled even among economists specializing in development issues, and prided herself on having gained much knowledge of her field from personal experience. Her hobbies of botany and drawing were fed by her travels, as she would obtain special permits to bring in plants from the various countries she visited and make sketches wherever she went, some of which were used to illustrate the couple's Christmas cards.

As well as Ursula's direct influence on commonwealth policy through her consultancies, she had great indirect influence on commonwealth governance through her Oxford association. She taught public finance at Oxford for 18 years, training a generation of civil servants. Her penultimate book, *Development Finance, Planning and Control* (1965), is based on the lecture notes from her annual course of lectures on 'Financial Problems of Emergent Countries', along with factual information derived from her various consultancies. Her duties at Oxford included the training of overseas officers in local government finance. She was associated with the Institute of Commonwealth Studies at Oxford, which included a lodging-house, Queen Elizabeth House, for students, scholars and public officials from Commonwealth countries, and was greatly involved in the social life surrounding this institute. Her students were drawn from a multitude of countries, as can be seen from the contributors to her Festschrift (David, 1973).

A final word should be said about the Hickses marriage, which was truly a partnership, both intellectual and social. While John, whose single-authored work was generally in the area of economic theory, received more public acclaim, including a knighthood and the Nobel prize, Ursula received her share of accolades as well. She received an honorary D.Sc.Econ. from Queen's University, Belfast, and was made a Fellow of the Institute of Social Studies at The Hague, which she visited regularly. And, notably, their research agenda was set by both, but leaned more and more towards Ursula's interests in applied public finance as the years went on. While many economists have married other economists and carried out parallel careers, it is rare to find a match as nearly equal as this one.

It is challenging to assess the lasting impact of Ursula Hicks's work on the field of public finance. In general, her research strengthened the analytical underpinnings of the field, moving it away from a primarily descriptive focus, but also stressed the importance of empiricism. However, her works are not often cited today, perhaps because the principles she espoused are so basic to the way public finance is nowadays taught that it is not considered necessary to cite references for them.

JOYCE P. JACOBSEN

Note

1. The author gratefully acknowledges the assistance provided by Frank and Catherine King.

Bibliography

Selected writings by Ursula Hicks

(1938), *The Finance of British Government, 1920–1936*, Oxford: Oxford University Press.
(1941), *The Taxation of War Wealth* (with J.R. Hicks and L. Rostas), Oxford: Clarendon Press.
(1943), 'Standards of local expenditure: a problem of the inequality of incomes' (with J.R. Hicks), National Institute of Economic and Social Research Occasional Paper no. 3, Cambridge: Cambridge University Press.
(1944), 'The problem of valuation for rating' (with J.R. Hicks and C.E.V. Leser),' National Institute of Economic and Social Research Occasional Paper no. 7, Cambridge: Cambridge University Press.
(1945), 'The incidence of local rates in Great Britain' (with J.R. Hicks), National Institute of Economic and Social Research Occasional Paper, Cambridge: Cambridge University Press.
(1946), 'The terminology of tax analysis', *Economic Journal*, **56**(221), March, 38–50.
(1947), *Public Finance*, Cambridge: Cambridge University Press.
(1954), *British Public Finances: Their Structure and Development 1880–1952*, Oxford: Oxford University Press.
(1955), *Report on Finance and Taxation in Jamaica* (with J.R. Hicks), Kingston, Jamaica: Government Printer.
(1961), *Federalism and Economic Growth in Underdeveloped Countries: A Symposium* (with F.G. Carnell, J.R. Hicks, W.T. Newlyn and A.H. Birch), London: George Allen & Unwin.
(1961), *Development from Below: Local Government and Finance in Developing Countries of the Commonwealth*, Oxford: Clarendon Press.
(1965), *Development Finance, Planning and Control*, Oxford: Oxford University Press.
(1978), *Federalism: Failure and Success, A Comparative Study*, Oxford: Oxford University Press.

Other sources and references

David, Wilfred L. (ed.) (1973), *Public Finance, Planning and Economic Development: Essays in Honour of Ursula Hicks*, New York: St Martin's Press. This *Festschrift* contains a biographical essay and a comprehensive bibliography of Ursula Hicks's works.

Elizabeth Ellis Hoyt (1893–1980)[1]

Elizabeth Ellis Hoyt, pioneer in consumption economics, was both economist and anthropologist. She was born on 27 January 1893 in Augusta, Maine, to William Adams and Fannie (Ellis) Hoyt. She attended the Boston Latin School for Girls and took an AB degree from Boston University in 1913. From 1917 to 1921 she worked for the National Industrial Conference Board in Boston doing field interviews for a cost-of-living index, predecessor of today's consumer price index. Because the Board consisted only of employers, she chose to meet also with labour unions. She was Instructor at Wellesley College 1921–23. Hoyt's graduate work in economics at Harvard (Radcliffe) led to an AM degree in 1924 and a Ph.D. in 1925.

Elizabeth Hoyt's doctoral dissertation analysed Harvard's collection of anthropological field reports from across the world to determine how market trade arose from gifts and other exchanges between peoples, some of whom were hostile to each other. Published as a book in 1926 under the title *Primitive Trade: Its Psychology and Economics*, it was reprinted in 1968 as an economics classic.

Elizabeth Hoyt joined the all-male economics faculty of Iowa State College (now University) in 1925 as an associate professor, becoming Full Professor in 1928. Besides teaching, she published *Consumption of Wealth* (1928), an early text in the new field of consumption economics. Her book was different from others because she emphasized the anthropological concept of culture with illustrations from across the world.

From 1926 to 1929 Hoyt supervised a survey of the value of living of 147 Iowa farm families. Her study was unique because, in addition to the usual account of expenditures, she sought information on intellectual, aesthetic, social and leisure activities. With regard to health care she found that cost and lack of availability led to instances such as the mother who set her child's arm when it was broken.[2]

A second woman, Margaret G. Reid (*q.v.*), joined the economics faculty of Iowa State in 1930. Her doctoral dissertation, completed under Hazel Kyrk at the University of Chicago, was published in 1934 as *Economics of Household Production*. I was in Reid's class when she first used it.

It soon became obvious that Margaret Reid was empirically minded and worked within received economic theory. Elizabeth Hoyt, on the other hand, was a visionary seeking to see the whole picture and entering into questions of values, but each appreciated the approach of the other, as shown when they were two of the four authors of *American Income and Its Use* (1954), a book sponsored by the National Council of Churches. Hoyt wrote Part One on 'The ethics of consumption' and Margaret Reid wrote Part Two on 'Distribution of income and consumption'.

Both women were well regarded by the Iowa State economists and also maintained a cordial relationship with the home economists. Hoyt attributed the early growth of consumption economics at Iowa State to encouragement of home economics. She wrote in the preface of her book, *Consumption in Our Society* (1938, vi), 'Dean Anna E. Richardson of Iowa State College perceived that home economics must take account of the principles of economics as they relate to the use of goods and services, that home economics itself is, to a large degree, applied consumption ...'. Most schools of home economics at that time emphasized food and clothing, but Richardson went further.

At Iowa State all second-year students on campus, no matter what their majors, were required to take two courses in principles of economics. Home economics students had their own classes in economics separate from the rest of the campus but used the same textbook. Following their two courses in principles they then took a third course, in consumption economics. In this way Hoyt and Reid could encourage student interest in their new field.[3]

Theodore W. Schultz had just become department head when I arrived in 1934. He gave constant encouragement to Elizabeth Hoyt and Margaret Reid. Schultz's departure for the University of Chicago in 1943 and Margaret Reid's later acceptance of an appointment there were a great loss to Elizabeth Hoyt but the close friendship between Hoyt and Reid would continue throughout their long lives.

In the late 1940s Hoyt wrote an introductory economics text, *The Income of Society* (1950). In its preface she wrote that her text placed economics in a social setting and she noted that it gave more space than most to the economics of food, health and housing. She also noted its many references to the economies of other countries and to the international economy.

Elizabeth Hoyt, with her continuing interest in anthropology, is considered to be the first economist at Iowa State to undertake international work. Encouraged by the spirit of President Truman's Point Four programme, over a period of four years in the 1940s, Hoyt, together with her students and with the help of the Inter-American Institute of Agricultural Sciences in Terrialba, Costa Rica, studied different large-scale investments and their social effects, particularly in Guatemala. Later she did this in Jamaica (see Hoyt, 1951b). Hoyt saw mistakes made from lack of understanding of local cultures and urged greater cooperation among social scientists.

In 1950–51 Hoyt was in British East Africa on a Fulbright scholarship and four years later established an African Libraries project, sending books and other materials to English-using libraries together with her two-page typed newsletter called *Our Africa*, which contained her candid insights. More than a hundred libraries south of the Sahara were involved and at least one was named after her.

In 1957–58 a Ford Foundation grant made possible her research on workers' reactions to employers' policies in the Caribbean area of Central America (see Hoyt, 1960).

Hoyt pulled together concepts of integration of culture for an article in *Current Anthropology* (1961). Integration by dominance of leading idea, integration by relationship of parts, and other concepts are incomplete, she wrote, but necessary 'to understanding the nature of other cultures, and the issues which we confront in our own'. Her history of concepts and her list of references are impressive.

Hoyt received the Distinguished Service Award from Radcliffe College and the Faculty Citation from the Alumni Association of Iowa State University, a citation which paid tribute to her lifetime 'devoted to humanitarian economics'. At a time when few academic women were listed in *Who's Who in America* Elizabeth Hoyt appreciated being listed in the first edition of *Who's Who of American Women* (1958–59).

Elizabeth Hoyt retired in 1963 but maintained an office on campus and continued her research and writing, publishing *Choice and the Destiny of Nations* (1969) in which she recognized humanity's fascination with technology but also saw its threat to world peace. She continued the African Libraries project. The Economics Department honoured her 50 years on its faculty on 16 May 1975 with a warm and appreciative celebration.

Never married, Elizabeth Hoyt was part of her nephew's family, whose five children in a sense became her children too. William and Muriel Hoyt lived on the west coast and she spent the final weeks of her life there. Elizabeth Hoyt died at Glen Eden Beach, Oregon on 22 November 1980, aged 87. She is buried in Ocean Hill cemetery at Round Pond, Maine near the ancestral Ellis farm where she spent most of her summers.

Elizabeth Hoyt bequeathed to Iowa State and its Economic Department $800 000, the second largest bequest up to then to be made by a faculty member. This money is used for international programmes and for scholarships for international students who are in need. The Elizabeth Ellis Hoyt papers are archived at the Iowa State University Library.

After completing my graduate work I wrote this memory of Elizabeth Hoyt:

> On entering her office you will find a brown haired woman with large blue eyes, arched with dark brows, sitting at her desk with arms folded so a hand is on each elbow. She leans a bit forward on her arms and seems to be thinking about the manuscript in front of her, a manuscript in her handwriting. She is thinking, not reading. People read too much and think too little, she believes.

My memory doesn't include what she was thinking about, but I suspect it was standards of living. In all her years Elizabeth Hoyt remained an extraordinarily courageous, warm-hearted person who yearned to see talents, organizations and academic disciplines brought together to improve the conditions in which people live.

ALISON COMISH THORNE

Notes

1. The author is indebted to Eleanor Parkhurst and Barrie Thorne for reading an early version of this essay and making helpful suggestions, and I appreciate Evelyn Forget's encouragement and thoughtful editing.
2. *Iowa Agricultural Experiment Station Bulletin*, 281, p. 223. See also *Consumption in Our Society* pp. 291, 358, 386.
3. I describe Elizabeth Hoyt's and Margaret Reid's mentoring in *Women of Value*, pp. 60–70.

Bibliography

Selected writings by Elizabeth Ellis Hoyt

(1926), *Primitive Trade: Its Psychology and Economics*, London: Kegan Paul, Trench, Trubner. Economics Classics Reprint, New York: Augustus M. Kelley, 1968.
(1928), *The Consumption of Wealth*, New York: Macmillan.
(1931), 'Value of family living on Iowa farms', *Iowa Agricultural Experiment Station, Bulletin* 281, Ames, Iowa.
(1938), *Consumption in Our Society*, New York and London: McGraw-Hill.
(1950), *The Income of Society: An Introduction to Economics*, New York: Ronald Press.
(1951a), 'Tiquisate: A call for a science of human affairs', *Scientific Monthly*, **72**(2), 114–19.
(1951b), 'Want development in undeveloped areas', *Journal of Political Economy*, **59**(3), 194–202.
(1954), *American Income and Its Use* (with Margaret G. Reid, Joseph L. McConnell and Janet M. Hooks), New York: Harper and Brothers.
(1960), 'Voluntary unemployment and unemployability in Jamaica with special reference to the standard of living', *British Journal of Sociology*, **11**, 129–30.
(1961), 'Integration of culture: a review of concepts', *Current Anthropology*, **2**(5), 407–26.
(1969), *Choice and the Destiny of Nations*, New York: Philosophical Library.

Other sources and references

Reid, Margaret Gilpin (1934), *Economics of Household Production*, New York: John Wiley and Sons and London: Chapman and Hall.
Thorne, Alison Comish (1995), 'Women mentoring women in economics in the 1930s', in Mary Ann Dimand, Robert W. Dimand and Evelyn L. Forget (eds), *Women of Value: Feminist Essays on the History of Women in Economics*, Aldershot, UK and Brookfield, US: Edward Elgar, pp. 60–70.

B.L. Hutchins (1858–1935)

Elizabeth Leigh Hutchins preferred to be known as Bessie, and most of her writing was signed Miss B.L. Hutchins. Though little is known of her early life, she was associated with the new London School of Economics from 1896 to 1906 as a student and lecturer on social science and administration (Banks, 1990, p. 109). An active member of the Fabian Society, she also made several important research contributions under the auspices of the Women's Industrial Council. Hutchins's strength was empirical work. She examined, as she titled two of her most important books, *The Working Life of Women* (1911) and *Women in Modern Industry* (1915). She contributed to the social investigations that were so influential in Britain during the first two decades of the twentieth century.

Hutchins challenged the traditional views that 'the proper sphere for women is the home' and the assumption 'that a decree of Providence or a natural law has marked off and separated the duties of men and women' (Hutchins, 1911, p. 3). She elaborated the discontinuity that marked the working life of women. Women's industrial life 'is not continuous, but is split in two' by marriage (p. 9). Unfortunately, 'their work is usually not permanent, but is abandoned on marriage, precisely at the time of life when the greatest economic efficiency may be looked for' (Hutchins, 1915, p. 88).

Hutchins argued that working women 'pass from one plane of social development to another' and that this may occur several times during their life (Hutchins, 1911, p. 12). She distinguished 'these planes as status and contract, or value-in-use or value-in-exchange'. Children are 'are born into a world of value-in-use' where they are not 'valued for what their services will fetch in the market'. When a young girl begins work, entering the value-in-exchange plane, 'she sells her work for what it will fetch' (p. 12). Hutchins called this second plane 'the stage of the cash nexus' (p. 13). 'If she marries and leaves work, she returns at once into the world of value-in-use: the work she does for husband, home, and children is not paid at so much per unit, but is done for its own sake' (p. 13). Usually, working families were unable to save enough to provide for their dependants. Yet women's 'superior longevity and the greater risks to which men are exposed, leave many women widows and unprovided for in middle or even early life' (Hutchins, 1915, p. 88). 'A certain proportion of women, therefore, … are forced to re-enter the labor market by widowhood, or by other economic causes – illness of the husband, desertion, and so on' (1911, p. 9). Other women are driven back into the labour market because they 'are unfortunate in marriage, the husband turning out idle, incompetent, of feeble health or bad habits' (1915, p. 88).

Hutchins believed that when women were forced back into the labour market, they were placed at an economic disadvantage. Since 'value-in-use is subordinated to value-in-exchange,' therefore, 'a woman may possess all the domestic virtues in the highest possible degree, but she cannot live by them' (1911, p. 13). Regardless, then, of any romantic visions of a 'natural law of non-labour' for women, Hutchins demonstrated that 'it is absurd to tell women that their work as mothers is of the highest importance to the State' (ibid.). In fact, the 'special anomaly of the woman's position' is that social pressure and tradition 'induce her to cultivate qualities that … are a positive hindrance to success in competitive industry' (p. 14). However, when forced into the labour market by circumstances beyond her control, 'there is little or no social attempt made to compensate her for her deficiencies. Her very virtues are often her weakness' (p. 14). So, 'having lost the habit of industrial work, having very usually children to look after and a home to find, she has to compete with girls and young women for wages' (p. 9). The wages paid to women are 'based upon a single woman's requirements' rather than the requirements of a woman with a family to support (1915, p. 89). The discontinuity in the working life of women also explains that the 'inferior technical skill often attributed to women as compared with men is largely due to this fact, that while a man gives his best years to his work, a woman gives precisely those years to other work, and therefore returns to industry under a considerable handicap.' She concluded that 'this is the chief cause of pauperism' among working women (1911, p. 9).

In her work, *Women in Modern Industry*, Hutchins used both the Census and the Registrar-General's Report to show that the 'female working population' is divided into 'three great groups: the domestic group [which included servants, charwomen and laundresses], the textile and clothing group, and other miscellaneous occupations' (1915, p. 84). This grouping of occupations gives 'illuminating testimony to the strength of the fundamental human instincts' and 'illustrates both the deeply rooted conservatism of women and … the modifying tendency of modern industry,' since 'the largest groups of women's trades are still traditional activities of household work' (pp. 83 and 84). While two-thirds of the women worked in 'the domestic group and the textile and clothing group', 'the newer occupations, the non-textile industrial processes that have been transformed by machinery and brought within the capacity of women, are, though much smaller in numbers, increasing at a rapid rate' (p. 84).

Those who believed that the proper sphere for women is the home must be 'struck by the fact that it is sad and in some cases even disastrous for a woman to go out to work and leave her infant children unprotected and untended' (Hutchins, 1915, p. 89). This led to recurring proposals to prohibit married women's employment – 'but many persons, even those who dislike the employment of married women, think that when a woman is left a widow, the best thing is to take her children' and get her a position as a domestic servant (p. 90). Hutchins alleged that 'the servant-keeping class often shows a tendency to regard social questions mainly from the point of view of maintaining the supply of domestic servants'. She pointed out that working wives and widows with children were not in a position to give their children the proper 'care and attention if she is without the means of subsistence'. She challenged those who sought to prohibit the employment of married women to consider two questions. First, 'how the prohibition should be applied in cases where the male head of the family is not competent or sufficiently able-bodied' to support the family, and second, 'whether the children of widows can flourish on neglect any better than the children who have a living father, and, if not, why it is more desirable for a widow than for a married woman to go to work outside her home and away from her children' (pp. 90–91).

Bessie Hutchins was strongly committed to the basic principles of the Fabian Society. Not only did she contribute careful empirical studies of the working life of women in modern industry, but she was also expert in factory legislation, especially as it served to protect working women. Though her publications ceased after World War I, Banks informs us that 'she remained politically concerned and served for a time on the Committee of the League of Nations' (Banks, 1990, p. 109).

JAMES P. HENDERSON

Bibliography

Selected writings by B.L. Hutchins

(1903), *A History of Factory Legislation* (with Amy Harrison), Westminster: P.S. King & Son.
(1906), *Labour Laws for Women in Australia and New Zealand*, London: Women's Industrial Council.
(1906), *Women's Wages in England in the Nineteenth Century*, London: Women's Industrial Council.
(1907), *Labour Laws for Women in France*, London: Women's Industrial Council.
(1907), *Home Work and Sweating, the Causes and Remedies*. January. Fabian Tract no. 130. London: The Fabian Society.
(1908), *Home Industries of Women in London* (with Margaret Ethel Gladstone Macdonald), London: Women's Industrial Council.
(1909), *The Public Health Agitation, 1833–1848*, London: A.C. Fifield.
(1909), *Working Women and the Poor Law*, London: Women's Industrial Council.
(1909), 'Gaps in our factory legislation', in Mrs. Sidney Webb, B.L. Hutchins and the Fabian Society, *Socialism and the National Minimum*, London: A.C. Fifield.
(1910), *What a Health Committee can do*. Fabian Tract no. 148. London: The Fabian Society.
(1911), *The Working Life of Women*, London: The Fabian Society.
(1912), *Robert Owen: Social Reformer*. Fabian Tract no. 166. The Fabian Society Biographical Series no. 2. London: The Fabian Society.
(1913), *Conflicting Ideas: Two Sides of the Women's Question*, London: T. Marby. Reprinted as *Conflicting Ideals of Women's Work* (1916). Fabian Tract no. 157. Fabian Women's Group Series no. 1. London: Women's Industrial Council.
(1915), *Women in Modern Industry*, London: G. Bell.
(1917), *Women in Industry after the War*. Social Reconstruction Pamphlet no. III. London: The Athenaeum.

Other sources

Banks, Olive (1990), 'Hutchins, Elizabeth Leigh, 1858–1935', *The Biographical Dictionary of British Feminists, Vol Two: A Supplement, 1900–1945*. Brighton: Wheatsheaf Books. pp. 109–111.

Mary Quayle Innis (1899–1972)

Mary Quayle Innis, Canadian historian and economic historian, was born Mary Emma Quayle in St Mary's, Ohio, on 13 April 1899. Her parents were Frederick R. Quayle, who installed telephone units for a livelihood, and Effie Lloyd Quayle, a home-maker. Mary was the oldest of four children; the other three were boys. Because of her father's job, the family moved every few years, so that she grew up in a number of small American towns. She finished her secondary schooling as an honour student at New Trier High School in Winnetka, Illinois (Pell, 1989).

Mary studied at the University of Chicago from 1915 to 1919, graduating with a Ph.B. degree in English. She took a variety of courses besides 11 in English language and writing, among them six in political economy and seven in history. During her final year at university she became acquainted with Harold Adams Innis (1894–1952), her economics teacher, who was studying for his Ph.D. They became engaged in 1920 and married in 1921, settling in Toronto where her husband would be a professor at the University of Toronto for the rest of his life.

Even before her marriage, Mary helped her fiancé with his Ph.D thesis, *A History of the Canadian Pacific Railway*, finally published as a book in 1923. In 1922, she accompanied her husband on a research trip to Europe and England to gather information for the book he was writing, published as *The Fur Trade in Canada*. The following year they collected more data on trips to Kingston, Montreal, and British Columbia. From 1924, when she had the first of four children, Innis was less able to become involved in her husband's research. She continued, however, to write stories and articles at this time and later, publishing them mostly in *Canadian Forum*, *Saturday Night*, and *The United Church Observer*. Some stories became part of her 1943 novel, *Stand on a Rainbow*.

Although she had four young children, she decided to write *An Economic History of Canada*, urged by her husband, who needed a book on this subject for the use of his students. There was as yet no book on this topic. The eminent economist James Mavor had planned to write such a text, but he died in 1925 before he could do so (Mavor, 1923, p. 312). In 1929, Harold Innis had edited and published *Select Documents in Canadian Economic History, 1497–1783*, in which he noted that 'the economic history [of Canada] is, for the most part, an uncharted sea' (1929, p. vii). These documents and others, Harold Innis notes in the preface to his wife's book, show that 'sufficient research has been done to indicate the main lines of development, to warrant an outline and to suggest obvious gaps'. Mary Innis's pioneering study was published in 1935 with remarkable speed; as late as June 1935, Harold Innis urged her in a letter to go immediately to the Ryerson Press to work on the references for the book which were not yet complete (letter, University of Toronto archives).

In her book, Mary Quayle Innis successfully followed the main line of development up to 1914 and filled in many of the gaps, attempting 'to advance from the geographic and technological approach toward work done in the constitutional field and to stake out a broad field for the study of Canadian cultural growth'. Her English background enabled her to write clearly and well; one reviewer notes that 'a ray of light is thrown into difficult matter by such crystal phrases as "a three-decker tariff", the "mosaic of nationalities" in Nova Scotia, and "railway gridiron"' (Henson, 1936).

An *Economic History of Canada* received favourable reviews and became a bestselling textbook for the next 20 years. One reviewer wrote (Trotter, 1936):

> Mrs Innis has made a real contribution to Canadian studies by weaving into a connected pattern the economic history of Canada from the earliest coming of Europeans. Her book gives fresh meaning and larger consistency to the story of this nation's origins and the foundations of its present character. It is largely a story of pioneering. The approach is geographical and technological, and follows the actual activities of men in a material environment. The development of means of transportation is one thread. Another follows the dependence of the community upon one staple export after another for the means of securing from the outside world those things for which a young and growing society must perforce be dependent upon others. Fish, furs, lumber, wheat, minerals, successively dominate the picture. Migration, settlement, and the development of an organized economy are worked into the pattern.

Mary built on the staples thesis postulated by her husband which argued that the Canadian economy had been based on the export of natural resources, or staples, to more advanced economies. He feared that the export of staples would lock Canada into a dependent relationship as a resource hinterland for more mature economies. Mary revised the book in 1943, and a new and enlarged edition which carried forward Canada's economic history from 1914 was published in 1954. It remained as a primary university textbook until at least 1956, when *Canadian Economic History* by W.T. Easterbrook and Hugh G.J. Aitken was published.

Following the completion of her book, Innis wrote articles on related Canadian topics – John Galt, Philip Henry Gosse, and an incident of the plague. She also published in 1937 'The industrial development of Ontario 1783–1820'. This is a detailed study, district by district, of the primitive industry that developed to meet the needs of a pioneer society – such as grist mills and sawmills. Its republication nearly 40 years later in a collection of classic historical essays on Upper Canada was a welcome and well-deserved recognition of the continuing importance of her research. Later, she was asked to write several books on Canadian history for children: *Changing Canada* came out in two well-illustrated books for early grades. The first, subtitled *Fish, Fur and Exploration*, appeared in 1951 and the second, *New France and the Loyalists*, in 1952. *Living in Canada* was an exceptionally successful school text co-written by Innis and two teachers (Cameron et al., 1954). It was reprinted a number of times – 1956, 1958 (twice), 1963, 1964, 1966 – and republished in 1968. During this time she also wrote and edited other books of history dealing with the YWCA, Canadian women and nursing education (see Bibliography).

In 1956, Innis's *Travellers West* was published; it describes the early journeys of three expeditions westward across Canada. In 1859–60 the Earl of Southesk explored areas of the Rocky Mountains that had never before been visited by Europeans in his pursuit of big game. The party of Viscount Milton and his tutor, Dr Cheadle, several years later, was so badly organized that the members almost starved to death in the Rocky Mountains before reaching the goldfields of British Columbia. Sandford Fleming and George Grant crossed Canada in 1872 while choosing a route for the Canadian Pacific Railway. The materials for her book were taken from the journals and diaries of these adventurers.

In 1965, Innis published the first complete edition of *Mrs Simcoe's Diary*. This diary was begun in 1791, when Mrs Simcoe came to Upper Canada as the wife of its first governor, and continued until 1796, when they returned to England.

After Harold Innis died in 1952, Mary Quayle Innis took on the large task of collecting a number of his articles into one volume, called *Essays on Canadian Economic History* (1956), and of editing three of his books for republication. Innis updated and improved these books in two ways: by adding references, alone or with notes, that had appeared after the date of publication of the book, and by adding Harold Innis's own questions and comments which had occurred to him since the book was published. These addenda were difficult because the poor writing and cryptic notations used by Harold Innis made them hard to decipher and track down to the source. She also prepared the indexes for all three books.

For the revised edition of *The Cod Fisheries* (1954), Innis was the main editor, seeking advice from her two co-editors, professors S.D. Clark and W.T. Easterbrook. The revised *The Fur Trade in Canada* (1956), was dedicated to Mary Quayle Innis (as the original book had been) as well as edited by her, again with the assistance of Clark and Easterbrook. In her editor's preface, she thanked them because they had 'studied every added note [which she had prepared from Harold Innis's marginalia] and weighed the problem of placing it in the text. The work of reconstructing and arranging the notes has depended on their knowledge and judgment.' This revised edition was reprinted (and not further revised) in 1962 by Yale University Press. Paradoxically, although the foreword by Robin Winks notes that the 1956 revision appeared 'through the efforts of Mary Quayle Innis, Samuel D. Clark, and W.T. Easterbrook – all members of the University of Toronto', the title page of the reprint incorrectly states it was 'prepared by S.D. Clark and W.T. Easterbrook', with Innis's name omitted. Innis also edited the revised edition (1972) of Harold Innis's *Empire and Communications*, again painstakingly incorporating and checking notes and marginalia that he had made over 20 years before.

Innis had a successful life and career on several levels. She raised a family of four who all completed graduate studies and themselves had fulfilling lives; as Dean of Women at University College, University of Toronto, she was a successful university administrator for nine years; she was the only Canadian woman delegate to the Commonwealth Conference on Education held at Oxford in 1959; she was recognized as a woman of erudition in that she took part several times in a Canadian radio programme of general knowledge called 'Beat the Champs' and succeeded in beating them; and she received two honorary degrees from Canadian universities for her literary and academic achievements (from Queen's University, 1958, and the University of Waterloo, 1965).

As her daughter, however, I know that she felt frustrated as a serious writer and academic, the areas of greatest importance to her, probably because of the way she felt marginalized by others. I do not remember her ever being treated as an academic – she did not attend daytime academic events at the university (although she and my father together attended many social university gatherings in the evenings), nor was she invited to attend sessions or lunches with professors to discuss academic interests. When I talked to a renowned woman professor who had known her for 40 years about Innis's accomplishments in academia, she could only recall that Innis had once told her about preparing an index by covering the rug around her with slips of paper listing subject headings.

Despite the success of her textbook on economic history, Innis always disparaged textbook-writing as an activity for a real academic, an attitude she probably picked up from her husband. As the wife of the Head of the Department of Political Science and Economics at the University of Toronto, for many years she baked and served tea every Sunday during term for other faculty couples and graduate students. During these afternoons, as would have been expected of her, she spent virtually all of her time serving her guests and socializing with the wives rather than joining in academic talk. Yet many students were greatly impressed by her book. In 1971 I saw one literally start back in astonishment and pleasure when he realized that the woman he was talking to was the same person who had written the text which meant a great deal to him.

All her life Innis remained unassuming about her accomplishments. When she became Dean of Women at University College in 1956, she was offered a position in the Department of English, but refused it because she felt she was not well enough qualified, despite having a vast knowledge of literature and being the author of many books and stories. One wonders if her work on the revised edition of *The Fur Trade in Canada* could have been overlooked as it was on the title page of the 1962 reprint if she had had the self-confidence that suitable academic recognition would have given her.

ANNE INNIS DAGG

Bibliography

Selected writings by Mary Quayle Innis

(1935, 1943, 1954), *An Economic History of Canada*, Toronto: Ryerson.
(1936), 'The record of an epidemic', *Dalhousie Review*, **16**, 371–5.
(1937), 'Philip Henry Gosse in Canada', *Dalhousie Review*, **17**, 55–60.
(1937), 'The industrial development of Ontario 1783–1820', *Ontario Historical Society, Papers and Records*, **32**, 104–13. Reprinted in J.K. Johnson (ed.), *Historical Essays on Upper Canada*, The Carleton Library no. 82, Toronto: McClelland and Stewart, 1975, pp. 140–52.
(1940), 'A Galt centenary', *Dalhousie Review*, **19**, 495–501.
(1949), *Unfold the Years: A History of the Young Women's Christian Association in Canada*, Toronto: McClelland and Stewart.
(1951, 1952), *Changing Canada*, 2 vols, Toronto: Clarke, Irwin.
(1956), *Travellers West*, Toronto: Clarke, Irwin.
(1965) (ed.), *Mrs Simcoe's Diary*, Toronto: Macmillan.
(1966) (ed.), *The Clear Spirit: Twenty Canadian Women and Their Times*, Toronto: University of Toronto Press for the Canadian Federation of University Women.
(1970) (ed.), *Nursing Education in a Changing Society*, Toronto: University of Toronto Press.

Other sources and references

Cameron, Alex Alfred, Mary Quayle Innis and J. Howard Richards (1954, 1968), *Living in Canada*, Toronto: Clarke, Irwin.
Henson, G. (1936), 'An economic history of Canada' (Book review), *Dalhousie Review*, **16**, 127–30.
Innis, Harold Adams (1923), *A History of the Canadian Pacific Railway*, Toronto: University of Toronto Press.
Innis, Harold Adams (ed.) (1929), *Select Documents in Canadian Economic History, 1497–1783*, Toronto: University of Toronto Press.
Innis, Harold Adams (1930, 1956), *The Fur Trade in Canada*, Toronto: University of Toronto Press.
Innis, Harold Adams (1940, 1954), *The Cod Fisheries*, Toronto: University of Toronto Press.
Innis, Harold Adams (1950, 1972), *Empire and Communications*, Oxford: Clarendon Press.
Innis, Harold Adams (1956), *Essays in Canadian Economic History*, Toronto: University of Toronto Press.
Mavor, James (1923), *My Windows on the Street of the World*, London: Dent.
Pell, Barbara (1989), 'Mary Quayle Innis', *Dictionary of Literary Biography*, **88**, 132–4.
Trotter, R.G. (1936), 'Pioneering and nation-building' (Book review), *Queen's Quarterly*, **43**, 213–18.

Alice Hanson Jones (1904–86)

Alice Hanson was born in Seattle on 7 November 1904 to Olof Hanson and Agatha Marie (Teigel) Hanson. She earned an AB in 1925 from the University of Washington where she served as a teaching fellow in 1927–28 and earned an MA in 1928. She married Homer Jones on 21 April 1930 and subsequently bore three children: Robert Hanson, Richard John and Douglas Coulthurst.

Her career included both academic appointments and work for various government agencies. In 1930, she served as assistant editor of *The Encyclopedia of the Social Sciences*, and then in 1931 became a researcher and writer for the President's Committee on Social Trends in New York City. She worked as an economist in the Cost of Living Division of the Bureau of Labor Statistics in Washington from 1934 until 1944, and then in the Bureau of the Budget from 1945 until 1948. In 1957 she became Secretary of the Committee on National Accounts at the National Bureau of Economic Research in Washington, and from 1958 until 1961 served as a supervising economist in the Consumer and Food Economics Research Division of the Department of Agriculture in Washington.

Jones became a lecturer in economics at Washington University in St Louis in 1963. After earning a Ph.D. from the University of Chicago in 1968, she became an assistant professor and an associate professor in 1971. In 1973 she became an adjunct professor at the University of Washington, a post she held until she retired in 1977. She served as an economic adviser to the Bank of Korea in 1967–68, and to the Agency for International Development during the same period.

Jones's most important academic work was in the area of American economic history and she served as Vice-President of the Economic History Association in 1976–77, President in 1982–83 and Trustee from 1983 until 1986. She died on 30 August 1986, five months after the death of her husband of 56 years.

Her most important publications include the three-volume *American Colonial Wealth: Documents and Methods* (1978) and *Wealth of a Nation to Be: The American Colonies on the Eve of the Revolution* (1980).

EVELYN L. FORGET

Bibliography

Selected writings by Alice Hanson Jones
(1970), 'Wealth estimates for the American middle colonies, 1774', *Economic Development and Cultural Change*, **18**(4), Part II.
(1972), 'Wealth estimates for the New England colonies about 1770', *Journal* of *Economic History*, **32**(1), 98–127.

(1978), *American Colonial Wealth*, 2nd edn, New York: Arno Press.
(1980), *Wealth of a Nation to Be: American Colonies on the Eve* of *the Revolution*, New York: Columbia University Press.
(1984), 'Wealth and growth of the thirteen colonies: some implications', *Journal of Economic History*, **44**(2), 239–54.
(1992), 'The wealth of women, 1774', in Claudia Goldin and Hugh Rockoff (eds), *Strategic Factors in Nineteenth-Century American Economic History: A Volume to Honor Robert W. Fogel*, Chicago: University of Chicago Press, pp. 243–63.

Other sources and references

Who Was Who in America? vol. IX: 1985–1989, Wilmette, IL: Marquis – Who's Who, 1989.

Florence Kelley (1859–1932)

Lawyer, social scientist and social reformer, Florence Kelley was best known for her activities as Executive Director of the National Consumers' League from the time of its founding in 1899 until her death in 1932. In that capacity she pursued labour legislation that achieved pathbreaking interventions in the relationship between employers and employees.

Kelley was born into a patrician Quaker and Unitarian family in Philadelphia, the daughter of William Durrah Kelley, a leading politician, and Caroline Bonsall Kelley, a descendant of John Bartram, the Quaker botanist. During a childhood plagued by illness she attended school only sporadically. Her intellectual development was nurtured by her father and her mother's aunt, Sarah Pugh. Her father, abolitionist, founding member of the Republican Party, Radical Reconstructionist, and US congressman from Philadelphia from 1860 until his death in 1890, became her chief mentor. Sarah Pugh, head of the Philadelphia Female Antislavery Society, close friend of Lucretia Mott, and correspondent of British reformers like Richard Cobden and John Bright, exemplified the ability of single women to devote their lives to reform causes. Florence often visited her grandparents' home, where Sarah Pugh lived, and heard about the women's rights activism of Pugh and Mott. For her, Sarah Pugh became 'conscience incarnate'.

During six mostly schoolless years before she entered Cornell University, Florence systematically read her father's library, imbibing the fiction of Dickens and Thackeray, Louisa May Alcott and Horatio Alger, the poetry of Shakespeare, Milton, Byron and Goldsmith, the writings of James Madison, histories by Bancroft, Prescott and Parkman, and the moral and political philosophy of Emerson, Channing, Burke, Carlyle, Godwin and Spencer.

Florence Kelley's childhood was also shaped by her mother's permanent depression, caused by the death of five of her eight children before they had reached the age of six. Two brothers but no sisters survived. Caroline Kelley developed a 'settled, gentle melancholy' that threatened to envelop her daughter so long as she lived at home.

At Cornell Florence studied history and social science, graduating in 1882. She spent her senior year in Washington DC, where she lived with her father and researched her honours essay in the Library of Congress. That essay, 'On Some Changes in the Legal Status of the Child since Blackstone', was published in 1882 in *The International Review*. Facing a very limited set of opportunities after college, and her application for graduate study rejected by the University of Pennsylvania on account of her sex, Kelley threw her energies into the New Century Working Women's Guild, an organization that fostered middle-class aid for self-supporting women. She helped found the Guild, taught classes in history, and assembled the group's library. Most importantly, perhaps, she escaped her mother's melancholy by developing a rage against social injustice, which she first expressed in an 1882 article, 'Need Our Working Women Despair?'

Remaining a dutiful daughter, in 1882 she accompanied her brother when his doctor prescribed a winter of European travel to cure temporary blindness. In Europe she encountered M. Carey Thomas, a Cornell acquaintance, who had just completed a Ph.D. at the University of Zürich, the only European university that granted degrees to women. From 1883 to 1886 Kelley also studied there, initially accompanied by her mother and younger brother. Her focus on government and law brought her into contact with the vital group of Russian emigrés, and in the autumn of 1884 she married Lazare Wischnewetzky, a Russian Jewish socialist medical student. The first of their three children, Nicholas, was born in July 1885.

She also joined the German Social Democratic Party. Outlawed in Germany, the Party maintained its European headquarters in Zürich, and Kelley met many of its leaders. Abandoning her pursuit of a postgraduate degree, she instead translated into English a classic work by Friedrich Engels, *The Condition of the Working Class in England*, published in German in 1845. This project launched a close but troubled relationship with Engels that persisted until his death in 1895.

Kelley returned to the USA in the autumn of 1886 with her husband and young son, taking up residence in New York City. Another child, Margaret, was born in 1887, and another son John, in 1888. In New York she found it impossible to continue the political commitments that she had begun in Zürich. Her Philadelphia friend, Rachel Foster Avery, then Secretary of the National Woman Suffrage Association, financed the publication of her translation of Engels's *Condition* (the book listed Avery as the copyright-holder), but Kelley's insistence on the importance of the writings of Marx and Engels led to her expulsion from the Socialist Labour Party in 1887. Party leaders resented Engels's preface to the *Condition*, which, at Kelley's urging, chastised the German-speaking majority of the Party for its isolation from the American labour movement.

Forced to pursue a new path, Kelley returned to her interest in child labour. She quickly became known as a sharp critic of state bureaus of labour statistics for their inadequate attention to child labour, and published articles on child labour in popular magazines.

Lazare, meanwhile, never found his footing in the USA. His medical practice dwindling to non-existence, he began beating her. At the end of 1891 she fled with their children to Chicago, going first to the 'Woman's Temple' headquarters of the Women's Christian Temperance Union, the WCTU having published her hard-hitting pamphlet, *Our Toiling Children* (1889). Her WCTU editor directed her to Hull House, the innovative social settlement founded by Jane Addams and Ellen Gates Starr in 1889. There she lived happily and productively until 1899.

Kelley exerted an immediate and dramatic influence on the generation of women reformers who clustered within the social settlement movement during the Progressive era. Her understanding of the material basis of class conflict and her familiarity with American political institutions, combined with her spirited personality, placed her in the vanguard of a generation of reformers who sought to make American government more responsive to what they saw as the needs of working people. In this way they were critical components in the process by which American governments, state and national, shifted from liberal *laissez-faire* policies to positive regulatory programmes. Kelley summarized her reform strategy in the phrase, 'investigate, educate, legislate, and enforce'. These tactics drew on her talents as a social scientist, a publicist, a lobbyist and an attorney. They also provided women reformers with a blueprint for revising the contours of government.

Soon after her arrival in Chicago Kelley resumed the law studies that she had begun in Zürich, completing her degree at Northwestern Law School in 1895. First, however, Addams helped Kelley place her children in the comfortable home of Henry Demarest Lloyd and Jessie Bross Lloyd in nearby Winnetka. Then she aided Kelley's appointment as a special agent of the Illinois Bureau of Labor Statistics. In that capacity Kelley completed one thousand schedules by 'sweaters victims' in the garment industry, first visiting them at work, then at home. Hearing of her reputation, Carroll Wright, Head of the US Department of Labor, hired her in the autumn of 1892 to direct a cadre of 'schedule men' who collected data from each house, tenement and room in the nineteenth ward, where Hull House was located. With the help of other Hull House residents, Kelley used these data to compile pathbreaking occupational and nationality maps later printed in *Hull House Maps and Papers* (1895). Sharing the podium with other civic leaders, including Henry Demarest Lloyd, Kelley often spoke at 'monster meetings' called to protest sweatshop working conditions. In the autumn of 1892 she wrote a sweeping report on the sweatshop problem and how to end it. The essentials of her recommendations were adopted in a bill passed by the Illinois legislature in June 1893, which limited women's and children's working hours to eight per day, prohibited commercial production in tenement homes, and provided for the law's enforcement with the creation of a Factory Inspector's office with a staff of 12, half of whom were required to be women. Illinois's reform-minded governor, John Peter Altgeld, promptly appointed Kelley Chief Factory Inspector.

As Chief Factory Inspector Kelley supervised manufacturing working conditions in an area two-thirds the size of Prussia. No other woman in the western world exercised equivalent power. She assembled a dedicated staff that included union organizers and socialists. Their vigorous enforcement of the law precipitated the formation of the Illinois Manufacturers' Association, which in 1895 obtained in Ritchie *v.* the People of Illinois an Illinois Supreme Court ruling that found unconstitutional the portion of the law mandating an eight-hour day for women. Kelley lost her office when Altgeld failed in his reelection bid in 1896. For three years she worked part-time at Crerar Library and paid her children's tuition bills by writing regularly for German social reform publications.

In 1899 Kelley agreed to serve as Secretary of the newly formed National Consumers' League, a position she held until her death. This took her to New York, where between 1899 and 1926 she lived at the Henry Street Settlement, Lillian Wald's 'nurses' settlement' on Manhattan's Lower East Side. Her children moved with her. Supported by aid from Jane Addams's life partner, Mary Rozet Smith, Nicholas Kelley graduated from Harvard in 1905 and then from Harvard Law School. Living in Manhattan, he became his mother's closest adviser. In a blow that caused her mother to spend the rest of the year in retirement in Maine, Margaret Kelley died of heart failure during her first week at Smith College in 1905. After this bereavement Kelley maintained a summer home on Penobscot Bay, Maine, where she retreated for periods of intense work with a secretary each summer. John Kelley never found a professional niche, but remained close to his mother and joined her in Maine each summer.

Kelley made the National Consumers' League into the nation's leading promoter of protective labour legislation for women and children. Between 1900 and 1904 she built 64 local consumer leagues – one in nearly every large city outside the south. Through a demanding travel schedule, which required her to spend one day on the road for every day she worked at her desk, Kelley maintained close contact with local leagues, urging them to implement the national organization's agenda, and inspiring them to greater action within their states and municipalities. Aiding the development of local leagues was the NCL's campaign to promote the adoption of a Consumers' White Label among local manufacturers. The NCL awarded its label to manufacturers who obeyed state factory laws, produced goods only on their own premises, did not require employees to work overtime, and did not employ children under 16 years of age. In determining whether local factories qualified for the label, league members learned a great deal about local working conditions. This prepared them for the next stage of league work – the promotion of state laws limiting women's working day to ten hours. The NCL also promoted its agenda through alliances with the mainstream women's organizations; within the General Federation of Women's Clubs between 1900 and 1902, Kelley chaired its standing committee on 'The Industrial Problem as It Affects Women and Children', and in 1903 she chaired the child labour committees in both the National Congress of Mothers and the National American Woman Suffrage Association. In her 1906 book, *Some Ethical Gains Through Legislation*, Kelley urged upon her readers the child's 'right to childhood', the working woman's 'right to leisure', 'the right to leisure of workingmen', along with 'the right of women to the ballot', and 'the rights of purchasers'.

The path for the NCL's legislative agenda on women's working hours was cleared in 1908, when the US Supreme Court upheld an Oregon ten-hour-day law for women. This case, Muller *v*. Oregon, pitted the NCL and its Oregon branch against a laundry owner who disputed the state's ability to regulate working hours in non-hazardous occupations. Louis D. Brandeis argued Oregon's case before the Supreme Court, based on research done by his sister-in-law, Josephine Goldmark, who was Director of Research at NCL. For what became known as the 'Brandeis Brief' Goldmark collected socio-logical rather than legal evidence, citing medical and other authorities to demonstrate that working days longer than ten hours were hazardous to the health of women. In accepting and basing their ruling on this data, the Supreme Court for the first time validated the use of sociological evidence.

Florence Kelley was deeply gratified by this ruling since it partially over-turned the Court's 1906 ruling in Lochner *v*. New York, which had found any regulation of hours in non-hazardous occupation unconstitutional, and defi-nitely overturned the Illinois Supreme Court's 1895 Ritchie ruling against the regulation of women's hours. Based on the Muller decision, inspired by Kelley's leadership, and joining with other groups, local consumer leagues gained the passage in 20 states of the first law limiting women's working hours. In response to the Muller decision, 19 other states revised their laws governing women's working hours.

The Court's 1908 opinion emphasized women's special legal (they did not possess the same contractual rights as men) and physiological (their health affected the health of their future children) circumstances, trying thereby to block the extension of such protections to men. Nevertheless, in 1917 Kelley and the NCL again cooperated successfully with the Oregon local league in bringing a case before the US Supreme Court, Bunting *v*. Oregon, in which the Court upheld the constitutionality of working hours laws for men in non-hazardous occupations. The Bunting case highlighted Kelley's commit-ment to labour legislation protecting men as well as women. She viewed laws for women as an entering wedge for achieving remedies for all working people.

After 1909 Kelley gave state minimum wage legislation a prominent place on the NCL agenda. Her goal was to prevent the downward spiralling of wages in some industries that paid workers less than what it cost to support themselves. Such workers then needed public relief, and such assistance seemed to her and other reformers to constitute an unfair public subsidy of employers who paid their workers poorly. Although new British minimum wage laws applied to all persons in certain poorly paid occupations, Kelley knew that the feasibility of wage regulations in the USA would have to be demonstrated first with regard to women and then extended to men. The NCL's campaign was remarkably successful: by 1919, 14 states and the District of Columbia and Puerto Rico had enacted minimum wage statutes for women. Their momentum stalled in 1923 when the US Supreme Court in Adkins *v.* Children's Hospital found Washington DC's wage law unconstitutional. Many state wage boards continued to function during the 1920s and 1930s, however, providing ample evidence of the benefits of the law, and serving as a basis for the inclusion of minimum wages for both women and men within the Fair Labor Standards Law of 1938.

At Henry Street Kelley continued to benefit from the same consolidation of female reform talents that had sustained her efforts at Hull House in Chicago. The creation of the US Children's Bureau in 1911 sprang from an idea generated by Kelley and Wald at Henry Street. That bureau was the only agency within governments in industrial societies that was run by women. Kelley herself thought that her most important social contribution was the passage in 1921 of the Sheppard–Towner Maternity and Infancy Protection Act, which first allocated federal funds to health care in a programme administered by the Children's Bureau to combat infant and maternal mortality. Kelley was instrumental in the creation of the coalition that backed the Act's passage, the Women's Joint Congressional Committee, and in the coalition's successful campaign for the bill in Congress.

By 1923 Kelley's strategy of using gender-specific legislation as a surrogate for class legislation had generated opposition from a new quarter – women who did not themselves benefit from gendered laws. The National Woman's Party (NWP), formed in 1916 by the charismatic leadership of Alice Paul and funded almost entirely by Alva Belmont, created a small coalition consisting primarily of professional women with some wage-earning women who worked in male-dominated occupations.

Despite Kelley's strong objections over the damage they would do to gender-specific legislation, including the Sheppard–Towner Act, in 1921 the NWP proposed an Equal Rights Amendment to the US Constitution. Although mainstream organizations like the General Federation of Women's Clubs and the League of Women Voters continued to support gender-specific legislation, the NWP's proposed amendment undercut the momentum of such gendered strategies. In some cases, as in their consultation with Justice George Sutherland who wrote the brief in the Adkins case, NWP leaders directly torpedoed women's labour legislation.

Florence Kelley spent the last decade of her life trying to repair the damage done by attacks on her agenda during the 'red scare' of the 1920s, both from the NWP and from virulent right-wing groups who called her Mrs Wischnewetzky and named her 'Moscow's chief conspirator.' Although she did not live to see it, many of her initiatives were incorporated into federal legislation in the 1930s under the leadership of her protegé, Frances Perkins, who, as the first woman cabinet member in the USA, served as Secretary of Labor.

KATHRYN KISH SKLAR

Bibliography

Writings and biography
Personal papers at the New York Public Library.
National Consumers' League papers at the Library of Congress.
Jane Addams papers at Swarthmore College.
Lillian Wald papers at New York Public Library and Columbia University.
Consumers' League of Massachusetts papers at the Schlesinger Library.
Henry Demarest Lloyd papers at the State Historical Society of Wisconsin.

Kelley's writings are voluminous. Her brief autobiography has been reprinted:
Sklar, Kathryn Kish (ed.) (1986), *Notes of Sixty Years: The Autobiography of Florence Kelley*, Chicago: Charles Kerr.
For the most complete account of Kelley's life before 1900 and for a bibliography of her writings before 1900 see:
Sklar, Kathryn Kish (1995), *Florence Kelley and the Nation's Work: The Rise of Women's Political Culture, 1830–1900*, New Haven: Yale University Press.
For the NCL's minimum wage work, see:
Sklar, Kathryn Kish (1995), 'Two Political Cultures in the Progressive Era: the National Consumers' League and the American Association for Labor Legislation', in Linda K. Kerber, Alice Kessler-Harris and Kathryn Kish Sklar (eds), *U.S. History as Women's History: New Feminist Essays*.

Other sources and references
Blumberg, Dorothy Rose (1964), '"Dear Mr. Engels": Unpublished Letters, 1884–1894, of Florence Kelley (Wischnewetzky) to Friedrich Engels', *Labor History*, **5**, Spring, 103–33.
Blumberg, Dorothy Rose (1966), *Florence Kelley: the Making of a Social Pioneer*, New York: Augustus M. Kelley.
Goldmark, Josephine (1953), *Impatient Crusader: Florence Kelley's Life Story*, Urbana: University of Illinois Press.
Kelley, Nicholas (1954), 'Early Days at Hull House', *Social Service Review*, **28**, December, 424–9.

Susan Myra Kingsbury (1870–1949)

Susan Myra Kingsbury was born on 18 August 1870, in San Pablo, California. She had one older brother and no sisters. Her parents, William Belmont Kingsbury, a physician, and Helen Shuler (De Lamater) Kingsbury, had relocated to California from Michigan. Kingsbury's father died by the time she was seven, and her mother supported herself and both children as Dean of

Women at the College of the Pacific in Stockton, California. In 1890, Kingsbury graduated from that college with honours. She subsequently taught in a rural school and then a boys' high school in San Francisco. In 1899, she received a master's degree in history from Stanford University and became a member of Phi Beta Kappa.[1]

In 1900, after her mother died, Kingsbury entered Columbia University to do graduate work in economics and history and became a university fellow in 1902–3. On a fellowship in 1903–4 she studied in England for a year, returning home armed with knowledge of the work of Beatrice Potter Webb and Seebohm Rowntree. Then, after a year in which Kingsbury was a history instructor at Vassar College, she received her doctorate from Columbia University in 1905. Her dissertation was entitled Introduction to the Records of the Virginia Company of London. In the next ten years, she made a short-term investigation on the relation of children to industries for the Massachusetts Commission on Industrial and Technical Education and taught at Simmons College in Boston, where she progressed through the ranks to Full Professor in Economics. During most of this time, she was the Director of Research at the Women's Educational and Industrial Union of Boston, where her mandate was 'to protect and improve the industrial conditions of women' (Kingsbury, 1911, p. xxii). This organization sponsored fellowships for graduate students; under Kingsbury's direction, these students published numerous studies, some of which appeared as collections, edited by her.

In 1912, M. Carey Thomas, the President of Bryn Mawr College, noted Kingsbury's address at a meeting of what was to become the American Association of University Women and invited her to become Chair of the newly created Carola Woerishoffer Graduate Department of Social Economy and Social Research at Bryn Mawr (named after a former student with the bequest she left to the school), the first professional social service school in the USA to have an academic affiliation. Kingsbury accepted and, after fulfilling prior commitments in Boston, she became Professor of Social Economy and Chair of the Graduate Department in 1915. She designed the graduate programme, which offered masters' and doctoral degrees in four areas, including social case work and industrial relations. She helped plan the Bryn Mawr Summer School for Women Workers in Industry and directed numerous doctoral theses. She was said by her colleague and co-author, Mildred Fairchild (Woodbury), to be an 'outstanding and beloved teacher' (Woodbury, 1971, p. 366). She was active in campus activities.

Kingsbury engaged in international travel, including trips to China and India. She travelled to Soviet Russia three times. On the basis of research undertaken during some of her travels, she co-authored two books on aspects of the post-Revolution socialization programmes in the Soviet economy. The first of these, *Employment and Unemployment in Prewar and Soviet Russia*, with Mildred Fairchild, presents data of Soviet Russia 'for a comparative study at the 1931 World Social Economic Congress' in the words of Mary Van Kleeck, who served as Chair of the Program Committee of the Congress (Kingsbury and Fairchild, 1931, Preface by Van Kleeck, p. 11). Given their work, the authors concluded that industrial production, employment, productivity and (real and nominal) wages were considerably higher in 1930 relative to 1913, although they noted a 'cataclysmic drop' in the figures during the 1920s (p. 101).

The second book (with responsibility for some of the chapters assumed by each author), *Factory, Family, and Woman in the Soviet Union*, with Mildred Fairchild, has a broader focus than the first. It is a provocative treatise covering the impact of the reorganization of Soviet Russia's economy on its society over the period 1915–32. Along with other material, it includes the authors' assessments of changes in the structure of women's lives and the family, given the government edicts of the times. They indicated the diversity of occupations in which women were found and, in part, attributed this to the fact that in the Soviet Union limitation of women's ability to engage in physical labour was determined on the basis of scientific research as opposed to tradition as in other countries; furthermore, they noted the explosive emergence of women into industry. Specifically, they concluded that 'women are not only in all types of industry; all types of women are in industry' (p. 263). They also examined men's and women's wages and concluded that they were similar within identical jobs, although women tended to have lower-paying jobs; none the less, they noted that women's wages due to the reorganization had, on average, increased from 50 per cent to 65–75 per cent of men's. Moreover, they felt that men and women received equitable opportunity to obtain training and jobs, and they were impressed with the possibility of promotion for women to significant positions. They did notice, however, that '[i]n Soviet Russia, as in America and Europe, … the woman … carries a double burden' (p. 269) of work outside and inside the home; they noted some easing of this burden by state provision of goods and services (for example, child and health care, laundry, meals). In summary, this book offers a detailed, fascinating view of the changes in economic organization that occurred in Soviet Russia, with specific attention paid to the impact on welfare of women and the family.

Kingsbury evidently was well known in professional circles. She served as Vice-President of both the American Economic Association in 1919 and the American Sociological Association. She was Chair of the National Committee on the Economic and Legal Status of Women of the American Association of University Women. She helped to found the American Association of Schools of Social Work. She received a number of honorary doctorates.

While Kingsbury's professional life was demanding, she managed outside activities as well. For example, she owned and helped to found a girls' camp in Maine. She enjoyed driving and horse-riding as hobbies.

Kingsbury officially retired in 1936, but participated in professional activities for some time thereafter. She died at her home in Bryn Mawr, Pennsylvania, on 28 November 1949.

Kingsbury was one of the earliest female Ph.D.s in the USA; at the time when she received her degree, less than a few hundred had been granted to women in the USA. She was one of the earliest female members of an academic economics department in the USA, and one of the few female chairs of a graduate department at the time.

SUSAN H. GENSEMER

Note

1. Biographical information on Kingsbury is taken from: Howes (1939), p. 488; Hutchinson (1930); Kingsbury entry in *Who Was Who in America: A Companion Biographical Reference Work to Who's Who in America* (1950); Meigs (1956); Woodbury (1971), pp. 335–6.

Bibliography

Selected writings by Susan Myra Kingsbury

(1905), *Introduction to the Records of the Virginia Company of London, with a Bibliographic List of the Extant Documents*, Ph.D. dissertation, Columbia University: Government Printing Office.

(1905), The Records of the Virginia Company of London, Government Printing Office, Introduction by Kingsbury.

(1910a), 'Opportunities for women trained in research', in Agnes Perkins (ed.), *Vocations for the Trained Woman: Opportunities Other Than Teaching*, New York: Longmans, Green, and Co., pp. 1–3.

(1910b), 'Economic research', in Agnes Perkins (ed.), *Vocations for the Trained Woman: Opportunities Other Than Teaching*, New York: Longmans, Green, and Co., pp. 28–9.

(1931), *Employment and Unemployment in Prewar and Soviet Russia* (with Mildred Fairchild), Schiedam, Holland: De Eendracht.

(1935), *Factory, Family, and Woman in the Soviet Union* (with Mildred Fairchild), New York: G.P. Putnam's Sons.

(1937), *Newspapers and the News, an Objective Measurement of Ethical and Unethical Behavior by Representative Newspapers*, New York: G.P. Putnam's Sons, 1937.

(1939), *Economic Status of University Women in the USA*, Report of the Committee on Economic and Legal Status of Women of American Association of University Women.

Women's Educational and Industrial Union, Department of Research Studies

(1911), *Labor Laws and Their Enforcement with Special Reference to Massachusetts*, by Charles E. Persons et al., edited and with an introduction by Kingsbury, New York: Longmans, Green, and Co.; Women's Educational and Industrial Union, Department of Research, Studies in Economic Relations of Women.

(1914), *Vocations for Trained Woman; Agriculture, Social Service, Secretarial Service, Business of Real Estate*, by Eleanor Martin and Margaret A. Post and Committee on Economic Efficiency of College Women, Boston Branch, Association of Collegiate Alumnae, directed by Kingsbury, New York: Longmans, Green, and Co., 1914; Women's Educational and

Industrial Union, Department of Research, Studies in Economic Relations of Women, vol. 1, pt 2.

(1915), *Licensed Workers in Industrial Home Work in Massachusetts: Analysis of Current Records* (with Mabelle Moses), Bureau of Research, Women's Educational and Industrial Union, Boston: Wright and Potter, State Printers.

(1916a), *Dressmaking as a Trade*, by May Allinson, directed by Kingsbury, Bureau of Research, Women's Educational and Industrial Union.

(1916b), *Opportunities for Women in Domestic Science*, by Marie Francke, directed by Kingsbury, Women's Educational and Industrial Union, Department of Research.

(1916c), *Millinery as a Trade for Women*, by Lorinda Perry, directed by Kingsbury, Women's Educational and Industrial Union, Department of Research, Studies in Economic Relations of Women, vol. 5, Bryn Mawr Thesis.

(1917), *Industrial Experience of Trade School Girls in Massachusetts*, by May Allinson, directed by Kingsbury, Bulletin of the US Bureau of Labor Statistics no. 215, Women in Industry Series no. 10; Women's Educational and Industrial Union, Department of Research, Studies in Economic Relations of Women.

Other sources and references

Howes, Durward (ed.) (1939), Kingsbury Entry in *American Women: The Standard Biographical Dictionary of Notable Women*, vol. III, 1939–40, Los Angeles: American Publications, Inc., p. 488.

Hutchinson, Emilie (1930), *Women and the PhD: Facts from the Experiences of 1,025 Women Who Have Taken the Doctor of Philosophy Since 1877*, Greensboro, NC: NC College for Women.

Meigs, Cornelia (1956), *What Makes a College?* New York: Macmillan.

Who Was Who in America: A Companion Biographical Reference Work to Who's Who in America (1950), vol. 2, Chicago: The A.N. Marquis Company.

Woodbury, Mildred Fairchild (1971), Kingsbury Entry in *Notable American Women, 1607–1950*, Cambridge, MA: Belknap Press of Harvard University Press, pp. 335–6.

Karin Kock (1891–1976)

Born in 1891, Karin Kock grew up in Stockholm in an upper-middle-class environment that allowed young girls to aspire to careers and accomplishments beyond the reach of girls of lesser social standing. She belonged to the small group of privileged women who, through access to a progressive part of the Swedish school system, could go on to gain a university degree, although that was a path of social pioneering on to which only girls of exceptional excellence would venture.

Kock's choice of subject, when she entered Stockholm University in 1910, was mathematics. However, after having completed one year of mathematical studies with distinction, she interrupted further academic work for a number of years and took a position with the Statistical Office of the City of Stockholm. When she resumed her studies in 1915 she pursued statistics as a minor and economics as a major addition to her previous mathematics and obtained a *fil.kand.*, the basic Swedish academic degree, in 1918.

In her pursuit of economics Kock had done very well. Becoming especially interested in issues of monetary economics, after having attended Gustav

Cassel's lectures, she decided to go on towards a higher degree in economics, with money and banking as her field of specialization. With her good experience in statistical work and with her excellent study record, she was, on Cassel's recommendation, able to secure a good financial and institutional basis suited for her plans. In 1918 she obtained a position in the statistical office and secretariat of the Skandinaviska Kredit AB, Sweden's largest commercial bank, where she remained employed for 15 years.

Kock completed her first year of graduate work in spring 1919 with a paper on the concentration tendencies in the Swedish banking sector. She then obtained, again with the backing of Cassel, a stipend that allowed her to study in England at the London School of Economics for the academic year 1919–20, while also spending part of her time working at Barclays Bank. After returning from England, Kock participated in the licentiate seminar at Stockholm University, conducted by the recently appointed Second Professor of Economics, Gösta Bagge. In 1923/24 she presented a paper to the seminar with the title 'Penningvärdets växlingar och räntan på korta och långa lån' ('Changes in the value of money and the short-term and long-term rate of interest'). As the title indicates, she had now arrived at the core theme for her subsequent research, which in modern theory would be classified under the heading 'the term structure of interest rates'. However, from the perspective of modern theory, she pursued this theme more generally as an inquiry into the relative interest rate structure in an imperfect capital market, also taking into account risks and institutional factors. In winding up her work for the *fil.lic.* degree she presented, in autumn 1924, an empirically focused paper on 'The development of the American credit market 1919–22' and after completing an oral examination for Bagge, she was awarded her degree in 1925.

As Kock had earned her licentiate degree 'with distinction', she felt encouraged to go on towards a doctor's degree. She began this enterprise with a second research period in England during the academic year 1925–26. Again she was supported partly by a grant which Cassel had endorsed. Her initial plan for the doctoral dissertation was to undertake a comparative study and to extend her licentiate thesis to cover not only the American but also the English loan market. However, as a result of her new study sojourn in England, she widened as well as deepened the scope of her dissertation work considerably and also gave special attention to international capital movements and to the influence of the trade cycle. In addition, she undoubtedly received new theoretical impulses from Gregory, Hawtrey and other leading economists she met in London and Cambridge. Now Swedish thinking also began to play a role in her research, with Gunnar Myrdal as probably the most important influence. After intense work in 1928 Kock's dissertation *A Study of Interest Rates* was finally published and defended for the doctor's degree at Stockholm University in February 1929 (Kock, 1929).

Basically because of Cassel's failure to appreciate its strengths, Kock's dissertation was not graded high enough to grant her a docentship in the Department of Economics immediately.[1] In the view of later assessors her study was underrated. But after a few years Kock had added enough to her publication list to qualify for a docent position (Kock, 1930, 1931c, 1932). These early postdoctoral works were mainly economic–historical, where her methodical and meticulous research paid off well. After receiving encouragement from Eli Heckscher, she made this type of research one of her intellectual priorities in the years to come. She was later, especially in her emeritus years, to make a number of economic–historical contributions of lasting value (Kock, 1937a, 1937b , 1944, 1959, 1961–62, 1969). Particularly interesting is her discussion of Torsten Gårdlund's dissertation (Gårdlund, 1941), where she raised several methodological points anticipating many of the later views of the cliometric school on how economic theory could and should be applied in historical writings (Kock, 1942).

Kock's early postdoctoral period coincided with the embryonic phase of the so-called Stockholm School. In that process Kock became for the local community of Stockholm economists something of a jack of all trades in providing her colleagues with many types of institutional and infrastructural services that an emergent academic profession requires. One such service was her contribution to the Political Economy Club, which in 1926 she became the first woman to enter. A notable occasion was a speech she gave in October 1931, a month after Sweden had left the gold standard, in which she surveyed the events that had lead to that decision. Her presentation was planned to be a background in a joint publication by the leading older and younger members of the club circle, with Heckscher and Myrdal as the main contributors (Henriksson, 1991). Their intention was to present a united front of informed professional views outlining the right action to be taken by the policy-makers. Heckscher, however, could not accept the first draft written by Myrdal and instead he rushed a book into print independent of the group project (Heckscher, 1931). Kock then helped Myrdal to have his manuscript published within a couple of weeks (Myrdal, 1931). Her own delivery in the club was entered as an appendix in that publication (Kock, 1931a).

Another, more logistically important activity was Kock's services in the Swedish Economic Society, where she held the position as secretary and editor of its proceedings through 1931–36. In the same capacity she was also in charge of the organizational arrangements that fell on that society as host to the important Meeting of Nordic Economists in the summer of 1931. She also served as both editor and contributor to the Cassel Festschrift, which appeared in 1933 (Kock, 1933c).

Formally appointed in 1933 as docent in economics at Stockholm University, Kock was now able to support herself fully through academic work; she had already left her position with the Skandinaviska Kredit AB in 1932. The following five years with the Department of Economics was a period of great theoretical as well as economic policy upheaval in Sweden, generating a number of interesting assignments for her. Although Kock was not in the front row of the Stockholm School in an analytical sense, she nevertheless assumed the school's policy stance and was a highly respected member of that group not only for her institutional services but also for her intellectual clarity. She delivered a number of reports on current issues pertaining to the national as well as to the international scene, and she was influential in employing the new theoretical outlook on the short-term as well as on the long-term development of the economy (Kock, 1933a, 1933b, 1934a, 1934b, 1935, 1936a, 1936b, 1938b).

Many of Kock's policy-oriented writings were done on the request of the government. Her first assignment was a minor statistical research project for the 1927 Unemployment Investigation (Kock, 1931b), but she was thereafter enlisted in several major tasks. An early notable appointment was her position as secretary to the Foreign Exchange Committee that was assembled in May 1933 to assess the price level stabilization norm that Sweden had assumed after having suspended its alignment with the gold standard in 1931. Among later similar assignments an important one was the task of preparing for the setting up of the Konjunkturinstitutet (KI), Sweden's economic survey and research institute, a brainchild of Dag Hammarskjöld (Henriksson, 1987). She also surveyed the importance of the forestry sector for the Swedish economy (Kock, 1938c) and analysed the position of women on the labour market (Kock, 1938a).

From 1938 to the end of the war, Kock was mainly preoccupied with teaching. She now served as acting professor and stand-in, sometimes for Bagge, and sometimes for Myrdal, when these professors were called to long-term preoccupations with other duties. At that time the teaching load imposed on the department had increased considerably due to the introduction of the popular *pol.mag.* degree, in which students could combine economics with statistics and political science. As the increased number of students was not met by a corresponding increase in faculty size, Kock could find less time than previously for research, but she was nevertheless quite productive. Her most important contribution in this period was her work on short-term capital movements, which had been one of the themes in her dissertation (Kock, 1939). Furthermore, she was again enlisted in government assignments; the Ministry of Finance, in particular, requested her assistance on various economic policy steps made necessary by the war (Kock, 1943).

As the war drew to a close, Kock was eventually, while still in charge of her professorial duties at Stockholm University, appointed to the important position of Head Secretary in the so-called Myrdal Commission, the formal government temporary peace planning body that was set up in 1944. Here Kock proved her salt for higher-level public service. At the end of 1945 she responded to a call to leave her university position permanently to assume important economic policy and research responsibilities with the Ministry of Trade, now headed by Myrdal. Earlier that year, in recognition of her long service at the highest level of teaching and research in the Department of Economics, she was awarded the title of Honorary Professor.

One of the preconditions for Kock's move from university to government work was that in the 1930s she changed her political allegiance from the Liberal Party to the Social Democrats. This was a notable switch, as she had been a parliamentary candidate of the Liberal Party in the 1932 election. She seems to have followed Myrdal and a number of other economists, who turned left politically after that year. However, she did not formally join the Social Democratic Party until the 1940s. It appears that she was never a very radical socialist and she seems to have preserved, even in her years of service for the Social Democratic government, some of the social liberalism that was her basic political belief in younger days.

In her new government service that started in 1946, Kock was initially stationed as an expert under Myrdal, but when Myrdal resigned from his ministerial post in early 1947 Kock was appointed member of the cabinet as a consultant expert closely related with the prime minister. One of her assignments was the post of government representative in postwar economic reconstruction efforts and restoration of economic cooperation and trade between countries that were now on the international agenda. In domestic affairs she was put in charge of structural industrial questions and various types of coordination efforts in the sphere of economic stabilization policy. The former type of issues she inherited from Myrdal, who in his period as Minister of Trade had tried to launch policy ideas worked out in the previously mentioned Myrdal Commission. However, Kock's efforts with efficiency-promoting industry cooperation schemes such as industrial councils and other projects in the central planning spirit of that commission were ill fated. Actually Myrdal's proposals had already foundered before he resigned, thus leaving Kock with a task that was bound to fail.

The short-term economic coordination attempts also turned out to be less successful in the end. Kock led a group of economists who worked on setting up a so-called national budget for the total economy. It was meant to be a comprehensive planning and forecasting tool to serve as a framing device for the social and economic policy reform ambitions of the Social Democrats. The national budgeting approach proved its usefulness in the disruptive balance-of-payments crisis and the related inflationary gap situation that arose in 1947–48. It made the government emergency regulations less *ad hoc*.

However, as the political opposition gained strength in the election of 1948, the annual setting up of national budgets lost its thrust as a key policy instrument for the government. Yet the annual calculation of a national budget remained a much-noted preoccupation of the Ministry of Finance for at least a decade.

Kock's formal position in the government was changed after the election of 1948. As the social democrats now had to revoke much of their previous push for economic policy interventions, Kock became Head of the 'Folk-hushållningsdepartementet'. This was the wartime Ministry for Supplies and related economic regulations which, although the war had long ended, was given an extended lease of life in the postwar years of economic crisis. However, this ministry was eventually to be terminated at the end of 1949, when Kock left the government. With such a dismantling task, contrasting with the type of forward planning that had previously been her mission in the government, Kock's new position as a cabinet member was less central in government life. However, she remained in the consulting group around the inner circle whenever difficult economic policy decisions had to be taken. One such occasion was the devaluation of the krona against the dollar in the autumn of 1949. As one of the voices behind that decision, Kock's had some authority, derived from her previous experience of exchange rate policy during the Depression of the 1930s.

When Kock left the government in 1950, after a tumultuous three-year period, she was appointed Head of the Central Bureau of Statistics, a post she held until 1958. This assignment did not offer her the quiet type of retreat she might have wanted. She continued to represent Sweden in the intense diplomatic debates at conferences on different levels that set the institutional stage for international economic cooperation in subsequent decades. Notable among her assignments was her position as Head of the Swedish delegation to the UN Economic Comission for Europe through 1947–60, where she served as chairman from 1950 to 1952. She also served on the board of Unesco's Institute for Social Sciences through 1950–58. One should add that an important part of her international involvements concerned questions of Nordic economic cooperation through the years 1950–54. In 1950–52 she chaired the Joint Economic Committee of the Nordic States.

However, Kock's new position at the Central Bureau of Statistics was the major challenge. She found herself confronted with the task of leading not only the bureau through a period of much organizational change; she was also in charge of centralizing the entire statistical system of the country. Sweden's official statistics had so far evolved as a system where each government agency had built up its own statistical services. Again Kock proved to be the competent type of skilful designer of workable solutions that the occasion demanded.

The position as Head of the Central Bureau of Statistics meant a great deal of international involvement in the field of statistics in addition to her continued government assignments abroad. As testimony to her many contributions to the field of statistics, not only nationally but also internationally, she was elected fellow of the American Statistical Association in 1956.

In her subsequent retirement period Kock resumed many of the lines of research which she had pursued before assuming government duties. As noted previously, she now reverted to economic–historical research and published a major survey of the history of Swedish credit market policy (Kock, 1961–62). She was also, through 1963–69, again aligned with Myrdal, who now chaired the newly established Institute of International Economics at Stockholm University. During this period Kock carried out a major study of the history of GATT (Kock, 1969).

A central preoccupation through Kock's life was her commitment to promoting the conditions and standing of women in the labour market. As mentioned earlier, she was a major contributor to the official committee that explored this question in the 1930s. Kock here presented an analysis (Kock, 1938a) which, aside from its importance in a gender perspective, has been regarded, next to the dissertation, as her analytically most accomplished work. But Kock's commitment to gender issues went much beyond her concerns as a professional economist. She had became personally involved as a result of her upbringing, but her commitment was no doubt reinforced by her experience as an employee of one of Sweden's major banks as well as by her later experience of being a woman in an academic career and, not least, by her having finally to contend with gender barriers in the limited opportunities at the highest political levels of the country.

Kock enrolled early in the women's equal rights movement, where she held many posts over the years. She was active in the trade union movement among women bank employees in the 1920s and later she participated in promoting cooperation between the various women's organizations in Sweden. She served as chairman in the committee set up for that purpose through 1936–45. However, her most important involvement concerned the rights of women with an academic degree like herself. From 1926 until 1933 she chaired the Swedish Organization of University Women. Subsequently she became its representative in the International Federation of University Women, where she served as Vice-Chairman for the period 1936–47.

Kock's husband was the renowned Swedish lawyer Hugo Lindberg (1887–1966), whom she married in 1936.

ROLF HENRIKSSON

Note

1.   Docent is a German and Scandinavian academic rank corresponding to lecturer in the UK or assistant professor in the USA.

Bibliography

Selected writings by Karin Kock

(1929), *A Study of Interest Rates*, London: P.S. King & Son.

(1930), *Svenskt bankväsen i våra dagar* (Contemporary Swedish banking), Stockholm: koop.förb.

(1931a), 'Hur Sverige tvingades överge guldmyntfoten' (How Sweden was forced to leave the gold standard), in G. Myrdal (1931), *Sveriges väg genom penningkrisen*, 141–60.

(1931b), 'Undersökning rörande kapitalbildningen i Sverige åren 1924–1929' (Capital formation in Sweden 1924–1929), in *Arbetslöshetsutredningens betänkande I*, (SOU 1931:20) 542–8.

(1931c), *Skånska privatbanken*, Stockholm: Norstedt.

(1932), *Skånska Cementaktiebolaget 1871–1931*, Uppsala: Almqvist and Wiksell.

(1933a), 'Budgeten och sparandet' (The budget and the savings), *Svensk Sparbankstidskrift*, **17**, 73–80.

(1933b), 'Förenta Staternas bankväsen' (The banking system in the United States), *Svensk Sparbankstidskrift*, **17**, 133–50.

(1933c), 'Paper currency and monetary policy in Sweden', in K. Kock (ed.), *Economic Essays in Honour of Gustav Cassel*, London: George Allen and Unwin, pp. 343–56.

(1934a), *Roosevelts program ur konjunktursynpunkt* (Roosevelt's program from a business cycle point of view), Ekonomiska debatten 3.

(1934b), *Sveriges handelsekonomiska läge* (The foreign trade position of Sweden), Stockholm: Bonnier.

(1935), *Konjunkturuppsvingets förlopp och orsaker 1932–34* (The course and causes of the business cycle upswing 1932–34), SOU 1935:16.

(1936a), 'Wirtschaftspolitik und Konjunkturaufschwung in Schweden 1933–1936', *Jahrbücher für Nationalökonomie und Statistik*, **144**, 708–29.

(1936b), 'PM rörande ekonomiska och sociala trendundersökningar' (Memo on economic and social trend investigations) *Riksdagens protokoll 1936. Bihang Saml 1, No 215 Bil. A*, 30–34.

(1937a), *Smålands bank 1837–1937*, Jönköping.

(1937b), together with E. Lindahl and E. Dahlgren, *National Income of Sweden 1861–1930*, Stockholm Economic Studies no. 5, 2 vols, London: P.S. King & Son.

(1938a), 'Kvinnoarbetet i Sverige' (Women's labour in Sweden), in *Betänkande ang. gift kvinnas förvärvsarbete m m.* avg. av Kvinnoarbetskommittén, Stockholm: I. Marcus boktryckeriaktiebolag, 1938:47 351–470.

(1938b), 'Crisis, Depression and Recovery in Sweden 1929–1937', in Hallendorff and Schück (eds), *History of Sweden*, commemorating the 300th anniversay of the Swedish 17th century American colony Delaware, Stockholm: Fritzes bokh, pp. 469–84.

(1938c), 'Skogsbruket och de skogsförädlande industriernas betydelse för folkhushållet' (The importance of forestry and forest industries for the economy), in *Utredning rörande skogsnäringens ekonomiska läge med förslag till åtgärder för höjande av näringens bärkraft Förberedande undersökningar och uttalanden. 1936 års skogsutrednings betänkande nr 1 avg. 25/11 1938*, SOU 1938: 53 69–103.

(1939), 'Några problem rörande definitioner och terminologi i teorin för de internationella kapitalrörelserna' (Some problems of definitions and terminology in the theory of international capital movernents), *Ekonomisk Tidskrift*, **41**, 311–24.

(1942), 'Review of Torsten Gårdlund (1941), *Industrialismens samhälle*' (The society of Industrialism), *Ekonomisk Tidskrift*, **44**, 286–96.

(1943), 'Swedish Economic Policy during the War', *Review of Economic Studies*, **10**, 75–80.

(1944), 'Nymalthusianismens genombrott i Sverige' (The breakthrough of neomalthusianism in Sweden), in *Studier i ekonomi och historia, tillägnade Eli F Heckscher 24/11 1944*, pp. 73–88.

(1959), *Statistiska centralbyrån 100 år* (The Central Bureau of Statistics 100 years), Stockholm: Statiskika centralbyrån.

(1961–62), *Kreditmarknad och räntepolitik 1924–1958* (Credit market and interest rate policy 1924–1958), 2 vols, Stockholm: Sveriges allmanna hypoteksbank.

(1969), *International Trade Policy and the Gatt 1947–1967*, Acta Universitatis Stockholmiensis, Stockholm Economic Studies New Series XI, Stockholm: Almquist & Wiksell.

Other sources and references

Gårdlund, T. (1941), *Industrialismens samhälle* (The society of industrialism).

Heckscher, E. (1931), *Sveriges penningpolitik Orientering och förslag* (Sweden's Monetary Policy Orientation and Proposals).

Henriksson, R. (1987) (ed.), *Konjunkturinstitutet på Erik Lundbergs tid* (Konjunkturinstitutet in Erik Lundberg's time).

Henriksson, R. (1991), 'The Political Economy Club and the Stockholm School, 1917–1951', in L. Jonung (ed.), *The Stockholm School Revisited*, Cambridge, New York, Melbourne: Cambridge University Press 41–74.

Myrdal, G. (1931), *Sveriges väg genom penningkrisen* (The Swedish road through the money crisis), Stockholm: Natur och Kultur.

Nationalekonomiska Föreningens Förhandling (The Transactions of the Swedish Economic Society) 1931–36.

Anna Koutsoyiannis (1932–86)

Anna Koutsoyiannis was born in Athens, Greece, in 1932 and died, prematurely and tragically by her own hand, in Ottawa, Canada, in September 1986. Left behind to grieve for her were a son Peter, her ex-husband Costas, colleagues at her final affiliation (the Department of Economics of the University of Ottawa), and her many students, with whom she had an excellent rapport.

Anna's career path can be easily traced. After a BA at the Athens School of Economics in 1954 (during which she won the Distinguished Student Award), she headed to England and the University of Manchester, where she received her Ph.D. in 1962; her last two years at Manchester were divided between her own research and teaching at lecturer rank. Returning to Greece, she served as Lecturer at the Graduate School of Business Studies in Athens from 1962 to 1964 and then at the University of Thessaloniki from 1964 through 1968, first as Assistant Professor of Economics and then as Associate Professor (1965–68). Anna then returned to England, to the University of Lancaster, where she held the rank of Senior Lecturer from 1968 to 1973 and then received promotion to the rank of Reader in 1974. However, she held this more senior position in Lancaster for only another year, as she moved to the University of Waterloo (as a Full Professor) in 1975, remaining there until 1983. In 1983 she moved to the University of Ottawa as (Full) Professor and Departmental Chairperson. Somewhat overwhelmed by the stresses of this demanding job, she decided to step down as Departmental Chair in 1985, after only two years; thus her final year at the University of Ottawa was as a regular professor in the Department.

Anna's gifts as a teacher of economics were considerable. The record shows that, during her eight years at the University of Waterloo, she won the Distinguished Teaching Award for the entire university (in 1978). One of her ex-students (Ellie Sayadi, whom I interviewed by telephone for this note) describes her as 'engaging', 'animated', and (especially) 'caring'. 'Professor Koutsoyiannis could make an 8:30 class come to life as no other professor with whom I have ever studied; she was more stimulating at that hour of the morning than the strongest cup of coffee!' Ellie Sayadi also noted that the texts in Professor Koutsoyiannis's class (generally written by herself) were generally available in paperback, thus sparing strained student book budgets. This could be interpreted as an illustration of her concern for her students, although a cynic might consider that it simply showed an applied price theorist's better awareness of demand elasticities in practice! At the time of her death, Anna was hard at work on an introductory text, which was designed to incorporate her vision of appropriate pedagogy at this level.

Anna's research (which was strong enough to merit her an entry in Marc Blaug's citation-based *Who's Who in Economics*, 1986) can be summarized briefly. The book on *The Leaf Tobacco Market of Greece* (1963) is a nice application of econometric techniques of the day, combined with considerable institutional knowledge, to study a challenging problem in agricultural economics, in the tradition of Henry Schultz. 'Demand functions for tobacco' (1963) is in this same tradition and was presumably a spin-off from the same predoctoral research. Anna's gifts as an expositor of received theories are well illustrated in *Theory of Econometrics* (1973, 1977), an undergraduate text, written to be accessible to undergraduate students (for example, the theory is developed in terms of summation signs instead of matrix algebra) . However, Anna's creativity really blossomed in the field of microeconomic theory and industrial organization. At this point, it will serve to allow Anna to speak for herself:

> In later years, I became increasingly preoccupied with the content of standard microeconomics textbooks, which largely ignore the changed economic conditions of countries of the Western world, dominated as they are by large oligopolistic conglomerates. In *Modern Microeconomics* [1975, 1979] and *Non-Price Decisions* [1982], oligopoly is treated as the general case rather than the exception in the contemporary business world.[1]

The final article published during her lifetime (to the best of my knowledge), 'Goals of oligopolistic firms' (1984), is a little gem in which Anna takes three possible hypotheses about firm behaviour (profit maximization, sales maximization, or pricing to limit entry of potential oligopolistic competitors) and then subjects them to econometric testing. She finds considerable evidence to suggest that large firms often set prices in the *inelastic* region of the demand curve, which in turn suggests pricing to limit the entry of possible competitors.

Finally, a word about Anna's reputation among her fellow economists. As noted above, Anna was one of roughly 1275 living and dead economists included in Mark Blaug's *Who's Who in Economics* (1986); such an inclusion might already be considered a major professional accomplishment. Perhaps the credit due to her increases even more when one realizes that there were only (roughly) thirty-one women economists recognized among the total of roughly 1275 entries.[2] (These thirty-one women economists, some of whom, like Joan Robinson and Rosa Luxemburg, are well known to the profession, are listed in the Appendix.) Finally, one can ask how Professor Koutsoyiannis's work has been regarded more than a decade after her death.

Although a cursory scan of two recent texts in microtheory and in industrial organization failed to turn up any citations, Marc Lavoie's recent book (1992) on Post-Keynesian economics cites *Modern Microeconomics* four times, according to the index.

RONALD G. BODKIN

Appendix: List of 31 identified women economists in *Who's Who in Economics*

Irma Adelman
Elizabeth E. Bailey
Caroline Shaw Bell
Barbara R. Bergmann
Mary Jean Bowman
Anne P. Carter
Christine Anne Greenhalgh
Anna Koutsoyiannis
Anne O. Krueger
Elisabeth Landes
Marie Lavigne
Arleen Leibowitz
Cynthia Brown Lloyd
Rosa Luxemburg
Jane Marcet
Mary Paley Marshall

Harriet Martineau
Donald Nansen (now Deidre) McCloskey
Cynthia Taft Morris
Selma Mushkin
Sharon Oster
Karen R. Polenske
Barbara Ruth Benton Reagan
Alice M. Rivlin
Joan Robinson
Anna Jacobson Schwartz
Frances Julia Stewart
Barbara M. Ward
Beatrice Webb
Anne Douglas Williams
Ann Dryden Witte

Notes

1. Koutsoyiannis (1986), p. 476.
2. The qualification 'roughly' is used advisedly. If I knew the individuals personally, then there was no question about gender (with one exception, discussed below). If not, I had to rely on the given name or other material in the entry, a not always perfect manner of deciding. (Thus names like 'Robin' in English or 'Claude' in French can refer to either men or women, while the name 'Jean' is generally a woman's name in English but a man's name in French. Also, with Oriental names, I was less than perfectly certain. Finally, there is the interesting case of Deidre (then Donald) McCloskey, who underwent a sex-change operation in the early 1990s; how should one classify her/him? Controver-

sial; but if we believe in individual preference, 'female' would appear to be the appropriate classification.

Bibliography

Selected writings by Anna Koutsoyiannis

(1963), *An Econometric Study of the Leaf Tobacco Market of Greece*, Athens: Papadimitropoulos Press.

(1963), 'Demand functions for tobacco', *Manchester School*, **33**(1), January, 1–20.

(1973), *Theory of Econometrics*, London and Basingstoke: Macmillan. Second edn 1977.

(1975), *Modern Microeconomics*, London and Basingstoke: Macmillan. Second edn 1979.

(1982), *Non-Price Decisions: The Firm in a Modern Context*, London and Basingstoke: Macmillan.

(1984), 'Goals of oligopolistic firms: An Empirical Test of Competing Hypotheses', *Southern Economic Journal*, **51**(2), October, 540–67. (Note: the journal reference and date are incorrect in her biographical entry – see below.)

(1986), Biographical entry, written by her, in Mark Blaug, *Who's Who in Economics: A Biographical Dictionary of Major Economists, 1700–1986*, 2nd edn, Cambridge, MA: MIT Press.

Other sources and references

Blaug, Mark (ed.) (1986), *Who's Who in Economics: A Biographical Dictionary of Major Economists, 1700–1986*, 2nd edn, Cambridge, MA: MIT Press.

Lavoie, Marc (1992), *Foundations of Post-Keynesian Economics*, Aldershot, UK and Brookfield, US: Edward Elgar.

Sayadi, Ellie, telephone interview with the author, 17 May 1999.

Hazel Kyrk (1886–1957)

Hazel Kyrk was born on 19 November 1886 in Ashley, Ohio, the only child of Jane (Benedict) Kyrk, who died when Hazel was in her teens, and Elmer Ellsworth Kyrk, who worked as a drayman. Once she had completed high school, Hazel supported herself as a teacher. She entered Ohio Wesleyan University in 1904 and was employed as a domestic helper in the home of an economics professor, Leon Carroll Marshall. When he moved to the University of Chicago, Kyrk accompanied the family and continued her undergraduate studies on a part-time basis (Nelson, 1980, p. 405). She completed her Ph.B. degree at the University of Chicago in 1910.

Kyrk spent the 1911–12 academic year as an Instructor at Wellesley College and then returned to Chicago to pursue doctoral studies in economics under the direction of James Alfred Field, a noted specialist in population economics (Dorfman, 1959, pp. 565–6, 572). In 1914 she accepted a position as Instructor and then as Assistant Professor of Economics at Oberlin College, and continued her doctoral studies as best she could. On leave from Oberlin during 1918–19, she contributed to the war effort as a statistician in London for the Allied Maritime Transport Council (Nelson, 1980, p. 405).

Following her return to Oberlin, she completed her thesis which was accepted in 1920, awarded the thousand-dollar Hart Schaffner and Marx prize for research in economics (Dorfman, 1959, p. 572), and, following revision, was subsequently published (Kyrk, 1923).

During 1923–24 Kyrk was an associate at Stanford University's Food Research Institute where she undertook research leading to a monograph on the American baking industry (Kyrk and Davis, 1925). She was at Iowa State College during 1924–25. In the autumn of 1925 she accepted a joint appointment in the Department of Economics and the Department of Home Economics at the University of Chicago. She was promoted to Full Professor in 1941 and remained at Chicago until her retirement in 1952.

Along with a few others, Hazel Kyrk pioneered what Joseph Dorfman has called the special area of 'consumption economics', the empirical study of household spending patterns among various cultural and economic groups within society (Dorfman, 1959, p. 570). In her 1923 book *A Theory of Consumption* and in her 1929 study *The Economic Problems of the Family*, Kyrk argued that household consumption patterns, and the wants and desires which underlay those patterns, were determined more by social influences than by individual differences and preferences. These social influences take the form of 'standards of consumption', levels of consumption which are in some sense socially acceptable, and which vary from period to period, from country to country, and from class to class. Of particular concern to Kyrk was the possibility that these 'standards of consumption' might involve such a high valuation of saving that a form of Hobsonian underconsumption would be inevitable:

> The problem is, how can this capital fund, which comes from a very unequal distribution of income and incapacity of owners to spend, be invested profitably? If it goes, without improvements in technical methods which will lower the cost, into the production of the staple necessities, there may be an 'oversupply'. The poor cannot buy more, the rich will not. To the production of what new goods or luxuries then shall it be applied? Can the producers invent new activities and new interests which will increase the will to spend of those who are able to do so? Unless they do, overinvestment will arise. (Quoted in Dorfman, 1959, p. 573)

And the only way to evaluate this danger was by detailed, empirical investigation of actual expenditures by households in different circumstances.

Accordingly, Kyrk took a special interest in the applied work of several government agencies. She served as principal economist in the Bureau of Home Economics of the US Department of Agriculture in the summers between 1938 and 1941. Her contribution to the massive survey of household expenditures (Kyrk et al., 1941) was crucial to the formulation of base-year prices for the official consumer price index. During World War II, Kyrk served in the Office of Price Administration, and in 1945–6 she chaired a technical committee which advised the federal government on the revision of the consumer price index to reflect postwar inflation (Nelson, 1980, p. 406).

Throughout her academic career, Hazel Kyrk took a special interest in women. Several of her books were primarily concerned with women's roles in contemporary families (Kyrk, 1929a; Monroe, Kyrk and Stone, 1940; Kyrk, 1953). At Chicago she mentored other women faculty members and supervised a number of women graduate students. During several summers she taught at the Bryn Mawr Summer School for Women Workers. And for several years she served on the board of the Chicago Women's Trade Union League (Nelson, 1980, p. 406). Although she never married, she raised and educated a foster daughter.

Hazel Kyrk died at her summer home in West Dover, Vermont, on 5 August 1957.

RICHARD A. LOBDELL

Bibliography

Selected writings by Hazel Kyrk

(1923), *A Theory of Consumption*, New York and Boston: Houghton Mifflin.
(1925), *The American Baking Industry* (with Joseph Stancliffe Davis), *1848–1923*, Palo Alto, CA: Stanford University Press.
(1929a), *Economic Problems of the Family*, New York and London: Harper and Brothers.
(1929b), 'The economics of consumption: discussion', *Journal of Farm Economics*, **11**, 575–7.
(1937), 'Discussion of methods of measuring variations in family expenditures', *Journal of the American Statistical Association*, **32**, 47–9.
(1939), 'The development of the field of consumption', *Journal of Marketing*, **4**, 16–19.
(1940), *Food Buying and our Markets* (with Day Monroe and Ursula Batchelor Stone), New York: M. Barrows & Company.
(1941) et al., *Family Expenditures for Housing and Household Operation in Five Regions*, Miscellaneous publications of the United States Department of Agriculture, no. 432 and no. 457, Washington, DC: Government Printing Office.
(1950), 'The income distribution as a measure of economic welfare', *American Economic Review*, **40**, 342–55.
(1953), *The Family in the American Economy*, Chicago: University of Chicago Press.
(1955), *The Art of Making Political Decisions*, Federal Extension Service, Washington, DC: Government Printing Office.

Other sources and references

Dorfman, Joseph (1959), *The Economic Mind in American Civilization*, vol. 5, New York: Viking Press, Inc.
Nelson, Elizabeth (1980), 'Hazel Kyrk', in Barbara Sicherman and Carol Hurd Green (eds), *Notable American Women: The Modern Period*, Cambridge, MA: Belknap Press, pp. 405–6.

Käthe Leichter (1895–1942)

Käthe Leichter, born as Käthe Pick in Vienna on 20 August 1895, was murdered near Magdeburg in February of 1942. She was a student of Carl Grünberg and one of the most important protagonists of Austromarxism, who occupied administrative posts in the 'Red Vienna' during the interwar period and shaped social reforms as well as union policies.

Leichter began in 1914 with the study of *Staatswissenschaften* (state sciences) in Vienna, studying with the proponent of *Grenznutzentheorie* (marginal utility theory) Friedrich von Wieser and the *Kathedersozialisten* ('socialists of the chair') Eugen von Philoppovich and Karl Pribram. Carl Grünberg, who was considered 'like an outlaw in Vienna national economics' (Steiner, 1973, p. 364), introduced her to historical materialism and to Karl Marx as a sociologist. Since women were not admitted to doctorate programmes at Vienna University, Leichter continued her studies in Heidelberg in 1917, and got her doctorate degree one year later with Alfred Weber. Grünberg had continued to advise her on her dissertation (Leichter, 1918). In the winter of 1918–19, Leichter went back to Vienna and studied institutions, history of law, and private law with Pribram, Grünberg, von Mises and Kelsen.

In 1919, Leichter took part in the 'Rötebewegung' and from then on was part of the left wing of Austrian Social Democracy. In April of 1919, Otto Bauer appointed her as research assistant to the State Commission on Socialization, to which people such as J. Schumpeter, C. Grünberg, E. Lederer, R. Goldscheid, A. Ammon and O. Neurath were contributing. The same year, Minister of Finance Schumpeter called her to work as a consultant for his ministry. Leichter described her experiences in the Commission for Socialization in detail in the *Festschrift* for Karl Kautzky (Leichter, 1914). Beginning in May 1925, Leichter was employed at the Workers' Council of Vienna. There, she cooperated with the womens' department of the unions as well as with the Social Democratic party, and built up the commission on women. She was the first to put together a systematic collection of material on womens' work, and started in 1927 with her own surveys on the protection of women workers and on the situation of Viennese home workers (Leichter, 1928). In the *Handbook of the History of the Austrian Union Movement*, she contributed an article on socialization and crisis, as well as on problems of rationalization and stabilization (Leichter, 1928). In the *Festschrift* for her teacher Grünberg, she analysed extremism and its political ambivalence in the union context, taking the concrete examples of Italian and Russian syndicalism (Leichter, 1932c). Leichter prepared her final major scholarly work in Switzerland in 1934. Commissioned by the Frankfurter Institut für Sozialforschung in the context of their 'studies on authority and the family', she had conceptualized and carried out a survey with 1000 Swiss youths.

Paul Lazarsfeld, who knew Leichter from the times of the youth movement, contributed the introduction on methods and a partial analysis of her data (Leichter, 1936a and 1936b). After February 1934, Leichter, like Bruno Kreisky, was busy organizing illegal socialist youth groups, and supported relatives of those persecuted. In August of 1936 she appeared in public for the last time, giving a talk on the unions and fascism under the pseudonym of Maria Mahler at the Congress of the International Women's Committee of the Socialist *Arbeiterinneninternationale* (Women Workers' International) in Brussels. While preparing herself to emigrate, she was arrested by the Gestapo in May 1938 and accused of high treason. The Philosophy Faculty of Heidelberg University revoked her doctorate degree in December of the following year. In January 1940 Käthe Leichter was deported to Ravensbruck. Together with 1500 other Jewish women she was murdered in the course of a 'gas-trial' experiment in a railway car.

Leichter was one of the most important figures of the First Republic who attempted within political institutions and from administrative posts to develop concrete concepts for legislation on the protection of workers and their insurance rights. Furthermore, she realized a form of praxis-oriented social research, which from the perspective of social politics – such as her studies on women's work and home employment – ranked among the most important of the interwar period.

THERESA WOBBE

Bibliography

Selected writings by Käthe Leichter
(1918), 'Die handelspolitischen Beziehungen Österreich-Ungarns zu Italien', Diss. Phil., Heidelberg, manuscript.
(1924), 'Erfahrungen des österreichischen Sozialisierungsversuchs', in *Der lebendige Marxismus. Festgabe zum 70. Geburtstag von Karl Kautsky*, Jena.
(1926) (author and editor), *Handbuch der Frauenarbeit in Österreich*, Vienna: Kammer für Arbeiter und Angestellte.
(1927), *Frauenarbeit und Arbeiterinnenschutz in Österreich*. Vienna: Kammer für Arbeiter und Angestellte and Verlag 'Arbeit und Wirtschaft'.
(1928), *Wie leben die Wiener Heimarbeiter? Eine Erhebung über die Arbeits- und Lebensverhältnisse*, Vienna: Verlag 'Arbeit und Wirtschaft'.
(1932a), *So leben wir – 1320 Industriearbeiterinnen berichten über ihr Leben. Eine Erhebung*, Vienna: Verlag 'Arbeit und Wirtschaft'.
(1932b), 'Sanierung und Krise', in Julius Deutsch (ed.), *Geschichte der Österreichischen Gewerkschaftsbewegung im Weltkrieg und in der Nachkriegszeit*, vol. 2, Vienna: Wiener Volksbuchhandlung, pp. 144–258.
(1932c), 'Vom revolutionären Syndikalismus zur Verstaatlichung der Gewerkschaften', in *Festschrift für Carl Grünberg. Zum 70. Geburtstag*, Leipzig: pp 243–81.
(1936a), 'Erhebung bei Jugendlichen über Autorität und Familie' (together with Paul Lazarsfeld), in *Studien über Autorität und Familie*, Forschungsberichte aus dem Institut für Sozialforschung (=Schriften des Instituts für Sozialforschung, ed. M. Horkheimer), Paris, pp. 353–415.

(1936b), 'Interviews mit Schweizer Sachverständigen', in *Studien über Autorität und Familie*, Paris, pp. 416–40.

Other sources and references
Steiner, Herbert (1973), *Käthe Leichter. Leben und Werk*, Vienna: Europaverl.
University Archiv Heidelberg, HB 1
Wiggershaus, Rolf (c1986), *Die Frankfurter Schule. Geschichte, theoretische Entwicklung, politische Bedeutung*, Munich: C. Hanser.
Knoll/Majce/Weiss/Wieser, in M. Rainer Lepsius (ed.), *Soziologie in Deutschland und Österreich 1918–1945. Materialien zur Entwicklung, Emigration und Wirkungsgeschichte* (Special Issue 23: *Kölner Zeitschrift für Soziologie und Sozialpsychologie*).

Charlotte Leubuscher (1888–1961)

Charlotte A.P. Leubuscher was born on 24 July 1888 in Jena, and died on 2 June 1961 in London. Leubuscher was a student of Heinrich Herkner, the successor of Schmoller in Berlin and a strong supporter of women's access to universities, who counted among his students in Zürich Rosa Luxemburg, Alexandra Kollontay, Frieda Duensing and others. Leubuscher was the first woman economist to earn her Habilitation at the University of Berlin and the first German woman to receive a professional position as an Associate Professor of Economics. Her domain was social policy, and she gained recognition as an expert on British social and trade policies.

After graduating from the Humanistisches Gymnasium in Meiningen, Leubuscher studied political science, philosophy and history in Cambridge, Gieben, Munich and Berlin. She wrote her thesis in Berlin at Professor Herkner's on the topic of the workers' struggle of English railway employees in 1911 (Leubuscher, 1913). She had collected the data for this study with the help of Lujo Brentano during a ten-week excursion to Great Britain in the summer of 1912. During the war, she was working for the Central Acquisition Company/Department for Statistics and Reports, for a small association on *Kriegshilfe* (war aid) in Stuttgart, as a lecturer at the women's college in Leipzig and at the Royal Statistical Institute in the winter of 1918–19. Beginning on 1 November 1919, she was employed as Herkner's assistant at the University of Berlin, where in 1921 she finished her Habilitation on socialism and socialization in England (Leubuscher, 1921). In the winter term of 1922–23 she was an associate at the Office for Social Policy. In 1923, she began to give classes as a Privatdozent on social policy, social movements and socialism at the University of Göttingen. In the winter term of the following year, she started lecturing at the Department of Economics and Statistics of Berlin University, focusing on foreign social policy with an emphasis on England and Russia.

Due to the initiative of her department – those who spoke on her behalf were, among others, H. Herkner, L. von Bortkiewicz, F. von Gottl-Ottilienfeld – she was made 'Extraordinary' Professor/Associate Professor of Economics at the University of Berlin in 1929. Besides her regular lecturing she also took over some of the lectures of Professor Herkner, for example on financial science (and tutored some of his students). She was among those who were discussed in relation to succeeding to his Chair in 1930. With the Nazi law on the 'Wiederherstellung des Berufsbeamtentums' ('restoration') taking effect in September 1933, she lost the right to teach due to the Jewish descent of her father's parents.

Leubuscher emigrated to Great Britain in summer 1933, where she had more than her old student contacts to build on. As an expert on British social policy and socialization she was fortunate in that her academic work focused on issues relating to Great Britain. Furthermore, she was personally known in many academic and state institutions due to countless research trips to Great Britain since 1910. From 1933 to 1936 she received research scholarships from her old College, Girton in Cambridge, which allowed her a living, while she was working in London with the huge colonial project of Lord Hailey and the Royal Institute for International Affairs, the 'African Survey'.

During the following six years she did research on African colonial policies (Leubuscher, 1944). A scholarship was provided for her by Lady Margaret Hall, Oxford. In 1942, she received a two-year grant at the London School of Economics, where in the mid-1920s she had conducted research for her study on liberalism and protectionism, and afterwards a short scholarship at Nuffield College. From 1945 to 1951, she was with the Colonial Office, where she conducted a number of studies on colonial raw materials (Leubuscher, 1951) as well as some smaller studies on colonial economics. After that she held a position as Research Fellow at the University of Manchester for three years, during which she worked on a study in cooperation with the Royal Institute (Leubuscher, 1956).

In 1956, Leubuscher received from the West German government the title of Professor Emeritus, honouring her academic teaching and excellent publication record, as well as a pension which allowed her to retire. Although she had travelled several times to the Continent after the war, she remained in Great Britain and took British citizenship in 1946.

Leubuscher was part of the first generation of women social scientists who were able to earn their Habilitation degree in Germany after 1920 and succeed in an academic career. She was also among the few whose academic career was supported by a mentor. She earned recognition when she wrote the sections on England and Russia for the seventh and eighth editions of Heinrich Herkner's *Die Arbeiterfrage*. From 1913 on she published three studies that dealt with British social and trade policies (Leubuscher, 1913;

1921; 1927). Leubuscher also wrote for the recognized journals on social policy and was active in the Verein für Sozialpolitik (Association for Social Welfare Policy). In her writings, she defended a social–liberal position, with an understanding of social policy that was based on the protective duties of community and state in the tradition of 'open' theory. In her writings on British social policy (Leubuscher, 1927), she opted for the controlled strengthening of free trade against the model of interventionism which increasingly dominated British debates during the 1920s due to the influence of J.M. Keynes.

In the late 1920s Leubuscher found herself a new subject in colonial economics. Her interest developed from her work on empire trade policies. She wrote a much-recognized analysis of the social and economic situation in South Africa which relied on her field studies in 1929 (Leubuscher, 1931). With this study she succeeded in bringing a new approach to German colonial science.

After emigrating, Leubuscher increasingly concentrated on this second issue of hers, colonial research, because there was a demand for it in Britain and it allowed her to earn a living from science. Leubuscher was not able to attain the same reputation and academic post in Britain as she had held in Germany, but she was able after her emigration to remain focused on the same research topics and to benefit from her old contacts for her professional integration.

Until her death in June 1961 Leubuscher worked as a social scientist; her last study was finished in spring 1961 (Leubuscher, 1963).

THERESA WOBBE
PHILINE SCHOLZE

Bibliography

Selected writings by Charlotte Leubuscher

(1913), 'Der Arbeitskampf der englischen Eisenbahner im Jahre 1911. Mit einem einleitenden Überblick über die allgemeinen Entwicklungstendenzen in der heutigen englischen Arbeiterbewegung', in G. Schmoller and M. Sering (eds), *Staats- und sozialwissenschaftliche Forschungen*, vol. 174, Munich/Leipzig: Duncker & Humblot.

(1921), *Sozialismus und Sozialisierung in England. Ein Überblick über die neuere Entwicklung der sozialistischen Theorien und über die Probleme der Industrieverfassung Englands*, Jena: Verlag von Gustav Fischer.

(1924), 'Die Nationalökonomin', *Die Frau*, **32**, 219–20.

(1925), 'Die Berufslage der deutschen Hochschuldozentinnen', *Die Frau*, **33**, 533–7.

(1927), *Liberalismus und Protektionismus in der englischen Wirtschaftspolitik seit dem Kriege*, Jena: Verlag von Gustav Fischer.

(1931), *Der südafrikanische Eingeborene als Industriearbeiter und als Stadtbewohner. Mit einer einleitenden Übersicht über die afrikanische Eingeborenenfrage*, Jena: Verlag von Gustav Fischer.

(1931–32), 'Heinrich Herkner zum Gedächtnis', *Die Frau*, **39**, 641–4.

(1951), 'Colonial Office. The Processing of Colonial raw materials. A Study in Location', London: H.M. Stationery Office.

(1956), *Bulk Buying from the Colonies. A Study of the Bulk Purchase of Colonial Commodities by the United Kingdom Government*, issued under the auspices of the Royal Institute of International Affairs, London.

(1963), *The West African Shipping Trade 1900–1959*, Leyden: Sythoff.

Other sources and references
University Archiv Humboldt-Universität zu Berlin
University Archive, Girton College Cambridge
Hochschullehrer der WiWi
Public Record Office (Colonial Office Bestand)
Royal Institute of International Affairs
Thüringisches Staatsarchiv Meiningen
Bundesarchiv.

Helene Lieser (1898–1962)

Helene Lieser was born in Vienna on 16 December 1898. She died in Paris, probably in 1962. Her father was a manufacturer. She was a pupil of the Schwarzwaldschen Schulanstalten and the Privat-Mädchen-Obergymnasium of the organization for women's development. Lieser submitted her doctorate to the Political Science Department in April 1920. Her thesis bears the title 'Währungspolitische Literatur der österreichischen Bankozettelperiode' (monetary policy writings of the Austrian Bankozettelperiode). The thesis was supervised by Ludwig Edler von Mises and Othmar Spann. Lieser starts out from the assumption that the Bankozettelperiode has a literature comparable with that of England at the beginning of the nineteenth century. The Austrian literature is, however, of inferior quality. In England a money theory developed due to the currency depreciation as a result of the coalition wars. In Austria such an economic theory was lacking, and was only developed in the 1870s. Lieser introduces different contemporary documents relating to the areas of currency depreciation, fighting inflation, and foundation of central banks. After this she turns in detail to the papers of Adam Mueller. She sets the monetary relevance for Mueller's theorem into parallel with the banking theory thereof. She comes to the conclusion that Mueller's theory of paper money presupposes elasticity in the circulation of money.

Spann saw a remarkable contribution to the history of the national economy in Helene Lieser's thesis in Austria. Lieser was not only the first woman to be conferred a doctorate at the University of Vienna –the *Dr. rer.pol.* She also presented the first thesis in political science which was registered at that university. In his memoirs Mises pointed out that it was only because of the bad economic conditions of 1920 that Lieser's thesis was not published. The monetary reform projects discussed in Europe around 1920 made Lieser's work highly topical. Lieser contributed some explanatory remarks to a reprint of Mueller's 'Versuche einer neuen Theorie des Geldes' (Tests of a new theory of money) two years later. This volume was published in the series 'Die Herdflamme' (The Stove Flame) edited by Othmar Spann.

Helene Lieser was a member of the Mises circle. At first she worked for the 'Vereinigung österreichischer Banken und Bankiers' (Association of Austrian banks and bankers) in Vienna between the wars. She had to leave Austria in 1938. For this reason she had married a man named Berger. In Switzerland Lieser devoted herself to victims of the Nazi aggression. According to Margit von Mises (1976, p. 52), Lieser was 'one of the gifted participants in [Ludwig von Mises's] seminar in Vienna. She was highly intelligent, practical minded and efficient ... She must have been good looking when she was young. When I met her, times and circumstances had greatly changed her'.

For many years, Helene Lieser was the secretary of the International Economic Association, based in Paris. She represented the organization at many international meetings.

JÜRGEN NAUTZ

Bibliography

Selected writings by Helene Lieser
(1920), 'Währungspolitische Literatur der österreichischen Bankozettelperiode', MS, University of Vienna dissertation.
(1922), Adam H. Müller, Versuche einer neuen Theorie des Geldes. Mit erklärenden Anmerkungen versehen von Dr Helene Lieser (in the series *Die Herdflamme. Sammlung der gesellschaftswissenschaftlichen Grundwerke aller Zeiten und Völker*, edited by Prof. Dr Othmar Spann, 2 vols), Jena: G. Fischer.

Other sources and references
Archives of the University of Vienna Inskriptionsbogen.
Promotionsakte Prot. Nr. 6551 Dr. rer.pol. Universitätsmatrikel
Haag, John (1981), 'The Spann Circle and the Jewish question', in Leo Baeck Institute Yearbook, vol. 18.
Mises, M. von (1981), *Ludwig Mises. Der Mensch und sein Werk*, München. German translation of Margit von Mises (1976), *My Life with Ludwig von Mises*, New Rochelle, NY: Arlington House.
Nautz, J. (1997), 'Zwischen Emanzipation und Integration. Die Frauen der Wiener Schule für Nationalökonomie', in L. Fischer and E. Brix (eds), *Die Frauen der Wiener Jahrhundertwende*, Vienna, Cologne and Weimar: Boehlau Verlag.

Gertrud von Lovasy (1902–74)

Gertrud von Lovasy was born on 17 December 1902 in Vienna, lived in Baden later and attended the Realgymnasium (high school). She entered the legal faculty of the University of Vienna in April 1924, where she remained for six semesters up to the winter semester 1926–27. She wrote a thesis with the title 'Die rechtliche Stellung der Kartelle unter besonderer Berücksichtigung der österreichischen Eisenindustrie' ('The legal position of the cartels with special consideration of the Austrian iron industry'). The oral examination for the doctor's degree took place on 18 December 1928. She acquired the title *Dr. rer.pol.* She then published, among other places, in the *Österreichischen Zeitschrift für Bankwesen* (Austrian Journal for Banking). In 1938 she had to leave Austria. At first she emigrated to Great Britain, from where she entered the USA in 1939, staying, among other places, in Princeton. She became a staff member of the International Monetary Fund in Washington, DC. She brought out publications on questions of monetary policy and finance, as well as on foreign trade. She died in 1974.

JÜRGEN NAUTZ

Bibliography

Selected writings by Gertrud von Lovasy
(1937), 'Zur Entwicklung des wirtschaftlichen Kapitalverkehrs in den letzten zehn Jahren', *Zeitschrift für Bankwesen*, **2**, 206–18.
(1941–42), 'International Trade under Imperfect Competition', *Quarterly Journal of Economics*, **55**, 567–83.
(1953), 'Rise in U.S. Share of World Textile Trade', International Monetary Fund, *Staff Papers*, **3**, April, 47–68.
(1953), 'Short Run Fluctuations in U.S. Imports of Raw Materials, 1928–39 and 1947–52' (with H.K. Zassenhaus), IMF *Staff Papers*, S. 270–89.
(1956), 'Price of Raw Materials in the 1953–54 U.S. Recession', IMF *Staff Papers*, **5**, 47–73.
(1962), 'Inflation and Exports in Primary Producing Countries', IMF *Staff Papers*, **9**, 37–69.
(1962), 'The International Coffee Market: A Note', IMF *Staff Papers*, **9**, 226–41.
(1964), 'The International Coffee Market' (with Lorette Boissonneault), *IMF Staff Papers*, **11**, 367–86.
(1965), 'Survey and Appraisal of Proposed Schemes of Compensatory Financing', IMF *Staff Papers*, **12**, 189–221.

Other sources and references
Archives of the University of Vienna, Inskriptionsbogen; Prot. Nr. 6551 Dr. rer.pol.
IWK Dokumentations- und Forschungsstelle österreichische Wissenschaftsemigration, Vienna.
Nautz, J. (1997), 'Zwischen Emanzipation und Integration. Die Frauen der Wiener Schule für Nationalökonomie', in L. Fischer and E. Brix (eds), *Die Frauen der Wiener Jahrhundertwende*, Vienna, Cologne and Weimar: Boehlau Verlag.

Rosa Luxemburg (1871–1919)

Rosa Luxemburg's intellectual work was closely tied to her constant and intense engagement in the socialist politics of Germany, Russia and Poland, and must be read against that backdrop. The following account is drawn from J.P. Nettl's two-volume biography, the best available guide. Luxemburg was born in 1871 in a part of Poland that had been under Russian control since 1815. After a nationalist insurrection in 1863–64, the area was Russified and its Polish élite destroyed. Matters worsened when, after the 1881 assassination of Alexander II, police repression and Russian domination of the empire's minorities were greatly increased. Opposition to the tsarist regime intensified. In Russia, the terrorist organization People's Will emerged and in Poland two socialist parties were established in 1882. One of these, the Proletariat, was at the height of its influence among students during Luxemburg's high-school years. By the time she graduated in 1887, she was probably an active member of its successor, the Second Proletariat (the leaders of Proletariat were executed or imprisoned by the Russians in 1886). During the next two years she became acquainted with the works of Marx and Engels. In 1889, to escape arrest for her revolutionary activities, Luxemburg was smuggled into Western Europe.

With financial support from her family, she opted to attend the University of Zürich. She first pursued courses in the natural sciences and mathematics, but in 1892 switched to the Faculty of Law, which then also encompassed politics and economics. During the next five years, in opposition to the liberal economics of her professors, she further developed her own Marxist stance. At the same time, she became heavily involved in the politics of *émigré* socialism, of which Switzerland was an important centre. Her main contribution in this respect came in 1893, when she helped form a new party, Social Democracy of the Kingdom of Poland (SDKP). It was in part a reaction to the programme of the Polish Socialist Party (PPS) – a mildly Marxist group which stressed national independence as a precondition for improving the condition of Polish workers. Luxemburg and her lover Leo Jogiches insisted that the restoration of historic Poland was a lost cause that would only sidetrack the socialist agenda. Luxemburg later argued the point at length in her doctoral dissertation, *The Industrial Development of Poland* (*Die industrielle Entwicklung Polens*, published in 1898). Unable to persuade a majority of the PPS to their view and marginalized within that party, Luxemburg, Jogiches and two others started the strongly Marxist SDKP. The new party was always small but lasted until World War I, after which it took the lead in forming the Polish Communist Party. Luxemburg remained active in the SDKP to the end of her life, serving as its central intellectual force and main public voice. During her university years she also began attending congresses of the Second International, where she distinguished herself by her fiery and outspoken presence. In fact, at the 1896 congress, having previously convinced German leaders of its relevance for the socialist movement as a whole, she forced the issue of Polish self-determination on to the agenda and fought vigorously to win the International to her position. Though the decision ultimately went against her, Luxemburg's political stature was enormously increased; she had drawn the greatest authorities of German Social Democracy (SPD) into public debate and won unquestioned recognition for the SDKP. Her name was now recognized by many SPD party workers and key German socialist periodicals began soliciting contributions from her pen.

Frustrated with the limited opportunities offered by a Polish *émigré* movement and eager to capitalize on her growing reputation within the SPD (the undisputed leader of European socialism), Luxemburg moved to Germany in 1898. She offered her services to the local SPD office as an agitator among the Silesian Poles in the coming Reichstag elections and was immediately handed the job. The move was strategic; she was out to build her influence in the SPD, and since no Germans relished a stint in the backwaters of Silesia, the party was now under an obligation to her. She also became a regular contributor to two East German socialist papers, the *People's Newspaper of Leipzig* (*Leipziger Volkszeitung*) and the *Saxon Workers' Newspaper* (*Sächsische Arbeiterzeitung*). Here too Luxemburg acted strategically; in writing on the issue of revisionism, then current in Germany, she saw an opportunity to speed her way into the top circles of influence in the SPD.

As Engels's former secretary, Eduard Bernstein was a powerful figure in the SPD and European socialism generally. Over the years 1896–98, in the pages of the party's main theoretical journal, *New Age* (*Neue Zeit*), he argued that the political strategy of German Social Democracy was due for a drastic overhaul. Socialism was never going to be attained by revolutionary means, since capitalism was not going to collapse from internal causes as Marx had thought. So the party should abandon the struggle for parliamentary predominance and instead join hands with reform-minded bourgeois radicals to help secure piecemeal improvements for German workers. From this alliance the momentum for a cooperative mode of production would gradually build. The party press expressed guarded approval or, at most, mild criticism. But in early 1898, Parvus, editor of the *Saxon Workers' Newspaper*, issued a long series of vehement criticisms; by their apparent warm reception (the paper's circulation grew tremendously) the SPD was forced to begin the process of taking a formal stand on the controversy. Luxemburg entered the fray at this point, writing for the *People's Newspaper of Leipzig* a series of articles in which she sought to undermine Bernstein's position while defending Marxist orthodoxy and the ideal of a revolutionary overthrow. She later followed this up with a critical review of Bernstein's 1899 book, *The Presuppositions of Socialism and the Tasks of Social Democracy* (*Die Voraussetzungen des Sozialismus und die Aufgaben der Sozialdemokratie*; the English translation was titled *Evolutionary Socialism*).

In 1899, Luxemburg's two sets of articles were republished as a pamphlet under the title, *Social Reform or Revolution?* (*Sozialreform oder Revolution?*).

Her views were front and centre at the 1898 SPD party congress, where the leadership, hoping to calm internal divisions, opted to put off a decision until the next congress. Luxemburg was invited (by Bebel himself) to speak on the matter at the 1899 congress, and though she provoked much opposition, a resolution was carried expressing the party's formal rejection of revisionism. Still, strong revisionist elements remained, causing a slow erosion of party discipline and cohesion. The executive saw in the theory of orthodox Marxism, which decisively rejected bourgeois-style reformism, the means to cement its control. So in 1901 it enlisted Parvus to contribute an article to *New Age* and Luxemburg to speak at the annual party congress. The strategy paid off; another resolution was passed condemning revisionism, this one much more sharply worded. The SPD decisively reiterated this stance at its 1903 congress; for a while revisionist voices in the party were all but silenced. Kautsky and Luxemburg combined forces at the 1904 Amsterdam congress of the Second International to carry the same victory over Jaurès and French revisionism.

The whole debate served to bring Luxemburg to the highest levels of influence in the SPD and into close personal contact with its principal leaders. Precisely because of her radicalism, Wilhelm Liebknecht recommended her for an editorial post at the party's main proceedings journal, the relatively stodgy *Onward!* (*Vorwärts*). Kautsky made his complete support for her anti-revisionist position a matter of public record. And she became a regular contributor to, and an associate editor of, *New Age*. By 1903, she parlayed her new influence, and her continued and very successful fieldwork in Silesia, into the right to speak as the party's chief authority on Polish matters. She used this office to turn the SPD against the PPS programme of Polish nationalism and greatly weaken ties between the two parties. Unfortunately for Luxemburg, her lofty rank in the SPD hierarchy was not to last, stemming as it did from a merely passing convergence between her constant commitment to revolution and the momentary political needs of the party.

Luxemburg threw herself into the events touched off by the Russian Revolution in 1905 with great energy and commitment. In Germany the Revolution heightened tensions between employers and workers. The idea of a general strike began to be seriously debated, drawing anarchists and syndicalists out of the woodwork and into the ranks of the SPD. Luxemburg, despite poor health and the already heavy demands of her Polish agenda, entered on an extraordinary period of campaigning in Germany. In numerous articles and public speeches, she urged German socialists to emulate the Russian example, peddling the mass strike as the appropriate political weapon; in contrast with the traditional, plodding organizational efforts of the SPD, it offered the chance to radicalize German workers overnight. For this strategy she won the guarded approval of Bebel and the 1905 SPD congress, though also the derision of revisionist trade union leaders, who sarcastically urged her to follow words with action and join the revolution in Russia. With regard to Russian Poland, Luxemburg's initial priority was to supply an intellectual focus for rising opposition to the tsarist regime. She unleashed a steady stream of publications intended to mould the emerging class-consciousness of the thousands of new recruits to the SDKP – since 1899 the Social Democratic Party of the Kingdom of Poland and Lithuania (SDKPiL). But she soon came to regard residence in Berlin as an insurmountable barrier to effective revolutionary action; it induced in her a sense of isolation and impotence and gave to her Polish journalism a pale, abstract quality. So, to the great surprise and worry of her German colleagues, in December 1905 she left for Warsaw under a false identity. There she set to work trying to convince socialist leaders, after the collapse that month of the revolution's third mass strike, that the logical next step was not a military *coup* but a continued effort to induce in the proletariat a class-consciousness capable of spilling over into a spontaneous, mass armed uprising. She pursued the latter course through the SDKPiL by means of a steady round of analysis, writing, printing and distribution. Luxemburg was arrested and imprisoned in March 1906 as the momentum for revolution slowly faded. Friends bribed officials to get her released from gaol, whereupon she made her way to Finland for discussions with the Russian revolutionary leaders gathered there.

Upon her return to Germany in September 1906, Luxemburg found the political climate altered very much to her distaste. At the SPD congress late that year, the executive showed clear signs of wanting to increase the power of trade union leaders within the party. Since the latter were traditionally a conservative force, Luxemburg strongly but unsuccessfully resisted the trend. Then came the Reichstag elections of 1907, in which the SPD dropped from 81 to 43 seats. The executive attributed its losses to the party's more revolutionary tone since 1905 and took steps to present a more conservative front to the electorate. The mass strike and the whole left wing of the party were suddenly out of official favour. Luxemburg uncharacteristically backed away from a struggle, withdrawing instead into relative political silence until 1910. This was made easier by her appointment in October 1907 to the Faculty of the new Central Party School at Berlin, a task which kept her occupied six months out of every year until World War I. There she established a reputation as a natural teacher, able to present the most difficult material with clarity and verve.

In 1910, a shift in the political wind forced the SPD executive to come out openly and aggressively against Luxemburg's activist position. Demonstrations and street clashes broke out across Prussia when it became apparent that the government was not going to make any meaningful reforms to a highly unrepresentative suffrage system. Political protest meshed with strikes in the mining and building trades to create a revolutionary atmosphere in which the mass strike was very much back in favour. Luxemburg swung back into action: during the next few months she spoke continuously all over Germany in an effort to radicalize the campaign for suffrage reform. She also submitted to *Onwards!* and then to *New Age* an article urging the SPD leadership to encourage the mass-strike movement and begin agitating for a republic. Both journals turned it down, the latter in a deceitful and hurtful manner. In the stable political environment of the first years of the century, the executive had been able to afford a rhetorical appeal to radicalism. But in a period of very real revolutionary potential, this was no longer an option; the party's whole political position rested on its pretended ability to keep the teeming masses under control. Luxemburg publicly castigated the leaders, her former ally Kautsky in particular, for their treachery, and entered into a period of open opposition to SPD policy that was to last the rest of her life. The suffrage issue petered out by May and at the SPD congress in June it became apparent that Luxemburg and the radicals were a very small minority in the party. This was emphasized again in 1911 when, despite her best efforts, the SPD executive, with an eye to the upcoming Reichstag elections, refused to issue a public criticism of the government's imperialist (and, after an English diplomatic protest, very popular) intervention in Morocco. In the elections the SPD increased its number of seats from 43 to 110; it was now the largest political party in Germany. The executive was ecstatic; parliamentary politics had been proven the true road to power and the radicals could now be put in their place. Luxemburg was increasingly marginalized; for instance, even though it had earlier commissioned her to write them, the *People's Newspapers of Leipzig* now refused to accept her articles. For the next few years Luxemburg once more largely withdrew into intellectual work; it was during this period that she wrote her celebrated theoretical study of capitalist imperialism, *The Accumulation of Capital* (*Die Akkumulation des Kapitals*, published in 1913).

With the sudden resurgence of industrial and political unrest in Germany and Russia in the first half of 1914, Luxemburg swung back into action. She spoke and wrote on the mass strike with great frequency, urging mass pressure on the SPD leadership to shake them loose from their conservative attachments. She began to speak also on the growing issue of German militarism, pleading for international solidarity of the working classes in the event of war. In February, for one such speech the previous autumn, she was handed a one-year prison sentence. Her trial had been closely reported (even in liberal and conservative papers) and the verdict won her immediate and widespread sympathy. Since an appeal was pending, she embarked on a tour of West Germany, seeking to use the militarism issue and her sudden enormous popularity to radicalize workers and win them to the party. The government paid close attention to her public pronouncements and in the summer brought her to trial on a new charge of having made false accusations against the German army. The SPD, in view of her sudden popularity a fervent supporter again, enlisted all its resources in her defence; the state eventually decided not to push the case to a verdict. Her standing with the masses reached new heights. At her instigation and against the warnings of the executive, in July the Berlin wing of the SDP adopted a resolution declaring the mass strike the only possible means to equal suffrage in Prussia.

But Luxemburg's renewed influence within the party as well as her dreams of revolution were quickly dashed by the outbreak of war in August. A sudden surge of patriotism among German workers meant declaring opposition to the war would have been political suicide for the SPD. So despite the pleas of the Second International and the party's own long-standing formal commitments to the contrary, on 4 August SPD representatives to the Reichstag joined all other parties in voting the necessary war credits. Luxemburg was horrified and at first close to suicide. She spent the next few months trying to organize a group of party members prepared to speak out against official SPD policy and the war: what came to be the left-wing socialist group Spartakus. In this connection, she spearheaded the creation of a new paper, *Die Internationale*. For these efforts she was arrested in February 1915 and taken to a women's prison in Berlin. Through the good offices of a sympathetic guard, she was able to continue writing for *Die Internationale*. She also used the time in prison to compose two longer works: her reflections on the war – *The Crisis of Social Democracy* (*Die Krise der Sozialdemokratie*, published at Zürich in 1916 under a pseudonym), and a reply to the critics of her views on imperialism – *The Accumulation of Capital or what the Disciples have made of Marxist Theory. An Anti-Critique* (*Die Akkumulation des Kapitals oder was die Epigonenen aus der Marxschen Theorie gemacht haben. Eine Antikritik*, posthumously published in 1921). From her release in January 1916 until her re-arrest six months later, Luxemburg, jointly with Karl Liebknecht (the first and for a while the only *Reichstag* representative to vote against war credits), entered upon a period of intense political activity. In a series of monthly *Spartacus Letters* (*Spartakusbriefe*) they vigorously attacked the position of both the SPD executive and, more so, a breakaway group, consisting of centrist SPD members now also opposed to the war, that in 1917 was to become a new party, Independent German Social Democracy (USPD). They agitated and heavily advertised for a May Day rally in Berlin, but were among the few actually to attend. At the rally, Liebknecht shouted 'Down with the government and the war!' and was promptly arrested; he was later sentenced to two and a half years' hard labour. For the next two months Luxemburg attended numerous political meetings trying to get radical resolutions passed. Arrested again in July (apparently to silence her, since no charges were laid), she was first kept at a harsh prison in Berlin, then transferred in October to a comfortable old fortress in Poznan and again in July

1917 to a much more regimented prison in Breslau. Once more she was able to get written material smuggled out, including numerous contributions to socialist newspapers. Especially important for her subsequent reputation was an article in the September 1918 *Spartacus Letter* offering a critical appraisal of Bolshevik rule. That same month she drafted her famous pamphlet, *The Russian Revolution* (*Die russische Revolution*), which for political reasons was not published until 1922. Her final two years in prison were also the occasion for larger intellectual projects: she translated into German the autobiography of the Russian novelist Korolenko and worked on revising her school lectures for publication. The surviving parts of the latter, unfinished manuscript were published in 1925 as *Introduction to Political Economy* (*Einführung in die Nationalökonomie*).

On 9 November 1918, the same revolutionary wave that brought the final collapse of the German imperial regime and its replacement with an SPD-led ministry also caused Luxemburg to be freed from prison. Spartakus, under the leadership of Liebknecht, Luxemburg and Jogiches, refused to cooperate with the new government, which it knew to be thoroughly revisionist. Instead, the group published an independent political programme (drafted by Luxemburg) and set about trying to increase its public support with the objective of moving Germany along to the next stage of revolution. After having failed to take over leadership of the USPD, Spartakus opted in late December to create the German Communist Party (KPD). Meanwhile, Luxemburg contributed a steady stream of articles to the new Spartakus organ, *Red Flag* (*Rote Fahne*), in which she sought to interpret the latest political trends along class lines and thus build the mass support she believed essential to a successful revolution. On 4 January 1919, the Berlin chief of police, a known revolutionary, was sacked by the SPD government. This touched off a series of large public demonstrations which the Revolutionary Shop Stewards, Berlin USPD leaders, and the KPD executive jointly tried to escalate into an armed uprising. The government sent in troops and the revolt gradually died out. By 6 January, USPD leaders and a section of the Shop Stewards were urging negotiation with the government. The KPD executive attributed defeat to poor leadership rather than lack of revolutionary sentiment among the Berlin populace. It declared through *Red Flag* that negotiations were a complete betrayal of the masses and refused to participate. On 15 January, Liebknecht, Luxemburg and one other Spartakus leader, then all in hiding, were arrested by a contingent of soldiers. Later that night, Liebknecht and Luxemburg were unceremoniously executed; Luxemburg's body was dumped in a canal, not to be recovered until May. Though the murders were thought to have been plotted by the socialist government and were widely protested, the only official reckoning took the form of gaol terms for one soldier and one junior officer (of two years and four months respectively).

Of Luxemburg's voluminous writings, only a few books qualify for discussion in an economics dictionary: *The Industrial Development of Poland, Social Reform or Revolution?*, *The Accumulation of Capital* and its follow-up *Anti-Critique*, and *Introduction to Political Economy*. The first work is a short history of the economy of nineteenth-century Russian Poland and of tsarist policy toward that region. It was addressed to the debate current within Polish and European socialism whether to make the quest for national independence the main basis of socialist agitation in the three regions of Poland. This explains why it had the distinction of being published – then very unusual for a doctoral dissertation in the social sciences – and was widely reviewed in Germany and in the Polish and Russian *émigré* press. In Part I, 'The History and Present State of Polish Industry', Luxemburg argued that the industrialization of Russian Poland had been caused by and continued to require its close political and economic ties with the Russian empire. During a period of Prussian rule (1796–1806) Polish agricultural estates sank deep into debt, ending their capacity to furnish tax revenues. Therefore the Kingdom of Poland, Russia's diplomatic spoils from the 1814 Vienna Congress, laboured from the outset under a chronic budget deficit. Seeking new sources of revenue, the tsarist government immediately set about encouraging industrial activity in the region. German craftsmen were lured with the offer of subsidies and legal privileges. New laws (for example the abolition of entails) and institutions (such as the Polish Bank) created a more favourable climate for investment. And the tariffs of 1822 and 1824 made for essentially free trade between Poland and Russia. The 1820s witnessed a dramatic rise in Polish textile exports to Russia. But after the Polish uprising of 1831, when the Russian border was closed, exports fell off dramatically and the pace of industrialization slowed to a crawl. The reopening of the customs barrier between Russia and Poland in 1851, together with the blockade of Russia's coasts during the Crimean War and Russian and Polish serf emancipation after 1861, brought about a complete revolution in Polish industry, transforming handicraft manufacturing into large-scale factory production. Polish output and profits rose still further during the 1880s, after Russia introduced a protectionist tariff policy *vis-à-vis* the rest of Europe. By 1890, Russian Poland had been transformed into a bustling industrial region, third largest in the empire (after the Moscow and Petersburg districts). Luxemburg stressed Polish industry's dependence on the Russian market, to which in the 1880s it sold more than half its output. In Part II, 'Russia's Economic Policy in Poland', she sought to counter the popular belief that Russia, driven by the protectionist interests of its own industrialists, would soon cut the Polish economy adrift by closing its customs border again. Such a belief mistakenly supposed that there was some monolithic capitalist interest in Russia united in its desire to oppress Polish industry. Because of a substantial division of labour between the two countries, the economic interests of Russian industries often ran counter to one another. Russian raw-materials producers, for instance, could be counted upon to oppose higher tariffs on Polish goods, since Polish industrialists were among their biggest customers. Moreover, Russia had first introduced free trade to weaken Polish nationalism (by creating a segment of Polish society interested in retaining ties with Russia) – and nothing had changed politically to make the imperial regime want to alter such an arrangement. The book never once mentions the PPS, but the implications for its nationalist stance are clear. Independence would cripple existing industries and halt further industrialization in Russian Poland, setting back the cause of socialist revolution in that country perhaps for decades. This cleared the way for the view of the SDKPiL that socialist agitation in the Kingdom of Poland had much better concentrate on a Russia-wide appeal to the industrial proletariat. It is difficult to tell whether the book influenced the eventual decision of the SPD to abandon the cause of Polish independence. Its main effect may have been indirect: the simple fact of its being accepted for publication, as well as Kautsky's very favourable review in *New Age,* served to raise Luxemburg in the esteem of her SPD colleagues and so perhaps eased her later triumph over the PPS. The latter group of course attacked it vigorously (see especially Perl, 1907) and Lenin dismissed its basic argument in his 1914 pamphlet on self-determination: from the fact of Poland's need for its Russian markets nothing could be decided about the *right* to national independence (Lenin, 1950, p. 21).

The first and by far the more lively half of *Social Reform or Revolution?*, 'The Opportunist Method', is a review of Bernstein's theoretical case for revisionism as first presented in the pages of *New Age*. According to Bernstein, capitalism was now unlikely to collapse from internal causes because it had developed new adaptations since Marx wrote *Capital*. He concluded that a socialist future would have to be built not by waiting for a grand sociopolitical crisis, but by piecemeal reforms leading progressively to cooperative production. But, asserted Luxemburg, to abandon the principle of a looming capitalist collapse is to admit that socialism is not historically necessary and thus to surrender the whole foundation and hope of social democracy. So she set out to prove Bernstein wrong on this point. On his view, the main post-Marx capitalist adaptations were credit and cartels. The former he supposed would aid capitalism by extending production (the share system was giving capitalists access to more capital) and facilitating exchange among producers (commercial credit). But given that capitalist crises are caused by the tendency of production to outrun consumption, credit will only increase their likelihood. Credit also paves the way for a socialist future by separating ownership from production, concentrating immense productive forces in the hands of a few. Bernstein thought trusts and cartels would help capitalism adapt by ending anarchy in production and so eliminating crises. But this would be the case only if cartels became the dominant form of production – something their very nature precludes. Cartels try to increase the profits of one industry at the expense of others – an aim which cannot be generalized. Luxemburg turned next to Bernstein's thesis that socialism could be achieved gradually through trade unions, social reforms, and the evolution of the state. He expected unions gradually to reduce the capitalists' control over production until finally they would be excluded entirely and a collective management substituted. But trade unions would only tend to arrest technical innovation and increase prices, substituting a battle between producer and consumer interests for a genuine class struggle. Furthermore, unions were destined to diminish rather than increase in power as capitalism spread; for as extra-capitalist markets became increasingly scarce, the demand for labour power would start to slacken. Bernstein supposed social reforms would likewise progressively diminish the scope for capitalist control. But being the product of capitalist societies, they would always serve the interests of capital alone. The case for state-led socialism was mistaken in assuming that governments function in the interest of society as a whole. In fact, especially in recent decades (for example protectionism, militarism), the state had begun imposing policies of benefit only to the bourgeois class (or even just segments of it) at the expense of society in general. The extension of democracy could not be expected to change this trend because in practice parliaments are just a tool of the ruling class. Luxemburg drew out the implications for the political practices of the SPD. Bernstein was advising the SPD to use its influence with trade unions and the Reichstag only to win immediate, concrete improvements for workers. But in the long run this descent into political horse-trading and diplomatic conciliation, since it could never give rise to socialism, would only disillusion German workers with the party. So at all costs the SPD needed to keep to its traditional strategy, using trade union and parliamentary struggles to prepare workers to take control of the state.

Part II of the book, 'Economic development and socialism', is Luxemburg's response to Bernstein's *Presuppositions of Socialism*. It lacks the coherence and flow of the first half and descends more into piecemeal rebuttal and close textual commentary. In the new book, Bernstein added to the case for revisionism in three main ways. First, in new evidence of the rising number and size of share-holding societies, he found further grounds for rejecting Marx's prediction of increasing concentration of capital. Second, he spelled out more clearly the path by which social reform would lead to socialism; trade unions and cooperatives would gradually suppress industrial and commercial profit respectively. Finally, he tried to show that capitalism made democracy historically inevitable. On the first point, Luxemburg countered that the growth of share-holding societies actually confirmed Marx's theory; it represented the unification of small fortunes into one large capital, and the separation of production from capitalist ownership. Bernstein failed to realize this because he saw the world in terms of relations between individuals (rich versus poor) rather than between classes (capital versus labour). Luxemburg thought her views in the first half of *Social Reform or Revolution?* sufficient to dispense with Bernstein's latest thoughts on trade unions. Production cooperatives could never lead to socialism because, being subject to competition from capitalist enterprises, they would have to behave like them. Their real possibilities could emerge only if they were able to assure themselves beforehand of a constant circle of consumers. But this meant that production cooperatives would always be limited in scope to small local markets and to necessities, especially food. As this excluded the most important branches of capitalist industry, they could never be the means of a general social transformation. Finally, a short survey of history sufficed to show capitalism was compatible with many different types of political rule besides democracy. Such democratic institutions as did accompany the rise of capitalism had already exhausted their usefulness to the bourgeoisie. In fact, in some respects liberalism had become a direct impediment to capitalism – namely in opposing imperialism and permitting the rise of working-class political parties. Hence Germany's current democratic institutions, few as they were, might easily disappear at any time. So, far from democracy being the means to the socialist world of the future, socialism was actually democracy's last hope. Luxemburg added a few reflections of her own. Historically, reform had always been the prelude to a revolution in which the rising class seized political power. So those who were pushing reform *in place of* revolution were opting not for a slower road to the same ultimate goal but for a different goal: a merely superficial modification of the old society. It was impossible to abolish capitalism merely by reforming German laws. The capitalist system rested not on human law, but on an economic necessity deriving from the current institutional regime. Similarly, wages were kept low not by statute but by unavoidable economic factors. Socialism could be attained only by overthrowing existing socioeconomic institutions, which in turn demanded the masses be brought consciously to desire this end.

In her magnum opus, *The Accumulation of Capital*, Luxemburg furnished a theoretical platform from which she could more effectively attack the opportunism then rampant in German Social Democracy. Though poorly organized in places, it is a unique and most catholic book. Its three sections roughly correspond to the fields of economic theory, the history of economic thought and economic history, and it is informed throughout by a keen sensitivity to the great political issues and forces of the nineteenth and early twentieth centuries. In Section One, 'The Problem of Reproduction', Luxemburg maintained that a fundamental problem is concealed in the growth process of capitalist economies. In the second volume of *Capital*, Marx developed a two-sector (producer and consumer goods), three-input (the famous c, s and v) model which appeared to show the perfect feasibility of a continuous and smooth process of capital accumulation. While the model would be perfectly applicable to a socialist economy, in a capitalist setting, Luxemburg charged, it has a fundamental flaw: it cannot explain why capitalists would ever be motivated to increase output. Specifically, whence the new sources of demand needed to absorb the increasing supply of consumer goods at which capital accumulation aims? They cannot come from workers, whose wages are fixed at subsistence throughout. Increased luxury consumption by capitalists cannot be the solution, since capital accumulation occurs only when they save, that is, when they *reduce* their consumption. There can be no appeal to civil servants, soldiers, clerics and the like since, mere parasites upon workers and capitalists, they have no independent means of purchasing power. Some of the extra output, it is true, can go as means of production to other capitalists; but this only pushes the problem back a step, since we still have not found the extra markets for consumer goods that would justify increased spending on means of production. Marx himself, Luxemburg asserted, was aware of the problem, and made several unsuccessful attempts to resolve it. In the end he settled on the monetary sector as his solution; this was a mistake, since the problem is a purely physical one and needs to be solved in physical terms. (For this she took care to excuse Marx, pointing to his poor health and the fact that he never actually finished the second volume.)

Though its specific contribution to Luxemburg's broader argument isn't clear, Section Two, 'Historical Exposition of the Problem', features a fascinating style of doctrinal history in which politics and sociological analysis are front and centre. It consists of a running commentary on the reflections of other economists, before and after Marx, about the problem disclosed in Section One. Sismondi was a far-seeing critic of capitalism who unfortunately came to the mistaken conclusion that capital accumulation was always harmful and should be discouraged as much as possible. All the same, he stood head and shoulders above his contemporaries McCulloch, Ricardo and Say, who all insisted that general gluts were impossible simply because supply always creates its own demand. (In disagreeing with them, Malthus was just trying to carve out a niche for a parasitic aristocracy.) Sismondi correctly countered that unless new production were matched to existing purchasing power, it would actually worsen the plight of workers by increasing unemployment and lowering wages. Rodbertus thought economic crises were the result of rising labour productivity; using a labour theory of value, he showed that this would automatically translate into a reduced share of total output going to labour. His proposed solution was therefore for governments to legislate a fixed share of total output for workers. This is foolishness, Luxemburg charged, because a fixed wage rate would bring capital accumulation to a halt; Marx had shown that profit rates were only kept up by the historical tendency of capitalism to increase the share of surplus value in the total payment going to workers and capitalists. Much more radical surgery than a fixed wage rate would be needed to end workers' woes. The Russian populists Vorontsov and Nikolayon believed that capitalism was inherently unstable, tending to overproduction, crises and unemployment. They drew the mistaken policy conclusion that capitalist development in Russia must be halted in favour of an economic system built upon communal farming. Their analyses were nevertheless to be preferred to those of the three Russian Marxists, Struvé, Bulgakov and Tugan Baranovski, who staked their political commitment to capitalism on the premise of its inherent sustainability. Struvé claimed that capitalist accumulation would be able to draw on rising demand from the professional classes. Bulgakov thought perpetual expansion possible owing to an ever-growing demand of capitalists for capital goods. Both positions Luxemburg had already given grounds for rejecting. Tugan Baranovski pointed to the smooth progression of numbers in Marx's model of economic growth as itself the proof that ongoing capital accumulation is possible. But in Section One Luxemburg had already shown that no plausible real-world causality was available for the numbers Marx had used.

In the first two chapters of Section Three, 'The Historical Conditions of Accumulation', Luxemburg offered her theoretical solution to the problem of capital accumulation. She began by adding another wrinkle to the problem. In his model of capitalist economic growth, Marx implicitly assumed a constant ratio of capital to labour power (c:v). But his principle of the increasing organic composition of capital requires the output of producer goods (capital) be rising faster than that of consumer (wage) goods. This is inconsistent with another prominent feature of the model (and of actual capitalist production): the need for mutual coordination and balance between the two output sectors and their respective input requirements. So capitalism needs extra markets not just to absorb rising output but also to sustain general equilibrium. Therefore the 'accumulation of capital, as an historical process, depends in every respect upon non-capitalist social strata and forms of social organisation' (Luxemburg, 1951, p. 366); capitalism is forced to pillory them for the needed new sources of demand. Certain passages in the third volume of *Capital* and in *Theories of Surplus Value*, she suggested, show that Marx himself recognized that the problem had to be solved this way.

In the remaining chapters of Section Three, by far the most readable and entertaining part of the book, Luxemburg aimed to give empirical content to her theory. She posited a basic schema for the progressive invasion by 'capital' of non-capitalist societies, illustrating its various stages with stimulating but highly polemic interpretations of the history of modern European colonialism. In the first stage, the struggle against 'natural economy', capital seeks to acquire property in natural resources and 'liberate' (in other words, destroy the traditional forms of livelihood of) indigenous populations to serve as wage labourers. Thus the British and French in India and Algeria respectively first forced communally held lands to be parcelled out as private property and then purchased or impounded huge tracts, driving on to the labour market the peasants who formerly worked them. Capital also forces the introduction of a 'commodity economy' – production for sale rather than use (an essential step in creating the necessary new markets for the excess production of capitalist countries). In the Opium Wars, for instance, Britain compelled China by military means to purchase opium from its Indian plantations. Finally, capital takes care to separate handicraft manufacturing from agriculture, transforming farmers into consumers of factory-manufactured goods. For example, after the Civil War, American politicians deliberately induced mid-western farmers to begin purchasing machinery in large quantities and producing surpluses of grain and livestock for sale (by raising taxes, subsidizing railroads and settlement, and erecting a protective tariff barrier for eastern industrial manufacturers). The second stage of capital's invasion of non-capitalist societies, as in an earlier part of Europe's own history, is the ruin of independent craftsmanship and its replacement with large-scale factory production. Without giving her reasons, Luxemburg opted not to discuss this stage (see Luxemburg, 1951, p. 416), perhaps in deference to Marx's own work on the subject. The third and final stage is imperialism: the 'industrialisation and capitalist emancipation of the hinterland where capital formerly realised its surplus value' (ibid., p. 419). One of its most common manifestations, loan-financed railway construction, further illustrates the contradictions inherent in capitalism. Its inner cause was the need to transfer output for which no markets existed in Europe to countries where it could be sold (to realize the surplus value contained in it) or invested. In the end, foreign peasants paid for the loans through forced extortion of their labour power, as for instance with the cotton and sugar plantations of the Khedive of Egypt. Another facet of imperialism was the recent global trend to protectionism, designed to close domestic and colonial markets to the manufactures of other European nations. England could afford to retain free trade only because of her immense possessions in non-capitalist areas of the world. Finally, militarism arises from the competitive struggle between capitalist nations to win control over their share of the ever-dwindling number of remaining non-capitalist countries. The obvious conclusion: the capitalist regime cannot possibly endure. Overproduction and economic crises must sooner or later become frequent and widespread; even before that time nations will be brought to armed conflict in the desperate and hopeless attempt to secure the constant supply of new markets needed to stave off declining profit rates.

> In its living history it [capitalism] is a contradiction in itself, and its movement of accumulation provides a solution to the conflict and aggravates it at the same time. At a certain stage of development there will be no other way out than the application of socialist principles. The aim of socialism is not accumulation but the satisfaction of toiling humanity's wants by developing the productive force of the entire globe. (Luxemburg, 1951, p. 467)

Luxemburg liked to think of *The Accumulation of Capital* as a scientific work written with the objectivity and detachment of the scholar. She told friends she had been drawn to the subject by an interest in higher mathematics and wrote the book in a dream-like trance during four months of total disengagement from the world of affairs. Allegedly, she handed the first draft to her publishers without even once rereading it. Nevertheless, seen against the backdrop of SPD policy and her own weak position within the party in the years just before World War I, it must be regarded as an intensely political work. Showing clear signs of the political opportunism it was to exhibit so clearly at the beginning of the war, the SPD executive refused to take a clear stand on the issue of German militarism. Luxemburg counselled building the party's entire political strategy around it. A firm declaration of its opposition to imperialist wars would greatly intensify bourgeois opposition to German socialism, putting an end to the opportunist dithering of the SPD executive. And if the masses could be brought to perceive imperialism in terms of class conflict, the party might exploit the issue to marshal the forces needed for a socialist revolution. For this radical political programme *The Accumulation of Capital* laid the necessary theoretical groundwork. It interpreted imperialism as the direct consequence of production for profit, part of the same historical dynamic that was oppressing workers in the form of low wages, cyclical and rising unemployment, pressure to work faster or for longer hours, and so forth. Section Three sought to portray colonialism as just the extension into other countries of the same capitalist rapacity with which European workers were already familiar at home. Nor should the masses be duped into thinking the acquisition of new foreign markets might bring economic relief; imperialism was only the last in a long succession of strategies by which capitalism was hoping to stave off its own inevitable collapse.

There have been three distinct phases in the history of the book's reception. It first achieved notoriety in connection with the politics of German socialism. Stolid party members immediately perceived its radical implications and were horrified; the socialist press was flooded with harsh negative reviews. The book had no effect on SPD policy; it served only to increase Luxemburg's political isolation, especially after socialist Reichstag representatives voted in favour of war credits. *The Accumulation of Capital* came to prominence for a second time in the mid-1920s as a result of political developments in Russia. After a second failed communist insurrection in Germany (1923), Lenin's death and Stalin's rise to power, the Bolshevik Party stopped trying to foment a European revolution and moved to a policy of 'socialism in one country'. Through the auspices of the Communist International, the new strategy filtered down to all European communist parties, including the KPD. So party writers in Russia and Germany (see especially Bukharin, 1925 and Fischer, 1925) were called out to refute once more *The Accumulation of Capital*, the perceived cornerstone of the former revolutionary tradition in German communism. Finally, in the mid-twentieth century, Luxemburg's *magnum opus* gained a measure of acceptance and even popularity as an early anticipation of the underconsumptionist theories of Kalecki, Sweezy and others. It is no accident an English translation appeared in the 1950s and with an introduction by Joan Robinson.

As its title suggests, the *Anti-Critique* was a reply to critics of *The Accumulation of Capital*. Written in 1915 while Luxemburg was in gaol, it was first published only in 1921 as an appendix to a new edition of the original book. The timing was deliberate. In 1920, Paul Levi, then leader of the KPD, had publicly criticized his party colleagues for ignoring his advice and attempting an insurrection in Germany. For this he won the hostility of Lenin and the Comintern and was made an outsider in the party. On the counter-attack, using his position as Luxemburg's literary executor, he published her draft manuscript on the Russian Revolution. Its forceful criticisms of the Bolshevik regime made Luxemburg's position a central issue in European socialism again and attracted renewed criticisms of her work in general. For this reason it became advisable for Levi to publish the *Anti-Critique* as well. Apart from its initial political ramifications, the pamphlet has attracted little interest. It began with a summary restatement of her position in *The Accumulation of Capital*; entirely non-mathematical and to the point, the exposition is vastly improved over that given in the original work. Luxemburg quickly dismissed the critics' main objection to her case: that in *Capital* Marx himself had already shown that the problem of capital accumulation was perfectly soluble. This was Tugan Baranovsky's argument, which she had already shown to be misguided. The rest of the book is devoted to the more original criticisms of Otto Bauer (published in 1913 in two successive issues of *New Age*). Bauer developed a mathematical model in which he claimed to have solved the problem of capital accumulation. His solution turned on the assumption that new demand would be created by the growth of population within capitalist societies themselves. But the alleged solution had been attained only by using numbers which would be impossible in any actual capitalist economy. Population growth could not be the solution, since the empirical record shows that capital always grows more rapidly than population. In the closing section, 'Imperialism' she objected to the practical consequences of Bauer's theoretical standpoint – since imperialism was an accidental aberration of capitalism, socialists should appeal to the uncorrupted part of the bourgeoisie for joint action against the few capitalists who benefited from the system. This was merely a cover for the SPD's inaction and cowardice, as became clear when the war broke out.

The *Introduction to Political Economy* is a fragment of a work Luxemburg never completed; of the ten chapters she planned, the drafts of only six survived the burning of her papers by German soldiers in 1919. Levi edited the work and published it in 1925, perhaps as a protest against the new anti-revolutionary trend of German communism. It passed largely without comment at the time and has since attracted attention only in connection with more recent developments in Marxist economic theory (a French translation was published in 1971 with a preface by Ernest Mandel; it has never been translated into English). Conceived as a popular work, ironically it is of all her writings the most dry and academic. It offers a grand philosophy of history on the Hegelian plan of thesis (a universal state of primitive communism), antithesis (humanity's fall into slavery, serfdom and capitalism) and synthesis (the planned and organized economy of the future – communism at a higher level). The initial chapters would have put off most popular readers, dwelling as they do on the fine points of competing definitions of 'political economy', debates among nineteenth-century European anthropologists on the nature and origins of primitive communism in Asia, Africa and South America, and capital's relentless assault on communal institutions during the medieval and early modern periods. The fourth chapter, 'Production for the market', was a little more topical. Consisting in large part of a theory of the origin of money, it finished by raising the question: how is it that the market system, which seems to conform to the highest moral principles of liberty (abolition of serfdom and guild restrictions), equality (exchange of equals for equals) and fraternity (absence of personal domination), nevertheless gives rise to systematic inequality? Chapter Five, 'Wage Labour', answers the question with a highly simplified version of Marx's theory of value and then proceeds to trace the most pressing woes of the proletariat to the capitalist's endeavour to extract surplus value from his employees: efforts to increase the length of the working day, constant downward pressure on wages, and large-scale unemployment (the deliberate preservation of an industrial reserve army). Against these afflictions trade unions are powerless; their only legitimate function is to help raise the revolutionary consciousness of workers. In the final chapter, 'Tendencies of the Capitalist Economy', Luxemburg gave her answer to the 'fundamental question of political economy': how does a capitalist economy function without planning or deliberate organization? Only by (a) exchange and money, which impose a global division of labour; (b) free competition, which assures technical progress but also transforms small producers into proletarians; (c) the capitalist law of wages, which prevents workers from escaping their proletarian state and at the same time permits a constant accumulation of capital; (d) an industrial reserve army that lets capital extend itself at will; and (e) price fluctuations and economic crises, by which a blind and chaotic balance is achieved between production and society's needs. She closed with an offer of hope for the future, based squarely upon her analysis in *The Accumulation of Capital*. Capitalism is only a transitional historical phase, containing the seeds of its own dissolution. It requires a normal profit, which rests in turn on a relationship between supply and demand that is being progressively undermined as capitalism floods world markets ever more quickly with ever more commodities. Industrial and commercial crises are looming; the final demise of capitalism is at hand.

RICHARD KLEER

Bibliography

Selected writings by Rosa Luxemburg

(1898), *Die industrielle Entwicklung Polens. Inaugural Dissertation zur Erlangung der staatswissenschaftlichen Doktorwürde der hohen staatswissenschaftlichen Fakultät der Universität Zürich*, Leipzig: Duncker & Humblot.

(1899), *Sozialreform oder Revolution? Mit einem Anhang: Miliz und Militarismus*, Berlin: Dietsch.

(1906), *Massenstreik, Partei und Gewerkschaften*, Hamburg: E. Dubber.

(1908), *Sozialreform oder Revolution?*, 2nd edn, Leipzig: Leipziger Buchdruckerei Antiengesellschaft.

(1913), *Die Akkumulation des Kapitals. Ein Beitrag zur ökonomischen Erklärung des Imperialismus*, Berlin: Buchhandlung Vorwarts, Paul Singer.

(1916), *Die Krise der Sozialdemokratie. Anhang: Leitsätze über die Aufgaben der internationalen Sozialdemokratie*, Zürich: Verlagsdruckerei Union.

(1918), 'Die russische Tragödie', *Spartakusbrief*, **11** (September), 2–4.

(1921), *Die Akkumulation des Kapitals oder was die Epigonen aus der Marxschen Theorie gemacht haben. Eine Antikritik*, Appendix to new edn of *Die Akkumulation des Kapitals*, Leipzig: Frankes Verlag.

(1922), *Die russische Revolution. Eine kritische Würdigung*, ed. and intro. Paul Levi, Berlin: Verlag Gesellschaft und Erziehung.

(1925), *Einführung in die Nationalökonomie*, ed. Paul Levi, Berlin: E. Laub.

(1951), *The Accumulation of Capital*, trans. Agnes Schwarzschild, intro. Joan Robinson, London: Routledge & Kegan Paul.

(1970), *Reform or Revolution*, 2nd edn, intro. Mary-Alice Waters, trans. Integer, New York: Pathfinder Press.

(1971), *Introduction à l'économie politique*, trans. J.B., pref. Ernest Mandel, Paris: Editions Anthropos.

(1972), *The Accumulation of Capital – An Anti-Critique*, ed. and intro. Kenneth Tarbuck, trans. Rudolf Wichmann, New York: Monthly Review Press.

(1973), *The Industrial Development of Poland*, intro. Lyndon LaRouche, trans. Tessa DeCarlo, New York: Campaigner Publications.

Other sources and references

Bernstein, Eduard (1899), *Die Voraussetzungen des Sozialismus und die Aufgaben der Sozialdemokratie*, Stuttgart: Dietz.

Bukharin, Nikolai (1925), *Imperializm i nakoplenie kapitala: teoreticheskii etiud*, Berlin and Vienna. English trans., *Imperialism and the Accumulation of Capital*, ed. and intro. Kenneth Tarbuck, trans. Rudolf Wichmann, New York: Monthly Review Press, 1972.

Fischer, Ruth (1925), 'Our most important task', *Die Internationale*, **8**(3), 105–11.

Lenin, Vladimir Ilich (1950 [1914]), *The Right of Nations to Self-Determination*, Moscow: Foreign Publishing House.

Nettl, J.P. (1966), *Rosa Luxemburg*, 2 vols, London: Oxford University Press.

Perl, Feliks (1907), *Kwestia polska w oswietleniu 'Socialdemokracji' polskiej* (*The Polish Question as Illuminated by Polish 'Social Democracy'*), Cracow.

Jane Haldimand Marcet (1769–1858)

Jane Haldimand Marcet was the oldest of ten children of Anthony (Antoine) Haldimand, a Swiss citizen, and Jane Pickersgill, an English woman. She grew up in London where her father was a very prosperous banker and real-estate developer. She was educated at home by tutors and was taught the same subjects as were her brothers. Due to her mother's death in childbirth, she was catapulted into adulthood at the age of 15. Her new role required that she supervise a large household and act as hostess for her father's frequent and lavish parties. He entertained at least twice a week and invited bankers, scientists, writers, politicians and visitors to London. At these opulent gatherings, she became conversant with the important ideas and events current at the turn of the nineteenth century. Here she also met her future husband, Alexander Marcet, a London physician and Swiss citizen.

Jane Haldimand had been engaged to a cousin in the British navy, but broke off the engagement due to her father's continuing disapproval of her fiancé's character. Thus, she found herself a 30-year-old spinster with no marriage plans. Her father disapproved of men who left large bequests in their wills to male heirs and much smaller amounts to females. Accordingly, she stood to inherit a full share of the Haldimand banking empire and this made her a very rich woman. As word spread that her engagement had been renounced, many men presented themselves. Her father allowed her to choose among them, although this was not the universal custom at the time. Several men wrote to her father describing their circumstances and prospects, including Alexander Marcet. Anthony Haldimand's response to the other men is unknown, but Alexander Marcet was told that he would have to press his own case to Jane and that the final decision would be hers. Although Marcet had no independent means, Jane accepted his proposal of marriage, seeing in him some of the qualities she admired in her father. They had a one-month engagement and were married in December 1799.

It was a new life in a new century which awaited her. Alexander Marcet's hobby was chemistry, a study much in vogue at the time. Jane was also interested in chemistry and decided to continue her studies with Humphrey Davy, then lecturing in London. Frequently she reviewed the lecture and repeated the experiments with her husband in his own laboratory at home. When Davy's course of lectures was over, Alexander and the publisher Longman encouraged her to put together an introductory book on experimental chemistry. This was the *Conversations on Chemistry* (1806) and there was no similar book at the time. The book was a great success, going to 16 editions and selling more than 160 000 copies in the USA alone. One of the early readers was the then bookseller's apprentice, Michael Faraday, who always credited Marcet as his 'first teacher'.

In the second decade of the century, Jane's younger brother, William Haldimand, was appointed at the age of 25 the youngest ever Director of the Bank of England. William Haldimand and her father had made their home with the Marcets after Jane's marriage and her brother's appointment to the Bank reinforced her ties with the London financial community. She and her husband, Alexander, had earlier made the acquaintance of the financier, David Ricardo, and the Marcet–Haldimand home became the setting for intense discussion on current monetary issues, particularly the Bullion Controversy. Ricardo, Haldimand and Jane Marcet took the position that the Bank of England should be forced to return to redemption in specie and a sound currency. The agricultural interests and many of the officers of the Bank favoured mild inflation and easily available credit. At the same time, the issue of the Corn Laws – protection for the grain industry – was the subject of contentious debate in Parliament. Jane Marcet was also much concerned with 'the condition of the people', particularly the well-being of the labouring classes. She became convinced that what was needed was a wider under-standing of the principles of political economy so that what was known only to a *few* could be known to *all*. This time independent of her husband's interests, but again encouraged by Longman, she prepared a second elemen-tary book, *Conversations on Political Economy* (1816). Even though the author stated in the preface that it was intended for 'young persons', the book was read by many, many adults. It covered capital, wages, population, rent, interest, value, price, money and foreign trade. The reader was exposed to the economic issues of the day without the necessity of reading the work of a writer such as Adam Smith.

The book contained a series of 22 dialogues between Mrs B, the teacher, and Caroline, her pupil. The market mechanism was presented in a simple straight-forward way and the harmony of interests of all classes was emphasized. The duties of the employing and labouring classes were discussed: capitalists were to save and labourers to work diligently. Marcet detailed the process of capital accumulation and the necessity of capital to pay labour. Wages were seen to be determined by the number of workers in relation to the goods available to pay them. The benefits of a free market were proclaimed repeatedly. The book avoided controversy and omitted contrary views. On one subject, her writing differed from the usual presentation; that was the theory of value. Instead of following the traditional labour theory of value explanation, she presented the argument of intrinsic value, or 'utility'. She avoided the claim that the labour required to produce a good determined its value and argued in favour of value as a reflection of a good's appeal to the buyer. Later, she credited this argument to J.B. Say, the French economist. A reader who took the trouble to read the book carefully and consider the contents would receive a basic grounding in classical economics as it was understood in the early nineteenth century.

Marcet's economics was not the 'dismal science' of Malthus and Ricardo. She was more optimistic about the future of the nation than either of these two writers for two reasons: first she saw no limit to growth of output, income and wealth, as did Ricardo; and second, she was not convinced, as was Malthus, that the working class would erode all increases in the standard of living by having more children. She believed in the benefits of economic growth for all and in the fairness of the existing income distribution. Speaking through her pupil, Caroline, she wrote, 'Formerly I imagined that whatever addition was made to the wealth of the rich was so much subtracted from the pittance of the poor, but now I see that it is, on the contrary an addition to the general stock of wealth of the country, by which the poor benefit equally with the rich' (Marcet, 1816, p. 469).

Jane Marcet's contemporaries recognized her contribution as an author and educator. *The Conversations on Political Economy* was recommended by Malthus and Ricardo. Other high-ranking critics also acclaimed her work. Macaulay wrote in 1825 that 'Every girl who has read Mrs. Marcet's little dialogues on political economy could teach Montagu or Walpole many lessons in finance' (Macaulay, 1851, p. 3). J.B. Say complimented her when he wrote that she was 'the only woman who has written on political economy and shown herself superior even to men' (*DNB*, 1899, vol. 36, p. 123). Maria Edgeworth, the author, described a social occasion at Ricardo's, saying, 'It has now become high fashion with blue ladies to talk to Political Economy. Mean time fine ladies now require that their daughters' governesses should teach political economy' (Colvin, 1971, p. 364).

Other introductory books followed and Marcet published texts on a variety of subjects including astronomy, botany, mineralology and physics. In between publications on new topics, she revised her previous books for new editions.

Her writing career did not keep the couple from raising the family that both wanted. Between 1803 and 1809, Jane gave birth to four children: two boys and two girls. Jane was able to employ nursemaids and governesses for her children. Nevertheless, she was particularly close to her growing children and took great pleasure in their accomplishments. As her family had arranged when she was a girl, the two sexes studied the same subjects with the best tutors available. Later, Marcet would write a number of books for children. Jane Marcet's happy marriage ended in 1822, when her husband died suddenly and unexpectedly. She fell into a severe depression.

It was two years before Jane Marcet could return to her usual activities of writing and publishing. She credited her Christian faith for sustaining her after her husband's death. As she neared recovery, she prepared a book on a new topic – religion. The book was titled *Conversations on the Evidences of Christianity* (1826) and concerned the circumstances of the writing of the New Testament. The subject explored was whether the gospels were of divine inspiration and were a proof of the divinity of Jesus Christ. The book contains some analysis of the language in which the various accounts were written and shows that she did a considerable amount of research with religious scholars. Thereafter, Marcet added new subjects to her publications: history, literature and humanities.

Over 15 years passed between the first publication of the *Conversations on Political Economy* and her next book on that subject. In the autumn of 1830 there had been many disturbances in the English countryside between farmers and their agricultural labourers. Rick-burning and machine-breaking spread and farmers who used threshing machines received threats. Some farmers in south Wales, who were concerned lest the riots in England spread to their own workers, organized a society to 'educate their workers'. Jane was approached to write a group of stories for the society which would illustrate the principles of political economy in an easy and familiar way. Earlier she had been opposed to teaching political economy to the working classes, but her desire for peace changed her mind.

In 1833 she published *John Hopkins's Notions on Political Economy*, a collection of nine original stories on economic themes which were intended 'for the improvement of the laboring classes' (Marcet, 1833, advertisement). The stories explored the economic questions thought to be relevant to a person near the bottom of the economic ladder. The topics were not treated as comprehensively in this book as in the *Conversations on Political Economy*, but the tales were more entertaining. The book centres on John Hopkins, an agricultural worker, who supported a large family on very meagre wages. He had a simple, inquiring mind and held many distorted views on political economy which the stories were designed to correct.

Hopkins believed that 'rich men by their extravagance deprive us poor men of bread' (Marcet, 1833, p. 1) and requests an obliging fairy to do away with luxuries. Disastrous employment consequences occur for Hopkins and his friends and he can hardly wait to ask the fairy to reverse his previous wish. Similarly serious results occur when Hopkins asks the fairy to double wages. As a result of his meddling, he requests no more from the fairy and concludes 'the interest of the rich and poor go hand in hand, like a loving man and wife, who though they may fall out now and then, jog along together till death parts them' (Marcet, 1833, p. 120). The stories continue in a similar vein to cover the benevolence of nature, emigration, Poor's Rate, capital goods, protection for agriculture, and the benefits of free international trade. While this book was less successful than the *Conversations on Political Economy*, it was favourably received and Malthus wrote to Marcet approvingly and revealed that he planned to purchase several copies.

Eighteen more years passed between *John Hopkins's Notions on Political Economy* and Marcet's last book on the subject, *Rich and Poor* (1851). This was a simple, 75-page work for children. The setting was a school in a country village, taught by a popular master, Mr B., who undertook to teach political economy to a group of six eager young boys. The topics of labour, profits, capital, wages, machinery, price, trade, money and banks are treated in 13 lessons. Perhaps because the book was targeted at children, it seems too simplified and self-serving. While some of the books Marcet wrote for children were clever and imaginative, this work did not so qualify; in it Marcet appears to have lost touch with what people believed about economic questions at mid-century.

By the end of her life, Jane Marcet had published 30 books on a variety of subjects – an almost unbelievable accomplishment for her day. She had maintained a strong interest in the scientific and intellectual concerns of her time and she had succeeded in communicating knowledge at an introductory level to her readers. She was the perfect popularizer. Her work may be judged in retrospect to have been too optimistic. Yet, she was a pioneer of economic education and perfection is rarely achieved by the pathbreakers.

Marcet died at the age of 89 in the London home of her daughter and son-in-law. She could look back with satisfaction to a half-century of writing and to an improvement in the circumstances of the people and the nation that she loved.

BETTE POLKINGHORN

Bibliography

Selected writings by Jane Haldimand Marcet
(1816), *Conversations on Political Economy*, London: Longman; 3rd edn, 1818.
(1826), *Conversations on the Evidences of Christianity*, London: Longman.
(1833), *John Hopkins's Notions on Political Economy*, London: Longman.
(1851), *Rich and Poor*, London: Longman.

Other sources and references
Colvin, Christina (1971), *Maria Edgeworth: Letters from England 1813–1844*, Oxford: Clarendon Press, p. 364.
Dictionary of National Biography (1899 edition) Sir Leslie Stephen and Sir Sidney Lee (eds), London: Smith, Elder, p. 123.
Macaulay, Thomas Babington (1851), *Critical and Historical Essays*, London: Longman, Brown, Green and Longmans, p. 3.

Mary Paley Marshall (1850–1944)[1]

Mary Paley was born on 24 October 1850 in Ufford, a village near Stamford, Lincolnshire, UK, about forty miles northwest of Cambridge. Her parents were Thomas Paley, Rector of Ufford, and Ann Judith Wormald. Thomas

Paley was grandson of Archdeacon Paley, the author of renowned works of theology that sought to prove the existence of God with reference to the order and complexity of nature. Within the confines of the rectory and in academic circles, this lineage compensated for the strictness of Thomas Paley's political and religious views – a 'strict Evangelical' and a 'staunch Radical' – that otherwise prevented social intercourse between the rectory and families of suitable social standing in the district (Marshall, 1947, pp. 8, 10). There were few opportunities for Mary Paley to meet young people of her own age. This was possibly to her advantage since her urge to study arose indirectly from boredom with her situation as a young woman.

Encouraged by her father, she studied for the Cambridge Higher Local Examinations for Women over Eighteen that had recently been set up to test standards among women entering the teaching profession. Her good results led to the award of a scholarship on condition that she came to Cambridge and took advantage of a 'Lectures for Women' scheme which had started there in the Easter Term, 1870, in which Cambridge lecturers offered teaching in the subjects of the Cambridge Higher Local Examination. Mary Paley described this scheme, whereby young, single women lived apart from their parents in Cambridge and followed lectures given by male university lecturers, as 'an outrageous proceeding' and this was undoubtedly what all but the most progressive people thought about it. Initially she attended lectures in 'safe' subjects for general cultivation – Latin, literature, history and so on – but a close friend persuaded her to attend a political economy lecture. She went, and went to stay, first as a student and then as teacher (ibid., p. 50).

Alfred Marshall, who had been closely involved in the scheme from its inception in January 1870, lectured in political economy. At that time, he saw no objection to women pursuing advanced studies and persuaded his two best women students, including Mary Paley, to study for the Moral Sciences Tripos, the degree examination that included papers in political economy. She sat her Tripos examinations, on an informal basis, in December 1874. The Tripos examiners marked her papers, placing her between the first and second class. Her achievement was astonishing compared with that of many of the male students taking honours degrees at that time. Not only did women students lack the disciplined habits of study and practice in writing examination papers familiar to most men, but society persistently fed women negative signals as to the wisdom, propriety and need for them to study beyond an elementary level. The companionship of like-minded women and the encouragement of their male teachers were of enormous importance and helped to combat social and often family disapproval. However, they lacked the all-important role-models of women who had tried and succeeded in the quest for academic recognition. Thus Mary Paley's first and probably most important legacy to women academics in general and to women economists in particular was to show that formal qualifications could be attained by a woman, and with distinction.

After her degree examination, Mary Paley returned home where she took the remarkable step of giving a series of public lectures in the nearby town of Stamford, a bold move for a young, unmarried woman. As a result of her enterprise, so Mary Paley believed, she was invited to return to Newnham College from October 1875 as Resident Lecturer, thus beginning a long career as a teacher of economics. She married Alfred Marshall in 1877. On marriage, Alfred Marshall had to resign his College Fellowship and find other means of support. Mary Paley Marshall, as she now signed her written work and letters, had inherited some money from her family, but her income, she records, was insufficient to support them. The University College in Bristol had opened in the spring of 1876, and was now looking for a principal who would forward the stated ideals of quality education not only for the sons of local businessmen but also the working class and women. The post was offered to Alfred Marshall, who was a known supporter of working-class and female education, together with a chair in political economy. His arrival marked an upswing in the number of students attending economics lectures but his wife was also a major attraction. She had written the papers for 'the Moral Sciences Tripos and shown ... her brains were equal to those of the men ... we felt indeed honoured to have her amongst us' (Pease, 1942, pp. 6–8).

Both Alfred and Mary were anxious that she be allowed to help in the work in the first college to start mixed education. In May 1878, she was appointed to take over Marshall's morning lectures at his request (Council Minutes, 15 May 1878). The decision to give her a teaching post was not an emergency arrangement; it was made a year before Marshall's illness obliged him to cut down on his teaching. Overall, Mary Marshall did more teaching, and more advanced teaching, than her husband did during their years at Bristol. Mary Paley Marshall's work was long remembered. Two years after Marshall's death, she was honoured for her life-long work as a teacher of economics with the award of the degree of D. Litt. by the University of Bristol. In presenting her for the degree, the Dean of the Faculty of Arts described her as 'A distinguished scholar in her own right, who has devoted the best of her powers to collaboration with her husband in researches which have brought economics out of the cloud of surmise into the daylight of true science' (reported in the Newnham College Roll *Letter*, January 1928).

In 1883, Marshall was appointed to a lectureship at Balliol College, Oxford. Mary Marshall became a successful teacher of economics for the scheme of extra-mural lectures that prepared women for the Oxford Examination for Women over Eighteen Years. She enjoyed Oxford and felt that the couple's future lay there, but after only four terms her husband was appointed to the

Chair of Political Economy in Cambridge. It might be assumed that on her return to Cambridge as an experienced lecturer in economics and wife of the professor, Mary Marshall would assume a high profile as a lecturer at Newnham. This was not the case; it becomes quite difficult to trace her work as a lecturer in economics from this point. She lectured in moral science subjects from 1885 but did not participate significantly in other college teaching matters. One reason for this may be that the number of Newnham students taking economics as a Tripos subject was small, another her wish not to embarrass her husband who had become one of the chief spokesmen for the anti-women faction in the university. With the foundation of the Economics Tripos in 1904, Mary Paley's role as teacher assumed a new significance. The number of women opting to take an economics degree was still small in the early days, but they now had a three-year course of study in economics in which they required teaching and guidance. From 1904 to 1916, Mary Paley steered 55 women through the new examination, gaining an outstanding success in 1908 when two of her students were alone in gaining first-class degrees (McWilliams Tullberg, 1993a). This was the year of Marshall's retirement and, though officially retired herself, Mary continued to advise students in their studies, set papers and provide any other assistance that was needed. She acted as Director of Studies for all students reading economics, whether as a whole Tripos or a paper in the History Tripos acting in an honorary capacity after 1910. This meant that she organized their teaching, especially extra teaching or coaching, advised them on their choice of subjects, guided their reading, looked over weekly and term papers, and assessed their progress. The outbreak of war in 1914 and subsequent staff shortages postponed any plans that she may have had for complete retirement. She finally retired in 1916.

After the turn of the century, Newnham students began to have access to a new breed of women teachers who had gone through the Cambridge Tripos mill and who were actively pursuing and publishing their own research work. Some members of the women's colleges felt that their academic goals needed to be reconsidered. This must not be exaggerated – the university gave women no scholarships or facilities for research work and their own colleges had very little money for research fellowships. Mary Marshall was still much liked and respected by her students as a 'pioneer', yet to these young women of the twentieth century, her teaching lacked the glamour of independent scholarship. Some complained that she followed her husband's texts too slavishly, regarding the *Principles* as verbally inspired. In her defence, it might be argued that the style and content of her teaching lacked vision and originality not simply because of her identification with Marshall's work, but also because she had herself been taught in a Cambridge tradition that had encouraged personalized *coaching*, in the sense of cramming a specific syllabus for the purpose of passing a necessary examination or achieving a high position in a competitive Tripos. Throughout her teaching career, she had spent her energies in helping women gain a foothold on the first rungs of the academic ladder and teaching the schoolteachers of the next generation of students. Her teaching career, stretching as it did over 40 years, was devoted to grounding women students in the fundamentals of economic theory and analysis as laid down by her husband. She contributed significantly to the rapid progress made in women's education, which in turn made her own teaching practices obsolete. Yet her own lack of independent scholarship cannot be explained away so simply. It still might be argued that, married as she was to a man with a secure income, with no children, with access to books and a taste for the simple life, she might have achieved more. It is therefore necessary to examine further aspects of her life before her apparent lack of originality can be explained.

Mary Paley Marshall's first excursion into authorship remains her most controversial. Shortly after returning to Newnham as lecturer, she was approached by the University Extension Lectures scheme that wanted a simple and cheap textbook in economics for its students. Mary Paley Marshall would later claim that she could not have completed the book herself: 'However, Mr Marshall came to the rescue and the book gradually became almost entirely his. In fact, its Book II contains the germ of his Theory of Distribution' (Newnham Notes: Talk, pp. 19–12). *The Economics of Industry* was published in 1879 and reprinted nine times, with minor revisions in 1881. In the early 1890s, Marshall, in his own words, 'had the book suppressed', and he continued to condemn it for many years. Keynes said of the original *Economics of Industry*: 'It was, in fact, an extremely good book; nothing more serviceable for its purpose was produced for many years, if ever' (Keynes, 1985 [1944], p. 239). It seems probable that Mary Marshall's contribution to the book was two-fold: first, a large share in the authorship of the early and probably some of the later chapters of the book; and second, editorial work throughout the book. Book I deals with the agents of production, the law of diminishing returns, the organization of industry, the division of labour and the tenure of land and is largely definitional and descriptive. The analytical core of the book is in Book II, covering normal value, demand and supply, rent, wages and profits and the earnings of management, while Book III examines market values, market fluctuations and their causes, and contains the discussions on trade unions and cooperatives. There is a clarity of style and directness in *The Economics of Industry*, sorely missing from the *Principles*, which must in large measure be attributed to Mary Marshall. Left to his own devices, it seems unlikely that Marshall would have or could have produced *The Economics of Industry* alone. The record of the production of the eight editions of the *Principles,* of *Industry and Trade* and

Money, Credit & Commerce, not to mention the abandoned second volume of the *Principles*, demonstrates his incapacity for producing books on time and of limited length. Extension Lecture students, candidates for the Higher Local and Bankers' Examinations and those of limited means and leisure no doubt had reason to thank her for the little book's existence. In the debate over who wrote what, perhaps the most apt description of the book is as the 'interaction between ... two facets – the keen student expositor and the original theorist' (O'Brien, 1994, p. xviii).

The part that she played in the production of her husband's 'big books' is unclear. In the preface to the first edition of the *Principles* Marshall wrote: 'My wife has aided and advised me at every stage of the MSS and of the proofs, and it owes a very great deal to her suggestions, her care and her judgement.' He was less generous in his thanks in the next three editions, but from the fifth edition he returned, in content, to the original acknowledgement. However, these tributes could mean that Mary Paley was primarily concerned with secretarial and sub-editorial matters, not with drafting or determining structure or content. Professor Austin Robinson had the impression that she was used as a sounding-board for Marshall's written work – if she could catch his point, then so could the general reader (Private conversation, September, 1990). There is no record anywhere that he asked her advice as an economist.

The aid and advice given by his wife was also acknowledged by Marshall in both editions of *Industry and Trade* (1919 and 1921). This latter work included material which had been typeset as far back as 1904, but in view of Marshall's declining health and mental powers, the completion of the book must owe a great deal to her skill in bringing coherence to Marshall's many drafts, notes and previously printed pieces. This is even more the case with *Money, Credit & Commerce* that was published in 1923, one year before Marshall's death. She seems to have understood the decline in his mental faculty before it was confirmed by Marshall's doctor; she began making notes 'Recollections of Alfred' as early as January 1920 (Newnham Notes: Talk, p. 52). As she explained: 'After [*Industry and Trade*] came out [1919] his health began to fail, though he did not know it. On this account, I did all I could to hasten the appearance of [*Money, Credit & Commerce*], especially as Dr. Bowen told me in 1921 that his working life was over and that he was incapable of constructive work.'

For 15 years after the publication of *The Economics of Industry*, Mary Marshall published nothing on economics. She had great facility as a writer, but chose to use her pen non-controversially, only once during Marshall's lifetime publishing views with which he disagreed. She made three review contributions to the *Economic Journal*, all concerned with labour economics. The third of these, a review of a collected edition of Clara Collet's papers, shows Mary Paley Marshall at her most independent, willing to draw conclusions about Collet's data that Alfred Marshall preferred to ignore or deny (1902). Collet's research found that qualified middle-class women were given and accepted low wages on the assumption that their work filled only a temporary interval before marriage. Her analysis of demographic data showed that while almost all women in the poorer classes could expect to marry, this was not the case in the middle and upper classes. Nor could the unmarried woman simply turn to the overcrowded profession of teaching. Collet's analysis of the 'Expenditure of middle-class working women' revealed that many high-school teachers did not earn the efficiency wages that permitted 'the necessary rest and recreation in an occupation requiring freshness, vitality, and energy, and ... provision in old age' (Marshall, 1902, p. 255). An increasing number of careers were opening to the well-educated girl and Mary Paley quoted approvingly Collet's suggestion that men in business should train their daughters as they did their sons; there was much scope in business for them as designers, chemists, foreign correspondents and factory managers. In April 1902, Marshall had written his *Plea for the Creation of a Curriculum in Economics* in which he proposed a Cambridge education in economics for businessmen's sons. Later the same year, his wife suggested in her review article that the same education should be given to their daughters. To become at least capable of economic independence was good for a woman's character: 'A fine character needs self-respect and it is impossible for a woman to have much self-respect if she has to marry for a living' (ibid.). In the early days of the women's higher education movement, education had been seen as an 'insurance policy' for middle-class girls. Only later in the century were education and a career beginning to be regarded as offering an *alternative* to marriage, giving women a choice. Such views were strongly opposed by those who felt it was a woman's duty to entertain and obey a man. Others argued woman's duties on eugenic grounds and, like Alfred Marshall, held that women should be schooled in motherhood for the benefit of the race.

Mary Paley Marshall had talents not only as a descriptive writer (1884, 1947) but was a gifted amateur painter (McWilliams Tullberg, 1994). She spoke in public on a number of occasions, though always to private audiences. After her husband's death, she gave a number of talks about Marshall to private gatherings, making no mention of her own contribution to his work. She did, however, single out as his greatest achievement not his analytical work but the founding of the Economics Tripos, an educational reform that could be enjoyed by men and women alike. It had also re-established her importance as teacher of economics at Newnham and, through spectacular Tripos successes, provided proof of her teaching skills.

She was an active member of the Charity Organization Society (COS) committees in both Oxford and Cambridge. When questioned before the

Royal Commission on the Aged Poor, 1893, Alfred Marshall was able to claim a 'good deal of indirect experience of the working' of the Society, not only through careful reading of the Society's journal, but also through discussions with his wife at mealtimes following her attendance at a committee meeting (Keynes, 1926, p. 217). She declared that she was happy in this auxiliary role, writing to John Maynard Keynes in 1922 that 'to have been for so many years his companion, and to have helped, however little, such a life as his is an enviable and delightful lot'. She had, perhaps, hoped for a partnership rather than the job of amanuensis and nurse.

When Archbishop Benson died in 1896, his widow wrote of her emptiness: 'he had it all, and his life entirely dominated mine. Good Lord, give me a personality ...' (Moore, 1974, p. 89). Mary Paley Marshall did not suffer this appalling fate when Alfred Marshall died in 1924; she certainly did not find herself without a personality. She had never surrendered completely to his preaching, never accepted his views on the intellectual capacities of women nor his repudiation of the need for educational opportunities for women at the highest possible level. Through her art, she had also carved out a space in her life that Marshall had not been able to invade and take over. Claude Guillebaud, in an unpublished obituary of his aunt, gave an admirable summary of the situation:

> Until [Marshall's] death in 1924, she lived only for him collaborating with him in his writing and tending him with a self-sacrificing devotion that could hardly be exceeded. She was 74 years of age when he died, but instead of resigning herself to the inactivity of old age, her individuality blossomed forth in what became for her a real St Martin's summer. ... Age never warped the kindly, tolerant and humorous attitude towards life which made her such a delightful companion. (Guillebaud, 1944)

Keynes completed the picture by describing the use to which she put her new freedom – by generously devoting time and money to ensure that students might have access to that prerequisite of good scholarship – a well-stocked library and a knowledgeable librarian. Marshall had donated many books for the use of students during his lifetime. On his death, his private library was handed over to the university and formed the core of the Marshall Library of Economics. Mary Marshall sat in the library each morning, advising students in their reading, and compiling a remarkable subject index of current economic periodicals. She ended her days doing what she thought was most important – helping young students, male and female, make the best use of their educational opportunities.

RITA MCWILLIAMS TULLBERG

Note

1. The author is grateful to the Fellows of Newnham College and the Faculty of Economics and Politics, Cambridge for permission to publish material from their archives; and to the Provost and Scholars of King's College, Cambridge for permission to quote from material from the J.M. Keynes archive.

Bibliography

Selected writings by Mary Paley Marshall

(1884), 'The growth of Newnham', Newnham College Club *Letter*.

(1895), '*Viertehalb Monate Fabrikarbeiterin* by M. Wetterstein-Adelt', Review, *Economic Journal*, **12**, 401–44.

(1896), 'Conference of Women Workers', *Economic Journal*, **6**, 107–9 (review of *The Official Report of the Conference of Women Workers*, 1895).

(1902), '*Educated Working Women* by Clara E. Collet', Review, *Economic Journal*, **12**, 252–7.

(1922), Letter to J.M. Keynes, 27 July 1922, Keynes Collection, King's College, Cambridge, JMK EJ/6.4.

(1940), Obituary of Mary Wright (Kennedy), 1871–75, Newnham College Roll *Letter*, January.

(1947), *What I Remember*, Cambridge: Cambridge University Press.

Other sources and references

Groenewegen, P.D. (1995), *A Soaring Eagle: Alfred Marshall 1842–1924*, Aldershot, UK and Brookfield, US: Edward Elgar.

Guillebaud, C.W. (1944), Unpublished obituary, Keynes Collection, King's College, Cambridge, EJ/6.4.

Keynes, J.M. (1985 [1944]), 'Mary Paley Marshall', in D. Moggridge (ed.), *Essays in Biography, Collected Writings of John Maynard Keynes*, London: Macmillan for the Royal Economic Society, vol. 12, ch. 15. Originally published in the *Economic Journal*, June–September, 1944.

McWilliams Tullberg, R. (1992), 'Alfred Marshall's attitude to *The Economics of Industry*', *Journal of the History of Economic Thought*, **14**, Fall, 257–70.

McWilliams Tullberg, R. (1993a), 'Marshall's final lecture, 21 May 1908', *History of Political Economy*, **25**, Winter, 605–16.

McWilliams Tullberg, R. (1993b), 'Marshall papers in the Newnham College Archive', *Marshall Studies Bulletin*, **3**, 36–47.

McWilliams Tullberg, R. (1994), 'Art and economics in Cambridge', *Marshall Studies Bulletin*, **4**, 23–33.

McWilliams Tullberg, R. (1995a), 'Mary Paley Marshall, 1850–1944', in M.A. Dimand, R. Dimand and E.L. Forget (eds), *Women of Value*, Aldershot, UK and Brookfield, US: Edward Elgar.

McWilliams Tullberg, R. (1995b), 'The women's education movement at Cambridge', in 'Alfred Marshall's contribution to the women's education movement', in T. Raffaelli, E. Biagini and R. McWilliams Tullberg (eds), *Alfred Marshall's 'Lectures to Women', 1873*, Aldershot, UK and Brookfield, US: Edward Elgar.

Moore, K. (1974), *Victorian Wives*, London: Allison & Busby.

Newnham College Roll *Letter*, January 1928.

O'Brien, D. (1994), Introduction to *The Economics of Industry*, Bristol: Thoemmes Press.

Pease, M.F. (1942), Manuscript: 'Some reminiscences of University College Bristol', University of Bristol Archives.

Pigou, A.C. (ed.) (1925), *Memorials of Alfred Marshall*, London: Macmillan.

Harriet Martineau (1802–76)

Harriet Martineau was born at Norwich on 12 June 1802, the sixth of eight children of Thomas Martineau, a textile manufacturer, and Elizabeth Rankin Martineau. The family was Unitarian and belonged to the literary society of which William Taylor was head. Harriet was educated at home, learning Latin from her eldest brother, until 1813 when she was sent to a school run by the Reverend Isaac Perry where she studied French, Latin and English composition. When Perry left town in 1815, she left school but continued her classical study at home.

Her health was never good. As a young child she suffered from indigestion and nervous weakness. Her deafness, which would later increase significantly, began to show itself at school. She claims never to have possessed the senses of taste or smell. Beginning in 1817, she spent 15 months at her maternal uncle's home in Bristol where she had been sent, for her health, by her parents. There she became a disciple of the Unitarian minister Lant Carpenter and, through his influence, began to read philosophy, including especially Joseph Priestley and David Hartley. From these, she adopted the materialist and determinist doctrine of 'philosophical necessity' which substantially modified her religious beliefs. Her first literary effort was an article on 'Female Writers on Practical Divinity' which she submitted to the *Monthly Repository*. The praise that followed that effort induced her to begin writing *Devotional Exercises* and to attempt a theological novel.

After the financial difficulties faced by her family in the crisis of 1825, and the subsequent death of her father in 1826, Harriet became engaged to a man named Worthington who was a student with her brother James. His family objected to the union because of false reports that she had previously been engaged to another. Her fiancé died before a marriage could take place, in any case. During 1827, her health suffered and she distracted herself by writing a few short pieces including a story, 'The Rioters', which dealt with the wages question.

A long illness followed, which was treated by her brother-in-law at Newcastle. While there, she met William Johnson Fox, who was the new editor of the *Monthly Repository* and who would play a large role in her later literary employment. At the same time, she wrote a life of Howard for the Society for the Diffusion of Useful Knowledge, a work which somehow vanished in the archives of the society and brought her no income. Because of the failure of some investments in 1829, she was forced to earn a living partly by needlework. Fox gave her 15 pounds a year for writing reviews for the *Repository*, and encouraged the publication of *Traditions of Palestine*.

Martineau's financial difficulties undoubtedly led her to enter, in 1829, a contest sponsored by the Central Unitarian Association which offered prizes for essays intended to convert Catholics, Jews and Muslims. She was awarded all three prizes, a sum of 45 guineas, which allowed her to visit her brother James in Dublin in 1831. While there, she mapped out a plan for a series of stories designed to illustrate doctrines of political economy, the principles of which she had learned from the *Conversations* of Jane Marcet and James Mill's *Elements of Political Economy*. After many struggles to find a publisher, she negotiated an arrangement with Charles Fox, brother of William Fox, to publish her stories. The series was begun in February 1832 and by 10 February the first edition of 1500 copies had been sold out, inducing Fox to print 5000 more.

Twenty-five stories were produced, along with four 'poor-law' tales, for the Society for the Diffusion of Useful Knowledge. In 1834, she wrote five supplementary *Illustrations of Taxation*. Chiefly memorable for their illustration of the contemporary zeal for popularization, her tales were didactic and so intense that they were easily caricatured. They were less read by the working classes than she had hoped, but much admired by the already converted. Her celebrity brought her into contact with many of the major figures of the period: Brougham, Sidney Smith, Malthus and Carlyle, among others. Cabinet ministers sought her advice. Brougham, as chancellor, supplied her with private papers in order that she might write effectively on behalf of the projected Poor Law reforms. Robert Owen sought, unsuccessfully, her support for his socialist theories.

Her overwork had again injured her health and Martineau decided to travel to America for a change of scene. She had already written about abolition and used the opportunity to make the acquaintance of the leaders of the movement. She returned in 1836 and accepted an offer from Saunders and Otley for a book entitled *Society in America*, a title imposed by her publisher instead of her own suggested *Theory and Practice of Society*. This work included a chapter on the status of women in America, contrasting their low wages and limited property rights with the American ideology of equality (see Frawley, 1992). The lighter and more personal *Retrospect of Western Travel* was published the same year. *How to Observe. Morals and Manners* (1838), a companion piece, was an innovative work of comparative ethnology. Turning down editorship of the proposed *Economic Magazine*, she published a novel entitled *Deerbrook* and continued contributing to periodicals.

In 1839 she travelled to Venice where she again became ill and returned to her brother-in-law's care in Newcastle. In 1840, she published *The Hour and the Man* and a series of children's stories called *The Playfellow*; in 1843, she wrote *Life in the Sick Room*. Her poor health made her incapable of any work, and her friends raised money for an annuity in 1843 because she had taken the position that she could not accept a government pension that might compromise her independence. Such an offer had been broached by Lord

Grey in 1835, and made by Lord Melbourne in 1841. She declined a similar offer from Gladstone in 1873. Her health difficulties led her to mesmerism, under the influence of which she made a rapid cure. She recounted her experience in *Letters on Mesmerism*, which caused great public controversy and alienated her mother and eldest sister.

By 1845, she decided to have a house built in Westmorland and turned her attention to *Forest and Game-Law Tales*. She travelled to Egypt and Palestine in 1846 and returned to write *Eastern Life, Past and Present* (1848). That same year, she began a *History of the Peace* (1849) which presented the views of the philosophical radicals. In 1851, she published with H.G. Atkinson *Letters on the Laws of Man's Nature and Development*, which alienated her from her brother James and caused much controversy for their anti-theological views. In 1852, she began a translation and abridgement of Comte's *Philosophie positive*, which was published in 1853. Before beginning the translation, she had begun writing articles for the *Daily News*. This association lasted until 1866, by which time she had published over 1600 articles.

In 1855, she published an autobiography in anticipation of her death due to heart disease. She did not, however, die until 27 June 1876.

Martineau's genius is that of a diligent writer and expositor. Her efforts in political economy were not original, but were rather attempts to make the 'truths' of the discipline broadly known and understood. Her *Illustrations of Political Economy* (1823–24) were a didactic and extreme polemic in favour of *laissez-faire*. But Martineau's experience with the abolitionists in America challenged her views on property, and in later life she was prepared to give qualified support to workers' cooperatives and to advocate state intervention in the economy under certain very limited circumstances (Webb, 1987, p. 366). Indeed, in her biography she distanced herself from her best-selling *Illustrations of Political Economy*, writing that she had 'not the courage to look at a single number – convinced that [she] should be disgusted by bad taste and metaphysics in almost every page' (Martineau, 1877, vol. I, pp. 194–5). In her personal life she was a philanthropist, despite her relatively modest income, and started a building society and other schemes. Her lectures at Workingmen's Institutions illustrated her profound belief in education as a remedy for most social ills.

EVELYN L. FORGET

Bibliography

Selected writings by Harriet Martineau

(1823), *Devotional Exercises ... with 'A Guide to the Study of the Scriptures'*, London: R. Hunter.

(1830), *Traditions of Palestine*, London: Longman, Rees, Orme, Brown and Green.

(1831), *Five Years of Youth, or Sense and Sentiment. A Story for the Young*, London: Harvey and Darton.

(1831), *Essential Faith of the Universal Church, etc.*, London: Unitarian Association.

(1832), *The Faith as Unfolded by Many Prophets.* London: Unitarian Association.

(1832), *Providence Manifested through Israel*, London: Unitarian Association.

(1832–34), *Illustrations of Political Economy*, 9 vols, London: C. Fox.

(1833), *Poor Laws and Paupers, Illustrated*, London: C. Fox.

(1834), *Illustrations of Taxation*, London: C. Fox.

(1837), *Society in America.* London: Saunders and Otley.

(1838), *Retrospect of Western Travel*, 3 vols, London: Saunders and Otley.

(1838), *How to Observe. Morals and Manners*, London: C. Knight.

(1838), *Addresses, with Prayers and Original Hymns*, London: C. Fox.

(1839), *Deerbrook, a Novel*, 3 vols, London: E. Moxon.

(1841), *The Playfellow, a Series of Tales*, London: G. Routledge.

(1841), *The Hour and the Man, an Historical Romance*, London: E. Moxon.

(1843), *Life in the Sick Room: Essays by an Invalid*, London: E. Moxon.

(1845), *Letters on Mesmerism*, London: E. Moxon.

(1845), *Forest and Game-Law Tales*, London: E. Moxon.

(1845), *Dawn Island, a Tale*, published for the Anti-Corn Law League, Manchester: J. Gadsby.

(1846), *The Billow and the Rock*, London: C. Knight.

(1848), *Eastern Life, Past and Present*, London: E. Moxon.

(1849), *History of England During the Thirty Years' Peace*, London: C. Knight.

(1849), *Household Education*, London: E. Moxon.

(1851), *Introduction to The History of the Peace.* London: C. Knight.

(1851), *Letters on the Laws of Man's Nature and Development* (with H.G. Atkinson), London: J. Chapman.

(1852), *Letters from Ireland, from the Daily News*, London: J. Chapman.

(1853), *The Positive Philosophy of Comte, freely translated and condensed*, Chicago and New York: Belford, Clarke & Co.

(1855), *A Complete Guide to the English Lakes*, Windermere: J. Garnett.

(1855), *The Factory Controversy, a Warning against 'Meddling Legislation'*, Manchester: Ireland & Co. and the National Association of Factory Operators.

(1857), *Corporate Traditions and National Rights. Local Dues on Shipping*, London: G. Routledge.

(1857), *British Rule in India, an Historical Sketch*, London: Smith, Elder.

(1858), *Suggestions towards the Future Government of East India*, London: Smith, Elder.

(1859), *England and Her Soldiers. Written to Help Miss Nightingale*, London: Smith, Elder.

(1861), *Health, Husbandry, and Handicraft, an Account of Her 'Farm of Two Acres'*, London: Bradbury.

(1869), *Biographical Sketches, from the Daily News*, London: Macmillan.

(1877), *Harriet Martineau's Autobiography. With Memorials by M.W. Chapman*, London: Smith, Elder.

Other sources and references

David, D. (1987), *Intellectual Women and Victorian Patriarchy: Harriet Martineau, Elizabeth Barrett Browning, George Eliot*, New York: Cornell University Press.

Frawley, Maria H. (1992), 'Harriet Martineau in America: Gender and the Discourse of Sociology', *Victorian Newsletter*, no. 81, pp. 13–20.

Henderson, Willie (1992), 'Harriet Martineau or "When Political Economy was Popular"', *History of Education*, **21**: 383–403.

Hunter, S. (1995), *Harriet Martineau: The Poetics of Moralism*, Aldershot, UK: Ashgate Publishing Co.

McDonald, Lynn (1998), *Women Theorists on Society and Politics*, Waterloo, Ontario: Wilfrid Laurier University Press.

O'Donnell, Margaret (1983), 'Harrier Martineau: a popular early economics educator', *Journal of Economic Education*, **14**(4): 59–64.

Pichanick, V. (1980), *Harriet Martineau: the Woman and Her Work*, Ann Arbor, MI: University of Michigan Press.

Polkinghorn, B. and D.L. Thomson (1998), *Adam Smith's Daughters*, revised edn, Cheltenham, UK and Northampton, US: Edward Elgar.

Shackleton, J.R. (1990), 'Jane Marcet and Harriet Martineau: pioneers of economics education', *History of Education*, **19**: 283–97.

Webb, R.K. (1960), *Harriet Martineau, a Radical Victorian*, London: Heinemann.

Webb, R.K. (1987), 'Harriet Martineau', in J. Eatwell, M. Milgate and P. Newman (eds), *The New Palgrave: A Dictionary of Economics*, London: Macmillan.

Jean Trepp McKelvey (1908–98)

Jean Trepp McKelvey was an innovative teacher–scholar–practitioner of economics, whose commitment to social change and to education influenced all aspects of her professional life. This interplay between learning, thinking and doing not only led McKelvey to a distinguished career as an economist, but also provides contemporary feminist economists with ideas for reconceiving economic practice and education.

Jean Carol Trepp was born on 9 February 1908 in Saint Louis, Missouri, to Samuel and Blanche (Goodman) Trepp. In 1925, she entered Wellesley College, where she majored in economics. While at Wellesley, Trepp received numerous college honours, including the Phi Beta Kappa Sophomore Prize, the New York Times Current Event Prize, a Durant Scholar award and Phi Beta Kappa induction in her junior year. Additionally, Trepp earned Honors in Economics and was awarded the prestigious Hart, Shaffner & Marx Prize for Undergraduate Essay in Economics for her paper 'Trade-Union Interest in Production', written under the direction of Professor Henry Mussey. Trepp's receipt of the prize was, according to Economics Department Chair Elizabeth Donnan, 'the most gratifying occurrence of the year' for the department (Donnan, 1930, p. 2). After her 1929 graduation, Trepp continued her association with Wellesley College by serving as the college's first alumnae trustee at large (1947–52) and by returning often to speak to Wellesley students about her work. In 1975, Trepp received a Wellesley Alumnae Achievement Award for her efforts 'in the public interest' ('Jean Trepp McKelvey "29"').

After leaving Wellesley, Trepp entered the graduate programme in economics at Radcliffe College, where she received her master's degree in 1931 and her Ph.D. degree in 1933. Trepp's dissertation, *Trade Union Interest in Production*, expanded on her Wellesley honours essay. Supported by a Wellesley College Trustee Fellowship (1929) and the Fanny Bullock Workman Fellowship (1931–32), Trepp travelled 'to a large number of industrial centers in the United States to collect first-hand material' for her study ('Jean Trepp McKelvey elected Alumnae Trustee at large', p. 320). This travel not only extended her interest in labour problems, but also exemplified her belief in the importance of incorporating the experiences of actual people into economic analysis.

In 1932, Trepp joined the Social Sciences Faculty at Sarah Lawrence College, which was making the transition from a junior college to a four-year institution and was gaining recognition for offering a unique environment for women's progressive education and experiential learning (Horowitz, 1984). By emphasizing individualized programmes of study, courses 'defined by problem, rather than by discipline' (Horowitz, 1984, p. 328), non-hierarchical learning communities and the use of fieldwork and group activities in its curriculum, Sarah Lawrence also provided an excellent environment for Trepp to extend her real-world approach to economics into the classroom. In 1939, Trepp published a statement of her philosophy, which was to inform her subsequent work in economics, in *The Uses of Field Work in Teaching Economics*.

Trepp's book, the first in a series recording the pedagogical experimentation taking place at Sarah Lawrence, elaborated how fieldwork – defined to include individual or group trips, extended on-location research and special jobs with organizations off campus – represented an integral component in the education of students who would be participants in responsible social relations. Indeed, Trepp argued that a valid education required not only that students learn how to read and to think; it also required that students learn to participate in the world in which they lived and to use this knowledge to develop their own abilities and interests, a result encouraged through the systematic use of fieldwork in the economics curriculum. And as Trepp discovered, this pedagogical method also significantly affected how she taught the subject-matter of economics and even what constituted economics itself. As she explained,

> The traditional college courses in economics had been largely academic in character, stressing abstract principles and their application to static situations. That economics ought fundamentally to be concerned, not with the behavior of Ricardo's economic man, but with the customs, social habits, beliefs and activities of real human beings engaged in the process of making a living was then a very unorthodox notion which only a few economists, following Veblen, had ventured to develop. Very early in my teaching experience I discarded the classical texts and while I was engaged in the search for new reading materials I was also casting about for other ways in which the traditional forms of instruction might be modified to serve the needs and interests of the students. I had noted a fear on the part of prospective students that economics would be a dry and statistical subject which only the promptings of parents could lead them to elect. And yet most of these girls were genuinely interested in current events, eager to learn more about

the world around them, and almost desperately anxious to find fields of activity
which called for their participation in the future. (Trepp, 1939, p. 6)

This lengthy statement reflects both the Sarah Lawrence (and Trepp's)
philosophy of women's education as well as Trepp's belief that 'the proper
concern of the social sciences is with the institutions, attitudes and behavior
of individuals and social groups and that *the teaching objectives inherent in
this approach are bound up with preparing students for intelligent and effective participation in the civic life of their communities*' (Trepp, 1939, pp. 38–9;
italics added).

This educational approach meant that Trepp chose current economic issues
for study and encouraged her students to reflect on their own experiences and
to develop their critical thinking and analytical skills *vis-à-vis* these issues. In
her industrial relations course, for example, Trepp combined readings from
the economics and popular literature with 'visits to factories, courts, hearings, legislatures, union meetings, etc., and … interviews with public
administrators, employers and trade unionists' (Trepp, 1939, p. 37), so that
students gained 'an understanding of the human, as well as the economic,
side of industrial relations', drew 'their conclusions from observation and
contacts rather than from abstract contemplation of the categories, "capital
and labor"' and learned about 'the actual processes and functional operations
of the organization and institutions which deal with labor problems' (ibid.,
p. 29). This interplay of thinking, observation and experience not only
informed all Trepp's courses at Sarah Lawrence but also all aspects of Trepp's
professional life that followed.

In 1944, Trepp, now McKelvey,[1] took a war-related leave of absence from
Sarah Lawrence, and worked first as a shop steward at Delco Appliance
Division of General Motors, where she 'learned more about industrial prob-
lems and relations than she had ever gained from mere academic research'
('Jean Trepp McKelvey elected Alumnae Trustee at large', p. 320), and then
as a public panel member, hearing officer and arbitrator for the National War
Labor Board. After World War II, she formally resigned from Sarah Lawrence
and became a founding faculty member of Cornell University's New York
State School of Industrial and Labor Relations (ILR) in 1946. Beginning as
an assistant professor, McKelvey achieved the rank of professor in 1951 and
was named Professor Emeritus in 1976.

During her tenure at the ILR school, McKelvey developed the school's first
curriculum, which she viewed as 'a unique opportunity … to experiment with
teaching methods applicable to the training of young men and women for
professional work in industrial relations' (McKelvey, 1961, p. 221). She taught
courses in arbitration, labour practices and labour law even after retirement,
and she was actively involved with establishing and coordinating the

off-campus graduate courses offered through the ILR's extension programme. In 1994, the School of Industrial and Labor Relations honoured her contributions by creating its first endowed Chair, the Jean McKelvey-Alice Grand Professor of Labor Management Relations.

While at Cornell, McKelvey continued as an active academic scholar. Author of dozens of articles and *AFL Attitudes Toward Production, 1900–1932* (1952), as well as the editor of several volumes, McKelvey was an acknowledged authority on labour relations and arbitration, in part due to her multidisciplinary and 'real-world' understanding of historical and contemporary labour relations. For example, while one reviewer of her 1952 book praised it as an 'outstanding historical study' in which the 'original and profound analysis' detailed how nascent union–management cooperation was affected by changes in AFL and management attitudes (Dale, 1953, pp. 445–6), another considered McKelvey's excellent discussion of the '"why" as well as the "what"' of the AFL's policies toward production to be 'significant not only for understanding the labor policies of the first third of the century, but equally in evaluating the activities and attitudes of organized labor today' (Rosenbloom, 1952, p. 312). McKelvey's historical work also explored the interplay between arbitration and gender. In her 1971 National Academy of Arbitrators presidential address, 'Sex and the Single Arbitrator', McKelvey's study of arbitration decisions since the time of the War Labor Board clearly showed that 'the male-dominated world of industrial relations and arbitration wore "blinders" when women's jobs were compared with men's jobs' (Newman, 1982, p. 49) and led McKelvey to argue that 'if the institution of arbitration is to survive and to be "relevant" to the emerging needs of a new social and economic order it cannot afford simply to remain as a part of "the Establishment"' (McKelvey, 1971, p. 353). McKelvey also frequently commented on the state of arbitration education and challenged a long-held belief that 'arbitrators are born, not made. That McKelvey has never subscribed to this mindset is reflected in the many arbitrators she has trained and the key role she has played in the Academy (of Arbitration) and arbitrator development programs' (Nowlin, 1988, p. 4). As further analysis of citations of her work revealed, McKelvey was widely respected for her ability to identify and explain complex interactions between economic and other factors, for her working knowledge of labour relations and for challenging the *status quo* in both the practice and education of arbitrators.

McKelvey may be best known, however, as a practising labour mediator and arbitrator. She was a 'much sought after arbitrator resolving disputes in a number of fields, especially the airline industry' (*Chronicles*, 15 January 1998). In addition, McKelvey was appointed to numerous city, state and federal mediation panels, including the New York State Board of Mediation (1955–66) and the Federal Service Impasses Panel (1970–90) along with several presidential committees on employee–management relations, and she served on the United Auto Workers' Public Review Board from 1960 up until her death on 5 January 1998. Perhaps most notable, McKelvey broke ground for women, often in an impressive fashion, in fields traditionally characterized as the province of men. In 1953, she was the only woman appointed by the Secretary of Labor to a special Labor Department Advisory Committee formed to study changes in the Taft–Hartley Law. She was both the first female member of the National Academy of Arbitrators (1947) and its first female president (1970). In 1975, she was awarded the first special award for 'distinguished service in labor–management relations' by the Federal Mediation and Conciliation Service, and after serving on the national panel of the American Arbitrator Association, she was awarded its Distinguished Arbitrator Award in 1985.

For McKelvey, her professional life reflected the interplay between teaching, scholarly academic writing and professional practice that she believed was crucial for gaining and expanding economic knowledge. In a 1961 statement of her educational goals and methods, McKelvey reiterated the importance of incorporating 'three good instruments of discovery: the Document (original research), Personal Observation (field work), and the Interview' in an industrial and labour relations curriculum. Lamenting that an economics concerned with the process of making a living was 'still unfortunately an heretical notion in too many of our colleges and universities', McKelvey then wondered how, 'unless students are given an opportunity to learn something first-hand about actual union functions, … can they appraise the worth of the abstractions currently being circulated as true coin in the learned economic journals?' (McKelvey, 1961, p. 221). She continued by noting that 'my own activity as a practitioner in … mediation, arbitration and internal union disputes settlement has been valuable to me chiefly as an aid to learning and to teaching, for it has provided my students with opportunities to supplement reading with first-hand observation and analysis of actual labor relations cases, to combine formal education with some practice in the field' (ibid.). By remaining true to the philosophy established at the beginning of her professional life in which she so completely integrated learning and doing, Jean Trepp McKelvey deserves recognition both as an important economic educator and contributor to the field of labour relations and as a role-model for contemporary economists concerned with creating an economics grounded in human action.

MARGARET LEWIS

Note

1.   Trepp married Blake F. McKelvey in 1934 and began to use his name professionally after leaving Sarah Lawrence.

Bibliography

Selected writings by Jean Trepp McKelvey

(1933), 'Union–management co-operation and the Southern Organizing Campaign', *Journal of Political Economy*, **41**(5), 602–24.

(1939), *The Use of Field Work in Teaching Economics*, Bronxville, NY: Sarah Lawrence College.

(1952), *AFL Attitudes Toward Production, 1900–1932*, Ithaca, NY: ILR Press.

(1952), 'Trade union wage policy in postwar Britain', *Industrial and Labor Relations Review*, **6**(1), 3–19.

(1953), *Dock Labor Disputes in Great Britain*, Ithaca, NY: ILR Press.

(1957) (ed.), *Critical Issues in Labor Arbitration: Proceedings of the 10th Annual Meeting, National Academy of Arbitrators*, Washington, DC: Bureau of National Affairs, Inc.

(1959) (ed.), *Arbitration and the Law: Proceedings of the 12th Annual Meeting, National Academy of Arbitrators*, Washington, DC: Bureau of National Affairs, Inc.

(1960) (ed.), *Challenges to Arbitration*, Washington, DC: Bureau of National Affairs, Inc.

(1961), 'College teaching in colleges and universities here and abroad', *Wellesley Alumnae Magazine*, May, p. 221. (From collections in the Wellesley College Archives.)

(1967), 'The role of state agencies in public employee labor relations; address before joint meeting of the Association of Labor Mediation Agencies and the National Association of State Labor Relations Agencies', *Industrial and Labor Relations Review*, **20**(2), 179–98.

(1969), 'Fact finding in public employment disputes: Promise or illusion?', *Industrial and Labor Relations Review*, **22**(4), 528–43.

(1971), 'Sex and the single arbitrator', *Industrial and Labor Relations Review*, **24**(3), 335–53.

(1977) (ed.), *The Duty of Fair Representation; Papers from the National Conference on the Duty of Fair Representation*, Ithaca, NY: ILR Press.

(1985) (ed.), *The Changing Law of Fair Representation*, Ithaca, NY: ILR Press.

(1988) (ed.), *Cleared for Takeoff; Airline Labor Relations Since Deregulation*, Ithaca, NY: ILR Press.

(1998), *Industrial Relations at the Dawn of the New Millennium* (edited with Maurice F. Neufeld), Ithaca, NY: New York State School of Industrial and Labor Relations, Cornell University.

Other sources and references

American Men and Women of Science; Social and Behavioral Sciences (1978), 13th edn, New York: Bowker.

Dale, Ernest (1953), 'Review of *AFL Attitudes Toward Production, 1900–1932*', *Industrial and Labor Relations Review*, **6**(3), 445–6.

Donnan, Elizabeth (1930), 'Report to Wellesley president'. (From Collections in the Wellesley College Archives.)

Horowitz, Helen Lefkowitz (1984), *Alma Mater*, Boston: Beacon Press.

'Jean Trepp McKelvey elected Alumnae Trustee at large', (1947), *The Wellesley Alumnae Magazine*, July, p. 320. (From collections in the Wellesley College Archives.)

'Jean Trepp McKelvey "29"' (1975), *The Wellesley Alumnae Magazine*, Spring, p. 32. (From collections in the Wellesley College Archives.)

'Jean Trepp McKelvey' (1998), http://www.news.cornell.edu/Chronicles/1.15.98/obits.html.

Newman, Winn (1982), 'Pay equity emerges as a top labor issue in the 1980s', *Monthly Labor Review*, April, 49–51.

Nowlin, William A. (1988), 'Arbitrator development: Career paths, a model program, and challenges', *Arbitration Journal*, **43**(1), 3–13.

Peck, Virginia Gould (1986), 'Labor of love', *Wellesley Alumnae Magazine*, Winter, p. 55. (From Collections in the Wellesley College Archives.)

Rosenbloom, Hilda (1952), 'Review of *AFL Attitudes Toward Production, 1900–1932*', *Wellesley Alumnae Magazine*, July, p. 312. (From Collections in the Wellesley College Archives.)

Who's Who of American Women (1989–90), 16th edn, Chicago: Marquis Who's Who, Inc.

Theresa Schmid McMahon (1878–1961)

Theresa Schmid grew up on Mercer Island, at that time an isolated island in Lake Washington. After attending an 'ungraded' school on Mercer Island, she entered the University of Washington's sub-freshman class in 1894, at the age of 16. She graduated in 1899, and received an AM in English in 1901. In 1900, she married Edward McMahon, a University of Washington history graduate who died shortly before their fiftieth wedding anniversary. They had no children. In 1901, they went to California for a year of graduate study. They then taught in Seattle before going in 1906 to the University of Wisconsin, where Edward took an AM in history in 1907 and Theresa a Ph.D. in sociology in 1909 (economics and sociology formed a single department at Wisconsin). Her feminist doctoral dissertation, *Women and Economic Evolution*, was published by the University of Wisconsin in 1912. She studied with John R. Commons, and was influenced by the writings of Charlotte Perkins Gilman (*q.v.*).

After graduation, Theresa McMahon spent a year at Hull House, as statistician for the Associated Charities of Chicago, studying infant mortality. In 1910 she joined the University of Washington (where her husband already taught) as an assistant in political science (despite her Ph.D., and despite having taken only a single, elementary course in political science). She became an instructor in 1911, Assistant Professor in 1914, Associate Professor in 1926 (after publication of her book on *Social and Economic Standards of Living*), and Full Professor in 1929, retiring in 1937. She went with the economists when the Department of Political and Social Science was split into three departments in 1916. In the autumn of 1917, during a period of wartime witch-hunting. McMahon, who came from a German family, took a year's leave from the University of Washington, and conducted research in New York. A university rule against employing both husband and wife was made retroactive, an action which she denounced:

> About two years ago, President Sieg had Mr. McMahon in his office and told him how the governor was bringing pressure to bear to remove one member of the family if two were on the payroll. He reassured Mr. McMahon that the ruling would not be retroactive but he made it clear that my resignation would be welcome. I have always been discriminated against in my salary. Whether it was because I was a progressive or because both of us were working, I do not know. If it is because I am a progressive my academic freedom has been worth whatever financial price 1 have had to pay. (Quoted by Howe, 1989, p. 233)

In her delightful autobiography, McMahon ([1958] 1989, p. 256) recalled that early in her career, 'When I got back to campus [after defending the eight-hour work day for women before a legislative committee], acting

President Landis called me to the office and said, "The Regents are going to meet this afternoon and ask me to fire you. What shall I do?" I answered him impertinently, "Tell them to do their damnedest!"'

She declined an offer from Paul Douglas (formerly her colleague at the University of Washington) to join the University of Chicago, but her student George Stigler later moved there. Theresa McMahon taught innovative courses on women in industry, vocational opportunities for women in the Pacific Northwest, the economics of consumption, and social and economic standards of living, drawing on her own research, as well as courses on elements of economics, history of the American labour movement, modern labour problems, immigration and labour, European labour problems, American labour problems, labour legislation, labour in industry, and a seminar on labour. Florence Howe (1989) reports typescripts and correspondence indicating that McMahon began work on another book, on the economics of consumption. McMahon sympathized with the labour movement (unlike the university administration, which was strongly pro-business) and was the leading figure on Washington's state minimum wage commission, to which she was appointed on the recommendation of Florence Kelley (*q.v.*). Although McMahon used A.C. Pigou's *Economics of Welfare* as well as John R. Commons's *Institutional Economics* in her graduate courses, she resisted pressure to move into teaching economic theory and out of her controversial courses on labour issues.

In 1957, Ewan Clague, then US Commissioner of Labor Statistics, wrote to McMahon that

> It was you who wrote back to John R. Commons at the University of Wisconsin and obtained the fellowship which made it possible for me to go there. It was you who advanced the money which I needed in order to get through the first year. And it was you who put me firmly over into the field of labor economics, which is where I really belonged. I have always considered that this was the real turning point in my career. (Quoted by Howe, 1989, p. 231).

ROBERT W. DIMAND

Bibliography

Selected writings by Theresa Schmid McMahon
(1912), *Women and Economic Evolution*, Madison: University of Wisconsin Bulletin no. 496.
(1915) et al., 'Public regulation of wages: discussion', *American Economic Review: Supplement*, **5** (March), 278–99.
(1925), *Social and Economic Standards of Living*, Boston: D.C. Heath.
([1958] 1989), 'My story', in Geraldine Jonçich Clifford (ed.), *Lone Voyagers: Academic Women in Coeducational Institutions, 1870–1937*, New York: The Feminist Press at The City University of New York, pp. 238–80.

Other sources and references

Howe, Florence (1989), 'Practical in her theories: Theresa McMahon 1878–1961', in Geraldine Jonçich Clifford (ed.), *Lone Voyagers: Academic Women in Coeducational Institutions, 1870–1937*, New York: The Feminist Press at The City University of New York, pp. 223–8.

Page, Alfred N. (1976), 'Teresa McMahon's "Women and Economic Evolution": a retrospective review', *Journal of Economic Literature*, **14**(1): 63–5.

Mary Meynieu (d. 1877)

Between 1837 and 1860, Mary Meynieu is credited with a number of works in religion and in economics. Her economic writing takes three forms. She is, in the style of Jane Marcet (*q.v.*), a textbook author, publishing in 1839 *Elements d'économie politique, exposés dans une suite de dialogues entre un instituteur et son élève, à l'usage des écoles normales primaires* (Elements of political economy, illustrated by a series of discussions between a teacher and a student, to be used in primary schools). She is a policy commentator, publishing in 1841 *Du paupérisme anglais* (On English pauperism). She is a critic and reviewer of the work of others, publishing in 1859 in the *Journal des économistes* 'Observations sur l'économie politique, à propos du Manuel de M. Baudrillart' (Observations on political economy, relevant to Baudrillart's *Manuel*) and in 1860 *Quelques mots sur le travail des femmes, à l'occasion d'un article de M. Jules Simon* (A few words on women's work, occasioned by an article by Jules Simon).

Her theological interests are illustrated by another book aimed at young readers entitled *Histoire du peuple juif, mêlée de réflexions à l'usage de la jeunesse* (A history of the Jewish people, reflections for the use of youth) (1837), by her response to Larroque's article on slavery in Christian nations published in 1857, and by her 1856 article 'De l'esprit actuel de l'Eglise anglicane (The real spirit of the Anglican church).

Evelyn L. Forget

Selected writings by Mary Meynieu

(1837), *Histoire du peuple juif, mêlée de réflexions à l'usage de la jeunesse*, Paris: A. Cherbuliez.

(1839), *Eléments d'économie politique, exposés dans une suite de dialogues entre un instituteur et son élève, à l'usage des écoles normales primaires*, Paris. A. Cherbuliez.

(1841), *Du paupérisme anglais*, Paris: A. Cherbuliez.

(1856), 'De l'esprit actuel de l'Eglise anglicane', *Disciple de Jésus-Christ* (November).

(1857), 'Le christianism et l'esclavage: réponse à un article de P. Larroque, intitulé "De l'esclavage chez les nations chretiennes"', *Disciple de Jésus-Christ* (March).

(1859), 'Observations sur l'économie politique, à propos du Manuel de M. Baudrillart', *Journal des économistes*, no. 65 (May).

(1860), *Quelques mots sur le travail des femmes, à l'occasion d'un article de M. Jules Simon*, Paris: Impr. Du Corps léglislatif, A.H. Noblet.

Harriet Hardy Taylor Mill (1807–58)

Harriet Hardy was the daughter of Thomas Hardy, an austere surgeon whose relative wealth must have meant access to education for his children. She married John Taylor at 18 and became part of the Unitarian Radical group of William J. Fox. She contributed poetry and essays to the *Monthly Repository* which he edited.

Harriet Taylor and John Stuart Mill met in 1830. They developed an intense friendship characterized by intellectual collaboration and a presumably platonic romantic attachment until their marriage in 1851, two years after John Taylor's death. Their union was short-lived and plagued by Taylor's ill-health. She died in 1858 while travelling in the south of France.

Harriet Taylor's life and contributions have traditionally been eclipsed by those of John Stuart Mill. Her ideas, when and if mentioned, have been discussed as reflections of or influences on Mill's rather than in their own right.[1] Yet a comparative analysis of Taylor's and Mill's writings and a survey of their published correspondence and of the variations in Mill's published works reveal Taylor as an independent thinker who often held the more radical and insightful views.

There are few writings from Harriet Taylor's hand, and these have not been the object of a 'collected works' edition to date. Hayek reprinted a short essay on the tyranny of conformism and public opinion, from the *Monthly Repository* (Hayek, 1951, pp. 271–9). Her early essay on marriage and divorce, part of an 1832 dialogue with Mill, has been published by Hayek (1951, pp. 75–8) and Rossi (1970, pp. 84–7). Her better-known 1851 essay 'The enfranchisement of women' has been reprinted both by Rossi (1970, pp. 89–121) and more recently Taylor (1983).

Whereas the exact extent of Taylor's contribution to John Stuart Mill's *Principles of Political Economy* (1848 [1965]) cannot be ascertained due to insufficient archival documentation, her own discussion and elaboration of elements of political economy can be identified in her writings. Harriet Taylor's thought is positioned within the liberal and utilitarian traditions, but she used her feminist and socialist beliefs to extend these philosophies beyond their dominant patriarchal and bourgeois interpretations. Hence Taylor developed an analysis of women's economic and social position, denouncing the lack of options for economic independence available to them, identifying the socially constructed and maintained power imbalances between the sexes as the roots of this situation, and proposing reforms towards the enfranchisement of women.

Utilitarian principles were particularly put to use by Taylor to support her argument for women's rights to equality, liberty and self-determination: liberty of choice, freedom to achieve individuality and self-development, are necessary to attain happiness. The greatest happiness for the greatest number can only be achieved if all, including women, have self-determination and are free to engage in activities they deem will bring them happiness. And, Taylor added, these choices cannot be made for women.

She strongly denounced the division of humanity 'into two castes, one born to rule over the other', where the power of one caste is maintained through the exclusion of the other from most occupations and life activities (Taylor, 1851 [1970], p. 97). The severe restrictions society imposes on women's liberty of choice and access to opportunities prevent them from maximizing their happiness and deny them control over their own lives and livelihoods.

Taylor advocated complete freedom of access by women to the labour market, thus using liberal philosophy not only to argue in favour of women's political equality but also to support women's economic equality. In an open and competitive labour market, individuals will be matched to occupations in an optimal fashion. Provided with free entry (along with access to education and training), women will offer their labour in competition with men at the going price, and the market will sort out who will be employed in what occupations on the basis of the skills offered (Taylor, 1851 [1970], pp. 100–101) . Efficiency and general welfare will increase, since 'the world will have the benefit of the best faculties of all its inhabitants'. To achieve this situation would require not only abrogating customs, traditions and specious rationales against women's employment, but also all existing legislation which impeded their free entry, such as the Factory Acts.

Taylor condemned the practice of reserving lucrative employments 'as the exclusive domain' of men (Taylor, 1851 [1970], p. 97). She argued that 'so long as competition is the general law of human life, it is tyranny to shut out one-half of the competitors', identifying here a substantial exception to the ostensible 'law' of free competition' (Taylor, 1851 [1970], p. 105). She especially exposed the irony of the argument that women's employment would create excessive levels of competition, in the age of orthodox liberal extolling of the virtues and necessity of free competitive markets. Having identified male control over the labour market as a 'monopoly', Taylor confronted those who supported the maintenance of this monopoly and the resulting higher wages and non-optimal market outcomes. Analysing the worst possible scenario (under a wage-fund hypothesis), where 'a man and a woman could not together earn more than is now earned by the man alone', she asserted that society would still witness a net improvement, as the woman would have gained access to her own earnings: she 'would be raised from the position of a servant to that of a partner' (Taylor, 1851 [1970], pp. 104–5).

Breaking down men's monopoly over employment will potentially reduce the difference between men's and women's wages. Taylor saw wage inequality as another effect of patriarchy: not only do men control most of the labour market, they receive a 'family wage' which assumes and reinforces the dependent status of women and gives men a dominant status in the home. The gendered structure of the labour market is thus linked to the power relations in the private realm.

The scope of Taylor's analysis of skills and productivity goes beyond the labour market setting to which political economists have restricted themselves. She recognized the distinct skills involved in women's ability to perform a multitude of tasks (both manual and mental) in quick succession while maintaining high levels of productivity. These observations challenge the prevailing Smithian doctrine on the division of labour and productive efficiency. For Taylor, it is 'habit' or training, rather than the specific nature of the task, that is essential to the achievement of efficiency. Taylor's observations could contribute to the revolutionizing of theories of labour processes, and their biased applications to women's skills and productivity.

Taylor reviewed the origins and manifestations of the sexual division of labour and of sex roles through history and across cultures to support her argument for sex equality. Her analysis, although marred by Eurocentric bias, led her to conclude that sex roles were not natural but socially developed, and were imposed upon women either by force or, in the presumably more refined society of her time, 'by sedulous inculcation of the mind' (Taylor, 1851 [1970], p. 108). She also established the economic aspect of this coercion, women being denied any form of economic support other than by being a man's wife and mothering his children.

Taylor identified and denounced the dominant sex-role ideology used to justify the sexual division of labour, whereby women are constructed as naturally subservient and loyal to men. She uncovered the power relations behind this ideology: 'power makes itself the centre of moral obligation, ... a man likes to have his own will, but does not like that his domestic companion should have a will different from his' (Taylor, 1851 [1970], p. 108). Hence it is not nature and destiny that have placed women in a position of servitude towards men, but men's power: the existing division of labour works for the exclusive benefit of men, and through it their needs are serviced and their power further reinforced.

Taylor showed how women's exclusion from the public realm reinforced their confinement to the private realm and their seclusion into economic dependence. She exposed male agency in the exclusion of women from the market sphere to ensure their availability in the home. For her, it was very clear that marriage was both the end and the means of a socioeconomic arrangement which maintained the subservience of women. Consequently, she advocated unconditional rights to divorce on demand and predicted that the institution of marriage would be cast off once women achieved economic independence (Taylor, 1832 [1970], p. 85).

The 'sedulous inculcation' of women's minds denounced by Taylor comprises depriving them of any formal education, and erecting for them the social norms of femininity. Women were not encouraged to develop independent thought, and any criticism or rebellion towards their condition was impressed upon them as unfeminine. Taylor insisted that women must have access to education on equal terms with that received by men. They must be 'educated for themselves and for the world' rather than for the needs of the other sex, as proposed by some reformers of her time. Education should 'form strong-minded women' rather than 'prevent them from being formed' (Taylor, 1851 [1970], pp. 112–13).

Women's access to education, employment and equality were also proposed as part of the solution to the problem of population growth. Combining socialist and feminist insights, Taylor linked excessive population growth to the harsh competitive conditions of the capitalist labour market, and to the dependent status of both the poor and women in capitalist society. For her, change towards a more socialist arrangement was necessary, as well as imminent. Social progress was also associated with the merger of the public and the private spheres, without which there would be limits to women's influence and social improvement.

In the *Enfranchisement*, Taylor developed an insightful and precursory analysis of the nature of patriarchal hegemonic ideology. She showed how women were made to internalize this ideology and argued against those who used this as evidence of women's acquiescence in their social position. Taylor pointed to the social conditioning women were subjected to from infancy as the cause of their compliance with their assigned feminine role. She compared this process to that of the subjection of colonized people, tenants and labourers, and identified apparent acquiescence as a survival mechanism. The quasi-universal acceptance of the concept of femininity worked to deny women any agency and disempowered them from taking action in their own personal, economic, and political interest.

Belief in women's right to autonomy, in their individually separate claim to economic well-being and to physical and intellectual liberty, was a persistent theme in Taylor's writings. Women must have access to all freedoms: freedom of education and occupation, freedom of thought, and freedom of disposing of their own person without putting someone else's interests first. To attain this goal, women must have access to the means to exert these freedoms.

Taylor's feminist standpoint was grounded in her analysis of her own experience as a woman. It allowed her to elaborate a pathbreaking analysis of gendered power relations, sex roles and the sexual division of labour, and the mechanisms – economic, political, legal and ideological – which maintain the material subjection of women.

Her materialist feminist analysis took her beyond the male-centred, idealistic reform proposals of the most enlightened liberal thinkers (including John Stuart Mill). She criticized these proposals as meaningless because they did not come from a woman's perspective, but from that of the 'rulers' over women, who, at best, only wanted to soften the impact of their rule. By applying a (pre-Marxian) class analysis to the power relations between the sexes, she could ascertain that the rulers would never emancipate those whose lives they controlled, because it was against their interests.

Taylor stands on her own as an original and insightful feminist thinker and as an economist and political theorist. Her ideas were well ahead of her time and recognition of her contributions to feminist economic theory is long overdue.

MICHÈLE A. PUJOL

Note
1. For more on scholars' treatment of Taylor, and on the differences between Taylor's and Mill's views, see Pujol (1995).

Bibliography
Hayek, F.A. (1951), *John Stuart Mill and Harriet Taylor, Their Correspondence and Subsequent Marriage*, London: Routledge and Kegan Paul.
Mill, John Stuart (1848 [1965]), *Principles of Political Economy, with some of their Applications to Social Philosophy*, vols II and III of *The Collected Works of John Stuart Mill*, ed. by J.M. Robson, Toronto: University of Toronto Press.
Pujol, Michèle (1995), 'The Feminist economic thought of Harriet Taylor (1807–58)', in Mary Ann Dimand, Robert W. Dimand and Evelyn Forget (eds), *Women of Value: Feminist Essays on the History of Women in Economics*, Aldershot, UK and Brookfield, US: Edward Elgar, pp. 82–102.
Rossi, Alice S. (ed.) (1970), *Essays on Sex Equality*, by John Stuart Mill and Harriet Taylor Mill, Chicago: University of Chicago Press.
Spender, Dale (1982), 'Harriet Taylor (1807–1858)', in *Women of Ideas (And What Men Have Done to Them)*, London: Pandora.
Taylor, Harriet (1832), 'Early essay on marriage and divorce', in Rossi (1970), pp. 84–7.
Taylor, Harriet (1851), 'Enfranchisement of women', in Rossi (1970), pp. 89–121.
Taylor Mill, Harriet (1851 [1983]), *Enfranchisement of Women* (with J.S. Mill's *The Subjection of Women*, and introduction by Kate Soper), London: Virago.

Ilse Schüller Mintz (1904–78)

Ilse Schüller was born in Vienna on 19 June 1904. She died in Washington, DC in 1978. Her parents were Richard Schüller and Erna, née Rosenthal. Her father was a favourite student of Carl Menger's, the founder of the Viennese School of economics. Before World War I, Schüller quickly advanced to become an important official in the trade department. After the war Schüller was, despite his Jewish faith, one of the most influential federal officials of the First Austrian Republic. In 1926 Ilse married the lawyer Max Mintz.

Ilse studied at the Faculty of Political Science of the University of Vienna from 1922 to 1927. She gained her doctorate there in 1927 (*Dr. rer. pol.*). According to Machlup, at first she was without permanent position. During the years 1927 to 1928 she worked at the Institut für Konjunkturforschung in Vienna. Hayek managed the institute, founded on 1 January 1927. At first there were only two employees apart from Hayek. In March 1938 Ilse Schüller emigrated with her family via Switzerland to the USA. There she enrolled at the Economic Faculty at Columbia University. After studying statistics she gained her Ph.D. in 1951. From 1948 to 1969 she was member of the Faculty of Economics at Columbia. She was part of the senior staff of the National Bureau of Economic Research from 1951 to 1973. She finished her career as an adjunct professor at the Catholic University of America in Washington, DC. Ilse Schüller Mintz was in the forefront with her studies on the business cycle theory and on foreign trade questions.

JÜRGEN NAUTZ

Bibliography

Selected writings by Ilse Schüller Mintz
(1951), 'Deterioration in the Quality of Foreign Bonds Issued in the United States, 1920–30', New York: Publications of the National Bureau of Economic Research, no. 52.
(1959), 'Trade Balances during Business Cycles: U.S. and Britain since 1880', New York: National Bureau of Economic Research, Occasional Paper 67.
(1961), 'American Exports During Business Cycles, 1879–1958', New York: National Bureau of Economic Research, Occasional Paper 76.
(1967), 'Cyclical Fluctuations in the Exports of the United States since 1879', New York and London: National Bureau of Economic Research.
(1969), 'Dating Postwar Business Cycles: Methods and their Application to Western Germany, 1950–67', New York and London: National Bureau of Economic Research, Occasional Paper 107.
(1973), 'U.S. Import Quotas: Costs and Consequences', American Enterprise Institute for Public Policy Research, Domestic Affairs Study 10, Washington, DC. 2nd edn 1974.

Other sources and references
American Men and Women of Science, vol. 2, S. 1717.
Biographisches Handbuch der deutschsprachigen Emigration, vol. 2, S. 820.
Craver, Earlene (1986), 'The emigration of Austrian economists', *History of Political Economy*, **18**(1): 1–32.
Hagemann, Harald and Claus-Dieter Krohn (eds) (1999), *Biographisches Handbuch der deutschpragigen wirthschaftswissenschaftlichen Emigration nach 1993*, 2 vols, Munich: K.G. Saur Verlag.
Machlup, Fritz, in Margit von Mises, *Der Mensch*, S. 261.
Nautz, J. (1990), *Unterhändler des Vertrauens. Aus den nachgelassenen Schriften von Sektionschef Dr. Richard Schüller*, Vienna and Munich.
Nautz, J. (1997), 'Zwischen Emanzipation und Integration. Die Frauen der Wiener Schule für Nationalökonomie', in L. Fischer and E. Brix (eds), *Die Frauen der Wiener Jahrhundertwende*, Vienna, Cologne and Weimar: Boehlau Verlag.

Natalie Moszkowska (1886–1968)[1]

Born in Warsaw on (appropriately enough) 1 May 1886, to Jewish parents, Natalie Moszkowska was an original and analytically ambitious socialist economist who made significant contributions to the Marxian theory of crisis, the concept of monopoly capital, and the economic interpretation of military expenditure. She wrote her doctoral thesis on workers' savings banks in the Polish coal and steel industries; it was published by Dietz in 1917. Six years later Moszkowska moved to Switzerland, where she worked as a private tutor and wrote for the trade union and socialist press. She lived in or near Zürich from 1923 until her death on 26 November 1968. Never married, she was survived by her sister Gustava.

Apart from her dissertation, Moszkowska published three books. The first, *Das Marxsche System*, appeared in 1929. Moszkowska begins by defending the labour theory of value from a perspective very similar to that of Ladislaus von Bortkiewicz, employing an unusually elaborate array of numerical examples of the transformation of values into prices of production. Her debt to Bortkiewicz is also apparent in the second part of the book, where she criticizes Marx's volume III treatment of the falling rate of profit (Schoer, 1976). Moszkowska argues that capitalists will introduce a new machine only if it saves at least as much paid labour as it costs to produce. Thus all genuine technological advances increase the productivity of labour; their effect on the rate of profit depends on whether they raise productivity by more or less than the increase in the quantity of means of production per worker. Although her technical analysis is defective, Moszkowska deserves great credit for her early statement of what was later described as the Okishio Theorem: viable innovations which reduce the rate of profit are associated with rising (not constant, still less falling) real wages (Groll and Orzech, 1989). She concludes that the falling rate of profit theory must be interpreted as taxonomic rather than as historically predictive. It 'only expresses a functional relationship' between the rate of surplus value and the rate of profit, 'and could as well be called "the law of the tendency for the rate of profit to fall" as "the law of the tendency for the rate of exploitation to rise". In reality the second tendency, not the first, has prevailed' (Moszkowska, 1929, p. 118).

In the third section of *Das Marxsche System*, Moszkowska applies these conclusions to crisis theory, dismissing the volume III rate of profit model as irrelevant and objecting also to the notion that disproportionalities between different branches of production were the underlying cause of the business cycle. If there was indeed a fundamental disproportionality in the capitalist economy, she maintained, it was in the sphere of distribution. An excessive profit share encourages the over-accumulation of capital and gives rise to crises of underconsumption, while if real wages were to rise rapidly in a boom, as unemployment fell, the consequent fall in profitability would also bring prosperity to an end. This points towards a 'knife-edge' model like that attributed to Marx by Bronfenbrenner (1965), but Moszkowska does not develop it formally. Already she appears to regard underconsumption as much the more powerful force, citing the increasing importance of selling costs and other expenses of circulation as evidence of a chronic deficiency of aggregate demand (Moszkowska, 1929, pp. 115–17).

Moszkowska's second book, *Zur Kritik Moderner Krisentheorien* (1935) represents a significant shift in focus. Whereas *Das Marxsche System* had drawn heavily on the pre-1914 literature, the new work criticized the more recent Marxian crisis theories of Adolph Löwe, Henryk Grossmann, Otto Bauer and others. By now Moszkowska was – understandably, perhaps, in the depths of the world depression – an unqualified underconsumptionist. She argues that macroeconomic equilibrium requires real wages to rise at the same rate as labour productivity, holding the share of wages constant. In fact the rate of exploitation tends to rise in 'late capitalism' (Moszkowska, 1935, p. 26), since growing monopoly power means downward price rigidity and widening profit margins, the power of capital is greater in the more concentrated industries, and selling costs increase inexorably. Attacking Grossmann's attempts to resuscitate the volume III falling rate of profit model, Moszkowska affirms even more clearly than in 1929 her view that technical progress will increase the profit rate unless it is offset by realization difficulties or by increasing costs of circulation. In late capitalism, excess capacity and unproductive expenditures make both the rate of exploitation and the rate of profit appear much lower than their actual (potential?) magnitudes.

In a depression the rate of surplus value increases even further, because money wages and raw material prices fall faster than the prices of manufactured goods. In this way the costs of a crisis are passed from cartelized to competitive industries, from industrial to agrarian nations, and from all of these to the working class. Moszkowska identifies a number of counteracting tendencies, which serve to prevent consumption from falling as rapidly as production in a downturn. These include the relatively greater burden of fixed costs, the continued consumption of unemployed workers, and the steady growth of selling costs. Despite all this, the gap between production and consumption is at its greatest in late capitalism, and with it grows the danger of a 'structural' or 'permanent crisis'. The Great Depression, for Moszkowska, was evidence not of a mere downturn in a 'long wave' of economic activity, but rather of the 'downfall [*Niedergang*] of capitalism' itself (1935, pp. 101, 102; cf. Howard and King, 1992, ch. 1).

In *Zur Dynamik des Spätkapitalismus* (1943), Moszkowska takes her critique of the falling rate of profit theory even further. She now distinguishes between 'under-accumulation' and 'over-accumulation' approaches to crisis theory. Under-accumulation refers both to contemporary bourgeois cycle models in which an upswing is brought to an end by a shortage of savings, and the Marxian (volume III) analysis of the falling rate of profit, which bears the scars of its classical origins and purports to be a 'natural' or 'eternal' economic law. Any genuinely socialist theory of crises must instead rest on social and historical laws, Moszkowska argues, and only over-accumulation theories qualify. It is necessary to purge Marxian political economy of the remaining elements of alien, under-accumulationist thinking (Moszkowska, 1943, pp. 9–12). There is an additional reason for doing so, since only a crisis theory emphasizing difficulties specific to the institutions of capitalism offers any hope that socialism can improve the living standards of the working class. Humanity can overcome historical laws, not ahistorical natural laws of the under-accumulationist type (ibid., pp. 49–50, 56–8, 79–80).

Moszkowska again traces underconsumption – which is what she means by 'over-accumulation' – back to the tendency for labour productivity to grow faster than real wages. In fact she claims that real wages were now more likely to fall than rise, given the increase in the bargaining power of capital in an era of Fascism and permanent mass unemployment (ibid., pp. 46, 89–93). Her 'law of the rising surplus' is supported by a detailed analysis of the *faux frais* or *tote Kosten* (that is, wasteful expenditures) which in late capitalism fill the gap between society's power to produce and its capacity to consume. These include excess capacity and unemployment; selling costs and the associated unproductive labour of sales personnel; the global misallocation of resources due to import controls and dumping of exports; armaments expenditures; and the enormous economic and social costs of war (ibid., pp. 98–128). These *faux frais* develop a momentum of their own, and tend to grow even more rapidly than is necessary to close the gap in effective demand (ibid., p. 136). Bourgeois liberalism and social democratic reformism are no longer viable, Moszkowska concludes. Fascism, imperialism and war have become the only conceivable alternatives to socialism (ibid., pp. 147–9).

This was the last of Moszkowska's books, but she continued after 1945 to write for trade union and socialist journals in Switzerland, Germany and Austria; well into her seventies, she published three academic papers in the prestigious *Schmoller's Jahrbuch*. In the 1950s she defended Marxian theory in the Swiss socialist party's *Rote Revue*, insisting against her revisionist critics that US capitalism had been saved from underconsumption only by massive armaments spending, which amounted to a new and more rational form of Fascism. Military expenditures benefited big business much more than small, accelerating the process of the centralization and concentration of capital; they stimulated economic growth in underdeveloped countries; and, through the civilian spin-offs from weapons research, they encouraged technical progress in advanced capitalist nations. Thus Heraclitus's statement was especially true of late capitalism: 'War is the Father of all things' (Moszkowska, 1954, p. 123). 'War capitalism', she claimed in 1958, had falsified Marx's expectations for capitalism, weakening the system's underconsumptionist tendencies and preventing further social polarization, but also 'dashing the reformists' hopes of increasing liberalization'.

Writing for a more academic audience, Moszkowska contrasted Marx and Keynes, entirely to the latter's disadvantage. Keynes's analysis was methodologically weak, she argued, since it placed most emphasis on ahistorical human nature, not on historical capitalist society. It ignored distributional factors, and offered an eclectic, multi-causal theory of crisis rather than the more rigorous and consistent monocausal explanation provided by Marx (Moszkowska, 1959). Her last two articles consisted of a methodological critique of marginal utility theory and a more general attack on subjectivism in modern political economy (Moszkowska, 1963, 1965).

Moszkowska's direct influence was never particularly great. She was not part of any academic network, and the Austro-German political tradition to which she belonged was, of course, destroyed in 1933. Like Grossmann, Bauer and several others, Moszkowska fell between two political stools, being neither a respectable reformist *à la* Kautsky nor a Communist. None of her work has appeared in English, and the introduction to the Italian translation of *Zur Kritik*, by Sergio Bologna, is unscholarly and excessively polemical. Moszkowska's work is acknowledged in several places by Paul Sweezy in his seminal *Theory of Capitalist Development* (1942, pp. 122n, 161n, 211n), and there are certainly clear parallels between her ideas and the Baran – Sweezy conception of monopoly capital, including the 'law of rising surplus' and the surplus-absorbing role of selling costs and armaments expenditure. Almost certainly Joan Robinson never read Moszkowska, yet there are strong echoes of her in the *Essay on Marxian Economics*. Robinson describes Marx's law of the tendency for the rate of profit to fall as a 'tautology', argues that a falling profit rate implies rising real wages, and develops the relationship between capital per worker, output per worker, the profit rate and real wages similarly to Moszkowska's treatment (Robinson, 1942, pp. 36–7). This is not to suggest plagiarism, though Moszkowska did once complain of it, without naming the (US) offender (Moszkowska, 1943, p. 6, n2). After all, these ideas were in the air – and Moszkowska played an important part in putting them there.

M.C. HOWARD

J.E. KING

Notes

1. The authors are grateful to Harald Hagemann for valuable biographical information on Moszkowska.

Bibliography

Selected writings by Natalie Moszkowska

(1929), *Das Marxsche System: ein Beitrage zu Dessen Aufbau*, Berlin: Verlag Hans Robert Engelmann.
(1935), *Zur Kritik Moderner Krisentheorien*, Prague: Michael Kacha Verlag.
(1943), *Zur Dynamik des Spätkapitalismus*, Zürich and New York: Verlag 'Der Aufbruch'.
(1954), 'Kleinhaltung des Massenkonsums und Wirtschaftliche Entwicklung', *Rote Revue*, **33**(4), 116–23.
(1958), 'Kapitalistische Wirtschaftswunder', *Gewerkschaftliche Monatshefte*, **9**(4), 224–8.
(1959), 'Das Krisenproblem bei Marx und Keynes', *Schmoller's Jahrbuch*, **79**(6), 665–701.
(1960), 'Erwartung und Wirklichkeit', *Periodikum für Wissenschaftlichen Sozialismus*, **16**, 5–16.
(1963), 'Wandlung der Methode und des Erkenntnisobjektes der Nationalökonomie', *Schmoller's Jahrbuch*, **83**(3), 269–83.
(1965), 'Methodologischer Subjektivismus in der Nationalökonomie', *Schmoller's Jahrbuch*, **85**(5), 513–24.

Other sources and references

Bronfenbrenner, M. (1965), '*Das Kapital* for the Modern Man', *Science and Society*, **29**(4), 419–38.
Groll, S. and Z.B. Orzech (1989), 'From Marx to the Okishio Theorem: a Genealogy', *History of Political Economy*, **21**(2), 253–72.
Howard, M.C. and J.E. King (1992), *A History of Marxian Economics. Volume II: 1929–1990*, Princeton: Princeton University Press and London: Macmillan, chs 1, 4, 6–8.
Robinson, J. (1942), *An Essay on Marxian Economics*, London: Macmillan.
Schoer, K. (1976), 'Natalie Moszkowska and the falling rate of profit', *New Left Review*, **95**, 92–6.
Sweezy, P.M. (1942), *The Theory of Capitalist Development*, New York: Oxford University Press.

Selma J. Mushkin (1913–89)

Mushkin made major contributions as both a government economist and as a scholar. Her research interests included issues of public finance, urban economics, the economics of education, and health economics. She was the author of several books; in addition, her scholarship was published in journals, such as the *Review of Economics and Statistics* and the *National Tax Journal*.

Mushkin received her BA in economics from Brooklyn College in 1934 and her MA from Columbia University in 1935. After a few years of working as an economics instructor at Brooklyn College, she went to Washington, DC to join President Roosevelt's New Deal Administration. In 1937 she found a job in the Division of Financial Services at the Social Security Administration and at a party met her husband-to-be, Israel Weissbrodt. Their three children, David, Amy and Ellen, were born in 1944, 1948 and 1951. With the help of live-in child care Mushkin continued to work full-time as she raised her children. She was promoted to chief of the Division of Financial Studies and then in 1949 took a position at the Public Health Service, where she remained until 1960. During that period Mushkin provided the principal financial support of her family because her husband started a law firm in 1947 and it took several years before the firm was self-sustaining.

Realizing that further advancement in her career as an economist required a doctorate, she completed language training and her thesis at the New School for Social Research in 1956. In 1960–61 she served as an economist at the Office of Education. In 1962 she took her children to Paris, where she completed a study of programme budgeting systems in education at the OECD. From 1963 through 1968 she was the Director of the State–Local Finances Project at George Washington University. During that time Mushkin won a grant from the Ford Foundation to project approximately one hundred components of state and local government expenditures and approximately fifty sources of state and local government revenues for each of the 50 states and the District of Columbia to 1970. In previous research, she had estimated federal tax incidence and the distribution of federal expenditures by state.

In 1970 Mushkin joined the Faculty at Georgetown University where she established the Public Service Laboratory (PSL), a research facility in public policy. While at Georgetown University, Mushkin won a grant from the National Science Foundation to assess the ability of city governments to provide and manage the human resources required for effective and efficient delivery of services to the public.

Mushkin also took several leaves of absence from the PSL to serve, for example, as an economist with the Office of Management and Budget during the Nixon/Ford Administration and as Fellow at the Woodrow Wilson International Center for Scholars during 1978–79.

Throughout her career, Mushkin addressed challenging and policy-relevant issues in her applied microeconomic research. For example, she addressed the question of whether the public interest is met by providing states with block grants for broad programme areas. She used state-level data to conclude, 'to the extent that the grant mechanism is used to pinpoint a national objective and to encourage state and local action in a specific direction, block grants are not a substitute for categorical aides' (*National Tax Journal*, September 1960, pp. 202–3).

Mushkin advocated a total re-evaluation of the intergovernmental fiscal structure. Like other economists she argued for the estimation of 'benefit spillovers' in order to make grants available where spillovers are large and to eliminate grants where spillovers are negligible. In addition, she argued for formulating the fiscal structure to (1) achieve economies of scale in administration, operation, and in the use of innovational and governmental skills and (2) maximize the responsiveness of government to the voter-consumer preferences for differentiated public goods and services. She recognized that these objectives or goals could not be met simultaneously and thus advocated the design of 'alternative plans of fiscal federalism, out of which appropriate combinations must be chosen' (*National Tax Journal*, September 1966, p. 246).

Mushkin also addressed challenging issues in the area of health economics and policy. For example, in *Health: What Is It Worth? Measures of Health Benefits*, she examines the following questions:

(1) What are the most important and relevant gradations in levels of health and well-being that represent outcomes or benefits of health programs? (2) What is the value of desirable outcomes? What would the public be willing to pay for improved chances of being in a higher functional level upon contracting a chronic disease? Practically, how can this willingness be measured? (3) Given public preferences, how should health funds, including biomedical research funds, be distributed among disease problems? (1979, p. 315)

Mushkin advocated shifting the basis for health benefits measurement (and the basis for costs-of-illness measurement) from the human capital model to measures of consumer preference or willingness to pay. Her position was based, in part, on the human capital model's failure to reflect the preferences of individuals to improve their own chances for a longer life or a higher quality life and the human capital model's tendency to under-evaluate women and children.

In *Consumer Incentives for Health Care*, Mushkin (with Alan Discuillo) discussed the allocation of scarce health care resources and estimated that more than 20 per cent of all non-psychiatric hospital and nursing home expenditures go toward care of the terminally ill. She was an early advocate of the idea that new institutional arrangements are required to give patients access to termination of care and to means of death.

Mushkin died of cancer on 2 December 1989.

DEBORAH HAAS-WILSON

Selected writings by Selma J. Mushkin

(1945), 'A formula for social insurance financing' (with Anne Scitovsky), *American Economic Review*, **35**: 646–52.
(1951), 'Social insurance finance under the Social Security Act amendments of 1950', *Public Finance*, **6**: 255–65.
(1957), 'Distribution of federal expenditures among the states', *Review of Economics and Statistics*, **39**: 435–50.
(1962) (ed.), *The Economics of Higher Education*, Washington, DC: US Department of Health, Education, and Welfare.
(1972) (ed.), *Public Prices for Public Products*, Washington, DC: Urban Institute.
(1974) (ed.), *Consumer Incentives for Health Care*, Neale Watson Academic Publications.
(1979) (ed.), *Health: What Is It Worth? Measures of Health Benefits* (with David W. Dunlop), New York: Pergamon Press.

(1979), *Personal Management and Productivity in City Government* (with Frank H. Sandifer), Lexington, MA: Lexington Books.
(1979), *Biomedical Research: Costs and Benefits*: Cambridge, MA: Ballinger Books.
(1979) (ed.), *Proposition 13 and Its Consequences for Public Management*, Cambridge, MA: Council for Applied Social Research with the assistance of ABT Books.

Margaret Good Myers (b. 1899)

The published works of Margaret G. Myers evidence exclusive scholarship in the complementary areas of money and financial institutions. Notably, her 1981 biographical information on record with the American Economics Association lists 'population' as a research focus.

There exists little personal or even professional information on Myers. She gained her AB from Barnard College in 1920 and we know from the 1981 American Economics Association biography brief that she attended Columbia University as a graduate student, gaining her MA there in 1922. She was Director of Statistics, E. Harlem Nursing and Health Demonstration from 1923 to 1925. Her next position for which we have information is that of Professor of Economics at Vassar College, 1934–64, and then Professor Emeritus at the same institution from 1964 onwards. In the preface to her 1931 monograph, Myers acknowledges an intellectual debt to Professor H. Parker Willis (in whose seminar her work on the New York money market was carried forward). This book was prepared under the auspices of the Columbia University Council for Research in the Social Sciences and the supervision of the subcommittee on economics (composed of Professors R.C. McCrea, W.C. Mitchell and E.R.A. Seligman). This work served as her Ph.D. dissertation and was published as the first volume in a four-volume series edited by B.H. Beckhart. At the time of printing, Professor Beckhart was an associate professor of Banking in Columbia University. In the acknowledgements section of later work, we find Myers thanking her husband.

The *New York Money Market* (1931) covers the origins and development of the money market, broadly conceived, from the period immediately following the American Revolution through to 1913 and the passing of the Federal Reserve Act. The shift from colonial financing to the domestic financing of American economic development and geographic expansion – encouraged by the withdrawal of British financial resources in the wake of the Revolution – shaped and was shaped by the development of the American money market. By broadening the working definition of the 'money market' from its narrowest definition (colloquially referring only to the call loan market) to include the market for all borrowed funds, Myers traces the evolution of several specialized markets including the market for investment funds, commercial credit, foreign exchange, foreign credit, bankers' balances, and, of course, call loans. This work fruitfully combines structural with functional elements of the markets and weaves together explanations of economic and political forces. The result is an informative history of America's formative financial period. And this approach of blending together the technical and mechanical with the historical, analytical and political to explain New York as a financial centre is a methodology that she adopts in all of her subsequent known work.

Margaret Myers then applies herself to a study of Parisian and, more generally, French financial institutions and markets. *Paris as a Financial Centre* (1936) devotes attention to the following: developments in the principal financial institutions of France, their interrelations and relation to the government, and their influence on the financial markets largely after 1928 and the stabilization of the franc. A historical context aids the reader's understanding of the 1930s French financial system and issues of the day. As with her earlier study of the *New York Money Market*, influence and development are cast in terms of both their structural and functional elements, facilitating a clearer understanding of the policy issues.

Four years later, Myers published a shorter book on monetary reform. Polemical in its tone – appealing as much to emotion as logic – *Monetary Proposals for Social Reform* (1940), sets out to discredit the social credit proposals of such 'heretics' as Major C.H. Douglas. The operative feature of social credit is the social dividend – government payment of cash to citizens at large. Given a presumption that such monies would be spent (rather than saved), combined with a belief that economic recessions or depressions are the result of underconsumption, the essence of social credit policy turns on the presumption of the non-passiveness of money. While there may be some reasonable grounds for holding such a position, Major Douglas and others were generally dismissed as monetary cranks. In fact, Myers goes even further and hints at their deliberate intellectual dishonesty.

Three decades elapse between *Monetary Proposals* and her final known monograph, *A Financial History of the United States* (1970). Clearly, she remains active during these years teaching at Vassar and reviewing at least 12 books for the *American Economic Review* and the *Journal of Economic History*.

A Financial History is a Herculean effort to distill over 300 years of financial history into 451 pages. The result is an interesting and accessible non-technical overview of the many key financial developments that mark American financial history. With this said, it is not without benefit to the specialist. Myers weaves together into an informative history the unfolding of government (local, state and federal) finances and the evolution of a wide variety of financial institutions and markets together with the economic philosophies and empirical (including political) forces that affected that evolution. The references are historical; nothing by way of scholarly context is proffered. As one reviewer comments (Miller, 1971) the two principal shortcomings of the book are the absence of empirical content (by which he presumably means empirical data) and inadequate recognition of 'newer points of view in monetary matters'. The incorporation of modern analytical approaches into the work of Milton Friedman and Anna Schwartz (1963) may explain why this book, and not Myers's, has become – in the minds of the orthodox – the pioneering work in American monetary history.

As Myers states in her preface, however,

> Any attempt to trace within the limits of one volume the financial history of the United States, ... involves difficult choices of method and treatment. A strictly chronological presentation has some advantages, but loses the thread of development for any one institution, while a study of one institution after another makes it difficult to see interrelationships. On another level, evaluation presents problems if not dangers, yet complete objectivity – if there is such a thing – is lifeless and cowardly. I have tried to steer a middle course among these dangers.

This excerpt captures well the essence of Myers's scholarly approach to the complex task of studying financial institutional history.

BRENDA SPOTTON VISANO

Bibliography

Selected writings by Margaret Good Myers

(1922), 'Monthly production of pig iron, 1884 to 1903', *Journal of the American Statistical Association*, **18** (June): 247–9.

(1931), *Origins and Development, vol. 1 of The New York Money Market*, ed. Benjamin Haggott Beckhart, New York: Columbia University Press, 1931. Reprinted New York: AMS Press, 1971.

(1936), *Paris as a Financial Centre*, London: P.S. King & Son.

(1940), *Monetary Proposals for Social Reform*, New York: Columbia University Press. Reprinted New York: AMS Press, 1970. Note: 'Published in celebration of the seventy-fifth anniversary of Vassar College and in honour of Henry MacCracken in the twenty-fifth year of his presidency'.

(1959), 'The attempted nationalization of banks in Australia, 1947', *Economic Record*, **35** (August): 170–86.

(1970), *A Financial History of the United States*, New York and London: Columbia University Press.

Other sources and references

Friedman, M. and A. Schwartz (1963), *A Monetary History of the United States 1867–1960*, Princeton, NJ: Princeton University Press.

Miller, E. (1971), 'Review of *A Financial History of the United States*', *Journal of Economic History*, **31**(3), September, 719–20.

Maria Negreponti-Delivani (b. 1933)

Maria Negreponti-Delivani was born on 9 June 1933 in Thessaloniki. After completing her primary education, she entered the School for Law and Economic Services of the University of Thessaloniki. She distinguished herself as a student and after four years of study took her first degree in economics ('ptichion') with distinction. After her graduation she went with a scholarship from the French government to the University of Paris–Sorbonne, where, in 1959, she obtained a state Ph.D. (Doctorat d'Etat) in economics. During her postgraduate studies she spent a year at the London School of Economics preparing her thesis.

Shortly before her return to Greece she became engaged and later married her Greek mentor, Professor Demetrios Delivanis (1909–97), with whom she shared a happy life. In 1965 she gave birth to their only child, a daughter, who later became an economist too.

After returning to Thessaloniki, Negreponti-Delivani started preparing a research monograph ('ifigessia') that would enable her to seek an academic career. Her marriage to a prominent academic might have given rise to the expectation that she would have an easy time; in reality, however, she had to struggle very hard to overcome the reservations of an all-male conservative electoral body, that finally approved her 'ifigessia' in 1961.

She started teaching at the University of Thessaloniki and at the Graduate School for Industrial Studies in Thessaloniki (later the University of Macedonia). In 1970 she was elected Full Professor there, a post that she holds to this day.

Negreponti-Delivani was the first woman to be elected rector of a Greek university in 1974. She was re-elected in 1984 and in 1985–88. Her many honours include consulting posts in the Greek government and in the OECD. She has been a visiting professor at the University of California at Berkeley and the European University in Florence. She is also very active in the Association of French-speaking Economists, and in Greek politics, local and national. She has published numerous books and articles in Greek, French and English.

The importance of Negreponti-Delivani for the development of economics in post-1945 Greece lies in the fact that she was one of the few economists to obtain an academic appointment in the 1960s. Up to then professors who occupied chairs in economics at Greek universities had done their Ph.D.s in the 1930s and 1940s, mostly in Greece, and to a lesser extent in Germany. Negreponti-Delivani was one of the few economists who started teaching economic analysis, meaning micro- and macroeconomic theory. Her first textbooks, published between 1969 and 1972, used mathematical analysis and helped Greek students cope with recent developments in economic theory, when older textbooks were descriptive and of a historicist–encyclopaedic nature. As the selection of her works in the bibliography shows, Negreponti-Delivani has an interest not only in economic theory, but also in applied economics. She wrote books about the economic development of Northern Greece, a chance for her to expand her research in regional development and in public finance. She analysed the structure of Greek industry, the shadow economy, the Greek public debt and unemployment in the country. In these publications she focused on the structural weaknesses of the Greek economy and rejected monetarist and neoclassical policies to reduce Greek inflation in the 1980s and early 1990s. At the beginning of her career she taught and researched in the history of economic thought.

Recently she has edited the diaries of her late husband that reveal some glimpses of Greek academic life between 1935 and 1985.

MICHALIS PSALIDOPOULOS

Selected writings by Maria Negreponti-Delivani

(1960), *L'influence du développement économique sur l'allocation des revenues*, Paris.
(1962), *Le développement de la Grèce du Nord depuis 1912*, Thessaloniki Greek edition, 1964.
(1962), *The pressure on the dollar*, Leyden: Martinus Nijhoff.
(1965), *Lectures on the history of economic thought*, Thessaloniki (in Greek).
(1966), *Kaldor's expenditure tax as a modern restatement of relevant mercantilist positions*, Thessaloniki (in Greek).
(1966), *A comparison of the views of older and modern authors on the stages of economic growth*, Athens (in Greek).
(1969), *Economic analysis*, Thessaloniki (in Greek).
(1969), *The distribution of national income during take-off*, Thessaloniki (in Greek).
(1970), *La contribution des investissements publics au développement régional de la Grèce*, The Hague.
(1971), *The three fathers of the church and economic thought*, Thessaloniki (in Greek).
(1972), *The contribution of I. Kapodistrias on the economic rise of Greece*, Thessaloniki (in Greek).
(1974), *Artisans and small enterprises in Northern Greece*, Athens (in Greek).
(1976), *Problèmes et structures du développement économique de la Grèce*, Thessaloniki.
(1986), *The Greek economy*, Athens (in Greek).
(1991), *The economics of the shadow economy in Greece*, Athens (in Greek).
(1994), *The Greek public debt*, Thessaloniki (in Greek).
(1995), *Unemployment: A pseudoproblem*, Athens (in Greek).

Mabel Newcomer (1891–1983)

Mabel Newcomer's career in economics spanned the five decades between 1917 and 1957 – decades which saw the passage of women's suffrage, the Great Depression, and two world wars. These were also decades of change in the education of women, government activism in economic policy (perhaps brought about by the increasing activity of economists in government), and a period of increasing professionalization for the American Economics Association. Mabel Newcomer established a rather commanding position in each of these arenas during her long career in the profession, navigating her way through barriers presented by higher education, government, and the organizational ranks of the AEA, as a professor of economics at Vassar College. Her research and publications, including ten books and over 30 articles, were recognized by appointments to local, state and federal government panels, while her enthusiasm for teaching found her promoting the education of women – to take their place in society not only as home-makers, but as educated productive workers. She was elected Vice-President of the American Economics Association, only the third woman to hold such a position since its founding in 1885. (Edith Abbott [*q.v.*, Chicago] was elected to this position in 1911 and Jessica B. Peixotto [*q.v.*, California] served as AEA Vice-President in 1928. As the only woman of the nine representatives President Roosevelt sent to the United Nations Monetary Conference in Bretton Woods, New Hampshire, in 1944, Newcomer spent the following year travelling through the country lecturing on the role women could and would play in the new world order. Throughout her career, Newcomer was able to avoid many of the 'cultural myths' that defined the position of women in US society in the late nineteenth and early twentieth centuries and attained what then, and now, must be viewed as a remarkable career in economics.

Newcomer received her AB in 1913 and her MA in 1914 from Stanford University and her Ph.D. from Columbia in 1917. Her Ph.D. thesis was published as a monograph, *Separation of State and Local Revenues in the United States in 1917*, by Columbia University Press and reprinted by AMS Press in 1968.

During her career as a professional economist she published over 30 scholarly pieces in the area of public finance and corporations, including four books, one bibliography and numerous articles on taxation or the impact of government policies on the economy. Her articles were published in the Columbia-based *Political Science Quarterly*, which in its early days was partially devoted to economics, the *Journal of Political Economy*, the *American Economic Review*, and the *National Tax Journal*.

Newcomer's work is summative and empirical. She collects and analyses data, and assesses the resulting theoretical and policy implications. Her 1940 book, *Taxation and Fiscal Policy*, was part of a series published by Columbia University Press to address 'those economists interested in an expert's overview of her particular subject and ... those who have an intelligent interest in and a genuine concern for the problems that confront them as citizens'. Newcomer also wrote a number of articles for the general public, educating them on taxation issues related to property taxes, war financing and peace financing. Newcomer moves easily from one audience to the next, intent on both informing and educating her peers on results of her research and the general public on the importance of economic research in their roles as citizens and voters.

Newcomer's work has endured through time. The *Social Science Citation Indexes* (*SSCI*) between 1971 and 1993 shows continued references to many of her books and articles. Her later work on the *Big Business Executive* (1955) and *A Century of Higher Education in America* (1959) are her works most often cited in the past two decades. As late as 1976, however, several of her earlier taxation articles from 1921, 1924, 1931 and 1953 are cited.

Between 1920 and 1947, Newcomer served on a number of research teams and panels. While her work on taxation and finance made her a likely and obvious candidate for these local, state and federal appointments, there was one appointment which she attributed to 'politics and luck, not special expertise'. This was her appointment by President Roosevelt to the United Nations Conference at Bretton Woods, New Hampshire, an appointment made not without some mild intervention on the part of several academic and professional women. When told that there were no women qualified to represent the country in the postwar negotiations, a 'Committee on Participation of Women in Post-War Planning' formed, and promptly recommended three women with impressive credentials to be a part of this project. Newcomer was one of the three whose names were prescribed to the President by the Committee. Shortly thereafter, Newcomer was named to the US delegation to Bretton Woods. After the Bretton Woods Conference, Newcomer travelled throughout the country addressing women's groups and the press on the importance of the IMF and IBRD. This appears to have been part of the job that came with appointment to the conference – selling the results to American women.

Today, despite her impressive career in economics, Newcomer's name is more often recognized and referenced as a primary resource in women's studies. Her *Century of Higher Education for Women* remains a benchmark in examining and assessing the movement of women into colleges and universities. Newcomer used this opportunity to extend the then socially accepted notion of educating women for 'educated motherhood' beyond these bounds. She wrote,

> First we were teaching for leadership, and we assumed all of our students were superior material. During the depression there wasn't much to lead so we trained for leisure. There was plenty of that and we featured the arts. With the beginning of the war we trained for service, which I believe is a sounder approach. Today we try to give girls training by which they can earn a living, have a happy family life, profitable leisure and be of community service.

In the 1960s Newcomer's research and analysis provided an economic foundation for fundamental issues of succeeding women's movements.

JEAN SHACKELFORD

Bibliography

Selected writings by Mabel Newcomer

(1917), *Separation of State and Local Revenues in the United States*, New York: Columbia University Press.

(1924), 'Vital statistics for Vassar College' (with Evelyn S. Gibson), *American Journal of Sociology*, **24**.

(1930), 'The general property tax and the farmer', *Journal of Political Economy*, **38**: 62–72.

(1932), 'Taxation of land values in Canada' (with Ruth Gillette Hutchinson), *Journal of Political Economy*, **40**: 366–78.

(1936), 'Equalization of local government resources in Germany and England', *American Economic Review Supplement*, **26**: 182–7.

(1937), 'Analysis of the nature of American public debts, federal, state, and local', *American Economic Review Supplement*, **27**: 49–57.

(1937), *Central and Local Finance in Germany and England*, New York: Columbia University Press.

(1938), 'A study in business mortality: length of life of business enterprises in Poughkeepsie, New York, 1843–1936' (with Ruth Gillette Hutchinson and Arthur R. Hutchinson), *American Economic Review*, **28**: 497–514.

(1939), 'Price variations among Poughkeepsie grocers' (with Margaret Perkins), *Journal of Marketing*, **4**: 39–44.

(1940), *Taxation and Fiscal Policy*, New York: Columbia University Press.

(1944), 'Congressional tax policies in 1943', *American Economic Review*, **34**: 734–56.

(1946), 'Undergraduate teaching of economics – report of the Subcommittee on the Undergraduate Economics Curriculum and Related Areas of Study,' *American Economic Review*, **36**(4): 845–7.

(1948), 'War and postwar developments in the German tax system', *National Tax Journal*, **1**: 1–11.

(1952), 'The chief executive of large business corporations', *Explorations in Entrepreneurial History*, **5**: 1–33.

(1953), 'The decline of the general property tax', *National Tax Journal*, **6**: 38–51.

(1953), 'The growth of property tax exemption', *National Tax Journal*, **6**: 116–28.

(1954), 'State and local financing in relation to economic fluctuations', *National Tax Journal*, **7**: 97–109.

(1955), 'Professionalization of leadership in the big business corporation', *Business History Review*, **29**: 54–63.

(1955), *The Big Business Executive: The Factors That Made Him, 1900–1950*, New York: Columbia University Press.

(1959), *A Century of Higher Education for American Women*, New York: Harper & Brothers.

Other sources and references

Marshall, Natalie (n.d.), 'Mabel Newcomer', Department of Economics, Vassar College, Poughkeepsie, NY.

Musgrave, Richard A. (ed.) (1965), *Essays in Fiscal Federalism*, Washington, DC: The Brookings Institution.

Musgrave, Richard A. and Carl S. Shoup (eds) (1959), *Readings in the Economics of Taxation: Selected by a Committee of the American Economic Association*, Homewood, IL: Richard D. Irwin, Inc.

Jessica Blanche Peixotto (1864–1941)

Jessica Blanche Peixotto was born in New York on 9 October 1864, to Myrtilla Jessica (Davis) Peixotto and Raphael Peixotto. Within a few years her family moved to San Francisco where Raphael soon established himself as a prominent merchant and leading citizen. Jessica graduated from high school in 1880 and had hoped to enter the University of California at Berkeley. But Raphael opposed his only daughter's desire, apparently convinced that 'university life was not appropriate for a young girl to whom were available the rich opportunities within a cultured home circle' (Hatfield, 1935, p. 5). Instead, he arranged a series of tutors who privately instructed Jessica in a wide variety of subjects (Chambers, 1971, p. 42).

At the age of 27, Peixotto enrolled at Berkeley as a special student not seeking a degree. After an undistinguished first year, she became serious about her studies and completed a four-year Ph.B. degree in the spring of 1894. In the next academic year, she began graduate studies in the Department of Political Science, and pursued a special interest in economics even thought she had completed only two economics courses as an undergraduate. She spent 1896–97 at the Sorbonne conducting research for her thesis, 'A Comparative Study of the Principles of the French Revolution and the Doctrines of Modern French Socialism', which was subsequently published under a slightly different title (Peixotto, 1901). In May 1900, Peixotto became the second woman to be awarded a doctoral degree by the University of California.

In 1904 Peixotto was appointed Lecturer in Sociology at Berkeley. She was primarily responsible for teaching two courses: 'Contemporary Socialism' and 'History of Socialism'. In 1907 she joined the Department of Economics as a regular member of the faculty, first as Assistant Professor of Sociology and then somewhat later as Assistant Professor of Social Economics. She was promoted to Full Professor in 1918, the first woman appointed to that rank in any field at Berkeley (Cookingham, 1987, p. 52; Hatfield, 1935, p. 9). Peixotto remained in that post until she retired in 1935.

Within the Economics Department at Berkeley the sub-field social economics was very largely the creation of Jessica Peixotto, with the help of her colleagues Lucy Stebbins and Emily Huntington. Students pursuing this specialization were expected to complete courses in economic theory, the control of poverty, theories of social reform, constructive philanthropy, the care of dependants, the child and the state, crime as a social problem, and studies in the standard of living (Cookingham, 1987, p. 50). It was in this last area that Peixotto made her most important contributions to what Dorfman has called 'consumption economics', the empirical study of household spending patterns among various cultural and economic groups within society (Dorfman, 1959, pp. 570–78).

Peixotto and her Berkeley associates on the Heller Committee for Research in Social Economics, of which she was Chair from its establishment in 1923 until her retirement in 1935, undertook numerous empirical studies of household expenditures among various income groups in California. Peixotto was particularly interested in household expenditure patterns of professionals and skilled workers. On the basis of her own studies, Peixotto concluded that household spending tended to be standardized in different social, occupational and income groups. For example, she examined in detail the household budgets of 96 faculty members and their families at Berkeley (Peixotto, 1927b and 1928). By and large these households sought a material standard of living comparable to that enjoyed by other professionals such as lawyers and physicians. But because professors invariably earned less, they found it very difficult to achieve this goal and consequently they and their families often felt frustrated. By way of contrast, her subsequent study of 82 typographers' families in San Francisco showed this group to be reasonably content since their income more than accommodated the consumption patterns of their peer group, other skilled workers (Peixotto, 1929).

Peixotto acknowledged that all households are torn by the conflict between the need for savings and the desire for a rising standard of living. Overall, the latter impulse appears stronger in American households:

> The essential characteristic of the American standard of living is not belief in abstinence, but rather this exuberant creed that the scale of wants of individuals and families must and should increase in volume, in variety and intensity; that expanding and varying wants spell increase of permanent happiness and general well-being. (Quoted in Dorfman, 1959, p. 578)

Jessica Peixotto's commitment to social economics extended beyond her academic work. She was a founding member of the Berkeley Commission of Public Charities; she was a long-serving member of the California State Board of Charities and Corrections; she served in a variety of capacities on the Council of National Defense during World War I; and in 1931 she served on the Consumers' Advisory Board of the National Recovery Administration (Hatfield, 1935, pp. 10–13; Chambers, 1971, p. 43).

For 28 years Jessica Peixotto served with distinction in Berkeley's Department of Economics. As the first woman doctoral graduate and first tenured woman in that Department, and as the first female Full Professor in that university, she served as mentor for later women students and professors (Cookingham, 1987, pp. 64–5). With the help of a few colleagues, she made social economics a distinct sub-field within the undergraduate major; by the mid-1920s, students could choose to specialize in one of economic theory, labour, or social economics (ibid., p.62). She was greatly respected as a teacher of both undergraduates and graduate students, as evidenced by the essays published in her honour at the time of her retirement by her former students. And, as shown by her election as Vice-President of the American Economics Association in 1928, her scholarly work was highly regarded by her professional colleagues.

Jessica Blanche Peixotto died in Berkeley on 19 October 1941.

RICHARD A. LOBDELL

Bibliography

Selected writings by Jessica Blanche Peixotto

(1901), *The French Revolution and Modern French Socialism: A Comprehensive Study of the Principles of the French Revolution and the Doctrines of Modern French Socialism*, New York: T.Y. Crowell and Company.

(1904), 'Bourgain's examination of socialism', *Journal of Political Economy*, **13**, 98–108.

(1913), 'Relief work of the associated charities', Part V in *San Francisco Relief Survey: The Organization and Methods of Relief Used after the Earthquake and Fire of April 18, 1906*, New York: Survey Associates.

(1915), 'New ideals for the schools', *Child Labor Bulletin*, **4**, 118–22.

(1917), *The Economizer: An Efficient Household Account Book that does not Require Tedious Bookkeeping* (with O.A. Jeschien), Berkeley, California: The University of California Press.

(1919), 'Minimum wage', *Standards of Child Welfare*, Washington, DC: United States Children's Bureau, Government Printing Office.

(1923), 'The case for coeducation', *Forum*, **LXX**, 2059–66.

(1924), 'The business man and the consumer', *Commercia*, **V**, 2–9.

(1927a), 'Family budgets', *American Economic Review*, **17**, 132–40.

(1927b), *Getting and Spending at the Professional Standard of Living: A Study of the Costs of Living an Academic Life*, New York: The Macmillan Company.

(1928), 'Family budgets of university faculty members', *Science*, n.s., **LXVIII**, 497–501.

(1929), *How Workers Spend a Living Wage: A Study of the Income and Expenditures of Eighty-two Typographers' Families in San Francisco*, Cost of Living Studies II, University of California *Publications in Economics*, Berkeley, California: The University of California Press.

Other sources and references

Chambers, Clarke A. (1971), 'Peixotto, Jessica Blanche', in Edward T. James (ed.), *Notable American Women, 1607–1950*, vol. III, Cambridge, MA: The Belknap Press.

Cookingham, Mary E. (1987), 'Social economists and reform: Berkeley, 1906–61', *History of Political Economy*, **19**, 47–65.

Dorfman, Joseph (1959), *The Economic Mind in American Civilization*, vol. 5, New York: Viking Press, Inc.

Hatfield, Henry Rand (1935), 'Jessica Blanche Peixotto', in *Essays in Social Economics in Honor of Jessica Blanche Peixotto*, Berkeley, California: University of California Press, pp. 5–14.

Virginia Penny (b. 1826)

Born in Louisville, Kentucky, USA, on 18 January 1826, Virginia Penny graduated from the Female Seminary in Steubenville, Ohio in 1845. She taught there for some time, later holding teaching positions in Illinois and Missouri.[1]

After being denied financial backing by a publisher, Penny used her inheritance to fund the 1863 printing of her book, *The Employments of Women: A Cyclopaedia of Woman's Work*, subsequently retitled twice as *Five Hundred Occupations Adapted to Women; with the Average Rate of Pay in Each* and then *How Women Can Make Money, Married or Single*. This ambitious project was based on three years of her research; she sent out thousands of questionnaires, processed the responses, researched in libraries, read a wide variety of historical and current material, and personally interviewed shopworkers (sometimes initiating conversations by purchasing their goods) and newly made acquaintances in various cities.

Within this volume are listed over 500 possible occupations for women, typically with descriptions of some of their characteristics: wages, female versus male monetary compensation, time required to learn the job, education and skills necessary for the job, paid or unpaid apprenticeship, seasonality of employment, and availability of positions for women. The thoroughness with which she delineated possibilities for women is illustrated by the fact that she covered jobs ranging from practising medicine to beekeeping to artificial eye making. She regularly noted employers' explanations, as well as her own, for female–male wage differentials. She listed some employers' advantages (for example, women do not typically strike or drink) and disadvantages (for example, women are physically weaker) of hiring female over male workers. She noted barriers to entry for women in some occupational areas.

Penny seems to have had at least two purposes in writing the book, which was dedicated to 'Worthy and Industrious Women in the United States Striving to Earn a Livelihood'. One purpose was to provoke women's thought and action toward exploring and realizing their employment opportunities. In fact, she stated, 'There is a large amount of female talent lying dormant for the want of cultivation, and there has been a large amount cultivated that is not brought into exercise for want of definite plans and opportunities of making it available' (Penny, 1971a, p. vi). She accomplished this purpose through writing in a personal, persuasive, and informative style. She gave detailed depictions of just exactly what a worker must do in a particular job, what remuneration she could expect, and what education and training she must undergo. To emphasize that these were potentially tangible possibilities for women, she often cited particular women (sometimes women she had met or historical figures, for example inventors and scholars) who had succeeded in such jobs, and she even included illustrations of women engaged in remunerative employment. Her second purpose seems to have been to persuade people to reconsider the lack of labour market opportunities for women. She said, 'The false opinion that exists in regard to the occupations suitable to women must be changed ere women have free access to all those in which they may engage' (Penny, 1971a, p. vii). At times she offered candid reactions, often in parentheses. For example, in her frustration at the existence of a trade society which discouraged women from entering basket work, she exclaimed, 'Oh, what an injustice to women!' (Penny, 1971a, p. 283). To men engaged in sewing, one of the few occupations in which women engaged at the time, she said, 'Shame on the man that engages in such effeminate employment ... !' (Penny, 1971a, p. 408).

At the time of its first printing, the book was reviewed in both the *New York Times* and the *English Woman's Journal*. The *New York Times* reviewer, while seeming to admire the completeness of the work, expressed some displeasure at the author's 'cheap moralizing' and inclusion of information 'not strictly germane to [what the reviewer felt] the subject' was (Review of *Employments of Women*, 1863). The first criticism may have referred to Penny's attempts to sway public opinion toward acceptance of women's employment outside the domestic sphere and its remuneration. The second criticism may have referred to her including historical women with workforce participation. The reviewer for the *English Woman's Journal*, who noted occasional correspondence between Penny and the journal, welcomed the book, written with 'steadiness and thoroughness'; the reviewer appreciated its portrayal of her 'American sisters', something about whom 'little or nothing' was known by English women ('Our American Sisters', 1863, pp. 204–5).

At the time of its first printing, given lack of advertisement, Penny's book was not widely sold; however, in its second printing (by a publisher to whom Penny sold the plates and rights for $100 at a point when her personal funds were depleted by her expenses associated with broadening women's employment opportunities), it was retitled and sold well. In fact, it has been reprinted several times, and a German translation appeared in 1867.

Although her second book, *Think and Act: A Series of Articles Pertaining to Men and Women, Work and Wages* (1869), has been said to be 'more purely literary than its predecessor' (*A Woman's Sacrifice*, n.d., p. 3), close inspection reveals it to contain more economic analysis of some of women's labour market problems than does the first. As was the first book, this one, a compilation of almost 100 short essays, was a mammoth research undertaking, although Penny described the book as simply containing 'a few sober reflections on woman and her business interests' (Penny, 1971b, p. 6).

Most of the essays have considerable economic content. The following topics, among others, are covered: married women's property rights and desired changes, use-value of women in the domestic sphere, the undesirability of women's lack of non-marriage market opportunities, the importance of even a married woman possessing human capital given the possibility of her husband's death, poverty rate of women relative to men, and economic changes, especially for women, wrought by the Civil War. As is the style of the first book, the style in this book is personable, provocative and engaging.

Penny seems to have been motivated to write both books by her own experience. She related that 'her severe struggle in poor health for several years ... to obtain a livelihood among strangers, alone and unaided, [taught her] the bitter experience of a woman thrown upon her own resources' (Penny, 1971a, pp. 120–21).

While details of her life are sketchy, there are newspaper reports indicating that for a short time she operated and financed an employment agency at Bible House and lectured on fields of employment for women in New York City. She participated with her brother Alex in protests leading to an increase in teachers' salaries in her home town of Louisville. In later years Penny returned to teaching and worked for the US Census Bureau. In 1902 the *New York Times* reported that Penny, 'who has spent almost a lifetime in seeking occupations for women in the United States', was living destitute and 'helpless' in a tenement in New York City ('Woman Worker in Want', 1902).

Virginia Penny showed great determination and fortitude in the cause of bettering employment opportunities for women. Her first book, one of the earliest listings of possible occupations for women, is a distinguished accomplishment; it clearly represents the product of considerable and careful research. Her second book shows a refinement of thinking on economic issues, particularly those that were and still are relevant to women. With both books and her other activities, she stimulated people to think about how women could support themselves financially and take appropriate action.

SUSAN H. GENSEMER

Note

1. The biographical material for Penny is from: 'How Women Can Earn Money: Lecture by Miss Virginia Penny at the Cooper Union' (1892); *How Women Can Make Money* (1971a), introduction by Stein and Taft; 'Our American Sisters' (1863); 'Review of *Employments of Women* (1863); 'A Woman's Sacrifice', n.d.; 'Woman Worker in Want' (1902).

Bibliography

Selected writings by Virginia Penny

(1863 [1971a]), *The Employments of Women: A Cyclopaedia of Woman's Work*, Boston: Walker, Wise & Co. Reprinted as *How Women Can Make Money*, New York: Arno and the *New York Times*, 1971, with an introduction by Leon Stein and Philip Taft.

(1867), *Die Beschäftigung des weiblichen Geschlechts in der Hand-Arbeit: oder praktische Nachweisung det Thätigkeit der Frauen im Haushalte* (German translation and adaptation of *Employments of Women* by A. Daul with a foreword by Max Wirth), Altona: J.F. Hammerich.

(1869 [1971b]), *Think and Act: A Series of Articles Pertaining to Men and Women, Work and Wages*, Philadelphia: Claxton, Remsen, and Haffelfinger. Reprinted New York: Arno and the *New York Times*, 1971.

(1892), 'How Women Can Earn Money: Lecture by Miss Virginia Penny at the Cooper Union', *New York Times*, 20 February, p. 8, col. 3.

Other sources and references
'Our American Sisters' (1863), *English Woman's Journal*, **XI**, 204–9.
'Review of *Employments of Women*', *New York Times*, 25 January 1863, p. 2, col. 3.
'A Woman's Sacrifice: Miss Virginia Penny's Labors on Behalf of the Members of her Sex – What She Found Women Could Do', Chicago (n.d.). Copies at Library of Congress, Syracuse University, Rutgers University, New York University, State University of New York at Binghampton, Columbia University, Pennsylvania State University.
'Woman Worker in Want: Miss Virginia Penny, Who Spent a Fortune for Her Sex, In a Helpless Condition', *New York Times*, 1 August 1902, p. 5, col. 3.

Edith Tilton Penrose (1914–96)[1]

Economists responsible for new ideas and approaches are often acknowledged through eponyms; their names denote a mode of analysis or a way of looking at the world, as with 'Walrasian equilibrium' or 'Keynesian demand'. It is rare for a woman's name to be so distinguished within the discourse of economics. The 'Penrosian firm' is an exception. It immortalizes Edith Penrose. It might seem that Penrose is doubly honoured in that her name is associated with an institution that appears central to economic life. But 'the firm', while clearly the hub of economic activity in the real world, until recently was a 'black box' as far as economic theory was concerned. Penrose was a pioneer in terms of breaking open the firm and trying to understand how it worked. Today the Penrosian firm motivates an organizational perspective which is shared by a growing community of scholars from a range of disciplines. However, while Penrose's book, *The Theory of the Growth of the Firm* (1959; hereafter *TGF*), is read and cited among economists, it has had more influence among emergent schools of management. Edith's distinctive way of studying the firm has not been to the taste of modern economists. Why?

Our answer has three dimensions. First, Penrose's main research covered difficult terrain from the viewpoint of orthodox economics, located as it was within the problematic relationship between the firm and the market (Best and Garnsey, 1999; Pitelis, 1999). Second, Penrose developed a methodology to understand the growth of the firm which contrasts with the deductive logic preferred by modern theorists. Third, we suggest that Penrose's aims and achievements were structured and constrained by events in the real world and her own life. For Edith life and work were of a piece and one is hard to understand without the other.

Penrose had other research to her credit before *TGF*. She worked on wartime problems when a special assistant to the US Ambassador in London (1941–46). She published with her thesis adviser Fritz Machlup on the patent controversy in the nineteenth century (Machlup and Penrose, 1950), a topic that she also studied in her 1951 Johns Hopkins Ph.D. on *The Economics of the International Patent System*. After *TGF* she published extensively on the petroleum industry and on multinationals (see Penrose, 1968). But *TGF* is her best known work, as reference to her entries in the *Social Science Citation Index* confirms.

Edith's agenda was distinct from the static theory of the firm which focused on equilibrium size, factor proportions, output and pricing (Earley, 1960). She sought to develop a theory of the *growth* of the firm which she held was more relevant to the modern business enterprise operating in a world of product diversification, innovation, technological change and merger activities.

The firm, for Penrose, was a pool of resources organized in an administrative framework. To explain the growth of the firm, Penrose elaborated a *process* view of production and competition, which led her to distinguish between resources and productive services, and between productive services and productive opportunities. These distinctions enabled her to incorporate knowledge and technology into a dynamic theory of enterprise growth which anticipated the 'resource-based' perspective in strategic management (Teece and Pisano, 1994; Foss, 1999).

Penrose argued that it was not the homogeneous *resources* of conventional economic theory that were inputs into the production process but rather the *services* that these resources rendered (*TGF*, p. 25). The services which resources could render derived from the unique experience, teamwork and purposes of each enterprise; they were unique because of their individual evolution and this made the firm similarly unique. 'The services yielded by resources are a function of the way in which they are used – exactly the same resources when used for different purposes or in different ways and in combination with different types or amounts of other resources provides a different service or set of services' (*TGF*, p. 25). Experience involved making new productive services available to the firm in a knowledge-based process.

The process of production created new productive services as a by-product. But this meant a coordination problem: 'only by chance [will] the firm … be able so to organize its resources that all of them will be fully used' (*TGF*, p. 32). These unused resources remain available to the firm. Managers attempt to use them in other activities, which sets in motion the process whereby new knowledge is created, and with it unused resources with their further pressure on managers to find new activities. The process is endless.

If the unintended creation of unused services was one dimension of the production dynamic, managers' ability to recognize possibilities for action was another. In an uncertain world, management had to be able to identify and respond to opportunities. In turn the pursuit of opportunities through new experience reverberated back to create new productive services (*TGF*, p. 53). 'From the Penrosian perspective, the firm strategically shapes the market rather than reacting to it, but within a moving, historically contingent environment' (Best and Garnsey, 1999).

How did Penrose, who had after all experienced a conservative training in economics at Johns Hopkins under the tutelage of Machlup, escape from the confines of orthodox industrial organization to develop this dynamic vision of path-dependent growth? One crucial point here is that Penrose did not explicitly confront the orthodox paradigm, arguing instead that her interest was in a different topic. She eschewed the static concerns of mainstream theory to focus explicitly on the dynamic question of what determined the *growth* of the firm. It was a clever move to claim as her own this neglected territory where she was not forced by custom and practice to take a particular approach, or, alternatively, to defend a decision not to take that approach. Penrose avoided getting bogged down in the defence of an alternative approach in a discipline notorious for its methodological rigidity. To not use the standard methodology was after all to not really 'do economics' (Humphries, 1995). In fact, Penrose's vision of the firm was heavily influenced by an atypical research experience. In 1954 Penrose, through Machlup's good offices, had obtained a fellowship which allowed her to spend six weeks studying the Hercules Powder Company 'with the full cooperation of all of its personnel' (Penrose, 1960, p. 2). She produced the detailed case study of Hercules before she embarked on *TGF*. The study not only helps illustrate the argument of the book but it almost certainly had an influence on the arguments of the book in the first place (Kay, 1999).

Hercules Powder Company was formed as an anti-trust enforced de-merger of Du Pont. Penrose cites the importance of 'the creation of consumer demand as a consequence of entrepreneurial desire to find a use for available productive resources' (1960, p. 9). The impetus for new product development and moves to create new markets came from 'the extensive knowledge of cellulose chemistry possessed by Hercules [because it] provided a continuous inducement to the firm to search for new ways of using it'. This was the clue to the productive services and market opportunity dynamics: Hercules's technological base enabled it to enter new markets, which in turn led the company to refine its technological knowledge (Kay, 1999).

The pivotal role of the case study in the genesis of Penrose's ideas has been hidden because the publisher cut the chapter devoted to Hercules to economize on space and consequently it was not published until 1960 when it appeared in *Business History Review*. The 'missing chapter' won the Newcomen Award for the best article published in the *Review* that year. *TGF* was thus not the product of deductive logic applied to a limited number of axioms and subsequently 'tested' with reference to the 'real world'. Penrose generalized from the case she knew in such detail and saw that her ideas about growth were consistent with other descriptive material. Her incisive summary of the Hercules Powder case study neatly captures the message of her book.

> Growth is governed by a creative and dynamic interaction between a firm's productive resources and its market opportunities. Available resources limit expansion; unused resources (including technological and entrepreneurial) stimulate and largely determine the direction of expansion. While product demand may exert a predominant short-term influence, over the long term any distinction between 'supply' and 'demand' determinants of growth becomes arbitrary. (Penrose, 1960, p. 1)

Penrose's methodology is worth a closer look. For her the world is inherently complex; we need theory to make sense of it and to act sensibly within it. Penrose's research method involved close observation and detailed documentation of individual firms. But she used observation to refine her conceptual model, not to 'test' hypotheses. Brian Loasby suggests that Penrose developed 'connecting principles', as Adam Smith called them, invented patterns of knowledge that help us to understand what we observe and experience (Smith, 1795; Loasby, 1991, p. 6; Penrose, 1995, pp. xiii–xiv). In this sense Penrose's method was interpretative. Her aim was not how to know 'the truth', but how to endow experience with meaning. Her work denied the positivist dichotomies implicit in much economic research between theory and evidence, positive and normative, fact and value, theory and practice. For example, she argued against 'a distinction, far too commonly made, between a "real" world of history and a world of theory' (1989, p. 10). Theory and history are not in opposition; their relationship is 'one of genuine complementarity' (p. 11). Without theory it is impossible to 'isolate from the seamless web the facts relevant to the questions we want to ask' (p. 11). The 'facts' are not, however, freestanding but depend upon the questions being asked. 'But it is hard to ask questions without knowing why you ask them – that is to say without a theory' (p. 12). Penrose likened theory to a camera: 'Our picture is a moving one and the camera must so select the facts it puts together as to depict the undepictable: the causal, unobservable, relationship between facts' (p. 8). As we look closer, the gulf between Penrose's methodology and the standard approach of mainstream economics widens.

Moreover, Penrose's economics has many of the characteristics which recent writers suggested would improve economics (McCloskey, 1983, 1985; Klamer, McCloskey and Solow, 1988; Nelson, 1992). These authors, often writing explicitly as 'feminist economists', have suggested that economics has been socially constructed as hard, logical, scientific and precise, characteristics that evoke masculinity. So long as masculinity is associated with superiority, the idea that economics could be improved by becoming more 'feminine' makes little sense. For example, reasoning in economics is identified with formal logic, mathematics, and hence masculinity. A simple dualism collapses other forms of reasoning into 'illogic'. But a more sophisticated view might complement logic with 'feminine' ways of reasoning such as by analogy or by pattern recognition, and we might add here by *connecting principles*. Such a view might also recognize a masculine–negative dimension in terms of (say) a sterile and impoverished formalism. Thus Penrose's explicit and implicit criticisms of standard hierarchical dualisms, her own methodology, and her elevation of the case study as a means through which to know and understand, would find sympathy with contemporary feminist economists (Ferber and Nelson, 1993; Kuiper and Sap, 1995; England, 1993). The renewed interest in Penrose's work is undoubtedly associated with a return to those economic issues which concerned the classical economists; stability *and* growth; order *and* progress. But her work has also obvious resonance with very modern themes. We have already noted its links to the resource-based view of the firm and strategic management. Here we underline her potential appeal to feminist economists (see also Best and Humphries, 1999).

Edith Penrose did not spend all her time in the calm pursuit of knowledge within university libraries or faculty clubs.[2] She was caught up in, indeed part of, the economic and political turmoil of the twentieth century. She was married twice and the mother of four children. Her life had its tragedies as well as its triumphs and at times a less doughty spirit would have been defeated. Like the entrepreneurs of her own theory, she made productive resources out of her own experience and then sought new opportunities in which to deploy them.

Born in 1914, Edith spent her childhood in pioneering conditions, which may have contributed to her physical and mental toughness and her lack of pretension. Her father, George Tilton, was an engineer for the California Department of Public Works. She and her two brothers, later killed in the armed services, were brought up and educated in road camps as the family followed George in his survey of the new road network. Her mother, Hazel Sparling, who was directly descended from William Brewster, one of the senior pilgrims on the *Mayflower*, reputedly shot a rattlesnake that threatened Edith at play. Edith went to high school in the Californian town of San Luis Obispo, to whose English teacher she attributed her own clear prose style. At the age of 18 she married David Denhardt, an aspiring politician some years older than Edith, whom she had met as a student at the University of California at Berkeley. Within a year he was shot in a hunting accident. Still under 20, Edith was a widow with a baby son. None the less, she gained her BA in economics at Berkeley in 1936. Her first job was as a social worker.

Opportunity knocked in 1939 when Edith was offered an attractive post in Geneva at the International Labour Office, working with E.F. Penrose, ('Pen'), her former professor, and an Englishman by birth and education. With war brewing, these were strange times but it must have been hard for Edith to flout convention and leave her little boy with his grandmother. In Geneva, Edith and Pen were involved in helping Jews escape from Germany. As a German invasion of Switzerland threatened, ILO staff were evacuated. But in 1941, Pen became Economic Adviser to the American ambassador in London, John Winant, and Edith was made his Special Assistant, with a brief from Eleanor Roosevelt to investigate social conditions in wartime Britain. The ILO published Edith's *Food Control in Great Britain* in 1940.

In 1945 Edith and Pen were married, and Pen joined the US delegation to the United Nations. A year later Edith gave birth to a son, Trevan, who died in infancy, following a measles inoculation. Two other sons, Perran and Trevear, were born in 1947 and 1948. In 1947 they moved to Johns Hopkins University where Edith undertook graduate studies. Fritz Machlup directed her doctoral research and subsequently appointed Edith to a research fellowship in a college–business exchange programme he had been instrumental in setting up. Her fieldwork at the Hercules Powder Company (see below) was thus part of a wider undertaking, though it was Edith's decision to focus on the theory of the growth of the firm.

The Penroses were caught up in the cold war, as they had been by earlier hostilities. When Senator McCarthy's Committee for Un-American Activities targeted Owen Lattimore, the eminent Sinologist, Edith and Pen rallied to his defence. Pen's consequent disillusionment with the USA led him to take extended sabbatical leave. The Penroses went first to the Australian National University in Canberra in 1955, where Edith worked on *TGF* and developed her interest in multinational firms by observing an Australian subsidiary. In 1957 there were new upheavals as the Penroses moved to what became the University of Baghdad and the boys were sent to school in England.

The years in Baghdad, followed by time spent teaching in the American University of Beirut, in Cairo and in Khartoum, enabled Edith to develop unique expertise in the petroleum industry. *The Large International Firm in Developing Countries: The International Petroleum Industry* was published in 1968. Edith was an important influence on a generation of Iraqi economists, many of whom subsequently faced severe difficulties as a result of the political situation. Together, Pen and Edith wrote *Iraq: International Relations and National Development*, published in 1978. The Penroses were expelled from Iraq in the 1960s.

In 1959 Edith drove across the Syrian desert (Pen did not drive), through Turkey and on to England in an old Hillman estate car so that she could attend an interview at Cambridge University. Joan Robinson had read the page proofs of *TGF* and instigated the invitation. As the story goes, Austin Robinson was less impressed and nothing came of it.

Shortly thereafter, Edith obtained a joint readership at the London School of Economics and the School of Oriental and African Studies, becoming Professor in 1964, a position she held until 1978 when she became Professor of Political Economy at INSEAD, the business school in Fontainebleau. Her appointment to a chair at a British university is a considerable achievement given the few women professors there were or have been in economics. Perhaps it speaks less of the economics profession as the chair was in an interdisciplinary department.

Upon assuming an academic post, Edith did not pursue the growth of the firm research agenda or lecture on related subjects. In fact, she made little subsequent reference to her theory of the growth of the firm until writing and speaking invitations to do so poured in during the last years of her life. At LSE and SOAS her concerns focused on economic development. She continued to travel. In 1972 she was a visiting professor at the University of Dar es Salaam which included a sensitive mission to University College of Rhodesia where she was outspoken about the College's collusion with racial segregation. During these years she was very active on many policy-oriented bodies, national and international (Best and Garnsey, 1999).

Her years at INSEAD marked another shift of orientation, this time towards management studies. From 1982 to 1984 she was Associate Dean for Research and Development. She taught a range of courses but none on the theory of the growth of the firm. Pen died in Fontainebleau, at the age of 90, and Edith returned to the UK to live outside Cambridge, near her sons Perran and Trevear, until she died in 1996. During these years the surge of interest in Edith's 1959 book took her pleasantly by surprise. She enjoyed the satisfaction of seeing young scholars turning to her work with enthusiasm and appreciated the (albeit delayed) renown that her work so richly deserved. Perhaps Edith would have enjoyed more immediate success if her methodology had parted company with the mainstream of economic analysis less abruptly. It was strategic to depict her agenda as a complement to the mainstream, as a focus on the *growth* of the firm rather than its static equilibrium. But the downside of this self-presentation was to marginalize her contribution (Loasby, 1999). Perhaps Edith would have enjoyed more recognition at a younger age if she had persisted with and consolidated the original product after 1959 instead of pursuing new projects. But here we have to think of the peripatetic academic life that Edith experienced and the demands of the intellectual partnership she enjoyed with Pen. In the last analysis Edith Penrose sacrificed academic ambition for a more rounded intellectual and human existence. In our conversations with her she had no regrets.

MICHAEL H. BEST
JANE HUMPHRIES

Notes

1. The authors have drawn extensively on Michael Best's and Elizabeth Garnsey's obituary of Edith Penrose in the *Economic Journal* (1999). Perran Penrose kindly provided a bio-graphical summary of Edith's life. The authors have benefited from pre-publication access to several articles, which appeared in a special issue of *Contributions to Political Economy*, edited by Christos Pitelis. We have enjoyed conversations about Edith Penrose's life and work with Christos Pitelis, Perran Penrose, Elizabeth Garnsey, Stanley Engerman, William Lazonick, Jonathan Storey, and (most of all) Edith Penrose herself. The special issues recently devoted to Edith Penrose by *Contributions to Political Economy* (**18**, 1999) and *Oeconomia* (**33**(8), August 1999) are evidence of a recent resurgence of interest in Penrose's work.
2. In fact when Edith was at Johns Hopkins, for example, as a woman she was denied admittance to the Faculty Club!

Bibliography

Selected writings by Edith Tilton Penrose

(1940), *Food Control in Great Britain*, Geneva: International Labour Office.
(1951), *The Economics of the International Patent System*, Baltimore, MD: Johns Hopkins Press. Spanish edition, 1974.
(1959), *The Theory of the Growth of the Firm*, Oxford: Basil Blackwell and New York: John Wiley & Sons. 2nd edn, Oxford: Basil Blackwell and New York: St Martins, 1980. Revised edition, Oxford: Oxford University Press, 1995. Translated into Japanese, French, Spanish and Italian.
(1960), 'The growth of the firm – a case study: the Hercules Powder Company', *Business History Review*, **XXXIV**, 1–23.
(1968), *The Large International Firm in Developing Countries: The International Petroleum Industry*, London: George Allen and Unwin.
(1971), *The Growth of the Firm, Middle East Oil and Other Essays*, London: Frank Cass.
(1978), *Iraq: International Relations and National Development* (with E.F. Penrose), London: Benn.
(1985), 'The Theory of the Growth of the Firm Twenty-five Years After', Uppsala: Acta Universitatis Upsaliensis, *Studia Oeconomiae Negotiorum 20.*
(1989), 'History, the social sciences and economic "theory", with special reference to multina-tional enterprise', in A. Teichova, M. Levy-Leboyer and H. Nussbaum (eds), *Historical Studies in International Corporate Business*, Cambridge: Cambridge University Press; Paris: Maison des sciences de l'homme.

Other sources and references

Best, Michael and Elizabeth Garnsey (1999), 'Edith Penrose, 1914–1996', *Economic Journal*, **109**(453), F187–F201.
Best, Michael and Jane Humphries (1999), 'Edith Penrose: crafted opportunities', mimeo.
Early, J. (1960), 'Review of *The Theory of the Growth of the Firm*', *American Economic Review*, **L**(5), 1111–12.
England, Paula (1993), 'The separative self: androcentric bias in neoclassical assumptions', in Marianne Ferber and Julie A. Nelson (eds), *Beyond Economic Man: Feminist Theory and Economics*, Chicago: University of Chicago Press.
Ferber, Marianne and Julie A. Nelson (eds) (1993), *Beyond Economic Man: Feminist Theory and Economics*, Chicago: University of Chicago Press.
Foss, Nicolai J. (1999), 'Edith Penrose, economics and strategic management', *Contributions to Political Economy*, **18**: 87–104.
Humphries, Jane (1995), 'Economics, gender and equal opportunities', in Jane Humphries and

Jill Rubery (eds), *The Economics of Equal Opportunities*, Manchester: Equal Opportunities Commission, pp. 55–86.

Kay, Neil (1999), 'Hercules and Edith', *Contributions to Political Economy*, **18**: 67–86.

Klamer, Arjo, Donald N. McCloskey and Robert M. Solow (eds) (1988), *The Consequences of Economic Rhetoric*, New York: Cambridge University Press.

Kuiper, Edith and Jolande Sap with Susan Feiner, Notburga Ott and Zafiris Tzannatos (eds) (1995), *Out of the Margin: Feminist Perspectives on Economics*, London: Routledge.

Loasby, Brian J. (1991), *Equilibrium and Evolution: An Exploration of Connecting Principles in Economics*, Manchester: Manchester University Press.

Loasby, Brian J. (1999), 'The significance of Penrose's theory for the development of economics', *Contributions to Political Economy*, **18**: 3–22.

Machlup, Fritz and Edith T. Penrose (1950), 'The patent controversy in the nineteenth century', *Journal of Economic History*, **X**(1), 1–29.

McCloskey, Donald N. (1983), 'The rhetoric of economics', *Journal of Economic Literature*, **21**(2), 481–517.

McCloskey, Donald N. (1985), *The Rhetoric of Economics*, Madison: University of Wisconsin Press.

Nelson, Julie A. (1992), 'Gender, metaphor and the definition of economics', *Economics and Philosophy*, **8**(1), 103–26.

Penrose, P. and C. Pitelis (1999), 'Edith Elura Tilton Penrose: Life contributions and influence', *Contributions to Political Economy*, **18**: 3–22.

Smith, Adam (1795[1980]), 'The principles which lead and direct philosophical enquiries: illustrated by the history of astronomy', in W.P.D. Wightman (ed.), *Essays on Philosophical Subjects*, Oxford University Press: Oxford, 1795, pp. 33–105.

Teece, David and G. Pisano (1994), 'The dynamic capabilities of firms: an introduction', *Industrial and Corporate Change* (3), 537–56. Reprinted in G. Dosi, D. Teece and J. Chytry (eds) (1998), *Technology, Organization and Competitiveness*, Oxford: Oxford University Press.

The Philip Family (Elna Nygaard, 1879–1959; Grethe Philip, b. 1916; Bodil Philip, b. 1944; Signe Philip, b. 1973)

It is not unusual to see dynasties where many generations have been lawyers or clergymen – grandfather, father, son, and so on. But in Denmark there exists a quite remarkable dynasty of four generations of female economists.

In Denmark, women were first admitted to university in 1875. The first Danish female university graduate was Nielsine Nielsen, who received a master's degree in medicine in 1885 (the traditional degree at the Danish universities has always been the Master's degree; Bachelor's and Ph.D. degrees have been introduced only very recently). The first female graduate in economics was Meta Kristine Hansen, who was awarded her degree in 1893. The next degree in economics awarded to a woman came in 1900, and then there were three female graduates in economics in 1904.

One of these three was Elna Nygaard. She was appointed to a management post in the Danish Mortgage Bank, but then married and gave up her career. However, in 1916 she bore a daughter, Grethe Philip, who in 1941 became the first female economics graduate from Denmark's second university, the University of Aarhus (founded in 1936). She married her professor in economics, Kjeld Philip, and both became prominent politicians as members of the Social–Liberal Party. Kjeld Philip was Minister of Trade and Economic Affairs from 1957 to 1964, while Grethe Philip was a Member of the Danish Parliament from 1960 to 1979, and a member of the parliamentary finance committee from 1962 to 1978. She also served on a number of important commissions (for example on pensions in 1961, on social reform 1964–72, and on women's issues 1965–74). She was a member of the Board of the Danish Central Bank between 1968 and 1971.

In 1944 Grethe Philip had a daughter, Bodil Philip, who received her degree in economics from the University of Copenhagen in 1971. She has since worked in the Prisons Service and has since 1989 been governor of a prison. She has been member of a number of commissions on criminal policy and criminal research.

Bodil Philip had a daughter in 1973: Signe Philip. She is currently completing her degree in economics from the University of Aarhus, and thus represents the fourth generation of female economists in this family.

NIELS KÆRGÅRD

Vera Cao Pinna (1909–86)

Vera Cao Pinna was born in Siliqua (Sardinia) on 23 December 1909 and died in Rome on 11 June 1986. She spent most of her life in Rome, living with her mother and sister Maria because neither of the two sisters ever married. After receiving her degree in economics with a dissertation in economic statistics under the supervision of Professor Niceforo, she never returned to her native island.

She made a remarkable contribution to the development of applied economics and econometrics in Italy, where she introduced input–output analysis. However, she qualified for university teaching only in her late forties and was appointed Lecturer in Economic Statistics at the University of Rome in the academic year 1956–57. From this year until her retirement in 1975 she kept the same academic position. She taught economic statistics, applied economics and econometrics, and wrote more than 70 books and articles but never won a chair. It is worth mentioning that in Italy the first woman economist to become Full Professor of the history of economic thought did so in 1961 and a second woman economist won a chair in economic development only in 1975, when Vera Cao Pinna had already retired. Moreover, her works could not be easily classified within the existing disciplinary fields, because they were on the borderline between economics and statistics. (Econometrics started to be taught in Italian universities many years later and the first chairs were given only in 1975.)

The most important event in her life was her work in the programme division of the Mutual Security Agency created by the USA in Italy after the war to assist the Italian recovery and support the defence effort after the end of the ECA (European Cooperation Administration). Hollis Chenery was the chief and Paul Clark was the deputy chief, when Vera Cao Pinna headed the Italian staff of the division. Overcoming many difficulties arising from the almost complete lack of data, they built up the first unofficial Italian input–output table for the year 1950, according to the Leontief model.

The subsequent development of input–output analysis in Italy was led by Vera Cao Pinna with methodological contributions and research works in many applied areas.

She cooperated with the Italian Central Statistical Institute to build up the first official Italian input–output tables. The 1954 table was published as an adjunct to the Government National Economic Report and the 1959 table was completed only in 1965. In those years Vera Cao Pinna cooperated with the Statistical Institute of the European Communities to solve the problems of comparability of the national input–output tables.

Vera Cao Pinna contributed to the development of Italian economic thinking mostly through her work on the Leontief model. Many articles and books were written with didactic purposes, after her major work in this field, the essay on input–output analysis in the *Dizionario di economia politica* (*Dictionary of Political Economy*) edited by Claudio Napoleoni. She was the only woman to take a significant part in the collective effort made by the leading Italian economists of the postwar period to introduce in Italy the new economic theories developed in other countries during the Fascist epoch and during the war.

In the applied area she developed a wide range of applications of input–output analysis. The most remarkable is the biregional model of the Italian economy, which she presented at the first World Congress of the Econometric Society held in Rome in 1965. In fact, the model opened the way to the Italian policy of economic planning. However, the best known and widely quoted work is *I parametri del sistema produttivo italiano* (in collaboration with B. Ferrara). It is still a standard reference in any research work on Italian economic development.

A second turning point in Vera's life is connected with the centre-left governments that led Italy from the middle of the 1960s to the middle of the 1970s. These governments offered her the opportunity to contribute with her own professional experience to the new policy of indicative planning.

She had always been involved in the debate on Italian economic policy, with special attention to the development of the South, and she had been a consultant to the Italian Parliament and to other official agencies charged with regional policies for the South (SVIMEZ, IASM).

However, during the centre-left period (1963–75) her contributions to Italian economic policy covered a wider range of topics and were more visible than before. She was one of the research leaders at the Centro Studi e Piani Economici, a private association of economists charged by the government to support policy-making by elaborating appropriate econometric models. The experience was politically frustrating, because very poor results were achieved. Vera Cao Pinna retired and continued her specialized econometric research as a private consultant. She made a remarkable contribution to a better understanding of the energy requirements of the Italian economy in a book with a preface by Wassily Leontief and she applied the input–output method to the analysis of many industries, for example ship-building.

Regional economics was for Vera Cao Pinna another important field of research based on input–output analysis. She built a regional table for Sicily in 1958 – as a member of a team of experts led by another great Italian economist, Paolo Sylos Labini – and in the following decades she made intense efforts to build input–output tables for all the Italian regions, overcoming the problems of estimating interregional trade flows that were not yet statistically estimated. She worked hard at this project as a consultant to SVIMEZ, the Italian agency officially charged with the project, completed only after her death.

Input–output analysis was the prevailing but not the only research field for Vera Cao Pinna. She also acquired a good reputation in aggregate consumption analysis. Here again her contributions are both methodological and applied. The first official household budget analysis in Italy was completed by the Central Institute of Statistics in 1953, with the cooperation of Vera Cao Pinna, on the basis of the methodology she had previously developed for a special committee of the National Research Centre (CNR). In the following years she made many estimations of the aggregate consumption functions in Italy and in other European countries, employing different specifications, covering many consumption items and referring either to national or regional data in different periods of time.

She built up a good reputation in Europe as an expert in long-term projections of food and non-food, private and collective, consumption and worked in this field for many international institutions. Thanks to her international linkages she became a founder member of Asepelt (Association of Scientific Experts in Long-Term Economic Projection), and acted as Vice-President of the Association for many years.

She was never appointed by official agencies or bodies but always acted as a consultant both in Italy and abroad. In each position she performed a significant role in improving the methodology of collecting data. In the applied fields her work is characterized by meticulous care in understanding the deficiencies of the data and care in their use.

She wrote not only in Italian but also in French and in English, and some of her works in Italian were edited in other languages by the international organizations that were interested in diffusing them. It was not usual for Italian economists in those years to have such strong international scientific influence as she had and revealed in the organization of the first World Congress of the Econometric Society held in Rome in 1965.

No account of her contributions would be complete without mentioning her influence in educating generations of students and public officers about modern econometric techniques and in assisting many young researchers on the first steps of their academic career towards their actual positions as full professors in Italian universities.

The end of her life was tragic: she died two weeks after the deaths of her beloved sister and mother.

GRAZIELLA FORNENGO

Selected writings by Vera Cao Pinna

(1952), 'La costruzione del bilancio analitico dell'economia italiana', *L'industria*, no. 4.

(1954), 'Analisi delle relazioni interindustriali di singoli settori produttivi', *L'Industria*.

(1955), 'Interdipendenze strutturali: analisi', *Dizionario di economia politica*, ed. C. Napoleoni, Milan: Comunità.

(1955), 'Applicazioni ed esperienze del metodo input output in vari paesi', *Economia Internazionale*, no. 1.

(1956), 'National experiences: Italy', in *The Structural Interdependence of the Economy*, New York: Wiley.

(1958), 'Principali caratteristiche strutturali di due economie mediterranee: Italia e Spagna', *Rivista de Economia Politica*, Madrid.

(1958), *Analisi delle interdipendenze settoriali di un sistema economico*, Turin: Boringhieri.

(1960), *Struttura e prospettive dell'economia energetica italiana* (preface by W. Leontief), Milan: EtasKompass.

(1960), 'Méthodes de prévision statistique à long terme', Office Statistique des Communautées Européennes, Informations statistiques, no. 6, November–December.

(1962), 'Validité théorique et empirique d'une prévision globale de croissance de l'économie italienne de 1958 à 1970' in R. Geary (ed.), *Europe's Future Consumption*, Amsterdam: North-Holland.

(1966), *I parametri del sistema produttivo italiano* (with B. Ferrara) Turin: Einaudi.

(1969), 'An Industrial Complex Approach to the Compilation and Analysis of Interindustrial Programming Data', in *International Comparison of Interindustry Data*, New York: United Nations.

(1973), *Bilanci aziendali e contabilita nazionale*, Ciriec, F. Angeli, Milan.

(1975), 'A Comparative Analysis of Household Consumption Financed by Individual and Collective Resources in France and Italy', *Review of Income and Wealth*, series 21.

(1975), 'Regional Economic Policy in Italy' in N.M. Hansen (ed.), *Public Policy and Regional Economic Development. The Experience of Nine Western Countries*, Cambridge, MA: Ballinger.

(1975), 'La consommation élargie: cadre conceptuel et comptable' in L. Solari and J.N. Pasquier (eds), *Private and Enlarged Consumption*, Amsterdam: North-Holland.

(1979), *Consumption Patterns in Eastern and Western Europe: an Economic Comparative Approach* (with S.S. Shatalin), Oxford: Pergamon Press.

Michèle A. Pujol (1951–97)

The death of Michèle Pujol has deprived feminist economists, historians of economic thought, and Canadian economists of an inspiring colleague and friend, who will be sorely missed.

Born a French citizen, Michèle grew up in Tahiti, where her father was a colonial administrator, but she made her career in Canada. She brought dedication, insight and enthusiasm to her teaching in the Economics Department and Women's Studies programme at the University of Manitoba (1980–88) and the Women's Studies programme at the University of Victoria (1990–97). Michèle coordinated Women's Studies at the University of Manitoba from 1984 until 1988, when she was not rehired. Her dissertation was completed the next year, while she worked at the checkout of a department store. She also remained an activist beyond campus, helping, for example, to organize Winnipeg's first Gay/Lesbian Pride Marches and first Women's Music Festival. Michèle's eloquent published research touched an even broader audience than her teaching, community activism and conference participation. She combined meticulous scholarship with a profound commitment to illuminating the role of women in the economy and in economics. Her 1989 doctoral dissertation at Simon Fraser University formed the basis of her path-breaking book, *Feminism and Anti-Feminism in Early Economic Thought* (1992), and of her keynote address, 'Into the Margin!' (1995a), to the first Out of the Margin conference on feminist economics. This research greatly extended the scope of the history of economics in two directions. She shone a searchlight on the analysis of women's economic role in what she termed the 'malestream' of British classical political economy and early neoclassical economics from Adam Smith to Edgeworth and Pigou, a topic which malestream historians of economics tend to restrict to discussion of John Stuart Mill (the one among the central figures of classical and early neoclassical economics who emerges most honourably from such scrutiny). She also extended the canon of past economics, rescuing from neglect (and what E.P. Thompson called 'the crushing, condescension of posterity') fascinating feminist analytical contributions on economic inequality by Harriet Hardy Taylor (later Harriet Mill *q.v.*), Barbara Leigh Smith Bodichon (*q.v.*), Millicent Garrett Fawcett (*q.v.*), Eleanor Rathbone (*q.v.*) and William Smart. The discussant of 'Into the Margin!', Amartya K. Sen, agreed that 'There is much of interest and importance in all this, and the reader may well be inspired to go on to read her book.'

Writing on 'The feminist economic thought of Harriet Taylor (1807–58)' (1995b), Michèle established the 'materialist analysis that distinguishes Taylor from Mill's idealist and male-centred position. There cannot be any doubt that Taylor stands on her own as an original and insightful feminist thinker and as an economist and political theorist.' Michèle captivated the History of Economics Society annual meeting at the University of British Columbia in June 1996 with a presentation on her most ambitious project for extending the canon, a multi-volume anthology of women's contributions to political economy before 1900 which she was editing for publication by Routledge and Thoemmes Press. This major work is being completed by Janet A. Seiz, and promises to transform our knowledge of the history of women in economics.

In addition to pioneering feminist history of economics, Michèle was active in contemporary feminist economics, with particular attention to broadening research methodology. She was engaged in a study of the implementation of pay equity policies in Manitoba, which her friends are preparing for publication. An associate editor of *Feminist Economics* from its foundation, Michèle, along with Nancy Folbre, edited an 'Explorations' section in the Fall 1996 issue (vol. 2, no. 33) on feminist issues in national accounting and on research priorities on non-market production. Michèle guest-edited a five-paper 'Explorations' section on 'Broadening Economic Data and Methods' in the Summer 1997 issue of *Feminist Economics* (vol. 3, no. 2), and in 1995 presented 'Is This Really Economics? Using Qualitative Research Methods in Feminist Economic Research' to the International Association for Feminist Economics (IAFFE) conference in Tours. Michèle Pujol was a tremendously active, committed, articulate and productive scholar who challenged and was beginning to transform accepted views about the past and methodology of economics. She died on 2 August 1997, on Salt Spring Island, British Columbia, in the home of her partner Brook, after five months of battling cancer. The Spring 1999 issue of *Atlantis: A Women's Studies Journal* (vol. 23, no. 2) is a special issue on 'Sexual Economics' guest-edited by Marjorie Griffin-Cohen, celebrating the life and work of Michèle Pujol, and reprints four poems by her.

ROBERT W. DIMAND

Bibliography

Selected writings by Michèle Pujol

(1984), 'Gender and Class in Marshall's *Principles of Economics*', *Cambridge Journal of Economics*, **8**, 217–34.

(1992), *Feminism and Anti-Feminism in Early Economic Thought*, Aldershot, UK and Brookfield, US: Edward Elgar Publishing. Paperback edition, with a preface by Janet A. Seiz, Cheltenham, UK and Northampton, US: Edward Elgar Publishing, 1998.

(1995a), 'Into the Margin!', in Edith Kuiper and Jolande Sap, with Susan Feiner. Notburga Ott and Zafiris Tzannatos (eds), *Out of the Margin: Feminist Perspectives on Economics*, London and New York: Routledge, pp. 17–34. Reprinted in *Atlantis*, **23**(2), Spring, 1999, 124–36.

(1995b), 'The Feminist Economic Thought of Harriet Taylor (1807–58)', in M.A. Dimand, R.W. Dimand and E.L. Forget (eds), *Women of Value: Feminist Essays on the History of*

Women in Economics, Aldershot, UK, and Brookfield, US: Edward Elgar Publishing, pp. 82–102.

Other sources and references

Fulton, Keith Louise (1999), 'Michèle Pujol: Ways for Women to Be', *Atlantis*, **23**(2), Spring, 136–7.

St Peter, Christine (1999), 'Michèle Pujol, the University of Victoria and Beyond', *Atlantis*, **23**(2), Spring, 137–9.

Eleanor Rathbone (1872–1946)

Eleanor Rathbone devoted her life to feminist and social reform campaigns in Britain, and is best known for her advocacy of family allowances. She was born in Liverpool to a wealthy and prominent family with a long tradition of public service. Her father, William Rathbone VI, was a shipowner and merchant involved in many philanthropic activities including relief for the poor and improvement of nursing education. He was a Member of Parliament from 1869 to 1895. The Rathbones' prosperity left Eleanor in the rare position of needing to rely neither on a husband's income nor on obtaining paid employment herself.

Eleanor attended Somerville College, Oxford, receiving a degree in philosophy in 1896. Upon returning to Liverpool, she became active in both social work and the women's suffrage movement. Through this work she met Elizabeth Macadam, who became her lifetime companion. From 1909–1914, Rathbone served on the Liverpool City Council, the first woman elected to that position.

As a social worker, Rathbone also pursued social research, conducting extensive studies of the conditions of Liverpool dock labourers (1909) and widows (1913). Her observations led her to sympathize strongly with working-class women, especially with their difficulties in supporting children on husbands' low and irregular wages.

During World War I, Rathbone helped to administer the system of separation allowances paid to wives of men in the armed forces. This experience convinced her of the need for and practicability of family allowances, and she led the campaign for allowances for the rest of her life. Her writings on this issue are discussed below.

Soon after her return to Liverpool she became a leader in the National Union of Women's Suffrage Societies, the moderate or 'constitutional' wing of the suffrage movement. In 1919 she took over from Millicent Garrett Fawcett (*q.v.*) the presidency of the organization (renamed the National Union of Societies for Equal Citizenship after the achievement of limited female suffrage in 1918). She held this position until 1928, and sought to reorient the movement toward what she called 'new feminism', which would be less confined to the pursuit of formal equality between women and men and more attentive to the specific needs of women as mothers (including family allowances). The motto she wanted NUSEC to adopt, she said, was 'I am a woman, and nothing that concerns the status of women is indifferent to me' (Alberti, 1996, p. 49). In 1929 Rathbone was elected to Parliament as an Independent member representing British universities. For the rest of her life, in and outside Parliament, she led the family allowances movement and participated in other social change efforts as well, including housing reform, campaigns against child marriage and for women's suffrage in India and against female circumcision in colonial Kenya, aid to war refugees, and the fight against anti-Semitism.

Rathbone's campaign for family allowances was undertaken while feminists were pressing for 'equal pay for equal work' and the labour movement was demanding the payment of a 'living wage' (or family wage) to male workers. She devoted much of her writing to arguing that both those demands were deeply flawed, and that a family allowance system would be a more just and efficient means of achieving the movement's goals of economic equality for women and higher living standards for working-class families.

Rathbone's first extended presentation of the case for family allowances came in her 1917 *Economic Journal* article on 'The Remuneration of Women's Services'. The war, she states, has transformed women's position both as wage-earners and as mothers: women have been allowed entry into skilled industrial jobs formerly reserved for men, and the separation allowances paid to servicemen's wives have both improved working-class living standards and provided mothers with their first independent income. Restoration of the prewar *status quo* would be neither easy nor just. Although women's lack of political voice would impede their protection of their interests (showing the need for suffrage), many would resist giving up their wartime gains.

The war at last broke down barriers to women's employment against which 'the "women's movement" had beaten itself for half a century in vain' (1917, p. 55). If these barriers are to be re-erected, 'they will have to be based frankly upon the desire of the male to protect himself from competition, and no longer upon the alleged incapacity of the female to compete' (p. 56). However, she argues, feminist demands that women be allowed to enter all occupations and receive 'equal pay for equal work' are neither practicable nor just. The 'equal pay' formula takes account neither of women's lower productivity in some of the trades they share with men, nor of other disadvantages such as statutory restrictions on hours and, most important, the fact that most leave their jobs after only a few years, since 'the majority of women workers are only birds of passage in their trades. Marriage and the bearing and rearing of children are their permanent occupations' (p. 65). Unless these real differences are allowed for by appropriate reductions of women's wages relative to men's, the main effect of 'equal pay' would be to restore women's exclusion from skilled trades. Thus feminists might best reframe their demand as 'equal wages to workers of equal value' (p. 60).

In addition, since the 'equal pay' demand is generally taken to apply only to occupations containing both women and men, it excludes most women workers. 'Can one justify levelling up women's wages to men's in trades where they both work, while keeping them on an altogether lower scale in wholly feminine trades of equivalent difficulty?' (p. 65). And if all trades are to be covered, how are the comparative values of very different kinds of work to be measured?

The main obstacle to equal pay, Rathbone argues, is the assumption that, unlike women, male workers 'have families to keep'. Society has chosen to provide for future generations only 'by the indirect and extraordinarily clumsy method of financing the male parent and trusting to him somehow to see the thing through', leaving it to 'what it is fond of calling "blind economic forces" to bring it about that the wages of men shall be sufficient for the purposes of bringing up families', and trusting each man's 'goodwill' to ensure that his wages are shared appropriately with his wife and children (p. 61). In contrast, it is generally assumed that women's wages need only provide for their individual subsistence.

As a result, there is a deep conflict of interest between women workers and working-class home-makers: if women's entry into 'male' occupations causes men's wages to fall, it will lower the living standards of the men's families. Rathbone sees only one way to resolve this conflict and make both groups of women better off: the state must 'take upon itself the prime cost of rearing future generations' (p. 68). It is beyond the scope of her article, she says, to discuss specifics on how this might be done, but the wartime separation allowances provide a useful model. A system of state provision for families, she says in closing, would both remove the main cause of the wage gap and better ensure the well-being of wives and children, so that 'the services of women – not only in industry, but in the home – would be remunerated on their merits' (p. 68).

Rathbone elaborates these arguments in greater depth in *The Disinherited Family* (1924), in which 'ruthlessly logical argument, practical experience, sympathy for the problems of working class women and a sardonic feminist wit are combined into a devastating attack on male-dominated economic theory' (Macnicol, 1980, p. 21). This book deserves a prominent place in the feminist economics canon: it addresses many issues still central to feminist discussions, including remuneration of women's domestic labour, the notion of children as 'public goods', the intra-family allocation of consumption, psychic costs of economic dependence, the gender gap in wages, occupational segregation, and the case for basing wages on 'comparable worth'.

In the book's first section (which will be the focus here), Rathbone criticizes the 'equal pay' and 'living wage' demands and presents the case for family allowances. She begins by decrying the lack of attention paid, even by economists, to the family as an economic unit. In raising children, families perform 'the most essential of all the nation's businesses', yet economic writings as well as the popular imagination assume that caring for children 'concerns only individual parents and can be safely left to them' (1924, p. ix). Wives and children are widely viewed as mere 'dependants' of husbands, as if they were parasitic; yet dependence on husbands' earnings, far from being 'timeless', is 'less than a century old' in England and doesn't (yet) exist in many other societies (p. 1). One might think economists would be concerned about whether the wage is an adequate and efficient way to provide for families; but while a few, from Smith to Marshall, note that wages must enable workers' families to subsist, they rarely delve further. Indeed, Rathbone says, if the population consisted entirely of adult unmarried women and men, 'nearly the whole output of writers on economic theory during the past fifty years might remain as it was written, except for a paragraph or phrase here and there, and those unessential to the main argument' (p. 13).

The labour movement's call for a 'living wage' for male workers (generally taken to mean a minimum wage sufficient to provide subsistence for a man, his wife, and three children), Rathbone argues, is neither justified nor achievable. Data on family size suggest that at a given time, only 19 per cent of male workers have three or more dependent children (though the 10 per cent with more than three support 40 per cent of all children). Thus the 'living wage' would exceed the family subsistence needs of four-fifths of male workers (providing for millions of 'phantom' wives and children) while failing to meet those of the families responsible for 40 per cent of all children (pp. 16–20). As for practicability, a variety of studies suggest that achieving the 'living wage' for all male workers would require at least a doubling of national income (pp. 29–39). 'Any system of wages', Rathbone urges, 'must inevitably be either wasteful or socially disastrous so long as it is the only means of providing for families, yet does not adjust itself to their varying sizes' (p. 20). To set individual men's wages according to family size would clearly be unworkable, and would still leave wives and children wholly dependent on husbands' generosity. A far better solution would be to provide for families directly, leaving wages to be determined by workers' productivity independent of their family responsibilities.

Rathbone describes with considerable sympathy how working-class families suffer when wages are too low. It is usually women and children whose consumption is cut as families grow, since the male worker's health and strength must be preserved. The well-to-do people who blame the widespread poor health of the working class on the mothers' 'ignorance and carelessness' know nothing of the constraints such women face, and fail to recognize that

> if motherhood is a craft (as doubtless in a sense it is), it differs from every other craft known to man in that there is no money remuneration for the mother's task, no guarantee of her maintenance while she performs it and … no consequential relationship recognized by society between the quantity and quality of her product and the quantity and quality of the tools and materials which she has at her disposal. (p. 65)

Instead, what is available for a woman and her children is determined by 'her husband's occupational value to the community and his power of extracting that value from his employer' (ibid.) and by his goodwill.

As in her 1917 article, Rathbone argues that this system also creates obstacles to the achievement of equality between female and male workers. The continued exclusion of women from skilled trades despite the wartime demonstration of their competence is both unjust and inefficient: 'All the usual arguments in favour of free trade as against protection apply here. ... [T]he prosperity of the community will be best served if the productive capacities of its citizens are allowed to find their natural level' (pp. 114–15). Feminists' response to working women's problems, however, is highly problematic. 'Those who claim to speak for women usually couple together equal pay and equal opportunity, as though they were as inseparable as concave and convex' (p. 135). In reality, the woman worker's 'cheapness has been the one effective weapon she has possessed' to break down the employment barriers created by men's traditional domination, vested interests, better labour organization, and greater political influence (p. 136). Thus in the present system, equal pay and equal opportunity conflict with each other and with the need of working-class mothers for higher living standards for their families.

Men's opposition to opening their trades to women is not solely motivated by 'sheer sex prejudice' or selfishness. Male workers rightly fear that admitting more competitors will drive down wages, especially since women, having far less responsibility for supporting families, may settle for much lower pay, making their competition 'unfair'.

> *As things now are*, it is true that the presence of women in the same occupations with men is a menace to the wage standards of the men. *As things now are*, it is true that, on the whole, unemployment or low wages among men brings greater suffering and more social damage than unemployment and low wages among women; because although not all men have dependent wives and children, yet the vast majority of wives and children are dependent on men. (p. 115)

Feminists' demand for 'equal pay' (which, they argue, would prevent the undercutting of male wages) also neglects the various inherent disadvantages of women's labour to employers (as suggested in the 1917 article). Enforcing equal pay by occupation might in some cases (where there are too few qualified men) not preclude the employment of women. But in most cases it would strengthen the tendency toward occupational segregation, leaving women with even less equality of opportunity than they have at present: 'it will tend to be the men who disappear in the unskilled and the women in the skilled occupations' (p. 151).

Women workers will be allowed to compete freely with men, Rathbone argues, only if (1) wages can be set to provide equal pay for work of really equal value; and (2) opposition based on men's having 'families to keep' can be eliminated (ibid.).

The first condition is the less problematic one. Setting appropriate wages in mixed occupations would require measuring the disadvantages associated with women's shorter time in the labour force, restricted overtime, sometimes lower productivity, and so on. This would be difficult, but it could be done. Further, since the majority of women workers are in 'female' occupations, the claim to 'equal pay' would have to be extended to include 'occupations where the work of women is different from that of men but equivalent' (p. 155); here the measurement task would be much more complex but still not impossible.

The far greater obstacle is the second condition. Eliminating it would require a system of family allowances that provided adequately for family needs. This would remove employers' 'one valid excuse for paying women less than men' for equal work (p. 154) and thus clear the way for achieving equal pay and equal opportunity for women, while at the same time protecting the interests of the large majority of women and children who were not labour force participants.

The book's second section describes family allowance experiments in Britain and elsewhere, and then addresses additional arguments against family allowances, including fears that they will (1) bring about a reduction in the quantity or 'quality' of the population;[1] (2) weaken family relationships and reduce parents' incentives to work; (3) impose an excessive tax burden; and (4) adversely affect the distribution of income between labour and capital. Rathbone also discusses a rarely articulated but none the less powerful source of male resistance which she dubs the 'Turk complex'. Even a man with no intent to abuse his 'power of the purse' can derive satisfaction from knowing 'that his wife throughout her married life, his children till adolescence, would have nothing in the world but what he chose to give them' (p. 270). The good provider can congratulate himself on his generosity, and the selfish and tyrannical one can indulge his whims. This complex, she says, even 'befog[s] the minds of learned economists', so that 'when they touch on the subject of the family they commit themselves to statements of a vagueness, an ineptitude, a futility, of which they would be ashamed if they were discussing, say, the cost of rearing live-stock, or rationing an army' (p. 272).[2]

In the final chapter, Rathbone discusses forms a family allowance system might take, examining questions such as scope and finance (state vs industrial or occupational schemes and funding by taxes or worker contributions), whether payments should be flat-rate or graded by income or number of children, and whether payments should go to mothers or fathers. While she acknowledges that it may not be possible out of current national income to meet adequately all families' subsistence needs, she argues that allowances would clearly be a more efficient and equitable means toward this end than the 'living wage'.

Rathbone wrote two more books (1927, 1940) advocating allowances. She believed she understood why the struggle was such a long one: 'the economic dependency of the married woman', she wrote in 1934, 'is the last stronghold of those who, consciously or unconsciously, prefer women in subjection, and ... perhaps this is why the stronghold is proving so hard to force' (Rathbone, 1934, cited in Land, 1990, p. 121). She lived to see some degree of victory: the Family Allowances Act, which created a national system of (very modest) family allowances paid to mothers, was passed in 1945, less than a year before her death.

JANET A. SEIZ

Notes

1. Although Rathbone is careful here to avoid (or refute) the most offensive of eugenicists' arguments, she was not always above using such arguments herself. Her 1917 article, for instance, notes (p. 66) that since fertility rates are highest among the slum-dwelling poor, 'we are as a nation recruiting the national stock in increasing proportion from those who have sunk to the lowest strata because they are physically, mentally, or morally degenerate'. For more detail, including similarly problematic references to race and empire, see Macnicol (1980).
2. Rathbone attaches to this passage a footnote: 'See   . But I will leave the reader to supply his own references!'

Bibliography

Selected writings by Eleanor Rathbone

(1909), *How the Casual Labourer Lives: Report of the Liverpool Joint Research Committee on the Domestic Condition and Expenditure of the Families of Certain Liverpool Labourers*, Liverpool: Liverpool Women's Industrial Council.
(1913), *Report on the Condition of Widows under the Poor Law in Liverpool*, Liverpool: Liverpool Women's Industrial Council.
(1917), 'The remuneration of women's services', *Economic Journal*, **27**, March, 55–68.
(1920), 'The New South Wales scheme for the grading of wages according to family needs', *Economic Journal*, **30**, December, 550–53.
(1924), *The Disinherited Family: A Plea for the Endowment of the Family*, London: Edward Arnold & Co.
(1927), *The Ethics and Economics of Family Endowment: The Social Service Lecture, 1927*, London: Epworth Press.
(1934), 'Foreword' in E. Reiss, *Rights and Duties of Englishwomen*, Manchester: Sherratt and Hughes.
(1940), *The Case for Family Allowances*, Harmondsworth: Penguin Books.

Other sources and references

Alberti, Johanna (1996), *Eleanor Rathbone*, London: SAGE Publications.
Land, Hilary (1990), 'Eleanor Rathbone and the economy of the family', in Harold L. Smith (ed.), *British Feminism in the Twentieth Century*, Amherst, MA: University of Massachusetts Press.

Macnicol, John (1980), *The Movement for Family Allowances, 1918–45: A Study in Social Policy Development*, London: Heinemann.
Stocks, Mary D. (1949), *Eleanor Rathbone: A Biography*, London: Gollancz.

Margaret Gilpin Reid (1896–1991)

In 1980, Margaret Reid became the first woman designated Distinguished Fellow by the American Economics Association, and was honoured as:

> [One] of the pioneers in several areas of research on consumer and household behavior, each of which has now burgeoned into a major field of study of its own. For example, she did some of the earliest work on the concept and measurement of permanent income. Again, she was one of the first to see that one could systematically study the economics of the household use of time. And, of course, she has been a major contributor to the statistical analysis of the demand for housing. The empirical tradition at the University of Chicago owes much to Margaret Reid's example and teaching. She was a famous taskmaster in the art of applying critical thinking to data. Her reputation as a truly tireless researcher is well known and well deserved. Her warmth, her felicitous sense of humor are less widely known, but always cherished by those who worked with her. (*American Economic Review*, 1980)

This was a fitting tribute to a remarkable woman.

Margaret Reid was born in 1896 on a farm near Winnipeg, Canada. She trained as a schoolteacher and taught in rural schools until 1916, when she seized the opportunity to begin a five-year course of study in home economics at a new degree programme established at the Manitoba Agricultural College. Excelling in her academic work while serving in student government and winning awards in basketball, Reid graduated in 1921. Instead of returning to teaching in the high schools, as did most of her colleagues, Reid went on to create an academic life.

As a doctoral student working under the supervision of Hazel Kyrk (*q.v.*), Reid earned a Ph.D. in economics at the University of Chicago, submitting a dissertation entitled *The Economics of The Household* in 1931. After expansion and revision, this was published as *The Economics of Household Production* (1934). After lecturing in home economics at Connecticut College during the 1929 academic year, Reid went to Iowa State College where she lectured on consumption economics in the Departments of Economics and Home Economics along with Elizabeth Hoyt (*q.v.*), whom she met there.

Reid became a full professor of economics at Iowa State in 1940. In 1943–44, she worked as an economist in the Division of Statistical Standards in the Executive Office of the President, and between 1945 and 1948 she was head of the Family Economics Division of the Department of Agriculture.

Between 1948 and 1951, she was Professor of Economics at the University of Illinois at Urbana-Champaign. In 1951, she joined the University of Chicago as a full professor of economics. After her retirement in 1961, she continued working until the late 1980s on a book she would never finish on the relationship between health and income. Reid never married, and died in 1991 at the age of 96. She left much of her estate to the University of Chicago with the aim of encouraging the study of consumption economics by young economists.

Reid inspired several of her male colleagues at the University of Chicago, including Theodore Schultz, whom she first met when he arrived in Ames in 1930. Gary Becker's new home economics is, while distinct in many respects, an extension of work she conceptualized, although his 'Theory of the Allocation of Time' (1965) makes no mention of an intellectual debt (Reid, 1934, p. 160). Milton Friedman paid tribute to Reid's contributions to the development of the permanent income hypothesis:

> Miss Reid, with characteristic enthusiasm, persistence, and ingenuity, proceeded to put to a critical test the hypothesis that had been evolving out of the conversations [between Milton Friedman, Rose Friedman, Margaret Reid and Dorothy Brady]. When it seemed to be passing the test with flying colors, she pressed me to write up the underlying theory so that she could refer to it in a paper presenting her conclusions. (Friedman, 1957, p. ix)

Franco Modigliani cited Reid's contributions to the life cycle model in his 1985 Nobel lecture:

> [A] fundamental contribution was the highly imaginative analysis of Margaret Reid ('The relation of the within-group permanent component of income to the income elasticity of expenditure,' unpublished paper) which pointed to a totally different explanation for the association between the saving ratio and relative income, namely that consumption was controlled by normal or 'permanent,' rather than current, income. This contribution was an important source of inspiration, both for the Life Cycle and for the roughly contemporaneous Permanent Income Hypothesis (PIH) of Milton Friedman (1957). (Modigliani, 1985, p. 262)

But Margaret Reid contributed more to economics than inspiring a subsequent generation of Nobel Prize winners at the University of Chicago.

Reid's earliest work, along with that of Hazel Kyrk and Elizabeth Hoyt, was instrumental in changing the nature of home economics education in America, helping to bring about an increased focus on the economic well-being of families (Yi, 1996, p. 18). All three believed that home economists understood consumer issues better than other economists, and believed that consumer education would benefit the national economy while bettering the lives of ordinary families. In this spirit, Reid's *Consumers and the Market*

(1938) raised the consciousness of consumers about such issues as advertising, labelling, credit, legal protection and the responsibility of the state for ensuring consumer protection. By the time that Reid arrived back in Chicago in 1951, her focus on issues of primary concern to home economics had accommodated itself to mainstream economics and, from that date, her publications on consumer economics appear consistently in economics, rather than home economics, journals.

Reid's most original work was in the field of consumption economics, especially household production. She recognized, as early as her doctoral dissertation, that unless we understand housework as productive work with associated labour costs, we can understand neither the contribution women make to output, nor their labour market decisions. She recognized the conceptual difficulty of distinguishing between consumption and household production, arguing that although it was obvious that leisure activities and conspicuous consumption were not production, other activities such as playing with one's own children could be either consumption or production depending upon the utility one derives from the activity. She therefore chose to define household production as the provision of goods and services that could be substituted for by market-produced goods and services.

She considered four alternative methods of valuing such activities: opportunity cost, retail price, hired workers cost, and boarding service cost (Reid, 1934, pp. 160–69). All had some weaknesses. Opportunity cost measured the value of the potential earnings foregone because of time spent on household production. This method, Reid claimed, was particularly useful for understanding the labour market decisions of individual women, but somewhat limited as a measure of the economic contribution of unpaid household workers because it implied that the value of a service provided by an individual who could earn a great deal in a different field was much greater than an identical or even superior service provided by someone without such alternative earning opportunities. This was the method Becker later adopted in his 1965 'A Theory of the Allocation of Time', although he chose not to adopt Reid's distinction between household production and consumption and instead treated all unpaid activities identically as alternatives to market employment.

The retail price method, which Reid considered particularly useful as the market expands to provide a greater range of goods and services, attempts to estimate value-added by household production by subtracting the cost of purchased inputs from the prices of market substitutes for household-produced goods and services. This analysis was the foundation for *Food For People* (Reid, 1943, pp. 134–6).

The cost of hiring someone else to do the work typically provided by household producers is a third potential method of valuing household production. It carries with it the difficulty of ensuring that hired alternative workers provide the same quality of goods and services as a family member. The fourth alternative, the boarding service cost, suffers from the same limitation; it is unlikely that the goods and services provided in a boarding house are identical in quality to those provided by family members. Reid explained household production as a function of income, geographical differences, education, race, tastes and stages of the life cycle (Reid, 1943, pp. 93–117).

After her retirement, Reid devoted most of her time to a study of the relationship between income and health. The book, which included a detailed consideration of related variables such as education levels, income security, changes in health care techniques, changes in permanent income related to position in the life cycle, and so on, was never completed. Margaret Reid died after a long illness in 1991, leaving as a legacy to the profession her abiding commitment to consumption economics.

EVELYN L. FORGET

Bibliography

Selected writings by Margaret Gilpin Reid
(1929), 'An Estimate of the Number of Women Engaged in Homemaking' (with Hazel Kyrk), *Journal of Home Economics*, **21**, 424–6.
(1934), *The Economics of Household Production*, New York: John Wiley.
(1936), 'Variations in Retail Prices of Certain Branded Foods' (with E. Schickele), *Journal of Home Economics*, **28**, 691–5.
(1938), *Consumers and the Market*, New York: F. S. Crofts and Co.
(1939), 'The United States Housing Act of 1937', *Journal of Home Economics*, **29**, 687–736.
(1940), 'Marketing Rewritten from the Consumer's Point of View', *Journal of Marketing*, **4** (Part 2), 134–7.
(1940), 'Economics of Marketing and the Family', in Moses Jung (ed.), *Modern Marriage*, New York: F.S. Crofts and Company, pp. 99–139.
(1941), 'Farmers in a Changing World: The 1940 Year-Book of Agriculture (Review)', *Journal of Farm Economics*, **23**, 446–50.
(1942), 'Consumer–Business Relations', *Journal of Home Economics*, **34**, 655–8.
(1943), 'An Appraisal of the U.S. Bureau of Labor Statistics Cost of Living Index' (with Frederick Mills et al.), *Journal of the American Statistical Association*, **53**, 387–405.
(1943), 'Trends in the Work of Married Women', *Marriage and Family Living*, **5**(1), 80–83.
(1943), *Food For People*, New York: John Wiley.
(1943), 'The Standard of Living in 1860 (Review)', *American Economic Review*, **23**, 376–8.
(1944), 'Grade Labelling of Canned Food', *Journal of Home Economics*, **36**, 9–12.
(1945), 'Obstacles to Better Nutrition Despite the Large Supply of Food in Prospect', in T.W. Schultz (ed.), *Food for the World*, Chicago: University of Chicago Press.
(1947), 'Economic Contribution of Homemakers', *Annals of the American Academy of Political and Social Science*, May, 61–9.
(1948), 'Expanding Research in Family Consumption', *Journal of Home Economics*, **40**, 27–8.
(1950), 'The Income–Expenditure Patterns of Farm Families', presented at the Conference on Research in Income and Wealth, National Bureau of Economic Research.
(1950), 'The 1950 Census: What Will It Tell About Families?', *Journal of Home Economics*, **42**, 341–2.

(1951), 'The Role and Interest of the Consumer (discussion)', *American Economic Review*, **41**, 41–4.

(1952), 'Effect of Income Concept upon Expenditure Curves of Farm Families', *Studies in Income and Wealth*, **15**, New York: National Bureau of Economic Research.

(1953), 'Savings of Family Units in Consecutive Years', in Walter W. Heller et al. (eds), *Savings in the Modern Economy*, Minneapolis: University of Minnesota Press.

(1954), 'Inequality of Income Distribution (discussion)', *American Economic Review*, **44**, 270–78.

(1954), 'Distribution of Income and Consumption', in E.E. Hoyt (ed.), *American Income and Its Use*, New York: Harper, pp. 81–214.

(1955), 'Food, Liquor and Tobacco', in Frederik J. Dewhurst et al. (eds), *America's Needs and Resources*, New York: Twentieth Century Fund.

(1956), 'Survey of Ceylon's Consumer Finances', *American Economic Review*, **46**, 956–64.

(1956), 'Effect of Variability of Incomes on Level of Income Expenditure Curves of Farm Families' (with Marilyn Dunsing), *Review of Economics and Statistics*, February, 90–95.

(1957), 'Agriculture and the Health of the Nation – Economic Aspects', *Agricultural Institute Review*, September–October, 18–26.

(1958), 'What We Do and Do Not Know About Food Consumption of American Families', *Journal of Farm Economics*, December, 1301–11.

(1958), 'Effect of Varying Degrees of Transitory Income on Income Elasticity of Expenditures' (with Marilyn Dunsing), *Journal of the American Statistical Association*, June, 248–59.

(1959), 'Once More: Capital Formation in Residential Real Estate – Reply to Leo Grebler, David M. Blank and Louis Winnick', *Journal of Political Economy*, December, 619–26.

(1959), 'Families in a Changing Economy', *Journal of Home Economics*, September, 569–72.

(1959), 'Increase of Rent of Dwelling Units from 1940-1950', *Journal of the American Statistical Association*, June, 358–76.

(1962), *Housing and Income*, Chicago: University of Chicago Press.

(1962), 'Consumption, Saving and Windfall Gains', *American Economic Review*, **52**, 728–37.

(1963), 'Consumer Response to the Relative Price of Store Versus Delivered Milk', *Journal of Political Economy*, **71**, 182–6.

(1963), 'Income and Welfare in the United States (review)', *Journal of the American Statistical Association*, September, 824–9.

(1964), 'Statement: Misrepresentation of Poverty', *Hearings on the Economic Opportunity Act of 1964: Hearings*, Sel. Com. Poverty, Comm. (sen.), Lab. and Public Welfare, 88th Congress, 2nd session, pp. 291–4.

(1973), 'Comment: Education and Derived Demand for Children', *Journal of Political Economy*, **8**(2), Part II, 165–7.

(1974), 'Labor Force Participation, Income and Health', unpublished paper.

(1977), 'How New is the "New Home Economics"?', *Journal of Consumer Research*, **4**(3), 181–3.

(1979), 'Comments: The Household as Producer', in C. Hefferan (ed.), *The Household as Producer: A Look Beyond the Market*, Proceedings of a Workshop: American Home Economics Association.

(1985), 'Health, Age and Income of Populations: An Introduction and Preview', unpublished paper.

(n.d.), 'Relation of the Within-Group Transitory Component of Income to the Income Elasticity of Family Expenditures', unpublished paper.

Other sources and references

Becker, Gary S. (1965), 'A Theory of the Allocation of Time', *Economic Journal*, **75**, 493–517.

Becker, Gary S. (1976), *The Economic Approach to Human Behavior*, Chicago: University of Chicago Press.

Folbre, Nancy and Michèle Pujol (eds) (1996), *Feminist Economics: a special issue in honor of Margaret Reid*, **2**(3), Fall.

Forget, Evelyn L. (1996), 'Margaret Gilpin Reid: A Manitoba Home Economist Goes to Chicago', *Feminist Economics*, **2**(3), 1–16.
Friedman, Milton (1957), *A Theory of the Consumption Function*, Princeton: University of Princeton Press.
Modigliani, Franco (1985), *Life Cycle, Individual Thrift and the Wealth of Nations*, Stockholm: Nobel Foundation.
Yi, Yun-Ae (1996), 'Margaret G. Reid: Life and Achievements', *Feminist Economics*, **2**(3), 17–36.

Joan Robinson (1903–83)

Joan Robinson was born in 1903 to a well-educated and high-achieving upper-middle-class family in Surrey. Her family combined a characteristic seriousness and forthrightness in the pursuit of truth with a well-established history of dissent. Her mother Helen Marsh was the daughter of Jane Perceval Marsh, a nurse and the founder of the Alexandra Hospital for Children with Hip Disease, and Frederick Howard Marsh, Professor of Surgery and Master of Downing College, Cambridge. Her paternal grandfather, F.D. Maurice, was involved in fundamental controversies over religious questions and had been the author of philosophical works, sermons and a novel. He was involved in one of the first efforts in 1848 to establish higher education for women in England. Her father was a military historian, a biographer and a journalist. He was also the victim of the (in)famous Maurice debate in Parliament in 1918 which ended his military career. He instigated this debate by accusing Prime Minister Lloyd George of deceiving the country about the strength of the British army in an unprecedented open letter to *The Times*. Her uncle Edward Marsh was a scholar, supporter of the arts and a collector of sculpture and paintings under whose influence Joan Robinson developed an interest in art and became a collector herself.

Joan Violet Maurice's seriousness as a student made her eligible to attend the prestigious St Paul's School for Girls and to win the Gilchrist Scholarship to Girton College, Cambridge in 1921, at a time when it was unusual for a girl to attend the university even if she were from the upper classes. She finished her Economics Tripos Part I in 1924 and Part II in 1925 but did not earn her degree from Cambridge University until 1948 since the right to this degree was withheld from women until this year. The faculty of economics into which Joan Maurice entered as an undergraduate included A.C. Pigou, J.M. Keynes, G. Shove, D.H. Robertson, C. Guillebaud, W. Layton, and A. Robinson (Turner, 1989, pp. 227–8). The theoretical teaching in economics in Cambridge at this time was dominated by Marshall's ideas as interpreted and taught primarily by Pigou and Shove.

Joan Maurice married Austin Robinson in 1926 and lived in India with him where she became involved in support of the case of Indian States against the economic rights of the British government while he tutored the Maharaja of Gwailor. Austin Robinson recalled that 'Joan became involved with the foreign secretary and others in the presentation of the Indian case for the Indian States, and subsequently went back to London to help the foreign secretary present the case' (in Turner, 1989, p. 18). Her stay in India was her first-hand introduction to issues faced by underdeveloped countries, issues that she remained deeply concerned with in her writing and teaching. The Robinsons returned to Cambridge in 1929 to a life of active theoretical contemplation, writing, and teaching in the intense intellectual setting of the 'years of high theory'.

At the time of Joan Robinson's return to Cambridge the Economics Faculty also included Piero Sraffa and Richard Kahn, both of whom had a significant influence on the development of her thinking. Robinson credited Sraffa's 1926 article for beginning the revolution in value theory. Analysing the making of *Imperfect Competition*, Robinson quoted Sraffa:

> Business men, who regard themselves as being subject to competitive conditions, would consider absurd the assertion that the limit to their production is to be found in the internal conditions of production in their firm, which do not permit the production of a greater quantity without an increase in cost. The chief obstacle against which they have to contend when they want gradually to increase their production does not lie in the cost of production – which, indeed, generally favours them in that direction – but in the difficulty of selling the larger quantity of goods without reducing the price, or without having to face increased marketing expenses. (Sraffa, 1926, p. 543, quoted in Robinson, 1958, p. 239)

This was a considerable challenge to perfect competition and its elastic demand curve which implies that producers can sell all of their products without affecting the price and that each firm is simply constrained by its own internal conditions of production. For Sraffa, firms should be analysed as essentially monopolies which are constrained by falling demand rather than rising marginal costs.

True to the oral tradition in which she was raised and which was a strong part of the intellectual life at Cambridge, the origins of *Imperfect Competition* have been traced to a series of collaborations including the discussions in early 1930 between Joan Robinson, Richard Kahn and Austin Robinson of Charles Gifford's conceptualization of the marginal revenue curve (Turner, 1989, p. 25). This discussion and the broader context of Sraffa's 'pregnant suggestion that the whole theory of value should be treated in terms of monopoly analysis' were integrated by Robinson into the 'foundations built by Marshall and Pigou' and the teachings of Shove to solve, with the help of Kahn, what she saw as the problems in economic theory (Robinson, 1933, 1958, p. v).

One major problem facing perfect competition theory was its prediction that less efficient firms would close down as a result of a sustained fall in demand similar to the one that was being experienced in the late 1920s and 1930s. Under the assumption of perfect competition each firm faces a perfectly elastic demand curve, thus maximizing output where price (which in this case is equal to marginal revenue) is equal to marginal cost. In this case the representative firm is so small relative to the market that it can sell all that it produces at the prevailing price without affecting that price. In the depth of the economic slump of the 1930s Robinson found it harder and harder to accept the Marshallian orthodoxy à la Pigou that:

> Each firm continuously produces the amount of output of which the marginal costs is equal to price. There are internal economies of scale only up to a certain size, at which average cost (including normal profit) is at a minimum. When demand is such as to call forth output beyond this size from a particular firm, marginal cost, and therefore price, exceeds average costs. Super-normal profits call in fresh competition which brings down the market price and pushes back the output of the firm. When price is below average cost, some firms are driven out of business, and those that remain expand. Thus the optimum size of firm, with minimum average costs, is always tending to be established. (Robinson, 1933 [1969], pp. v–vi)

The real world, however, was made up mostly of imperfect markets with large firms and restricted entry. Moreover, most firms were operating below capacity at this time rather than closing down. In *Imperfect Competition* Robinson showed that large firms face downward-sloping demand curves and thus falling marginal revenue curves and maximize profits at the output level where marginal revenue is equal to marginal cost at a price above marginal cost. She had therefore found the explanation for firms operating below capacity during the Depression, rather than closing down as perfect competition theory had predicted.

Equilibrium in a perfectly competitive industry implies that the representative firm's horizontal demand curve is tangent to the minimum point on the U-shaped average cost curve and that therefore in equilibrium each firm is of optimum size. The equilibrium size of the imperfectly competitive firm, however, is not the optimum since the negatively sloped average revenue curve is necessarily tangent to a point above the minimum of the falling average cost curve. Thus perfect competition theory's claim that 'any plant that was working at all must be working up to capacity', was clearly inadequate in the conditions of the deep slump of the 1930s. For Robinson 'Imperfect competition came in to explain the fact, in the world around us, that more or less all plants were working part time' (Robinson, 1933 [1969], p. vi).

In the final two sections of *Imperfect Competition* Robinson analysed the issues of exploitation of labour and the welfare implications of monopolies. Interestingly, while quickly losing interest in the apparatus she had built for her analysis of imperfect competition, she remained interested throughout her life in the arguments she had made in these two sections. Thus, while dismissing her own approach as 'based on fudge', she was 'very well pleased to refute the orthodox theory of wages'. It is also interesting to note that while her analysis of the structure and mechanism of imperfect competition is quite similar to Edward Chamberlin's *The Theory of Monopolistic Competition* (despite Chamberlin's claims to the contrary), it is indeed these two sections that clearly distinguish her work and intentions from Chamberlin's.

In the section on exploitation she defined exploitation as

> a state of affairs in which the wage of a factor is less than the value of its marginal physical production ... and we have distinguished two types of exploitation, monopolistic exploitation which arises when the demand curve for the commodity is not perfectly elastic, and monopsonistic exploitation which arises when the supply curve of the factor is not perfectly elastic to the individual employer. (1933 [1969], pp. 310–11)

In perfectly competitive commodity markets, labour receives the value of its marginal product which is its marginal physical product multiplied by the price of the commodity. Under monopoly conditions, however, price is higher than the marginal revenue accruing to the firm and the workers receive their marginal physical product multiplied by this lower marginal revenue. In this case, then, monopolistic exploitation arises since 'earnings of the factors have been reduced in the ratio of marginal revenue to price'. Moreover, the 'extent to which the factors are exploited will depend upon the elasticity of demand for the commodities', and 'the smaller the elasticity of demand for the separate commodities the greater will be the degree of exploitation'. (Robinson, 1933 [1969], pp. 311–12). Finally, the 'smaller the number of firms producing any commodity the smaller will be the elasticity of demand for the output of any one of them' (p. 313).

In the case of exploitation arising as a result of a monopsonistic labour market rather than a monopolistic commodity market, Robinson observed that

> The amount of employment given by the monopsonist organization will be restricted to the amount at which the marginal cost of labour ... is equal to its demand price for each particular type of organisation. The wage will be equal to the supply price of labour, and this in each case, will be less than the value of the marginal physical product of labour. Thus exploitation will occur. (Robinson, 1933 [1969], pp. 294–5)

For Robinson a monopolist is also and necessarily a monopsonist, since 'when we say that a monopolist regulates his output by the marginal cost to him of the output, we have already implied that he is a monopsonist in respect of the factors of production which he uses' (ibid., p. 229).

In terms of the comparisons of the welfare implications of perfect competition versus monopoly, Robinson demonstrated that 'perfect competition not only in selling commodities, but in buying the factors of production, is advantageous to the factors, and that any increase in the size of the unit of control, by reducing the elasticity of supply of the factors to the employing agency, will increase the degree of exploitation' (ibid., p. 315). Next she examined the 'effect of monopoly upon the distribution of resources between various uses' (ibid.). Here she found that

> even when we abstract from the change in distribution of wealth brought about by the monopolist, it seems on the whole justifiable to say that the composition of the national dividend under monopoly will be even further from the ideal than it was under competition, since both will be subject to the maldistribution of resources due to unequal wealth, and the dividend under monopoly will be subject to a further maldistribution due to the different divergences of marginal revenue from price. (Ibid, p. 319)

Moreover, the monopolist will bring about a composition of national dividend different from that of perfect competition and this 'change in the composition of the national dividend brought about by the monopolist would then enhance and not mitigate the maldistribution of wealth' (ibid). She therefore concludes that 'monopoly may have an unfavourable effect upon the distribution of resources between different uses and must have an unfavourable effect upon the distribution of wealth between individuals' (ibid, p. 320).

The economic slump that had motivated the abandonment of perfect competition in favour of imperfect competition was ultimately responsible for Robinson's abandonment of imperfect competition itself as she became more and more involved in the Keynesian revolution. In 1930 she was one of a group of five economists known as the Circus who began to meet in order to discuss Keynes's ideas which led to the development of *The General Theory*. She interpreted the Keynesian revolution as the acknowledgement of the historical specificity of the capitalist free enterprise system and the consequent recognition that economic life in this system is the result of the decisions of individuals based on convention and guess-work. 'Since the future is essentially uncertain, strictly rational behavior is impossible; a great part of economic life is conducted on the basis of accepted conventions' (Robinson, 1973, p. 171). In this system the course which it is best for each individual to pursue in his own interests is rarely the same as the course best calculated to promote the interests of society as a whole, and if our economic system appears sometimes fantastic or even insane – as when foodstuffs are destroyed while men go hungry – we must remember that it is not surprising that the interaction of free individual decisions should lead so often to irrational, clumsy and bewildering results. (Robinson, 1937, p. 2)

It is clear, then, why Robinson considered the foundations of the revolution to be 'in the change from the conception of equilibrium to the conception of history; from the principles of rational choice to the problems of decisions based on guess-work or on convention' (Robinson, 1973, p. 170).

More specifically, Keynes saw the modern capitalist economy as a monetary economy, thus breaking down the dichotomy between the real and the monetary sectors. For Keynes a monetary economy is based on a specific set of rules and institutions which required a holistic analysis of production and money, with money playing a role beyond a simple medium of exchange as also the stock of wealth affecting production. Indeed, it is exactly the existence of money that creates the uncertainty inherent in this type of economy.

The existence of money is bound up with uncertainty, for interest earning assets would always be preferred to cash if there was no doubt about their future value. In this light, the nature of interest becomes clear. Keynes was able to resolve a deep-seated confusion in traditional teaching by emphasizing the distinction between the rate of interest, as the price of finance, and the rate of profit expected on an investment, ... – the marginal efficiency of capital. (Robinson, 1973, p. 171)

Keynes developed his liquidity preference theory in the context of the financial situation in England during World War I when British institutions were substituting liquid for illiquid assets, thus defeating the attempts of the Bank of England to increase reserves in order to maintain the prices of financial assets.

The concrete historical issue Keynes was concerned about was the causes and consequences of variations in employment. He showed that output depends on demand (defined as money expenditures versus need or desire) which itself is both determined by and determines income in the sense that 'One man's expenditure provides other men's incomes and one man's income is derived from other men's expenditure' (Robinson, 1937, p. 3). Individuals, however, only spend part of their income while also saving a portion. If this saving went directly to the demand for capital goods, then the fact that individuals save a portion of their income would not result in unemployment. 'But the demand for capital goods comes, not from saving, but from business concerns who use them in production, and no entrepreneur is inclined to acquire capital goods unless he can see a profit by doing so' (p. 4). Moreover, since the 'profitability of capital goods depends upon the demand for the consumption goods which they produce', individual saving in fact 'does nothing to encourage entrepreneurs to expect a greater profit from capital' (ibid.). If individual saving is higher than the demand of entrepreneurs for capital, then unemployment will result. The rate of investment, then, plays a crucial role in determining the level of employment in Keynesian theory and the rate of investment is in turn influenced by the rate of interest.

While employment can rise as a result of either an increase in investment or a decrease in private saving, a change in money wages will not lead to any significant change in employment. The increase in demand, and therefore the potential rise in employment, that will result from an increase in wages will actually be offset by the rise in the cost of production. A decrease in wages, on the other hand, while decreasing the cost of production, will also reduce demand with an ambiguous effect on employment. Therefore, 'any change in money wages will set up a number of complicated repercussions, which may lead to a change in employment, in one direction or the other, to some extent, but a change in money wages is not likely to lead to any great change in employment in either direction' (p. 41). Money wage rates, however, are considered in Keynesian theory as the primary determinant of the level of prices and are themselves the result of the relative bargaining power between workers and employers. Robinson referred to the recognition of the primary role of money wages in governing the level of prices in industrial economies as 'the other half of the Keynesian revolution' (Robinson, 1973, p. 173), and argued that this 'was a greater shock to notions of equilibrium even than the concept of effective demand governed by volatile expectations' (p. 174).

With the postwar boom Robinson's interest moved away from analysing the role of effective demand in the determination of output and employment to examining the conditions necessary for accumulation and growth. The decade of the 1950s, therefore, saw her intense interest in the causes and consequences of long-term development. This was the period of not only her initiation of the capital controversy with her famous 1953 article 'The Production Function and the Theory of Capital', but also her careful reconsideration of Marx in *On Re-reading Marx* (1953), as well as her *Accumulation of Capital* (1956). In 1962, the year before she turned 60, she also published her *Essays in the Theory of Economic Growth* and her *Economic Philosophy*.

The capital theory controversies can be identified as essentially controversies in value and distribution theory surrounding the origin and size of profit in the context of the relationship between the generation of surplus, accumulation, and income distribution in the capitalist economy. Robinson began the debate by asking what the unit of measurement of capital was, independent of value and distribution. More specifically, neoclassical theory's view of price as an index of scarcity implies that the rate of profit (the price of capital) will be high or low depending on the degree of scarcity of capital. Therefore, a measure of capital must exist before the rate of profit can be determined. Yet neoclassical theory does not have a measure of capital independent of the rate of profit.

The question of the measure and even more importantly the meaning of capital was a long-period question since in the short period there is a fixed and specific set of capital equipment in use and thus it is possible to talk of a specific quantity of capital and a specific rate of profit. But in the long period 'capital equipment changes in quantity and in design. So you come slap up to the question: what is the quantity of capital?' (Robinson, 1973, p. 261). What was particularly confusing for Robinson was the lack of distinction in the neoclassical production function between capital as the means of production and capital as the 'command over finance'. Moreover, for Robinson the concept of the marginal productivity of capital – the relative share of profits in distribution – itself would be incoherent if a meaningful quantity of capital could not be identified.

Robinson defined capital as a heterogeneous stock of produced means of production measured in terms of labour time. Given this definition of capital, the marginal product of capital has no relationship to the rate of profit and thus the return to the capitalist. For Robinson, then, the distribution of income in capitalist societies (that is, income from work versus income from property) is not determined by the same supply and demand principles that determine the price of commodities. Instead, the rate of profit is determined by the rate of technical progress and the nature of the accumulation process while the wage rate in Robinson's schema depends on the relative bargaining power of workers and capitalists and thus on exogenous institutional factors. In fact in Robinson's analysis the wage and profit rates, rather than being simply prices among many in a market economy, are the determinants of other prices.

Joan Robinson read Marx seriously after writing a critical review of John Strachey's *The Nature of Capitalist Crisis* in the June issue of the *Economic Journal* in 1936 and being criticized herself by Strachey for not having read *Capital* (Turner, 1989, p. 64). In *An Essay on Marxian Economics* she identified two distinctions between Marx and neoclassical economics on which she sympathized with Marx. The first was Marx's historical approach versus the a-historicism of orthodox theory. For Marx: the capitalist system 'is a passing phase' while for orthodox economists this system is 'part of the eternal order of Nature' (Robinson, 1942, p. 1). Secondly, 'orthodox economists argue in terms of a harmony of interests between various sections of the community, while Marx conceives of economic life in terms of a conflict of interests' (p. 1). Theoretically what was of particular interest to her in Marx was his long-period employment analysis, his emphasis on effective demand, and his schema of expanded reproduction. She rejected Marx's labour theory of value as a theory incapable of providing an analysis of prices and found his explanation of the falling rate of profit confused. She reserved, however, her most piercing critique not for Marx but for Marxists. She found Marxists' dogmatic and uncritical idolization of Marx as anathema to Marx's historical vision since for her a historical perspective requires the theorist to adapt the method and tools of analysis to changing circumstances.

In the *Accumulation of Capital* Robinson explored the dynamic long-run consequences of capital accumulation brought about by short-run investment. She started her analysis by carefully defining three economic states – the state of tranquillity where expectations are constantly fulfilled, the state of lucidity where there is perfect information, and the state of harmony where the rules of the game are perfectly understood and accepted by everyone. Then she pointed out that 'it is only necessary to describe these conditions to see how remote they are from the states in which actual economies dwell'. Despite the general confusion in the capitalist economy, however, 'certain principles of coherence are imbedded in its confusion' (Robinson, 1956, p. 60). In the *Accumulation of Capital*, then, Robinson attempted to discover and explore these 'principles of coherence' by developing models with increasing levels of complexity that analyse the relationship between the accumulation of capital and technical progress. At the simplest level she defined the golden age as 'when technical progress is neutral, and proceeding steadily, without any change in the time pattern of production, the competitive mechanism working freely, population growing at a steady rate and accumulation going on fast enough to supply productive capacity for all available labor, the rate of profit tends to be constant and the level of real wages to rise with output per man' (p. 99). An economic system in this mythical golden age faces no internal contradictions and, barring any political disturbances or changes in entrepreneurial expectations, accumulation will continue in this system at the same rate as in the past. More generally she concludes that the rate of growth and the rate of profit depend on technical progress and increases in productivity which themselves are determined by capital accumulation at appropriate rates.

In contrast to the neoclassical model in which investment and savings are simultaneously determined, investment on the demand side and savings on the supply side, Robinson's demand-side accumulation theory centred around the distributional effects of investment. Thus, while in the neoclassical approach investment cannot be determined independently of savings, for Robinson, investment decisions were not only independent from but were also logically prior to savings. In this Keynesian view, uncertain and often unstable expectations made investment the most volatile component of aggregate demand. Robinson compared the desired rate of accumulation (the growth path at which investment and savings decisions are in dynamic balance) with feasible growth. Through this comparison several other paths (ages) depicted the interaction of class relations, accumulation and technological change. In this model distribution is the long-run mechanism through which persistent discrepancy between investment and savings can be adjusted. This is so in the sense that when a persistent drive to invest and accumulate puts pressure on capacity utilization, the result is an inflationary spiral which culminates in a fall in real wages.

Joan Robinson elaborated further the discussion of *Accumulation of Capital* in her *Essays in the Theory of Economic Growth* (1963). Here she attempted to provide an analysis which was less difficult than that of *Accumulation of Capital* and 'to get economic analysis off the mud of static equilibrium theory' (1963, Preface, p. v). However, although looking at the concept of equilibrium with considerable discomfort and misgiving, at this stage she still considered it as having limited usefulness as a tool of analysis. Thus while admitting that the 'metaphor of equilibrium can be applied to economic affairs only with great caution' (Robinson, 1956, p. 57), she went on to devote a chapter to 'Meaning of Equilibrium', and ultimately to employ this method in her own analysis. In the chapter on the meaning of equilibrium she gave various definitions of equilibrium as states of tranquillity, corresponding to a condition of confident expectations; lucidity, implying full information and knowledge regarding market and technical conditions; and harmony, as the situation in which the rules of the game are understood, accepted, and followed in the economy. Though combining these definitions to describe an economy 'devoted to the production and consumption of wealth in a rational manner', she explained that

> It is only necessary to describe these conditions to see how remote they are from the states in which actual economies dwell. Capitalism, in particular, could never have come into existence in such conditions, for the divorce between work and property, which makes large-scale enterprise possible, entails conflict; and the rules of the game have been developed precisely to make accumulation and technical progress possible in conditions of uncertainty and imperfect knowledge. Yet too much disturbance, deception and conflict would break an economy to pieces. The persistence of capitalism till to-day is evidence that certain principles of coherence are imbedded in its confusion. (Robinson, 1956, p. 57)

The analysis of the relationship between the realized rate of profit and the realized rate of accumulation on the one hand and the planned rate of accumulation and expected profitability on the other is in a sense one of equilibrium since 'the accumulation that was induced by certain expectations in fact fulfils them so that in the absence of change in underlying conditions, the economy will tend to stay accumulation at this rate' (Harcourt, 1990, p. 53).

Joan Robinson's discomfort with using equilibrium analysis is more clearly demonstrated in her later more critical work as she became more and more explicitly interested in and involved with methodological questions in economics. The fundamental roots of this ultimate abandonment of equilibrium for history was her analysis of the difference between logical versus historical time. In her famous 1953–54 article 'The Production Function and the Theory of Capital', she distinguished between time and space and claimed that equilibrium analysis, while purporting to be able to work with time, actually applies a space metaphor in its place. Therefore, in a final departure from Marshallian methods of analysis and the neoclassical general equilibrium analysis, she levelled a serious attack against framing an analysis in terms of first existence and uniqueness and then local and global stability. For her, questions of local and global stability should never arise if the economy is already in equilibrium since being in equilibrium implies that the expectations have been and are being fulfilled. On the other hand, if the economy is out of equilibrium, then the questions of existence and uniqueness should not be raised since, given the present state of disequilibrium and the state of expectations of the future, there is no reason to believe that there exists a unique equilibrium in store for the future. Thus, while for the neoclassical economist the economy always tends towards an equilibrium position, for Robinson 'it is impossible for a system to *get into* a position of equilibrium, for the very nature of equilibrium is that the system is already in it, and has been in it for a certain length of past time' (Robinson, 1953, p. 120).

Thus as time goes on Robinson gets closer and closer to abandoning equilibrium analysis even as an analytical tool. Without equilibrium, and considering the long period as worthy of analysis, she adopts history in the sense that short-period analysis holds the current stock of capital, current distribution of income, and so on, as given; while long-period analysis has to delve into past history. Therefore, in 1974, in 'History versus Equilibrium' she objected to the neoclassical confusion between the comparison of different equilibrium positions and a historical analysis of the process of accumulation. In other words, a static analysis of the difference between stationary equilibria is not the same thing for her as a moving historical picture of the process of accumulation. Reliance on equilibrium not only does not permit any admission of uncertainty, it actually requires the existence of perfect foresight on the part of the producers and consumers. Thus not only is history ignored but, since individuals have perfect foresight, the future also does not pose a problem for equilibrium theory. Equilibrium models therefore operate in logical time and as such are closed and deterministic. While pretending to explain a sequence of events happening through time, equilibrium models are actually unable to explain the outcomes of historical and thus irreversible economic processes. For Robinson it is rather the out-of-equilibrium processes that should be the subjects of economic analysis and these require the analysis of open systems occurring in historical time, contingent on historical context and governed by historically specific structures, powers, tendencies and relations.

ZOHREH EMAMI

Bibliography

Selected writings by Joan Robinson

(1933), *Economics of Imperfect Competition*, London: Macmillan: 2nd edn, 1969.

(1936), 'Review of Strachey, *The Nature of Capitalistic Crisis*', *Economic Journal*, **46**, June, 298–302.

(1937), *Introduction to the Theory of Employment*, London: Macmillan; 2nd edn, 1969.

(1942), *An Essay on Marxian Economics*, London: Macmillan; 2nd edn, 1966.

(1953a), 'The Production Function and the Theory of Capital', in *Collected Economic Papers*, vol. II, Oxford: Basil Blackwell.

(1953b), *On Re-reading Marx*, Cambridge: Students' Bookshops Ltd.

(1956), *The Accumulation of Capital*, London: Macmillan.

(1958), 'Imperfect Competition Today', *Collected Economic Papers*, vol. II, Oxford: Basil Blackwell.

(1962), *Economic Philosophy*, London: Watts and Co.

(1963), *Essays in the Theory of Economic Growth*, London: Macmillan.

(1973), 'What Has Become of the Keynesian Revolution?', *Collected Economic Papers*, vol. V, Oxford: Basil Blackwell.

(1974), 'History versus Equilibrium', *Collected Economic Papers*, vol. V, Oxford: Basil Blackwell.

Other sources and references

Harcourt, G.C. (1990), 'On the Contributions of Joan Robinson and Piero Sraffa to Economic Theory', in Maxime Berg (ed.), *Political Economy in the Twentieth Century*, New York: Phillip Allan, pp. 35–67.

Turner, Marjorie S. (1989), *Joan Robinson and the Americans*, Armonk, NY and London: M.E. Sharpe.

Clémence-Auguste Royer (pseud. Opportune Fervent) (1830–1902)

The extraordinary productivity and range of this woman suggests that her 1902 letter on perpetual motion may have been the outline of an autobiography. The only specifically economic work for which she is responsible is the two-volume theory of taxation, published in 1862, but the *Journal des économistes* published a great deal of her work, including several articles on migration and a piece on the ill-fated French attempt to construct the Panama Canal.

Her major interests were clearly in the natural sciences, especially in evolutionary biology, and in anthropology. Royer's translation of Darwin's

Origin of Species was not uncontroversial (see Royer, 1873), nor could have been her ethnographic researches. Royer's magnum opus was *Natura rerum* (1900).

Royer merits a good deal more historical interest from economists than she has yet received.

EVELYN L. FORGET

Bibliography

Selected writings by Clémence-August Royer

(1859), *Introduction à la philosophie des femmes, cours donné à Lausanne. Leçon d'ouverture*, Lausanne: impr. A. Larpin.
(1872), 'Société d'éthnographie. Instructions ethnographiques. Projet de questionnaire concernant les caractères ethnographiques du système reproducteur chez les diverses races humaines et leur différence ou variations particulières' (et al.), *Actes de la Société d'éthnographie*.
(1861), *Ce que doit être une église nationale dans une république, par un esprit religieux*, Lausanne: impr. De J.-L. Borgeaud.
(1862) (tr.), *L'Origine des espèces*, by Charles Darwin. Paris.
(1862), *Théorie de l'impôt, ou la Dîme sociale*, 2 vols, Paris: Guillaumin.
(1864), *Les Jumeaux d'Hellas*, 2 vols, Paris: A. Lacroix, Verboeckhoven et Cie.
(1868), *Capitoli estratti dalla Teoria dell'imposta*. See Bibliotheca dell'economista, 2nd series. Trattati speciali. Vol. X. Torino.
(1869), *Origine de l'homme et des sociétés*, Paris: Guillaumin.
(1873), *Lettre à M. le président de l'Académie des sciences morales et politiques*, Magny-en-Vexin: impr. De O. Petit (on the subject of the criticisms of M. Charles Lévêque on Royer's translation of Darwin's *Origin of Species*).
(1874), *Lettre d'Opportune Fervent à Mgr. L'évêque d'Aire, à propos de son mandement*, Paris: E. Dentu.
(1874), 'Zoroastre, son époque et sa doctrine en rapport avec les migrations aryennes', *Philosophie positive*, March–April.
(1875), *Du Percement de l'isthme américain*, Paris: Guillaumin (extracted from *Journal des économistes – Société internationale d'obtention de concession du canal colombien*).
(1875), 'Le Feu chez les peuplades primitives', *Revue d'anthropologie*, no. 4.
(1875), 'Le Lac de Paris à l'époque quaternaire', *Bulletins de la Société d'anthropologie de Paris*, 5 August.
(1875), 'La Nation dans l'humanité et dans la série organique', *Journal des économistes*, November.
(1876), 'Les Ages préhistoriques: leurs divisions, leur succession, leurs transitions et leur durée', *Philosophie positive*.
(1876), 'Les phases sociales des nations', *Journal des économistes*, July.
(1876), 'Les Rites funéraires aux époques préhistoriques et leur origine', *Revue d'anthropologie*, no. 3.
(1877), *Le Lac de Paris, essai de géographie quaternaire*, Versailles: impr. De Cerf (extract from *Philosophie positive*).
(1877), *Deux hypothèses sur l'hérédité*, Paris: E. Leroux.
(1877), 'Du Groupement des peuples et de l'hégémonie universelle', *Journal des économistes*, May.
(1878), 'Causes internes de la dissolution des peuples', *Journal des économistes*, July.
(1878), 'Mémoire sur l'origine des Aryas et leurs migrations', *Compte rendu sténographique du Congrès international des sciences anthropologiques*, August. Published, Paris: Impr. Nationale, 1880.
(1879), 'De la nature du beau', *Philosophie positive*, January–February.

(1880), *Des Rapports des proportions du crâne avec celles du corps, et des caractères corrélatifs et évolutifs en taxonomie humaine*, Paris: Impr. Nationale (extracted from *Compte rendu sténographique du Congrès international des sciences anthropologiques*, August 1978).

(1881), *Le Bien et la loi morale: éthique et téléologie*, Paris: Guillaumin.

(1883), 'Attraction et gravitation d'après Newton', *Philosophie positive*.

(1886), 'La Vie politique de François Arago', *Revue internationale*.

(1892), *Recherches d'optique physiologique et physique*, Bruxelles: Impr. Veuve Monnom.

(1897), 'La Question religieuse', *L'Humanité nouvelle*.

(1900), *Natura rerum. La Constitution du monde, dynamique des atomes, nouveaux principes de philosophie naturelle*, Paris: Schleicher frères.

(1901), *Histoire du ciel*, Paris: Schleicher frères.

(1902), *Une lettre à M. Laisant*. Paris: C. Naud (on perpetual motion and heat, extracted from *L'Enseignement mathématique*, **4**(1), January.

Other sources and references

Fraisse, Geneviève (1985), *Clémence Royer: Philosophe et femme de sciences*, Paris: La Découverte.

Lise Salvas-Bronsard (1940–95)

Lise Salvas-Bronsard received her MA in economics in 1965, from Laval University in Quebec. After working for a year at the Bureau d'aménagement de l'est du Québec, she went to Belgium to study at the University of Louvain. She took her doctorate in economics at Louvain in 1972, with a dissertation published as *Les techniques quantitatives de la planification.* While a graduate student, she published in *Econometrica* with her dissertation adviser, Anton Barten (Barten and Salvas Bronsard, 1970). She began publishing as Lise Salvas Bronsard, latter adding a hyphen. From 1970 until her death in August 1995, Salvas-Bronsard taught econometrics and macroeconomics at the Université de Montréal, where her husband and frequent co-author, Camille Bronsard, was a colleague. They had two children.

In the words of her colleague Marcel Dagenais (1996),

> During her twenty-five years of teaching, Lise trained a large number of economists now practising in Canada and abroad. Her enthusiasm, availability and dedication, as well as the clarity of her econometric and macroeconomic teaching, were deeply appreciated by all her students. Her beneficial influence on students was magnified through the many pedagogical responsibilities she took on through those years.

Lise Salvas-Bronsard was president of the Société Canadienne de Science Économique in 1984–85 and an associate editor of *L'Actualité Économique*, to which she contributed (Salvas-Bronsard, 1985; Bronsard and Salvas-Bronsard, 1980, 1988b, 1992; Allard, Bronsard and Salvas-Bronsard, 1994; Forest, Gourieroux and Salvas-Bronsard, 1997). She was also a member of the executive council of the Canadian Economics Association and an associate editor of the *Canadian Journal of Economics*, in which she published in both French and English (Salvas-Bronsard, 1980; Salvas-Bronsard and Bastien, 1984; Bronsard and Salvas-Bronsard, 1988a). Internationally, she published in the *Journal of Econometrics*, *Journal of Applied Econometrics* and *European Economic Review*. She retained close contacts with economics in francophone Europe, as a visiting scholar at the Centre for Operational Research in Economics (CORE) at Louvain and at the Institut de la statistique et des études économiques (INSEE) in France, and as a member of the editorial boards of *Annales de l'INSEE*, *Études Internationales*, and *Recherches Économiques de Louvain* (see Dagenais, 1996).

This European connection was evident in the exposition of some of Maurice Allais's contributions (Bronsard and Salvas-Bronsard, 1988b) and in research influenced by Edmond Malinvaud's fixed-price approach to Keynesian unemployment equilibrium (Bronsard and Salvas-Bronsard 1987, 1992; Morisette and Salvas-Bronsard, 1993). As an econometrician, Lise Salvas-Bronsard worked primarily on the estimation of complete systems of demand equations. Studies on estimating systems of demand functions subject to rationing in goods markets and to quantity constraints in the labour market (Bronsard and Salvas-Bronsard, 1980, 1986) linked this econometric research to the research in disequilibrium macroeconomics. In keeping with the title of her dissertation, her theoretical and empirical research was motivated by a concern for the application of quantitative methods to economic policy.

Robert W. Dimand

Bibliography

Selected writings by Lise Salvas-Bronsard

(1970), 'Two Stage Least Squares Estimation with Shifts in the Structural Form' (with A.P. Barten), *Econometrica*, **48**, November: 938–41.

(1977), 'Estimating Demand Functions: The Converse Approach' (with D. Leblanc and Camille Bronsard), *European Economic Review*, **21**, August: 301–21.

(1980), 'Notes sur l'utilisation des variables duales en politique économique', *Canadian Journal of Economics*, **13**, February, 35–45.

(1980), 'Econometrie des fonctions de demande avec et sans rationnement' (with Camille Bronsard), *Économie Appliquée*, **33**: 767–85.

(1984), 'On Price Exogeneity in Complete Demand Systems' (with Camille Bronsard), *Journal of Econometrics*, **24**: 235–47.

(1984), 'A Note on the Estimation of Complete Demand Systems from Canadian Household Budget Data' (with Ernest Bastien), *Canadian Journal of Economics*, **17**, February: 48–61.

(1985), 'L'information *a priori* en econometrie', *L'Actualité Économique*, **61**, September: 287–98.

(1986), 'Commodity and Asset Demands with and without Quantity Constraints in the Labour Market' (with Camille Bronsard), *Journal of Applied Econometrics*, **1**: 185–208.

(1987), 'Growth, Desirability, Profitability, and Unemployment' (with Camille Bronsard), *Annales d'Économie et de Statistique*, **6–7**, April–September: 13–35.

(1988a), 'Anticipations rationnelles, fonctions d'anticipations et structure locale de Slutsky' (with Camille Bronsard), *Canadian Journal of Economics*, **21**, Novermber: 846–56.

(1988b), 'Sur trois contributions d'Allais' (with Camille Bronsard), *L'Actualité Économique*, **64**, December: 481–92.

(1993), 'Structural Unemployment and Disequilibrium' (with René Morisette), *European Economic Review*, **37**, August, 1251–8.

(1992), 'De la varieté de Patinkin–Malinvaud à l'optimum macroéconomique de court term' (with Camille Bronsard), *L'Actualité Économique*, **68**, March–June: 205–24.

(1994), 'Reflexion numérique sur le phenomenon des anticipations', *L'Actualité Économique* (with Marie Allard and Camille Bronsard), **70**, September.

(1995), 'Singular Demand Systems as an Instrument of Scientific Discovery' (with Camille Bronsard and P. Michel), *Tijdschrift voor Economie en Management*, October.

(1997), 'D'une analyse de variabilités à une modele d'investissement de firmes' (with Danielle Forest and Christian Gourieroux), *L'Actualité Économique*, **73**, March–June–September.

Other sources and references

Dagenais, Marcel (1996), 'Obituary: Lise Salvas-Bronsard 1940–1995', *Canadian Journal of Economics*, **29**, August: 757–9.

Koko (Takako) Sanpei (1903–78)

Koko (Takako) Sanpei was born in Fukushima in 1903. She graduated from Tokyo Woman's Christian University in 1928 and then studied in the Department of Economics at Waseda University from 1928 until 1931. In 1931, she became a researcher (an economic historian) in Takahashi Institute for Economic Research, which was run by the influential economic journalist, Kamekichi Takahashi. Sanpei left the Institute in 1939 and joined the Japan Institute of Labor Science in 1940. She did fieldwork in rural villages and factories with the aim of improving working conditions. After World War II, Sanpei became a member of the Employment Security Council at the Tokyo Prefectural Labor Office in 1948, and a member of the Minimum Wage Council at the Ministry of Labor in 1952. Sanpei not only published several scholarly books on Japanese economic history, but also a couple of enlightening books for working women to improve their social status in the male-dominated Japanese society.

Sanpei published her first book, *The Historical Development of the Cotton Spinning Industry in Japan*, in 1941. This was known as the first masterpiece produced by a Japanese woman in the field of Japanese economic history and gained a high reputation. Sanpei uncovered the fact that women were the main workforce in Japan's cotton-spinning industry, which was the key sector in Japan's early capitalist economy. In other words, Japanese women participated in the workforce in the process of modernization and played a large part in light industries, including the modern textile industry in Japan. In the book, Sanpei traced the historical development of the spinning industry from its birth until its mature stage in the 1930s. The spinning industry was regarded as the foremost industry of Japan until the 1950s. She started with the introduction of a modern spinning technique into Japan by the government during the country's take-off stage around 1870. She observed that the gradual spread of modern techniques and machines was accompanied by a fall in home manufacturing of cotton handicraft and the decline of hand looms in rural areas. The production of cotton in Japan decreased as imports from India increased.

Sanpei discussed in detail the fierce competition between Lancashire (England) and Japan over India's cotton cloth market, especially in the early 1930s. India was a huge market for every advanced country because it was a relatively rich country in Asia until the 1950s and the second most populous in the world. Before World War I, Japan mainly exported raw cotton yarns to avoid the rivalry with Lancashire's fine yarns. When the war broke out in Europe, Britain and other participating countries stopped their exports. Japan gained increasing access to India's market, increased the production of fine yarns, and began to export cotton cloth to India and other regions. After Japan abandoned the international gold standard and reduced the exchange rate of the yen in 1931, cotton textile fabrics became Japan's most important export in spite of a fierce tariff battle with South Africa, Britain and France. This was thanks to the successful rationalization of the industry and the cheapest labour in the world, as documented by Sanpei. India was importing more cotton textile fabrics from Japan than any other country before the British government's breaking of the Japan–India Treaty of Commerce in 1933.

In the 1930s, however, the Japanese government put its emphasis on heavy industries and the development of staple fibres such as rayon ahead of promotion of light industries. Japan started the war against China in 1937 and World War II began in Europe in 1939. The Japanese government passed a mobilization law in 1938 and began to control its economy. The production of cotton cloth was only allowed for export to earn foreign exchange. It could not be sold to meet domestic demand, because the government decided to allocate as many resources to heavy industry as possible in order to wage the war efficiently. The production of cotton goods in Japan shrank drastically in the late 1930s.

In 1944, Sanpei published *The Rise and Fall of Home Manufacturing and Industries in Japan*. She researched the historical changes in Japan's six major traditional industries from the pre-modern, closed-door era (1639–1854) to the modernization period. Each industry was seriously affected by the open-door policy after 1854. First, Sanpei traced the historical changes in the production of Japanese indigo blue. She estimated that indigo plants were introduced into Japan from China and India around the fifth century. Only the noble people and those living in cities like Kyoto and Edo (now Tokyo) demanded cotton cloth in indigo blue before the dye began to be sold in the market in the first half of the nineteenth century. In other words, ordinary people in rural areas including peasants (80 per cent of Japan's population) usually wore white cotton clothes. Sanpei pointed out that the production cost of indigo blue was higher than that of other agricultural products. After Japan opened its door to the rest of the world in 1854, the producers of Japanese indigo blue were thrown into confusion due to the imports of cheaper natural indigo blue from India and various chemical colours from other advanced countries. Yet thanks to the deregulation of domestic trade of indigo blue, as well as the increase in demand after the end of the feudal era, the production of Japanese indigo blue was increased until around 1900. Then it gradually decreased as the domestic production of chemical blue and other colours increased.

Second, the production of Japanese paper seemed to have begun around the seventh century. The city of Kyoto was the biggest consumer of paper in Japan until around 1600, because it was the centre for both Japanese noble culture and politics. After the capital was moved to Edo in the seventeenth century, more paper was produced and distributed in urban areas. After 1854, the government promoted the rapid introduction of European and American culture into Japan, and this was accompanied by the introduction of modern printing techniques and paper manufactured with the use of machines. This caused a massive import of western paper, which was more suitable for modern printing than Japanese paper. The Japanese government protected traditional Japanese paper manufacturing, whose production was labour-intensive. It did this through the use of simple tools such as supporting the export of Japanese paper and by requiring its use for textbooks at the elementary level. After it was decided to use western paper for these textbooks in 1903, the decline of Japanese paper manufacturing was unavoidable.

Third, the production of lacquer trees and sap was developed alongside rice production in rural areas. Sanpei estimated that it started around the seventh century and was developed with the production of lacquered ware and Buddhist lacquered ceremonial tools. During World War I, the increase in labour demand in modern industries promoted the division of labour in Japan's economy, marked the end of the rural self-sufficient economics, and reduced the production of lacquer sap. Lacquered handicrafts have been typically used for special occasions, but not for everyday use in Japan.

Fourth, the custom of tasting and drinking green tea was introduced into Japan with the advent of Buddhism around the thirteenth century. Its production was rapidly developed after 1854. Japanese tea was an important export good, especially to America, thanks to the Japanese government's promotion policy, although the US government sporadically restricted its import.

Fifth, the production of rapeseed oil was very important for lamplight in the pre-modern period. Soon after 1854, oil lamps were imported and rapeseed was replaced by paraffin oil.

Sixth, the home manufacturing of china and porcelain was developed where kaolin or china clay occurred. After 1854, china and porcelain became important export goods.

In 1961, Sanpei published *The History of Weaving in Japan*, a work 630 pages long including statistical data and a chronological table of the weaving and textile industry in Japan. This book includes topics on the development of weaving technology from hand looms to automated looms, the development of cloth and textile manufacturing, the development of management since the introduction of machines in the post-1854 era, and the working conditions in the textile industry. Sanpei covered the period from the fourth century through the 1950s, and found two major turning points in the history. The first was the period that followed the end of the isolationist policy in 1854. The second was during the 1930s when the Japanese government began to emphasize the rapid development of heavy industries ahead of light industries. The government controlled the Japanese economy (and reduced the production of consumer goods in general to the subsistence level) to wage wars first against China after 1937 and then against the Allies after 1941. As a result, Japan's textile industry drastically reduced its production and stopped its exports to the rest of the world. In comparing the conditions in Japan's textile industry before and after World War II, Sanpei found changes in raw materials from natural fibres to synthetic ones, and changes in the industrial relations from a feudalistic master–apprentice to a modern labour–management relationship.

Sanpei's *The History of Working Women* (1956) was one of the best books for enlightening women. It was published with the strong encouragement of Kikue and Hitoshi Yamakawa. She traced the process of women's participation in the labour force and their conditions before, during and after World War II. When Japan started the war against China in 1937 and restricted the production of cotton goods for private use, many women lost their jobs in the textile industry. At the same time, men were drafted and off to war. As a result, women had to fill the positions that had been occupied by men. Twenty per cent of the jobless women from the textile industry began to engage in farming in their home villages. The remaining 80 per cent plus many housewives were forced to work in the munitions factories and in heavy industry. This was work which had been believed to be impossible for women to engage in. None the less, these women were removed from their jobs after the war was concluded and men came back home. Sanpei (1956, p. 134) writes:

> The war brought women from the house to the workplace, and a new variety of workplace at that. This was a tremendous experience for women. The prejudice that women were neither good at nor able to work outside the home had been overcome. Women themselves learned from their experience that they can do many things that men can if only they get the relevant training and the doors are open to them. Women can become liberated by getting themselves jobs and earning a wage. This was the major turning point in the history of Japanese women. This was a precious experience at the price of war. [Author's translation]

AIKO IKEO

Bibliography

Selected writings by Koko Sanpei (all in Japanese)
(1941), *The Historical Development of the Cotton Spinning Industry in Japan*, Tokyo: Keio Shobo. Reprint, Tokyo: Iwasaki Shoten, 1947.
(1943), *A Record of a Village*, Tokyo: Keio Shobo.
(1944), *The Rise and Fall of Home Manufacturing and Industries in Japan*, Tokyo: Ito Shoten.
(1956), *The History of Working Women: History and Status Quo*, Tokyo: Nihon Hyoronshinsha.
(1958), *Autobiography: Half Life of a Woman*, Tokyo: San-ichi Shobo.
(1961), *The History of Weaving in Japan*, Tokyo: Yuzankaku.
(1962), *The History of Dyeing in Japan*, Tokyo: Shibundo.

Other sources and references
Ikeo, Aiko (1997), 'Three women economists in Japan', *Nihonbunka Kenkyusho Kiyo*, **79**.

Elizabeth Boody Schumpeter (1898–1953)

Romaine Elizabeth Boody was born on 16 August 1898 to Hulda Hokansen Boody and Maurice Boody in Lawrence, Massachusetts, where she lived with her family until the autumn of 1916 when she was admitted to Radcliffe College. There she majored in economics, pursuing a special interest in labour problems. In the spring of 1920, she was awarded the College's first *summa cum laude* AB degree in economics.

After a short period working as an assistant labour manager for a clothing firm in Rochester, New York, Elizabeth Boody returned to Radcliffe for graduate studies in economics. It was a time when academic economists were increasingly interested in quantitative data and statistical techniques. Accordingly, her graduate training included courses in statistics as well as economics. Having completed her MA, Elizabeth joined the Harvard University Committee on Economic Research, where she was particularly interested in the statistical analysis of time series data and their use in forecasting business cycles. She became the first woman to serve as a contributing editor of the *Review of Economic Statistics*, in which she published her first scholarly article (Boody, 1924). Thereafter, she resumed doctoral studies at Radcliffe, and spent 1926 and 1927 collecting English trade statistics for her thesis in London, where she was strongly influenced by Harold Laski and others at the London School of Economics.

Work on her thesis was delayed after her return to Boston on three accounts: her appointment as Assistant Professor of Economics at Radcliffe; her eight-year marriage to Maurice Firuski, 'a radical bookseller and teacher', whom she divorced in 1933 (Swedberg, 1991, p. 122); and the discovery that she was a severe diabetic. According to her friend Elizabeth Waterman Gilboy (*q.v.*), although Boody 'was eventually able to lead an almost normal life, there is little doubt that the impact of the disease made it more difficult for her to carry on professional activities' (Gilboy, 1960, p. vi). In March 1934, Elizabeth Boody submitted her thesis (Boody, 1934) which was accepted by Radcliffe on the advice of her two supervisors, A.P. Usher and J.A. Schumpeter.

In 1935 Elizabeth Boody was employed by the Bureau of International Research at Harvard and Radcliffe to investigate Japan's economic recovery from the Depression. Based on this work, Elizabeth subsequently published four articles (Schumpeter, 1938b, 1939a, 1939b, 1940b) and edited a book in which she authored three chapters as well as an introduction and conclusion (Schumpeter, 1940a). Her overall conclusion was that Japanese economic recovery had been 'probably more rapid and more extensive than in any other country in the world' (Schumpeter, 1939b, p. 214), and 'that Japan is much stronger economically than is commonly supposed and that the present war could not be stopped by economic action on the part of the United States within shall we say two years' (quoted in Swedberg, 1991, p. 142). These conclusions attracted the particular attention of J. Edgar Hoover, Director of the Federal Bureau of Investigation, who ordered a thorough investigation to determine if Elizabeth was a national security risk; nothing illegal was uncovered, but a file of more than three hundred pages was assembled (ibid., pp. 142–3).

During these same years, Elizabeth collaborated with Gilboy and others on another research project, also sponsored by the Bureau of International Research, investigating English trade statistics and business fluctuations in the eighteenth century. Based on this work, Elizabeth published an important article entitled 'English Prices and Public Finance, 1660–1822' (Schumpeter, 1938a). This presents annual price indexes for consumer goods from 1660 to 1822 and for producer goods from 1660 to 1800, and annual data on British public finance and debt from 1689 to 1816. This article and these data are now regarded as standard sources for economic historians of eighteenth-century Britain.

Joseph Schumpeter arrived at Harvard in 1932 and must have made Elizabeth Boody's acquaintance soon thereafter. They were certainly known to each other well before 1934 when he examined Elizabeth's thesis. By the summer of 1936, Schumpeter was regularly invited to Elizabeth's country house in Taconic, Connecticut. They married in New York on 16 August 1937.

For the first three years of her marriage to Joseph, Elizabeth carried on with her own research and writing. But increasingly thereafter she took on the role of making life pleasant (or at least less miserable) for Joseph. She assisted with the research behind his Lowell Lectures in 1941 and his enormously popular *Capitalism, Socialism and Democracy* published in 1942 (Swedberg, 1991, p. 143). More generally, according to her friend Gilboy, Elizabeth 'provided the agreeable and hospitable background which was essential to her husband'; her own work was 'deliberately put aside in order that she might devote more time to her husband's interests' (Gilboy, 1960, p. vi). Elizabeth herself claimed to have undertaken everything she could to accommodate Joseph's 'nerves and health' (quoted in Swedberg, 1991, p. 123). It was a role understood by his colleagues; Arthur Smithies, for example, wrote after Schumpeter's death: 'Without [Elizabeth's] companionship and single-minded devotion [Joseph] might well have sunk into a state of intolerable melancholy and loneliness' (Smithies, 1951, p. 15). 'I could not go on without her', Joseph wrote in his diary at the time of Elizabeth's surgery for breast cancer the autumn of 1948 (quoted in Swedberg, 1991, p. 190).

When Joseph Schumpeter died suddenly in January 1950, his *History of Economic Analysis*, upon which he had worked for much of the previous decade, took the form of incomplete manuscripts located in his Harvard office, Boston home, and Connecticut country house. Some of these were typed and corrected, others were typed but uncorrected, and yet others were merely in Schumpeter's difficult longhand. There was no table of contents, and no discernible preferred order of presentation. In a few cases there existed alternative versions of entries. And he had not completed an introduction or conclusion to his book. Elizabeth undertook to edit this mass of materials into a publishable manuscript, notwithstanding the financial cost which required her to sell their Boston home and despite her own ill health. It was a enormous task, completed just before her own death in 1953, and gratefully acknowledged in subsequent reviews of the published work (see, for example, Robbins, 1955).

In the last years of her life, Elizabeth Schumpeter returned to the problem of eighteenth-century English trade statistics and hoped to correct what she believed to be some unsatisfactory aspects of her 1934 thesis. In particular, her thesis had relied on data taken at five-year intervals, and these obviously were inadequate for assessing short-term fluctuations inherent in business cycles. Accordingly, in the late 1930s she had returned to London to gather annual data on some one hundred export commodities and fifty import commodities during the period 1697–1808. But this research had been put aside during the 1940s, as Elizabeth became increasingly occupied with Joseph Schumpeter's health and work.

In 1952, T.S. Ashton visited Elizabeth in Connecticut and found her planning to revive her research on eighteenth-century English trade statistics, after she had completed work on Joseph's *History*. But Elizabeth was obviously very ill and, before she died, Ashton assured her that her statistical tables would be published by the Clarendon Press. In 1960 Elizabeth's statistical tables appeared as *English Overseas Trade Statistics, 1697–1808*, with an introduction by T.S. Ashton. This remains today one of the sources most frequently cited by economic historians of the eighteenth century, who, 'freed from the burden of transcription and calculation, which bore heavily on their predecessors' are now 'able to bring fresh minds to the task of interpreting the trends and fluctuations [of trade in particular commodities] revealed by Mrs. Schumpeter's tables' (Ashton, 1960, p. 14).

Elizabeth Boody Schumpeter died of cancer at her home in Taconic, Connecticut, on 17 July 1953. Most of her papers are to be found in the Schlesinger Library at Radcliffe College, but some of her letters are in the Schumpeter Collection at the Harvard University Archives.

RICHARD A. LOBDELL

Bibliography

Selected writings by Elizabeth Boody Schumpeter

(1924), 'Cyclical Fluctuations in the Volume of Mining, 1913–1923', *Review of Economic Statistics*, **6**, 77–92.

(1934), 'Trade Statistics and Cycles in England, 1697–1825', unpublished Thesis, Radcliffe College.

(1938a), 'English Prices and Public Finance, 1660–1822', *Review of Economic Statistics*, **20**, 21–37.

(1938b), 'How Strong is Japan?', address to the Institute of Public Affairs, the University of Virginia, Charlottesville, Virginia.

(1939a), 'Is There an Open Door to China?', address sponsored by the Massachusetts League of Women Voters, Cambridge, Massachusetts.

(1939b), 'Recovery in Japan', Papers and Proceeding's of the Fifty-first Annual Meeting of the American Economic Association, *American Economic Review*, **29**, 214–16.

(1940a), *The Industrialization of Japan and Manchuko, 1930–1940: Population, Raw Materials and Industry*, New York: Macmillan.

(1940b), 'The Problem of Sanctions in the Far East', New York: Japan Institute.

(1950), 'Bibliography of the Writings of Joseph A. Schumpeter', *Quarterly Journal of Economics*, **64**, 373–84.

(1951), 'Forward' in Joseph A. Schumpeter, *Ten Great Economists from Marx to Keynes*, New York: Oxford University Press.

(1960), *English Overseas Trade Statistics*, Oxford: Clarendon Press.

Other sources and reference

Ashton, T.S. (1960), 'Introduction', in Schumpeter (1960), pp. 1–14.

Gilboy, Elizabeth Waterman (1960), 'Elizabeth Boody Schumpeter, 1898–1953', in Schumpeter (1960), pp. v–vii.

Robbins, Lionel (1955), 'Schumpeter's History of Economic Analysis', *Quarterly Journal of Economics*, **69**, 1–22.

Schumpeter, Joseph A. (1954), *History of Economic Analysis*, edited from manuscript by Elizabeth Boody Schumpeter, New York: Oxford University Press.

Smithies, Arthur (1951), 'Memorial: Joseph Alois Schumpeter, 1883–1950', *American Economic Review*, May. Reprinted in Seymour E. Harris (ed.) (1951), *Schumpeter; Social Scientist*, Cambridge, MA: Harvard University Press.

Swedberg, Richard (1991), *Schumpeter: A Biography*, Princeton, NJ: Princeton University Press.

Anna Jacobson Schwartz (b. 1915)

Anna Schwartz has contributed significantly to our understanding of the role of money in propagating and exacerbating business cycle disturbances. Schwartz's collaboration with Milton Friedman in the highly acclaimed money and business cycle project of the National Bureau of Economic Research (NBER) helped establish the modern quantity theory of money (or monetarism) as a dominant explanation for macroeconomic instability. Her contributions lie in the four related areas of monetary statistics, monetary history, monetary theory and policy, and international arrangements.

Born in New York City, she received a BA from Barnard College in 1934, an MA from Columbia in 1936, and a Ph.D. from Columbia in 1964. Most of

Schwartz's career has ben spent in active research. After a year at the US Department of Agriculture in 1936, she spent five years at Columbia University's Social Science Research Council. She joined the NBER in 1941, where she has remained ever since. In 1981–82, Schwartz served as Staff Director of the United States Gold Commission and was responsible for writing the Gold Commission Report.

Schwartz's early research was focused mainly on economic history and statistics. A collaboration with A.D. Gayer and W.W. Rostow from 1936 to 1941 produced a massive and important study of cycles and trends in the British economy during the Industrial Revolution, *The Growth and Fluctuation of the British Economy, 1790–1850*. The authors adopted NBER techniques to isolate cycles and trends in key time series of economic performance. Historical analysis was then interwoven with descriptive statistics to present an anatomy of the development of the British economy in this important period.

Schwartz collaborated with Milton Friedman on the NBER's money and business cycle project over a period of 30 years. This research resulted in three volumes: *A Monetary History of the United States, 1867–1960, Monetary Statistics of the United States*, and *Monetary Trends in the United States and the United Kingdom, 1875–1975*.

The theoretical background to the project is the modern quantity theory of money. Based on the interaction of a stable demand for money with an independently determined money supply, the key proposition of the modern quantity theory is that changes in the rate of monetary growth produce corresponding but lagged changes in the growth of nominal income. At first, changes in money growth lead to changes in real output, but in the long run they are fully reflected in changes in the price level. Long-run historical evidence for the modern quantity theory is provided in *A Monetary History*, short-run cyclical evidence in 'Money and Business Cycles', and long-run econometric evidence in *Monetary Trends*.

The overwhelming historical evidence gathered by Schwartz linking economic instability to erratic monetary behaviour, in turn a product of discretionary monetary policy, has convinced her of the desirability of stable money brought about through a constant money-growth rule. The evidence of particular interest to the student of cyclical phenomena is the banking panics in the USA between 1873 and 1933, especially from 1930 to 1933. Banking panics were a key ingredient in virtually every severe cyclical downturn and were critical in converting a serious but not unusual downturn beginning in 1929 into the 'Great Contraction'. According to Schwartz's research, each of the panics could have been allayed by timely and appropriate lender-of-last-resort intervention by the monetary authorities. Moreover, the likelihood of panics ever occurring would be remote in a stable monetary environment.

MICHAEL D. BORDO

Selected writings by Anna Jacobson Schwartz

(1953), *The Growth and Fluctuation of the British Economy, 1790–1850: An Historical, Statistical, and Theoretical Study of Britain's Economic Development* (with A.D. Gayer and W.W. Rostow), 2 vols, Oxford: Clarendon Press.

(1963), *A Monetary History of the United States, 1867–1960* (with M. Friedman), Princeton: Princeton University Press.

([1963]1987), 'Money and Business Cycles' (with M. Friedman), in A.J. Schwartz, *Money in Historical Perspective*, Chicago: University of Chicago Press, ch. 2.

(1970), *Monetary Statistics of the United States* (with M. Friedman), New York: Columbia University Press.

(1982), *Monetary Trends in the United States and the United Kingdom: Their Relations to Income, Prices and Interest Rates, 1867–1975* (with M. Friedman), Chicago: University of Chicago Press.

([1983]1987), 'The Importance of Stable Money: Theory and Evidence' (with M.D. Bordo), in A.J. Schwartz, *Money in Historical Perspective*, Chicago: University of Chicago Press, ch. 10.

([1986]1987), 'Real and Pseudo-Financial Crises', in *Money in Historical Perspective*, Chicago: Chicago University Press, ch. 11.

(1987), *Money in Historical Perspective*, Chicago: University of Chicago Press.

(1988), 'Financial Stability and the Federal Safety Net', in S. Haraf and R.M. Kushmeider (eds), *Restructuring Banking and Financial Services in America*, Washington: American Enterprise Institute, pp. 34–62.

Nancy L. Schwartz (1939–81)

Nancy Lou Schwartz began her academic career in 1964 at Carnegie-Mellon University's Graduate School of Industrial Administration. She was part of the wave of young faculty that Dick Cyert, the school's dean, hired between 1963 and 1965. They included Tren Dolbear, Mel Hinich, Bob Kaplan, Lester Lave, John Ledyard, Mike Lovell, Bob Lucas, Ken MacCrimmon, Tim McGuire, Dick Roll and Tom Sargent. By the time she left Carnegie-Mellon in 1970 for Northwestern University she was a tenured associate professor and had been awarded a Ford Foundation Faculty Research Fellowship.

Nancy had come to Carnegie-Mellon fresh out of Purdue University's fabled economics department. Ed Ames, Lance Davis, George Horwich, Chuck Howe, John Hughes, Jim Quirk, Stan Reiter, Nate Rosenberg, Rubin Saposnik and Vernon Smith were among her teachers, while Pat Henderschott, Tom Muench, Don Rice, Gene Silberberg and Hugo Sonnenschein were among her classmates. Her Ph.D. dissertation, supervised by Chuck Howe and Stan Reiter, dealt with the optimal scheduling of towboats and barges along a river with multiple branches. It involved a generalization of the standard transportation problem in which a single conveyance is employed to haul cargo to two complementary conveyances. The optimal coordination of the two conveyances adds a layer of computational complexity to this transportation problem. Nancy developed a simulation routine to approximate its optimal solution.

Nancy was a first-rate graduate student by all the conventional measures, such as grades, passing of qualifying examinations, and timely writing of a dissertation. The outstanding characteristic for which she was known to her teachers and classmates was an uncanny ability to spot logical flaws in an argument. And the manner in which she would point out the flaw was also special in that it always came in the way of a seemingly innocent clarifying question. Nancy was too shy and too polite to point out a flaw directly. However, in time, her instructors and classmates came to realize that when she claimed not to understand a step in an argument, typically a critical one, it meant almost certainly that it was wrong. All this, of course, created a certain amount of dread among the instructors when her hand went up to ask a question, and some merriment among her classmates.

When Nancy joined Northwestern's Graduate School of Management in 1970 as a full professor, after considerable coaxing by John Hughes and Stan Reiter, it was hardly the world-class institution it eventually came to be. The physical facilities were abysmal. There was no dedicated management school building on the Evanston campus, and the bulk of the master's programme teaching was on the Chicago campus. Office space consisted of wooden partitions in the old library building that did not reach the ceiling. The Department of Managerial Economics and Decision Sciences, MEDS, did not yet exist. Its predecessor was a combination of three departments: Managerial Economics, Quantitative Methods and Operations Management. There were a few bright young faculty already there, including Dave Baron, Rich Khilstrom, Mark Walker, Tony Camacho and Matt Tuite, but much remained to be done. And so Nancy became one of the three senior faculty members instrumental in building the department. She participated in the hiring of John Roberts, Mark Satterthwaite, Arik Tamir, Ted Groves, Bala Balanchandran, Roger Myerson, Ehud Kalai, Eitan Zemel, Bob Weber, Nancy Stokey, Paul Milgrom, Bengt Holmstrom, Yair Tauman and Dov Samet.

Nancy headed the department's Ph.D. programme and chaired the department from 1977 to 1979 and then became the director of the entire school's Ph.D. programme. She was involved in guiding numerous students through their Ph.D. dissertations, including Raffi Amit, Raymond DeBondt, Eitan Muller, Jennifer Reinganum and Esther Gal-Or. In addition to attending to these internal administrative responsibilities, Nancy served on the Council of the Institute of Management Sciences, on the editorial board of *American Economic Review*, and as an associate editor of *Econometrica*. In 1981 Don Jacobs appointed her the Morrison Professor of Managerial Economics and Decision Sciences. She was the first woman to hold a chaired professorship at the School of Management.

Nancy's research beyond her dissertation was focused on theoretical issues in industrial organization. The earliest was inspired by J.R. Hicks's theory of induced technical advance, in which he claimed that firms directed their research efforts toward reducing the employment of a relatively more expensive factor of production. This theory was criticized on two grounds. The first was that it ignored the relative costs of achieving each type of technical advance. The second was that it was more relative factor shares than relative factor prices that induced the direction of technical advance.

Nancy was involved in a series of papers that dealt with all these issues through the analysis of the behaviour of a firm seeking to maximize profits over time by choosing both the levels of its factors of production and the focus of its research efforts, taking all costs into account. The analyses suggested that both relative factor prices and relative factor shares played a role in inducing the direction of technical advance. In the long run, technical advance tended toward neutrality; no one factor was targeted for reduction relative to the others.

Nancy's next major research project dealt with how rapidly firms developed new products or methods of production in the presence of rivals. This work eventually led to the theory of patent races. It was inspired by Yoram Barzel's claim that the quest to be the first to innovate led firms to over-invest in research and development from society's standpoint. This claim appeared to challenge the conventional wisdom that firms tended to under-invest in research and development from society's standpoint because they could not capture all the benefits. Barzel's result was driven by the assumption that the winner of the race to innovate would capture all the realizable profits and that the quest to edge out rivals would force the firm to accelerate development to the zero profit point. This would lead to higher than optimal investment in research and development in which the marginal cost of advancing development only slightly equals the marginal benefit of earlier access to the profit stream. Barzel supposed that each innovator knew who the rivals were. The critical feature of the work in which Nancy was involved was the opposite assumption, namely, that the innovator did not know at all who the rivals were. However, the innovator knew that they were out there and took account of them through the hazard rate, the conditional probability of a rival's introduction of a similar invention at the next instant of time given that it had not yet been introduced. In this model the innovating firm faced a sea of anonymous rivals, any one of whom might introduce a similar invention in the very next instant of time. The large number of rivals assumption meant that the individual firm's level of expenditure on research and development did not elicit an expenditure reaction from its unknown rivals, to whom it, too, was unknown. Rival imitation was allowed in this model and it was shown that when it was immediate, investment in research and development would cease in conformity with the conventional wisdom. Moreover, increasing intensity of competition in the form of a higher hazard rate could not force a firm to accelerate development of its innovation to the break-even point, as the decline in the probability of winning would cause firms to drop out of the race short of it. Thus the model allowed for increases in a firm's research and development expenditure with increasing intensity of rivalry up to a certain point and a decline thereafter, a feature consistent with empirical findings that industries in which the intensity of competition is intermediate between monopoly and perfect competition are the ones with the most research intensity. It was precisely this feature of the model that led to Loury's first formal patent race paper, in which the hazard rate became endogenously determined by Cournot-type interactions among the rival firms through their research expenditures. Lee and Wilde's paper followed, then the Dasgupta and Stiglitz papers, and then Reinganum's fully dynamic patent race model.

The works on the timing of innovations in the presence of rivals naturally led to the question of how a successful innovator might adopt a price strategy to retard rival entry and to the next major project in which Nancy was involved. The major theories of entry retardation at that time were the limit pricing ones proposed by Bain and by Sylos-Labini, as synthesized by Modigliani. The crux of this theory is that the incumbent firm sets a price and supplies the corresponding quantity demanded so that the residual demand function faced by the potential entrant just allows him or her to realize no more than a normal profit. Implementation of this limit pricing strategy requires that the incumbent know the average cost function of each potential entrant. The project in which Nancy participated involved dropping this assumption and replacing it with the supposition that the conditional probability of entry given that no entry had yet occurred, the hazard rate, was a monotonically increasing function of the incumbent's current market price. This assumption led to the formulation of the incumbent firm's problem as an optimal control problem with the probability of entry on or before the present time the state variable and the current price the control variable. The firm's objective was to maximize the present value of expected profits, where its pre-entry profits are at least as high as its post-entry profits, which are determined by whatever market structure emerges after entry. It was implicitly assumed that by lowering its price, the firm sought to divert a potential entrant to entry into another industry. The analysis of this model disclosed that the incumbent firm optimally chose a price below its immediate monopoly price but above the price it would take to deter entry altogether. In other words, it is optimal for the firm to delay entry rather than postpone it indefinitely. It is in this sense that the incumbent firm engages in limit pricing.

This model of limit pricing under uncertainty eventually led to Esther Gal-Or's dissertation and the Milgrom–Roberts paper in which the incumbent firm's current price is used to signal a potential entrant about the type of competitor he or she will face after entry. Its original vision as a game among incumbents seeking to divert entrants away from themselves was realized in Bagwell's work.

Beyond these major projects, Nancy was involved in a number of less prolonged excursions. There was a widely cited paper on the optimal maintenance and sale date of a machine subject to an uncertain time of failure. There were analyses of a growth model involving an essential exhaustible resource and endogenous development of a technology to replace it; of whether competition leads firms to produce more durable products; of the effect of health maintenance organizations on the delivery of care services; of the consequences for a firm seeking to maximize profits over time by producing a durable good by means of labour and capital, of the irreversibility of capital investment; of a firm's adoption of new technology when it anticipates further improvements in technology; of the consequences of technical advance for international trade; of the consistency of conjectural variations; and of the role of exclusion costs on the provision of public goods.

Apart from the individual articles, Nancy co-authored two books: *Dynamic Optimization: Calculus of Variations and Optimal Control in Economics and Management Science* and *Market Structure and Innovation*. The first was the outgrowth of an intense use of techniques for optimization over time in many of the analyses she conducted. The focus of the book was to expose to the student the tricks that were employed in the application of these techniques rather than provide a rigorous treatment of the theory behind them. The second was the culmination of all the work in technical advance in which Nancy had been involved. It was the direct result of a survey article on the same subject that she had co-authored.

Nancy led a full and successful academic life and interacted with many of the best economists in her cohort, the older generation of economists who were her teachers, and the younger generation that she taught or hired. She provided a role model for younger women who contemplated becoming academic economists.

MORTON I. KAMIEN

Bibliography

Selected writings by Nancy L. Schwartz
(1966), 'Asymmetry between Bribes and Charges', with M.I. Kamien and F.T. Dolbear, *Water Resources Research*, 147–57.
(1966), 'Asymmetry between Bribes and Charges: Reply', with M.I. Kamien and F.T. Dolbear, *Water Resources Research*, 856–7.
(1968), 'Optimal "Induced" Technical Change' with M.I. Kamien, *Econometrica*, January, 1–17.
(1968), 'Discrete Programs for Moving Known Cargoes from Origins to Destination on Time at Minimum Bargeline Fleet Cost', *Transportation Science*, May, 134–45.

(1969), 'Determination of Equipment Requirements for the Bargeline: Analysis and Computer Simulation', Charles W. Howe (ed.), *Inland Waterway Transportation: Studies in Public and Private Management and Investment Decisions*, Washington: Resources for the Future, Inc., Johns Hopkins Press, 1969, ch. 4, pp. 50–72.

(1969), 'Induced Factor Augmenting Technical Progress from a Macroeconomic Viewpoint', with M.I. Kamien, *Econometrica*, October, 668–84.

(1969), 'A Naive View of the Indicator Problem' with M.I. Kamien in Karl Brunner (ed.), *Targets and Indicators of Monetary Policy*, Chandler Publishing Company.

(1970), 'Market Structure, Elasticity of Demand and Incentive to Invent', with M.I. Kamien, *Journal of Law and Economics*, April, 241–52.

(1970), 'Factor Augmenting Technical Advance in a Two Sector Economy', with N.C. Miller, *Oxford Economic Papers*, November, 338–56.

(1970), 'Revelation of Preference for Public Good with Imperfect Exclusion', with M.I. Kamien, *Public Choice*, Fall, 19–30.

(1971), 'Expenditure Patterns for Risky R and D Projects', with M.I. Kamien, *Journal of Applied Probability*, March, 60–73.

(1971), 'Optimal Maintenance and Sale Age for a Machine Subject to Failure', with M.I. Kamien, *Management Science*, April, B495–504.

(1971), 'Limit Pricing and Uncertain Entry', with M.I. Kamien, *Econometrica*, May, 441–54.

(1971), 'Sufficient Conditions in Optimal Control Theory', with M.I. Kamien, *Journal of Economic Theory*, June, 207–14.

(1971), 'Theory of the Firm with Induced Technical Change', with M.I. Kamien, *Metroeconomica*, September–December, 233–56.

(1972), 'Timing of Innovations Under Rivalry', with M.I. Kamien, *Econometrica*, January, 43–60.

(1972), 'Market Structure, Rivals' Response and the Firm's Rate of Product Improvement', with M.I. Kamien, *Journal of Industrial Economics*, April, 159–72.

(1972), 'A Direct Approach to Choice Under Uncertainty', with M.I. Kamien, *Management Science*, April, B470–77.

(1972), 'Exclusion Costs and the Provision of Public Goods', with M.I. Kamien, *Public Choice*, Spring, 43–55.

(1972), 'Some Economic Consequences of Anticipating Technical Advance', with M.I. Kamien, *Western Economic Journal*, June, 123–38.

(1972), 'Uncertain Entry and Excess Capacity', with M.I. Kamien, *American Economic Review*, December, 918–27.

(1973), 'Exclusion, Externalities, and Public Goods', with M.I. Kamien and D.J. Roberts, *Journal of Public Economics*, August, 217–30.

(1973), 'Payment Plans and the Efficient Delivery of Health Care Services', with M.I. Kamien, *Journal of Risk and Insurance*, September 1973, 427–36.

(1974), 'Risky R&D with Rivalry', with M.I. Kamien, *Annals of Economic and Social Measurement*, January, 267–77.

(1974), 'Patent Life and R&D Rivalry', with M.I. Kamien, *American Economic Review*, March, 183–7.

(1974), 'Product Durability Under Monopoly and Competition', with M.I. Kamien, *Econometrica*, March, 289–391.

(1975), 'Cournot Oligopoly and Uncertain Entry', with M.I. Kamien, *Review of Economic Studies*, January, 125–31.

(1975), 'Market Structure and Innovation: A Survey', with M.I. Kamien, *Journal of Economic Literature*, March, 1–37.

(1976), 'On the Degree of Rivalry for Maximum Innovative Activity', with M.I. Kamien, *Quarterly Journal of Economics*, May, 245–60.

(1977), 'Technology: More for Less?', with M.I. Kamien, in Sidney Weintraub (ed.), *Modern Economic Thought*, University of Pennsylvania Press, 501–15.

(1977), 'A Note on Resource Usage and Market Structure', with M.I. Kamien, *Journal of Economic Theory*, August, 394–7.

(1977), 'Disaggregated Intertemporal Models with an Exhaustible Resource and Technical Advance', with M.I. Kamien, *Journal of Environmental Economics and Management*, 271–88.

(1977), 'Optimal Capital Accumulation and Durable Goods Production', with M.I. Kamien, *Zeitschrift für Nationalokonomie*, **37**, 25–43.

(1978), 'Optimal Exhaustible Resource Depletion with Endogenous Technical Change', with M.I. Kamien, *Review of Economic Studies*, February, 179–96.

(1978), 'Potential Rivalry, Monopoly Profits, and the Pace of Inventive Activity', with M.I. Kamien, *Review of Economic Studies*, October, 547–57.

(1978), 'Self-Financing of an R&D Project', with M.I. Kamien, *American Economic Review*, June, 252–61.

(1980), 'A Generalized Hazard Rate', with M.I. Kamien, *Economics Letters*, Vol. 5, 245–9.

(1981), *Dynamic Optimization*, with M.I. Kamien, Amsterdam: Elsevier–North Holland; 2nd edn 1991.

(1981), *Market Structure and Innovation*, with M.I. Kamien, Cambridge: Cambridge University Press; Spanish edition, 1988.

(1981), 'Technical Change Inclinations of a Resource Monopolist', with M.I. Kamien, in G. Horwich and J.P. Quirk (eds), *Essays in Contemporary Fields of Economics*, Purdue University Press, pp. 41–53.

(1982), 'Role of Common Property Resources in Optimal Planning Models with Exhaustible Resources', in V.K. Smith and J.V. Krutilla (eds), *Explorations in Natural Resource Economics*, Resources for the Future.

(1983), 'Conjectural Variations', with M.I. Kamien, *Canadian Journal of Economics*, 191–211.

Other sources and references

Bagwell, K. (1992), 'A Model of Competitive Limit Pricing', *Journal of Economics and Management*, 585–606.

Barzel, Y. (1968), 'Optimal Timing of Innovations', *Review of Economics and Statistics*, 348–55.

Dasgupta, P. and J. Stiglitz (1980), 'Industrial Structure and the Nature of Innovative Activity', *Economics Journal*, 266–93.

Dasgupta, P. and J. Stiglitz (1980), 'Uncertainty, Industrial Structure and the Speed of R&D', *Bell Journal of Economics*, 1–28.

Gal-Or, E. (1980), 'Limit Price Entry Prevention and Its Impact on Potential Investors – A Game Theoretic Approach', Ph.D. dissertation, Northwestern University.

Hicks, J.R. (1932), *The Theory of Wages*, London: Macmillan.

Lee, T. and L. Wilde (1980), 'Market Structure and Innovation: A Reformulation', *Quarterly Journal of Economics*, 429–36.

Loury, G.C. (1979), 'Market Structure and Innovation', *Quarterly Journal of Economics*, 395–410.

Milgrom, P. and J. Roberts (1982), 'Limit Pricing and Entry Under Incomplete Information: An Equilibrium Analysis', *Econometrica*, 443–60.

Modigliani, F. (1958), New Developments on the Oligopoly Front', *Journal of Political Economy*, 215–32.

Reinganum, J. (1981), 'Dynamic Games of Innovation', *Journal of Economic Theory*, 21–41.

Reinganum, J. (1982), 'A Dynamic Game of R&D: Patent Protection and Competitive Behavior', *Econometrica*, 671–88.

Hannah Robie Sewall (1861–1926)

Hannah Robie Sewall was one of the earliest American women to earn a Ph.D. in economics. Her enduring contribution to the discipline is her monograph, *The Theory of Value Before Adam Smith*, considered a classic in the field and the standard reference on pre-Smithian value theory.

Sewall was born in Boston in 1861 to Mary Vashon Wright and Joseph S. Sewall. She was raised in St Paul, Minnesota and educated at the newly founded University of Minnesota, earning her BA in 1884, her MA in 1887, and her Ph.D. in 1898 at the age of 37. After earning her master's she was a Fellow in History at Bryn Mawr from 1888 until 1890. She returned to the University of Minnesota by 1892 when she was appointed Assistant in Political Science, a title she retained until 1902. (Economics at that time was part of the Department of Political Science.) In addition to her teaching responsibilities at Minnesota, Sewall served as assistant to economist William Watts Folwell, the president of the University. She was also an active member of the Association of Collegiate Alumnae, a group founded by Marion Talbot at the University of Chicago to expand opportunities for women college graduates, and was instrumental in establishing a consumers' league under its auspices.

In 1901 the American Economic Association published her dissertation entitled *The Theory of Value Before Adam Smith*. It was reissued in 1968 and again in 1971 in the Reprints of Economic Classics series of the Adam Smith Library. After almost a century, it remains known among historians of economic thought as 'an excellent survey' (Hutchison, 1988, p. 385) and 'still the standard reference work on the subject' (Blaug, 1985, p. 35).

The monograph traces the evolution of the theory of value from its beginnings in Aristotle through Sir James Steuart and shows how its development was linked to contemporary economic conditions. Its publication filled a 'long felt want', according to reviewer Wesley C. Mitchell (1902, p. 144), because of its comprehensiveness and because it made the ideas of nascent economic writers before Adam Smith accessible to students who did not read Italian, German and French.

Reviewing the writings on value before the sixteenth century, Sewall, in the first chapter, argues that the incipient attempts to understand value by ancient Greeks and Romans were halted by the plunge of Europe into the primitive economy of the Middle Ages. Not until a money and trading economy was again thriving by the eleventh century would philosophers return to questions of value. Christian theologians, the main thinkers of the time, approached the issue seeking to determine principles of justice in buying and selling that would guide human conduct. Sewall recounts the development of the concept of just price in the writings of St Thomas Aquinas, John Nider of Swabia, St Anthony of Florence and St Bernard of Siena.

Chapter 2 is devoted to the writers of the sixteenth and seventeenth centuries who gradually turned away from considering value as an ethical issue (what value should be) and began to understand value as an economic problem (what value is). Sewall characterizes the work of ethical jurists Grotius and Pufendorf as the bridge between Aquinas and the theologians and the new empiricists including Davansati, Montanari and Barbon. She shows how the increasingly complex economies of the time coupled with current theories of mercantilism influenced these writers to replace the idea of true value with the idea of value-in-exchange; goods came to be seen to have value in relation to each other, not absolutely.

In chapter 3 Sewall deals with Petty, Locke and Steuart, and the physiocrats Quesnay, Condillac, Turgot and Galvani. She shows how their writings advanced a conception of exchange value as well as a subjective theory of value. She concludes that while these early efforts to understand value were not completely satisfactory, significant progress was made. Significant enough, she argues, 'that there is scarcely any proposition of importance in the modern discussion of value which was not either stated or suggested ... before Adam Smith' (p. 124).

In the same year that her dissertation was published, economist Carroll D. Wright, the first commissioner of the US Bureau of Labor, appointed Sewall as special agent to investigate child labour. For her report published by the Bureau in 1904, she gathered data from 215 businesses in 13 states on the demographic, wage and employment conditions of working children. Her report also included a compendium of laws relating to child labour enacted in the USA and in force by the year 1903.

Little is known about the remainder of her life. In 1914, when she was 53, *Women's Who's Who* (Leonard, 1914) described her as an economist, a member of the Just Government League of Maryland and the National Child Labor Committee, an influential group of academics and business, church and government leaders dedicated to reform of child labour practices in the USA. Sewall's chief activity was listed as keeping bees. Sometime after 1914, she married the University of California geneticist John Bellings. She died in 1926.

CLAIRE HOLTON HAMMOND

Bibliography

Selected writings by Hannah Robie Sewall
(1901), *The Theory of Value Before Adam Smith*, New York: The Macmillan Company for the American Economic Association. Reprinted in 1968 and 1971 in Reprints of Economic Classics/The Adam Smith Library, New York: Augustus M. Kelley.
(1904), 'Child labor in the U.S.', *U.S. Bureau of Labor Bulletin*, **52**, May, 485–637.

Other sources and references
(1901, 1902), Minnesota *Alumni Weekly*, various issues. University of Minnesota Archives.
(1969), 'Review of Hannah Sewall's *The Theory of Value before Adam Smith*', *Choice*, **5**, February, 1612.

Blaug, Mark (1985), *Economic Theory in Retrospect*, 4th edn, Cambridge: Cambridge University Press.

Hammond, Claire (1993), 'American women and the professionalization of economics', *Review of Social Economy*, **51**, Fall, 347–70.

Hutchison, Terence (1988), *Before Adam Smith: The Emergence of Political Economy. 1662–1776*, Oxford: Basil Blackwell.

Leonard, John (ed.) (1914), *Women's Who's Who in America: A Biographical Dictionary of Contemporary Women of the U.S. and Canada, 1914–1915*, New York: American Commonwealth Co.

Mitchell, Wesley C. (1902), 'Review of Hannah Sewall's *The Theory of Value Before Adam Smith*', *Journal of Political Economy*, **11**, December, 144–5.

Kate Sheppard (Catherine Wilson Sheppard, née Malcolm) (1847–1934)

Brief biography

Kate Sheppard, born in Liverpool, was one of five children of lawyer and musician, Andrew Wilson Malcolm, and Jemima Crawford Souter, both of Scottish ancestry. Widowed young, Jemima emigrated to New Zealand with Kate, then aged about 21, and other family members, to join her older married daughter. Kate married businessman Walter Sheppard two years later, spending the remainder of her 86 years based in Christchurch, although with several trips back to England for both personal and international suffrage and women's movement business. Kate and Walter had one son, Douglas, born in 1880.

From 1885 onwards, following a visit to New Zealand by Mary Leavitt representing the women's Christian Temperance Union of the USA, Kate Sheppard devoted most of her energy over 40 years to the battles for equality for women, including a large body of journalism and other writing, and tireless work for associated organizations. Women's suffrage was the major early target, with the work of Sheppard and others ensuring that New Zealand became in 1893 the first country in the world where women won the vote in national parliamentary elections. However, she saw suffrage not only as an important end in the struggle for equality, but also a means whereby other economic and social policies of importance to women's equality would be more likely to be achieved – as well as allowing influence on the full range of policy issues, all of which she saw as needing women's input.

Sheppard vehemently countered a male account (by William Pember Reeves) of women having been handed the vote on a plate and the effects being largely negative, with the contention that 'by the enfranchisement of women an immense impetus was given to the social and moral forces at work in the colony. The effect was speedily seen in Parliament. Reform followed reform in quick succession. Especially was this so in matters affecting the welfare of women and children' (Sheppard, 1903). Her examples included greater gender equality and economic rights of women in the areas of divorce, separation and maintenance, adoption and infant protection reform, the institution of old-age pensions for both sexes, admission of women to the legal profession, and amendments to Factory Acts to improve health and safety and increase the wages of female apprentices. She had always seen it as essential to persuade and obtain the support of male decision-makers and to use a great range of strategies including the media, petitions, active organizing and advice from male allies to push through key changes.

Kate Sheppard was clearly 'the central figure in the suffrage movement' (Lovell-Smith, 1992, p. 12) and in the first wave of feminism in all its manifestations in New Zealand. Her voluntary, lobbying public work, including running organizations and campaigns, speaking, writing and editing, absorbed almost all her time over several decades, particularly if overseas trips for a combination of family reasons and making international contacts with the feminist movement (1894–6 in England/Europe, 1903–4, 1908 for her son's wedding, and 1912–13) are included.

New Zealand followed the USA in the links between the national and regionally organized temperance movement, in which Sheppard became active, and the suffrage/equality causes. Editing the women's page in the temperance movement's fortnightly newspaper the *Prohibitionist* (claimed to have 25 000 readers, according to Lovell-Smith, 1992) from 1891 to 1894 was her first opportunity to promote all these causes and publicize the activities of feminist movements in other countries. This was followed by editing *White Ribbon*, a monthly women's newspaper, from 1895 (initially sending reports on the world Women's Christian Temperance Union (WCTU) convention in London) to 1903. In Christchurch, the Canterbury Women's Institute (CWI), founded in 1892, became the vehicle for the fight for franchise, and Sheppard convened its Economics Department which worked on employment matters and suffrage.

The most influential lobby group for women's rights to this day, albeit having survived periods of inactivity, is the National Council for Women (NCW), founded in 1896 following Sheppard's experience of the International Council while in London. Her influential presidential addresses and articles in *White Ribbon*, with suffrage already won, covered many areas of social reform and women's rights. In addition to those mentioned elsewhere in this article, she promoted reform of the political process with enhancements to the democratic process, together with health, education and dress reform. However, the comparative lack of political success in the 1890s contributed to the decline of participation in women's rights organizations, with the NCW going into recess in 1906, although some feminist activities continued, with the CWI opposing conscription during World War I.

Kate Sheppard's personal life is much less documented in detail than the public activities and is the subject of controversy. There are parallels with other suffrage figures, such as Charlotte Perkins Gilman (*q.v.*), *inter alia*, in the likelihood that a not totally happy marriage accentuated the priority accorded economic independence for women. Her biographer suggests that her questioning of traditional views on family matters came partly from this personal experience (Devaliant, 1992), although she continued to spend most of her time with Walter until 1905. She advocated education towards responsible marriage choices, but recognition of the inevitability of some divorces, with the consequent need for the Church to be willing to remarry divorced people.

Ill health, including a nervous breakdown, and the desire of her husband to live in England provoked Sheppard's withdrawal from her political activities in 1903. Although she followed him to England, their relationship was by then strained (Devaliant, 1992, p. 174). Her special bond with William Lovell-Smith, whom she married in 1925 a year after the death of his wife Jennie, was already well established. She returned from England in 1905 and went to live with the Lovell-Smiths. Devaliant discusses what can be established, together with the gossip, controversy, and earlier writings about these relationships. It was both sad for Kate Sheppard and a cause of the lack of conclusive evidence on these matters that she predeceased most of her family and had no surviving direct descendants: Walter died in 1915, and their only son Douglas in 1910, two years after his marriage, while Douglas's widow and daughter Margaret died before Kate.

While Kate Sheppard's public activities slowed with bad health in her sixties and later, she nevertheless maintained her international connections and was a key figure in the 1917 revival of the NCW. Her 1917 presidential speech (read for her) shows ongoing vision prioritizing peace and the desire for social justice, internationally through the new League of Nations and locally. Among women's rights issues not mentioned elsewhere in this article, she advocated women serving as police, jurors and Justices of the Peace, and receiving equal guardianship rights over children. The latter two reforms were achieved in 1926–27, but the first two not until after her death.

Kate Sheppard's economic ideas

Kate Sheppard clearly recognized the damage done by the public/private worlds distinction and the associated sharp dichotomy of roles between men and women, as illustrated below. She also argued strongly for economic independence for women, the sharing of income in the household, the recognition and valuation of unpaid work, and equality in the labour market.

> Our strong conviction is that until a true and perfect equality is recognised between men and women that will apply to any and every relation in life, the highest

happiness cannot exist ... But this will never be accomplished while they live such separate lives as they do so largely at present; while men are supposed to have little or nothing to do with 'home,' and women nothing at all to do outside it; while coarseness is condoned in the one sex, and helplessness encouraged in the other, and entitled 'womanliness'; and while the one sex assumes superiority and accords to the other tacitly, if not openly, inferiority. (Sheppard, 1892, p. 6)

On economic independence, she asserted it was just, necessary for her own protection and that of the children, for protection of a man from himself, to improve the position of married women and provide them with freedom and justice as 'mothers of the race' (Sheppard, 1899, p. 18). She, like others of her day, made strategic use of possibly conflicting notions of women's equality to and difference from men to advocate suffrage and other causes. However, differences in position and needs between groups of women were as poorly acknowledged as in most countries, with suffrage fights led by white middle-class women. Marital status differences and consequences for policy were dealt with, but class and ethnic issues were largely ignored. There were some Maori branches of the WCTU, but writing by Maori women or on Maori women's status in the suffrage-inspired media was non-existent.

In advocating economic independence for women, one principle argued by the 1890s' suffragists was that a married woman should have a legal right to a part share, or even an equal share, of her husband's income. In 1896 the National Council of women passed the following motion: 'That in all cases where a woman elects to superintend her own household and to be the mother of children, there shall be a law attaching a certain just share of her husband's earnings or income for her separate use, payable, if she so desired it, into her separate account' (Malcolm, 1989, pp. 7–8). Kate Sheppard translated this proposal into a Bill introduced into Parliament incorporating the principle that if only the husband is in paid work, the earnings shall form 'a common fund appropriated to the maintenance of their household and family expenses and to the education and outfit in life of the children of the marriage'. It also provided that the wife 'shall be entitled if she sees proper to do so' to require half such earnings to be paid to her. It is hardly a surprise that the Bill was not successful (ibid., pp. 8–9).

All the arguments for properly valuing unpaid work familiar today were used, in the language of the time. They included recognition of the opportunity costs in foregone income of being a full-time housewife and mother, the fact that unpaid work is real work and that the wife's work frees the husband to be active in the paid workforce, and concern over many wives having to plead for adequate housekeeping allowances, let alone personal money. Also argued were the desirability of personal fulfilment through a career, the need for women to have adequate education and training in case they stayed single or became single through death of the spouse, and the hopes that it would prevent the situation of undertaking or staying in unsatisfactory marriages, as well as providing greater bargaining power within marriage.

In arguing that household work was real work and should be valued, Sheppard discussed the statistical categorization of women into 'breadwinners' and 'dependents or non-breadwinners' in the 1892 Census. She noted that 124 454 of the 248 364 women in the latter category were described as 'persons performing domestic duties for which remuneration is not paid'. She went on: 'As we suppose that wives are included in this latter category, we feel inclined to take exception to their being classed as "dependent", for she earns her living, in many cases far more hardly than her husband does, although he is the actual wage receiver' (Sheppard, 1892, p. 6, reprinted in Lovell-Smith, 1992, p. 108).

Both equal opportunity for women to receive appropriate education and training to enter any area of the paid labour force they chose, and equal pay with men doing the same work were on the agenda of women active in the New Zealand suffrage movement, including Sheppard. Noting that the Canterbury Board of Education paid 20 per cent less to an assistant master [*sic*] if a female teacher was employed, she commented that 'There is no difference in the work to be done. The same standards have to be taught and the same examinations passed ... How manifestly unfair then to have two rates of pay for the same work, merely because one of the workers is a woman' (Sheppard, 1892, p. 6). However, equal pay for equal work in the private sector was not legislated until 1972, and the fight for pay equity continues (Hyman, 1994).

Kate Sheppard's ideas – reception and influence

Sheppard's work, along with that of many other suffragists, was critical in achieving female suffrage, despite the comments of Reeves touched on above. Without her individual leadership, writing and other media involvement, it is unlikely that success would have come so quickly. She considered crucial the links between suffrage (and women sitting in Parliament, which was not enacted until 1919 and actualized until 1933) and the active ongoing fights for other economic and social rights. Her claims that welfare, family and labour market improvements for women were at least partly a result of suffrage seem well-based. The reaction to her ideas was naturally better among more liberal opinion than elsewhere – while the more radical proposals, such as the common fund or separate account for married women, met a frosty reception.

With the quieter period for feminist activity, or at least public attention to it, from the 1920s to recent decades, and the lack of documentation in histories and school texts, generations could grow up in Aotearoa/New Zealand totally ignorant of Kate Sheppard. Judith Devaliant, her biographer, who started work on the 1992 book in 1978, 'came across' her in that year, when seeking a woman with a strong personality to study. She was:

hitherto unknown to me as to so many other New Zealanders who were brought up on English history at school. We knew more about the activities of the suffragettes, the militant wing of the English suffrage movement, than we did about the lengthy campaign for women's franchise in New Zealand, led by Kate Sheppard … it seemed tragic that a woman who was so well known in her own time should have been so largely forgotten. (Devaliant, 1992, pp. 3–4)

The resurgence of feminist activism, together with its theory and history wing, the appearance of the biography, and the centenary of suffrage which inspired and part-funded much feminist history and other writing, mean that Sheppard is now a household name. During the 1980s and 1990s a feminist bookshop and a street have come to bear her name, while a memorial was among the suffrage projects. But many of the reforms she advocated remain to be implemented and many of the economic ideas she espoused are as fresh and necessary as they were in her day.

PRUE HYMAN

Bibliography

Selected writings by Kate Sheppard
(1892), 'Economics', *Canterbury Times*, 15 December, p. 6; reprinted in Lovell-Smith (1992), pp. 106–9.
(1899), 'Economic Independence of Married Women', reprinted with an introduction by Tessa Malcolm, 1989 in *Women's Studies Journal*, **5**(1), 3–24.
(1903), 'Editorial' in *White Ribbon*, February, pp. 6–7.

Other sources and references
Devaliant, J. (1992), *Kate Sheppard – A Biography: The Fight for Women's Votes in New Zealand – The Life of the Woman Who Led the Struggle*, Auckland, NZ: Penguin.
Hyman, P. (1994), *Women and Economics: a New Zealand Feminist Perspective*, Wellington, NZ: Bridget Williams Books.
Lovell-Smith, M. (1992), *The Woman Question – Writings by the Women who Won the Vote*, Auckland, NZ: New Women's Press.
Malcolm, T. (1989), 'Kate Sheppard: Economic Independence of Married Women', introduced by Tessa Malcolm, *Women's Studies Journal*, **5**(1), 3–24.
Malcolm T. (1993), 'Sheppard, Katherine Wilson 1847–1934' in 'The Suffragists – Women Who Worked for the Vote': Essay from *The Dictionary of New Zealand Biography*, with an introduction by Dorothy Page, Bridget Williams Books and Dictionary of New Zealand Biography, pp. 120–28

Irene M. Spry (1907–98)

Irene Spry was born at Standerton, Transvaal, South Africa of British parents. Her father, Evan E. Biss, ran a teachers' training college and was later an inspector of schools. Before Irene turned three, the family moved to Bengal. Three years later, Irene's mother took the children to England, leaving them with an aunt. When World War I broke out, Irene and the other Biss children were caught in England – her parents still in India.

Irene's own early career goals included 'being the Prime Minister of Britain, and I wrote an essay to that effect when I was at school'. Luckily, she says, that career dream did not come true. Once she became an academic, she was hooked: 'I always wanted to find out about things.'

As a teenager, she studied economics by correspondence, then, at 17, was admitted to the London School of Economics, where she was greatly influenced by the economic historian, Eileen Power. One year later she gained admission to both Oxford and Cambridge, opting for Cambridge on a scholarship. After completing three years there, she moved on to graduate studies at Bryn Mawr in the USA, accepting a day before receiving notice of admission to the University of Toronto, in Canada. Irene's curriculum in social research and social work included working on the conveyor belt at a factory, touring a coalmine, and working as a sales clerk at an up-market retail store in New York.

In 1929, 'Toronto very kindly renewed its offer', so Irene headed north, lecturing in the Department of Political Economy and also acting as a residence don. In Toronto, Irene said that she was lucky enough to get to know Harold Innis, who was tremendously important to her intellectual development.

Spry's long working life can be broken into three parts. During the first period, she worked as a junior academic and government economist in Canada (1929–45). The second period (1945–67) was spent mostly in Great Britain, where Spry engaged in self-styled 'miscellaneous lecturing, writing and reviewing'. Finally, the third period (1969–94) was spent as a mature academic, working as an associate, full professor and finally professor emeritus at the University of Ottawa, again in Canada.

Spry began her working life as a young instructor at the University of Toronto, where she was a colleague of Innis, a political economist and some say the father of a distinctly Canadian economics. She was also an emerging theorist and economist in her own right, pursuing her own interests in economic and social theory. She met her husband-to-be – Graham Spry – at a skating party organized by the League for Social Reconstruction. Irene described the meeting: 'I fell down at every step, because 1 couldn't skate, and as he propped me up, this was a good beginning'. Graham and Irene were married at Chelsea Old Church, London, England, in 1938. The couple lived in England, then Irene returned to Toronto for the duration of the war. She worked for one year as an economic consultant for the national YMCA of Canada, then in Ottawa, first with the Wartime Prices and Trade Board (WPTB) and then the Commodity Prices Stabilization Corporation.

Between 1930 and 1950, Canada (along with the rest of the world) suffered a depression, a world war and the rigours of reconstruction. During this time economics became a discipline in its own right, separate from political economy. Economic analysis began to be applied to pressing societal problems. It was the era of Keynes[1] and the time of a concerted attempt to set up internationally comparable systems of national accounts. Most discussions we find of this time mention only the men who were involved in these endeavours. For example, the biography of Donald Gordon, a deputy governor of the Bank of Canada and Chairman of the WPTB, gives a scant half-page to women. In fact, many women worked within the government during the war years, undoubtedly filling places that would otherwise have gone to men whose energies were now focused on direct war work. A cadre of women worked in the government, at both the Dominion Bureau of Statistics (DBS) and at the Bank of Canada.[2] A sprinkling worked at the universities. During the war, the research division of the WPTB employed at least three other women economists, besides Irene Spry and Phyllis Turner: Frances Keith-MacLean, Helen Aikenhead-Buckley and Beryl Plumptre.[3]

After World War II, Graham was appointed Agent General for the Province of Saskatchewan in the United Kingdom and Europe. At Saskatchewan House, Irene's and Graham's New Year's parties were famous, and it became the place for students (and others) to be on 31 December. In this second stage of her career, Irene became passionately interested in Captain John Palliser's expedition to British North America and produced two books on the Palliser expedition, one a scholarly compilation and the other a popular account. The popular account is entitled *The Palliser Expedition: An Account of John Palliser's British North American Exploring Expedition 1857–1860* (Spry, 1963). The book certainly is not economics (nor does it pretend to be), but it is a rollicking good story. The scholarly book, *The Papers of the Palliser Expedition* (Spry, 1968), reports Palliser's record of his three years spent exploring what is now Canada west of Winnipeg. This research also resulted in at least five published papers.

Irene was also involved with an international women's group, The Associated Countrywomen of the World, work that took her all over the world. She put it on record that she went into this 'very reluctantly and with a very haughty sort of academic view of these poor amateur volunteers', but then had the grace to say that she soon changed her mind.[4] Irene's essentially urban background, despite a youth spent in India, may have coloured her views, but she learnt quickly and gave the association sterling service. In 1959, she was appointed chair of its executive committee. She remained active with the group until the 1990s.

Irene and Graham returned to Canada in 1967, and to Ottawa in 1968, settling into their final home in Rockcliffe. (Irene spent one year at the University of Saskatchewan and then accepted a post at the University of Ottawa.) In 1985 the University honoured her with a book of essays in economic history. That book is divided into three parts, one on political economy, one on resource development and the final part on 'Canadian Community', effectively covering her work on the west and Palliser. Despite her poor eyesight she continued to work right to the time of her death. Irene has also received two honorary doctorates (Toronto and Ottawa) and has been appointed an Officer of the Order of Canada. She can be classified as a Canadian economist, by virtue of her long association with Canada and her contribution to the Innis tradition and to Canadian economics.

Spry first worked with Harold Innis in the 1930s. She was also a member of the League for Social Reconstruction, a group formed by Frank Underhill and the lawyer and poet, F.R. Scott, in the early 1930s. The League was critical of monopoly capital and sought social change through parliamentary means. The influence of Innis is reflected in Spry's interest in resources, including energy, and her unflagging awareness of the cultural and humane dimensions of our society (see, for example, Spry, 1936, 1937, 1938). This interest continued throughout her career (see Spry, 1980, 1981 and Crabbe and Spry, 1973). In October 1994, Spry spoke at the Innis centenary conference held at Concordia University, in Montreal.

Spry could also be called the dean of Canadian women economists, as she is one of the most senior of those women who practised economics in the 1930s and 1940s. What is most impressive about her work is the breadth of her interests. She did not confine herself to narrow economics – indeed, another academic of our acquaintance, a historian, did not even know that Irene was an economist, she said she knew her only as a historian. Historians know Spry's work on the Palliser expedition well, and it is highly respected. Although Spry specialized in economic history and resource economics, she also has to her credit several theoretical articles that attest to her analytic turn of mind (Spry, 1977, 1980, 1981, 1981a). The essays in her honour also include a bibliography of her work.

Finally, a personal digression on the hiatus that appears in her academic work between 1949 and 1967, when she reappears in Canada. For both women and men we must view their lives as an intertwining of the professional and the personal. We cannot always extricate the public person from the private, although it usually easier to distinguish the public from the private man than the public from the private woman. It is impossible to understand Irene Spry without knowing something of her personal life and the life of her husband. The demands of Graham Spry's career forced Irene to give up her career in Canadian academia during the middle period of her life. Of course, during those years she also reared their three children, so it is hard to say, and in fact not particularly useful to speculate, on what might have happened had they not left Canada. The Sprys were in essence exiles from Canada for over 20 years, Graham from his native land and Irene from her adopted home.

Graham Spry, who was the Manitoba Rhodes scholar for 1922, returning to Canada in 1924, also belonged to the League for Social Reconstruction. He was involved in the Co-operative Commonwealth Federation, a coalition of progressive socialist and labour interests in Calgary in 1922, running unsuccessfully in 1933 in the Broadview riding in Toronto. He was also instrumental in setting up the Canadian Fabian Society. Through his connections he also was active in the Canadian efforts for the Spanish Civil War. These activities led by 1937 to his being, in the bleak words of Joe Atkinson, 'finished in Canada', on account of his political affiliations and activities.[5] It turned out that he was, indeed, unemployable in Canada and the Sprys left the country.

In 1938 Graham Spry succeeded in finding employment as an executive for California Standard Oil and was stationed in England. Later he became the trade representative for the Saskatchewan government and was also an assistant to Sir Stafford Cripps. From his letters it appears that he would dearly have loved to return to Canada and campaigned hard, but unsuccessfully, to be appointed to the Board of Broadcast Governors, the predecessor of the Canadian Broadcasting Commission, The Sprys returned to Canada only at the end of Graham's working life.

JUDITH A. ALEXANDER
KAREN SHOPSOWITZ

Notes

1. Keynes visited Canada in the early 1940s.
2. See Schull (1979), p. 66. Phyllis Turner-Ross, the Oils and Fats Administrator of the Board, is described at work, as 'hip-booted and oilskinned, the glamorous young widow with the stamp of Bryn Mawr [who] ... toured the ports of the Maritimes persuading sceptical fishermen to save the codfish livers they had usually thrown away'. Schull also describes the volunteer women, an 'army of snoopers', sixteen thousand strong, who tracked prices across the country, who were, in his opinion, the real muscle of the Board.
3. I owe this information to Gideon Rosenbluth of the University of British Columbia, who also worked at the WPTB during the war.
4. Quoted from Gerald Friesen (1985), p. 326. Friesen also includes a bibliography of Spry's work.
5. See Potvin (1992), p. 100, '[Joe Atkinson of the Toronto Star] said to me, "You're finished in Canada. Your only alternative is to leave the country". He said, "You're labeled now, you haven't a chance of getting satisfactory employment". Well this turned out to be the case. It was very cutting advice, hard to take.'

Bibliography

Selected writings by Irene M. Spry

(1936), 'The Contracts of the Hydro-Electric Power Commission of Ontario', *Economic Journal*, **XLVI**(183), September, 549–54.
(1937), 'Recent Power Legislation in Quebec', *Canadian Journal of Economics and Political Science*, **III**(4), November, 550–58.

(1938), 'Economic Aspects of National Unity', *Annual Review, The Commerce Journal*, March, 36–40.

(1963), *The Palliser Expedition: An Account of John Palliser's British North American Palliser Exploring Expedition 1857–1860*, Toronto: Macmillan.

(1968) (ed.), *The Papers of the Palliser Expedition*, Toronto: Champlain Society.

(1973) (eds) *Natural Resource Development in Canada* (with Philippe Crabbe), Ottawa: University of Ottawa Press.

(1977), 'Consumer Interests and the Future of the Economy', *Conserver Society Notes* (Science Council of Canada), **II** (3), Summer, 19–22.

(1980), 'Innis, the Fur Trade and Modern Economic Problems', in Carol M. Judd and Arthur J. Ray (eds), *Old Trails and New Directions: Papers of the Third North American Fur Trade Conference*, Toronto: University of Toronto Press, pp. 291–307.

(1981), 'Overhead Costs, Rigidities in Productive Capacity and the Price System', in William H. Melody, Liora Salter and Paul Meyer (eds), *Culture, Communication and Dependency: The Tradition of H.A. Innis*, Norwood, NJ: Ablex Publishing, pp. 155–66.

Other sources and references

Babe, Robert E. (1998), 'Graham Spry' in Mel Hurtig (ed.), *The Canadian Encyclopedia*, Edmonton: Mel Hurtig Publishing, p. 2064.

Cameron, Duncan (1985) (ed.), *Explorations in Canadian Economic History: Essays in Honour of Irene Spry*, Ottawa: University of Ottawa Press.

Freisen, Gerald (1988), 'Irene Spry' in Mel Hurtig (ed.), *The Canadian Encyclopedia*, Edmonton: Mel Hurtig Publishing, pp. 2064–5.

Potvin, Rose (1992), *Passion and Conviction: The Letters of Graham Spry*, Winnipeg: Hignell Printing, Ltd.

Schull, Joseph (1979), *The Great Scot, A Biography of Donald Gordon*, Montreal: McGill-Queens University Press.

Maria Szecsi (1914–84)

Maria Szecsi was born in Budapest. Her parents left Hungary in 1919 and emigrated to Austria. Under the influence of her uncle, Karl Polanyi, she engaged herself in socialist ideas very early. She became a member of the Social Democrat youth organization 'Rote Falken' and later of the Socialist Highschool Group. After the Austrian Civil War in 1934 and the prohibition of the Social Democrat Party she worked for the underground organization. Captured, she was sentenced to gaol and dismissed from the University of Vienna.

The German occupation of Austria enforced her emigration to the USA. There she continued her studies in history, economy and political science at the Universities of Cincinnati and Chicago, and achieved her MA. She became Lecturer and later Instructor at Roosevelt College of Chicago University.

In 1948 she returned to Austria and became a member of the Communist Party. She worked in the department for social policy in the Communist World Trade Union. But her critical approach made it impossible for her to adopt its political attitude. After the Hungarian Revolution in 1956 she left the Communist Party. In the letter to the Central Committee she explained her reasons for leaving. It is worth quoting at some length because of the clarity and honesty of her thinking:

> My opinion is that it is necessary to revise the thesis of the proletarian dicatorship and the leading role of the party. This thesis has now become, I fear, an obstacle to the socialist conscience of workers. The labour force of developed capitalist countries, whose situation is in no way 'unbearable' today (in the sense of Lenin), nor in all probability will become so in the future, has no reason to aspire to socialism, at the price of being deprived of its rights and of making the sacrifices that the Central Committee demands. Although I wish that socialism would become reality, I do not want it at any price and certainly not at the price that has been and still is paid daily in the Soviet Union, in Hungary and in the CSSR. Therefore workers must have the opportunity to control the legal power, which they themselves have created and to throw out a government in which they no longer trust. (Szecsi, 1979, p. 6 – translation by the author)

In 1960 Szecsi entered the Austrian Chamber of Labour, the official forum for representation of workers and employees, where she worked in the economics department until her retirement in 1974. There she dealt mainly with problems of income distribution, prices, private consumption and income levels. In 1971 she was – as the first woman – delegated to the Council of Economic and Social Questions, a central organization of the Austrian Social Partnership. Here she did studies on the grey markets and the reduction of working hours. She also contributed to the reform of the Austrian cartel law and became assessor at the court of cartels.

During her later years in the Chamber of Labour she engaged herself in the creation of a publication which would discuss economic and social concerns of trade unions, but at a scholarly level and on an empirical basis. She was successful in 1975, when *Wirtschaft und Gesellschaft* began publication. After her retirement until 1978 she remained chief editor of this journal, which became a respected one among the scholarly publications in the German language (though English articles are, of course, included).

The work and intellectual development of Maria Szecsi can be regarded as typical of an academic in postwar Austria in several respects. She was part of the considerable group of Austrian emigrants who were engaged in socialist groups. After having studied in the USA she returned to Austria to fulfil her political ambitions. In contrast to many others, she had a tendency to the extreme left. But her break with the Communist Party was fundamental. From that time forward she became an advocate of impartial scientific research, a position which fitted well with the aims of the Austrian Social Partnership, where scientific analysis was in high esteem. And she defended this position energetically against the revolution of the so-called 'New Left' after 1968. She not only exerted considerable influence on the theory and policy of the Austrian trade unions, but also on the Social Democrat Party. Her contribution is helpful in an understanding of the specific development of the Austrian governance structure after 1945.

FELIX BUTSCHEK

Bibliography

Selected writings by Maria Szecsi

(1958), 'Kapitalismus der letzten Etappe', *Arbeit und Wirtschaft*, no. 2.
(1958), 'Geistige Wandlungen im Sozialismus', *Arbeit und Wirtschaft*, no. 7.
(1963), 'Adam Schaff über Toleranz und Unversöhnlichkeit', *Zukunft*, no. 5.
(1965), 'Der Aufstieg der österreichischen Wirtschaft', *Arbeit und Wirtschaft*, no. 4.
(1966), 'Pluralismus und Klassengesellschaft', *Arbeit und Wirtschaft*, no. 6.
(1967), 'Parteiprogramm und Pluralismus', *Zukunft*, no. 4.
(1967), 'Sinn und Unsinn von Wohlstandsvergleichen', *Arbeit und Wirtschaft*, no. 3.
(1967), 'Art and Coexistence. On Ernst Fischer', *Mosaic*, October.
(1969), 'Arbeitszeit und Wirtschaftswachstum', *Arbeit und Wirtschaft*, no. 3.
(1969), 'Manipulierte Bedürfnisse?', *Zukunft*, no. 11.
(1969), 'Arbeitszeit als politische Entscheidung', *Wirtschaftspolitische Blätter*, nos 2/3.
(1970), 'Jenseits der Vierzigstundenwoche', *Arbeit und Wirtschaft*, no. 9.
(1972), 'Kartelle', *Arbeit und Wirtschaft*, no. 10.
(1974), 'Plädoyer für eine aktive Verteilungspolitik', *Arbeit und Wirtschaft*, no. 4.
(1975), 'Zur Frage des gedrosselten Wachstums', *Wirtschaft und Gesellschaft*, no. 3.
(1977), 'Rückblick auf die Great Transformation', *Wirtschaft und Gesellschaft*, no. 4.
(1979), 'Looking back on the Great Transformation', *Monthly Review*, New York, January.
(1979), 'Randbemerkungen zum Parteiprogramm der SPÖ', *Wirtschaft und Gesellschaft*, no. 2.
(1979), 'Wirtschaftspolitik zwischen Weltanschaung und Sachzwang. Festschrift für Maria Szeczi', Sondernummer von *Wirtschafts und Gesellschaft*, vol. 5.

Setsu Tanino (b. 1903)

Setsu Tanino (Setsuko Ochiai) was born in Chiba Prefecture in 1903, and graduated from the Department of Social Work at Japan Women's University in 1926. She hoped that she would find work in social welfare, but unexpectedly found a job in the Ministry of Home Affairs, the most powerful ministry in pre-World War II Japan. She became the first woman probationary factory supervisor in 1928. At that time, night work and long hours of work in Japan were notorious around the world. Japan was always criticized at international conferences of the International Labour Organization (ILO) since its establishment in 1919, even though Japan participated in the creation of the ILO by sending two Japanese to the Committee of International Labour Legislation. For example, at the 1926 general assembly of the ILO, an Indian employers' representative criticized Japan for increasing production by women's night work on a two-shift basis and driving India's products from the world market, because night work was prohibited in India. A British employees' representative pointed out that unless Japan forbade women's night work, China would remain reluctant to improve their conditions, which were worse than Japan's. He demanded that Japan fully approve all the clauses of the Constitution of the ILO because he believed that Japan was in an important position regarding the international cooperation for improvement of working conditions promoted by the organization. Inside Japan, the necessity of a female factory supervisor was realized not only by male factory supervisors, but also by scholars and workers based on their voluntary inspection of textile factories. They found that it was difficult for men to observe the real working and living conditions of women workers, especially in the textile industry, where 80 per cent of workers were from remote villages and lived in the factory residence. The Japanese government had to take some action and so appointed a woman, Tanino, as a probationary factory supervisor.

Tanino was the only woman (probationary) factory supervisor during the 1930s when the function of the factory supervisor was becoming more and more important in Japan's rapidly developing industrial society. Several international inspectors were sent to Japan to investigate women's working conditions because Japan's export of cheap textile goods was a target of reproach by the rest of the world. Every time such inspectors visited Japan, Tanino was invited to meet them as evidence of an incumbent woman factory supervisor doing her job in Japan. Therefore, Kitagawa (1985, vol. 1, p. 28) was right to judge that Japan's government appointed a woman factory supervisor mainly because it had to keep up appearances as 'a first-class country' in the light of external condemnation, not because of internal considerations.

Tanino made detailed reports on the conditions of the working women based on documents sent from factories. She also stayed in the residence of a spinning factory (usually overnight and once for a month) to experience night work with women workers. She sometimes conducted 'surprise' inspection of factories to investigate the real working conditions of women. Her reports and articles appeared in several governmental journals such as *Industrial Welfare* (*Sangyo Fukuri*), *Social Works* (*Shakai Jigyo*), and *Welfare Japan* (*Kosei no Nippon*). Yet some important reports were not published until 1985. Tanino's writings reflected the current problems of working women and minors, and showed Japan's changing situation from rationalization of industry to mobilization towards war.

Women's and minors' night work was legally prohibited in Japan in July 1929, 13 years after the passage of the Factory Law in Japan in 1916. The civil engineer Ryuji Suzuki investigated the effect of this prohibition on the textile industry, including its production and the workers' physical conditions during September and December 1929, and Tanino summarized the results in her report 'On the Effect of the Prohibition of Night Work' in 1931. The textile industry had resisted most strongly the prohibition of night work in Japan. The report first examined production in the factories which had practised ten-hour days on a two-shift basis before the prohibition of night work, but subsequently shifted to eight-and-a-half-hour days. In general, production did not decrease as much as the reduction in working hours of 15 per cent, that is, the reduction from 10 to 8.5 hours, although the productivity per spindle was reduced everywhere. The actual results crucially depended on the operating speed of spindles and crankshafts, the dexterity of workers, the quality of raw materials, and the environment of working rooms. The production of silk yarn decreased most, by 8 per cent per day. On the other hand, labour productivity actually increased by 18 per cent in the spinning industry and by 1.5 per cent in woollen manufacturing, because workers began to handle more spindles than before. Second, the number of ill workers was reduced by 64.4 per cent among men and by 34.0 per cent among women. Fewer workers had trouble with digestive or respiratory organs, and cases of flu were also reduced. However, the injury rate remained unchanged.

In 1933, Tanino compiled a report entitled 'The Participation of Women in the Labour Force during the Past Five Years', in response to a request by the ILO. During the severe economic depression of the early 1930s, it was surmised in many countries that the unemployment of male workers was – at least partially – caused by women's participation in the labour force. Tanino made a careful investigation of this hypothesis in the period from 1927 to 1932, during which time the Japanese economy was beset by depression triggered by the financial panic of 1927. Tanino found not only that the respective number of men and women workers decreased, but also that the ratio of women to men workers declined during this period. A few more women began to work in the textile industry and machine manufacturing than before, whereas the number of women working in coal mines conspicuously decreased because the legal prohibition of women's underground working was scheduled to start in September 1933. With regard to work during the day, the number of men labourers increased much more than that of women. With the development of the public transportation system, including motor buses, more women than men were newly employed, mainly as conductresses, in the transportation and communications industry. As Tanino found from the employers' responses to her questionnaires, in hotels and restaurants more women were employed because they impressed the customers favourably. In addition, women substituted for men not only because their wages and salaries were lower than men's, but also because the employers believed that women were too gentle and obedient to become involved in labour disputes with them. Tanino concluded that women workers did not have bright futures for promotion and professional occupations, and that male wages would go down due to women's further participation in the labour force.

Tanino also compiled three reports for submission to the ILO in order to respond to the severe criticism from the rest of the world of Japan's 'poor' working conditions. They were 'Welfare Facilities in the Mining Industry in Japan' (1933), 'Examples of Retirement Grants in the Mining Industry in Japan' (1934), and 'The Examination of the Contribution of Employers to the Cost of Welfare Facilities in Mines' (1935). These reports were based on the 1932 investigation of the welfare facilities in 2267 companies and 117 mines that employed more than 100 workers. Japan's exports surged thanks to the depreciation of the Japanese yen immediately after it left the international gold standard in December 1931. Japan was fiercely criticized for 'social dumping' at the 1933 general assembly of the ILO and further condemnation was expected at the 1934 assembly. In 1934, Fernand Maurette the Deputy Secretary-General of the ILO, was sent to Japan to inspect conditions. When he visited a new textile factory, he unexpectedly found good education facilities for the women workers who lived in the residence of the factory. In fact, employers had to provide better welfare facilities and fringe benefits (to make up for low wages) because it was becoming harder for them to secure new women workers as the poor working conditions gradually became known in remote (farming) areas (Kitagawa, 1985, vol. 1, pp. 257–9; Taikakai, 1971, pp. 450–52).

Tanino contributed her 'The Protection of Women Workers in Japan's Industries' (1935) to *Labor Legislation (Rodo Rippo)*. This was the occasional journal for the promotion of the legislation of labour laws by a non-governmental institution, the Institute of Labour Legislation. The journal was circulated for less than two years from January 1934. Based on her reports for governmental journals, Tanino included her own opinion on the protection of motherhood. The journal was discontinued because of fears that the secret police might suspect socialist tendencies in the discussion of 'social' problems. In fact, the police had been encroaching on the right of a free press, especially since the establishment of the puppet state of Manchukuo in the northeast region of China in 1931 (Kitagawa, 1985, vol. 1, p. 287).

Tanino's 'A Note of A Woman Probationary Factory Supervisor' (*c.* 1936) was first published in 1985. This was the record of the unannounced inspection of small factories, which were the basis for Japan's export industries in pre-World War II Japan. In small bulb-making factories, Tanino found 5–15 pale boys and girls working without clothes in hot, dimly lit workplaces. Both employers and employees had dim futures and were working hard in depressing circumstances. They received orders from their parent companies erratically, and therefore they sometimes worked both day and night while at other times they were laid off for half a day. The parent companies often 'sincerely asked' the small factory owners to supply at a lower price. In textile factories, Tanino was surprised to see women workers competing fiercely, both at individual and at group level. She witnessed a poor girl with flu and a fever forced to work by her team-mate, with the expectation of gaining an award for the team. With regard to the remittances of young workers in large factories to their parents in remote villages, the parents tended to believe that the company which allowed the children to remit the most money was the best. Tanino lamented this and remarked that the parents did not usually notice how low the children's pocket money was. She also called attention to the fact that women were entering machine manufacturing and expected that this would be a threat to male workers with respect to both jobs and wages.

Tanino's 'New Working Clothes for Women' (1937) is an interesting report on the history of dress culture in Japan. In July 1936 she investigated a bulb factory in Tokyo that had newly introduced light western clothes for women workers instead of the heavy traditional *kimono* with tight *obi* belt. The company made the switch in July because it thought the women would be more comfortable wearing new western-style clothes in the summer heat, and it was satisfied with the lower ratio of absent and ill workers that summer compared with the previous year. From the 26 women responding to her questions, Tanino also found that most of them liked the western-style working clothes better than the Japanese *kimono*, and that only three did not like them. Before the introduction of western clothes in factories, women in *kimonos* operated machines 'with drops of sweat'.

Japan's military force began to fight with China in July 1937. This was called 'the Sino-Japanese Conflict' at the time in order to make it appear as a mere skirmish and avoid international criticism, but it is now rightly called the 'Sino-Japanese War'. Many men in the prime of life were drafted to the battlefields and women had to fill the vacant positions on Japan's mainland. According to Tanino's 'Women's Advance into Machine Shops and Their Adaptability', women began to work in machine manufacturing including munitions plants at an accelerating pace, not only because of the shortage of male workers, but also because women received lower wages than men for the same job, and gave a better performance (in the inspection of product quality). The wage differentials between men and women became wider with age. According to Tanino, it was expected that after the end of the war, when Japan returned to normal conditions, women would lose their jobs and resume concentrating on housework.

In a series of reports including her 'Women's Working Conditions in Factories and Their Protection during the Sino-Japanese Conflict' and 'Working Women and Welfare Facilities' (1939), Tanino called attention to the need for immediate improvement of working environments for women because women were suddenly working in machine shops and munitions factories which were designed specifically with men in mind. She also maintained that in general the physical constitution of women should be improved, and that the protection of motherhood, including the care of pregnant women and infants, was necessary. Tanino was worried about the result of women workers' self-diagnosis which revealed that around 80 per cent of them had health problems in 1940. She also found that the turnover rate of women in machine manufacturing was very high and that many women did not like 'mannish' working environments in heavy industry. In 1943, Tanino and others prepared the 'Material' for the Seminar on Women Labour Management, which was organized by the Ministry of Health and Welfare. Further mobilization of women, that is, more housewives, became necessary in various places because more men were sent to the battlefields.

Japan surrendered unconditionally in August 1945, and the Allies began their occupation in September. The Allies destroyed Japan's military forces and implemented several measures to democratize Japan. In December 1947 they broke up the Ministry of Home Affairs, which was believed to share the major responsibility for initiating and waging the war along with Japan's military forces and the Ministry of Finance. The Ministry of Home Affairs was unable to alter the occupation policy because it had no one who could speak English fluently enough to rebut the Allies' reform plan, whereas the Ministry of Finance managed to emasculate the initial dissolution plan and survives with immense power to the present day (Noguchi, 1995).

In September 1947 Tanino became the section chief at the Bureau of Women and Minors in the newly established Ministry of Labour and began to work under Director-General Kikue Yamakawa. Tanino became the third Director-General in the Bureau in 1955 and held the position for a decade. In

1965 she retired from the Ministry of Labour and became a member of the Judging Committee of Labour Insurance. In 1985 a collection of her articles was published by Nobu Kitagawa under the title *The Record of the Woman Factory Supervisor.*

AIKO IKEO

Bibliography

Selected writings by Setsu Tanino (all in Japanese)

(1931), 'On the Effect of the Prohibition of Night Work' (with Ryuji Suzuki), *Industrial Welfare*, June.

(1933), 'Welfare Facilities in the Mining Industry in Japan', Industrial Welfare, October (for the ILO).

(1934), 'Examples of Retirement Grant in the Mining Industry in Japan', *Industrial Welfare*, May (for the ILO).

(1935), 'The Examination of the Contribution of Employers to the Cost of Welfare Facilities in Mines', *Industrial Welfare*, March (for the ILO).

(1935), 'The Protection of Women Workers in Japan's Industries', *Labor Legislation*, **2**(2/3) and **3**(2).

(*c.* 1935), 'Problems Relating to the Protection of Women Workers' (unpublished).

(1936), 'The Participation of Women in the Labour Force during the Past Five Years', *Industrial Welfare*, September (for the ILO).

(*c.* 1936), 'A Note of A Woman Probationary Factory Supervisor' (unpublished).

(1937), 'New Working Clothes for Women', *Industrial Welfare*, January.

(1937), 'The Record of Inspection in the Factory at the Headquarter of Gunze Spinning Corporation', *Industrial Welfare*, May.

(1937), 'The Lives of the Women who Retired from Spinning Work', *Industrial Welfare*, November.

(*c.* 1938), 'On the Recruiting of Women and Minors', *Industrial Welfare*.

(1939), 'Women Works and Music', *Industrial Welfare*, February.

(1939), 'Women's Advance into Machine Shops and Their Adaptability', *Industrial Welfare*, September.

(1939), 'Women's Working Conditions in Factories and Their Protection during the Sino-Japanese Incident', *Social Works*, October.

(1939), 'Working Women and Welfare Facilities', *Welfare Japan*, November.

(1940), 'Women's Labors and Vocational Guidance', *Scientific Industry*, April.

(1940), 'The Current Situation of Working Women', published, but journal unknown.

(1940), 'The Report on Working Women', paper presented at a meeting of Showa Kenkyukai, November.

(1942), 'An Observation of the Factory of Japanese Figured Mat Maker (in Okayama)', *Industrial Welfare*, July.

(1943), 'A Few Considerations about Women Labour Management', Sanpo, March.

(1943), 'Problems of Working Women', *Industrial Welfare*.

(1943), 'Material for the Seminar on Women Labour Management (with Hirokazu Kachi, Touru Mitsui, and Koroku Kurokawa)

(1985), *The Record of the Woman Factory Supervisor: The Collected Articles of Setsu Tanino*, 2 vols, edited by Nobu Kitagawa, Tokyo: Domes Shuppan.

Other sources and references

Ikeo, Aiko (1997), 'Three women economists in Japan', *Nihonbunka Kenkyusho Kiyo*, **79**.

Kitagawa, Nobu (1985), Introduction to Tanino (1985) (in Japanese).

Noguchi, Yukio (1995), *The Regime of 1940* (in Japanese), Tokyo: Toyo-keizai-shimposha.

Sanpei, Koko (1956), *The History of Working Women: History and Status Quo* (in Japanese), Tokyo: Nihon Hyoron-shinsha.

Taikakai, The Editorial Committee of the History of the Ministry of Home Affairs (1971), *The History of the Ministry of Home Affairs* (in Japanese), vol. 3, Tokyo: Taikakai.

Maria da Conceição Tavares (b. 1931)

Biographical sketch

Maria da Conceição Tavares, a leading Brazilian economist, was born in Portugal in 1931. After getting a degree in mathematics at the University of Lisbon in 1953, Tavares immigrated to Rio de Janeiro in 1954 and became a Brazilian citizen in 1957. In the mid- and late 1950s she worked as a statistician at government institutions and was trained as an economist at the Universidade do Brasil (now the Universidade Federal do Rio de Janeiro, UFRJ). The turning point in her professional life came in 1960–61, when she attended a postgraduate programme at the Economic Development Centre set up jointly by ECLA (United Nations' Economic Commission for Latin America, known as CEPAL in Latin American countries) and BNDE (the Brazilian National Bank for Economic Development) in Rio. At ECLA, Tavares was heavily influenced by well-known Latin American structuralist economists such as Raul Prebisch, Celso Furtado and especially Aníbal Pinto. Tavares's work has been very much in the tradition of ECLA's structural–historical approach, without any traces of her mathematical background (see the interview with Tavares in Biderman, Cozac and Rego, 1996, pp. 133–4). In 1961 she was invited to join the Economic Development Centre, which she did; she also did some part-time lecturing at the Department of Economics of UFRJ.

During the 1960s and early 1970s Tavares produced for ECLA a few essays on the development of the Brazilian economy (collected in Tavares, 1972), which soon became classics and established her reputation as one of the main interpreters of import-substituting industrialization in Brazil. After spending four years at ECLA headquarters in Santiago de Chile, she returned to Brazil in 1972 and, upon leaving ECLA in 1974, became deeply involved with the creation of economics postgraduate programmes at UFRJ and Universidade de Campinas (UNICAMP). As part of her new position as full-time university lecturer and researcher, Tavares wrote two long pieces on the cyclical pattern of economic growth in Brazil in the 1970s (Tavares, [1975] 1986; 1978). She has participated intensively in the debates about economic development and economic policy in Brazil, including the 1970s controversy on the causes and effects of unequal income distribution, and the reactions to the debt crisis and the recessive adjustments of the 1980s. Tavares retired from her university positions in the mid-1990s and, as a member of the Labour Party, was elected for the Brazilian Congress in 1995.

Import-substituting industrialization

Tavares's most influential contribution to the literature on Brazilian industrialization can be found in her first essay, published in English and Spanish in ECLA's *Economic Bulletin for Latin America* (Tavares, 1964a; 1964b; translated into Portuguese in Tavares, 1972, pp. 27–124). It is worth noting that, apart from a footnote, the authorship of the 1964 essay was not attributed (see Tavares, 1964a, p. 1). Hence, Hirschman (1968, p. 3, n. 4) referred to the 1964 article as an 'influential' one, without mentioning the name of the author, but rectified that in the 1971 reprint (cf. Hirschman, [1968] 1971, p. 88, n. 4). Tavares's 1964 piece has been regarded as the first systematic analysis of the dynamics of the import substitution process in Brazil and Latin America and, particularly, of its exhaustion in the early 1960s (see Hirschman, 1981, p. 106; Bielschowsky, 1988, p. 30; Love, 1994, pp. 431–2).

According to Tavares (1964a, p. 5), the dynamics of the process of development through import substitution may be regarded as 'a series of responses to the successive challenges presented by the restrictions in the external sector, as a result of which the economy gradually becomes less quantitatively dependent on external sources, and also effects a transformation in the nature of this dependence'. Historically, the import substitution process in Latin America started as a reaction to the external bottlenecks imposed by the world depression in the 1930s. In its first phase, substitution is concentrated on the domestic production of previously imported non-durable consumer goods, as the technological requirements are simpler and less capital-intensive in that sector, and, more importantly, there is a larger unexploited market for those goods. Given the income distribution pattern prevailing at the start of import-substituting industrialization, domestic industrial production was in the main directed to meeting the unsatisfied demand of high-income groups. In the initial stages of the process, the market expanded through the increase in the income of those groups and through incorporation of the workers employed in the new dynamic sectors. However, as Tavares (p. 8) explains, when import substitution is extended to durable consumer goods its growth is decided basically by the purchasing power of high-income brackets only, since the now higher capital–output ratio prevents massive absorption of labour, and, furthermore, large sectors of the population cannot participate in the durable consumer goods market because of their high relative price. At the same time, the import structure changes by a decline in the proportion of consumer goods and an increase in the proportion of intermediate and capital goods.

Another important feature of the industrialization process is that, given its substitutive nature, the technology adopted is imported from developed countries. This poses obstacles for the continuation of the process when it becomes necessary to embark on substitution in production sectors with increasing problems of scale and technological complexity, to wit the intermediate goods and capital goods sectors. As Tavares (p. 57) points out, the external bottle-neck stimulated the industrialization process only to the extent that there was untapped internal demand for consumer goods imports, which led to expansion of the domestic market and an ensuing demand for capital and intermediate goods, followed by another round of external bottleneck and substitution. Once the process reaches a stage when the imports not yet replaced consist mainly of capital and intermediate goods, and, furthermore, the consumption goods sectors have exhausted the market created by the external bottleneck, 'the latter ceases to act as an incentive to investment and hence to growth, and becomes merely an obstacle, removal of which can no longer be the motive underlying the dynamics of the economy'. From this perspective, the strategic problem faced by the Brazilian economy in the early 1960s according to Tavares was how to make the transition from an import substitution model to a self-sustained growth model. She suggested that the increasing capital–output ratio observed in the Brazilian economy would lead (under the assumption of fully used capacity) to decreasing returns in the industry as a whole, followed by a slow-down in the rate of economic growth (see 1964a, pp. 41, 56, 58).

Beyond stagnation

The stagnationist flavour of the concluding sections of Tavares (1964a) was widespread in Latin American structuralist thought at the end of the import substitution period in the mid-1960s (see, for example, Furtado, 1966) and was reinforced by the development of 'dependency theory' at the time (see Palma, 1987). However, the Latin American economy and especially the Brazilian economy started to grow again swiftly in the late 1960s. This was accompanied by a short period of crisis in the ECLA school of thought, as stagnationist theories had overlooked the cyclical pattern of capitalist development and the transformations in the world capitalist system (see also Tavares, 1972, pp. 20–24). It was in that context that Tavares and Serra wrote in 1971 (translated into Portuguese in Tavares, 1972, pp. 153–207, and into English in Petras, 1973, ch. 3) an essay that has been described as 'the first substantial critique of stagnationist theories' in Latin America (Palma, 1987, p. 804).

Tavares and Serra (1973, p. 62) claimed that, instead of a sign of a long-range structural stagnation, the crisis that followed the decline of the substitution process in Latin American economies should be interpreted as a transitory condition toward a new pattern of capitalist development, with the reinforcement of some features of the substitutive growth model (such as unequal income distribution) but also presenting dynamic characteristics absent from the latter. In order to understand the new model, Tavares and Serra (1973, pp. 64–70) first of all attempted to dispel the notion that stagnation was a necessary consequence of an increasing capital–output ratio. They pointed out that the capital–output ratio is an *ex post* (not an *ex ante*) variable, that is, a result and not a determinant of the economic process (cf. Tavares's footnote to the Portuguese translation of her 1964 essay, 1972, p. 120, n. 45). Accordingly, the relevant variable in the determination of investment demand is the expected rate of profit. The Brazilian economic downswing of the mid-1960s had been provoked by the impossibility of the rate of investment sustaining economic growth after the exhaustion of import substitution. The lack of massive new investments was explained by problems related to the composition of demand (highly concentrated income distribution and low consumption demand from the middle sectors) and to the lack of finance (wage–surplus relationship), which were solved through upward distribution of income in favour of the middle and upper groups and reduction of real wages of low-skill workers. The financial reforms introduced in the mid-1960s were instrumental in the transfer of the 'surplus' (corporate profits) to the financing of the purchase of durable consumer goods by the middle classes (Tavares and Serra, 1973, p. 80; see also Wells, 1977) and are behind the establishment of what Tavares (1972, pp. 213–18) calls 'financial capitalism' in Brazil.

The main characteristics of the new phase of economic growth of the Brazilian economy in the 1960s and 1970s (after the decline of the import substitution process) consist in the growing importance of durable consumer goods in the production structure accompanied by changes in the distributional trends and by investment demand carried out basically by modern sector foreign corporations in response to the growth in the demand for 'luxury' goods. The process of incorporation and dissemination of technical progress led by multinational firms brings about cycles of modernization in the dynamic sectors and accentuates the economy's structural heterogeneity (Tavares and Serra, 1973, pp. 81–5). The interactions between income distribution, investment demand and production structure put forward by Tavares and Serra have been formalized by Bacha and Taylor (1976) in a three-sector model with elastic supply of unskilled labour, leading to an unequalizing growth spiral (see also Taylor, 1991, pp. 19 and 256–60).

The peculiarities of the process of capital accumulation in dependent and underdeveloped economies like Brazil were further examined by Tavares in several studies carried out in the 1970s (Tavares, 1974, 1975 [1986] 1978), where she claimed that, besides the general wage–profit contradiction, underdeveloped economies are beset by a specific contradiction between 'capitalist consumption' (that is, modern sector workers with high wages) and 'worker consumption' (see Tavares, 1974, p. 39; 1975 [1986], pp. 29 and 143). At this stage, Tavares became attracted by the well-known Kaleckian division of the economy into three departments, which she applied to investigate the 'dynamic disproportions' between the demand composition and the production capacity of the economic system. She argued that (following the stylized facts mentioned above and adopting a Kaleckian framework of analysis) a continuous growth of profits at a speed higher than the growth in wages is possible only if the rate of investment is accelerated, that is, the capital goods sector must expand continuously ahead of the other sectors. Hence, despite the increasing rate of profit, the rate of investment will eventually decline because of excess capacity generated in the capital goods sector (and, by that, the rate of profit will also decline in the end), which provides an explanation for the upper turning point (see also the article by Tavares's former research students at UNICAMP, Possas and Baltar, 1981, pp. 156–9). The lower turning point is decided, as before, by the recovery in the sector producing durable consumer goods for 'capitalist consumption' (1975 [1986], pp. 142–3). As pointed out by Tavares and Serra (1973, p. 98), the growth cycle in dependent countries such as Brazil is shorter than in the economies of the developed 'centre', as the infeasibility of domestic generalization of technical progress together with the unequal income distribution 'abbreviates the periods during which the exchange surplus must be even more intensively reoriented' and provokes short and intense cycles of growth in productive capacity and consumption.

Debt crisis and recessive adjustment

After the early 1980s, Tavares changed the focus of her analytical efforts from the study of the process of uneven economic development of the 1960s and 1970s to the discussion of economic policy alternatives during the period of 'stagflation' in the Latin American economy. The dollar crisis and the first oil shock in the early 1970s were the first symptoms that the long boom in postwar capitalist expansion had come to an end. The breakdown of the US hegemony at the time was accompanied by the introduction of a floating exchange rate system and international financial liberalization, which, together with the oil shock, brought about a period of debt-led growth in Brazil, largely based on indebtedness by state enterprises (Tavares and Teixeira, 1981, pp. 100–101). According to Tavares (1985), the economic policies pursued by the USA since 1979 (the so-called 'Volcker shock'), with a combination of an expansionary fiscal policy and a restrictive monetary policy, resulted in higher interest rates and the attraction of financial flows to that country. This marked the beginning of what Tavares (1985) called the 'revival of the American hegemony', which led other industrialized countries to redirect their own policies to bring them into line with the American centre. This, together with the sudden halt in foreign loans in 1982, forced Brazil (and other Latin American countries) to implement a drastic adjustment process and to carry out profound changes in its trade structure (Tavares, 1985, pp. 144–5; see also Tavares and Gomes, 1998, p. 216).

The dramatic reduction in the rate of growth of the Brazilian economy in the 1980s and early 1990s, together with the intense inflationary process, resulted from the macroeconomic policies adopted in the attempt to reverse the growing domestic and internal imbalances, as discussed by Tavares (1993) in a paper presented at a meeting held in Washington at the Inter-American Development Bank in January 1993. Tavares argued that the restrictive monetary policy implemented through increasing government debt was ineffective in Brazil, as the debt issued by the government in the open market works as 'indexed money' with high liquidity, in what she described as a 'financial merry-go-round'. Moreover, devaluations of the exchange rate did not usually affect the relative prices of tradable goods, but, instead, had a strong impact on the debt of state enterprises and on the domestic price level because of the increasing prices of imported intermediate goods. More importantly, as pointed out by Tavares (1993, pp. 101–2), the rate of interest and the exchange rate work as 'reference prices' for the formation of expectations and for the average level of mark-ups over costs by producers, which means that increasing interest and exchange rates have a perverse effect in inflationary economies without a reliable monetary standard. After the resumption of a positive net inflow of foreign resources in the early 1990s, and the consequent increase of reserves, the Brazilian government successfully untangled the indexation mechanism that perpetuated inflation and achieved stabilization through the creation of a new currency and the use of the exchange rate as a nominal 'anchor'. Tavares, however, has been critical of Brazil's recent excessive exposure to cyclical movements of short-term capital, which she has described as a 'new form of dependency' (Tavares and Melin, 1997). In a methodological reflection on the crisis of economic theory, Tavares (1990) criticized orthodox economics for neglecting the fact that capital accumulation and technological progress are not conducive to human happiness in the present state of instability and unpredictability of the world economy. As far as the Latin American countries are concerned, the basic question, according to Tavares (1990, pp. 218–19), is not the gap between growth and stagnation, but the fact that several decades of 'conservative modernization' have not affected the unequal structural matrix of capitalism in their economies.

MAURO BOIANOVSKY

Bibliography

Selected writings by Maria da Conceição Tavares

(1964a), 'The Growth and Decline of Import Substitution in Brazil', *Economic Bulletin for Latin America*, **9**(1), 1–59.

(1964b), 'Auge y declinación del proceso de sustitución de importaciones en el Brasil', *Boletín Económico de America Latina*, **9**(1), 1–62.

(1971), 'Más allá del estancamiento: Una discusión sobre el estilo del desarrollo reciente en Brasil' (with J. Serra), *El Trimestre Económico*, no. 152.

(1972), *Da Substituição de Importações ao Capitalismo Financeiro: Ensaios sobre Economia Brasileira* (*From Import Substitution to Financial Capitalism: Essays on the Brazilian Economy*), Rio: Zahar.

(1973), 'Beyond Stagnation: A Discussion on the Nature of Recent Developments in Brazil' (with J. Serra), in J. Petras (ed.), *Latin America: From Dependence to Revolution*, New York: John Wiley & Sons.

(1974), 'Distribuição de Renda, Acumulação e Padrões de Industrialização: Um Ensaio Preliminar' ('Income Distribution, Accumulation and Industrialization Patterns: A Preliminary Essay'), in R. Tolipan and A.C. Tinelli (eds, *A Controvérsia sobre Distribuição de Rende e Desenvolvimento*, Rio: Zahar.

([1975] 1986), *Acumulação de Capital e Industrialização no Brazil* (*Capital Accumulation and Industrialization in Brazil*), Campinas: UNICAMP.

(1978), 'Ciclo e Crise: O Movimento Recente da Industrialização Brasileira' ('Business Cycle and Crisis: The Recent Phase of Brazilian Industrialization'), unpublished manuscript.

(1981), 'Transnational Enterprises and the Internationalization of Capital in Brazilian Industry' (with A. Teixiera), *CEPAL Review*, **14**, 85–105.

(1985), 'The Revival of American Hegemony', *CEPAL Review*, **26**, 139–46.

(1990), 'Economics and Happiness', *CEPAL Review*, **42**, 211–20.

(1993), 'As políticas de ajuste no Brazil: os limites da resistencia' ('The adjustment policies in Brazil: the limits of resistance'), in M.C. Tavares and J.L. Fiori, *Desajuste Global e Modernização Conservadora*, S. Paulo: Paz e Terra.

(1997), 'A Desordem Globalizada e a Nova Dependencia' ('Globalized Disorder and the New Dependency') (with L.E. Malin), *Revista ANPEC*, **2**, 9–30.

(1998), 'La CEPAL y la integración económica de America Latina' (with G. Gomes), *Revista de la CEPAL*, Special Issue, 213–28.

Other sources and references

Bacha, E. and L. Taylor (1976), 'The Unequalizing Spiral: A First Growth Model For Belindia', *Quarterly Journal of Economics*, **90**(2), 197–218.

Biderman, C., L.F. Cozac and J.M. Rego (1996), *Conversas com Economistas Brasileiros* (*Conversations with Brazilian Economists*), S. Paulo: Editora 34.

Bielschowsky, R. (1988), *Pensamento Economico Brasileiro: O Ciclo Ideológico do Desenvolvimentismo* (*Brazilian Economic Thought: The Ideological Cycle of Developmentalism*), Rio: IPEA.

Furtado, C. (1966), *Development and Stagnation in Latin America*, New Haven: Yale University Press.

Hirschman, A.O. (1968), 'The Political Economy of Import-Substituting Industrialization in Latin America', *Quarterly Journal of Economics*, **82**(1), 2–32.

Hirschman, A.O. (1971), *A Bias for Hope: Essays on Development and Latin America*. New Haven: Yale University Press.

Hirschman, A.O. (1981), *Essays in Trespassing: Economics to Politics and Beyond*, Cambridge: Cambridge University Press.

Love, J.L. (1994), 'Economic Ideas and Ideologies in Latin America since 1930', in L. Bethell (ed.), *The Cambridge History of Latin America*, vol. 6. Cambridge: Cambridge University Press.

Palma, G. (1987), 'Dependency', in J. Eatwell et al. (eds), *The New Palgrave: A Dictionary of Economics*, vol. 1. London: Macmillan.

Possas, M. and P. Baltar (1981), 'Demande Efetiva e Dinamica em Kalecki' ('Kalecki on Effective Demand and Economic Dynamics'), *Pesquisa e Planejamento Economico*, **11**(1), 107–60.

Taylor, L. (1991), *Income Distribution, Inflation and Growth: Lectures on Structuralist Macroeconomic Theory*, Cambridge, MA: MIT Press.

Wells, J. (1977), 'The Diffusion of Durables in Brazil and its Implications for Recent Controversies concerning Brazilian Development', *Cambridge Journal of Economics*, **1**(3), 259–79.

Marguerite Thibert (1886–1982)

Marguerite Thibert was born Marguerite Javouhey, the daughter of a hardware wholesaler on 31 January 1886 at Chalon-sur-Saône (Saône-et-Loire), France. She earned her *brevet supérieur* at a Dominican school and then, with her sister, prepared privately for her *baccalauréat* examination. She married Georges Thibert, an architectural student, in 1912. When he was appointed architect of the National Assembly, she moved with him to Paris, where he died in 1915.

Thibert continued her study of philosophy, and after earning her licence began to teach at Sévigny College in 1917. She decided to write a doctoral thesis entitled *Le féminisme dans le socialisme français, de 1830 à 1850* under the direction of Célestin Bouglé. This she completed in 1926, becoming the fourth woman *docteur ès-lettres* in France. From that time, she was in contact with the feminist lawyer Marcelle Kraemer-Bach and Cécile Brunschvicg, president of the Union française pour le suffrage des femmes. Thibert joined the Union in 1922 and contributed to its review *La paix par le droit*.

In 1926, Thibert joined the International Labour Office at the invitation of Bouglé, studying the issue of international migration. She worked on this topic for three years, but remained with the ILO until 1965. In 1929, at the request of Albert Thomas, she became head of the division concerned with working women and children, and stayed with this division until 1957. During the 1930s, she wrote against limitations on working women in periods of unemployment. She was sent as an expert observer to many nations.

During her first visit to the United States in 1935, she became acquainted with Eleanor Roosevelt and made contact with trade unionists in the garment industry, especially the International Ladies' Garment Workers' Union. Between 1935 and 1939, she travelled widely in Europe and participated in a number of conferences devoted to the issue of women's rights.

She remained in Geneva until 1941, when she followed the ILO to Canada and the USA where she supported the issue of a free France. After the war, she worked as an international expert and undertook missions to China, the

Middle East, India and Central America. She returned to France in 1957, but maintained contact and continued to undertake studies on behalf of the ILO.

Thibert joined l'Union de la gauche socialiste, then the Convention des institutions républicaines and finally the Parti socialiste in 1972.

EVELYN L. FORGET

Bibliography

Selected writings by Marguerite Thibert
(1921), *Féminisme et socialisme d'aprés Flora Tristan*, Paris: M. Rivière.
(1923), 'Saint-simoniennes et pacifistes [Eugénie Niboyet and Pauline Roland]', *La paix par le droit*, **23**(6), June.
(1925), '*Le Rôle social de l'art d'après Saint-Simon*, Paris: M. Rivière.
(1926), 'Le Rôle social de l'art d'après les saint-simoniens', thèse complémentaire pour le doctoral ès lettres, présentée à la Faculté des lettres de l'Académie de Paris, Paris: M. Rivière.
(1926), 'Le Féminisme dans le socialisme français, de 1830 à 1850', thèse principale pour le doctorat ès lettres, présentée à la Faculté des lettres de l'Université de Paris, Paris: M. Giard.
(1930), *L'Émigration (Immigration et migrations)*, Paris: Sirey.
(1933), 'Crise économique et travail féminin', *Revue internationale du travail*, **27**(4-5), April–May.
(1948), 'Training problems in the Far East. Report on technical and vocational training in the Far East, prepared for the International Labour Organisation and the United Nations Economic Commission for Asia and the Far East', preface by David A. Morse, Geneva: International Labour Office (Studies and reports), new series, no. 11.

Other sources and references
Maitron, Jean and Claude Pennetier (1992), *Dictionnaire biographique du mouvement ouvrier Français*, quatrième partie: 1914–1939, vol. 42, Paris: les éditions ouvrières.

Mabel Frances Timlin (1891–1976)

Mabel Frances Timlin was born on 6 December 1891 in Forest Junction, Wisconsin. After studying at the Milwaukee State Normal School and teaching in Wisconsin and rural Saskatchewan, Mabel Timlin joined the University of Saskatchewan as a secretary in 1921. She initially intended to study economics at the University of Saskatchewan, but, upon closer acquaintance with the Department of Economics and Political Science, she decided (correctly) that she could learn more economics on her own, and decided to take her degree in English. After taking her BA with great distinction in English in 1929, Timlin directed correspondence courses in economics until 1942, and became instructor in economics in 1935, after completing graduate course work at the University of Washington during summers and a six-month leave. She became Assistant Professor in Economics at the University of Saskatchewan and a member of the executive committee of the Canadian Political Science Association (CPSA) in 1941 in her fiftieth year, when she received her Ph.D. from the University of Washington for *Keynesian Economics* (1942). She was promoted to Associate Professor in 1946 and Full Professor in 1950, although her salary remained low. She retired as Professor Emeritus in 1957, and never married. Timlin was elected a Fellow of the Royal Society of Canada in 1951, then the only female fellow in the social sciences or humanities, and was named to the Order of Canada in 1976. In 1959–60, she was the first woman president of the CPSA (then including economics). Timlin served on the executive committee of the American Economic Association (1958–60), and was one of very few Canadian economists to take part in International Economic Association round tables. She received an honorary doctorate from the University of Saskatchewan, which has established an annual Timlin Lecture in economics or political science. She died on 19 September 1976, in Saskatoon.

Timlin's study of Keynesian economics began in 1935, before publication of Keynes's *General Theory*, when Benjamin Higgins came to teach at the University of Saskatchewan for a year, bringing a copy of Robert Bryce's seminar paper based on Keynes's lectures. Her major work, *Keynesian Economics*, presented a static 'Keynes–Lange system' restating Keynes in Walrasian general equilibrium terms, and then advanced two 'supplementary models' of shifting equilibrium in sequence economies, extensively illustrated with innovative diagrams. She adapted the process analysis of D.H. Robertson and Bertil Ohlin to track the shifting equilibrium of a Keynesian system, in which the equilibrium for one week creates new conditions for the next. When Keynes died, Timlin organized a Canadian Political Science Association memorial session at the annual Learned Societies conference. Harry Johnson described Timlin's *Keynesian Economics* as the first work of economics to establish 'a Canadian claim to competence ... in pure theory ... a remarkable personal achievement which extended the Keynesian model by replacing the long-term interest rate by an analysis of the structure of interest rates and its role in the general equilibrium of the system' (quoted by Ainley, 1999, p. 29). Warren Young has argued that the neglect of Timlin (1942) has led to unwarranted attributions of originality:

> To be brief, they [Robert Clower and Axel Leijonhufvud] have restated the link that Lange made between Keynes and Walras some thirty years earlier, which was subsequently developed by Timlin more than twenty years prior to Clower's 1965 paper. ... Leijonhufvud did not pay attention to the fact that his proposed FIM [full information macroeconomic] model is similar, if not identical, to the Keynes–Lange system developed by Timlin [in her Fundamental Model] over forty years earlier. (Young, 1987, pp. 155–6)

A Guggenheim Fellowship in 1945 to study welfare economics led to her next importation of theory into a largely atheoretical Canadian economics profession, with an article arguing for the policy relevance of general equilibrium analysis and three review articles on Lerner, Lange and Myint, in the *Canadian Journal of Economics and Political Science* (1945–49). She then turned from theory to policy: Timlin's *Does Canada Need More People?* (1951) held that increased immigration would raise output per capita, and she concluded a decade of writing on immigration policy with a historical review in her 1960 CPSA presidential address. In the *American Economic Review* (1953), she blasted the Bank of Canada for neglecting countercyclical stabilization during the Korean War boom.

Her last publication (Timlin, 1968) was a monograph on the financing and organization of the social sciences in Canada, commissioned in 1964 by the Social Science Research Council of Canada. She concluded that

> Under-support or fear of the social sciences is a sign of immaturity in a society. ... [T]he maturity which finds dissent tolerable is not enough to ensure the quality of the decision. But if the society is one which has also a concern for and an understanding of both the nature of justice and the conditions which can create equality of opportunity for human beings, it will be able in its decision-making to utilize the services of its social scientists in a manner which improves the quality of life. It may even be able under such conditions to escape much, if not most, of the violence of our violent age.

An inspiring teacher, Timlin promoted Keynesianism in Canada and expounded modern economic theory to Canadian economists. Devoted to the University of Saskatchewan, where she was the only economic theorist, she rejected offers from the University of Toronto and elsewhere. The first tenured woman among Canadian economists and a former secretary who first published at the age of 50, Timlin broke barriers.

ROBERT W. DIMAND

Bibliography

Selected writings by Mabel Frances Timlin

(1942), *Keynesian Economics*, Toronto: University of Toronto Press; reprinted, with biographical note by A.E. Safarian and introduction by Lorie Tarshis, Toronto: McClelland and Stewart, Carleton Library, 1977.

(1945), 'Review article on *The Economics of Control* by Abba Lerner', *Canadian Journal of Economics and Political Science*, **11**, February, 285–93.

(1946a), 'Review article on *Price Flexibility and Employment* by Oscar Lange', *Canadian Journal of Economics and Political Science*, **12**, May, 204–13.

(1946b), 'General Equilibrium Analysis and Public Policy', *Canadian Journal of Economics and Political Science*, **12**, November, 483–95, and rejoinder, **13**, May 1947, 285–7.

(1947), 'John Maynard Keynes', *Canadian Journal of Economics and Political Science*, **13**, August, 363–5.

(1949), 'Review article on *Theories of Welfare Economics* by Hla Myint', *Canadian Journal of Economics and Political Science*, **15**, November, 551–9.

(1950), 'Economic Theory and Immigration Policy', *Canadian Journal of Economics and Political Science*, **16**, August, 375–82.

(1951), *Does Canada Need More People?*, Toronto: Oxford University Press.

(1953), 'Recent Developments in Canadian Monetary Policy', *American Economic Review: Papers and Proceedings*, **43**, May, 42–53.

(1955), 'Monetary Stabilization Policies and Keynesian Theory', in Kenneth R. Kudhara (ed.), *Post-Keynesian Economics*, London: George Allen & Unwin, pp. 59–88.

(1958), 'Canadian Immigration with Special Reference to the Post-War Period', in International Economic Association, *International Migration*, London: Macmillan, ch. 11.

(1960), 'Canada's Immigration Policy, 1896–1910', *Canadian Journal of Economics and Political Science*, **26**, November, 517–32.

(1968), 'The Social Sciences in Canada: Retrospect and Potential', in Mabel F. Timlin and Albert Faucher, *The Social Sciences in Canada: Two Studies (Les Sciences Sociales au Canada: Deux Etudes)*, Ottawa: Social Science Research Council of Canada, pp. 25–136.

Other sources and references

Ainley, Marianne Gosztonyi (1999), 'Mabel F. Timlin, 1891–1976: A Woman Economist in The World of Men', *Atlantis: A Women's Studies Journal*, **23**(2), Spring, 28–38.

Neill, Robin F. (1991), *A History of Canadian Economic Thought*, London and New York: Routledge.

Rymes, T.K. (1995), 'Mabel Timlin and Keynesian Economics', in A *Tribute to Mabel Timlin, Canadian Women Economists Network Newsletter* (November).

Spafford, Duff (1977), 'In Memoriam: Mabel F. Timlin', *Canadian Journal of Economics*, **10**, May, 279–81.

Spafford, Shirley (forthcoming), Draft history of economics and political science at the University of Saskatchewan.

Young, Warren (1987), *Interpreting Mr. Keynes: The IS–LM Enigma*, Cambridge: Polity Press and Boulder, CO: Westview Press.

Cläre Tisch (1907–?41)

Cläre Tisch was born on 14 January 1907 in Wuppertal-Elberfeld, Germany, and it is presumed that she died in the Holocaust, Minsk, November 1941. Between 1926 and 1929 Tisch, who was descended from a Jewish merchant family, studied economics at the Universities of Bonn, Geneva, Berlin and again Bonn where she took her diploma exam in July 1929. Afterwards she began to write her Ph.D. thesis under the supervision of Joseph A. Schumpeter who also suggested the topic, 'Economic calculation and distribution in a centralized socialist commonwealth'. Two years later Tisch finished her doctoral thesis and gained her Ph.D. with the successful oral exam from the University of Bonn on 31 July 1931. Subsequently she became a research assistant of Arthur Spiethoff until she was dismissed by the Nazis in 1933. She earned her living as a shorthand typist in Cologne and a clerk in a shoeshop in Solingen before she became the head of the central office for orphans of the Jewish Women League in Wuppertal in 1936. She sacrificed several possibilities to emigrate so that she could take care of Jewish orphans.

She was probably killed immediately after arrival in the Jewish ghetto in Minsk at the end of 1941.

In the two years as a researcher at Bonn University Tisch wrote two books on the cartel question. In the first one she analysed the jurisdiction of the German Cartel Court since the passing of the law against the abuse of economic power in November 1923 (1934a). In the other volume (1934b) she dealt with the role of small and medium-sized firms in German industry, particularly in sectors producing final products where they dominated. Although she argued against price cartels from a liberal point of view, she nevertheless favoured cartels among these small firms as a means to challenge the dominance of big business on the suppliers' side, in industries such as iron, coal, steel and electricity, as well as the group of powerful department stores on the demand side. But she clearly saw the limitations of this 'second-best' solution. The emphasis on dynamic issues demonstrated her Schumpeterian views which come out, for example, when she argues against a *Kartellrentnertum*, that is, cartel rentiership, which would undermine the speed of technical progress and thus would generate welfare losses (1934b, pp. 143–4).

However, there can be no doubt that Tisch's most important scientific contribution was her doctoral thesis *Wirtschaftsrechnung und Verteilung im zentralistisch organisierten sozialistischen Gemeinwesen* [Economic calculation and distribution in the centrally organized socialist community] (1932). Whereas her work was recognized as an important contribution to the contemporary debate, as emerges, for example, in Hayek, who testified that Tisch had put together a useful collection of different allusions to the problem of economic calculation in the socialist community from Marx's writings (Hayek, 1935, p. 13), or in Hoff (1949), her contribution has almost fallen into oblivion nowadays. Nevertheless, even from a critical modern perspective it has to be noted that Tisch's contribution as well as Marschak's early critique of Mises (Marschak, 1924) contradicts the commonly made sweeping statement that the opponents of Mises in continental Europe were blinded by Marxism and completely lacking in economic theory; this only changed after the socialist calculation debate was transferred to the Anglo-Saxon language area after 1933. Tisch's doctoral thesis deploys serious economic analysis which is not distorted by political prejudices. Her critique of barter socialism is as well founded as her own solution of the socialist calculation problem which is based on a Walrasian general equilibrium system in the version of Cassel.

Tisch can be regarded as a forerunner of the so-called 'neoclassical socialists', like H.D. Dickinson, Oskar Lange and Abba Lerner, who dominated the debate in the 1930s (see Vaughn, 1980, pp. 540 ff.). Thus it is no accident that Hayek in his later confrontation with these authors also referred to Tisch's work (Hayek, 1940, p. 128). The later debate and the development of modern input–output and activity analysis have shown that efficient production within the framework of quantity planning is possible and that the result coincides with the solution in the price system under the conditions of the duality theorem (as constant returns to scale). In this respect Tisch was right in her critique of Mises's thesis that economic calculation in a socialist common-wealth is impossible. However, her procedure, like the more elaborated approaches later developed by Lange and Lerner, was decisively static, and she underestimated the full implications of dynamic phenomena for the viability and efficiency of socialist economies in the long run. Although she agreed with Mises that a monetary system is a prerequisite for calculation and made a survey of the discussion of money in Marxist literature, she held a limited conception of the nature of a monetary economy, in which the role of money is reduced to its accounting and means-of-payment functions, despite the fact that the store-of-value function was as decisive for Marx in his critique of Say's law as was later the case for Keynes. In this context she also did not see the importance of efficient capital markets and of the property-rights argument for the adoption of risk, responsibility and decision-making and for the long-run evolution of technical progress.

It should be pointed out that Mises only fully developed his essential argument that the economy is in a process of permanent change and that therefore the data necessary for efficient planning are not available in the second edition of his *Gemeinwirtschaft* (1932, pp. 182 ff.), which Tisch could not have known when she wrote her thesis. All the more so this holds for Hayek's important writings since 1935 in which he developed the argument on the dispersion of knowledge and the problem of decision-making with uncertainty and incomplete information (see Streissler, 1994). Against Hayek's later argument that a central planning office does not use the necessary information to guide economic activities efficiently, Tisch had not much to say. Nevertheless her work was at the forefront of the contemporary debate and must be seen as an eminent precursor of the subsequent writings of the neoclassical socialists whose critique of Mises, valid only for a static system, prepared the ground for the shift and the pungency of the critique of the socialist economic system by Hayek. Unfortunately, political circumstances prevented Tisch from participating in the later debate.

Tisch was highly esteemed by the other outstanding fellow students in Schumpeter's seminar at the University of Bonn – like August Lösch, Hans Singer (1997, p. 130) and Wolfgang F. Stolper (1994, pp. 12 and 358) – in the late 1920s and early 1930s. Being about three years more advanced than most of the others, she was one of the most devoted students of Schumpeter, who repeatedly sent affidavits during the Nazi period and with whom she corre-sponded until the end. Tisch not only made accurate notes on Schumpeter's lectures but also of his valedictory address 'Das Woher und Wohin unserer

Wissenschaft' ('The Origin and Destination of our Science') delivered to the Faculty of State Sciences in Bonn on 20 June 1932 before he left for Harvard, in which he emphasized that he never tried to bring about a Schumpeter School but instead saw his function as 'opening doors' (1952, p. 600). Schumpeter wanted to open the American door for his early favourite student in Bonn to enable Tisch to escape the Nazi regime. In her last letter to Schumpeter, dated 8 November 1941, Tisch mentioned that she would leave Wuppertal soon and that she neither knew her new address nor whether she could inform her former teacher in due course. This remained the last sign of her life. From a deportation list, located in the archive of the city of Wuppertal, it is evident that on 11 November 1941 Cläre Tisch was carried off to Minsk, where it is presumed she was killed.

HARALD HAGEMANN

Bibliography

Selected writings by Cläre Tisch
(1932), *Wirtschaftsrechnung und Verteilung im zentralistisch organisieren sozialistischen Gemeinwesen*, Wuppertal-Elberfeld: Scheschinski.
(1934a), *Der wirtschaftliche Sinn der bisherigen Rechtsprechung des deutschen Kartellgerichts*, Frankfurt: Vittorio Klostermann.
(1934b), *Organisationsformen der deutschen Mittelindustrie*, Frankfurt: Vittorio Klostermann.

Other sources and references
Hayek, F. A. (ed.) (1935), *Collectivist Economic Planning*, London: Routledge.
Hayek, F.A. (1940), 'Socialist Calculation: The Competitive Solution', *Economica*, 7, 125–49.
Hoff, T.J.B. (1949), *Economic Calculation in the Socialist Society*, London, Edinburgh and Glasgow: William Hodge; Engl. transl. of the 1938 Norwegian original.
Marschak, J. (1924), 'Wirtschaftsrechnung und Gemeinwirtschaft. Zur Mises'schen These von der Unmöglichkeit sozialistischer Wirtschaftsrechnung', *Archiv für Sozialwissenschaft und Sozialpolitik*, 51, 501–20.
Mises, L.v. (1920), 'Die Wirtschaftsrechnung im sozialistischen Gemeinwesen', *Archiv für Sozialwissenschaft und Sozialpolitik*, 47, 86–121; English transl. 'Economic Calculation in the Socialist Commonwealth', in Hayek (1935), pp. 87–130.
Mises, L.v. (1922), *Die Gemeinwirtschaft. Untersuchungen über den Sozialismus*, Jena: Gustav Fischer; 2nd edn 1932.
Schumpeter, J.A. (1952), 'Das Woher und Wohin unserer Wissenschaft', in E. Schneider and A. Spiethoff (eds), *Joseph A. Schumpeter. Aufsätze zur ökonomischen Theorie*, Tübingen: J.C.B. Mohr (Paul Siebeck), pp. 598–608.
Singer, H.W. (1997), 'The Influence of Schumpeter and Keynes on the Development of a Development Economist', in H. Hagemann (ed.), *Zur deutschsprachigen wirtschafts- wissenschaftlichen Emigration nach 1933*, Marburg: Metropolis, pp. 127–50.
Stolper, W.F. (1994), *Joseph Alois Schumpeter. The Public Life of a Private Man*, Princeton: Princeton University Press.
Streissler, E. (1994), 'Hayek on Information and Socialism', in M. Colonna, H. Hagemann and O.F. Hamouda (eds), *Capital, Socialism and Knowledge. The Economics of F.A. Hayek*, vol. 2, Aldershot: Edward Elgar, pp. 47–75.
Vaughn, K.J. (1980), 'Economic Calculation under Socialism: The Austrian Contribution', *Economic Inquiry*, 18, 535–54.

Flora Tristan (1803–44)

The writings of Frenchwoman Flora Tristan have yet to be explored in discussions of early economic thought. Feminists, however, rediscovered Tristan's work in the 1920s, and again in the 1990s, and have examined her writing in the contexts of the intellectual development of feminist thought, social theory and socialist and Utopian thought. Although she wrote numerous pamphlets and petitions, a novel (*Mephis*), three travel narratives (*Peregrinations of a Pariah 1833–1835, Promenades dans Londres*, or, *The London Journal*, and *Le Tour de France*), and a political treatise calling for an international workers' union (*L'Union Ouvrière*), Tristan's work has remained outside the borders of classical political economy. Yet, in 1963, G.D.H. Cole declared Tristan's plan in *L'Union Ouvrière* to be 'the first published project of a world-wide Workers' International, … she was the first person to put forward a definite plan for an all-inclusive Proletarian International'.

In many of her writings Tristan dealt with perspectives on political economy and capitalism in particular, and on developing her theory linking women's inequality to economic forces. *The London Journal* initiated her political and historical critique of capitalism and foreshadowed Marx's discussions of worker alienation and exploitation. In *The London Journal*, Tristan put forth her theory that gender inequality is a cornerstone of both capitalism and patriarchy, arguing that capitalism fosters sexism and exploits both workers and women. She saw these two forms of exploitation as interconnected and pointed out that equality for women without economic transformation would only help upper-class women, and that improvements for the working class would not ensure gender equality. In *The London Journal*, Tristan's analysis of classical political economy was fundamental to her positions on gender and worker equality. She draws heavily on the traditions of the Utopian socialists, German philosophers and early political economists (1972, p. 169). *The London Journal* remains primarily a social critique grounded in a parallel critique of industrial capitalism attacking aspects of industrial and bourgeois capitalism at every turn, particularly discussions of economic factors responsible for worker alienation and exploitation. Tristan links falling wages to manufacturers' desire to reduce the cost of production so that products will continue to dominate domestic and international markets.

She links higher taxes to the state's need to maintain imperial connections, and higher tariffs (in a heated exhortation on the Corn Laws) as necessary to protect domestic agriculture. And, without the traditional 'scientific' explanation, Tristan, none the less puts forth a classical labour theory of value, noting that institutions enforce the necessary labour relations to maintain this production of wealth.

Her disdain of the English economists' views on the poor is apparent throughout her work. She notes that the callousness of the views of Malthus towards the poor are shared by Ricardo and the entire school of English economists, and attacks them.

In her critique of capitalism and the industrial system, Tristan's rhetoric resembles various Utopian socialists from Owen (whom she at one point admires) to the Fourierists and Saint-Simonians. In studying Tristan's feminism, Marie Cross and Tim Gray point out that in Tristan's time the word 'socialism' referred not to a political agenda, but to 'a method of analysis incorporating a critical perspective by which to make sense of social phenomena' (1992, p. 67). Still, Tristan proposes reforms that include both liberal and socialist ideas. She writes of individual freedom, liberty and enfranchisement as well as civil and civic responsibility. At the same time as she deplores the social conditions of workers and women, she calls for reforms of existing capitalist structures. In her analysis of capitalism she acknowledges the positive effects of the Industrial Revolution and seeks a social revolution to enable all social classes to enjoy the fruits of these discoveries. While supporting changes in working conditions and an overhaul of capitalism through worker organization and associations, she recognizes that a worker-inspired revolution will do little for women.

In *The London Journal*, Tristan not only bases her analysis of worker alienation and exploitation on capitalism, but also puts the case that these same economic forces are the primary cause of women's inequality. She notes that this inequality is rooted in both property relations and in economic discrimination in education and work. Women are denied education, training and jobs, and until these patriarchal and market relations are changed women will continue to be unequal. While initially Tristan believed that workers' rights and women's rights could be pursued together and were complementary to one another, she ultimately concluded that women's rights were a precondition for workers' rights. The emancipation of women was essential to the emancipation of all workers. While issues of women's inequality are raised throughout *The London Journal*, two chapters are devoted to examining the plight of two classes of English women.

In an earlier work Tristan calls for the abolition of property – particularly women as property. In 1837 she wrote in 'Petition pour le rétablissement du divorce a Messieurs les deputés', 'that all property is theft – of land, capital, women, men, children, family – of ideas ... A terrible curse must be called down on property' (Dijkstra, 1991, p. 152). In *The London Journal*, however, revolutionary reform is suggested to ameliorate injustices of the existing economic forces. Her analysis of the causes of sexism and discrimination against women is clear, and Tristan has offered us more than observation; she has offered us an economic analysis of class structure and its interrelationship with women's inequality, capitalism and patriarchy.

While her writing about economic issues was important and interesting, her life resembles a 1990s soap opera. Born Flora Celestine Therese Henriette Tristan Moscoso in 1803 in Paris, her mother had been a refugee in Spain during the French Revolution where she met and married Don Mariano de Tristan Moscoso, a colonel in the Spanish Army and member of a prominent Peruvian family. The Tristans settled in France after the war, entertaining their family friend, Simon Bolivar, on occasion and enjoying the privilege of the aristocracy. This prosperity lasted only until her father's death in 1807. In settling his estate French authorities discovered that the Tristans had failed to obtain a French marriage certificate, making the marriage illegal. The French government confiscated the family home and possessions. Tristan Moscoso's Peruvian family refused to provide for the family. Flora grew up in relative poverty in the French countryside without a formal education, moving to Paris when she was 15. Forced to work to support her family, she was employed by the painter and lithographer André Chazal. Flora's mother arranged her daughter's marriage to Chazal – which Flora opposed – in 1821. A violent and abusive marriage caused Flora to leave Chazal in 1825, and begin her life-long petitioning of government officials to allow women to divorce under French law.

By chance, Flora overheard a ship captain talking of her Peruvian family and she discovered that her grandmother was still alive, as was Uncle Pio, who refused to support Flora's family. Flora sent her children to stay with her mother, well out of Chazal's reach, and journeyed to Peru to claim her birthright. Her grandmother died just as Tristan reached South America and Don Pio, charmed by Flora, consented to a small allowance. Tristan returned to France and wrote of her adventure in an autobiographical narrative, *Peregrinations of a Pariah* (1838). While the book was a success in France, Don Pio had all copies in Peru burned and revoked Flora's newly won allowance.

On her return to France, Chazal demanded Flora's return and the return of the children. Chazal was so provoked by Flora's resistance that he shot her. Flora survived, and Chazal's trial only generated more publicity for Flora and her book. Chazal was sentenced to 20 years' hard labour.

Influenced by Robert Owen, Saint-Simonians, Fourierists and other socialists, Flora turned her attention to social issues, particularly to the status of women. She regularly invited French intellectuals and workers to her parlour for provocative discussions. Her small apartment became a popular gathering-place for conversations of critical social issues.

After publishing *L'Union Ouvrière*, Flora travelled throughout France meeting workers and promoting the international union. She kept a log of these journeys which were published after she died in 1844 at the age of 41, suffering from typhoid fever and a stroke. Her Tour of France was published in 1844, and her notes for *L'Emancipation de la femme, ou le Testament de la paria*, were rewritten and published by Alphonse Constant in 1845.

After Flora's death, her daughter Aline married Clovis Gauguin and gave birth to a son, Paul, who would grow up to be an artist (Paul Gauguin).

JEAN SHACKELFORD

Bibliography

Selected writings by Flora Tristan

(1835), *Nécessité de faire un bon accueil aux femmes étrangères*, Paris: Imprimerie de Mme. Huzard.

(1838), *Peregrinations of a Pariah 1833–1835*, edited and translated by Jean Hawkes, Boston: Beacon Press, 1986.

(1838), *Mephis*, Paris: A. Betrand.

(1840–42), *The London Journal of Flora Tristan 1842 or the Aristocracy and the Working Class of England*, translated by Jean Hawkes, London: Virago, 1984.

(1843), *Union ouvrière*, Paris: Prevot.

(1845), *L'Emancipation de la femme: Ou, la testament de la paria*, Paris: Guarin.

(1984), *The London Journal of Flora Tristan 1842*, or *The Aristocracy and the Working Class of England*, trans. Jean Hawkes, London: Virago.

(1986), *Peregrinations of a Pariah 1833–1835*, ed. and trans. Jean Hawkes, Boston: Beacon Press.

Other sources and references

Beik, Doris and Paul Beik (1993), *Flora Tristan, Utopian Feminist: Her Travel Diaries and Personal Crusade*, Bloomington, IN: Indiana University Press.

Cross, Maire and Tim Gray (1992), *The Feminism of Flora Tristan*, Oxford: Berg Publishers Limited.

Desanti, Dominique (1972), *A Woman in Revolt: A Biography of Flora Tristan*, trans. Elizabeth Zelvin, New York: Crown Publishers, Inc.

Dijkstra, Sandra (1991), *Flora Tristan: Feminism in the Age of George Sand*, London: Pluto Press.

Mary Abby Van Kleeck (1883–1972)

Born in Glenham, New York in 1883 and dying of a heart attack in Kingston, New York, in 1972, not long before her 89th birthday, Van Kleeck graduated from Flushing High School in 1900 and received her AB from Smith College in 1904. Her father was an Episcopal minister and her mother the daughter of one of the founders of the Baltimore and Ohio Railroad. In her AB, Van Kleeck concentrated on economics and social work and subsequently undertook graduate studies in social economy at Columbia University under the supervision of Edward T. Devine and Henry R. Seager.

While at Columbia, Van Kleeck joined a group of social investigators and women reformers which included Lillian Brandt, Florence Kelley (*q.v.*) and a number of other feminists associated with the Women's Trade Union League of New York. She was a fellow of the College Settlements Association and during 1905–6 conducted research on child labour in the factories and tenements of New York City. Following this experience, as Industrial Secretary of the Alliance Employment Bureau, Van Kleeck launched her pioneering investigations into women's employment.

The Russell Sage Foundation began supporting her studies in 1908, and in 1910 integrated them into the work of its newly established committee on women's employment chaired by Henry Seager. Van Kleeck's studies were characterized by the use of rigorous statistical methods – which involved collection and analysis of data from factory records, payroll sheets and other official documents – attention to the relationship between wage levels and the standard of living enjoyed by workers, and the effects of labour legislation on women's working conditions and employment opportunities. These studies enabled her to produce several books: *Artificial Flower Makers* (1913), *Women in the Bookbinding Trade* (1913), *Working Girls in Evening Schools* (1914), and *A Seasonal Trade: A Study of the Millinery Trade in New York* (1917). Van Kleeck's studies influenced the drafting of protective labour legislation in New York State and judicial opinion when such legislation was tested in the courts.

One of the most important findings of Van Kleeck's studies was that the problems experienced by women at work were largely brought about by the same social, economic and industrial factors as determined the conditions under which men worked. Receptive to Van Kleeck's insight that common influences shaped men's and women's participation in the labour market, in 1916 the Russell Sage Foundation established and put under her directorship the Department of Industrial Studies which investigated social and other factors affecting the employment of men and women. Except for a brief period of government service during 1918–19, she remained in this position until her retirement in 1948.

While continuing to work for the Russell Sage Foundation, between 1914 and 1917 Van Kleeck gave courses on industrial problems and industrial research at the New York School of Philanthropy. It was at the School of Philanthropy that she first came into contact with the ideas of Frederick Winslow Taylor and the scientific management movement. In 1915, she told her social work students that perhaps the most significant lesson they could draw from scientific management was the importance of detailed, scientific study of working conditions. As with other Taylorists, she held that the management of human resources was just as important to the performance and smooth operation of the enterprise as the management of capital, plant and equipment. In keeping with this sentiment, Van Kleeck believed that social workers should be trained to assume personnel management positions in industry, and that the industrial audit was a fundamental element in sound personnel management.

In 1915, Van Kleeck and Edward Devine undertook a study of positions available to women in private social agencies in New York. This study was conducted for the School of Philanthropy and the Intercollegiate Bureau of Occupations of which Van Kleeck was President. The Intercollegiate Bureau helped educated middle-class women find employment in occupations other than teaching. She remained active in the Bureau's successor organization, the National Social Workers' Exchange. In the prewar years Van Kleeck also served on New York Mayor John P. Mitchel's Committee on Unemployment.

The influential research and investigative work Van Kleeck conducted for the Russell Sage Foundation, Intercollegiate Bureau and other private and public agencies gave her a well-deserved reputation as one of the nation's leading experts on women's employment. Accordingly, when the USA entered World War I in late 1917 she was engaged as an adviser on the employment of women by the army's Ordnance Department, and at the beginning of 1918 was appointed the director of the women's branch of the Department's Industrial Service Section. This presented her with an opportunity to put the personnel management principles of the scientific management movement into practice in the interests of women employed in government service.

At the request of Dean Herman Schneider, who headed the Labor Division of the Ordnance Department, her first assignment as director was to assess the feasibility of employing women in the ordnance storage plants. Drawing on similar work which Morris Cooke of the Taylor Society and AFL head Samuel Gompers had undertaken for Ordnance, Van Kleeck later developed a set of standards for the employment of women in that department. In July 1918, she took up the position of Director of the Department of Labor's Women in Industry Service, the forerunner of the Women's Bureau. In that position, Van Kleeck set standards for the employment of women in industry and the professions. These standards were adopted by the War Labor Policies Board, a body on which she served as the only woman member in the years 1918–19.

Van Kleeck returned to the Russell Sage Foundation in 1919. Even before her brief absence, the Department of Industrial Studies had begun investigating large-scale factors affecting the employment of both men and women. While she continued with this line of investigation when she resumed her position of Director, she also took the Department in new directions that were consonant with her growing commitment to the principles of scientific management, particularly friendly cooperation between workers and management.

Thus a new field for investigation and analysis were the many experiments in improving employer–employee relationships then being conducted in numerous industries and workplaces around the country. These included trials of schemes for workers' participation in management, the operation of company unions, and other plans. Van Kleeck was particularly interested in the schemes and plans that were at the time undergoing trial in the coal industry. In 1924, she published, with Ben Selekman, *Employees' Representation in Coal Mines*, which was a detailed study of the employee representation plan operating in the Colorado Fuel and Iron Company. In investigating the plan, Van Kleeck and Selekman employed the methods of investigation she had developed at the Russell Sage Foundation. All relevant documents were studied, interviews with both employees and managers conducted, and a draft report submitted to company and union officials for review before final publication.

In addition to undertaking studies in union–management cooperation, in the mid- to late 1920s Van Kleeck also developed expertise in the interpretation and use of unemployment statistics as part of an overall analysis of macroeconomic conditions. She maintained her concern with women's unemployment and kept in close touch with the Women's Bureau. Indeed, Van Kleeck drafted the bill which in 1920 created the Bureau. In its investigations, the Women's Bureau employed the methods of investigation and analysis which she had instituted at the Women in Industry Service. As did other labour feminists, she opposed the Equal Rights Amendment on the grounds that it would undermine labour laws that protected working-class women and close off many of the possibilities that had emerged with the winning of adult woman suffrage.

Van Kleeck devoted considerable time and energy to infusing social work with the principles and perspectives of scientific management. She helped to organize the American Association of Social Workers, also serving on several of its committees. Her strong commitment to scientific management was reflected in the fact that in the early 1920s she was elected to the Nominating Committee and Board of Directors of the Taylor Society. Her efforts to promote the merging of social work and scientific management moved her to the centre of the movement for management reform. She also became heavily involved in President Hoover's forums promoting national economic planning. In 1921, she served on the President's Conference on Unemployment and in 1922–23 on the Committee on Unemployment and Business Cycles. She wrote a chapter of the latter committee's final report, *Business Cycles and Unemployment*, which was published in 1923, and was credited with helping to dampen the business cycle during the middle years of the 1920s.

In 1926, she was appointed to the Technical Consulting Committee which oversaw the Women's Bureau investigation of labour laws for women and the effect of these laws on women's employment opportunities. Lillian Gilbreth was also a member of the Technical Committee. The Committee's landmark report, *The Effects of Labor Legislation on the Employment Opportunities of Women*, was published in 1928. It concluded that protective labour legislation for women did not restrict their employment opportunities. Van Kleeck and Gilbreth ensured that the investigation was conducted in accordance with the painstaking details and rigour of scientific management, showing that this methodology was well suited to the impartial measurement of the effects of gender-specific labour legislation. In addition to these numerous activities and her work at Russell Sage, Van Kleeck was trustee of Smith College (1922–30) and chaired the National Interracial Conference (1928).

In 1933 she was appointed to the Federal Advisory Council of the US Employment Service but resigned after one day in opposition to the National Recovery Administration's failure to support collective bargaining and the labour movement more generally. In *Miners and Management: A Study of the Collective Agreement* (1934), Van Kleeck began by examining the union–management cooperation scheme in the Rocky Mountain Fuel Company, a study which was one of the major themes in her work during the 1920s. In the second part of the book she surveyed the American coal industry. Finding that the industry was characterized by chronic waste and inefficiency, she urged that it be put under the control of the federal government and operated according to the principles of scientific management.

Van Kleeck broadened her perspective in *Creative America: Its Resources for Social Security* (1936), which focused on how technological progress and social development could be harmonized in the common interest. She presented a case against private ownership of the means of production, and sought to find a more secure economic future for the workers of the USA. This involved macroeconomic planning as a means of avoiding recurrent recession and depression. To this end, she also advocated a strong labour movement and a moderate form of collectivism.

In 1928 Van Kleeck had become Associate Director of the International Industrial Relations Institute (IRI), a position which she retained until 1948.

IRI was formed in 1922 at the First International Welfare Conference. The Conference was attended mainly by women personnel management specialists, but others like Van Kleeck were also present. Their aim in forming IRI was to foster closer links between industrial relations and scientific management. By the late 1920s, Van Kleeck and Mary Fledderus, IRI Director, had converted IRI into a vehicle for the promotion of the international coordination of social economic planning. Accordingly, the 1931 triennial conference of IRI, held against the background of the plunge into depression and the Soviet Union's experiments in central planning, took as its theme international economic cooperation and the planned development of productive capacity in order to raise levels of employment and the standard of living. Titled the World Social Economic Congress, the meeting sought in effect to further the fusion of social welfare and scientific management on a world-wide basis.

The Congress was attended by a diverse collection of Taylorists, academics, socialists and trade unionists. Among the delegates from the USA were Harlow Person, Edward A. Filene and Lewis Lorwin (Brookings Institution). Also in attendance was a delegation from the State Planning Commission of the USSR (Gosplan), whose presence attracted a great deal of attention to the Congress. The Soviet delegates discussed their nation's experience of social economic planning under the Five-Year Plans. In the wake of the Amsterdam Congress, Van Kleeck and Fledderus worked to establish a World Commission for the Study of Social Economic Planning under the auspices of IRI which would be a clearing-house for statistical and other data necessary for international social economic planning. Despite the determined efforts of Van Kleeck and Fledderus, IRI failed to live up to their aspirations.

In 1932 Van Kleeck presided over the Second International Conference of Social Work held in Frankfurt-am-Main. In the years leading up to World War II, she also became a member of the executive committee of Hospites, an organization which assisted refugee social workers from Nazi Germany with financial relief and in finding employment, and served on the executive committee of the Social Workers' Committee to Aid Spanish Democracy.

In the midst of all this international activity, Van Kleeck turned the Sage Foundation's Department of Industrial Studies to the study of natural resource industries, the social and economic impact of technological change, and measures to increase the standard of living of American workers. She also participated in the movement for the creation of a National Economic Council, a body which would coordinate national social economic planning. In 1937 Mary Fledderus joined the Department of Industrial Studies and there, in collaboration with Van Kleeck, expanded on the Department's investigations of the impact of technological change. Their joint efforts culminated in 1944 with the publication of *Technology and Livelihood*. Drawing heavily on National Resource Committee reports, the first part of the book analysed the process of technological change in basic industries such as agriculture, construction and transportation. It also looked at the power and chemical industries. The second part considered the impact on employment levels of technological change and development in the context of World War II, noting that increasing productivity was not necessarily matched by a commensurate increase in employment.

In the years leading up to her retirement from the Russell Sage Foundation in 1948, Van Kleeck broadened her already wide array of interests and began to write and lecture on disarmament, the peaceful uses of atomic energy and the possibilities of community organization, while continuing to promote the benefits of social economic planning. In the year of her retirement she threw her support behind Henry A. Wallace's run for the presidency and, as the candidate of the American Labor Party, unsuccessfully ran for the New York State senate. Retaining an interest in the development of the Soviet Union, in 1953 she was subpoenaed by Senator Joseph McCarthy's Senate Permanent Subcommittee on Investigations.

Throughout her life Van Kleeck remained a deeply committed Christian Socialist. She retained a life-long affiliation to the Episcopal League for Social Action and had a long and active involvement with the Church League for Industrial Democracy. She was a member of the Society of the Companions of the Holy Cross, an Episcopal women's organization whose members combined contemplation and prayer with a concern for the study and amelioration of social problems.

Mary van Kleeck was a leading social investigator and labour feminist. She was a recognized expert on women's employment, but always worked for the advancement of both women and men workers. Throughout her career, she remained committed to the view that the quantitative methods of the applied social sciences could play an important ameliorative and moderating role in the resolution of social problems. In keeping with this view, she believed that detailed, scientific study of social problems could assist in the just settlement of disputes over, for example, the effects of sex-specific labour legislation on women's employment opportunities and the ability of union–management co-operation schemes to create a more harmonious industrial relations environment in industry. Van Kleeck never drew back from her conviction that ascertaining the facts was the first step in the movement for social reform.

CHRIS NYLAND
MARK RIX

Bibliography

Alchon, Guy (1992), 'Mary van Kleeck and Scientific Management', in Daniel Nelson (ed.), *A Mental Revolution: Scientific Management Since Taylor*, Columbus, OH: Ohio State University Press, pp. 102–29.

Gordon, Gertrude (1931), 'Interview with Mary van Kleeck', *The Independent Woman* (December) reprinted in Mary R. Beard (ed.) (1933), *America Through Women's Eyes*, Macmillan Co., reprinted Westport, CT: Greenwood Press, 1961.

Lewis, Eleanor Midman (1980), 'Mary Van Kleeck', in Barbara Sicherman, Carol Hurd Green, Ilene Kantrov and Harriette Walker (eds), *Notable American Women, the Modern Period: A Biographical Dictionary*, Cambridge, MA and London: The Belknap Press of Harvard University Press, pp. 707–9.

Moore, Dahrl Elizabeth (1986), *Mary van Kleeck: A Biographical Sketch and Annotated Bibliography of Her Writings*, unpublished master's thesis, Florida Atlantic University, Boca Raton, Florida.

Nyland, Chris and Mark Rix (2000), 'Mary van Kleeck, Lillian Gilbreth and the Women's Bureau Study of Gendered Labor Law', *Journal of Management History*, forthcoming.

Who's Who in America: A Biographical Dictionary of Notable Living Men and Women 1950–51, Chicago, IL: The A.N. Marquis Company.

Priscilla Wakefield (1751–1832)

The Quaker philanthropist and author Priscilla Wakefield (née Bell) was born in Tottenham, England, on 31 January 1751, and married the London merchant Edward Wakefield on 3 January 1771. She established several savings banks (then called 'thrift banks'). According to the *Dictionary of National Biography*, 'She resided at Tottenham, and almost the first savings bank in existence was that founded by her there, in what is now the Ship Inn Yard. It was commenced under the auspices of a friendly society established by her at Tottenham on 22 Oct. 1798 ... She also formed in Tottenham a charity for lying-in women in 1791.' She was a successful children's author: *The Juvenile Travellers*, an imaginary tour of Europe first published in 1801, reached its nineteenth edition in 1850, while *A Family Tour through the British Empire*, first published in 1804, appeared in 15 editions by 1840. Eleven editions of Wakefield's *An Introduction to Botany in a Series of Familiar Letters* were published from 1796 to 1841, and it was translated into French in 1801. Kathryn Sutherland (1995) draws attention to the striking critique of Adam Smith's *Wealth of Nations* in Wakefield's *Reflections on the Present Condition of the Female Sex, with Suggestions for its Improvement* (1798).

Wakefield objected that Smith ignored the exclusion of women from dignified and well-paid work, which forced women into poverty and prostitution. She proposed that, to counteract that phenomenon, male workers should be excluded from midwifery and from shops that catered to female purchasers. Wakefield (1798, pp. 1–2, 150–53), quoted by Sutherland 1995, pp. 104–5) wrote that

> It is asserted by Doctor Adam Smith, that every individual is a burthen upon the society to which he belongs, who does not contribute his share of productive labour for the good of the whole. The Doctor, when he lays down this principle, speaks in general terms of man, as a being capable of forming a social compact for mutual defence, and the advantage of the community at large. He does not absolutely specify, that both sexes, in order to render themselves beneficial members of society, are equally required to comply with these terms; but since the female sex is included in the idea of the species, and as women possess the same qualities as men, though perhaps in a different degree, their sex cannot free them from the claim of the public for their proportion of usefulness. ...
>
> Men monopolize not only the most advantageous employments, and such as exclude women from the exercise of them, by the publicity of their nature, or the extensive knowledge they require, but even many of those, which are consistent with the female character. Another heavy discouragement to the industry of women, is the inequality of the reward of their labour, compared with that of men, an injustice which pervades every species of employment performed by both sexes. ...
>
> In employments which depend upon bodily strength the distinction is just; for it cannot be pretended that the generality of women can earn as much as men, where

the produce of their labour is the result of corporal exertion; but it is a subject of great regret, that this inequality should prevail, even where an equal share of skill and application are exerted. Male stay-makers, mantua-makers, and hair-dressers are better paid than female artists of the same professions; but surely it will never be urged as an apology for this disproportion, that women are not as capable of making stays, gowns, dressing hair, and similar arts, as men; if they are not superior to them, it can only be accounted for upon this principle, that the prices they receive for their labour are not sufficient to repay them for the expense of qualifying themselves for their business, and that they sink under the mortification of being regarded as artizans of inferior estimation, whilst the men, who supplant them, receive all the encouragement of large profits and full employment, which is ensured to them by the folly of fashion.

Wakefield died on 12 September 1832 in Ipswich, at the home of her daughter. The prison reformer Elizabeth Fry was Wakefield's niece. Her grandson was Edward Gibbon Wakefield, the theorist of colonization among the classical political economists, closely connected with the Durham Report in Canada and with the colonization of South Australia and New Zealand.

ROBERT W. DIMAND

Bibliography
E.I.C., 'Wakefield, Mrs. Priscilla (1751–1832)', in Sir Leslie Stephen and Sir Sidney Lee (eds), *Dictionary of National Biography*, vol. XX, pp. 455–6.
Sutherland, Kathryn (1995), 'Adam Smith's Master Narrative: Women and the *Wealth of Nations*', in Stephen Copley and Kathryn Sutherland (eds), *Adam Smith's Wealth of Nations: New Interdisciplinary Essays*, Manchester: Manchester University Press, pp. 97–121.
Wakefield, Priscilla (1798), *Reflections on the Present Conditions of the Female Sex, with Suggestions for its Improvement*, London: J. Johnson, and Darton and Harvey; 2nd edn London: Darton, Harvey, and Darton, 1817.

Phyllis Ann Wallace (1923?–93)

Phyllis Wallace was born and raised in Baltimore. State law at that time prevented African-American students from attending the all-white University of Maryland, but provided out-of-state expenses for those students whose chosen major was not offered at all-black Morgan State College. She chose economics as her major after comparing the Morgan State catalogue with that of the University of Maryland, and went on to graduate *magna cum laude* and Phi Beta Kappa from New York University in 1943 (Malveaux, 1994, p. 93). She planned to teach high school in Baltimore, but was encouraged to apply to Yale, where she earned a master's degree in 1944 and became the first African-American woman to earn a doctorate in economics from Yale in 1948 (Anderson, 1994, p. 91). At Yale, she was denied employment as a teaching assistant because of departmental regulations, but she was employed as a research assistant and received fellowship support from the Rosenwald

Foundation and the Sterling Fund (Malveaux, 1994, p. 94). She left Yale with proficiency in German, Russian, Spanish and French.

Wallace is renowned for her work on race and, especially, the experiences of minority women in the labour market. Her earliest work, however, was in the area of international trade. Her dissertation examined commodity trade, specifically international sugar agreements. After receiving her Ph.D. from Yale, she taught at City College of New York while doing research on international trade and productivity at the National Bureau of Economic Research. She also spent some time as a researcher with 'a defense-related federal agency', likely an intelligence agency, in the late 1940s and early 1950s (Malveaux, 1994, p. 94). In 1953, she accepted a position with the Economics Department at Atlanta University, where she remained until 1957.

In 1957, she accepted employment as an economic analyst with the CIA. During that period, she co-authored 'Industrial Growth in the Soviet Union' (1959) for the *American Economic Review* and testified on 'Dimensions of Soviet Economic Power' (1962) before the Joint Economic Committee. Wallace was already somewhat isolated as an African-American woman economist and her intelligence work forced her to limit her social interactions because she was not free to discuss her work with friends and family (Malveaux, 1994, p. 95). Her professional life during this period reflected the limitations posed by racial relations; she had difficulty attending American Economics Association meetings when they were held in cities that restricted access of African-Americans to various public venues, and her written protest was largely responsible for the 1958 decision of the Executive Committee not to hold meetings in New Orleans (ibid., p. 94).

The civil rights movement of the 1960s induced Wallace to shift her research focus. She began working as Chief of Technical Studies for the Equal Employment Opportunity Commission in 1965, and worked closely with Lester Thurow, Orley Ashenfelter, James Heckman, Ray Marshall and Robert McKersie in preparation for the pivotal discrimination case against AT&T (Wallace, 1976).

In 1968, she joined the Metropolitan Applied Research Center as Vice-President to work on issues affecting young black women. While there, she began writing *Pathways to Work: Unemployment among Black Teenage Females* (1974), which challenged contemporary thinking about the aspirations of young women and revealed the pervasive labour market discrimination that limited their access to white-collar jobs. She examined the impact of training programmes, and considered the relationship between race and poverty in urban settings.

In 1972, Wallace joined the Sloan School at MIT where she was tenured as a full professor in 1974, thereby becoming its first African-American professor (Anderson, 1994, p. 92). She continued her work on employment discrimination and began to investigate labour–management relations. She also worked hard to attract and develop the talents of African-American students at the Sloan School. *MBAs on the Fast Track* (1989) was a longitudinal study of Sloan School graduates that demonstrated the gaps between salaries earned by men and women, and between minority and white MBAs, and documented trends such as commuter marriages and 'glass ceilings' (Malveaux, 1994, p. 96).

The organizing principle of Wallace's work is a pervading interest in the ways that women and people of racial minorities move through the workplace. She tried to shift the research agenda of labour economists and corporate human-relations specialists to examine the barriers to the advancement of minorities and women in internal labour markets, and recognized that employment and training programmes may be the critical factor in maintaining the position of America in the world economy. Wallace always emphasized the importance of case studies, and always recognized that research is only part of the task (ibid.). Perhaps her most enduring legacy is the many women, African-American, and other students in economics and the arts that she mentored (Anderson, 1994, p. 92).

Phyllis Wallace made her contributions in a quiet, yet very determined, way. For her accomplishments, she was awarded honorary degrees from Wellesley and Atlanta University among others. She was elected President of the Industrial Relations Research Association (again the first woman and the first African American to head that organization). In 1982, she was awarded the Samuel Z. Westerfield Award by the National Economic Association. She served on many corporate boards and on the board of the Boston Bureau of Fine Arts where she was instrumental in developing its Nubian Gallery.

Phyllis Ann Wallace, through her academic research, her leadership and her activism, worked tirelessly to banish the barriers that impede African Americans and women in the workplace.

EVELYN L. FORGET

Bibliography

Selected writings by Phyllis Ann Wallace
(1959), 'Industrial Growth in the Soviet Union: comment' (with R.V. Greenslade), *American Economic Review*, **49**(4), 687–95.
(1962), *Dimensions of Soviet Economic Power*, testimony before the Joint Economic Committee, US Congress, Washington, DC: US Government Printing Office.
(1971), 'Economic Position and Prospects for Urban Blacks', *American Journal of Agricultural Economics*, **53**(2), 316–18.
(1974), *Pathways to Work: Unemployment among Black Teenage Females*, Lexington, MA: Lexington Books.
(1975), 'Public Policy and Black Economic Progress: A Review of the Evidence' (with B.E. Anderson), *American Economic Review (Papers and Proceedings)*, **65**(2), 47–52.

(1976) (ed.), *Equal Employment Opportunity and the AT&T Case*, Cambridge, MA: MIT Press.

(1977) (eds), *Women, Minorities, and Employment Discrimination* (with A.M. Lamond), Lexington, MA: Lexington Books.

(1980), *Black Women in the Labor Force*, Cambridge, MA: MIT Press.

(1982) (ed.), *Women in the Workplace*, Boston, MA: Auburn House.

(1984), 'Motivation and New Technologies: comment', in M.L. Wachter and S.M. Wachter (eds), *Removing Obstacles to Economic Growth*, Philadelphia: University of Pennsylvania Press, pp. 171–5.

(1985–86), 'A Research Agenda on the Economic Status of Black Women', *Review of Black Political Economy*, **14**(2–3), 293–5.

(1987), 'Minority Women in the Workplace' (with J. Malveaux), in K.S. Koziara, M.H. Moskow and L.D. Tanner (eds), *Working Women: Past, Present, Future. Industrial Relations Research Association Series*, Washington: Bureau of National Affairs, pp. 265–98.

(1989), *MBAs on the Fast Track*, New York: Harper and Row.

Other sources and references

Anderson, B.E. (1994), 'The Economic Status of African-American Women: Special Session in Honor of Phyllis A. Wallace, Introduction', *American Economic Review (Papers and Proceedings)*, **84**(2), 91–2.

Malveaux, J. (1994), 'Tilting against the Wind: Reflections on the Life and Work of Phyllis Ann Wallace', *American Economic Review (Papers and Proceedings)*, **84**(2), 93–7.

Rivlin, A. (1990), 'Phyllis Ann Wallace, scholar/activist', in K. Abraham and R.B. McKersie (eds), *New Developments in the Labor Market: Towards a New Institutional Paradigm*, Cambridge, MA: MIT Press, pp. ix–xiv.

Barbara Ward (1914–81)

Biography

Barbara Mary Ward was born in York, England on 23 May 1914 and died on 21 May 1981 in Lodsworth, England. Her parents were Walter Ward (a solicitor) and Teresa Mary Burge. At age 15 she went to the Continent to study, first in Paris for two years (Lycée Molière and the Sorbonne), then for one year in Germany (Jugenheim). In 1932 she entered Oxford (Somerville College) as an exhibitioner. In 1935 she graduated, taking a first in Modern Greats (philosophy, politics and economics). In her more than four-decade career, she would take many 'firsts'.

Barbara Ward's nonpareil career was inspired in part by another Oxford graduate and ex-Principal of Somerville College, the well known penal reform advocate, Margery Fry. Ward related to an interviewer that she heard Fry talk on 'the challenge of armaments' when Hitler was coming to power. She said: 'Margery Fry spoke so well and with such energy that, suddenly, the penny dropped for me.' Ward was spoken of as an economist throughout her life, but she never professed to be one. It was, perhaps, convenient for the non-academic public to view her as an economist as much of her writing dealt with economic concerns such as European postwar recovery, economic development, environmental questions, and so on. Ward would marshal her writing and speaking skills with a persuasive, attractive personality to campaign for policies she championed. Ward possessed a fourth asset, that of her faith. As a devout Roman Catholic throughout her life she was concerned with her Church and its policies.

Her initial focus was the problem of postwar Europe, but this focus broadened, early on, to global proportions. She had anticipated that the USA would need to aid the recovery of Europe and shared Jean Monnet's vision of a unified Europe. She recognized that the post-colonial world was one of extreme imbalance and that the 'rich nations' should facilitate the development of the 'poor nations'. She came to see the complicating imperative wherein economic growth, of both developed and developing areas, must not be allowed to so damage the environment that future growth could not be sustained. Much of her later writings were attempts to sort out the problems of this global dilemma and fashion a strategy for overcoming them.

The venues through which Ward worked or had influence were many and varied: *The Economist*; the Sword of the Spirit movement; the Council of the Royal Institute of International Affairs; the British Ministry of Information; the BBC; *The New York Times Magazine*; W.W. Norton & Co.; the White House; the UN Secretariat; The Catholic Women's League; Harvard and Columbia Universities; the Pontifical Commission on Peace and Justice; the Audubon and Conservation Societies; the World Bank; the Columbia Conference on International Development; the Stockholm Conference on the Human Environment; the Synod of Bishops on World Peace; the Pearson and Brandt Commissions; the International Institute of Environment and Development. Her ultimate influence is impossible to gauge; clear, however, is the industry and ingenuity with which she pursued her ideals.

Fittingly, Ward began her career as a university extension lecturer on foreign affairs at Cambridge. A Vernon Harcourt scholarship allowed her to travel to Italy, Austria and the Balkans for three summers. In 1938 her first book was published, *The International Share-Out*, and Geoffrey Crowther asked her to freelance for the *Economist*. She joined the staff of the periodical and became, at age 26, its foreign editor. Barbara Ward clearly wished to become an influential voice in international affairs. The international prestige of a Geoffrey Crowther or a Walter Lippmann may have encouraged her to take up journalism in lieu of politics or academics. Roland Bird reported that she and Donald Tyerman 'largely maintained' the magazine during the war. This responsibility appeared to have lightly burdened her. She wrote books on Italian and Russian foreign policy and a third on Turkey as well as a chapter on Yugoslavia in the Fabian Society's *Hitler's Road to Baghdad*, all between 1939 and 1943. In this period she was also active speaking and writing for the Sword of the Spirit movement. For her war service she was assigned to the Ministry of Information and on its behalf travelled to the USA, Sweden and postwar Berlin to give speeches promoting British policies.

Ward wrote not only on foreign affairs for the *Economist*, but also on domestic conditions in other journals. Assessing the mood of 'Young' Britain in 1943, she found it to be 'radical' but not leftist in the Marxist sense; 'radical' in that younger people were calling for large social reforms over and above that offered by the Beveridge Plan. She further speculated on the 1945 elections. She felt that Labour had failed to become a true national party. Hopeful signs for effective leadership were the emergence of Herbert Morrison of Labour and Quintin Hogg of the 'young' Tories.

In a 1944 article, 'Women in Britain', in *Foreign Affairs* Ward explored the position of and prospects for women in Britain. She noted the hopes of some that the marked disruptions to family and work life wrought by the war were a harbinger of a radical improvement for women in their economic status, much as the first war had brought suffrage. She noted that the 1920 promises of reform to the civil service had not been fulfilled. There, limited opportunities, discriminatory wages and enforced termination of employment upon marriage set a poor standard for the private sector. Before the war the wage differential in general was about 50 per cent. She found this 'incredibly unfair' in a time when many women would be unable or choose not to marry. (Ward's favourite aunt was a spinster and she herself did not marry until age 36.) Ward opined that the case for equal pay and opportunity as a norm was unanswerable. She warned, however, that the creation of a bias against the household vocation was 'dangerous and disastrous'. She concluded: 'The lasting answer lies in part with the educational system, in part with the political and economic reconstruction of this country. The war has opened up some new opportunities, cast down some old barriers and created some problems of it own. But the issues of women's work and women's rights and women's place in society all lie ahead, still to be solved' (Ward, 1944, p. 576). Twenty-four years later Ward commented in a 1967 interview by *McCall's*: 'One of the pleasant things I shan't live to see will be the day when it's not remarkable for a woman to be doing things, and then she'll have a greater psychological ease and ability to do things for their own sake' (1967, p. 48).

Ward, who had seriously considered singing opera, was elected Governor of Sadler's Wells and Old Vic Theatres in 1943. That same year she joined the staff of BBC's popular *Brains Trust* radio programme to become one of its stars and gained national recognition (at the price of having to respond to thousands of letters seeking personal advice). In the 1945 elections, she was asked to stand for Labour, but refused. She did speak for Ernest Bevin and Herbert Morrison. Anecdotes about her speaking abilities abound. In one instance she held the audience for 100 minutes when she had been asked to speak for five. In another, Donald Tyerman reports that her oratory on the need for full employment and the policies which would achieve it brought Bevin, a from-the-ranks trade unionist, to tears. Triumphant Labour named her a governor of the BBC in 1946.

In the next ten years Ward was engrossed with cold war policies and European unity. In the *Economist* and the *New York Times Magazine* she waged a campaign for a rapid implementation of the Marshall Plan. She would often refer back to the Plan which she called an 'Unsordid Act' as embodying key elements for an unprecedented, peacetime, aid programme. For the USA the Plan was bold in its magnitude, undeniably generous and at the same time self-interested. For its recipients it was a challenge to work in a cooperative manner to determine its successful implementation which should encourage future cooperation. Her books, *The West At Bay* (1948), *Policy for the West* (1951) and *The Interplay of East and West* (1957), were widely read and reviewed, for they represented up-to-date analyses of international affairs and provided general policy prescriptions.

Ward's marriage in 1950 to Robert G.A. Jackson, who was beginning a distinguished career as international development adviser, helped bring about a transformation in her hierarchy of concerns. She and her husband lived briefly in Australia and India, then began a six-year formal residence in Ghana in 1956, although for many of these years she taught the winter term at Harvard and Radcliffe. Their only child, Robert, was born in 1956. The couple were legally separated in 1966.

Ward's shift from questions of the cold war to those of world development can be traced in her books: *Faith and Freedom* (1954), *Five Ideas that Changed the World* (1957), *India and the West* (1964). At Harvard she was introduced to Adlai Stevenson by John Kenneth Galbraith. She became a close friend and adviser to Stevenson. John F. Kennedy, whom she had met in 1945, welcomed her advice. Warmer still was her relationship with the Johnson White House. Lyndon ordered that she be received and schedules altered, if she were visiting Washington. Lady Bird commented in her published diary that Lyndon listened to her 'which he doesn't always do, especially to women'. From 1964 to 1968 with Harold Wilson in Great Britain and Lester Pearson in Canada in power she enjoyed simultaneous ready access to three administrations. Wilson once, in talks with Johnson, recognized that the brief they were discussing was the work of Barbara Ward. In 1965 Secretary-General U Thant asked her to draft a mid-term report on developmental progress which became *The Decade of Development: A Study in Frustration?* The President of the World Bank, George Woods, sought her help to revitalize commitment to developmental aid and she wrote his last speech as President, 'Grand Assize', in 1967. This speech became the inspiration for the Pearson Commission. It was Wood's successor with whom Ward was most influential,

Robert McNamara. She helped to convince him that the Bank could develop programmes that would effectively reach the lower 40th percentile of the world's population. She was encouraged to do so by her friend, William Clark, while technical expertise was provided by another friend, the economist Hollis Chenery.

Ward's academic career began in 1957 as a visiting scholar and Carnegie Fellow at Harvard University and Radcliffe College. She taught classes on government and economics the second semester of each year up to 1967. Her publishing continued to flourish: *Spaceship Earth* (1966), *Nationalism and Ideology* (1967) and *The Lopsided World* (1968). Ward was made Albert Schweitzer Professor of International Development at Columbia University in December of 1967. Her appointment was controversial because this was an appointment to the Department of Economics whereas at Harvard she had taught mainly in the Graduate School of Public Administration. She organized the 1970 Columbia Conference on International Economic Development. Ward persuaded McNamara, Paul Hoffman, Johannes Wittveen and Maurice Strong to attend representing respectively the World Bank, the UN Development Programme, the International Monetary Fund and the Canadian aid programme. She also invited radical voices such as Mahbub ul Haq, the brilliant Pakistani economist, to challenge conventional foreign aid wisdom. *The Widening Gap*, a collection of essays from the conference edited by Ward, reflected these challenges. Ward resigned her chair at Columbia in 1973.

In her tenure at Columbia she became increasingly aware of environmental concerns. She served as President of the Conservation Society in 1972. Maurice Strong commissioned her and René Dubos to prepare a preliminary report for the 1972 Stockholm Conference on the Human Environment. Ward was particularly cognizant that environmental concern should be made equally relevant to affluent countries and poorer ones. *Only One Earth: The Care and Maintenance of a Small Planet* was the published result of her collaboration with Dubos. Although Ward and other participants were disappointed with the results of the conference, it was, in hindsight, path-breaking. Ward assumed the directorship of the International Institute of Environmental Affairs which she had helped to found in 1971. On her insistence the title of the institute was altered to the International Institute of Environment and Development. The Institute would play a significant role in UN conferences on population, food, the law of the sea, human settlements, desertification, water and technology. For the Rome Conference on Food in 1974, at the request of Sayed A. Marei, Secretary-General of the conference, she convened and chaired a pre-conference forum and wrote the foreword to *Hunger, Politics and Markets*. For the Vancouver Conference on Human Settlements she wrote *The Home of Man* (1976), dedicating it to Constantinos Doxiadis. The last major work she was able to complete was *Progress For A Small Planet* (1979). She advocated, successfully, that Willy Brandt spearhead a successor to the Pearson Commission. She praised the Brandt Report when it appeared without betraying what her behind-the-scenes role may have been.

Throughout her career Ward played an active role in her Church and Church-related organizations. In the 1940s she spoke and wrote for the Sword and Spirit movement led by Cardinal Hinsley. This movement, which was Catholic, but ecumenical in spirit, emphasized points which would foreshadow Ward's concerns. Following Pius XII, it protested against extreme inequality of wealth and the lack of equal opportunity in education. Further, it stressed unity in international relations, a sharing of resources and their employment in a manner that did not prejudice future generations. In 1941 Ward wrote a book reflecting these ideals, *A Christian Basis for the Post-war World*. She served as President of the Catholic Women's League (1948–50). In 1953 she wrote *Are Today's Problems Basically Religious?* In 1967 she was appointed to the Pontifical Commission for Justice and Peace and wrote a commentary on the *Encyclical Letter of His Holiness Pope Paul VI On the Development of Peoples*. That same year she helped draft a resolution advocating the end of the Church's ban on birth control on the part of the World Congress of Roman Catholic Laymen. She later made clear that she was not advocating birth control as a solution to world population questions. In 1971 she became the first woman to address a synodal session at the Vatican (Synod of the Bishops on World Justice). Under the aegis of pontifical commissions she produced three works: *A New Creation: Reflections on the Environmental Issue* (1973), *The Angry Seventies* (1976) and *Peace and Justice in the World* (1981). Being a devout Catholic did not impede her from campaigning for change within her Church or from speaking to all Christians, or furthermore from sincerely attempting to understand and find affinity among the great religions.

Barbara Ward received many honours for her efforts. Between 1949 when Fordham University and Smith College granted her honorary doctorates and 1976 when the London School of Economics made her an honorary fellow, many universities and colleges likewise honoured her. She was the recipient of the Campion and the Christoper Awards for her books. She was named the 18th Audubon Medallist, the second woman named after Rachel Carson. In 1974 she won the Jawaharlal Nehru prize for work against illiteracy. The Royal Institute of British Architects made her a fellow in 1975. After being proclaimed Dame of the British Empire in 1974, she was made life peer by Elizabeth II, becoming Baroness Jackson of Lodsworth in 1976. In 1980, too ill to accept it in person, she was given the Royal Society of the Arts Gold Medal.

From the mid-1950s Lady Jackson suffered from cancer of the throat and endured several major operations. It is, in a sad way, ironic that two of her great gifts were impaired in her later years. She found that writing, which she once jokingly called her 'fatal facility', had become an exhausting burden. And, of course, due to the cancer which would result in her death in May 1981, her speaking abilities were diminished as well. In 1980 she turned the directorship of the IIED over to her long-time friend, William Clark. Perhaps, in the end, her greater gifts were those that could not be taken away: her determination, her intelligent compassion and her faith.

Faith and Freedom

Barbara Ward's writings and speeches display a remarkable continuity that spans the four decades of her activity as an intellectual champion of a variety of causes: US leadership of the non-communist world; Western European unity; economic assistance to the developing countries of Asia and Africa; the moral unity of humankind compassionately expressed with a commitment to freedom; and the need to preserve the fragile ecology of the planet for posterity. In developing her themes, Ward was not only telling a story in an inimitable way; she was also advocating goals and policies which she felt were indispensable for securing a harmonious, peaceful and prosperous world.

All the themes that were to resonate in her many articles, speeches and books in the 1950s and 1960s were developed in her *Faith and Freedom* (1954). Western civilization, based on the Greek heritage and the idea of a Supreme God bequeathed to it by the Jewish and Christian religions, ensured that freedom of choice was available as an alternative to compete against the deterministic elements of material and moral existence. It never gave up the search for the ideal, even when overwhelmed by the constraints of the actual. Moreover, writes Ward, the ideal was never divorced from the Good. Freedom has the possibility of transcending necessity.

The Greek heritage ensured the primacy of reason and engendered the belief that we live in an intelligible universe. Reason, in turn, 'established the notion of Law behind the flux of phenomena ... Reason, further, can grasp by direct intuition the highest of all realities, which is the idea of the Good' (Ward, 1954, p. 45).

The external world is permeated with Law. Law implies reason and reason is the basis of understanding all reality. Human beings, capable of knowledge, have therefore the capacity and the right to govern themselves, according to Law.

The Jewish faith gave to western civilization the concept of a progressive unfoldment of the Divine Plan for humanity. In contrast to the world-denying propensity of the east, western man sees the world as an assertion of God's will. It is an outpouring of God's energy. While this left unresolved the reasons for and implications of man's suffering, the triumph of the Christian faith, the rise and sacrifice of the 'Second Adam', as Barbara Ward terms the phenomenon, ends the alienation of man from God. God is made incarnate in human history by Christ's sacrifice.

Ward's understanding of Western European history centres around the existence of independent centres of power in the Christian church and the temporal authority of kings and lords under feudalism. The struggle of each of these to ensure their own sovereignty produced the division of power at the very apex of authority that enabled subordinate institutions to assert their own autonomy. Economic evolution, the growth of trade and eventually of manufacturing, reinforced the checks from below to the checks from above of absolute power. This strengthened the foundation of freedom in the evolution of western societies.

Together the egalitarian tendencies of Christianity, and the emphasis on man as the pinnacle of creation in scholastic philosophy, constrained the centralizing tendencies of the fifteenth and sixteenth centuries, first in the United Kingdom and later in the USA and France. The strong Calvinistic element in Britain and the USA played a key role in the victory of limited government.

Simultaneously, there was taking place in the sixteenth century an enormous growth in global trade which laid the foundations both of the nation state and the economic revolution that transformed the United Kingdom and then the rest of Western Europe and North America. Ward regards the nation state as one of the great 'political' innovations of the period. She believed that the circumstances in which the nation state arose were conducive to the maintenance of liberty as well as the eventual evolution to democracy.

In the economic sphere, the scholastic view of property as a social convenience gave place to the Lockean concept of property as the right to the fruits of one's labour and eventually to the concept of property as a right free from all constraints. Nationalism and the new view of property reinforced the political and economic revolutions that enthroned the cult of work, money-making and economic success under the aegis of the nation state. Society was freed of all restraints and responsibilities in the pursuit of individual goals.

Ward's view of capitalist evolution emphasizes the primacy of technological change and the role of science. Further, this view stresses the simultaneity of innovations in agriculture and industry so that what is regarded as the Industrial Revolution in Britain is an agricultural–industrial revolution. Finally, the vital part played by the entrepreneur in the revolution and the importance of the 'primitive accumulation' of capital for the process are pointed out. It was a necessary evolution, but it had the effect of worsening the plight of the poor, who were no longer regarded as worthy of Christian charity but deserving of condemnation for their lack of initiative.

The unleashing of national ambition and economic enterprise led from the sixteenth to the nineteenth centuries to the colonization of the entire globe by the white race. In the subtropical regions of Africa and Asia, this process led to imperial rule and the appropriation of the resources of these continents for European development. Barbara Ward's view of colonialism was that, while it was not necessarily a result of premeditation, the impoverishment of what became the world's underprivileged areas was a direct consequence. The west must bear the responsibility for it.

The English and American political revolutions of the seventeenth and eighteenth centuries, with their defence of constitutional liberties inherited from medieval times and their increasing emphasis on other freedoms such as the right to free speech, assembly and worship, provided the route back from the centralized nation state to free, democratic societies subject to the rule of law. They invigorated the process of reform that restored the sense of responsibility of the state to the deprived and impoverished masses.

The French Revolution, based on the primacy of the 'general will' with its loyalty to the abstract concepts of liberty and equality, did not have any long-range ill-effects on the political evolution of France itself. It did present an alternative vision of the embodiment of the 'general will' in the totalitarian states of the twentieth century. It presented the dangers of a concept of equality pursued as a levelling down of all to uniformity. The bureaucracy would in this event not only take over the state but might make of the community itself the private property of the bureaucrat. The vision became a nightmare reality as the determinism of Marx found its realization in the Russian Revolution and the unbridled assertiveness of western nationalism found its extreme manifestation in the Nazi state.

Barbara Ward put herself squarely against the unlimited freedom of the market and the absolutism of the state, whether in the name of class or nation. To the extent that *laissez-faire* capitalism creates the poor or accentuates their plight, it needs the remedy of social policy to correct its excesses. The government also needs to institute policies to correct the excessive fluctuations of the business cycle and prevent inflation or unemployment. The democratic capitalistic state, in performing these necessary tasks, had reconciled class interests, created a compassionate society, and produced a stake in freedom and the existing order in the domestic economies of the western world. Freedom, democracy and government reinforced each other in western societies.

The answer to the appeal of communism to the underprivileged societies of the newly independent countries of the post-colonial world lies first in recognizing the responsibility of the western world for their situation, and second in extending to these societies the concept of welfare so successfully applied domestically. Nationalism could not be allowed to limit the concept of welfare to domestic frontiers. Less developed societies had to be increasingly incorporated in a system of economic aid, provided as a matter of right. This was both a moral imperative and a strategic necessity.

Barbara Ward fully supported the policies of the western military alliance and containment against the threat of Soviet expansion. But she was certain that it was necessary to underpin these policies to ensure economic stability and growth in the west, and assist development in the newly independent states of Asia and Africa. She reiterated the Christian view of wealth as a trust and the responsibility of those who are wealthy to the larger national community and the responsibility of wealthy nations toward the less developed ones. She was sustained in the possibility of evolution to a better global society by her faith that after four hundred years of rationalism and science, western man will return to his roots in religion. Christianity, which in dividing power between the secular and the sacred had ensured freedom, could provide the possibility that out of the disharmonies and injustices of the present, humankind has the ability to make the choices that produce the Good.

Ward on the postwar era
In the aftermath of World War II, Ward's concerns were more immediate, namely, the plight of Western Europe after the devastation inflicted by the war, and the future of Western Europe in the face of the Soviet threat. Her analytical abilities, her prescience in anticipating problems and potentialities, and the remarkable clarity of her writing, made her books both popular and influential in policy discussions. In her first American publication, *The West at Bay* (1948), Ward concerned herself with the problems involved in uniting Western Europe and enhancing the cohesiveness of the Atlantic alliance. On the title page she quoted Edmund Burke: 'When bad men combine, the good must associate.' This was not so much a commentary on Stalinism as a strident challenge to the western powers. Ward argued persuasively that Britain belonged in Europe and should not allow the Commonwealth connection to keep her out. The argument continued for the next two decades as Britain first chose not to join the European Economic Community, and France under De Gaulle later vetoed its entry when it did apply for admission. Ward discussed the nature of the union, whether it should be close to a federal structure from the beginning or should involve a cautious movement from association in a free trade area, greater defence cooperation and consultation to eventual economic and political union. She confronted the uniqueness of the problem of agriculture in Europe and Britain, and the difficulties inherent in some surrender of national sovereignty by all concerned. *The West at Bay*, written in six weeks in an attempt to be timely, was, yet, both a first-rate political–economic analysis as well as a pragmatic policy prescription.

Policy for the West (1951) was in a sense an update of *The West at Bay*, with its major themes re-examined in the light of changing conditions. Ward details the fears that rearmament of the west will prove inflationary. She found in Keynesian economics the means to maintain high employment and to avoid the extremes of the business cycle, and believed that they were equally applicable to governments with extensive planning and those with no planning efforts. Ward's interest in economic theory was a practical one in that she gleaned from it what appeared to have hopeful policy implications. She proposed a somewhat vague practical federalism for Europe. This book, as well as her other books and articles on policy, was an exercise in diplomacy. Knowing full well that any concrete proposal for European unity would be immediately divisive, she was content to push only the general issue. She argued that the 'facts' of Stalin's aggressions since 1945 were sufficient to justify the policy of containment and was thus allying herself with the American point of view.

In 1957 Ward presented a series of three lectures on East–West relations to an audience of over 2500 students and faculty members of McGill University and townspeople of Montreal. She argued that the East had largely experienced disruption and exploitation at the hands of the West. With the fading of western domination Ward saw the East facing a choice in its necessary drive for modernization between adopting a mixed economy or following the Soviet model. Despite the East's suspicions of its former colonizers, she urged them to elect the mixed economy and not be deluded by the Soviet success in industrialization, for this overlooked its failures in agriculture which for the populous East could result in calamity. To the bargain Ward added the possibility, almost unknown in the history of the East, of personal freedom. Noting the tumultuous changes to come in the East, she pleaded for cooperative aid from the West to effectively meet its enormous needs. Edwin O. Reischauer, in commenting on the book, concluded in agreement with Ward: 'Our dilemma is not basically military, economic or political, back of all these aspects lies the need for what she calls "moral unity" without which all our efforts may miscarry.'

Ward on development
The 1950s was a period of the break-up of the European imperial system, the rise of new nation states, the emergence of the problems of industrialization, development and communism in the context of the emerging Third World, and the rise of internationalism around the poles of the USA and the Soviet Union. Barbara Ward examined these issues in a series of lectures published as *Five Ideas that Changed the World* (1957), *The Rich Nations and the Poor Nations* (1962), *India and the West* (1964) and *Nationalism and Ideology* (1967).

In *Five Ideas that Changed the World*, Ward set the present-day problems in their historical context. Nationalism, reinforced by industrialization, had created the powerful nation states of Western Europe. The evolution of American nationalism from what at the beginning was only an American government, and the emergence of Russian nationalism in the Soviet state, both represented the triumph of nationalism over ideology. To the extent that nationalism had evolved in a context of increasing democratization, it had been a liberating force in the metropolitan countries. It also compelled imperial regimes to grant political freedom to their colonies. Ward was uncertain whether nationalism would prove as potent in breaking up the Russian and Chinese empires. She was, however, fully cognizant of the dangers to peace from the existence of multi-ethnic, multilingual states, should the sub-nationalisms become strong. The dangers, she was certain, stretched from Eastern Europe through the Middle East, South and Southeast Asia to China.

One of Barbara Ward's best-known books was *The Rich Nations and the Poor Nations*. Lyndon Johnson called it his 'other Bible'. She declared 'the gap between the rich and the poor has become … the most tragic and urgent problem of our day' (1962, p. 36). Perhaps, more powerfully than in her other works, Ward decries the West's lack of vision, of a grand strategy and of urgency in the face of global poverty. She calls for a long-term, generous and creative commitment from the West, not so much to meet the challenge of communism, but to live up to its own purported values of openness, freedom and liberty.

Ward demonstrated analytical clarity in her lectures to an Indian audience on Indian planning, published in the 1964 (revised) edition of her *India and the West*. The work contrasts the recovery of Europe under Marshall Aid with the failure of Marxist–Leninist prognostications about the capitalism of the western world and the increasing unrealism of Leninist doctrine with regard to both capitalism and colonialism. In the lectures on Indian planning, she noted the difficulty of realizing 'primitive accumulation' in a democratic setting. At the same time, a democratic society has the advantage of proceeding by consensus. She emphasized the importance of agricultural development for successful over-all development and was highly critical of the Indian neglect of agriculture in the first decade of planning. She stressed the importance of entrepreneurship. Prejudice against entrepreneural capitalism was unwarranted. The state had an appropriate role in ensuring the provision of an adequate infrastructure and in directing foreign investment into desired channels, but it must not over-extend itself. A country of small businesses and middle farmers such as India needed to operate in an entrepreneural environment with its appropriate incentives. Entrepreneurship, big and small, was vital, and disapproval of people getting rich should not kill it. She cautioned against over-expansion of the public sector, as it deprived the private sector of both needed capital and management. She warned against increasing the bureaucratic stranglehold, even though the serious scarcity of foreign exchange necessitated some controls. She was highly critical of the vast disparity between the rhetoric of Indian planning and the achievement of specific targets. The lectures which were given to an Indian audience represent a remarkable trait of Ward's – the ability to speak the truth as she saw it, with conviction and grace, and without offence.

In *Nationalism and Ideology*, Barbara Ward confronted a different set of questions. Despite its enormous contribution to economic growth, industrialism, extension of markets, technological advances, and democratization of the polity in the western setting, nationalism had failed to provide to non-western states a sense of either cohesion or of economic function. It had created an extraordinary assortment of more than one hundred states of all sizes, in proximity and interdependent, which yet proclaimed their identity on the basis of keeping others out. In the context of modern technology, present-day modern states are too small to underpin full economic development. Western capitalism had built an incredibly productive global economy. The latter has outgrown the nation state, but has failed to supersede it. In her view, the USA and the Soviet Union are post-national states that have failed to transcend the narrowness of nationalism. The reality of human existence – that of the planetary present – is defeated by the particularist past to which humans cling. There has been a failure of imagination.

This contradiction between the physical oneness of the whole of humanity and its moral and social division is stressed by Ward in her commentary on the encyclical of Pope Paul VI, *On the Development of Peoples* (1967), which she perhaps had a part in helping to draft. The encyclical described the consequences of colonialism in the distorted nature of development which colonial countries experience, the semi-modernization it produced, and the consequent runaway problems of population growth and unemployment. It called upon the rich – nations and individuals – to assume their responsibility to turn the 'brute fact of our planet's physical neighbourhood into the moral and social fact of genuine community' (1967, p. 11).

Ward had made the same plea in the Sir Robert Falconer Lectures at the University of Toronto (published as *Toward a World of Plenty*, 1964). In these lectures, she emphasized the political factors that had transformed the early capitalism that Marx knew into a humane society in which government had taken the responsibility to redistribute income through taxation, without stifling innovation. She pleaded for a cooperative, integrated, international effort on the part of affluent nations for 'a more energetic, joint attack on the economic deadlocks among the developing peoples' (1964, p. 41). Her justification was that the USA and the European colonial powers had created the 'dependence' which had resulted in their present economic situation. In her Christian Herter Lectures at Johns Hopkins University (published as *The Lopsided World*, 1968), she made the argument in greater detail. Earlier in the George P. Peagram Lectures at Columbia University (published as *Spaceship*

Earth, 1966), she had spoken of 'Patriotism for the world itself' that made possible 'the moral unity of our human experience' (1966, p. 148).

The decade of the 1960s ended with a none-too-helpful confrontational posture on the questions of assistance to less developed countries. The donor nations questioned the effectiveness of aid, even when some of them, in their bilateral giving, intended some of it as bribes to ruling élites and instruments of leverage over policies. The recipients shifted to a posture that aid was a right that was owed to them by past wrong. Ward tried to bring understanding and goodwill into the debate.

Ward on the environment
Only One Earth was the title of the report prepared by Barbara Ward and René Dubos, eminent biologist, for the United Nations Conference on the Human Environment at Stockholm (1972). Commissioned by the World Bank and the Ford Foundation, the report provided basic information on the consequences of specific types of human activity such as sewage and solid waste disposal produced by urban agglomerations, the exponential growth in generation of electric power, and the extraordinary growth of agricultural output heralded by the Green Revolution involving the use of new seed varieties, fertilizer, pesticide, and so on. They provide historical perspective to the problem of environmental pollution and a survey of solutions such as those attempted in the Ruhr valley, where a combination of effluent standards, user fees, and so on helped to clean up the highly polluted Ruhr river. The report emphasized the finite nature of the earth's resources. It confronted the difficult problems of equity stemming from the rising costs of producing pollution-free goods and cleaning up the environment, on the one hand, and the aspirations of the developing countries for higher living standards which could be stymied by such costs.

Along with environmental degradation, and not unrelated to it, is the question of the huge urban concentrations of the developed world and the increasing number of such vast urban agglomerations in the developing countries. One of the final accomplishments of Barbara Ward was another book commissioned by the United Nations to serve as a keynote to the global conference on Human Settlements (Habitat) in Vancouver in 1975. Published as *The Home of Man* (1976), this report examines the evolution of the city as it has been forced to absorb enormous numbers of assimilable and unassimilated migrants since the time of the Industrial Revolution, the problems (as of yet unresolved) in old, large cities such as Paris and New York, and the explosion of unliveable new cities in the less developed countries. She pleads for political will and planning to deal with housing, sanitation, food, water, basic medical services, education (especially for women) and infant mortality. She urges rural development and revitalization to stem the push factor. She condemns the indiscriminate 'automobilization' of societies with its ravenous appetite for land and energy. She presents evidence from countries like France, Belgium and Germany, confronting these issues and seeking to resolve them creatively. She asks that developed countries provide the financing that less developed countries need to begin to confront their urban problems.

Ward's last major book was *Progress for a Small Planet: New Directions for the Industrial Order* (1979). In a magisterial prologue Ward draws up a balance sheet for planet earth. She concludes: 'In this "morning's war" between hope and destruction, between insight and despair, the forces are not all on the side of night.' Although her air is that of a prophet, she turns to the task of meticulously examining the practical, albeit incomplete, possibilities for finding a planetary balance that allows one to imagine a humane future. In doing this she demonstrated again her 'determined optimism' which was in no sense quixotic.

Barbara Ward thus remained until the end of her life a scholar and a publicist with a conscience, at the frontier of issues confronting humankind. She brought to her task great analytical ability, clear and incisive writing, passion and compassion. She was a mentor of leaders, a counsellor for policy-makers, and an activist whose Christianity embraced all mankind. She was a force for unity in a divided world. She helped men and women who led many countries and international institutions to see and share her vision of a world united in its moral concern for all. She pushed herself as she tried to help others to act on the most important issues of her time. In the issues she raised, and the plea for action she sustained over many decades, she remains relevant. Her voice speaks with concern and compassion to an ever-present future.

CHRISTOPHER K. RYAN
RAMAKRISHNA VAITHESWARAN

Bibliography

Selected writings by Barbara Ward
(1948), *The West at Bay*, New York: W.W. Norton.
(1951), *Policy for the West*, New York: W.W. Norton.
(1954), *Faith and Freedom*, New York: W.W. Norton.
(1957), *Five Ideas that Changed the World*, New York: W.W. Norton.
(1957), *The Interplay of East and West*, New York: W.W. Norton.
(1962), *The Rich Nations and the Poor Nations*, New York: W.W. Norton.
(1964), *India and the West*, New York: W.W. Norton.
(1964), *Toward a World of Plenty?* Toronto: Toronto University Press.
(1966), *Spaceship Earth*, New York: Columbia University Press.
(1967), *Nationalism and Ideology*, New York: W.W. Norton.
(1968), *The Lopsided World*, New York: W.W. Norton.
(1972), *Only One Earth: The Care and Maintenance of a Small Planet* (with René Dubos), New York: W.W. Norton.

(1976), *The Home of Man*, New York: W.W. Norton.
(1979), *Progress for a Small Planet*, New York: W.W. Norton.

Other sources and references

Beloff, Nora (1981), 'Ward, Barbara Mary', *Dictionary of National Biography*, pp. 410–11.
Bird, Roland (1981), 'Barbara Ward,' *Economist*, 6 June, 35–9.
Gladish, Kenneth Leroy (1985), *Barbara Ward Jackson and the Postwar World: The Ethic of Interdependence*, Ph.D. dissertation, Woodrow Wilson Department of Government and Foreign Affairs, University of Virginia.

Caroline Farrar Ware (1899–1990)

Caroline Ware was an economic and social historian who was also a consumer activist, involved in community development work, concerned with the status of women in American society, and a founding member of the National Organization of Women. She was born in Brookline, Massachusetts, the daughter of Henry and Louisa Wilson Ware, a distinguished Unitarian family quite active in community affairs. Ware attended private schools and graduated from Winsor School in Boston (1916), and then went on to Vassar College (1916–20), Oxford University (1922–23), and finally to Harvard (Radcliffe) where she earned both a master's degree in 1924 and a doctorate in 1925 in history. In her studies, she was influenced by Lucy Salmon, James Harvey Robinson and Frederick Jackson Turner, especially in regard to their broad conception of history, the use of primary sources, attention to regional study, and the experience of common people. In fact, because Ware adopted the Salmon approach to history and the teaching of history – look at the evidence, order it logically, and then draw conclusions – she could not teach from textbooks and did not think that students could learn history from them. Ware did her dissertation work under the noted economic historian Edwin Gay, who suggested that she use the papers of the Boston Manufacturing Company recently acquired by the Harvard Business School to write something on the Industrial Revolution.

Ware taught history at Vassar from 1925 to 1934, social science at Sarah Lawrence (1935–37), and, from 1936 to 1944, taught social economy and history at American University. In the autumn of 1942 she joined the faculty of the Howard University School of Social Work, where she stayed until she retired in 1961. Aside from her academic career, Ware also had a career as a consumer activist. From 1934 to 1946 she worked for the Consumer Advisory Board of the National Recovery Administration, the consumer division of the National Emergency Council, and the Consumer Commission of the National Defense Advisory Board which later became part of the consumer division of the Office of Price Administration. Later she was a member of the consumer advisory committee to Truman's Council of Economic Advisors and of the Consumer Advisory Council which reported directly to Kennedy. Throughout this entire period, Ware represented the Association of American University Women on consumer issues before Congressional committees.

Beginning in 1945, Ware became increasingly drawn into the area of community development. While involved in Puerto Rico's efforts at development in the late 1940s, she wrote a manual on how to study a community which was later adapted for more general use and widely distributed throughout Latin America. In addition, between 1962 and 1976, she was a technical adviser in community development and cultural affairs for the United Nations, with missions in Central and South America. The final major area in which Ware was an activist was that of women's status and rights. From 1961 to 1963 she was a member of Kennedy's President's Commission on the Status of Women, and from 1963 to 1968 she was a member of the Citizen's Advisory Council on the Status of Women. In 1966, she undertook the initial spadework which eventually resulted in the founding of the National Organization of Women. Later, in 1975, she was involved with a number of committees celebrating International Women's Year.

Ware published books on a variety of subjects, most distinctively on economic and sociocultural history and on consumer economics. Her doctoral dissertation, which was published as *The Early New England Cotton Manufacture: A Study in Industrial Beginnings* (1931), received the prestigious Hart, Schaffner & Marx award. She also edited *The Cultural Approach to History* (1940) for the American Historical Association. In addition, she published *Greenwich Village. 1920–1930: A Comment on American Civilization in the Post-War Years* (1935) for the Columbia University Council for Research in the Social Sciences; *The Consumer Goes to War: A Guide to Victory on the Home Front* (1942) and *The Consumer in the Postwar Economy* (1945); and *Labor Education in Universities: A Study of University Programs* (1946) for the American Labor Education Service. She was a co-author and editor for UNESCO of *The Twentieth Century*, which appeared in the six-volume *History of the Scientific and Cultural Development of Mankind* (1966); a co-editor of and contributor to *Consumer Activists: They Made a Difference* (1982); and contributed several articles to the *Encyclopaedia of the Social Sciences* (1934). Finally, as a contributor to *The Structure of the American Economy* (1939), which was published by the National Resources Committee, she was responsible with Grace Knott for preparing 72 maps showing the location of different types of farms, ranches, orchards, manufacturing plants, pipelines, oil fields and quarries.

Ware's work as a historian centred on social and cultural history, especially on the lives of non-élite, ordinary people and specific cultural groups. Her dissertation examined the transformative role and costs of industrialization, studying both the entrepreneurs and the workers as well as large-scale social forces and conditions. Her contribution to *A Cultural Approach to History* emphasized shifting the focus from institutions and élites to the lives of the 'inarticulate and semi-articulate' masses. But it also emphasized recognition of the diminished role of the individual in the modern urban, industrial world; the interdependence of social, economic and cultural forces; class formation; and the culture of industry and work. Ware's study of Greenwich Village exemplified ethnic and community study and identified the *anomie* of urban life. Altogether, Ware pursued the integration of ethnicity, industrialism, urbanism, gender and class in both national identity and the study of its history.

Ware was the wife of Gardiner Coit Means (8 June 1896 – 15 February 1988) who was the co-author of *The Modern Corporation and Private Property (1932)*, one of the most important books published in the twentieth century, and a leading heterodox economist. Although she had already embarked upon an academic career teaching history at Vassar in 1925, Ware married Means on 2 June 1927 with the very clear intention of combining a career with marriage and children (although for physical reasons the marriage remained childless). She long believed that women did not have to choose between children and a career. Indicative of her desire to combine marriage and a career, Ware retained her maiden name, a very unusual, but not unheard of, practice then. Apropos of this, she later reported that she then had more status than her husband and did not want to set aside her own name; and that when her husband achieved more status than she, she did not want to ride on his coat-tails. Their relationship was complex, although she reported that they lived in mutually supportive harmony for 60 years. She felt that neither competed with nor intruded on the academic field of the other. She felt that she was an intellectual midwife of *The Modern Corporation and Private Property*, working to restate the ideas of an economist and a lawyer to each other. Ware and Means wrote one book together, *The Modern Economy in Action* (1936), with a dedication which reads, 'by Caroline F. Ware to Gardiner C. Means who furnished the basic analysis, and by Gardiner C. Means to Caroline F. Ware who actually wrote the book'. And they read and critiqued each other's work. After Means's death in 1988, Ware worked assiduously to promote the memory and historical professional standing of her late husband.

In 1935, Ware and Means purchased for their residence a 70-acre farm and apple orchard near Vienna, Virginia. Most of the land was donated to the Northern Virginia Regional Park Authority in 1988. The result is the Meadowlark Gardens Regional Park, a fitting memorial to two individualists with social consciences.

Ware was a member of the Washington Urban League, the American Historical Association, and the National Association of Social Workers. She received many honours and citations, including the Radcliffe College Graduate Achievement Award (1967), the National Consumer League's Trumpeter Award (1978), and the Urban League's Community Service Award (1987).

Ware had an active and successful career as an historian and as an activist and expert in consumer affairs, community development and the status of women. Her work has been the subject of scholarship and acknowledged by writers in the fields of labour, industrial and gender history (Fitzpatrick, 1991) and her career in government has been recorded on tape and deposited at the Schlesinger Library, Radcliffe College (Ware, 1983). Ware's papers are at the Franklin Delano Roosevelt Library, Hyde Park, New York. Although legally blind in the last years of her life, she continued to be active, assisted by a succession of secretaries and by friends, and was regarded by all who knew and respected her as a grand lady with a marvellous and penetrating intellect who had no compunction in speaking her mind.

FREDERIC S. LEE
WARREN J. SAMUELS

Bibliography

Selected writings by Caroline Farrar Ware

(1925), 'The Industrial Revolution in the New England Cotton Industry', Ph.D. dissertation, Radcliffe College.

(1926), 'The Effect of the American Embargo, 1807–1809, on the New England Cotton Industry', *Quarterly Journal of Economics*, **40**, August, 673–88.

(1931), *The Early New England Cotton Manufacture: A Study in Industrial Beginnings*, Boston: Houghton Mifflin.

(1935), *Greenwich Village, 1920–1930: A Comment on American Civilization in the Post-war Years*, New York: Octagon Books.

(1936), *The Modern Economy in Action* (with Gardiner C. Means), New York: Harcourt Brace.

(1940), *The Cultural Approach to History*, New York: Columbia University Press.

(1942), *The Consumer Goes to War: A Guide to Victory on the Home Front*, New York: Funk & Wagnalls.

(1945), *The Consumer in the Postwar Economy*, Washington, DC: American Association of University Women.

(1946), *Labor Education in Universities: A Study of University Programs*, New York: American Labor Education Service, Inc.

(1949), 'Trends in University Programs for Labor Education', *Industrial and Labor Relations Review*, **2**, October, 54–69.

(1966), *The Twentieth Century* (edited with K.M. Panikkar and J.M. Romein), New York: UNESCO.

(1982), *Consumer Activists: They Made a Difference* (edited with E. Angevine, M.D. Keyserling and S.H. Newman), New York: Consumers' Union Foundation.

(1983), 'Interview', History of Women in America: Women in Federal Government Project. Schlesinger Library, Cambridge: Radcliffe College.

(1992), 'Academic Resistance to Administered Prices', in F.S. Lee and W.J. Samuels (eds), *The Heterodox Economics of Gardiner C. Means: A Collection*, Armonk, NY: M.E. Sharpe.

Other sources and references
Fitzpatrick, E. (1991), 'Caroline F. Ware and the Cultural Approach to History', *American Quarterly*, **43**, 173–98.

Beatrice Potter Webb (1858–1943)

Martha Beatrice Potter Webb was born on 2 January 1858, the eighth daughter of Richard and Laurencina Potter. She grew up at Standish House on the River Severn in Gloucestershire. Though she had little formal education, she 'was educated at home by governesses; by extensive travel on the continent; and by a wide and serious range of reading' (Hamilton, 1959, p. 936). The works of Herbert Spencer and Auguste Comte were early influences on her thought.

Alfred Marshall too had an influence. On 8 March 1889, Beatrice Potter noted in her diary several long talks she had with Marshall. After baiting Potter with his nettlesome views on women's place in marriage, Marshall turned to her research interests. Potter recounts his advice:

> 'There is one thing that *you*, and only *you* can do – an inquiry into that unknown field of female labour. You have (unlike most women) a fairly trained intellect, and the courage and capacity for original work, and yet you have an insight into a woman's life. There is no man in England who could undertake with any prospect of success an inquiry into female labour ... if you devote yourself to a study of your own sex as an industrial factor, your name will be a household word two hundred years hence.' (Webb, 1982–85, vol. 1, p. 274).

At the end of this diary entry she made a vow: '"Female labour" *shall* be one of the principal inquiries of my life' (p. 275). Several years before this encounter with Marshall, she 'joined the Charity Organization Society (COS), a group that sought to provide Christian philanthropy to the downtrodden and assuage the consciences of the upper classes' in 1883 (Fiala, 1988, p. 845). In 1886, she had published a short article entitled 'A Lady's View of the Unemployed', in the *Pall Mall Gazette* (1886, p. 154). Later that spring, she joined Charles Booth's survey of the people and conditions of the East End working district of London and published her findings in 'The Pages of a Workgirl's Diary', in the *Nineteenth Century* in October, 1888. She soon 'abandoned her belief in the individual and individual effort', seeing a more important role for state intervention in treating the social and economic problems facing society (Fiala, 1988, p. 845).

Much of her work was co-authored with her husband, Sidney Webb. They married in 1892, and referred to themselves thereafter as 'the firm of Webb'. She claimed that 'We are both of us second-rate minds; but we are curiously combined. I am the investigator and he the executant; between us we have a wide and varied experience of men and affairs' (quoted in Hamilton, 1959, p. 936). The two were leading lights in the Fabian Society. Their work was empirical. Social investigations such as theirs provided the foundation for policy proposals in the Fabian tradition. 'Their fifty year partnership in research, publication, and disinterested public service had a profound impact on English social and political institutions' (Fiala, 1988, p. 844). They jointly authored *The History of Trade Unionism* (1894) and followed this with an analytical sequel, *Industrial Democracy* (1897). Her most important contributions in economics focused on women's pay and working conditions and on Poor Law reform.

In 1896, she published a Fabian Tract (number 67) titled 'Women and the Factory Acts' (1896). Here she identified the basis of the central conflict between the feminists and the trade unionists. The trade unions, comprised mostly of men, wanted job protection. What they feared most was that women would take jobs away from their own members by offering to work for lower wages. Union members believed that requiring equal pay for men and women for equal work would limit the substitution of women and men. On the other hand, the feminists demanded equal job opportunities, at whatever wages women could obtain. The feminists, led by Millicent Fawcett (*q.v.*) and Ada Heather-Bigg, opposed those aspects of the Factory Acts which regulated women's labour, believing that such regulation diminished the demand for women in the labour market which resulted in a lowering of their wages (Webb and Webb, 1902, p. 83).

In 1897, *Industrial Democracy* was published. Their treatment of the problem of gender-based occupational segregation is particularly important. Their empirical work revealed that men and women rarely hold the same jobs. They pointed out that union members, almost all of whom were men, resented and abhorred the idea of women entering their trades because they undercut men's wages, the standard rate, established by the trade unions. Consequently, wherever trade unions had the power, they prohibited women from taking men's jobs.

Growing acceptance of the notion of 'equality of the sexes' pressured the unions to change tactics. They dropped their overt sexual discrimination in favour of the 'maintenance of a Standard [Wage] Rate for each grade of labour' for piece-work (Webb and Webb, 1902, p. 498). The outcome was not surprising, for the standard rate caused 'a real, though unobtrusive, segregation' of jobs by gender (p. 501). In return for adopting these standard rates, the unions agreed to allow a woman to do a man's job, 'but she must win her way by capacity, not by underbidding' (ibid.). This was an important source of gender-based occupational segregation – the adoption of the standard rate for piece-work tended 'to segregate into virtually non-competing groups' the jobs performed by women and men.

Women are not engaged at the men's jobs, because the employers, having to pay them at the same high rate as the men, find the men's labour more profitable. On the other hand, the ordinary man does not offer himself for the woman's job, as it is paid for at a rate below that which he can earn elsewhere, and upon which, indeed, he could not permanently maintain himself. But there need be no rigid exclusion of exceptional individuals. (p. 507)

This magnified the strife between trade unionists and the 'women's advocates', and put the feminists on the horns of a dilemma. 'Within the world of manual labour, at any rate, "equality" between the sexes leads either to the exclusion of women from men's trades, or else to the branding of the whole sex as blacklegs' (p. 505).[1] Most surprisingly, the Webbs recommended that this dilemma be avoided by segregating manual jobs by gender. They insisted that, within the category of manual labour, gender-based job segregation is the natural result of the differences between the sexes. 'To keep both sexes in the same state of health and efficiency – to put upon each the same degree of strain – implies often a differentiation of task, and always a differentiation of effort and subsistence' (ibid.). While they did not suggest that 'either men or women need to be explicitly excluded from any occupation in virtue of their sex', none the less such gender-based job segregation 'comes automatically into existence, and needs no express regulation' in the majority of cases (p. 506). Of particular concern to the Webbs was the need to prevent 'under-bidding of individuals of one sex by individuals of the other' (ibid.). In the few cases where both 'men and women compete directly with each other for employment, on precisely the same operation, in one and the same process', unless 'definite Standard Rates are settled for men's work and women's work respectively', the very survival of the union movement was threatened (ibid.).

Beatrice Webb recognized that the power of the employer far outweighs that of the individual worker. Workers had two methods of defending themselves: 'the method of collective bargaining – in short, Trade Unionism. The other method is the settlement by the whole community ... Factory legislation' (Webb and Webb, 1902, p. 89).

She noted that the Factory Acts improved women's ability to compete for jobs since the regulations relating to safety, sanitation, employers' liability and age apply to both men and women. 'The only restriction of any importance in our Labour Code which bears unequally on men and women is that relating to the hours of labour' (p. 92). Turning to the alleged competition between men and women for the same jobs, she 'found it very difficult to discover any trade whatever in which men and women did the same work' (p. 94). She continued to believe that men's jobs reflected genuine physical differences between the sexes. Thus men had an advantage in those cases where 'the physical strength or endurance required, or the exposure involved, puts the work absolutely out of the power of the average women' (ibid.). Women have 'certain qualities not possessed by the average working-man' (p. 95). Women's qualities stemmed from social and cultural factors: 'they eat little, despise tobacco, and seldom get drunk; they rarely strike or disobey orders; and they are in many other ways easier for an employer to deal with' (ibid.). These qualities, combined with 'their standard of expenditure', make women attractive employees. Thus, in Fabian terminology, men have a 'rent of superior strength and endurance', while women possess a 'rent of abstemiousness' (ibid.). Since the limitations imposed by the Factory Acts on women's hours did not affect their ability to compete with men for jobs, these laws did not reduce occupational opportunities for women.

In 1914, Beatrice Webb published a series of articles on 'Personal Rights and the Woman's Movement' in *The New Statesman*; the last two examined equal job opportunity and equal pay. There she concluded that women ought not to demand equal pay, but instead ought to insist on 'an adequate Standard Rate for their own needs, and the opportunity to enter other [occupations] now artificially closed to them' (Webb, 1914a, p. 526). She was anxious that her position not be misunderstood: 'I hope that no one will take this argument against the demand for identity of earnings as any discouragement to women, in any occupation whatever, to press for higher pay' (ibid.). In fact, she listed five demands that women ought to press: (i) higher standards, wages and better working conditions; (ii) membership in trade unions; (iii) better nutrition and clothing; (iv) more thorough technical training; and (v) the opening of other occupations to women (pp. 526–7).

In 1919, she published a pamphlet, *The Wages of Men and Women: Should They Be Equal?*, as a Minority Report to the findings of The War Cabinet Committee on Women in Industry. Here she specified ten 'principles on which wages have hitherto been determined' (Webb, 1919, p. 8). These were: the principle of individual bargaining, the principle of the 'national minimum' wage, the 'principle of collective bargaining and of the occupational rate leading ... to a male rate and a female rate', the principle of adjusting money wages to the cost of living, the principle of determining wages by family obligations, 'the principle of the vested interest of the male' (by which she meant the enforcement of the concept of 'men's work' with high wages and 'women's work' with much lower remuneration), 'the principle of a definite [technical] qualification for employment', 'the principle of limiting wages by foreign competition', the principle of profit-sharing, and finally, 'the formula of equal pay for equal work' (ibid., pp. 8, 9, 11, 13, 15, 17, 20, 24, 25 and 31). She identified three different meanings attached to the formula of equal pay for equal work: '(1) equal pay for equal efforts and sacrifices; (2) equal pay for equal product; (3) equal pay for equal value to the employer' (ibid., p. 46). First, 'equal efforts and sacrifices' refers to 'the physiological and mental' efforts put forth by the workers (ibid., p. 21). She claimed that 'we have not yet learned how to measure [efforts and sacrifices] with any accuracy, apart from the time the wage-earner has to place at the disposal of the employer and the character of the work performed' (ibid.). In the second case, 'equal pay for equal product', the intention was that wages reflect 'the quantity and quality of the product, irrespective of the effect' of the work effort upon the workers themselves, 'or of the net value of the service to the employer' (ibid.). Webb maintained that employers preferred the third interpretation, 'equal pay for equal value to the employer'. They argued that wages were only a part of their costs of production. Believing that women were less productive than men, employers concluded that employing women increased their costs due to 'their different demands in the way of time and space, involving greater ... "overhead charges" for rent and repairs, lighting and heating, interest on cost of machinery and its annual maintenance or renewal' (ibid., p. 22). Employers also complained that women workers were inflexible and could not easily be switched from one task to another, which reduced their value and increased costs. Employers adopted two common tactics for evading the payment of equal pay to men and women. First, they paid piece wages to workers of one gender, while those of the opposite sex were paid time wages. Second, employers would make 'some alteration in the process, or in the machinery employed, or in the arrangement of the tasks of the operatives, or in the way the labour was divided', then substitute women for men at a lower wage rate (ibid., p. 24). She charged that 'if an employer is in some way required to give "Equal Pay for Equal Work," he habitually takes care to make some change in the work, so as to escape from the obligation' (ibid.).

In 1905, Beatrice Webb was appointed to serve on the Royal Commission on the Poor Laws and the relief of distress. Unable to sway the majority, she and Sidney drafted the famous minority report in 1909. This marked the beginning of a propaganda campaign involving conferences, summer schools, the Fabian Research Department, and a weekly newspaper aimed at reforming the old 1834 Poor Law, designed originally by Nassau Senior. She blamed the old Poor Law for creating, rather than relieving, much of the nation's poverty. She developed a comprehensive programme for reforming the system – including transferring the administration of the Poor Law to local authorities and 'establishment of a ministry of labour to deal with unemployment' (Fiala, 1988, p. 847). Beatrice wrote a number of books on the subject: *The Relation of Poor Law Medical Relief to the Public Health Authorities* (1906), *A Crusade Against Destitution* (1909), *Socialism and the National Minimum* (1909), *A New Crusade Against Destitution* (1909), *Complete National Provision for Sickness: How to Amend the Insurance Act* (1912), and *The Abolition of the Poor Law* (1918). Though the campaign failed, 'the fabric of the old Poor Law was gradually dismantled and the new system of social insurance took its place' (Hamilton, 1959, p. 938).

Beatrice Potter Webb died on 30 April 1943 and Sidney on 13 October 1947. The ashes of 'the firm' were buried in Westminster Abbey.

JAMES P. HENDERSON

Note

1. 'Blackleg' was a term of derision aimed at those who offered to work at lower wages than current employees.

Bibliography

Selected writings by Beatrice Potter Webb

(1886), 'A Lady's View of the Unemployed', *Pall Mall Gazette, 18 February*.
(1891), *The Co-operative Movement in Great Britain*, London: S. Sonnenschein & Co.
(1892), *The Relationship between Co-operation and Trade Unionism*, Manchester: Co-operative Union Ltd.
(1894), *The History of Trade Unionism* (with Sidney Webb), London: Longmans, Green.
(1896), 'Women and the Factory Acts', Fabian Pamphlet, also ch. IV in *Problems of Modern Industry* (1902), London: Longmans, Green and Co., pp. 82–101.
(1896a), 'The Method of Collective Bargaining' (with Sidney Webb), *Economic Journal*, **6**(1): 1–29.
(1896b), 'The Standard Rate' (with Sidney Webb), *Economic Journal*, **6**(3): 356–88.
(1897), *Industrial Democracy* (with Sidney Webb), 2 vols, London: Longmans, Green.
(1898), *Problems of Modern Industry* (with Sidney Webb), London: Longmans, Green.
(1902), *Problems in Modern Industry* (with Sidney Webb), London: Longmans, Green.
(1903–29), *English Local Government from the Revolution to the Municipal Corporations Act* (with Sidney Webb), 11 vols, London: Longmans, Green. Reprinted with additional essays by B. Keith-Lucas, G.J. Ponsonby, L. Radzinowicz and W.A. Robson, London: Frank Cass, 1963.
(1904), 'The Assize of Bread' (with Sidney Webb), *Economic Journal*, **14**(2): 196–218.
(1906), *The Relation of Poor Law Medical Relief to the Public Health Authorities*.
(1909), *A Crusade Against Destitution*, [?] London: National Committee for the Prevention of Destitution.
(1909), *Socialism and the National Minimum* (with B.L. Hutchins and the Fabian Society), London: A.C. Fifield.
(1909), *Minority Report of the Poor Law Commission* (with Sidney Webb), 2 vols, London: Fabian Society.
(1910), *The Minority Report in its Relation to Public Health and the Medical Profession*, [?] London: National Committee for the Prevention of Destitution.
(1910), *A New Crusade Against Destitution*,[?] London: National Committee for the Prevention of Destitution.
(1910), *The State and the Doctor* (with Sidney Webb), London: Longmans, Green.
(1912), *Complete National Provision for Sickness: How to Amend the Insurance Act*, London: Standing Joint Committee of the Independent Labour Party and the Fabian Society.
(1914a), 'Personal Rights and the Woman's Movement: Equal Remuneration for Men and Women', *The New Statesman*, **3**, August, 525–7.
(1914b), 'Personal Rights and the Woman's Movement: The Right of Women to Free Entry into all Occupations', *The New Statesman*, **3**, July, 493–4.
(1916), *A Woman's Appeal: Personal Expenditure in Wartime*.
(1918), *The Abolition of the Poor Law*, London: Fabian Society (Fabian Tract 185).

(1919), *The Wages of Men and Women: Should They Be Equal?*, London: Fabian Society.
(1926), *My Apprenticeship*, London: Longmans, Green.
(1928), 'The Discovery of the Consumer', in *Self and Society, First Twelve Essays: Social and Economic Problems from the Neglected Point of View of the Consumer*, London: Ernest Benn.
(1931), *A New Reform Bill*, London: Fabian Society (Fabian Tract 236).
(1948), *Our Partnership*, Barbara Drake and Margaret I. Cole (eds), London: Longmans, Green.
(1978), *The Letters of Sidney and Beatrice Webb* (with Sidney Webb), N. Mckenzie (ed.), 3 vols, Cambridge, UK: Cambridge University Press.
(1982–85), *The Diary of Beatrice Webb*, N. Mackenzie and J. Mackenzie (eds), 4 vols, London: Virago.

Other sources and references

Beilharz, Peter and Chris Nyland (eds) (1998), *The Webbs, Fabianism and Feminism: Fabianism and the Political Economy of Everyday Life*, Aldershot, UK: Ashgate.
Cole, G.D.H. (1943), 'Beatrice Webb as an Economist', *Economic Journal*, **53**(4): 422–37.
Fiala, Robert D. (1988), 'WEBB, Martha Beatrice Potter (1858–1943)', in *Biographical Dictionary of Modern British Radicals Vol. 3: 1870–1914, L–Z* ed. Joseph O. Baylen and Norbert J. Grossman, Brighton: Wheatsheaf.
Hamilton, Mary Agnes (1959), 'WEBB, (Martha) Beatrice (1858–1943)', under 'WEBB, Sidney James', *Dictionary of National Biography*, Oxford: Oxford University Press.
Radice, Lisanne (1984), *Beatrice and Sidney Webb*, New York: St Martin's Press.

Helen Laura Sumner Woodbury (1876–1933)

Helen Laura Sumner was born in Sheboygan, Wisconsin, on 12 March 1876, the only daughter and second child of Katherine Eudora (Marsh) Sumner and George True Sumner, a lawyer. Five years later the family moved to Durango, Colorado, when George was appointed a judge. The family subsequently relocated to Denver, where Helen graduated from high school. During her undergraduate studies at Wellesley College, Helen became interested in social and economic questions of the time and published a novel defending free silver during the Bryan presidential campaign, *The White Slave; or 'The Cross of Gold'* (Sumner, 1896). She was also active in the College Settlements Association. Helen graduated with an AB degree in 1898 (Olson, 1971, pp. 650–51).

In February 1902 Helen began graduate studies in economics at the University of Wisconsin. She also worked as secretary to Richard Ely. John Commons was instrumental in her appointment as an honorary fellow in political economy during 1904–6. She was co-author of a university textbook on labour problems (Adams and Sumner, 1905). In September 1906 she began a 15-month investigation of woman suffrage in Colorado; some years later, the results of her investigation were published as a book (Sumner, 1909). During 1907–8 Helen was a correspondence instructor at the University of Wisconsin, an experience that did not attract her to teaching as a career (Olson, 1971, p. 651).

Her doctoral thesis, 'The Labor Movement in America, 1827–1837', was accepted in 1908. In revised form, this constituted a segment of the pioneering *History of Labor in the United States* (Commons et al., 1918). Helen also helped edit the 11-volume *Documentary History of American Industrial Society* (Commons et al., 1910–11), and was largely responsible for the volumes dealing with the labour movement from 1820 to 1840. During these same years, she completed a study (Sumner, 1910) which was published as part of the Bureau of Labor Statistics' multi-volume *Report on Condition of Women and Child Wage-Earners in the United States.*

After 1909 Helen lived in Washington, DC, where she was employed in a variety of contract studies for federal agencies (for example, Sumner, 1912). In 1913 she joined the Children's Bureau, where she conducted policy research on a variety of topics involving children (for example, Sumner, 1914; Sumner and Merritt, 1915; Sumner, 1919; and – following her marriage to Robert Morse Woodbury in November 1918 – Woodbury, 1921, 1924). In 1924 she joined the Institute for Economics (before it became the Brookings Institution) from which she took early retirement in 1926.

Helen Sumner Woodbury's most notable contribution to scholarship are the many volumes on American labour history she wrote and helped edit, and her work in women's history. The works with John R. Commons and others are standard references in labour history. That two of her own books (Sumner, 1909 and Sumner, 1910) have been reprinted recently is a tribute to their enduring scholarly value.

Helen Laura Sumner Woodbury died on 10 March 1933 at her New York home just before her 57th birthday.

RICHARD A. LOBDELL

Bibliography

Selected writings by Helen Laura Sumner Woodbury
(1896), *The White Slave; or 'The Cross of Gold'*, Chicago: C.H. Kerr & Co.
(1905), *Labor Problems: A Textbook* (with Thomas Sewall Adams), New York: The Macmillan Company.
(1909), *Equal Suffrage: The Results of an Investigation in Colorado made for the Collegiate Equal Suffrage League of New York State*, New York and London: Harper & Brothers. Reprinted New York: Arno Press, 1972.
(1910), *History of Women in Industry in the United States*, vol. IX of *Report on Conditions of Women and Child Wage-Earners in the United States*, Bureau of Labor Statistics, Washington, DC: Government Printing Office. Reprinted New York: Arno Press, 1974.
(1910–11) (edited with John R. Commons, Ulrich B. Phillips, Eugene E. Gilmore and John B. Andrews), *A Documentary History of American Industrial Society*, 11 vols, Cleveland: The A.H. Clark Company.
(1912), *Industrial Courts in France, Germany and Switzerland*, US Labor Bureau, Washington, DC: Government Printing Office.
(1914), 'Vocation Education – Its Social Relationships', National Education Association, *Journal of Proceedings and Addresses*, 572–7.

(1915) (with Ella A. Merritt), *Child Labor Legislation in the United States*, Washington, DC: Government Printing Office.

(1918), *History of Labor in the United States* (with John R. Commons, David J. Saposs, E.B. Mittleman, H.E. Hoagland, John B. Andres and Selig Perlman), New York: The Macmillan Company.

(1919), *Standards Applicable to Child Labor*, US Children's Bureau, Washington, DC: Government Printing Office.

(1921), *The Working Children of Boston: A Study of Child Labor under a Modern System of Legal Regulation*, Washington, DC: Government Printing Office.

(1924), *Standards Applicable to the Administration and Employment-Certificate Systems*, Washington, DC: Government Printing Office.

Other sources and references

Olson, Frederick I. (1971), 'Helen Laura Sumner Woodbury', in Edward T. James (ed.), *Notable American Women, 1607–1950*, Cambridge, MA: Belknap Press.

Maxine Bernard Yaple Sweezy Woolston (b. 1911)

Maxine Woolston grew up in the Kansas City area, and was a granddaughter of Zachary Taylor, twelfth president of the USA. She received her BA and MA from Stanford, and her Ph.D. from Radcliffe/Harvard (1940); she also attended the London School of Economics. Woolston taught at various schools in the USA, including Sarah Lawrence, Tufts, Vassar, Simmons, Haverford, Swarthmore, Wellesley, University of Pennsylvania, University of New Haven, and, for the greatest length of time, Bryn Mawr. During World War II she worked in the Office of Price Administration and the Foreign Economic Administration. Her detailed knowledge of the structure of the German economy was apparently utilized when the USA attempted pinpoint bombing of German industrial targets during World War II. Woolston's first husband was Paul Sweezy, the eminent US Marxist economist; her second husband was William J. Woolston, a Philadelphia lawyer.

Her first article, 'The Burden of Direct Taxes as Paid by Income Classes' (1936) calculated federal personal income and corporation taxes in the years 1924, 1927, 1929, 1932 and 1933. Woolston concluded that these taxes were indeed generally progressive for all income classes, with the possible exception of the top class with income over one half million dollars.

In 1938 she published with six other economists *An Economic Program for American Democracy*. This is a Keynesian-based analysis arguing for broad liberal social democratic policies. The authors claim that after 1929 a basic change in the structure of the US economy occurred, leading to a continuing depression as a result of inadequate aggregate demand in general and inadequate private investment in particular.

The authors argued for general redistributive policies from relatively wealthy individuals to relatively poor individuals with a higher propensity to consume; higher minimum wages and unemployment benefits; encouragement to unionization; and, especially, increased government deficit spending on public investment to build low-cost public housing, schools, hospitals, highways, parks, dams and so on. The authors predicted continuing economic stagnation in the absence of liberal public policies to increase aggregate demand.

Work from her dissertation led to the publication of the book *The Structure of the Nazi Economy* (1941). This is a thorough, detailed institutional analysis of the Nazi economy, including separate chapters on transportation, corporations, cartels, industrial pricing policy, foreign exchange, financial markets, labour markets and farming. By Woolston's interpretation, Nazi Germany was a totalitarian state which either prepared for or was at war. The Nazis ended Germany's massive unemployment by rearmament and achieved a strong military state.

The government essentially set the tasks for industry to perform and required industry to carry them out. Nazi policies led to the increasing importance of big business and heavy industry, as well as an increased concentration of control and growth in the average size of corporations. Members of the Nazi Party élite were starting to organize their own firms, so that, for example, Hermann Goering, was half-political and half-industrial overlord.

The Nazi economy had effective wage and price controls and full employment with the rationing of many consumer goods. The government controlled foreign exchange and much of foreign trade as well as the stock market, and banking regulations were centralized. Trade unions were destroyed and collective bargaining abolished. According to Woolston, Germany basically created a modern equivalent to medieval feudalism, where the German worker (both industrial and agricultural) became attached and fixed to his job, it being a criminal offence for the workers to quit work without permission of the employment authorities. In agriculture, the Nazis reintroduced primogeniture, and controlled food imports and prices.

Women were at first forced out of the labour force, then forced back in as the economy went from a labour surplus to a labour shortage economy. Germans achieved more employment and worked longer hours; there were increases in the number of factory illnesses and accidents. More of the share of income went to property income, and less to wage income, generating increases in the inequality of wealth and income. None the less, living standards were not reduced below depression levels.

According to Woolston, the Nazis succeeded in building an efficient war machine, and, within severe limitations, the system of private ownership of the means of production still operated. The government largely controlled investment by its allocation of foreign raw materials and control over the capital market. Firms, however, could and did grow through the reinvestment of profits. Industrial cartels helped to enforce administered price controls. The Nazi regime was opposed to state ownership, and many undertakings were denationalized and demunicipalized. Woolston viewed the increase in the wealth and income of Nazi Party members as somewhat analogous to the loot and booty of feudal robber barons. Basically, the new industrialists of Germany were the Nazi Party members. None the less, Woolston sadly concluded that the Nazis had indeed succeeded in building an efficient, aggressive economic war machine: 'Tyranny in the age of machines presages the continuation of an economic system which is basically decadent but efficient and aggressive in war' (1941, p. 239).

Two sections from her dissertation/book appeared as journal articles. 'Distribution of Wealth and Income Under the Nazis' (1939) details the increase in inequality in wealth and income during the Nazi regime. 'German Corporate Profits: 1926–1938' (1940) calculates profit ratios of German corporations according to industrial classes. Woolston found that the demand for peacetime consumer goods was quite low, and that the heavy industry group did particularly well. The state was the largest customer of industry, and it granted contracts covering 5–10 years. These contracts guaranteed a price which ensured a reasonable profit. The role of the state in the economy was great: it absorbed private savings, monopolized foreign trade, controlled prices, completely regulated labour, allotted raw materials, determined in what sectors of the economy new investments would go, and decided upon new manufactures.

In 1945 the American Association of University Women published a pamphlet by Woolston entitled 'Medical Care for Everybody?' Woolston summarized the state of the health of the US population as well as the health care industry. She briefly outlined the rise of Blue Cross Plans, Medical-Society Plans, prepaid group practice plans, farm security administration medical care plans, and other voluntary medical plans. Woolston gave arguments for and against federal health insurance without stating her own position.

Woolston published another pamphlet with the AAUP in 1950, 'World Economy and Peace: A Study Guide'. After short descriptions of the World Bank, the International Monetary Fund, and the proposed International Trade Organization, Woolston discussed the international dollar shortage. She argued for, among other things, gradual reduction in US tariffs, the promotion of economic integration in Western Europe, ratification by the US Congress of the International Trade Organization, and greater support for the UN and its specialized economic agencies.

A book of readings to supplement elementary economics principles texts edited by Woolston appeared in 1953: *Basic Information on the American Economy*.

Woolston was active in regional economic planning and community and social affairs in the greater Philadelphia area for much of her adult life (Bryn Mawr College Archives). She currently resides in Connecticut.

SPENCER J. PACK

Bibliography

Selected writings by Maxine Bernard Yaple Sweezy Woolston
(1936), 'The Burden of Direct Taxes as Paid by Income Classes' *American Economic Review*, **26**: 691–710.
(1938), *An Economic Program for American Democracy* (with Richard V. Gilbert, George H. Hildebrand Jr., Arthur W. Stuart, Paul M. Sweezy, Lorie Tarshis and John D. Wilson).
(1939), 'Distribution of Wealth and Income under the Nazis', *Review of Economic Statistics*, **21**: 178–84.
(1940), 'German Corporate Profits: 1926–1938', *Quarterly Journal of Economics*, **54**: 384–98.
(1941), *The Structure of the Nazi Economy*, Harvard Studies in Monopoly and Competition, Boston, MA: Harvard University Press.
(1945), 'Medical Care for Everybody?', American Association of University Women.
(1950), 'World Economy and Peace: A Study Guide', American Association of University Women.
(1953) (ed.), *Basic Information on the American Economy*.

Other sources and references
Bryn Mawr College Archives.

Barbara Wootton (1897–1988)

Barbara Frances Adam (Barbara Wootton) was born on 14 April 1897 in Cambridge, England. Her father, James Adam, was Fellow and Senior Tutor of Emmanuel College, and her mother Adela was an accomplished scholar and linguist. As the daughter of classical scholars, she was expected to excel academically. She was raised in an intellectually stimulating atmosphere: she would read the New Testament aloud to her father in Greek and they even named their cat Plato. Wootton and her two older brothers Neil and Arthur were so successful academically that they were held up as examples to their classmates, and detested by these same classmates, much to Wootton's dismay. James Adam died when Wootton was ten, and thereafter, her mother became the dominant force in her life.

Wootton began to display some of the independent thinking that would characterize much of her later life in that she showed little interest in her mother's chosen field of study, classics, and instead gravitated towards economics. This greatly disappointed Adela, who would later refer to her daughter as someone 'who might have been distinguished'. Indeed, the two were never close and Wootton received more support from her nanny, Elizabeth Haynes.

Haynes was a friend of John Maynard Keynes's cook, Jenny, and Wootton often heard Jenny complaining about Keynes's laziness and that he would stay in bed until noon. Wootton formed the impression that Keynes was a 'hopeless ne'er do well', but in all likelihood he was up most of the night studying.

In 1915, Wootton entered Girton College, Cambridge, to study classics, but she also attended economics lectures, with an intention of studying economics after her first degree. In an effort to prepare for the lectures, she read Alfred Marshall's *The Economics of Industry* and *Principles of Economics* and was struck by the 'unnecessary fuss about the obvious'. She did not believe that such complex expositions were needed to explain why prices went up when quantity supplied went down and vice versa. Her suspicion of these works increased and resulted in *Lament for Economics* 24 years later. She did enjoy one book, however, and even referred to it as her 'emancipation', G.D.H. Cole's *World of Labour*.

It was at this time that she met her first husband, Jack Wootton. They were married on 5 September 1917, and a day and a half later he was recalled to his regiment in France, cancelling their honeymoon. Five weeks later, Captain John Wootton was shot through the eye and died 48 hours later. The couple had spent a total of 36 hours together. True to her upbringing, Wootton did not wallow in despair, nor did she use her misfortune to abandon her studies.

After John's death, Wootton moved back home to complete her studies at Cambridge. She became ill during final examinations and was unable to complete them, causing her to lose her first-class standing. She was awarded an aegrotat and, more importantly, she was able to pursue her economics studies. She earned a first with a special mark of distinction, an achievement of which she remained proud for the rest of her life. Her economics education continued with a research scholarship at the London School of Economics, but the research went unfinished as Wootton could not adapt to the unstructured environment. Despite this, she became Director of Studies in Economics at Girton, a position that provided material comfort and her first real difficulty as a woman in a traditionally male profession. She could not write the letters BA after her name because she could not be a member of the university, unlike the men who earned the same degree. (She eventually received honorary doctorates from 13 universities.) As her reputation as a lecturer grew, she was invited to give a series of lectures on the economic functions of the state, but the General Board of Studies refused to print her name on its list of lecturers; instead they announced that 'Mr. Hubert Henderson' would lecture, with Wootton's name mentioned in a footnote. Wootton resented this treatment for the rest of her life.

Life was comfortable but not wholly satisfying, so in 1922 she left Cambridge to become a researcher in London for the Joint Research Department for the Trades Union Congress and the Labour Party. Part of her dislike of studying the classics was that it was not applicable to the present day. She viewed economics as a way to improve conditions in a real and tangible way, and this position allowed her to use her skills for the social good. In 1924 she became the only female member of a departmental committee to study the national debt and existing taxation. In the same year, at the age of 29, she became a Justice of the Peace, ironic since women were not allowed to vote until the age of 30. Her service for more than 40 years as a lay magistrate in London led to her 1963 Hamlyn Lectures at Oxford on *Crime and the Criminal Law* and her 1978 book on *Crime and Penal Policy* (see the first volume of her *Selected Writings*, 1993).

She quickly realized there was little possibility of advancement at the Congress, so she left to become Principal of Morley College for Working Men and Women at the University of London. This job provided a better outlet for her socialist fervour, and the classes in adult education helped shape the politics of the time. She remained at the University for the next 17 years.

Now in her thirties, she had accomplished much by anyone's standards and she began to travel extensively. She found the Russians unwilling to face reality and admit the failures of socialism. She outlined her democratic socialist ideas in 1934 in *Plan or No Plan*, but events in Europe caused her to doubt her hopeful view of the future.

In 1935 she married George Wright and they settled in London. The couple made several trips to the USA and observed that everywhere but in Russia unemployment was at drastically high levels, and that governments' response was to reduce spending, the opposite of what she believed ought to be done. This is outlined in great detail by John Maynard Keynes in his *General Theory of Employment, Interest and Money* which Wootton describes as 'inordinately complicated'. She believed that economists tended to make things more difficult than necessary and that their language did not speak to the average person. In 1938 she published *Lament for Economics*, which was a response to Professor Lionel Robbins's *The Nature and Significance of Economic Science*. Wootton was disappointed by the inability of economists to solve economic problems and their habit of burying themselves in abstractions in order to avoid dealing with problems that really exist. This book was to mark the end of her interest in economics as a means of improving conditions, as she gradually realized that she no longer wanted to be an economist.

In 1944 she moved to Bedford College, London, where she obtained a readership (and in 1948 a professorship) and became the head of the Department of Economics, Sociology and Social Sciences, a difficult job as she was the target of resentment and jealousy. She resigned her chair in 1952 and received a five-year research fellowship from the Nuffield Foundation, after which she retired.

Her contribution to economics comes in the form of books she published, mostly outside the academic setting, because her interests lay in the real world. She discussed the political economy of socialism in *Plan or No Plan*, which was followed in 1945 by *Freedom Under Planning*, an emphatic but courteous social democratic response to Friedrich Hayek's anti-collectivist polemics. She was a governor of the British Broadcasting Corporation from 1950 to 1956, and served on Royal Commissions on Workmen's Compensation (1938–44), the Press (1947–49), the Civil Service (1953–55), and the Penal System (1964–66), chairing the Countryside Commission from 1968 to 1970. Her work as an arbitrator on the Civil Service Arbitration Tribunal resulted in *The Social Foundations of Wage Policy* in 1955 and *Incomes Policy: an Inquest and a Proposal* in 1975. She was an original thinker in that she disagreed with the commonly held belief that economics be practised independent of its effect on society. Economics had to disregard current constraints in order to be valuable to society. She demonstrated this in *The Social Foundations of Wage Policy*, where she showed how the theory of wages could be tested against the wages in the real world. She believed wages should be evenly distributed and controlled by the government, and that the demand side of the economy could be boosted, while keeping a check on inflation.

Wootton did not often mix with those who shared her economic beliefs, preferring to remain alone. Although she was an independent thinker, she attracted no followers and had little need for the support of her peers. She was one of a group who, in the 1930s, outlined the new economic policies of the Labour Party, and at times was even more radical than her peers; she never lost her belief in socialism, even when faced with its failures.

Wootton's career was unique in that she was an economist, social scientist, magistrate, writer, educator and Life Peer (as The Baroness Wootton of Abinger, from 1958) and made contributions in all these fields. She was the first woman to be president of the British Sociological Association and the first to preside over the House of Lords (as a Deputy Speaker from 1967). As an economist, she is remembered as an iconoclast, someone who endeavoured to bring practicality and humanity to a discipline removed from the average person. Before she eventually became disillusioned with her chosen profession, she added her voice to those who believed in demand-side economics and government intervention in the economy.

Barbara Wootton died on 11 July 1988.

INDRA HARDEEN

Bibliography

Selected writings by Barbara Wootton

(1920), 'Classical Principles and Modern Views of Labour', *Economic Journal*, **30**, March, 46–60.

(1929), 'Shavian Socialism', *Economic Journal*, **39**, March, 71–7.

(1934), *Plan or No Plan*, London: Victor Gollancz.

(1938), *Lament for Economics*, London: George Allen & Unwin.

(1943), *Full Employment*, London: Fabian Society.

(1945), *Freedom Under Planning*, New York: University of North Carolina Press.

(1950), *Testament for Social Science*, London: George Allen & Unwin.

(1955), *The Social Foundations of Wage Policy*, London: George Allen & Unwin.

(1963), *Crime and the Criminal Law*, Hamlyn Lectures no. 15, London: Stevens & Sons.

(1967), *In a World I Never Made*, Toronto: University of Toronto Press.

(1975), *Incomes Policy: An Inquest and a Proposal*, London: George Allen & Unwin.

(1993), *Barbara Wootton: Selected Writings*, 4 vols, ed. Philip Bean and Vera G. Seal, London: Macmillan.

Other sources and references

Bean, Philip and D. Whynes (eds) (1986), *Barbara Wootton: Social Science and Social Policy*, London and New York: Tavistock Publications.

Morris, Terence (1989), 'In Memoriam: Barbara Wootton 1897–1988', *British Journal of Sociology*, **40**(2), June, 310–18.

'Women of Our Century IV: Barbara Wootton – A Champion of the Impossible', *The Listener*, **112**, 1984, 10–12.

Frieda Wunderlich (1884–1965)

Frieda Wunderlich was born in Berlin on 11 November 1884. She studied at the University of Freiburg, where she received her doctorate in 1919. In 1933 she became one of the founding members of the 'University in Exile' – the Graduate Faculty of Political and Social Science in the New School for Social Research, New York – a faculty of outstanding *emigré* social scientists. Prior to her emigration, Wunderlich had been a member of the Prussian State Parliament and the Berlin City Council, and she had served as a judge of the German Supreme Court for Social Welfare. From 1923 to 1933 she was the editor of the important anti-Hitler political weekly magazine *Soziale Praxis*.

Wunderlich's research focused on labour markets, social problems and, after 1939, problems of allocating resources in a war economy. After the outbreak of war in Europe in 1939 the Graduate Faculty, with financial assistance from the Rockefeller Foundation, initiated the Peace Research Project and the project on Economic and Social Controls in Germany and Russia; Wunderlich was an active participant. The aim of the projects was to investigate the causes of war and the conditions necessary for lasting peace. Wunderlich's work on the methods adopted by totalitarian regimes, in particular Germany and the Soviet Union, for the allocation of resources during wartime ranks among the best in the field, and is probably her most important scientific legacy. Most of this work was published in the journal *Social Research* between 1940 and 1948. Over the course of her career, she was the author of numerous books, including *Farm Labor in Germany until 1945* (1961) and *German Labor Courts* (1946) and scientific articles.

Wunderlich died in East Orange, New Jersey on 19 December 1965.

GARY MONGIOVI

Bibliography

Selected writings by Frieda Wunderlich

(1920), *Hugo Münsterbergs Bedeutung für die Nationalökonomie*, Jena: G. Fischer.

(1925), *Die Bekämpfung der Arbeitslosigkeit in Deutschland seit Beendigung des Krieges*, Jena: G. Fischer.

(1926), *Produktivität*, Jena: G. Fischer.

(1927), 'Die Arbeitseitbestimmungen im Entwurf eines Arbeitsschutzgesetzes', *Archiv für Sozialwissenschaft und Sozialpolitik*, **58**: 375–99.

(1928), 'The German Unemployment Insurance Act of 1927', *Quarterly Journal of Economics*, **42** (February): 278–306.

(1932), *Versicherung, Fürsorge und Krisenrisiko*, Leipzig: Kommissions-Verlag von Lühe.

(1934), 'New Aspects of Unemployment in Germany', *Social Research*, **1** (February): 97–110.

(1935), 'Women's Work in Germany', *Social Research*, **2** (August): 310–36.

(1937), 'Health Insurance', *Social Research*, **4** (November): 509–14.

(1938), 'Germany's Defense Economy and the Decay of Capitalism', *Quarterly Journal of Economics*, **52** (May): 401–30.

(1940), 'Labour Under German Democracy, Arbitration, 1918–1933', *Social Research*, Supplement II.

(1941), 'British Labor and the War', *Social Research*, Supplement III.

(1943), 'The Beveridge Plan', *Social Research*, **10** (May): 233–45.

(1945), 'The National Socialist Conception of Landed Property', *Social Research*, **12** (February): 60–76.

(1946a), 'The National Socialist Agrarian Program', *Social Research*, **13** (March): 33–50.

(1946b), *German Labor Courts*, Chapel Hill, NC: University of North Carolina Press.

(1947), 'Social Insurance versus Poor Relief', *Social Research*, **14** (March): 75–94.

(1949), 'New Trends in Social Insurance', *Social Research*, **16** (March): 31–44.

(1950), 'Social Insurance in the United States', *Social Research*, **17** (March): 90–105.

(1952), 'Agriculture and Farm Labor in the Soviet Zone of Germany', *Social Research*, **19** (June): 198–219.

(1953), 'Codetermination in German Industry', *Social Research*, **20** (April): 75–90.

(1958), *Farmer and Farm Labor in the Soviet Zone of Germany*, with a foreword by Alvin Johnson, New York: New School for Social Research.

(1961), *Farm Labor in Germany 1810–1945. Its Historical Development within the Framework of Agricultural and Social Policy*, Princeton, NJ: Princeton University Press.

Other sources and references

Diehl, K. (1927), 'Zur Lehre von der Produktivität', *Schmollers Jahrbuch*, **51** (2): 533–44.

Meyer, J. (1966), 'In Memoriam: Frieda Wunderlich, 1884–1965', *Social Research*, **33** (1): 1–3.

Kikue Yamakawa (1890–1980)

Kikue Yamakawa was a feminist activist, commentator and writer, who was deeply interested both in changing society and in the economic problems caused by women's participation in the labour force in Japan. She was concerned about the working conditions of women and the changing role of women in family life. She joined a variety of activities such as the women's liberation movement and the socialist movement in the 1920s, the folklorist project around 1940, the civil service at the Bureau of Women and Minors in the Ministry of Labour from 1947 to 1951, and was a prolific writer her whole life. Yamakawa's short essays reflect the situation of the Japanese society in which she was living and writing, and she helped create a more liberal Japanese public opinion by publishing timely and mostly polemical commentaries in popular magazines. Her several books provide the historical records of the experiences of her family, her mother and herself in the transition of Japanese society from feudal to more liberal between the mid-nineteenth and the mid-twentieth century.

Kikue Yamakawa was more influenced by her mother's side than her father's. Her *Record of Women in Two Generations: Mother and Daughter* (1956) is an excellent biography of her mother and herself up to the 1940s and gives us vivid descriptions of the lives and experiences of her mother Chise Morita (1857–1947) and herself, reflecting the turbulent changes in Japanese society. Chise Morita was from the Aoyama family, who had long lived in Mito. Her father Enju Aoyama and three uncles were all noted scholars on what was called *Kangaku* (Chinese learning), and engaged in the editorial work on *The Grand History of Japan* (*Dai Nihon-shi*, 397 volumes, 1657–1906) in Mito and taught at *Kodokan* (The School of Mito). *Kangaku* was one of the most important disciplines in the pre-modern Japanese academy during the Edo era, with others being *Kokugaku* (Japanese classical learning) and *Rangaku* (Dutch learning). *Kangaku* covered many fields such as history, politics, economics, art, medicine, and natural and social sciences. The Mito domain was one of the most influential feudal clans both in political and academic respects during the Edo era, but the turbulent change of Japanese society after the end of the isolationist policy (1639–1854) brought a bloody civil war to Mito. In spite of the criticism by the central government, a number of young and old men of ability in the Mito domain were lynched, or executed for political crimes without legitimate trial by the local Mito government. Therefore, in some respect, Yamakawa's *Notes on Late-Tokugawa Mito* (1974) was a long-awaited book written by a woman whose mother and family survived the bloody turmoil in Mito.

In 1872 Chise Morita, Kikue's mother, moved to Tokyo when her husband Ryunosuke Morita took up a position there. A little later Chise's parents moved out of unstable Mito and settled in with Chise. Kikue was born to Ryunosuke and Chise Morita as their third child in Tokyo in 1890. When her grandfather Enju Aoyama died in 1906, Kikue Morita formally succeeded to the head of the Aoyama family and changed her family name to Aoyama. Kikue Aoyama tried several women's schools to get an adequate education. In 1908, Kikue Aoyama just passed the entrance examination to *Joshi Eigaku-juku* (Women's School for English Study), the school which later became Tsuda University. This was because one of her answers to the exam questions was a resolution to work for women's liberation, and this was not very welcome. In 1912 Kikue Aoyama graduated from the school a few weeks after her classmates did, because she had to attend classes, including physical education, which she had thought unnecessary and had not attended. In 1916 Kikue Aoyama was married to socialist Hitoshi Yamakawa (1880–1958). Hitoshi was known as an intellectual leader of the left wing and had already been jailed once for political crimes. Kikue had changed her family name back to Morita just before her marriage and changed it to Yamakawa upon her marriage. As expected, Hitoshi was arrested at every round-up of socialists, especially after the Universal Male Suffrage and the Peace Preservation Law became effective in 1925.

Kikue Aoyama became known as a feminist activist when she criticized Noe Ito's objection to the abolition of 'registered prostitution in whorehouses (*kosho*)' and urged the protection of women's rights. Ito argued that 'registered prostitution' would be 'safer' than 'unregistered prostitution on the street (*shisho*)', because the women in the house were forced to take tests for syphilis. Yet Ito soon confessed that she did not know much about the system of prostitution (in Japan). Kikue Aoyama contributed to a magazine *New Society* (*Shin Shakai*) and developed her objection to 'registered prostitution' and the abolition of forced tests for syphilis, urging the enlightenment of the people to eradicate poverty and unemployment, and the achievement of economic independence of women in society. Kikue Aoyama became involved in the socialist movement as well. She suffered from tuberculosis soon after her marriage and recuperated in the suburbs of Tokyo. Although she did not make a full recovery until 1925, she managed to deliver a boy and named him Shinsaku in 1917.

During World War I, Japan exported an increasing number of industrial goods to countries to which the fighting European countries had stopped their exports, such as India, and Japanese companies made enormous profits. In contrast, the working conditions for Japanese labourers deteriorated because their wages did not keep up with rapidly rising prices. Japanese workers began to feel sympathy with the socialist movement and gradually became class-conscious. The protection of women workers became an issue at the first Washington meeting of the International Labour Organization (ILO), which was established in 1919. All three representatives of Japan, that is, the government, the male employer, and the male 'labourer', who were chosen by the government, unanimously objected to the article of protection for women workers, maintaining the uniqueness of Japanese circumstances. At that time, Kikue Yamakawa was recovering from tuberculosis and studying socialist literature including the English version of V.I. Lenin's *State and Revolution* (1911).

During the period of her relatively good health, at the request of economist Tatsuo Morito, Kikue Yamakawa gave a talk on the problems of working women at a meeting of the Society of Social Policy in 1918. The society was established in Japan in 1896 following the German model of Verein für Sozialpolitike, which was organized by the German Historical School in 1873. Yamakawa's speech included a comparison between women's problems of the middle and working class, women's low wages, and problems relating to marriage. The transcript appeared in *Kokka-gakkai Zasshi*, the journal of the Law Department of the Imperial University of Tokyo (the University of Tokyo after 1947). It is noteworthy that the university did not allow any women to enrol as regular students before 1947.

In 1923 Tokyo metropolitan area was hit by major earthquakes. Many houses and buildings were damaged by the tremors and the fire caused by the earthquakes. Kikue, Hitoshi and Shinsaku Yamakawa survived although their house collapsed. Many women in the registered whorehouses were burned to death because they could not escape from the houses. This tragedy ignited the women's movement in its call for the abolition of registered prostitution. Kikue Yamakawa drafted the manifesto of the Women Allies for the Abolition of Registered Prostitution. The allied women were not satisfied just with the abolition of registered prostitution. Their manifesto stated that they would do their best to enhance the social status of women in general, to improve women's education and vocational training, and to establish social facilities for the protection of the rights of women and minors. All this was aimed at preventing women from becoming involved in prostitution. However, Kikue Yamakawa decided to move from Tokyo to Kobe to recuperate further when she managed to sell the lumber of her collapsed home.

Kikue Yamakawa finally came back to the forefront of the women's liberation movement in 1925. At the time, she had to fight with the socialist men who were arguing for the abolition of the women's divisions in trade unions and were objecting to the organization of the women's allies. She kept trying to persuade socialist men of the importance of the particular problems of women in the course of the proletarian movement toward a socialist revolution. In 1925 she proposed to add six articles for the protection of women's rights to the action programme for the Women's Department in the Kobe Branch of the Society of Political Study:

1. The abolition of the system of the head of the family, and the abolition of all the laws based on sexual inequality.
2. Equal opportunity for education and vocation.
3. The abolition of registered prostitution.
4. A demand for a uniform minimum wage rate without regard to sex or race.
5. Equal wage rates for the same job.
6. The protection of motherhood, that is, the protection of women before and after childbirth and a prohibition against firing pregnant women.

Initially the cadre of the society was indecisive about the abolition of registered prostitution and disapproved of all the rest because the proposals were anti-Marxist. Yet later her husband Hitoshi Yamakawa managed to persuade the cadre to approve all the proposals drafted by Kikue Yamakawa. From the late 1920s, Kikue Yamakawa began to make more efforts to increase awareness of the situation of women. She also translated feminist works by Mary Wollstonecraft, August Bebel and Edward Carpenter.

Kikue Yamakawa took care of her sick son from 1930 until 1935. At that time, the Japanese people were losing the freedom of speech and press. Kikue and Hitoshi Yamakawa could not live by writing any more. They began to keep quail, and sold their eggs to Mitsukoshi Restaurant every day and occasionally to others. In 1940 Kikue Yamakawa had a talk with folklorist Kunio Yanagita (1875–1962). Their meeting was arranged by a magazine publisher. Yanagita was eager to construct and preserve a record of the traditional life of Japanese women. Yanagita encouraged Yamakawa to write about common women's lives in Mito. Yamakawa had already collected materials for the historical study of ordinary people in Mito such as her grandfather's collection of books, his diary kept for more than 60 years, a copy (made by hand) of the record of current topics both public and private in mid-nineteenth century Mito, the private correspondence and poetry written by scholars, *samurais* (feudal warriors) and her relatives.

Yamakawa published her *Women of the Mito Domain* in 1943. She depicted the daily life of a *samurai* household vividly based on what she had heard from her mother and grandfather, the collected materials, and the related literature. The ordinary topics she covered were education, food, dwellings, amusements, relatives, marriage and divorce. Yamakawa also recorded 'the turmoil of 1864'. This was a bloody civil war in Mito initiated by the conflict over the implementation of the reform plan which emphasized military readiness, education, the encouragement of industriousness, and a reduction of extravagance after the end of the isolationist policy. In undertaking this reform plan, 'a policy of promoting men of ability under which incompetents of high rank were held in check and many people of low rank were singled out and awarded positions of central importance' aroused strong opposition among the upper ranks of domain retainers who eventually became opponents of the reforms (Yamakawa, 1992, p. 116). It can be said that the policy threatened the traditional Japanese view of a hierarchical social order. The story was expanded and published as her *Notes on Late-Tokugawa Mito* in 1974. The English version of *Women of the Mito Domain* was published by Kate Wildman Nakai in 1992.

Yamakawa was advised by Yanagita to write about the rural farming village, Okamura in Kamakura-gun, where she had lived since 1936. She knew nothing about farming and had no friends when she and her son had moved into the village which was filled with native farmers. She learned about farming, conducted hearings with the village people she met, and collected the materials in a facility to which a researcher in the Ministry of Health and Welfare had given her access. She published her *My Village Where I Live* in 1943. This book included both the description of the lives of the village people and the oral history narrated by them to her.

In 1945 World War II ended and the Allies, led by American forces, occupied Japan until 1952. The Allies eradicated Japan's fighting capability and conducted democratic reforms to bring Japan back to the world community. In 1947 they helped establish the Ministry of Labour which included the Bureau of Women and Minors. Kikue Yamakawa was appointed the first Director-General of the Bureau, and boldly decided to give the near 250 staff positions in prefectural offices only to women, after becoming irritated by receiving recommendations only for male candidates (Tanino, 1982). In 1952, Yamakawa agreed to resign from the position, when it was 'recommended' she do so because she did not pass the examinations for civil servants.

After that, Yamakawa participated in many activities for women's liberation. She published *The Record of Women in Two Generations: Mother and Daughter* in 1956 and *Notes on Late-Tokugawa Mito* in 1974. A few chapters from her *Notes on Late-Tokugawa Mito* are included in the English version of *Women of the Mito Domain* (1992). These chapters shed light on the economic life of *samurai* and marriage practices in Mito. *Samurais* received their salary based on a very complicated stipendiary system. Their life was supposed to be frugal enough to 'begrudge one drop of oil'. Yamakawa reported that abortion and infanticide were common practices in Japan until around the mid-nineteenth century.

Yamakawa died at the age of 91 in 1980. In 1981 ten volumes of her *Collected Works of Kikue Yamakawa* were published with one supplement. The assistant editor Yuko Suzuki has wisely placed Yamakawa's writings in chronological order to allow readers to fully understand the importance of Yamakawa's timely essays.

AIKO IKEO

Bibliography

Selected writings by Kikue Yamakawa (originally all in Japanese)
(1919), *The Victory of Women*, Tokyo: Nihon-Hyoron-sha.
(1919), *Modern Life and Women*, Tokyo: Sobunkaku.
(1919), *From the Standpoint of Women*, Tokyo: Mita Shobo.
(1919), 'On the Problems of Women at Work', *Kokka-gakkai Zasshi*, **33** (2–3).
(1922), *The Revolt of Women*, Tokyo: Santoku-sha.
(1923), *Russian in the Dawn*, Tokyo: Sobunkan.
(1925), *Women's Problem and Women's Movement*, Tokyo: Bunka Gakkai.
(1943), *Women of the Mito Domain*, Tokyo: Mikuni Shobo.
(1943), *My Village Where I Live*, Tokyo: Mikuni Shobo.
(1956), *The Record of Women in Two Generations: Mother and Daughter*, Tokyo: Nihon Hyoron-shinsha.
(1974), *Notes on the Late-Tokugawa Mito*, Tokyo: Iwanami Shoten.
(1981), *The Collected Works of Kikue Yamakawa*, 10 vols, edited by Sumiko Tanaka and Shinsaku Yamakawa, Tokyo: Iwanami Shoten.
(1984), *The Collected Essays on Women's Liberation by Kikue Yamakawa*, Tokyo: Iwanami Shoten.
(1990), *Selected Essays of Kikue Yamakawa*, edited by Yuko Suzuki, Tokyo: Iwanami Shoten.
(1992), *Women of the Mito Domain: Recollections of Samurai Family Life*, translated into English and with an introduction by Kate Wildman Nakai, University of Tokyo Press.

Other sources and references
Ikeo, Aiko (1997), 'Three women economists in Japan', Nihonbunka Kenkyusho Kiyo, **79**.
Nakai, Kate Wildman (1992), 'Introduction' to Yamakawa (1992).
Setani, Yoshihiko (1982), 'Bibliography' to the supplement volume to Yamakawa (1982).
Suzuki, Yuko (1982), 'Bibliography' to each volume of Yamakawa (1982).
Tanino, Setsu (1982), Yamakawa Director-General in the Women's and Minors' Bureau, advertisement to vol. 7 of Yamakawa (1982).
Tsurumi, Shunsuke (1982), 'Bibliography' to vol. 9 of Yamakawa (1981).

Anna Pritchett Youngman (d. 1974)

Anna Youngman received a Ph.B. from the University of Chicago in 1905 and a Ph.D. from the same institution in 1908. Her dissertation was entitled 'The Economic Causes of Great Fortunes', and published in book form in 1909. It was quite favourably reviewed by A.P. Winston in the *Journal of Political Economy*. The book examines the growth of the fortunes of John Jacob Astor, Jay Gould, the Standard Oil group and the Morgan group. In the book she tries to distinguish between the personal abilities of those under study and the economic forces which they used in order to amass their fortunes. She also examines the rise of the modern corporation and the stock market and how those under study responded to these developments. She concludes that while the personal element is still important in the process of fortune accumulation, the financial element is becoming increasingly important.

While a Ph.D. student at Chicago, she wrote articles on the growth of financial banking (1906) and a two-part article on the tendency of modern combination (1907). These articles are mainly composed of descriptive statistics with very little analysis, which was quite common in articles in the *Journal of Political Economy* of that time.

After she left Chicago, she took up a position at Wellesley where she stayed until approximately 1919. While at Wellesley she wrote several articles on public finance for the *Quarterly Journal of Economics* and two book reviews for the *American Economic Review (AER)*.

After she left Wellesley she was on the staff of the Division of Analysis and Research of the New York Federal Reserve Bank from 1919 to 1922 and the School of Business, Columbia University until 1923. In 1921 and 1922, she wrote two articles for the *AER* on the discount rate and credit which contain some very 'modern' ideas on these topics. Since she was working at the Federal Reserve Bank in New York during part of the time that these articles were written, it is interesting to speculate how much of the monetary activism proposed in these articles was a reflection of the ideas of the administration of the New York Bank. The first article (1921) discusses the effectiveness of the discount rate as a means of credit control and the relationship of the discount rate to various market rates. She concludes that the short-term interest rate is not an important element in business decisions during periods of prosperity but 'if goods do not move regularly, the burden of interest charges may be keenly felt, but it will then be felt even if rates are very low' (Youngman, 1921, p. 472). She then makes the point that even if short-term interest rates are important in the business decision-making process, the discount rate is irrelevant to this process, since the discount rate is not a market rate but is usually much below the market rate. This spread between the market interest rate and the discount rate allowed many banks to borrow at the discount window and relend in their communities. Youngman proposes that the discount rate be increased until it is above the market rate. This would then discourage borrowing, which would free up reserves and allow the Federal Reserve to use these reserves for open market operations in a wide variety of financial instruments to control the total amount of credit accommodation available.

The second paper looks at the whole issue of the ability of the central bank to control credit and what effect this control will have on the economy. It is a much more difficult paper to read since the definition of some of the terms has changed over time. This paper reflects the view that credit is something that can be controlled rather than being a 'reflex' of the demand for productive goods and services. She clearly rejects the idea that the supply of loanable funds is solely dependent on savings by individuals, arguing that it is in fact augmented by creating banking credits. Youngman also saw that there was little difference between long-term and short-term credit. 'It is easy to think of a long-time loan as a succession of short-time loans, renewed at intervals' (p. 430). This is almost the same discussion as can be found in most current money and banking texts. She discusses the relationship between credit and inflation and rejects the idea that some types of loans are non-inflationary but other types of loans are speculative in nature and should be discouraged.

She reiterates her earlier discussion of the desirability of a market-driven discount rate. She ties this to the gold standard by urging policy-makers to ignore minor gold movements and only raise interest rates if major movements occur because of domestic inflation. These gold movements are viewed as an indicator of the need for credit restriction within the country.

The final part of the article calls for the availability of information and economic forecasting so that more rational decisions can be made by both the suppliers and users of credit.

Both of these articles call for activism on the part of the central bank in the area of credit policy. They reject the idea that the bank is powerless in the determination of interest rates. In fact the bank is urged to use open market operations to control interest rates. In an interesting twist, both interest rates and credit are defined in terms of purchasing power.

From 1924 to 1932 she was an associate editor for the *Journal of Commerce*. She then went to work for the *Washington Post*, where she continued to work until her retirement in 1952. She died in 1974.

In 1945, while at the *Post*, she wrote *The Federal System in Wartime*, which describes how the Fed aided the federal government to finance World War II. She discusses the Fed policy of maintaining very low short-term interest rates and the implications of this policy in the postwar era. She continues her argument, made in her *AER* articles, that the Fed has the ability to control interest rates and credit. She also expresses concern over the inflationary pressures that are building in the economy and makes several suggestions on how the Fed should deal with these forces after the war.

BARBARA LIBBY

Bibliography

Selected writings by Anna Pritchett Youngman
(1906), 'The Growth of Financial Banking', *Journal of Political Economy*, **14**, 435–43.
(1907), 'The Tendency of Modern Combination', *Journal of Political Economy*, **15**, 193–208.
(1907), 'The Tendency of Modern Combination', *Journal of Political Economy*, **15**, 284–98.
(1908), 'The Fortune of John Jacob Astor', *Journal of Political Economy*, **16**, 345–68, 436–41, 514–30.
(1909), *The Economic Causes of Great Fortunes*, New York: The Bankers Publishing Co.
(1912–13), 'Frankfort-on-the-Main: A Study in Prussian Communal Finance. I, II', *Quarterly Journal of Economics*, **27**, 150–201, 329–72.

(1915), Book reviews of *Die Lohntheorien von Ad. Smith, Ricardo, J. St. Mill und Marx*, by Ferdinand von Degendeld-Schonburg, *American Economic Review*, **5**, 55.

(1917–18), 'The Revenue System of Kentucky: A Study in State Finance', *Quarterly Journal of Economics*, **32**, 142–205.

(1918), Book review of *The Conflict of Tax Laws*, by Rowland Estcout, *American Economic Review*, **8**, 831.

(1921), 'The Efficacy of Changes in the Discount Rates of the Federal Reserve Banks', *American Economic Review*, **11**, 466–85.

(1922), 'A Popular Theory of Credit Applied to Credit Policy', *American Economic Theory*, **12**, 417–46.

(1923), Book review of *Money, Banking and Exchange in India*, by H. Stanley Jevons, *American Economic Review*, **13**, 512.

(1945), *The Federal Reserve System in Wartime*, New York: National Bureau of Economic Research.

Other sources and references

A.P. Winston (1909), 'Review of Anna Pritchett Youngman: *The Economic Causes of Great Fortunes*', *Journal of Political Economy*, **18**.

Irini (Rena) Zafiriou (b. 1912)

Rena Zafiriou was born in 1912 in London. She entered the University of Athens in 1930 and took her first degree in Politics and Economics in 1934 and the degree in Law one year later. She worked in the Ministry of Finance as a civil servant for two years (1937–39).

Zafiriou participated in the competition for a 'Damereion' scholarship for postgraduate studies in economics and was the first woman to win the prize. She resigned her position in the Ministry of Finance and registered at the London School of Economics in October 1939. Through the intervention of her supervisor Lionel Robbins and because of the quality of her papers during her first year of study she registered for the Ph.D. degree. After the outbreak of the Second World War the LSE was evacuated to Cambridge. Most of the courses and seminars attended by Zafiriou were given by the Cambridge faculty. She heard Keynes's lectures and became a Keynesian. This proved to be a problem as after 1940 Robbins went to work for the government in London and F.A. von Hayek became Zafiriou's new supervisor. She disagreed with him on almost every issue and after various delays she received her Ph.D. in July 1945. Her external examiner was P. Rosenstein Rodan. Zafiriou is the first Greek woman economist to receive a Ph.D. in economics.

When the Greek government in exile arrived in London the Greek embassy contacted Greek students asking them to attend interviews at the embassy in order for them to get appointed to government positions. Zafiriou joined the staff of Professor Kyriakos Varvaressos who was the Governor of the Central Bank in exile and Minister of Finance. Zafiriou was responsible for following economic developments in Greece and reporting on them, and attended inter-allied meetings on war finances and postwar reconstruction. She was a member of the Greek delegation to the Food and Agricultural Conference in Hot Springs, Virginia and later participated on pre-Bretton Woods discussions in Washington as an assistant to Varvaressos. She was also present at the meetings of the United Nations Relief and Rehabilitation Administration and prepared memoranda on Greek post-war relief needs, on Greece's finances and on Greek economic conditions. She was the economist best qualified to do that for her country, for she had documented the looting of Greece under the German occupation and knew of the Greek government in exile's efforts to relieve the starving Greeks and plan post-war reconstruction. As an aide to Professor Varvaressos she interacted with high-ranking British civil servants who held her in high esteem as they found her well qualified and 'literate in Keynesian economics' (Lykogiannis, 1999).

After the liberation of Greece in October 1944 Zafiriou remained in London in charge of economic matters until February 1945 when she returned to

Greece and was appointed head of the Economic Studies department of the (Central) Bank of Greece. The economic situation of the country deteriorated however because of political instability and different agendas on policy issues between the two great men of Greek economics, Professor K. Varvaressos and Professor X. Zolotas.

Zafiriou stood next to Governor Varvaressos and reached the high echelons of policy making when Varvaressos became Deputy Prime Minister in June 1945. She assisted him in the so-called 'Varvaressos Plan', an effort to put a strong government in charge of the reconstruction of the country. The plan foresaw the immediate distribution of UNRRA supplies and raw materials to firms, the taxation of the profits of war and the provision of basics to the people through government authorities. The plan, the only comprehensive, well-argued attempt to solve the economic misery of the country, was abandoned in September 1945 because of lack of political support from both the right and the left. The net result was that the Greek currency came to be stabilized only seven years later.

Zafiriou was a member of the Greek delegation in the first United Nations session in London in early 1946. In June 1946 Zafiriou resigned from her post in the Bank of Greece and left for the United States where she joined the World Bank. She moved to the International Monetary Fund for two years before returning to the World Bank where she worked as a senior economist until her retirement. At the World Bank she was responsible for the Nordic countries within the European Department. She was also active in the annual Economic Research Report and in the Sector Analysis Department. She lives in Washington, DC.

The quality of her 1942 article in the theory of monopolistic competition and of her thesis demonstrates that, had Zafiriou opted to stay in Greece, she could have become an academic even if she was not particularly interested in teaching. As, however, she opted to emigrate to the USA, Zafiriou is today, unfortunately, hardly known in her native country.

MICHALIS PSALIDOPOULOS

Bibliography

Selected writings by Irini Zafiriou
(1942), 'The contemporary stand of the theory of monopolistic competition', *Epitheorissis Koinonikis ke Dimosias Oikonomikis* (Review of Social and Public Economics) (in Greek).
(1945), 'The concept of capital in economic theory', unpublished Ph.D. thesis, London School of Economics.

Other sources and references
Lykogiannis, A. (1999), 'Britain and the Greek economic crisis 1944–7: from liberation to Truman doctrine', unpublished Ph.D. thesis, London School of Economics.